Fodor's 92
Europe's
Great Cities

W9-CIL-137

Reprinted from *Fodor's Europe '92*

Fodor's Travel Publications, Inc.
New York and London

ISBN 0-679-02039-X

Fodor's Europe's Great Cities

Editor: Christopher Billy
Contributors: Barbara Walsh Angelillo, Anne Campbell-Lord, Nancy Coons, Donna Dailey, Melody Favish, Robin Gauldie, George Hamilton, Emma Harris, Simon Hewitt, Allanah Hopkin, Amanda B. Jacobs, Dennis Jaffe, Karin Kaminker, Helmut Koenig, Graham Lees, Alan Levy, Delia Meth-Cohn, Richard Moore, Chris Mosey, Anita Peltonen, Karina Porcelli, Mark Potok, Marcy Pritchard, Jon Sigurdsson, Eric Sjogren, Ulli Stadler, Lynda Stout, Robert Tilley, Julie Tomasz
Art Director: Fabrizio La Rocca
Cartographer: David Lindroth
Illustrator: Karl Tanner
Cover Photograph: Peter Guttman

Design: Vignelli Associates

Special Sales

Fodor's Travel Publications are available at special discounts for bulk purchases (100 copies or more) for sales promotions or premiums. Special editions, including personalized covers, excerpts of existing guides, and corporate imprints, can be created in large quantities for special needs. For more information write to Special Marketing, Fodor's Travel Publications, 201 East 50th St., New York, NY 10022, or call 1–800–800–3246. Inquiries from the United Kingdom should be sent to Fodor's Travel Publications, 20 Vauxhall Bridge Rd., London, England SW1V 2SA.

MANUFACTURED IN THE UNITED STATES OF AMERICA
10 9 8 7 6 5 4 3 2 1

Contents

Index   *445*

Maps

Foreword

While every care has been taken to assure the accuracy of the information in this guide, the passage of time will always bring change, and consequently, the publisher cannot accept responsibility for errors that may occur.

All prices and opening times quoted here are based on information supplied to us at press time. Hours and admission fees may change, however, and the prudent traveler will avoid inconvenience by calling ahead.

Fodor's wants to hear about your travel experiences, both pleasant and unpleasant. When a hotel or restaurant fails to live up to its billing, let us know and we will investigate the complaint and revise our entries where the facts warrant it.

Send your letters to the editors of Fodor's Travel Publications, 201 E. 50th Street, New York, NY 10022.

Highlights'92 and Fodor's Choice

Highlights '92

Throughout 1992 West European countries will continue to make adjustments in their economies as they prepare for the end of the year, the time when all trade barriers between the 12 member states of the European Community (or Common Market) are to be disbanded. This move will turn much of Europe into one huge tariff-free market, the largest economic grouping in the world. By 1993, we'll see fewer border checks between countries, freer airline competition (which should make flying within Europe less exorbitant), and a new burst of business and leisure travelers across the Atlantic. Europeans, too, will be enjoying greater prosperity and will be traveling their continent more freely.

Great Britain will be marking several significant anniversaries in 1992. In addition to celebrating the 500th anniversary of the sailing of Columbus to America, the nation will commemorate the 40th anniversary of Queen Elizabeth II's ascent to the throne as well as the 200th anniversary of the death of the great architect Robert Adam. Nineteen hundred and ninety two also marks the 50th anniversary of the arrival in Britain of the U.S. 8th Air Force to help win World War II. This celebration will be based in East Anglia—where the 8th had its headquarters—and will be marked by air shows, Glenn Miller–style concerts, street parties, and services to commemorate those who lost their lives.

For a good part of the year much of the world's attention will be focused on **Spain,** which will host two major events: the **1992 Summer Olympic Games** in **Barcelona** and the **1992 International Exposition** in **Seville.** And, as if that weren't enough, **Madrid** has been designated cultural capital of Europe for 1992. For Spain, 1492 was a pivotal year: The Catholic monarchs Ferdinand and Isabella defeated the last Moorish kingdom on the peninsula at Granada and sent Columbus off to discover the New World, making Spain the world's richest and most powerful nation. With the events of 1992, the Spaniards are hoping to recover some of the luster of that golden age.

Travelers visiting Spain in 1992 will see the best the country has to offer: carefully restored historic quarters, flowering gardens along scrubbed avenidas, and state-of-the-art facilities for the world's top sporting and cultural events. It will also be exhausting, both to the body and the pocketbook. Bring warm-weather clothing; the summer climate of Barcelona is notoriously hot and humid. Seville is drier but has temperatures that frequently soar above 100°F. Also bring lots of money. The strong peseta has made Spain an expensive tourist destination, especially for Americans who suffer as well from the weak dollar. Hotel rates will be very high during the Olympics and the Expo, but this happens with all world-class events. Up to 10 million foreign tourists are expected to visit Spain during 1992; the best way to cope is to make plans as early as possible.

Summer Olympic Games The Olympic flame will be lighted in Barcelona's Montjuïc Stadium the afternoon of July 25, signaling the start of the games, which run through August 9. Some 400,000 tourists are expected to crowd into the city for the big event, as are 10,000 athletes, 10,000 members of the Olympics administration, 10,000 reporters, and 40,000 guests of corporate sponsors. With so many visitors, there are concerns about a shortage of accommodations, transportation tangles, and security. But chances are all the problems will be ironed out by the time the Olympics open.

Most of the competitions will be held at four main Olympic areas within the city of Barcelona. The areas are not more than 6 miles apart, and traveling time between them is estimated at 20 minutes, whether by public transportation or private car. Though events are being held at various facilities throughout the city, the **Montjuïc Area,** on a hill overlooking the Mediterranean, is the nerve center of the games. Eleven sports are being played in this area in four venues that make up the so-called *Anillo Olimpico* (Olympic Ring). Opening and closing ceremonies are being held at the Montjuïc Stadium. Traffic is banned on Montjuïc hill, and access is by escalator and a remodeled funicular that can move 8,000 people an hour.

Only legal residents of Spain and companies operating within the country can buy Olympic tickets directly from Barcelona. Seats to the most popular events were distributed by lottery during 1991, but tickets are still available for some competitions. They are being sold in Spain through all branches of Banesto bank. In the United States tickets can be purchased through **Olson Travelworld** (100 N. Sepulveda Blvd., Suite 1010, El Segundo, CA 90245, tel. 800/874–1992, fax 213/640–1039). The official agent for tickets in Britain is **Sportsworld Travel** (New Abbey Court, Stert St., Abingdon, Oxon OX14 3JZ, tel. 0235/55–48–44, fax 0235/55–48–41). The agent for Canada is also **Sportsworld Travel** (287 MacPherson Ave., Toronto, Ontario M4V 1A4, tel. 416/924–7495). Both Sportsworld and Olson, a veteran of the Calgary and Seoul games, offer complete travel packages but sell tickets separately. Seats went on sale in early 1991, and it was not known at press time how long it would take for the allocations to sell out.

One of the hardest parts about seeing the Olympics will be finding a place to stay. The Olympic organizing committee has reserved 80% of the rooms at all of Barcelona's three-, four-, and five-star hotels. Foreign visitors and tour operators have been told to scrounge for lodging in beach towns along the Costa Brava north of Barcelona and the Costa Dorada to the south. Most of these overbuilt resorts have suffered a steep drop in business as tastes have changed over the past three summers, but they are holding out for one last hurrah during the games. Expect price gouging. The big advantage of these resorts is a railway line that links them with the central city. Independent travelers can try to snag a room at one of Barcelona's pensions or one- and two-star hotels. The tourist office will mail a list on request. Several companies have also sprung up to provide accommodations in private homes during the games. These range in quality from an entire luxurious house to an empty bedroom in a family apartment.

Expo '92 Leaving the competitive world of athletic achievement to their Catalan brothers, the extroverted residents of Seville are getting ready for a global block party. The Expo's theme, "The Age of Discoveries," fits neatly into the commemoration of the 500th anniversary of the "discovery" of America by Columbus, who spent time between voyages in Seville and was later buried there. But Expo '92 will also showcase the most recent human discoveries in technology and outer space. More than a world's fair, the Expo is a universal exhibition in the tradition of London's Crystal Palace Exhibition of 1851. The most recent similar events were in Brussels (1958), Montreal (1967), and Osaka (1970).

About 18 million visitors are expected to click through the turnstiles during the six-month run of Expo '92. It opens April 20 and closes on Columbus Day, October 12. Visitors could easily spend a week exploring the 538-acre fairgrounds and enjoying Expo's cultural offerings, but organizers acknowledge that most people will be happy with a two- or three-day stay.

No fiesta would be complete without entertainment, and Expo '92 will not disappoint on that count. An ambitious program of 50,000 shows featuring pop music, opera, dancing, and theater will unfold daily on 21 stages. Each day has been designated the national celebration of one of the participating countries, and performances featuring that country's music and dance will be held every 45 minutes in the Palenque, a cool white tent in the area of the international pavilions that can seat 2,000 spectators. Highlighting each day is the festival parade, featuring 15 floats and 300 performers reenacting all the fiestas that take place throughout a calendar year in Spain. Each day will be capped by a fireworks show at the lake and dancing to live music at the Palenque.

There are not enough hotel rooms in Seville to accommodate all the visitors expected each day at Expo '92, and that's one reason transportation links have been improved. Only about 20,000 rooms exist within Seville's metropolitan area, so the exhibition is expected to become a day trip for most people. Some of the best bets for commuters include Córdoba and the resorts along the Atlantic coast near Huelva and Cádiz, all of which are about an hour away by car. Expo can also be a long day trip from Madrid using the high-speed train.

Eastern Europe In 1992, Europeans, like their American counterparts, will be heading east in growing numbers for a look at the countries that until the (mostly peaceful) revolutions of late 1989 and early 1990 made up the East Bloc. Many travelers who earlier were intimidated by barbed wire and excessive bureacratic red tape are now curious to witness the emergence of fledgling governments and the transformation of long-repressed societies.

Though the tourist amenities in Eastern Europe are still not up to Western standards many of the difficulties of traveling there have been greatly reduced. Bulgaria, Czechoslovakia, Hungary, and Poland have eliminated their visa requirements, and the mandatory exchange of currency was abolished for most visitors in Czechoslovakia, Hungary, Poland, and Romania (*see* individual chapters for details). Some Eastern European currencies are still not convertible on the world market, which means that the East European money you have left at the end of your stay cannot in all cases be exchanged back into a hard currency such as dollars or Deutschmarks. Another consideration is the dramatic rate of inflation and devaluation in many of these nations. The best way to guard against fluctuating rates is to exchange small amounts of money.

Nonstop flights to Eastern Europe have largely been limited in the past. But last year airlines began adding more routes in response to the growth in tourist demand. Pan Am was the first U.S. carrier to provide nonstop routes to the region. American Airlines has signed an agreement with Malev Hungarian Airlines that will expedite connections through Zürich to Budapest. Foreign carriers have been slower to follow, but some have added new flights during the peak tourist season. Polish Airlines (Lot) last year added flights to their Chicago–Warsaw route and introduced two nonstop flights from Los Angeles to the Polish capital.

Air facilities in Eastern Europe are also being upgraded in anticipation of future traffic. **Prague's** Ruzyně Airport, which expects to handle more than 5.3 million passengers a year by the end of 1992, began a renovation last year that should be completed by spring 1992.

Rental cars, once rare behind the Iron Curtain, are generally easier to find now. Rates are higher than in Western Europe, however, and locating gasoline can be a problem. In most of these countries, stations are few and far between, and gas can only be purchased by tourists with coupons. Maps, too, may be somewhat outdated since newly elected governments have changed the names of towns, streets, squares, and subway stops. Communists are out; saints, pre–World War II heroes, and former dissidents are in.

Lodging in the former East Bloc countries has traditionally been tight, but the picture is changing somewhat as international hotel chains aggressively pursue development in the area. Most countries still require that foreign investments be run as joint ventures with national interests, but those restrictions, too, are loosening. Major chains, such as Hyatt International and Inter-Continental, are in the process of renegotiating existing franchise agreements so they can directly manage their East European properties and bring them up to Western standards.

One word of caution: With the downfall of the Communist party as the unifying power, resurfacing rivalries among nationalities has led to political unrest in Romania and Yugoslavia. At press time travelers were advised to avoid certain areas, particularly Croatia and the Kosovo region in Yugoslavia. Check with the U.S. Embassy or U.S. Consulate before departure for current information (*see* individual country chapters).

Transportation In the past year, both American and foreign carriers have launched a number of new flights into the heartland of Europe. At press time, travelers were able to take nonstop or direct flight to more than 45 European cities from the United States. An increasing number of flights were also departing from smaller and inland U.S. airports, such as Charlotte, North Carolina, and Cincinnati, Ohio, thus enabling travelers to avoid congestion at major U.S. gateways.

Another development, the **Channel Tunnel,** or Chunnel, is expected to alleviate air traffic as well. The $9.2 billion project, which was begun in February 1988, is slated for completion by mid-1993. At that time, double-deck railcars will shuttle up to 120 vehicles (and their passengers) from Folkestone, England, to Coquelles, France, in 35 minutes. High-speed trains also will use the tunnel to run from London to Paris in about three hours. Though travel between Britain and the Continent will be greatly facilitated, some fear that the long-awaited tunnel will be operating at peak capacity from the start, thus leading to inevitable delays. Expectations are that as many as 50,000 people a day will use the tunnel.

Apart from the Chunnel, the Continent boasts of other major rail developments. The Atlantic TGV, the newest French high-speed (186 miles per hour) rail line, will continue to expand its services over the next four years. In late 1990, French Railroads completed the track work between **Paris** and St. Pierre des Corps, and the company expects to connect the capital city with **Bordeaux** and **La Rochelle** on the Spanish border by 1993. Future plans include service from Paris to Avignon, Marseille, Nice, and Barcelona, Spain—a run that would take 4½ hours.

Not to be outdone by its northern neighbor, Spain is investing heavily in RENFE, the Spanish National Railway system. Currently, 24 high-speed luxury trains, which will cruise at 186 miles per hour, are under construction. The first high-speed route, between **Madrid** and **Seville,** is scheduled to begin operation in early 1992 in time for Seville's Expo '92.

With roughly 20 million visitors expected to visit Seville this year, the city is undertaking some structural improvements. Seven new multimillion-dollar permanent bridges, designed by leading architects and engineers, will connect the city with La Cartuja, the island on which Expo '92 will be held. Aside from providing passage to the island, the bridges will facilitate vehicular traffic within the greater metropolitan area. The Madrid–Seville N-IV highway is being upgraded, and many sections are already completed. Construction began in 1990 on a new 2,000-foot suspension bridge across the Guadian River, which will connect Ayamonte in the Spanish province of Huelva with Portugal's Algarve.

Improved public transport facilities and extended travel services are among the key new features of interest to tourists visiting **Germany.** Hot on the heels of faster Intercity Express (ICE) trains introduced in 1991 comes news of even better service between northern and southern Germany. In 1992 visitors will be able to travel the 675 kilometers (422 miles) between **Hamburg** and **Munich** in under six hours—cutting up to 30% off the old journey time.

Although Germany technically still has two separately administered state-owned rail systems—the Bundesbahn and former East Germany's Deutsche Reichsbahn—railroad links between the two "halves" of Germany will be considerably better in 1992. Several hundred new east–west services have been introduced since the middle of 1990, linking Berlin, Leipzig, and Dresden in the east with Hamburg, Frankfurt, Nürnberg, and Munich in the west.

A new international airport opens in Germany in 1992: The **Franz Josef Strauss Airport** (named after the late Bavarian state premier) replaces Munich's old and cramped **Riem Airport** sometime in early summer. The new airport, 10 years in the making, will be the biggest in southern Germany, capable of handling up to 14 million passengers a year. Situated 28 kilometers (17 miles) northeast of the city near the town of Freising, Franz Josef Strauss Airport is connected directly to Munich's downtown area by a new, fast train line.

Reunification has brought a big increase in air traffic to and from **Berlin.** The Tempelhof airfield in west Berlin and east Berlin's Schönefeld Airport are both being expanded to re-lieve the extra load on Tegel, Berlin's main airport. Though it probably won't catch on for a while, Tegel was recently renamed the Otto Lilienthal Airport, in honor of the Berlin engineer who was the first man to fly farther than 15 yards.

Fodor's Choice

No two people will agree on what makes a perfect vacation, but it can be fun and helpful to know what others think. In compiling this list, we've included choices from each of the 22 cities covered in the book, and we hope that you'll have a chance to experience some of them yourself. For more detailed information about each entry, refer to the appropriate chapters within this guidebook.

Hotels

Amsterdam	Golden Tulip Pulitzer (*Expensive*)
	Hotel de l'Europe (*Very Expensive*)
Berlin	The Grand (*Very Expensive*)
Florence	Monna Lisa (*Expensive*)
Munich	Vier Jahreszeiten (*Very Expensive*)
Paris	The Ritz (*Very Expensive*)
Rome	Hassler-Villa Medici (*Very Expensive*)
Stockholm	Clas på Hörnet (*Expensive*)
Zurich	Sonnenberg (*Moderate*)

Restaurants

Barcelona	Eldorado Petit (*Very Expensive*)
Brussels	Comme Chez Soi (*Very Expensive*)
Budapest	Kisbuda (*Moderate*)
London	Bibendum (*Expensive*)
Munich	Aubergine (for lunch) (*Very Expensive*)
Paris	Tour d'Argent (*Very Expensive*)
Rome	El Toulà (*Very Expensive*)
Vienna	Zu den Drei Husaren (*Very Expensive*)
Zurich	Bierhalle Kropf (*Moderate*)
	Kronenhalle (*Expensive*)

Monuments

Brussels	The Atomium, Laeken
Madrid	The Valley of the Fallen
Paris	The Arc de Triomphe
Prague	Starý Židovsky Hřbitov (Old Jewish Cemetery)

Rome   The Pantheon

Museums and Galleries

Amsterdam   Rijksmuseum Vincent Van Gogh

Berlin   Pergamon Museum

Lisbon   Gulbenkian Foundation

London   Queen's Gallery

Madrid   Prado Museum

Munich   Alte and Neue Pinakotheks

Festivals

Amsterdam   Holland Festival of Opera and Ballet

Dublin   St. Patrick's Day Parade

Munich   Oktoberfest

Venice   Venice Carnavale

Churches, Temples, and Mosques

Budapest   The medieval synagogue

Florence   San Lorenzeo

Munich   Asamkirche

Rome   St. Peter's

Vienna   Karlskirche

Parks and Gardens

London   Regent's Park and Queen Mary's Gardens

Prague   Vrtbovská Zahrada

For Children

Barcelona   Snowflake, the albino gorilla in the Barcelona zoo

Berlin   Zoologischer Garten (Zoo)

Brussels   Brupark

Copenhagen   Tivoli Gardens

London   The Whispering Gallery of St. Paul's

Paris   Le Jardin d'Acclimatation
Ride to the top of the Eiffel Tower

Rome   The view from the roof of St. Peter's

Shopping

Athens	Natural sponges
Brussels	Lace
Dublin	Donegal tweeds
Florence	Shoes
Munich	Nymphenburg porcelain
Paris	Chocolates from the Maison du Chocolat
Prague	Bohemian crystal

Europe

World Time Zones

| +12 | +13 | -9 | | | | -5 | -4 | -3 | | 25 |

Numbers below vertical bands relate each zone to Greenwich Mean Time (0 hrs.).
Local times frequently differ from these general indications,
as indicated by light-face numbers on map.

| +11 | +12 - | -11 | -10 | -9 | -8 | -7 | -6 | -5 | -4 | -3 | -2 |

Algiers, **29**   Berlin, **34**   Delhi, **48**   Istanbul, **40**
Anchorage, **3**   Bogotá, **19**   Denver, **8**   Jerusalem, **42**
Athens, **41**   Budapest, **37**   Djakarta, **53**   Johannesburg, **44**
Auckland, **1**   Buenos Aires, **24**   Dublin, **26**   Lima, **20**
Baghdad, **46**   Caracas, **22**   Edmonton, **7**   Lisbon, **28**
Bangkok, **50**   Chicago, **9**   Hong Kong, **56**   London (Greenwich), **27**
Beijing, **54**   Copenhagen, **33**   Honolulu, **2**   Los Angeles, **6**
                      Dallas, **10**   Madrid, **38**
                                                                     Manila, **57**

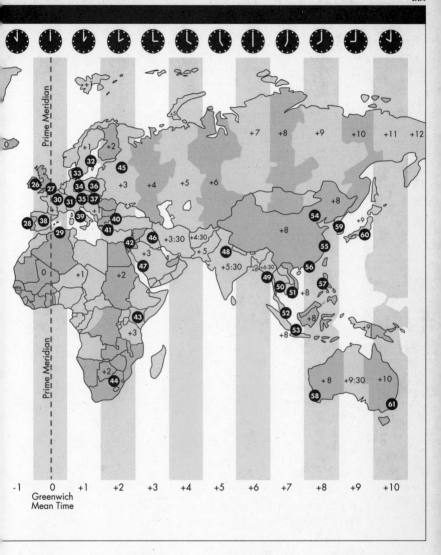

1 Essential Information

Before You Go

Government Tourist Offices

Austria Austrian National Tourist Office. **In the United States:** 500 Fifth Ave., 20th Floor, New York, NY 10110, tel. 212/944–6880; 500 N. Michigan Ave., Suite 1950, Chicago, IL 60611, tel. 312/644–5556; 11601 Wilshire Blvd., Suite 2480, Los Angeles, CA 90025, tel. 213/477–3332; 1300 Post Oak Blvd., Suite 960, Houston, TX 77056, tel. 713/850–9999.
In Canada: 1010 Sherbrooke St. W., Suite 1410, Montreal, Quebec H3A 2R7, tel. 514/849–3709; 200 Granville St., Suite 1380, Vancouver, British Columbia V6C 1S4, tel. 604/683–5808; 2 Bloor St. E., Suite 3330, Toronto, Ontario M4W 1A8, tel. 416/967–3381.
In the United Kingdom: 30 St. George St., London W1R OAL, tel. 071/629–0461.

Belgium Belgian National Tourist Office. **In North America:** 745 Fifth Ave., Suite 714, New York, NY 10151, tel. 212/758–8130.
In The United Kingdom: Premier House, 2 Gayton Rd., Harrow, Middlesex HA1 2XU, tel. 081/861–3300.

Czechoslovakia Czechoslovak Travel Bureau and Tourist Office (Cedok). **In North America:** 10 E. 40th St., New York, NY 10016, tel. 212/689–9720.
In the United Kingdom: 17–18 Old Bond St., London W1X 4RB, tel. 071/629–6058.

Denmark Danish Tourist Board. **In the United States:** 655 Third Ave., New York, NY 10017, tel. 212/949–2333.
In Canada: Box 115, Station N, Toronto, Ontario M8V 3S4, tel. 416/823–9620.
In the United Kingdom: Sceptre House, 169–173 Regent St., London W1R 8PY, tel. 071/734–2637.

France French Government Tourist Office. **In the United States:** 610 Fifth Ave., New York, NY 10020, tel. 212/315–0888; 645 N. Michigan Ave., Chicago, IL 60611, tel. 312/337–6301; 2305 Cedar Springs Rd., Dallas, TX 75201, tel. 214/720–4010; 9454 Wilshire Blvd., Beverly Hills, CA 90212, tel. 213/271–6665.
In Canada: 1981 McGill College, Suite 490, Montreal, Quebec H3A 2W9, tel. 514/288–4264; 1 Dundas St. W., Suite 2405, Box 8, Toronto, Ontario M5G 1Z3, tel. 416/593–4717.
In the United Kingdom: 178 Piccadilly, London W1V OAL, tel. 01/491–7622 or 071/499–6911.

Germany German National Tourist Office. **In the United States:** 747 Third Ave., New York, NY 10017, tel. 212/308–3300; 444 S. Flower St., Suite 2230, Los Angeles, CA 90071, tel. 213/688–7332.
In Canada: 175 Bloor St. E., Suite 604, Toronto, Ontario M4W 3R8, tel. 416/968–1570.
In the United Kingdom: 65 Curzon St., London W1Y 7PE, tel. 071/495–3990.

Great Britain British Tourist Authority. **In the United States:** 40 W. 57th St., New York, NY 10019, tel. 212/581–4700; 625 N. Michigan Ave., Suite 1510, Chicago, IL 60611, tel. 312/787–0490; World Trade Center, 350 S. Figueroa St., Suite 450, Los Angeles, CA 90071, tel. 213/628–3525; 2305 Cedar Springs Rd., Suite 210, Dallas, TX 75201, tel. 214/720–4040.

In Canada: 94 Cumberland St., Suite 600, Toronto, Ontario M5R 3N3, tel. 416/925–6326.
In the United Kingdom: Thames Tower, Black's Rd., Hammersmith, London W6 9EL, tel. 081/846–9000.

Greece **Greek National Tourist Organization: In the United States:** 645 Fifth Ave., New York, NY 10022, tel. 212/421–5777; 611 W. 6th St., Suite 2198, Los Angeles, CA 90017, tel. 213/626–6696; 168 N. Michigan Ave., Chicago, IL 60601, tel. 312/782–1084.
In Canada: 1233 Rue de la Montagne, Montreal, Quebec H3G 1Z2, tel. 514/871–1535; 1300 Bay St., Toronto, Ontario M5R 3K8, tel. 416/968–2220.
In the United Kingdom: 4 Conduit St., London W1R 0DJ, tel. 071/734–5997.

Hungary **Hungarian Travel Bureau (IBUSZ). In North America:** 1 Parker Plaza, Suite 1104, Fort Lee, NJ 07024, tel. 201/592–8585.
In the United Kingdom: Danube Travel Ltd. (authorized agent), 6 Conduit St., London W1R 9TG, tel. 071/493–0263.

Ireland **Irish Tourist Board. In the United States:** 757 Third Ave., New York, NY 10017, tel. 212/418–0800 or 800/223–6470.
In Canada: 160 Bloor St. E., Suite 934, Toronto, Ontario M4W 1B9, tel. 416/929–2777.
In the United Kingdom: Ireland House, 150 New Bond St., London W1Y OAQ, tel. 071/493–3201.

Italy **Italian Government Travel Office (ENIT). In the United States:** 630 Fifth Ave., Suite 1565, New York, NY 10111, tel. 212/245–4822; 500 N. Michigan Ave., Suite 1046, Chicago, IL 60611, tel. 312/644–0990; 360 Post St., Suite 801, San Francisco, CA 94108, tel. 415/392–6206.
In Canada: 1 Place Ville Marie, Suite 1914, Montreal, Quebec H3B 3M9, tel. 514/866–7667.
In the United Kingdom: 1 Princes St., London W1R 8AY, tel. 071/408–1254.

Netherlands **Netherlands Board of Tourism. In the United States:** 355 Lexington Ave., New York, NY 10017, tel. 212/370–7367; 225 N. Michigan Ave., Suite 326, Chicago, IL 60601, tel. 312/819–0300; 90 New Montgomery St., Suite 305, San Francisco, CA 94105, tel. 415/543–6772.
In Canada: 25 Adelaide St. E., Suite 710, Toronto, Ontario M5C 1Y2, tel. 416/363–1577.
In the United Kingdom: 25–28 Buckingham Gate, London SW1E 6LD, tel. 071/630–0451.

Portugal **Portuguese National Tourist Office. In the United States:** 590 Fifth Ave., New York, NY 10036, tel. 212/354–4403.
In Canada: 2180 Yonge St., Toronto, Ontario M4S 2B9, tel. 416/250–7575.
In the United Kingdom: 1–5 New Bond St., London W1Y 0NP, tel. 071/493–3873.

Spain **Spanish National Tourist Office. In the United States:** 665 Fifth Ave., New York, NY 10022, tel. 212/759–8822; 845 N. Michigan Ave., Chicago, IL 60611, tel. 312/642–1992; San Vicente Plaza Bldg., 8383 Wilshire Blvd., Suite 960, Beverly Hills, CA 90211, tel. 213/658–7188.
In Canada: 102 Bloor St. W., Suite 1400, Toronto, Ontario M5S 1M8, tel. 416/961–3131.
In the United Kingdom: 57–58 St. James's St., London SW1A 1LD, tel. 071/499–4593 or 071/499–0901.

Sweden Swedish Tourist Board. In North America: 655 Third Ave., New York, NY 10017, tel. 212/949–2333.
In the United Kingdom: 29–31 Oxford St., 5th floor, London W1R 1RE, tel. 071/437–5816.

Switzerland Swiss National Tourist Office. In the United States: 608 Fifth Ave., New York, NY 10020, tel. 212/757–5944; 260 Stockton St., San Francisco, CA 94108, tel. 415/362–2260.
In Canada: 154 University Ave., Suite 610, Toronto, Ontario M5H 3Y9, tel. 416/971–9734.
In the United Kingdom: Swiss Center, 1 New Coventry St., London W1V 8EE, tel. 071/734–1921.

Tour Groups

The range of tours to Europe is immense, with everything from fully escorted to almost entirely independent trips available, and at prices to suit almost every pocketbook. Whatever your budget, package tours often add value to your trip by providing lower airfares and hotel rates than you would get on your own. There can be trade-offs, of course—you may find yourself dining with 20 strangers and marching to the beat of a tour director's drum.

When considering a tour, be sure to find out (1) exactly what expenses are included, particularly tips, side trips, meals, and entertainment; (2) the ratings of all hotels on the itinerary and the facilities they offer; (3) the additional cost of single, rather than double, accommodations if you are traveling alone; and (4) the number of travelers in your group. Note whether the tour operator reserves the right to change hotels, routes, or even prices after you've booked, and check out the operator's policy regarding cancellations, complaints, and trip-interruption insurance. Many tour operators request that packages be booked through a travel agent; there is generally no additional charge for doing so.

It is beyond the scope of this book to provide a full listing of the many hundreds of tours to Europe currently catalogued. The following is only a sampling of packages from some of the most established, experienced operators. For more information, contact your travel agent.

General-Interest Tours American Express Vacations (Box 5014, Atlanta, GA 30302, tel. 800/241–1700 or, in Georgia, 800/282–0800) offers a veritable supermarket of tours. At last count, it had about 70 ways to see Europe, including 14 tours under the general title "Europe in Depth." "Tempo," for example, is a classic grand tour stopping in England, France, Switzerland, Italy, Austria, Germany, and Holland over a frenetic 15 days.
Globus-Gateway/Cosmos (150 S. Los Robles Ave., Suite 860, Pasadena, CA 91101, tel. 818/449–0919 or 800/556–5454) has a wide variety of high-quality tours from the mind-boggling "Super European"—a Globus-Gateway tour of 14 countries in 38 days—to regional and city tours. Cosmos is generally the more budget-minded of the affiliated companies.
Caravan Tours (401 N. Michigan Ave., Chicago, IL 60611, tel. 312/321–9800, weighs in with six grand tours and a variety of regional tours. Caravan's "Two Week Slow and Easy" is a welcome change of pace with only four countries—England, France, Switzerland, and Italy—over 17 days.

If you are willing to pay for luxury, **Abercrombie & Kent International** (1420 Kensington Rd., Oak Brook, IL 60521, tel. 708/954–2944 or 800/323–7308) offers some posh programs. Other popular operators include **Maupintour** (Box 807, Lawrence, KS 66044, tel. 913/843–1211 or 800/255–4266) and **Olson-Travelworld** (100 N. Sepulveda Blvd., Suite 1010, El Segundo, CA 90245, tel. 800/421–2255, in California 213/615–0711 or 800/421–5785).

In the United Kingdom, **Thomas Cook** (Box 36, Thorpe Wood, Peterborough PE3 6SB, tel. 0800–881234 or 0733/332255) offers a massive range of European vacations, either escorted tours or packages for the independent traveler, but with a representative on site to help out if needed.

Thomson Holidays (Greater London House, Hampstead Rd., London NW1 7SD, tel. 081/200–8733), another market leader, offers vacations in almost every resort in Europe. A similar company with a wide range of packages is **Enterprise** (Groundstar House, London Rd., Crawley, West Sussex RH10 2TB, tel. 0293/560777). Check out the brochures from these companies, particularly for fly/drive deals, which are often the best-value options for getting around Europe.

Special-Interest Tours
Art/Architecture

Esplanade Tours (581 Boylston St., Boston, MA 02116, tel. 617/266–7465) and **Exprinter Tours** (500 Fifth Ave., New York, NY 10110, tel. 212/719–1200) concentrate on Europe's rich heritage. **Olson-Travelworld's** (*see* General-Interest Tours, above) "From the Rijksmuseum to the Louvre" covers a staggering range of artistic treasures.

In the United Kingdom, **Prospect Music & Art Tours Ltd.** (454–458 Chiswick High Rd., London W4 5TT, tel. 081/742–2323 or 081/995–2163) offers a comprehensive range of art and architecture tours, including Great Britain, France, Spain, Italy, Austria, Holland, Germany, Turkey, and Switzerland.

Christmas/Culture

"Christmas in Europe and the Kaiserball" is one of **Olson-Travelworld's** (*see* General-Interest Tours, above) unique packages. The program includes a traditional white Christmas in the Swiss Alps, a performance at the marionette theater in Salzburg, and the exclusive Kaiserball in Vienna.

In the United Kingdom, **Swan Hellenic Art Treasures Tours** (77 New Oxford St., London WC1A 1PP, tel. 071/831–1616) has Christmas tours to several European cities.

Music

Dailey-Thorp Travel (315 W. 57th St., New York, NY 10019, tel. 212/307–1555) transforms the traditional grand tour into the "Grand Opera Tour of Europe." Stops on the deluxe program generally include Paris, Milan, Vienna, and London, although itineraries vary according to available performances. "Musical Heartland of Europe" features musical performances in Berlin, Dresden, and Prague, while "Prague, Budapest, Vienna" highlights the historic capitals of the Habsburg Empire. All tours are deluxe, with generally excellent seats for performances.

In the United Kingdom, **Brompton Travel Ltd.** (64–66 Richmond Rd., Kingston-upon-Thames, Surrey KT2 5EH, tel. 081/549–3334) will arrange tickets and book your flights and accommodations for musical events in Europe and offers several opera tours. **Prospect Music & Art Tours** (*see* Art/Architecture Tours) has many music tours.

Singles and
Young Couples **Trafalgar Tours** (21 E. 26th St., New York, NY 10010, tel. 212/689–8977 or 800/854–0103) offers "Club 21–35," faster paced tours for travelers unafraid of a little physical activity—from bike riding to discoing the night away.

Sports **Travel Concepts** (373 Commonwealth Ave., Suite 601, Boston, MA 02115, tel. 617/266–8450) gives you the choice of the British Open Golf Tournament, the Henley Royal Regatta, or, if you prefer to play rather than sit, the Rangitiki Polo School in Windsor, England, or the SAS Bjorn Borg Tennis Clinic in Stockholm.

In the United Kingdom, **Caravela Tours** (38–44 Gillingham St., London SW1V 1JW, tel. 071/630–9223) has tennis and golf vacations in Portugal.

Wine/Cuisine **Travel Concepts** (see Sports, above) serves up some exceptional food and drink in France, Germany, Italy, Switzerland, Scandinavia, England, and Ireland. Gracious living (and dining) is also available from **Floating Through Europe** (271 Madison Ave., New York, NY 10016, tel. 212/685–5600 or 800/221–3140) with deluxe barge cruises on inland waterways in England, France, Belgium, and Holland.

In the United Kingdom, **World Wine Tours Ltd.** (Drayton St. Leonard, Oxon OX10 7BH, tel. 0865/891919) has wine-tasting tours of Germany, along the Rhine, and France in the region of Alsace, as well as of other countries.

Package Deals for Independent Travelers

Globus-Gateway/Cosmos, DER Tours, American Express, and **Abercrombie & Kent** (see General-Interest Tours, above) all offer packages for independent travelers, with choices of hotels, air, ground transportation, and sightseeing. The international airlines are also good sources, particularly **TWA Getaway Vacations** (800–GETAWAY) and **Pan Am Holidays** (800–THE-TOUR). **CIE Tours** (122 E. 42nd St., New York, NY 10168, tel. 212/972–5600 or 800/CIE–TOUR) specializes in "fly/drive" tours, as does DER Tours.

In the United Kingdom, the companies mentioned in General-Interest Tours are good for the independent traveler, as well as for those who prefer to have their activities organized for them. These companies offer flights and accommodations; tours and activities are offered as optional extras once you arrive at your destination. Company representatives are usually on hand to help you organize anything that may not be covered in their programs.

Festivals and Seasonal Events

The following is just a sampling of the special events in Europe throughout the year; a complete list would fill an entire book. A good overall guide—*Major Events in Europe*—is available from the **European Travel Commission,** 630 Fifth Ave., Suite 565, New York, NY 10111, tel. 212/307–1200.

January **Austria.** Carnival in Vienna.
France. International Circus Festival.
Great Britain. International Boat Show, Earl's Court, London.
Greece. Epiphany celebrations (January 6) nationwide.
Italy. Epiphany celebrations (January 6) nationwide.

February **Great Britain.** Cruft's Dog Show, Earl's Court, London.
Hungary. Gypsy Festival, Budapest.

March **Austria.** Haydn Festival, Vienna.
France. Prix du Président de la République horse race, Paris; Paris Opera Season opens.
Germany. Fasching season or Carnival, nationwide; Munich Fashion Week.
Holland. Carnival celebrations nationwide; Amsterdam Arts Weeks, cultural events.
Hungary. Spring Festival, Budapest.
Ireland. St. Patrick's Week is celebrated in Dublin.
Italy. Carnival in Venice.
Portugal. Carnival of Portugal nationwide.
Spain. Carnival celebrations nationwide.

April **Austria.** International Music and Drama Festival, Vienna.
Belgium. International Fair, Brussels.
France. Le Mans 24-hour motorcycle race; major horse races, Paris.
Germany. Munich Ballet Days.
Great Britain. Camden Festival (London) and London Marathon.
Greece. Easter processions nationwide.
Italy. Explosion of the Cart, Easter folklore event, Florence; Good Friday procession, Rome.
Portugal. Festival of the Crosses.
Spain. Holy Week processions, nationwide.
Sweden. Walpurgis Night celebrations (April 30), nationwide.
Switzerland. Sechselauten Spring Festival, Zurich.

May **Austria.** International Music and Drama Festival, Vienna.
Czechoslovakia. Prague Music Festival.
Denmark. Ballet and Opera Festival, Copenhagen.
France. International Marathon, Paris; French Open Tennis Championship, Paris.
Great Britain. Chelsea Flower Show, London.
Holland. National Windmill Day, May 12.
Ireland. Royal Dublin Society Spring Show, Dublin.
Spain. San Isidro Festival, Madrid.

June **Austria.** Midsummer's Day celebrations nationwide; International Youth Music Festival, Vienna.
Denmark. Midsummer's Eve festivals nationwide.
France. Festival du Marais, Paris; Grand Steeplechase de Paris and Grand Prix de Paris; Tour de France Cycling Race begins.
Germany. Franco-German Folk Festival, Berlin; Munich Film Festival.
Great Britain. Derby Day, Epsom Racecourse; Royal Ascot Horse Race; Wimbledon Lawn Tennis Championships; Trooping the Colour at Whitehall, London.
Greece. Arts Festivals in Athens.
Holland. Holland Festival of International Performing Arts, Amsterdam.
Ireland. Festival of Music in Great Irish Houses, performed in several stately homes.
Italy. Regatta of the Great Maritime Republics, Venice.
Portugal. St. Anthony's Eve processions, Lisbon.
Sweden. Midsummer celebrations nationwide.
Switzerland. International Music, Theater, and Art Festival, Zurich.

July Belgium. Ommegang Pageant, Brussels.
Denmark. Rebildfest, since 1912, has been the largest celebration of America's independence (July 4) outside the United States; Jazz Festival, Copenhagen.
France. Festival Estival, Paris; Bastille Day (July 14) is celebrated nationwide.
Germany. Folk festivals nationwide; Munich Opera Festival.
Great Britain. City of London Festival; the Royal Tournament, Earl's Court, London.
Greece. Athens Festival, with opera, ancient drama, ballet, and concerts.
Italy. Gondolas gather for the Feast of the Redeemer, Venice; Festa de Noantri, with processions, parade of boats, and fireworks, Trastevere quarter, Rome.

August Belgium. Planting of the Mayboom Tree, Brussels.
Greece. Athens Festival at the Acropolis.
Ireland. Dublin Horse Show.
Italy. Venice Film Festival.
Switzerland. Swiss National Day (August 1).

September Austria. Harvest and wine festivities nationwide.
France. Festival of Autumn, Paris.
Germany. Oktoberfest, Munich.
Great Britain. Chelsea Antiques Fair, London.
Holland. The Boulevard of Broken Dreams is a potpourri of theatrical offerings in tents on Amsterdam's Museumplein.
Hungary. Budapest Arts Weeks.
Ireland. Dublin Theater Festival.
Italy. Two-oar gondolas compete in the Historic Regatta in Venice.
Portugal. Wine Vintage Festivals nationwide.
Spain. International Music Festival and Feast of the Merced, Barcelona.
Switzerland. Knabenschiessen festivities, Zurich.

October France. Prix de l'Arc de Triomphe, Longchamp Racecourse, Paris; International Auto Show, Paris.
Germany. Berlin International Marathon.
Great Britain. Horse of the Year Show, show jumping, Wembley Arena, London.
Greece. Athens Marathon.
Ireland. Dublin Theater Festival; Dublin International Marathon Road Race.
Italy. Wine festivals nationwide.

November Austria. Advent brings markets and exhibits in Vienna and performances by the Vienna Boys' Choir.
France. International Dance Festival, Paris.
Germany. Jazz Festival, Berlin; Antiques Fair, Berlin; International Six-Day Cycle Race, Munich.
Great Britain. London–Brighton Veteran Car Run; Lord Mayor's Procession and Show, London.
Italy. Feast of the Salute, Venice.

December Austria. The Imperial Ball, Imperial Palace, Vienna; "Silent Night, Holy Night" celebrations (December 24), nationwide.
Germany. Christmas markets in Munich, Berlin, and other cities.
Great Britain. International Show Jumping Championships, Olympia, London.

Italy. Feast of St. Ambrose celebrations, Milan; La Scala Opera Season opens, Milan; Christmas masses in Rome's basilicas.
Sweden. Santa Lucia Day (Dec. 13), Stockholm.

Climate

Current weather information on more than 750 cities around the world is only a phone call away. Dialing 900/370–8728 will connect you with the **WeatherTrak** computer, which you can access at the cost of 75¢ for the first minute and 50¢ per minute thereafter. A taped message will tell you to dial the three-digit access code to any of the destinations covered. The code is either the area code (in the United States) or the first three letters of the foreign city. For a list of all access codes send a stamped, self-addressed envelope to Cities, Box 7000, Dallas, TX 75209. For further information, phone 800/247–3282.

What to Pack

Pack light—porters and baggage trolleys are scarce. The luggage restrictions imposed on international flights help limit what you pack.

What you pack depends more on the season than on any particular dress code. In general, northern and central Europe have cold, snowy winters, and the Mediterranean countries have mild winters, though parts of southern Europe can be bitterly cold, too. In the Mediterranean resorts you may need a warm jacket for mornings and evenings, even in summer. The mountains usually are warm on summer days, but the weather, especially in the Alps, is unpredictable, and the nights are generally cool. The Pyrenees don't have much snow except in the higher elevations, but they have extremely damp, foggy weather and lots of rain year-round.

For European cities, pack as you would for an American city; formal outfits for first-class restaurants and nightclubs, casual clothes elsewhere. Jeans are as popular in Europe as they are in the rest of the world and are perfectly acceptable for sightseeing and informal dining. Sturdy walking shoes are appropriate for the cobblestone streets and gravel paths that fill many of the parks and surround some of the historic buildings. For visits to churches and cathedrals, especially in southern Europe, avoid shorts and immodest outfits. Italians are especially strict, insisting that women cover their shoulders and arms (a shawl will do). Women, however, no longer have to cover their heads in Roman Catholic churches.

To discourage purse snatchers and pickpockets, take a handbag with long straps that you can sling across your body, bandolier-style, and with a zippered compartment for money and other valuables.

You'll need an electrical adapter for hair dryers and other small appliances. The voltage in most parts of Europe is 220, with 50 cycles. If you stay in budget hotels, take your own soap: Many do not provide soap, and those that do often give guests only one tiny bar per room.

Taking Money Abroad

Traveler's checks and major U.S. credit cards—particularly Visa—are accepted throughout the major cities and resorts of Western Europe and in many cities of Eastern Europe. Even in Western Europe you'll need cash for some of the smaller cities and rural areas and for small restaurants and shops in the major cities. Although you won't get as good an exchange rate at home as abroad, it's wise to change a small amount of money into the currency of the country you're visiting (or the one you'll visit first) to avoid long lines at airport currency exchange booths. Most U.S. banks will exchange your money into foreign currency. If your local bank can't provide this service, contact **Deak International** (630 Fifth Ave., New York, NY 10111, tel. 212/635–0515).

For safety and convenience, it's always best to take traveler's checks. The most recognized traveler's checks are American Express, Barclay's, Thomas Cook, and those issued through major commercial banks such as Citibank and Bank of America. Some banks will issue the checks free to established customers, but most charge a 1% commission fee. Buy some of your traveler's checks in small denominations to cash toward the end of your trip. This will avoid having to cash a large check and ending up with more foreign money than you need. You can also buy traveler's checks in foreign currency, a good idea if the U.S. dollar is falling and you want to lock in the current rate. Remember to take along addresses of offices where you can get refunds for lost or stolen traveler's checks.

Banks and bank-operated exchange booths at airports and railroad stations are the best places to change money. Hotels and privately run exchange firms will give you a significantly lower rate of exchange.

Getting Money from Home

There are at least three ways to get money from home: (1) Have it sent through a large commercial bank with a branch in the European country you're visiting. The only drawback is that you must have an account with the bank; if not, you'll have to go through your own bank and the process will be slower and more expensive. (2) Have it sent through American Express. If you are a cardholder, you can cash a personal check or a counter check at an American Express office for up to $1,000; $200 will be in cash and $800 in traveler's checks. There is a 1% commission on the traveler's checks. American Express has a new service, American Express MoneyGram, that is now available in most major European cities. Through this service, you can receive up to $10,000 cash. To find out the American Express MoneyGram location nearest your home and the addresses of offices in Europe, call 800/543–4080. You do not need to be a cardholder to use this service. (3) Have it sent through Western Union (tel. 800/325–6000). If you have a MasterCard or Visa, you can have money sent for any amount up to your credit limit. If not, have someone take cash or a certified cashier's check to a Western Union office. The money will be delivered in two business days to a bank in the town where you're staying. Fees vary with the amount of money sent and the location of the recipient. For $1,000 the fee is $69; for $500, $59.

Passports and Visas

Americans All U.S. citizens need a **passport** to enter the 31 countries covered in this guide. Applications for a new passport must be made in person; renewals can be obtained in person or by mail (*see* below). First-time applicants should apply well in advance of their departure date to one of the 13 U.S. Passport Agency offices. In addition, local county courthouses, many state and probate courts, and some post offices accept passport applications. Necessary documents include: (1) a completed passport application (Form DSP-11); (2) proof of citizenship (either birth certificate with raised seal or naturalization papers); (3) proof of identity (unexpired driver's license, employee ID card, or any other document with your photograph and signature); (4) two recent, identical, two-inch-square photographs (black and white or color); (5) $42 application fee for a 10-year passport (those under 18 pay $27 for a 5-year passport). If you pay in cash, you must have the exact change. No change is given. Passports are mailed to you in about 10 working days.

To renew your passport by mail, you'll need a completed Form DSP-82; two recent, identical passport photographs; a recent passport (less than 12 years old from date of issue); and a check or money order for $35.

Many countries require **visas** for stays of three months or longer; apply at the country's embassy in Washington, DC.

Canadians All Canadians need **passports** to enter the 17 countries in this guide. Send the completed application (available at any post office or passport office) to the Bureau of Passports (Suite 215, West Tower, Guy Favreau Complex, 200 René Lévesque Blvd. West, Montreal, Quebec H2Z 1X4). Include $25, two photographs, a guarantor, and proof of Canadian citizenship. Applications can be made in person at the regional passport offices in Edmonton, Halifax, Montreal, Toronto, Vancouver, or Winnipeg. Passports are valid for five years and are nonrenewable.

Visas are required by Canadian citizens traveling to Hungary.

Britons All British citizens need **passports**; applications are available from travel agencies or a main post office. Send the completed form to your nearest regional passport office or to the Passport Office, Clive House, 70 Petty France, London SW1H 9HD (tel. 071/279–3434). The application must be countersigned by your bank manager or by a solicitor, barrister, doctor, clergyman, or justice of the peace who knows you personally. In addition, you'll need two photographs and the £15 fee. The occasional tourist may opt for a British Visitor's Passport. It is valid for one year and allows entry into other European Community (EC) countries only. It costs £7.50 and is nonrenewable. You'll need two passport photographs and identification. Apply at your local post office.

Customs and Duties

On Arrival Arrival formalities vary from country to country and are detailed in each chapter. In addition to specific duty-free allowances, most countries allow travelers also to bring in cameras and a reasonable amount of film and electronic equipment; most do not allow fresh meats, plants, weapons, and narcotics.

On Departure If you are bringing any foreign-made equipment from home, such as a camera, it's wise to carry the original receipt with you or to register such equipment with U.S. Customs before you leave (Form 4457). Otherwise you may end up paying duty on your return.

U.S. residents may bring home duty-free up to $400 worth of foreign goods, as long as they have been out of the country for at least 48 hours and they haven't made an international trip in 30 days. Each member of the family is entitled to the same exemption, regardless of age, and exemptions may be pooled. For the next $1,000 worth of goods, a flat 10% rate is assessed; duties vary with the merchandise for anything over $1,400. Included for travelers 21 or older are 1 liter of alcohol, 100 cigars (non-Cuban), and 200 cigarettes. Only 1 bottle of perfume trademarked in the United States may be brought in. However, there is no duty on antiques or art over 100 years old. Anything exceeding these limits will be taxed at the port of entry and may be taxed additionally in the traveler's home state. Unlimited amounts of goods from designated "developing" or GSP countries also may be brought in duty-free; check with the U.S. Customs Service (Box 7407, Washington, DC 20044). Gifts valued at under $50 may be mailed to friends or relatives at home duty-free, but not more than one package per day to any one addressee and not including perfumes costing more than $5 or tobacco or liquor.

Exemptions for returning **Canadians** range from $20 to $300, depending on the length of stay out of the country. For the $300 exemption, you must have been out of the country for one week. For any given year, you are allowed one $300 exemption. You may bring in duty-free up to 50 cigars, 200 cigarettes, 2.2 pounds of tobacco, and 40 ounces of liquor, provided these are declared in writing to customs on arrival and accompany the traveler in hand or checked-through baggage. Personal gifts should be mailed as "Unsolicited Gift—Value under $40." Request the Canadian Customs brochure "I Declare" for further details.

There are two levels of duty-free allowance for **Britons** returning to the United Kingdom: one, for goods bought outside the European Community (EC), or for goods bought in a duty-free shop within the EC; two, for goods bought in an EC country but not in a duty-free shop.

In the first category, you may import duty-free 200 cigarettes or 100 cigarillos or 50 cigars or 250 grams of tobacco, plus 1 liter of alcoholic drinks over 22% volume or 2 liters of alcoholic drinks not over 22% volume or fortified or sparkling wine, plus 2 liters of still table wine, plus 50 grams of perfume, plus 9 fluid ounces of toilet water, plus other goods to the value of £32.

In the second category, you may import duty-free 300 cigarettes or 150 cigarillos or 75 cigars or 400 grams of tobacco, plus 1.5 liters of alcoholic drinks over 22% volume or 3 liters of alcoholic drinks not over 22% volume or fortified or sparkling wine, plus 3 liters of still table wine, plus 75 grams of perfume, plus 13 fluid ounces of toilet water, plus other goods to the value of £265.

In addition, no animals or pets of any kind may be brought into the United Kingdom without a six-month quarantine. Penalties for evading this are severe and strictly enforced.

Traveling with Film

If your camera is new, shoot and develop a few rolls before leaving home. Pack some lens tissue and an extra battery for your built-in light meter. Invest about $10 in a skylight filter; it will protect the lens and also reduce haze.

Hot weather can damage film. If you're driving in summer, don't store film in the glove compartment or on the shelf under the rear window. Put it behind the front seat on the floor, on the side opposite the exhaust pipe.

On a plane trip, never pack unprocessed film in check-in luggage; if your bags get X-rayed, you can say good-bye to your pictures. Always carry undeveloped film with you through security and ask to have it inspected by hand (carry your film in a plastic bag for quick inspection). Inspectors at American airports are required by law to honor requests for hand inspection; abroad, you'll have to depend on the kindness of strangers.

The old airport scanning machines use heavy doses of radiation that can turn a family portrait into an early-morning fog. The newer models—used in all U.S. airports—are safe for anything from five to 500 scans, depending on the speed of your film. The effects are cumulative; you can put the same roll of film through several scans without worry. After five scans, though, you're asking for trouble.

If your film gets fogged and you want an explanation, send it to the National Association of Photographic Manufacturers (550 Mamaroneck Ave., Harrison, NY 10528). Experts will try to determine what went wrong. This service is free.

Photographing trains, junctions, or railway stations can land you in *serious* trouble in Eastern Europe. Turkish and, to a lesser extent, Greek authorities can also be sensitive. This is equally true of airports. Don't take pictures without making sure it is permitted.

Staying Healthy

There are no serious health risks associated with travel in Europe. However, the Centers for Disease Control (CDC) in Atlanta cautions that most of southern Europe is in the "intermediate" range for risk of contracting traveler's diarrhea. Part of this may be due to an increased consumption of olive oil and wine, which can have a laxative effect on stomachs used to a different diet. The CDC also advises that international travelers swim only in chlorinated swimming pools if there is any question about contamination of local beaches and freshwater lakes.

If you have a health problem that might require purchasing prescription drugs while in Europe, ask your doctor to prescribe the drug by its generic name. Brand names vary widely from one country to another.

The International Association for Medical Assistance to Travelers (IAMAT) is a worldwide association offering a list of approved English-speaking doctors whose training meets British and American standards. Contact IAMAT for a list of European physicians and clinics that belong to this network. **In the**

United States: 417 Center St., Lewiston, NY 14092, tel. 716/754–4883. **In Canada:** 40 Regal Rd., Guelph, Ontario, N1K 1B5. **In Europe:** 57 Voirets, 1212 Grand-Lancy, Geneva, Switzerland. Membership is free.

Shots and Medications Inoculations are not needed for Europe. The American Medical Association (AMA) recommends Pepto-Bismol for minor cases of traveler's diarrhea.

Insurance

Travelers may seek insurance coverage in three areas: health and accident, lost luggage, and trip cancellation. Your first step is to review your existing health and home-owner policies; some health insurance plans cover health expenses incurred while traveling, some major medical plans cover emergency transportation, and some home-owner policies cover the theft of luggage.

Health and Accident Several companies offer coverage designed to supplement existing health insurance for travelers:

Carefree Travel Insurance (Box 310, 120 Mineola Blvd., Mineola, NY 11501, tel. 516/294–0220 or 800/343–3149) provides coverage for emergency medical evacuation and accidental death and dismemberment. It also offers 24-hour medical phone advice.

International SOS Assistance (Box 11568, Philadelphia, PA 19116, tel. 215/244–1500 or 800/523–8930) provides emergency evacuation services, worldwide medical referrals, and optional medical insurance.

Travel Guard International, underwritten by Transamerica Occidental Life Companies (114 Clark St., Stevens Point, WI 54481, tel. 715/345–0505 or 800/782–5151), offers reimbursement for medical expenses with no deductibles or daily limits and emergency evacuation services.

Wallach and Company, Inc. (243 Church St. NW, Suite 100D, Vienna, VA 22180, tel. 703/281–9500 or 800/237–6615) offers comprehensive medical coverage, including emergency evacuation services worldwide.

Lost Luggage Airlines are responsible for lost or damaged property only up to $1,250 per passenger on domestic flights, and $9.07 per pound (or $20 per kilo) for checked baggage on international flights, and up to $400 per passenger for unchecked baggage on international flights. If you're carrying valuables, either take them with you on the airplane or purchase additional insurance for lost luggage. Some airlines will issue additional luggage insurance when you check in, but many do not. Insurance for lost, damaged, or stolen luggage is available through travel agents or directly through various insurance companies. Two that issue luggage insurance are **Tele-Trip** (Box 31685, 3201 Farnam St., Omaha, NE 68131, tel. 800/228–9792), a subsidiary of Mutual of Omaha, and **The Travelers Insurance Corporation** (Ticket and Travel Dept., 1 Tower Square, Hartford, CT 06183, tel. 203/277–0111 or 800/243–3174). Tele-Trip operates sales booths at airports and issues insurance through travel agents. Tele-Trip will insure checked luggage for up to 180 days; rates vary according to the length of the trip. The Travelers Insurance Corporation will insure checked or hand luggage for $500 to $2,000 valuation per person and for a maximum of 180 days. Rates for 1–5 days for $500 valuation are $10; for 180 days, $85.

Other companies with comprehensive policies include **Access America, Inc.,** a subsidiary of Blue Cross–Blue Shield (Box 1188, Richmond, VA 23230, tel. 800/334–7525 or 800/284–8300); and **Travel Guard International** (*see* Health and Accident Insurance, above).

In the United Kingdom, for free general advice on all aspects of holiday insurance, contact the **Association of British Insurers** (Aldermary House, 10–15 Queen St., London EC4N 1TT, tel. 071/248–4477). A provider of holiday insurance is **Europ Assistance** (252 High St., Croydon, Surrey CR0 1NF, tel. 081/680–1234).

Before you go, itemize the contents of each bag in case you need to file an insurance claim. Be certain to put your home or business address on each piece of luggage, including carry-on bags. If your luggage is lost or stolen and later recovered, the airline will deliver the luggage to your home free of charge.

Trip Cancellation Flight insurance is often included in the price of a ticket when paid for with American Express, Visa, and other major credit cards. It is usually included in combination travel insurance packages available from most tour operators, travel agents, and insurance agents.

Renting, Leasing, and Purchasing Cars

Renting It's best to arrange a car rental before you leave. You won't save money by waiting until you arrive in Europe, and you may find that the type of car you want is not available at the last minute. If you're flying into a major city and planning to spend some time there before using your car, save money by arranging to pick it up on the day of your departure. You'll have to weigh the added expense of renting a car from a major company with an airport office against the savings on a car from a budget company with offices in town. You could waste precious hours trying to locate the budget company in return for only a small financial saving. If you're arriving and departing from different airports, look for a one-way car rental with no return fees. If you're traveling to more than one country, make sure your rental contract permits you to take the car across borders and that the insurance policy covers you in every country you visit. Be prepared to pay more for a car with an automatic transmission; because they are not as readily available as those with manual transmission, reserve in advance.

Rental rates vary widely and depend on size and model, number of days you use the car, insurance coverage, and whether special drop-off fees are imposed. In most cases, rates quoted include unlimited free mileage and standard liability protection. Not included are Collision Damage Waiver (CDW), which eliminates your deductible payment should you have an accident; personal accident insurance; gasoline; or local taxes. European value-added taxes (VAT) vary from country to country, ranging from zero in Switzerland to a whopping 33.3% in France.

Rental companies usually charge according to the exchange rate of the dollar at the time the car is returned or when the credit card payment is processed. Three companies with special programs to help you hedge against the falling dollar, by guaranteeing advertised rates if you pay in advance, are: **Bud-**

get **Rent-a-Car** (3350 Boyington St., Carrollton, TX 75006, tel. 800/527–0700); **Connex Travel International** (983 Main St., Peekskill, NY 10566, tel. 800/333–3949); and **Cortell International** (17310 Red Hill Ave., Suite 360, Irvine, CA 92714, tel. 800/228–2535).

Other budget rental companies serving Europe include **Europe by Car** (1 Rockefeller Plaza, New York, NY 10020, tel. 212/245–1713, 800/223–1516 or in CA 800/252–9401); **Foremost Euro-Car** (Suite 306, 5430 Van Nuys Blvd., Van Nuys, CA 91401, tel. 800/423–3111); and **Kemwel** (106 Calvert St., Harrison, NY 10528, tel. 800/678–0678). Other major firms with European rentals include **Avis** (tel. 800/331–1212); **Hertz** (tel. 800/654–3001); and **National** or **Europcar** (tel. 800/CAR-RENT).

In the United Kingdom, there are offices of **Avis** (Hayes Gate House, Uxbridge Rd., Hayes, Middlesex UB4 0NJ, tel. 081/848–8733); **Hertz** (Radnor House, 1272 London Rd., London SW16 4XW, tel. 081/679–1799); and **Europcar/Godrey Davis Ltd.** (Bushey House, High St., Bushey, WD2 1RE, tel. 081/950–4080).

Driver's licenses issued in the United States and Canada are valid in Europe. Non-EEC nationals must have Green Card insurance (*see* By Car in Getting Around Europe, below). You might also take out an International Driving Permit before you leave in order to smooth out difficulties if you have an accident or as an additional piece of identification. Permits are available for a small fee through local offices of the **American Automobile Association** (AAA) and the **Canadian Automobile Association** (CAA), or from their main offices (AAA, 8111 Gatehouse Rd., Falls Church, VA 22047–0001, tel. 703/AAA–6000; and CAA, 2 Carlton St., Toronto, Ontario M5B 1K4, tel. 416/964–3170).

Britons driving in Europe should have a valid driver's license. Green Card insurance is a wise buy, though not compulsory for EEC nationals. All drivers must carry their car registration documents and a red warning triangle.

Leasing For trips of 21 days or more, you may save money by leasing a car. With the leasing arrangement, you are technically buying a car and then selling it back to the manufacturer after you've used it. You receive a factory-new car, tax-free, with international registration and extensive insurance coverage. Rates vary with the make and model of car and length of time used. Car-leasing programs are offered by Renault, Citroën, and Peugeot in France and by Volkswagen, Ford, Audi, and Opel, among others, in Belgium. Delivery can be arranged outside France and Brussels for an additional fee. Before you go, compare long-term rental rates with leasing rates. Remember to add taxes and insurance costs to the car rentals, something you don't have to worry about with leasing. Companies that offer leasing arrangements include Kemwel and Europe by Car, listed above.

Purchasing Given the weakness of the dollar on the international market and the logistical complexities of shipping a car home, the option of purchasing a car abroad is less appealing today than it was a decade ago. The advantage of buying a car in Europe is that you'll get what amounts to a free car rental during your stay in Europe. If you plan to purchase a car in Europe, be certain the prices quoted are for cars built to meet specifications set down by the U.S. Department of Transportation. If not, you will have to go through considerable expense to convert the car before you can legally drive it in the United States. You will also be subject to a U.S. customs duty. For more information, contact Kemwel or Europe by Car, both listed above, or ask your local car dealer to put you in touch with an importer.

Student and Youth Travel

The **International Student Identity Card (ISIC)** entitles students to youth rail passes, special fees on local transportation, Intra-European student charter flights, and discounts at museums, theaters, sports events, and many other attractions. If purchased in the United States, the $14 card also entitles the holder to $3,000 in emergency medical insurance, plus $100 a day for up to 60 days of hospital coverage. Apply to the **Council on International Educational Exchange** (CIEE, 205 E. 42nd St., 16th floor, New York, NY 10017, tel. 212/661–1414). In Canada, the ISIC is available for CN$12 from **Travel Cuts** (187 College St., Toronto, Ontario M5T 1P7, tel. 613/748–5638).

The **Youth International Educational Exchange Card** (YIEE), issued by the **Federation of International Youth Travel Organizations** (FIYTO, 81 Islands Brugge, DK-2300 Copenhagen S, Denmark), provides similar services to nonstudents under 26 years of age. In the United States, the card is available from CIEE (*see* above). In Canada, the YIEE card is available from the **Canadian Hostelling Association** (CHA, 1600 James Naismith Dr., Suite 698, Gloucester, Ontario K1B 5N4, tel. 613/ 748–5638).

An **International Youth Hostel Federation** (IYHF) membership card is the key to inexpensive dormitory-style accommodations at thousands of youth hostels around the world. Hostels provide separate sleeping quarters and are situated in a variety of locations, including converted farmhouses, villas, restored castles, and specially constructed modern buildings. There are more than 5,000 hostel locations in 68 countries around the world. IYHF memberships, which are valid for 12 months from the time of purchase, are available in the United States through **American Youth Hostels** (AYH, Box 37613, Washington, DC 20013, tel. 202/783–6161). The cost for a first-year membership is $25 for adults 18 to 54. Renewal thereafter is $15. For youths (17 and under) the rate is $10 and for senior citizens (55 and older) the rate is $15. Family membership is available for $35. Every national hostel association offers special reductions for members visiting its country, such as discounted rail fare or free bus travel, so be sure to ask for an international concessions list when you buy your membership. IYHF also publishes an extensive directory of youth hostels around the world. Economical bicycle tours for small groups of adventurous, energetic students are another popular AYH student travel service. For information on these and other AYH services and publications, contact the AYH at the address above.

In the United Kingdom, contact the **Youth Hostel Association** (YHA, Trevelyan House, 8 St. Stephen's Hill, St. Albans, Herts AL1 2DY, tel. 0727/45047).

Council Travel, a CIEE subsidiary, is the foremost U.S. student travel agency and specializes in low-cost charters and serves as the exclusive U.S. agent for many student airfare bargains and student tours. The 80-page *Student Travel Catalog* and *Council Charter* brochure are available free from any Council Travel office in the United States (enclose $1 postage if ordering by mail). Contact CIEE headquarters at the address above, or Council Travel offices in Amherst, Austin, Berkeley, Boston, Cambridge, Chicago, Dallas, La Jolla, Long Beach, Los Angeles, New York, Portland, Providence, San Diego, San Francisco, and Seattle, to name a few.

The **Educational Travel Center,** another student travel specialist worth contacting for information on student tours, bargain fares, and bookings, may be reached at 438 N. Frances St., Madison, WI 53703, tel. 608/256–5551.

Students who would like to work abroad should contact CIEE's **Work Abroad Department** at the address given above. The council arranges various types of paid and voluntary work experiences overseas for up to six months. CIEE also sponsors study programs in Europe, Latin America, and Asia, and publishes many books of interest to the student traveler, including *Work, Study, Travel Abroad: The Whole World Handbook* ($10.95 plus $1 book-rate postage or $2.50 first-class postage), and *Volunteer! The Comprehensive Guide to Voluntary Service in the U.S. and Abroad* ($6.95 plus $1 book-rate postage or $2.50 first-class postage).

The Information Center at the **Institute of International Education** (IIE, 809 UN Plaza, New York, NY 10017, tel. 212/984–5413) has reference books, foreign university catalogues, study-abroad brochures, and other materials that may be consulted by students and nonstudents alike, free of charge. The Information Center is open weekdays 10–4.

IIE administers a variety of grant and study programs offered by U.S. and foreign organizations, and publishes a well-known annual series of study-abroad guides, including *Academic Year Abroad, Vacation Study Abroad,* and *Study in the United Kingdom and Ireland.* The institute also publishes *Teaching Abroad,* a book of employment and study opportunities overseas for U.S. teachers. For a current list of IIE publications, along with prices and ordering information, write to the IIE Publications Service at the address given above. Books must be purchased by mail or in person; telephone orders are not accepted. General information on IIE programs and services is available from its regional offices in Atlanta, Chicago, Denver, Houston, San Francisco, and Washington, DC.

For information on the Eurail Youthpass, *see* Rail Passes.

Traveling with Children

Publications *A Capital Guide for Kids: A London Guide for Parents with Small Children* by Vanessa Miles (Allison & Busby, 6a Noel St., London W1V 3RB; £1.95). *Children's Guide to London* by Christopher Pick (Cadogan Books, 16 Lower Marsh, London SE1 7RJ; $8.50). *Family Travel Times* is an 8- to 12-page newsletter published 10 times a year by TWYCH (Travel with Your Children, 80 Eighth Ave., New York, NY 10011, tel. 212/206–0688). Subscription includes access to back issues and twice-weekly opportunities to call in for specific advice. *Kids' London* by Elizabeth Holt and Molly Perham (St. Martin's Press, $5.95). *Young People's Guide to Munich* is a free pamphlet available from the German National Tourist Office (747 Third Ave., New York, NY 10017, tel. 212/308–3300).

Family Travel Organizations   **American Institute for Foreign Study** (AIFS; 102 Greenwich Ave., Greenwich, CT 06830, tel. 203/869–9090) offers programs for college students and interested adults. For information on programs for high-school aged students and their families, contact the **Educational Travel Division, American Council for International Studies** (19 Bay State Rd., Boston, MA 02215, tel. 617/236–2015 or 800/825–AIFS).

Families Welcome! (Box 16398, Chapel Hill, NC 27516, tel. 800/326–0724) is a travel agency that arranges England and France tours brimming with family-oriented choices and activities.

The French Experience (370 Lexington Ave., New York, NY 10017, tel. 212/986–3800) is an organization that understands family needs.

Getting There   On international flights, children under two not occupying a seat pay 10% of adult fare. Various discounts apply to children two to 12 years of age. Regulations about infant travel on airplanes are in the process of changing. Until they do, however, if you want to be sure your infant is secure and traveling in his or her own safety seat, you must buy a separate ticket and bring your own infant car seat. (Check with the airline in advance; certain seats aren't allowed. Or write for the booklet "Child/Infant Safety Seats Acceptable for Use in Aircraft," from the Federal Aviation Administration, APA-200, 800 Independence Ave., SW, Washington, DC 20591, tel. 202/267–3479.) Some airlines allow babies to travel in their own car seats at no charge if there's a spare seat available; otherwise safety seats will be stored and the child will have to be held by a parent. (If you opt to hold your baby on your lap, do so with the infant outside the seatbelt so he or she won't be crushed in case of a sudden stop.)

Also inquire about special children's meals or snacks. *Family Travel Times* includes "TWYCH's Airline Guide," which contains a rundown of the children's services offered by 46 airlines.

Hotels   **Novotel** hotels in Europe permit up to two children to stay free in their parents' room. Many Novotel properties have playgrounds. (International reservations, tel. 800/221–4542.)

Sofitel hotels in Europe offer a free second room for children during July and August and over the Christmas holiday, depending upon availability. (International reservations, tel. 800/221–4542.)

Happy Family Swiss Hotels are 22 properties in Switzerland that have joined together to welcome families, offering outstanding programs for children at reduced prices. A brochure on these hotels is available from the Swiss National Tourist Office (608 Fifth Ave., New York, NY 10019, tel. 212/757–5944).

Club Med (40 W. 57th St., New York, NY 10019, tel. 800/CLUB–MED) has "Baby Clubs" (from age four months), "Mini Clubs" (for ages four to six or eight, depending on the resort), and "Kids Clubs" (for ages eight and up during school holidays) at many of its resort villages in France, Italy, Switzerland, and Spain.

In Germany, families should consider any one of the **Schloss** (castle) hotels, many of which are located on parklike grounds. United States representatives: **Europa Hotels and Tours** (tel.

800/523–9570 or, in Washington, 206/485–6985); **DER Tours, Inc.** (tel. 800/937–1234 or, in California, 213/479–4411).

CIGA hotels (Reservations, tel. 800/221–2340) has 22 properties in Italy, all of which welcome families.

Villa Rentals **At Home Abroad, Inc.** (405 E. 56th St., Suite 6H, New York, NY 10022, tel. 212/421–9165).
Villas International (71 W. 23rd St., New York, NY 10010, tel. 212/929–7585 or 800/221–2260).
Hideaways, Int'l (Box 1270, Littleton, MA 01460, tel. 508/486–8955).
B. & D. de Vogue (1830 S. Mooney Blvd., #113, Visalia, CA 93277, tel. 209/733–7119 or 800/727–4748).
Meeting Points (5515 S.E. Milwaukee Ave., Portland, OR 97207, tel. 503/233–1224).
Vacances en Campagne/Vacanze in Italia/Heritage of England (Box 297, Falls Village, CT 06031, tel. 203/824–5155 or 800/533–5405).
Italian Villa Rentals (Box 1145, Bellevue, WA 98009, tel. 206/827–3694).

Home Exchange Exchanging homes is a surprisingly low-cost way to enjoy a vacation abroad, especially a long one. The largest home-exchange service, **International Home Exchange Service** (Box 190070, San Francisco, CA 94119, tel. 415/435–3497) publishes three directories a year. Membership, which costs $45, entitles you to one listing and all three directories. **Loan-a-Home** (2 Park Lane, Apt. 6E, Mount Vernon, NY 10552) is popular with the academic community on sabbaticals and businesspeople on temporary assignments. There's no annual membership fee or charge to list your home, but one directory and a supplement costs $35. Loan-a-Home publishes two directories and two supplements each year. All four books cost $45 per year.

Baby-sitting To find out about recommended child-care arrangements, first
Services ask your hotel concierge. Also call the American embassy or consulate for a listing of child-care agencies with English-speaking personnel. Local tourist offices, especially in Germany, maintain an updated list of local baby-sitters.

Hints for Disabled Travelers

The Information Center for Individuals with Disabilities (Fort Point Place, 1st floor, 27–43 Wormwood St., Boston, MA 02210–1606, tel. 617/727–5540; TDD 617/727–5236) offers useful problem-solving assistance, including lists of travel agents who specialize in tours for the disabled.
Moss Rehabilitation Hospital Travel Information Service (1200 West Tabor Rd., Philadelphia, PA 19141–3009, tel. 215/456–9600, TDD 215/456–9602) provides information on tourist sights, transportation, and accommodations in destinations around the world for a small fee.
Mobility International USA (Box 3551, Eugene, OR 97403, tel. 503/343–1284) coordinates exchange programs for disabled people and offers information on accommodations and organized study programs around the world.
The Society for the Advancement of Travel for the Handicapped (26 Court St., Penthouse, Brooklyn, NY 11242, tel. 718/858–5483) offers access information. Annual membership costs $45, or $25 for senior travelers and students. Send a stamped, self-addressed envelope.

Travel Industry and Disabled Exchange (TIDE, 5435 Donna Ave., Tarzana, CA 91356, tel. 818/368–5648) is an industry-based organization with a $15 per-person annual membership fee. Members receive a quarterly newsletter and information on travel agencies and tours.

The Itinerary (Box 2012, Bayonne, NJ 07002, tel. 201/858–3400) is a bimonthly travel magazine for the disabled.

Access to the World: A Travel Guide for the Handicapped by Louise Weiss is available from Henry Holt & Co. for $12.95 plus $2 shipping (tel. 800/247–3912, order number is 0805 001417).

Hints for Older Travelers

The American Association of Retired Persons (AARP, 1909 K St., NW, Washington, DC 20049, tel. 202/662–4850) has two programs for independent travelers: (1) the Purchase Privilege Program, which entitles members to discounts on hotels, airfare, car rentals, and sightseeing, and (2) the AARP Motoring Plan, provided by Amoco, which offers emergency aid and trip routing information for an annual fee of $33.95 per couple. The AARP also arranges group tours, including apartment living in Europe. Contact **American Express Vacations** (Box 5014, Atlanta, GA 30302, tel. 800/241–1700 or, in Georgia, tel. 800/637–6200). AARP members must be 50 or older. Annual dues are $5 per person or per couple.

Elderhostel (75 Federal St., 3rd floor, Boston, MA 02110, tel. 617/426–7788) is an innovative educational program for people 60 and older. Participants live in dorms on some 1,200 campuses around the world. Mornings are devoted to lectures and seminars, afternoons to sightseeing and field trips. The all-inclusive fee for trips of 2–3 weeks, including room, board, tuition, and round-trip transportation, ranges from $1,800 to $4,500.

Saga International Holidays (120 Boylston St., Boston, MA 02216, tel. 800/343–0273) specializes in group travel for people over 60. A selection of variously priced tours allows you to choose the package that meets your needs.

The Discount Guide for Travelers over 55 by Caroline and Walter Weintz lists helpful addresses, package tours, reduced-rate car rentals, and so forth in the United States and abroad. To order, send $7.95 plus $1.50 shipping and handling to NAL/Cash Sales (Bergenfield Order Dept., 120 Woodbine St., Bergenfield, NJ 07621, tel. 800/526–0275).

Arriving and Departing

Because the air routes between North America and Europe are among the world's most heavily traveled, the passenger can choose from many airlines and fares. But fares change with stunning rapidity, so consult your travel agent on which bargains are currently available.

From North America by Plane

Be certain to distinguish among (1) nonstop flights—no changes, no stops; (2) direct flights—no changes but one or more stops; and (3) connecting flights—two or more planes, two or more stops.

Airlines The U.S. airlines that serve the major cities in Europe are **TWA** (tel. 800/892–4141); **Pan Am** (tel. 800/221–1111); **American Airlines** (tel. 800/433–7300); **Northwest** (tel. 800/447–4747); and **Delta** (tel. 800/241–4141).

Many European national airlines fly directly from the United States to their home countries. The biggest advantage in arriving on a home airline is that the landing privileges are often better, as are the facilities provided at main airports. Here are the U.S. telephone numbers of those airlines that have representation in the United States; most of the numbers are toll-free.

Austria: Austrian Airlines (tel. 800/843–0002)
Belgium: Sabena Belgian World Airlines (tel. 800/632–8050)
Czechoslovakia: Czechoslovak Airlines (CSA, tel. 212/682–5833)
Denmark: Scandinavian Airlines (SAS, tel. 800/221–2350)
France: Air France (tel. 800/237–2747)
Germany: Lufthansa (tel. 800/645–3880)
Great Britain: British Airways (tel. 800/247–9297); Virgin Atlantic (tel. 800/862–8621)
Greece: Olympic Airways (tel. 800/223–1226)
Holland: KLM Royal Dutch Airlines (tel. 800/777–5553)
Hungary: Malev Hungarian Airlines (tel. 212/757–6446)
Ireland: Aer Lingus (800/223–6537)
Italy: Alitalia (tel. 800/223–5730)
Portugal: TAP Air Portugal (tel. 800/221–7370)
Spain: Iberia Airlines (tel. 800/772–4642)
Sweden: Scandinavian Airlines (tel. 800/221–2350)
Switzerland: Swissair (tel. 800/221–4750)

Flying Time From New York: 6½ hours to London and 7–8 hours to Scandinavian capitals. From Chicago: 8½ hours to London, 10–11 hours to Scandinavian capitals. From Los Angeles: 10 hours to London, 12–13 hours to Scandinavian capitals.

Discount Flights The major airlines offer a range of tickets that can increase the price of any given seat by more than 300%, depending on the day of purchase. As a rule, the further in advance you buy the ticket, the less expensive it is and the greater the penalty (up to 100%) for canceling. Check with airlines for details.

The best buy is not necessarily an APEX (advance purchase) ticket on one of the major airlines, because these tickets carry certain restrictions: They must be bought in advance (usually 21 days); they restrict your travel, usually with a minimum stay of 7 days and a maximum of 90; and they also penalize you for changes—voluntary or not—in your travel plans. But if you can work around these drawbacks (and most travelers can), they are among the best-value fares available.

Travelers who are willing to put up with some restrictions and inconveniences in exchange for a substantially reduced air fare may be interested in flying as an air courier. A person who agrees to be a courier must accompany shipments between designated points. There are two sources of information on courier deals: (1) A telephone directory lists courier companies by the cities to which they fly. Send $5 and a self-addressed, stamped, business-size envelope to Pacific Data Sales Publishing, 2554 Lincoln Blvd., Suite 275-F, Marina Del Rey, CA 90291. (2) For a copy of a booklet called *A Simple Guide to Courier Travel*, send $14.95 (includes postage and handling) to Box 2394, Lake Oswego, OR 97035. For more information, call 800/344–9375.

Charter flights offer the lowest fares but often depart only on certain days, and seldom on time. Though you may be able to arrive at one city and return from another, you may lose all or most of your money if you cancel your trip. Don't sign up for a charter flight unless you've checked with a travel agency about the reputation of the packager. It's particularly important to know the packager's policy concerning refunds should a flight be canceled. One of the most popular charter operators is **Council Charter** (205 E. 42nd St., New York, NY 10017, tel. 212/661–0311 or 800/223–7402), a division of CIEE (Council on International Educational Exchange). Other companies advertise in Sunday travel sections of newspapers.

Somewhat more expensive—but up to 50% below the cost of APEX fares—are tickets purchased through consolidators, companies that buy blocks of tickets on scheduled airlines and sell them at wholesale prices. Here again, you may lose all or most of your money if you change plans, but at least you will be on a regularly scheduled flight with less risk of cancellation than on a charter. Once you've made your reservation, call the airline to confirm it. Among the best-known consolidators are **UniTravel** (Box 12485, St. Louis, MO 63132, tel. 314/569–2501 or 800/325–2222) and **Access International** (101 W. 31st St., Suite 1104, New York, NY 10001, tel. 212/465–0707 or 800/825–3633). Others advertise in Sunday newspaper travel sections.

A third option is to join a travel club that offers special discounts to its members. Three such organizations are **Moment's Notice** (425 Madison Ave., New York, NY 10017, tel. 212/486–0503), **Discount Travel International** (114 Forrest Ave., Narberth, PA 19072, tel. 215/668–7184), and **Worldwide Discount Travel Club** (1674 Meridian Ave., Suite 300, Miami Beach, FL 33139, tel. 305/534–2082). These cut-rate tickets should be compared with APEX tickets on the major airlines.

Enjoying the Flight If you're lucky enough to be able to sleep on a plane, it makes sense to fly at night. Many experienced travelers, however, prefer to take a morning flight to Europe and arrive in the evening, just in time for a good night's sleep. Because the air on a plane is dry, it helps, while flying, to drink a lot of nonalcoholic beverages; drinking alcohol contributes to jet lag, as does eating heavy meals on board. Feet swell at high altitudes, so it's a good idea to remove your shoes at the beginning of your flight. Sleepers usually prefer window seats to curl up against; those who like to move about the cabin ask for aisle seats. Bulkhead seats (in the front row of each cabin) have more legroom, but seat trays are attached to the arms of your seat rather than to the back of the seat in front.

Smoking You can request a nonsmoking seat during check-in or when you book your ticket. If the airline tells you on the day of the flight that there are no seats available in the nonsmoking section, insist on one: Department of Transportation regulations require U.S. carriers to find seats for all nonsmokers, provided they meet check-in time restrictions. These regulations apply to all international flights on domestic carriers; however, the Department of Transportation does not have jurisdiction over foreign carriers traveling out of, or into, the United States.

Luggage
Regulations Airlines allow each passenger two pieces of check-in luggage and one carry-on piece on international flights from North America. Each piece of check-in luggage cannot exceed 62 inches (length + width + height) or weigh more than 70 pounds. The carry-on luggage cannot exceed 45 inches (length + width + height) and must fit under the seat or in the overhead luggage compartment. On flights within Europe, you are allowed to check a total of 44 pounds, regardless of luggage size. Requirements for carry-on luggage are the same as for those on transatlantic flights.

For information on luggage insurance, *see* Insurance in Before You Go.

Labeling Luggage Put your home or business address on each piece of luggage, including hand baggage. If your lost luggage is recovered, the airline will deliver it to your home, at no charge to you.

From North America by Ship

Cunard Line (555 Fifth Ave., New York, NY 10017, tel. 800/221–4770 or 212/880–7545) operates four ships that make transatlantic crossings. One is the *Queen Elizabeth 2*, the only ocean liner that makes regular transatlantic crossings. The others make repositioning crossings twice a year, as one cruise season ends in Europe and another begins in North America. The *QE2* makes regular crossings April through December, between Baltimore, Boston, and New York City, and Southampton, England. Arrangements for the *QE2* can include one-way airfare. The *Sea Goddess I* and *Sea Goddess II* sail to and from Madeira, Portugal, and St. Thomas in the U.S. Virgin Islands, for their repositioning crossings. The *Vistafjord* sails to and from Marseilles, France, and Fort Lauderdale, Florida, on its repositioning crossings. Cunard Line offers fly/cruise packages and pre- and post-land packages. For the European cruise season, ports of call include Southampton, Madeira, Marseilles, Hamburg, Genoa, Rome, Venice, Naples, Monte Carlo, Malaga, Piraeus (Athens), Copenhagen, and Stockholm. Ports of call vary with the ship.

Royal Viking Line (750 Battery St., San Francisco, CA 94111, tel. 800/634–8000) has three ships that cruise out of European ports. Two of the ships make repositioning crossings to and from Fort Lauderdale and Lisbon, Portugal. Fly/cruise packages are available. Major ports of call, depending on the ship, are Copenhagen, Stockholm, Bergen, Hamburg, Leningrad, Barcelona, Venice, Dubrovnik, Villefranche, Corfu, and Lisbon.

American Star Lines (660 Madison Ave., New York, NY 10021, tel. 800/356–7677 and, in New York, 212/644–7900) makes transatlantic crossings in spring and fall to and from Greece and Barbados (in the British West Indies). The crossings are regular cruises, with ports of call in Portugal, Italy, Turkey, and the Greek islands. Summer cruises are from Piraeus (Athens), to the Greek islands, and Turkey. Fly/cruise packages are available.

Check the travel pages of your Sunday newspaper for other cruise ships that sail to Europe.

From the United Kingdom by Plane

Air travel from Britain to continental Europe has undergone a quiet revolution during the past few years. Thanks in part to the ever-growing demand for inexpensive charter flights, in part to the British government's determination to break down the cozy system of intergovernmental fare setting, and above all to a stronger sense of a shared European identity, more and more Britons regard flying as an everyday means of transportation rather than as an occasional luxury. The result, as expected, is more flights, greater choice, and lower fares.

But it isn't all good news. For one thing, not all European governments share Britain's enthusiasm for more competitive fares. Of long-term concern is the evident incapacity of European air networks to cope with an explosion in passenger numbers. And, at least at peak periods, more people traveling means more congestion and more delays.

It's not just those in the cheaper seats who suffer, either. Scheduled flights are just as likely to be delayed as charter flights, though they are, it's true, mostly spared the major delays that can afflict the summertime charter flights. Nonetheless, Europe's more militant air-traffic controllers have never been slow to grasp that the most effective way to draw attention to increased work loads and, in many cases, antiquated air-traffic control systems is to go on strike when maximum disruption is guaranteed—in other words, at the busiest times. Shots of beleaguered tourists gamely bedding down for another night at the airport have become a commonplace on Britain's TV screens. France, Spain, and Greece currently head the list of countries with the most strike-happy air controllers.

None of which is intended to suggest that flying from Britain to the Continent is something that can be recommended only to those who don't mind not sleeping for three days. And not least, of course, because everyone agrees that Europe's prosperity depends more than ever on good communications, with air travel well up there in the forefront.

Though some would certainly argue that it's all long overdue, the past two years have seen a welcome and widespread recognition that vastly increased investment and a determination to rethink the answers are crucial if Europe is to have the air networks it deserves. A unified European air-traffic control system in place of the current nationally operated systems may still be only a gleam in the eye of Utopian-minded Europhiles, but a new generation of air-traffic control systems is, at last, being installed in many countries. Once in place, they should improve dramatically the capacity of today's overworked machines. Likewise, in the certain knowledge that routine delays will eventually kill the goose that lays the golden egg, airlines, tour operators, and charter companies have exerted increasing pressure on governments to ensure that strikes become the exception, not the rule.

Scheduled Airlines If flying from a convenient airport, avoiding night flights at awkward hours, and relative reliability are more important to you than just finding the cheapest flight, scheduled flights are a better option than charters. London, with its two main airports—Heathrow and Gatwick—and three subsidiary airports—Luton, Stanstead, and London City—is Europe's biggest air hub. Frequent scheduled services connect it with virtually every major European city and resort. British Airways (BA) is the largest single operator, but all other leading international European airlines have flights to and from their own countries. There is never less than one flight a day to all the European capitals; in most cases, many more.

Competition from up-and-coming airlines such as British Midland, determined to grab customers from BA, has increased the options available to travelers. These smaller airlines have pioneered routes to European capitals from regional British airports. Manchester, for instance, has become a busy northern hub for several carriers, with shuttle flights to London and several flights a day to Amsterdam and other European points. Other major European airlines also have flights from several regional British airports. Air France, for example, has daily flights from Edinburgh to Paris. Similarly, SAS has a daily flight from Edinburgh to Copenhagen. (Both Glasgow and Edinburgh are linked to London by frequent shuttle flights operated by BA, British Midland, and others.)

Most airlines' weekday schedules cater principally to business flyers, who want to fly at clearly defined peak times (generally weekdays, first thing in the morning and late afternoon/early evening). As a result, lower fares are available outside these peak times. Look for better fares on midday flights, and check into weekend fares. Some are less than half the regular economy fares, though note that nearly all require that you spend at least one Saturday night at your destination. As a basic rule of thumb, remember that the cheaper a fare is, the more likely it is to carry restrictions. Always make sure you find out what these are before you buy your ticket.

The busiest routes also tend to be the cheapest. There are ever-more competitive fares on offer between London and Paris and London and Frankfurt. Likewise, fares between London and Brussels are also lower than the European average, mile for mile. Fares between London and Amsterdam can be a bargain, the cheapest in Europe. What's more, there are excellent onward connections from Amsterdam to other European cities.

Finally, remember, too, that few European flights are longer than four hours; the majority, in fact, rarely top two hours. Such short journeys make flying business-class or first-class, where it exists, an unnecessary luxury for most travelers. It's also worth bearing in mind that on most European airlines business class is open to anyone with a full-fare economy (coach class) ticket.

Charter Airlines   Charter airlines offer much cheaper fares to Europe than do the scheduled carriers, but the rules that bind them are more restrictive. While the British government turns a blind eye to sales of seat-only charter tickets, some European governments still require proof that you have bought an inclusive package vacation rather than just a flight. Most of the seat-only agencies will therefore give you a voucher stating that you have accommodations at a certain hotel. This is to comply with the rules—it won't necessarily get you a bed, even if you can find the hotel in question!

Greece specifically has expressed its determination to stamp out seat-only traffic by threatening passengers using such tickets with fines or deportation under international rules on charter sales. Its implementation of this rule has, though, been patchy so far.

Charter flights are by far the cheapest form of air transportation to main vacation destinations—particularly in the Mediterranean—and some of the charter fares available to last-minute buyers compare favorably even with bus or rail fares. Moreover, to destinations such as Spain, Greece, Turkey, and Italy, charter flights can give significant savings over scheduled fares. These are countries whose governments have vigorously resisted the introduction of cheaper scheduled fares and that remain zealously protective of their national airlines.

The main drawback of traveling by charter is rigid timetabling. Your return flight will be 7, 14, or 21 days from your departure date. The cheapest flights leave at inconvenient times—mainly in the early hours of the morning—and, in London, from airports a long way from the city center, such as Luton. The other major disadvantage is that charter flights are much more prone to delay than are scheduled flights. Delays of up to two days have been known, though these are admittedly exceptional. But on most flights it nonetheless makes sense to expect some delay, even if it's only an hour or so.

Arrival airports are often resorts rather than capital or major cities. In Spain, most charters fly to the Mediterranean coast rather than to Madrid or Seville; in Portugal, most flights arrive in the Algarve resort area rather than Lisbon. In Greece, this system can be an advantage rather than a drawback—most flights go to the islands rather than to Athens, so if your destination is, for example, Mykonos or Crete, you can fly there direct by charter without having to transfer to a domestic flight or ferry at Athens.

Charters bought at the last minute can be extremely cheap—check in travel agents' windows or in the classified sections of the *London Evening Standard* for cheap late-booking deals. Some of these may be so inexpensive that you may consider discarding the round-trip half of the ticket and traveling onward in Europe from your arrival point, rather than coming back to London.

From the United Kingdom by Car

Nearly all ferries from Britain to the Continent take cars. Which route you take, therefore, will be determined by a combination of your eventual destination and the amount of driving you want to do. The shortest routes are the fastest and the most popular: from Dover, Ramsgate, or Folkestone to Calais, Boulogne, and Ostend. These are the most convenient routes for much of France and Belgium, as well as central and southern Germany, Austria, Switzerland, Italy, and southeast Europe. If you're heading to western France or to Spain and Portugal, then Dieppe, Le Havre, Caen, Cherbourg, and St. Malo are better routes. Similarly, though the cost is much higher (though equally, the driving is greatly reduced) you should consider putting your car on the train in France or taking the ferry to Santander in northern Spain. The best routes to Holland and north Germany are from Dover and Felixstowe to Zeebrugge; from Sheerness to Vlissingen; and from Harwich to the Hook of Holland and Hamburg. If you're heading for Scandinavia, there are sailings from Harwich and Newcastle to Esbjerg in Denmark, Gothenburg in Sweden, and Stavangar and Bergen in Norway. There are regular sailings to Dublin from Holyhead and to Rosslare from Fishguard and Pembroke in Wales.

Unless you're traveling in the dead of winter, and sometimes even then, it's essential to book well in advance (*see* By Ferry/Ship below for addresses). Rates vary according to the length of your vehicle, the time of your crossing, and whether you plan to travel in peak, shoulder, or low season. Morning and evening crossings in the summer months are most expensive, and national holidays should be avoided where possible.

Both the **Automobile Association** (Fanum House, Basingstoke, Hants. RG21 2EA; tel. 0345/500600) and the **Royal Automobile Club** (RAC House, Box 100, South Croydon CR2 6XW, tel. 081/686–2525) operate on-the-spot breakdown and repair services across Europe. Replacement cars can be provided in case of accidents. Both companies will also transport cars and passengers back to Britain in case of serious breakdowns. The AA's 5-Star Cover costs £26.50 for up to 5 days, £34.50 for up to 12 days, and £42.95 for up to 31 days. Nonmembers are charged an extra £3; basic membership costs £41.75. The RAC's Euro-Cover costs £33.45 for up to 10 days and £42.85 for up to 31 days. Again, nonmembers are charged an extra £3; basic membership costs £31.

For advice on whether to bring your own car or to buy or rent one on your trip, *see* Renting, Leasing, and Purchasing Cars in Before You Go.

From the United Kingdom by Ferry/Ship

Ferry routes for passengers and vehicles link the North Sea, English Channel, and Irish Sea ports with almost all of Britain's maritime neighbors.

To France and Belgium By far the fastest and, for most visitors, the most convenient routes are those across the English Channel to France and Belgium. The principal routes are Dover–Calais (operated by **P&O European Ferries, Sealink,** and **Hoverspeed**); Dover–Boulogne (operated by P&O European Ferries and Hoverspeed); Dover–Zeebrugge (operated by P&O European Ferries); Dover–Ostend (operated by P&O European Ferries); Folkestone–Boulogne (operated by Sealink); and Ramsgate–Dunkirk (operated by **Sally Line**). Crossing times vary from 75 minutes for the Dover–Calais sailings to four hours for the Dover–Ostend sailings, depending on sea states. Make reservations well in advance for peak periods (Easter, July, and August).

The passengers-only Dover–Ostend Jetfoil (book through P&O European Ferries) is a good bet if you're traveling by train. It makes the crossing in only 100 minutes. But note that it is both more expensive than the regular ferries and much more liable to cancellation in bad weather.

There is a wide choice of other sailings to France: Newhaven–Dieppe (operated by Sealink); Portsmouth–Le Havre or Cherbourg (operated by P&O European Ferries); Southampton–Cherbourg (operated by Sealink); Portsmouth–Caen (operated by **Brittany Ferries**); Portsmouth–St. Malo (operated by Brittany Ferries); Poole–Cherbourg (operated by Brittany Ferries, summer only); and Plymouth–Roscoff (operated by Brittany Ferries). Journey times are longer (ranging from four hours for the Newhaven–Dieppe route to nine hours for the Portsmouth–St. Malo route) and fares higher, but you can avoid a great deal of unnecessary driving across northern France. Again, make reservations well in advance for peak periods.

To Spain and Portugal Brittany Ferries, which runs the St. Malo service, also sails from Plymouth to Santander in northern Spain. The crossing takes 24 hours and the line's cruise ferries offer economy and luxury cabins, as well as entertainment facilities that include a cinema and restaurants. If you are traveling by car and plan to tour Spain, this route offers you the option of looping back through France and returning to Britain without retracing your tracks. Onward travel into Spain without a car, however, will be time-consuming and is really an option only for those with plenty of time to spare.

Holland, North Germany, and Scandinavia There are excellent ferry routes linking British east coast ports with Europe's North Sea coast. Crossings are longer than English Channel routes, and most North Sea ferry lines have adopted the ferry-cruise concept, with cabins with various degrees of comfort and on-board facilities that can include duty-free shopping, bars, restaurants, discos, and casinos.

For Holland and north central Germany, the best routes are Sherness–Vlissingen (operated by **Olau Line**) and Harwich–Hook of Holland (operated by Sealink). If you're based farther north in England, the Hull–Rotterdam route (operated by **North Sea Ferries**) is also good. North Germany is best served by the Harwich–Hamburg route (operated by **Scandinavian Seaways**), the only direct ferry link with Germany. Services to Scandinavia include Harwich–Esbjerg, Denmark, and Newcastle–Esbjerg (both operated by Scandinavian Seaways); Harwich–Gothenburg, Sweden, and Newcastle–Gothenburg (both also operated by Scandinavian Seaways); Newcastle–Stavanger and Bergen, Norway (operated by **Color Lines** and Scandinavian Seaways).

To Ireland The principal ferry routes to Ireland are Holyhead–Dublin (operated by **B+I**); Holyhead–Dun Laoghaire (operated by Sealink); and Fishguard/Pembroke–Rosslare (operated by Sealink); and Pembroke–Rosslare (operated by B+I). There's a service between Swansea and Cork (operated by **Swansea Cork Ferries**) that runs from March through September. For Northern Ireland, take the Stranraer–Larne ferry (operated by P&O European Ferries and Sealink).

Useful Addresses For information on the services mentioned above, contact:

B+I Line UK Ltd. (East Princes Dock, Liverpool L3 0AA, tel. 051/236–8325).
Brittany Ferries (Mill Bay Docks, Plymouth PL1 3EW, tel. 0752/221321).
Color Line (Tyne Commission Quay, North Shields NE29 6EA, tel. 091/296–1313).
Hoverspeed (Maybrook House, Queens Gardens, Dover, Kent CT17 9UQ, tel. 081/554–7061).
North Sea Ferries (King George Dock, Hedon Rd., Hull HU9 5QA, tel. 0482/77177).

Olau Line (104 Anchor Lane, Sherness Docks, Sherness, Kent ME12 1SN, tel. 0795/666666).
P&O European Ferries (Channel View Rd., Dover, Kent CT17 9TJ, tel. 0304/210004).
Sally Line (Argyle Centre, York St., Ramsgate CT11 9DS, tel. 0800/636465).
Scandinavian Seaways (Scandinavia House, Parkeston Quay, Harwich, Essex CO12 4QG, tel. 0255/241234).
Sealink (Charter House, Park St., Ashford, Kent TN24 8EX, tel. 0233/647047).
Swansea Cork Ferries (Kings Dock, Swansea SA1 8RU, tel. 0792/456116).

From the United Kingdom by Train

Air travel may offer the fastest point-to-point service, car travel the greatest freedom, and bus transportation the lowest fares, but there is still an unparalleled air of romance about setting off for Europe by train from one of the historic London stations.

Boat trains timed to meet ferries at Channel ports leave London from Victoria, Waterloo, Paddington, and Charing Cross stations and connect with onward trains at the main French and Belgian ports. Calais and Boulogne have the best quick connections for Paris (total journey time about six to seven hours using the cross-Channel Hovercraft); the Dover–Ostend Jetfoil service is the fastest rail connection to Brussels (about 5½ hours, station to station) with good rail connections to Germany, northern France, and Poland.

Boat trains connecting with ferries from Harwich to the Dutch and Danish North Sea ports leave from London/Liverpool Street; there are good rail connections from the Dutch ports to Amsterdam and onward to Germany and Belgium and south to France.

For the Republic of Ireland, trains connecting with the ferry services across the Irish Sea leave from London/Paddington.

One-way and round-trip city-to-city tickets, including rail and ferry fares, can be booked in the United States through **BritRail**, either directly or through your travel agent. If you are traveling on one of the European rail passes bookable in the United States or in Britain, you may be entitled to free or discounted ferry crossings (*see* Getting Around Europe By Train, below).

If all international rail journeys have a certain glamour, none has the cachet of the **"Venice Simplon-Orient Express."** It's a reconditioned vintage train that, twice weekly from February through November, makes the 32-hour run between London/Victoria and Venice. Style and class abound. Prices are high. A peak-season one-way fare is £745; round-trip, £1,118. You can make reservations in Britain from **VSOE** (Sea Containers House, 20 Upper Ground, London SE1 9PF, tel. 071/928–6000). In the United States, contact **Orient Express** (Suite 2841, One World Trade Center, New York, NY 10048, tel. 800/223–1588).

Useful Addresses   For European rail information, contact **InterCity Europe,** the international wing of **BritRail,** at London/Victoria station: information, tel. 071/834–2345; reservations, tel. 071/828–9892.

Bookings can be made by phone using American Express, MasterCard, and Visa.

From the United Kingdom by Bus

Freeways (motorways) in the United Kingdom link London with the English Channel ferry ports and make bus travel—connecting with fast ferry, Jetfoil, or Hovercraft crossings—only a little slower than rail travel on the shorter routes into Europe.

Bus travel to cities such as Paris, Brussels, Amsterdam, Rotterdam, and Bruges is by fast and comfortable modern buses with reclining seats, air-conditioning, video entertainment, and airplane-style refreshment carts. There are frequent departures from central London pickup points. Fares by bus are a good deal less than the equivalent rail fare.

Eurolines—a consortium of bus operators that includes the British companies Wallace Arnold, National Express, and Grey Green—as well as Dutch, Belgian, and French lines—offers a range of day and night services linking London with Amsterdam, Paris, Antwerp, Brussels, and other points en route. Night services to Paris take about 10¼ hours; overnight journey time to Amsterdam is a little more than 13 hours.

Faster **Citysprint** daytime crossings use the Dover–Ostend Jetfoil service en route to Amsterdam, reducing journey time to a little more than eight hours. The fast Hoverspeed crossing to France cuts the day trip time to Paris to just under seven hours. There are also one-day round-trips to Antwerp and Brussels and "Eurobreakaway" holiday packages with accommodations for two or three nights in Paris, Amsterdam, and Brussels.

National Express uses Sealink ferries to the Republic of Ireland. A connecting bus service in Ireland is operated by **Bus Eireann.** Sailings are from Fishguard to Rosslare—a 3½-hour crossing. The onward service goes via Waterford and Cork to Killarney and Tralee.

There are summer buses to the Spanish vacation resorts, aimed mainly at British families on a tight vacation budget. If you, too, are on a budget, these can be an inexpensive way of getting to Spain. The same is true for the winter coaches that run to Europe's less expensive ski destinations, notably Andorra and some Italian resorts.

Longer-haul buses operate to Greece, aiming mainly at the student and backpacker market, but these tend to be less comfortable and, to a certain extent, less safe. Roads deteriorate rapidly once you leave Western Europe, and the overused and narrow main highway through Yugoslavia is to be avoided. Bus travel to Greece and Turkey is only for the really budget-conscious, and even then the savings on the lowest charter airfare are not very great; return bus fare to Athens, costing about £122, or to Istanbul at £175 (low season), is only £30 or so cheaper than the lowest airfare.

Both Eurolines and Hoverspeed City Sprint services are bookable in person at **National Express** offices at Victoria Coach Station (52 Grosvenor Gardens, London SW1, opposite Victoria Rail Station) and at the **Coach Travel Centre** (13 Regent St., London SW1, for credit card reservations, tel. 071/730–3499; inquiries, tel. 071/730–0202). Or book at any National Express agent throughout Britain.

Getting Around Europe

By Car

Touring Europe by car has tremendous advantages over other ways of seeing the Continent. You can go where you want, when you want, traveling at your own pace, free of the petty restrictions of timetables. But there are pitfalls, too. For the American driver, used to a uniform system of signs and traffic rules from coast to coast, and accustomed to being able to ask directions in English, Europe can be a bewildering experience. On the excellent freeways of northern and central Europe, it's possible to drive through three or four countries in less time than it would take to cross one of the larger of the U.S. states—which means that in one day you may have to cope with perhaps four different languages and four sets of traffic rules!

Road Conditions In general, the richer European countries—France, Germany, Holland, Denmark, the Benelux countries, the United Kingdom, and Italy—all have excellent national highway systems. In Spain, freeway building is proceeding rapidly, and roads are much better than they were even 10 years ago.

By contrast, Greece has just two stretches of freeway-type road—the Odos Ethnikos, or National Road, between Athens and Thessaloníki, and the main road between Athens and Patras.

The Irish Republic's nearest equivalent to freeways is its National Primary Routes, but the low speed limit of 55 mph reflects the fact that their general size and standard falls below the usual European freeway network. Of the Western European countries, Portugal still lags furthest behind in freeway building, but the factor that holds it back—it is the poorest country in Western Europe—also means that far fewer people own cars, so its relatively poor roads are also less crowded.

In Scandinavia, the roads vary according to how far north they are. The harsh winters crack road surfaces in the far north of Norway and Sweden. Minor roads have bumps and dips. Otherwise Scandinavia's main roads are well surfaced and refreshingly traffic-free.

Traffic Conditions On the freeway, U.S. drivers may find the pace of European traffic alarming. Speed limits in most countries are set much higher than those in the United States. Even on British motorways, where the upper limit is a very conservative 70 mph, it is not uncommon to be passed by vehicles traveling 15–20 mph faster than that. On German *autobahns*, French *autoroutes*, or Italian *autostrade*, cars in the fast lane are often moving at 100 mph. Much of the time traffic is heavier than is common on U.S. freeways outside major city rush hours.

Consequently, most tourists will find it more rewarding to avoid the freeways and use the alternative main routes. On these roads, where traffic moves more slowly, driving at a more leisurely pace is possible, and stopping en route is easier. This can also save money; many European freeways (such as those of

France, Spain, Italy, and Greece) are toll roads, and a day's drive on them can be expensive. If you break down on any of the European highways, you can expect to pay a hefty fee for towing unless you have prudently joined one of the motorist plans offered by one of the many national associations such as the AA or RAC in Britain (*see* From the United Kingdom by Car in Getting to Europe).

As in many U.S. states, traffic officers in most European countries (with a few exceptions, such as the United Kingdom) are empowered to fine you on the spot for traffic violations. The language barrier will not make your case any easier.

In Spain and Greece, make sure you carry insurance that provides bail bond in case of an accident. When driving a rental car in Greece, beware of damaging the underside of the vehicle on Greek roads, which are among the worst in Europe. Normal collision-damage waiver, even from one of the major international chains, may not cover such damage, and you could face a crippling fine.

In Eastern Europe, police and frontier officials will pay much closer attention to your papers than they do in the West, but roads are emptier and foreign drivers are still a novelty. The language barrier may be greater, but the novelty value has been known to lead to foreigners being let off with a warning when local drivers might be fined for minor offenses.

Road Signs In some European countries—Greece and parts of Yugoslavia—the language barrier is compounded by an alphabet barrier. Main road signs in Greece, for example, are written in the Greek alphabet. The only solution is to carry a good map.

Rules of the Road In the United Kingdom and the Republic of Ireland, cars drive on the left. In other European countries, traffic is on the right. Beware the transition when coming off ferries from Britain or Ireland to the Continent (and vice versa)!

Rush Hours During peak vacation periods, main routes can be jammed with holiday traffic. In the United Kingdom, try to avoid driving during any of the long bank-holiday (public holiday) weekends, when motorways, particularly in the south, can be totally clogged with traffic. In France and Italy, where huge numbers of people still take a fixed one-month vacation in August, avoid driving during *le depart*, the first weekend in August, when vast numbers of drivers head south; or *le retour*, when they head back.

Many German families drive to the Yugoslavian or Greek beaches for their summer vacation and, in the months of June and July, the main highways of Yugoslavia—which are at any time among Europe's worst roads—can also be horrendously over-crowded.

Frontiers You may be surprised at the relatively casual approach many European countries have toward border controls for drivers. At many frontiers, you may simply be waved through; it is quite possible, for example, to drive from Amsterdam to Germany, via Belgium and France, without once being stopped for customs or immigration formalities. There are, however, spot checks at all borders, and at some—particularly those check-points used by heavy commercial truck traffic—there can be long delays at peak times. Ask tourist offices or motoring associations for latest advice on ways to avoid these tie-ups. If you are driving a rented car, the rental company will have provided you with all the necessary papers; if the vehicle is your own, you will need proof of ownership, certificate of roadworthiness (known in the United Kingdom as a Ministry of Transport [MOT] road vehicle certificate), up-to-date vehicle tax, and a Green Card proof of insurance, available from your insurance company (fees vary depending on destination and length of stay).

By Train

European railway systems vary from the sublime to the ridiculous in terms of comfort and convenience. France, Germany, and the United Kingdom led the field in developing high-speed trains; although the latter has fallen behind the other two. The **French National Railroads'** (SNCF's) Train à Grande Vitesse (TGV), for example, takes just 4½ hours to cover the 540 miles from Paris to Marseille on the Mediterranean.

BritRail operates high-speed InterCity trains—with a top speed of 125 mph—on its north-south routes between London and Scotland. Normal fares apply on the BritRail high-speed services, but there is a supplementary fare for travel on French TGV services.

The German rail system **Deutsche Bundesbahn** (DB, known in the United States as GermanRail) last year wrested the world rail speed record from the French, and its high-speed InterCity trains make rail travel the best public transportation option within Germany.

Swiss trains are not the fastest in Europe, but they are the most punctual and reliable, making onward travel connections remarkably stress-free.

International trains link most European capital cities, including those of Eastern Europe; service is offered several times daily. Generally, customs and immigration formalities are completed on the train by officials who board when it crosses the frontier.

Most European systems operate a two-tier, sometimes three-tier, class system, with first class substantially the most expensive. The only outstanding advantage of first class is that it is likely to be less crowded on busier routes. Train journeys in Europe tend to be shorter than in the United States—trains are much faster and distances much shorter—so first-class rail travel is usually a luxury rather than a necessity. Some of the poorer European countries retain a third class, but avoid it unless you are on a rock-bottom budget.

A number of European airlines and railways operate fast train connections to their hub airports, and these can sometimes be booked through the airline's computer reservation service. The "Lufthansa Express" connects Frankfurt and Köln/Bonn airports and is a splendid two-hour scenic journey along the Rhine valley.

Trains in Sweden and Norway offer supreme comfort, but greater distances and the more rugged terrain make for longer journey times; if you are on a tight schedule, you may prefer to take internal flights.

In Italy, there are some excellent rail services between major cities—but be sure that the train you book *is* a main intercity service, not one that stops at every minor station. Off the major lines, Italian rail services are slower and less frequent.

Trains are generally to be avoided in Spain and Portugal as point-to-point transportation—though there are some attractive scenic routes and special tourist trains. In Greece and Turkey anyone but the most fanatical rail traveler will find the more frequent, modern, and comfortable buses preferable to the trains, which are slow, unreliable, crowded, and dirty.

Rail travel is vital to most Eastern European countries, and services within and between them are better and more comfortable than you might expect. Though usually much slower than the more modern western European trains, service is frequent and reliable.

Rail Passes Almost all European countries offer discount rail passes; details are given in the appropriate country chapter. Here is a listing of the rail passes available before you leave.

The **EurailPass,** valid for unlimited first-class train travel through 17 countries (Austria, Belgium, Denmark, Finland, France, Germany, Greece, Holland, Hungary, Ireland, Italy, Luxembourg, Norway, Portugal, Spain, Sweden, and Switzerland), is the best-value ticket for visitors from outside Europe. The ticket is available for periods of 15 days ($390), 21 days ($498), one month ($616), two months ($840), and three months ($1,042). For two or more people traveling together, a 15-day rail pass costs $280. Between April 1 and September 30, you need a minimum of three in your group to get this discount. For those under 26, there is the **Eurail Youthpass,** for one or two months' unlimited second-class train travel at $380 and $500. The pass must be bought from an authorized agent before you leave home. Apply through your travel agent, or one of the following: French National Railroads, GermanRail, or Italian State Railways (*see* Useful Addresses, below).

For travelers who like to spread out their train journeys, there is the **Eurail Flexipass.** With the 15-day pass ($198), travelers get five days of unlimited first-class train travel but they can spread that travel out over 21 days; a 21-day pass gives you 9 days of travel ($360), and a one-month pass gives you 14 days ($458).

For European travelers under 26, the **Inter-Rail card** is an unbeatable value. It is available to people who have been resident in Europe for at least six months, and for one calendar month gives unlimited rail travel in 22 countries—the same as the EurailPass with the addition of Morocco, Romania, European Turkey, Czechoslovakia, and Yugoslavia. It also gives half-price travel within the United Kingdom and discounts of up to 50% on some ferry services to and from the United Kingdom. The card costs £175 and is available from rail stations.

Useful Addresses Full information on rail services within the countries listed here is available from the addresses below. Otherwise, contact the national tourist office of the country concerned.

In the United States and Canada **Belgian National Railroads** (745 Fifth Ave., New York, NY 10151, tel. 212/758–8130).
BritRail Travel International Inc. (630 Third Ave., New York,

NY 10017, tel. 212/599–5400; 94 Cumberland St., Toronto, Ontario M5R 1A3; 409 Granville St., Vancouver, BC V6C 1T2).

French National Railroads (610 Fifth Ave., New York, NY 10020, tel. 212/582–2110; 9465 Wilshire Blvd., Beverly Hills, CA 90212; 11 E. Adams St., Chicago, IL 60603; 2121 Ponce de Leon Blvd., Coral Gables, FL 33114; 360 Post St., Union Sq., San Francisco, CA 94108; 1500 Stanley St., Montreal, Quebec H3A 1Re; 409 Granville St., Vancouver, BC V6C 1T2).

GermanRail (747 Third Ave., New York, NY 10017, tel. 212/308–3106; 625 Statler Office Bldg., Boston, MA 02116, 617/542–0577; 95–97 W. Higgins Rd., Suite 505, Rosemont, IL 60018; 112 S. Ervay St., Dallas, TX 75201; 11933 Wilshire Blvd., Los Angeles, CA 90025; 442 Post St., 6th Floor, San Francisco, CA 94102; 8000 E. Girard Ave., Suite 518S, Denver, CO 80231; 2400 Peachtree Rd. NE, Lenox Towers, Suite 1299, Atlanta, GA 30326, tel. 404/266–9555; and Bay St., Toronto, Ontario M5R 2C3).

Italian State Railways (666 Fifth Ave., New York, NY 10103, tel. 212/397–2667).

In the United Kingdom **Belgian National Railways** (Premier House, 10 Greycoat Pl., London SW1P 1SB, tel. 071/233–0360).

French Railways (French Railways House, 179 Piccadilly, London, W1V 9DB, tel. 071/491–1573).

German Federal Railways (18 Conduit St., London W1, tel. 071/499–0577).

Netherlands Railways (Egginton House, 25–28 Buckingham Gate, London SW1E 6LD; tel. 071/630–1735).

Norwegian State Railways Travel Bureau (21–24 Cockspur St., London SW1Y 5DA, tel. 071/930–6666).

Swiss Federal Railways (Swiss Center, 1 New Coventry St., London W1V 8EE, tel. 071/734–1921).

For information about rail networks in other European countries, contact their tourist boards in London.

By Plane

Licenses to operate on a given international or internal route are issued by governments, and international route licenses are in most cases still issued on the basis of bilateral agreements between the two countries in question. This means that bus stop–style services, like those so common in the United States, do not yet exist in Europe, though they may begin to appear in the near future. So-called fifth freedom licenses, which grant airlines the right to land and pick up passengers at intermediary points on a given route, are jealously guarded by governments and consequently are hard to come by. This makes touring Europe entirely by air a costly process, and the best bet, if you plan to visit a number of European countries, is to combine air travel with other transportation options.

Hub Airports As in the United States, airlines are developing hub and spoke-style services within Europe. The idea is that you take a transatlantic flight to an airline's hub, then continue on its intra-European services to other European cities. Thus, **SAS** is actively developing Copenhagen as a Scandinavian hub; the Dutch airline **KLM** is doing the same at Amsterdam's Schiphol; **British Airways** at London's Heathrow and Gatwick; and **Lufthansa** at Frankfurt. If you plan to fly to other European cities, one of these hubs is your obvious choice.

Domestic Services Most Western European countries have good internal services linking the capital city with major business and industrial centers and with more remote communities. In Germany, France, and Spain, regional flights tend to connect major business cities rather than areas of touristic interest—though in Spain there is a considerable overlap between the two.

In such countries as Sweden, Norway, Greece, and to some extent the United Kingdom, however, air services are a vital link between remote island and mountain communities and are often subsidized by the central government. In Greece, for example, you can fly very inexpensively between Athens and the islands—though not *between* islands.

Before booking an internal flight, consider the alternatives. Flights from London to Edinburgh take about one hour—airport to airport—while the competing BritRail InterCity train takes 4½ hours. But if you add in the hour needed to get from central London to the airport, the need to check in as much as one hour before departure, the inevitable flight delays, the time spent waiting for luggage on arrival, and the transfer time back into town from Edinburgh Airport—you'll find you may not have saved any more than an hour in travel time for a considerably higher fare. When looking into air travel as an option, remember that distances between European cities can be deceptively short to an eye accustomed to U.S. routings.

Formalities For scheduled flights, you will be asked to check in at least one hour before departure; for charter flights, generally two hours. These are guidelines; if you are traveling with just hand luggage, it is possible to check in as late as 30 minutes before takeoff time. European luggage allowances are based on the total weight of your checked luggage, not, as in the United States, on the number of bags. The usual allowance is 44 pounds.

You may be pleasantly surprised by the Green Channel/Red Channel customs system in operation at most western European airports and at other international frontier posts. Basically, this is an honor system: If you have nothing to declare, you walk through the Green Channel without needing to open your bags for inspection. There are, however, random spot checks, and penalties for abusing the system can be severe. If in doubt, go through the Red Channel.

Eastern Europe Eastern European countries need hard Western currency so badly that they try not to set airfares at intolerably high levels. Most routes are operated in tandem with Western carriers, however, and anyone with an eye to comfort and safety will prefer the latter.

Useful Addresses Major national airlines for the following European countries can be contacted at their London addresses:

Aer Lingus (Ireland) (Aer Lingus House, 83 Staines Rd., Hounslow, Middlesex TW3 3JB, tel. 081/569–5555).
Air France (158 New Bond St., London W1Y 0AY, tel. 071/499–9511).
Alitalia (Italy) (205 Holland Park Ave., London W11 4XB, tel. 071/602–7111).
Austrian Airlines (50/51 Conduit St., London W1R 0NP, tel. 071/439–0741).
British Airways (Box 10, Heathrow Airport, Hounslow, Middlesex TW6 2JA, tel. 081/897–4000).

Czechoslovak Airlines (72 Margaret St., London W1N 7LF, tel. 071/255–1898).

Iberia (Spain) (130 Regent St., London W1R, tel. 071/437–5622).

JAT Yugoslav Airlines (2nd floor, Prince Frederick House, 37 Maddox St., London W1R 0AQ, tel. 071/493–9399).

KLM Royal Dutch Airlines (8 Hanover St., London W1R 9HF, tel. 081/750–9000).

Lufthansa (Germany) (23–26 Piccadilly, London W1V 0EJ, tel. 071/408–0442).

Olympic Airways (Greece) (164 Piccadilly, London, W1V, tel. 071/493–3965).

SAS Scandinavian Airlines (52/53 Conduit St., London W1R 0AY, tel. 071/734–4020).

Swissair (Swiss Centre, 10 Wardour St., London W1V 4BJ, tel. 071/439–4144).

By Bus

If you have opted for land rather than air travel, the choice between rail and bus is a major decision. In countries such as Britain, France, Germany, and Holland, bus travel was, until recently, something of a poor man's option—slow, uncomfortable, and cheap. Today, though, fast modern buses travel on excellent highways and offer standards of service and comfort comparable to those on a train—but still at generally lower fares. Between major cities and over long distances, trains are still preferable and almost always faster, but buses will take you to places that trains often do not reach.

In several southern European countries—including Portugal, Greece, much of Spain, and Turkey—the bus has supplanted the train as the main means of public transportation, and is often quicker, more frequent, and more comfortable than the antiquated rolling stock of the national rail system. Choose the bus over the rail in these countries unless there is a particular scenic rail route or a special tourist train you want to use. But be prepared to discover that the bus is now more expensive than the lowly railway. Competition among lines is keen, so compare services such as air-conditioning or reclining seats before you buy.

Information Information on bus transportation in most countries is available from national or regional tourist offices. For reservations on major bus lines, contact your travel agent at home. For smaller bus companies on regional routes, you may have to go to a local travel agency or to the bus line office.

Note that travel agencies may be affiliated with a certain line and won't always tell you about alternative services—you may have to do some legwork to be sure of getting the best service.

By Ferry/Ship

Bounded by the sea on three sides and crossed by a number of major rivers, Europe offers an abundance of choices for anyone who loves water travel.

The Baltic In the north, ferries ply daily between most of the major Baltic ports in Western Europe, as well as between Finnish ports and those of the Soviet Union. Baltic crossings are not for those in a hurry—several of them last overnight—and shipping lines operate luxury cruise-ferry vessels with all kinds of entertainment facilities and duty-free shopping.

Major lines include **Silja,** which operates between Finland and Sweden/Germany (book through Scandinavian Seaways); **Viking Line,** which operates between Finland and Sweden (book through Scantours); **Color Line,** which operates between Sweden and Norway; **Stena Line,** which operates between Norway and Sweden (book through Sealink); and **TT-Line,** which operates between Sweden and Germany (book through Olau Lines).

Local ferries ply the Norwegian fjords and are an excellent way of seeing the country, whether you are traveling by car or on public transportation; a fjord trip in mid-summer, the time of the Midnight Sun in northern Norway, should not be missed.

Main international Baltic ports are Copenhagen, Gothenburg, Malmö, Stockholm, Helsinki, Kristiansand, and Oslo—also Travemunde in Germany.

Useful Addresses   **Viking Line** (Scantours, 8 Spring Gardens, Trafalgar Sq., London SW1A 2BG, tel. 071/930–9510).
For other Baltic ferry lines mentioned here, *see* From the United Kingdom by Ferry/Ship.

Greece   Interisland ferries play an important part in the Mediterranean, too, particularly among the Greek islands. Many island communities have formed cooperative companies to operate services linking their island with others and with Piraeus, the port of Athens. While all Baltic ferries offer high standards of comfort, even luxury—at commensurately high fares—Mediterranean ferry lines observe widely different standards. On Greek ships, for example, you can travel in a first- or second-class cabin or rough it in deck class for a much lower fare. The same is true for the international ferries plying between the Italian ports of Bari and Brindisi and the Greek ports of Corfu, Igoumenitsa, and Patras. The age of Greek ferry boats varies widely, too. Some are of pre–World War II vintage, while others—like the *Naxos,* which sails between Piraeus and Crete—are modern vessels. For Greek ferry information, contact the **National Tourist Organization of Greece** in New York or London.

Flying Dolphin Lines operates fast hydrofoil service from Piraeus to points popular with Athenian vacationers, including the Saronic Gulf islands and resorts on the eastern Peloponnese.

One luxury sea option in the eastern Mediterranean is the *Orient Express,* owned by the same company that operates the train. The ship connects with the train at Venice, sails to Piraeus, Istanbul, and Kusadasi (Turkey); returns via Patmos and Katakolon in Greece, then meets the train again in Venice. For details, contact **Venice Simplon-Orient Express** (Suite 2565, 1 World Trade Center, New York, NY 10048) or **British Ferries Orient-Express** (Charter House, Park Street, Ashford, Kent TN24 8EX, tel. 0233/647047).

River Travel   Major river systems crisscross Europe. Among the many attractive river trips available are a number of luxury cruises on the Rhine and Danube rivers.

The Danube passes through European countries in Western and Eastern Europe, and international cruises are possible.

Contact the **German National Tourist Office** for details. There is also an international hydrofoil service that operates several times a day on the Danube between Budapest in Hungary and Bratislava in Czechoslovakia. Information and booking are available through **Ibusz,** the Hungarian state travel agency, or **Cedok,** its Czech equivalent, in New York or London. For details of Rhine trips, contact **K.D. German Rhine Line** (170 Hamilton Ave., White Plains, NY 10601) or in the United Kingdom (28 South St., Epsom, Surrey KT18 7PF, tel. 03727/42033).

Though a great deal less spectacular than either the Rhine or the Danube, the smaller rivers of Belgium, Holland, France, and other Western European countries can also provide a relaxed and fascinating vacation. **Floating Through Europe** (271 Madison Ave., New York, NY 10016, tel. 212/685–5600) specializes in these kinds of tours.

By Bicycle

Bicycling in Europe can be sheer pleasure or unadulterated torment—depending on when you go, where you go, and what you try to do.

If you're planning a European bike trip, you are probably experienced enough not to need advice on equipment and clothing. But it needs to be said that some European countries are far more user-friendly than others toward bicyclists. In countries like Holland, Denmark, Germany, and Belgium, bikes are very much part of the landscape—mainly because the landscape tends to be uniformly flat. City streets and many main roads in these countries (as well as in Germany) have special bike lanes set aside, and car drivers are used to coping with large numbers of bicycle riders.

Cycling is a major sport in Italy, Spain, and Portugal, as well as in France, and there are regular "Tour" road races. Cyclists also get a good deal in the Eastern Bloc countries, where for economic reasons, the bicycle is still an everyday form of transportation.

Northern Scandinavia and Iceland, plus the Alpine countries Austria and Switzerland, with their steep terrain, are destinations only for the serious cyclist. The Scandinavian countries have plenty of excellent-value campsites. Ireland has emptier roads and a gentler landscape than Sweden or Norway and is a pleasant country to bicycle in, though the temptation to sample just one more Guinness at each wayside pub can be a hazard in itself.

Of the wealthier European countries, Britain has the most shameful record when it comes to providing facilities for bicyclists or considering their interests. Riding in London traffic is a stomach-churning experience requiring nerves of steel. Except in remoter areas—such as the north of Scotland—main roads are overcrowded and often dangerous to cyclists.

Bicycle Transport Transporting your bicycle from the United Kingdom to Europe holds no big problems—some ferry lines transport bicycles free, others charge a nominal fee. Shop around. Surprisingly, you can transport your bicycle by air as checked baggage—you won't have to pay extra so long as you are within the 44-pound total baggage allowance.

Most European rail lines will transport bicycles free of charge or for a nominal fee, though you may have to book ahead. Check with the main booking office. One of the joys of biking in Europe is being able to bike one way and return by train or to board a train with your bike when you need to cover long distances or simply when you need to take a rest. SNCF (French Railways) converted wagons on four of its Motorail services from Boulogne to carry bicycles for the first time in 1988. Transporting your bike by bus is also possible.

Renting Bicycles Bicycles can be rented by the day or week in most European capitals and are most readily available in cities like Amsterdam and Copenhagen, where cycling is part of the way of life. Local tourist boards are the best source of information on reliable rental agencies with safe bicycles to rent; remember to check on local traffic rules and make sure your insurance covers you in case of an accident. **GermanRail (DB)** rents bicycles at selected stations in summer—get further information from GermanRail or the German National Tourist Office in New York.

2 Amsterdam

Arriving and Departing

By Plane Most international flights arrive at Amsterdam's Schiphol Airport, one of Europe's finest. Immigration and customs formalities on arrival are relaxed, with no forms to be completed.

Between the Airport and Downtown The best transportation between the airport and the city center is the direct rail link, with three stops en route to the central station, where you can get a taxi or streetcar to your hotel. The train runs every 10 to 15 minutes throughout the day and takes about half an hour. Second-class fare is Fl. 4.40.

Taxis from the airport to central hotels cost about Fl. 50.

By Train The city has excellent rail connections with the rest of Europe. Fast services link it to Paris, Brussels, Luxembourg, and Cologne. The central station is conveniently located in the center of town.

Getting Around

By Bus, Streetcar, and Metro A zonal fare system is used. Tickets (starting at Fl. 2) are bought from automatic dispensers on the metro or from the drivers on streetcars and buses; or buy a money-saving **strippenkaart**. Even simpler is the one-day **dagkaart**, which covers all city routes for Fl. 9.50 (a two-day card costs Fl. 12.60). These discount tickets can be obtained from the main VVV office, along with route maps of the public transportation system. Recently introduced water buses in the city center also have day cards (Fl. 12.50) and two-day cards (Fl. 20).

By Taxi Taxis are expensive: A short 3-mile ride costs around Fl. 15. Taxis are not usually hailed on the street but are picked up at stands near stations and other key points. Alternatively, you can dial 777777. Water taxis are even more expensive (about Fl. 120 per hour).

By Car Thanks to the city's network of concentric canals, one-way systems, and lack of parking facilities, it isn't easy to drive in Amsterdam. It's best to put your car in one of the parking lots on the edge of the old center and abandon it for the rest of your stay. Expensive hotels often have private parking lots.

By Bicycle Rental bikes are readily available for around Fl. 7.50 per day with an Fl. 100–Fl. 200 deposit. Bikes are an excellent and inexpensive way to explore the city. Several rental companies are close to the central station, or ask at the VVV offices for details.

On Foot Amsterdam is a small, congested city of narrow streets, which makes it ideal for exploring on foot. The VVV issues seven excellent guides that detail walking tours around the center. The best are "The Jordaan," a stroll through the lively canalside district, and "Jewish Amsterdam," a walk past the symbolic remains of old Jewish housing and lone synagogues.

Important Addresses and Numbers

Tourist Information There are two VVV offices: one outside the central station in the Old Dutch Coffee House (Stationsplein 10, tel. 020/6266444), and the other at Leidsestraat 106. The VVV reserves for accommodations, tours, and entertainment, but reservations must be made in person. The Stationsplein office is open Easter–September, daily 9 AM–11 PM; October–Easter, weekdays 9–6, Saturday 9–5, Sunday 10–1 and 2–5.

Consulates **U.S.** (Museumsplein 19, tel. 020/6790321). **Canadian** (7 Sophialaan, The Hague, tel. 070/3614111). **U.K.** (Koningslaan 44, tel. 020/6764343).

Emergencies The general number for emergencies is 06–11, but note direct numbers. **Police** (tel. 020/222222); **Ambulance** (tel. 020/5555555); **Doctor Academisch Medisch Centrum** (Meibergdreef 9, tel. 020/5669111). **Central Medical Service** (tel. 020/6642111) will give you names of pharmacists and dentists as well as doctors.

English Bookstores **American Discount Book Center** (Kalverstraat 158, 020/6255537). **Athenaeum Boekhandel** (Spui 14, tel. 020/6233933). **English Bookshop** (Lauriergracht 71, tel. 020/6264230).

Travel Agencies **American Express** (Damrak 66, tel. 020/6262042, Van Baerlestraat 38, tel. 020/6714141); **Holland International** (Rokin 54, tel. 020/65512812); **Key Tours** (Wagon-Lits) (Dam 19, tel. 020/247310); **De Vries & Co.** (Damrak 6, tel. 020/6248174). **Thomas Cook** (Bureau de Change, 31a Leidseplein, tel. 020/2670000).

Guided Tours

Boat Tours The most enjoyable way to get to know Amsterdam is by taking a boat trip along the canals. Several operators run trips, usually in glass-top boats. There are frequent departures from points opposite the central station, by Smits Koffiehuis, beside the Damrak and along the Rokin and Stadhouderskade (near the Rijksmuseum). For a tour lasting about 1½ hours, costs range from Fl. 8 to Fl. 12, but the student guides expect a small tip for their multilingual commentary. On summer evenings, longer cruises include wine and cheese or a full buffet dinner. A few tours feature increasingly drunken stops for wine tastings in canalside bars. Costs range from Fl. 30 for wine and cheese tours to Fl. 135 for a candlelight dinner. Trips can be booked through the VVV.

Alternatively, you may want to rent a pedal-boat and make your own canal tour. At **Canal-Bike,** prices begin at Fl. 19 per hour; for details, tel. 020/6265574.

The **Museum Boat** capitalizes on the fact that the 12 major museums lie beside the canals. From April to September, a special boat ferries eager passengers between cultural landmarks. Tickets cost Fl. 12 for adults, Fl. 8 for children, and include a 40% discount on museum admission. Details and bookings are available from the VVV.

Bus Tours Guided bus tours around the city are also available and provide an excellent introduction to Amsterdam. Lindbergh's combined bus-and-boat tour includes the inevitable trip to a diamond factory. Costing Fl. 25, the comprehensive three-hour tour can be booked through **Lindbergh** (26 Damrak).

Exploring Amsterdam

Amsterdam is a gem of a city for the tourist. Small and densely packed with fine buildings, many dating from the 17th century or earlier, it is easily explored on foot or by bike. The old heart of the city consists of canals, with narrow streets radiating out like the spokes of a wheel. The hub of this wheel and the most convenient point to begin sightseeing is the central station. Across the street, in the Old Dutch Coffee House, is a VVV office that offers helpful tourist information.

Amsterdam's key points of interest can be covered within two or three days, with each walking itinerary taking in one or two of the important museums and galleries. The following exploration of the city center can be broken up into several sessions.

Around the Dam *Numbers in the margin correspond to points of interest on the Amsterdam map.*

1 Start at the **central station.** About three blocks away, at Haarlemmerstraat 75, a plaque commemorates the occasion, in 1623, when the directors of the Dutch West India Company planned the founding of Nieuw Amsterdam on the southernmost tip of the island of Manhattan. In 1664, this colony was seized by the English and renamed New York.

2 The street directly across from the station is Prins Hendrikkade. To the left is **St. Nicolaaskerk** (Church of St. Nicholas), consecrated in 1888. Of interest are the baroque altar with its revolving tabernacle, the swinging pulpit that can be stowed out of sight, and the upstairs gallery.

3 Around the corner from St. Nicolaaskerk is the **Schreierstoren** (Weeping or Criers' Tower), where seafarers used to say goodbye to their women before setting off to sea. The tower was erected in 1487, and a tablet marks the point from which Henrik Hudson set sail on the *Half Moon* on April 4, 1609, on a voyage that took him to what is now New York and the river that still bears his name. Today the Weeping Tower is used as a combined reception and exhibition center, which includes a maritime bookshop.

4 Three blocks to the southwest along the Oudezijds Voorburgwal you can see the **Oude Kerk,** the city's oldest church. Built during the 14th century but badly damaged by iconoclasts after the Reformation, the church still retains its original bell tower and a few remarkable stained-glass windows. From the tower, there is a typical view of old Amsterdam stretching from St. Nicolaaskerk to medieval gables and, if your eyesight is good, to glimpses of negotiations between a prostitute and a prospective client immediately below! *Admission free. Open May–Oct., Mon.–Sat. 11:30–4:30; Nov.–Apr., Mon.–Sat. 11–3. Tower open June–Sept., Mon. and Thurs. 2–5, Tues. and Wed. 11–2.*

5 Just beyond the Oude Kerk on the canal is the **Amstelkring Museum,** whose facade carries the inscription "Ons Lieve Heer Op Solder" ("Our Dear Lord in the Attic"). In 1578, Amsterdam embraced Protestantism and outlawed the church of Rome. So great was the tolerance of the municipal authorities, however, that secret Catholic chapels were allowed to exist; at one time there were 62 in Amsterdam alone. One such chapel was established in the attics of these three neighboring canalside houses, built around 1661. The lower floors were used as ordinary dwellings, while services were held in the attics regularly until 1888, the year St. Nicolaaskerk was consecrated for Catholic worship. *Oudezijds Voorburgwal 49, tel. 020/246604. Admission: Fl. 4. Open Mon.–Sat. 10–5, Sun. 1–5.*

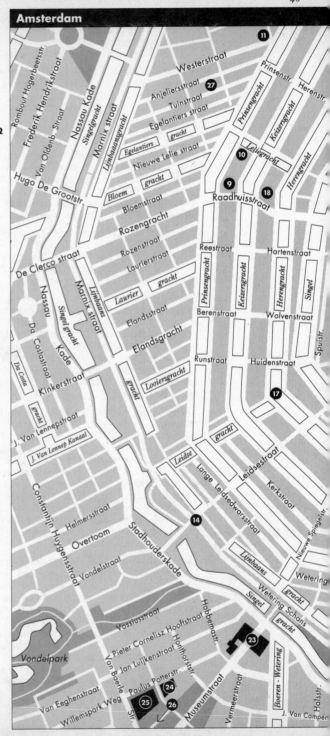

Amsterdam

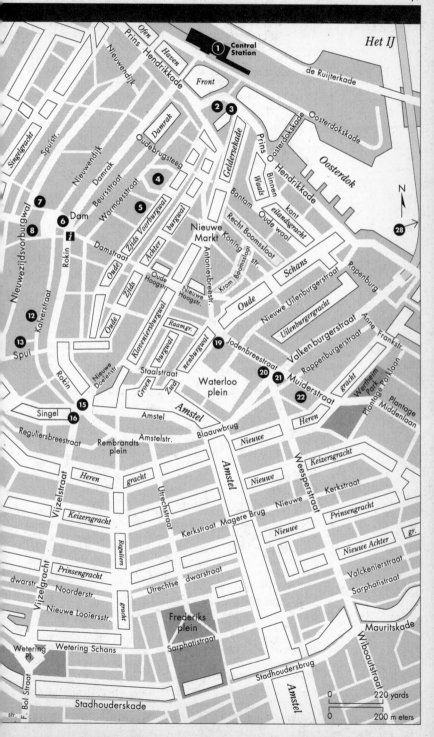

Het IJ

Ofen
Haven
Front
① Central Station
Prins Hendrikkade
de Ruijterkade

Nieuwendijk
Damrak
② ③
Geldersekade
Oosterdokskade
Oosterdokskade

Oosterdok

Singelgracht
Spuistr.
Nieuwendijk
Damrak
Oudebrugsteeg
Beursstraat
Warmoesstraat
④
⑤
Zijds Voorburgwal
Achter burgwal
Bantam
Prins Hendrikkade
Waals
Binnen
kant
eilandsgracht
Oude waal

⑦
⑥ Dam
Nieuwezijdsvorburgwal
⑧
ⓘ
Rokin
Damstraat
Oude
Zijds
Oude
Hoogstr.
Nieuwe
Hoogstr.
Nieuwe Markt
Antoniesbreestr.
Koning str.
Recht Boomssloot
Krom Boomssloot
Schans
Oude
Nieuwe Uilenburgerstraat
Uilenburgergracht
Rapenburg
Oude Schans

⑫
Kalverstraat
⑬
Spui
Rokin
Nieuwe Doelenstr.
Klovenniersburgwal
Raamgr.
Zuid burgwal
nenburgwal
⑲
Staalstraat
Groen
Zuid
Waterloo plein
Jodenbreestraat
⑳
㉑
Valkenburgerstraat
Roppenburgerstraat
Anne Frankstr.
gracht
Wertheim Park
Plantage Parklaan
Plantage Middenlaan

⑮
Singel
⑯
Reguliersbreestraat
Rembrandts plein
Amstel
Amstel
Amstelstr.
Blaauwbrug
Heren
Nieuwe
㉒
Muiderstraat
Heren

Vijzelstraat
Heren
Keizersgracht
gracht
Reguliers
Utrechtstraat
Amstel
Kerkstraat Magere Brug
Nieuwe
Nieuwe
Nieuwe
Weesperstraat
Keizersgracht
Kerkstraat
Prinsengracht
Nieuwe Achter
gr.
Volckenierstraat
Sarphatistraat

Vijzelgracht
Prinsengracht
dwarstr.
Noorderstr.
Nieuwe Looiersstr.
gracht
Utrechtse dwarstraat
Frederiks plein
Sarphatistraat
Mauritskade

Wetering Pl.
Wetering Schans
str. F. Bol Straat
Stadhouderskade
Amstel
Stadhoudersbrug
Wibautstraat

N
㉘

0   220 yards
0   200 meters

This area, bordered by Amsterdam's two oldest canals (Oudezijds Voorburgwal and Oudezijds Achterburgwal), is the heart of the *rosse buurt*, the red-light district. In the windows at canal level, women in sheer lingerie slouch, stare, or do their nails. Drawn red curtains above suggest a brisker trade. Although the area can be shocking, with its sex shops and porn shows, it is generally safe, but midnight walks down dark side streets are not advised. If you do decide to explore the area, take care; purse snatching is common.

6 Return to the Damrak and continue up to the **Dam,** the broadest square in the old section of the town. It was here that the fishermen used to come to sell their catch. Today it is jammed with shops, people, and traffic; it is also a popular youth center for outdoor concerts. To the left, you will notice a simple monument to Dutch victims of World War II. Eleven urns contain soil from the 11 provinces of Holland, while a 12th contains soil from the former Dutch East Indies, now Indonesia.

7 To the right of the square is the **Nieuwe Kerk** (New Church). A huge Gothic church, it was gradually expanded until 1540, when it reached its present size. Gutted by fire in 1645, it was reconstructed in an imposing Renaissance style, as interpreted by strict Calvinists. The superb oak pulpit, the 14th-century nave, the stained-glass windows, and the great organ (1645) are all shown to great effect on national holidays, when the church is bedecked with flowers. As befits Holland's national church, the Nieuwe Kerk is the site of all coronations, including the crowning of Queen Beatrix in 1980. But in democratic Dutch spirit, the church is also used as a meeting place and is the home of a lively café, temporary exhibitions, and concerts. Built into the north porch of the church are two of the smallest shops in Europe: One customer enters and the shop is full. *Open Mon.–Sat. 11–4, Sun. noon–3. Closed Jan. and Feb.*

Time Out   **De Drie Fleschjes** (The Three Bottles). Situated in a bell-gabled house on a crooked, medieval street behind the Nieuwe Kerk, this is one of the most typical 17th-century *proeflokalen* (wine- and spirit-tasting houses). The tone is set by the burnished wood interior, the candle-lit bar, and the profusion of kegs and taps. Brokers are big buyers here when the markets close. Although the main emphasis is on drink, light snacks are also available. *Gravenstraat 18. Open Mon.–Sat. noon–8.*

8 Glance at the **Koninklijk Paleis** (Royal Palace), or **Dam Palace,** a vast, well-proportioned structure on Dam Square that was completed in 1655. It is built on 13,659 piles, sunk into the marshy soil. The great pedimental sculptures are an allegorical representation of Amsterdam surrounded by Neptune and mythological sea creatures.

9 From behind the palace, Raadhuisstraat leads west across three canals to the **Westermarkt** and the **Westerkerk** (West Church), built in 1631. The church's 85-meter (275-foot) tower is the highest in the city. It also features an outstanding carillon (set of bells). Rembrandt and his son Titus are buried in the church. During the summer, you can climb to the top of the tower for a fine view over the city.

Opposite, at Westermarkt 6, is the house where Descartes, the great 17th-century French philosopher ("Cogito, ergo sum"—"I think, therefore I am") lived in 1634. Another more famous

⑩ house lies farther down Prinsengracht. This is the **Anne Frank Huis** (Anne Frank House), immortalized by the poignant diary kept by the young Jewish girl from 1942 to 1944, when she and her family hid here from the German occupying forces. A small exhibition on the Holocaust can also be seen in the house. *Prinsengracht 263, tel. 020/6264533. Admission: Fl. 6. Open June–Aug., Mon.–Sat. 9–7, Sun. 10–7; Sept.–May, Mon.–Sat. 9–5, Sun. 10–5.*

⑪ Continuing right up the Prinsengracht, you'll reach the **Noorderkerk,** built in 1623. In the square in front of the church, the Noorderplein, a bird market, is held every Saturday.

South of the Dam Turn down Kalverstraat, a shopping street leading south from the Royal Palace. You will notice a striking Renaissance gate (1581) that guards a series of tranquil inner courtyards. In medieval times, this area was an island devoted to piety. Today the bordering canals are filled in.

⑫ The medieval doorway just around the corner in St. Lucien-steeg leads to the former Burgerweeshuis (City Orphanage), once a nunnery but now the **Historisch Museum** (Museum of History). The museum traces the city's history from its origins as a fishing village through the 17th-century Golden Age of material and artistic wealth to the decline of the trading empire during the 18th century. The engrossing trail unfolds through a display of old maps, documents, and paintings, often aided by a commentary in English. *Kalverstraat 92, tel. 020/5231822. Admission: Fl. 5. Open daily 11–5.*

⑬ A small passageway and courtyard link the museum with the **Begijnhof,** an enchanting, enclosed square of almshouses founded in 1346. The *beguines* were women who chose to lead a form of convent life, often taking the vow of chastity. The last beguine died in 1974 and her house, No. 26, has been preserved as she left it. No. 34, dating from the 15th century, is the oldest and the only one to keep its wooden Gothic facade. *Tel. 020/6235554. Open weekdays 11–4.*

In the center of the square is a church given to Amsterdam's English and Scottish Presbyterians more than 300 years ago. On the church wall and also in the chancel are tributes to the Pilgrim Fathers who sailed from Delfthaven to New York in 1620. Opposite the church is another of the city's secret Catholic chapels, built in 1671.

Once back in Kalverstraat, you soon come to Spui, a lively square in the heart of the university area. It was a center for student rallies in revolutionary 1968. Now it is a center for bookstores and bars, including the cozy "brown cafés."

⑭ A right turn here would bring you to the Singel Canal and, following the tram tracks, to Leidsestraat, an important shopping street that terminates in the **Leidseplein.** Much farther along the Singel, on the left bank, just past the lock at Open Haven, is what is erroneously called the smallest house in Amsterdam. In fact, it is just a door opening onto a small alley. The real narrowest house is the art gallery **Den Gulden Fonteyn,** at Singel 166.

⑮ If you continue straight along Kalverstraat instead of turning, you'll soon reach the **Muntplein,** with its **Munttoren** (Mint Tower, built in 1620), a graceful structure whose clock and bells still seem to mirror the Golden Age. West from the Muntplein

16 is the floating **flower market** on the Singel Canal. *Open Mon.–Sat. 9:30–5.*

From the Singel, take Leidsestraat to the Herengracht, the city's most prestigious "Gentlemen's Canal." The stretch of canal from here to Huidenstraat is named The **Golden Bend** for its sumptuous patrician houses with double staircases and grand entrances. Seventeenth-century merchants moved here from the Amstel River to escape the disadvantageous byproducts of their wealth: the noisy warehouses, the unpleasant smells from the breweries, and the risk of fire in the sugar refineries. These houses display the full range of Amsterdam facades: from neck, bell, and step gables to grander Louis XIV–style houses with elaborate cornices and frescoed ceilings. In particular, look at Nos. 364–370, as well as No. 380, with its sculpted angels and Louis XIV facade; Nos. 390 and 392 display neck-shaped gables surmounted by statues of a couple in matching 17th-century garb. These houses are best seen from the east side of the canal. For more gables, turn left down Wolvenstraat into the Keizersgracht, the Emperor's Canal. Walk northward toward Westerkerk and the Anne Frank Huis.

Time Out On the corner of Keizersgracht and Reestraat is the well-restored **Pulitzer Hotel** and restaurant complex. Inside, you can wander around quiet inner courtyards and a modern art gallery before sitting down in the Pulitzer Coffeeshop for a well-deserved apple tart or pastry. *Keizersgracht 236. Open daily 11–11.*

---

18 Along Herengracht, parallel to the Westerkerk, is the **Nederlands Theater Instituut.** This theater museum is a dynamic find on such a genteel canal. Two frescoed Louis XIV–style merchants' houses form the backdrop for a history of the circus, opera, musicals, and drama. Miniature theaters and videos of stage productions are just two entertaining features. During the summer, the large garden is open for buffet lunches. *168 Herengracht. Admission: Fl. 3. Open Tues.–Sun. 11–5.*

Jewish Amsterdam Take the Museumboat or the metro to Waterlooplein and walk east to Jodenbreestraat. This is the heart of **Jodenbuurt,** the old Jewish district and an important area to all Amsterdammers. The original settlers here were wealthy Sephardic Jews from Spain and Portugal, later followed by poorer Ashkenazic refugees from Germany and Poland. At the turn of the century, this was a thriving community of Jewish diamond polishers, dyers, and merchants. During World War II, the corner of Jodenbreestraat marked the end of the *Joodse wijk,* (Jewish neighborhood) by then an imposed ghetto. Although the character of the street was largely destroyed by partial demolition in 1965, neighboring Muiderstraat has retained much of the original atmosphere. Notice the gateways decorated with pelicans, symbolizing great love; according to legend, the pelican will feed her starving young with her own blood.

19 From 1639 to 1658, Rembrandt lived at Jodenbreestraat No. 4, now the **Museum Het Rembrandthuis** (Rembrandt's House). For more than 20 years, the ground floor was used by the artist as living quarters; the sunny upper floor was his studio. It is fascinating to visit, both as a record of life in 17th-century Amsterdam and as a sketch of Holland's most illustrious artist. It contains a superb collection of his etchings and engravings.

From St. Antonies Sluis bridge, just by the house, there is a canal view that has barely changed since Rembrandt's time. *Jodenbreestraat 4–6, tel. 020/6249486. Admission: Fl. 4. Open Mon.–Sat. 10–5, Sun. 1–5.*

20 Visserplein is a square linking Jodenbreestraat with Muiderstraat. In the center is a burly statue of the **Dokwerker** (Dockworker), a profession that has played a significant part in the city's history. The statue commemorates the 1942 strike by which Amsterdam dockworkers expressed their solidarity with persecuted Jews. A memorial march is held every year on February 25.

21 Facing the Dokwerker is the 17th-century **Portuguese Synagogue.** As one of Amsterdam's four neighboring synagogues, it was part of the largest Jewish religious complex in Europe. The austere interior is still intact, even if the building itself is marooned on a traffic island. *Open Apr.–Oct., Sun.–Fri. 10–4.*

22 On the other side of the street is the intriguing **Joods Historisch Museum** (Jewish History Museum), set in a complex of three ancient synagogues. These synagogues once served a population of 100,000 Jews, which shrank to less than 10,000 after 1945. The new museum, founded by American and Dutch Jews, displays religious treasures in a clear cultural and historical context. Since the synagogues lost most of their treasures in the war, their architecture and history are more compelling than the individual exhibits. *Jonas Daniël Meijerplein 2–4, tel. 020/6269945. Admission: Fl. 7. Open daily 11–5.*

Time Out **Cafeteria Kosher.** Situated within the oldest part of the museum, the cafeteria is built above the former kosher meat halls that later became ritual baths. It still looks like part of a clandestine Catholic church, the original model for the synagogue. Jewish delicacies include fish cakes, cheese tarts, bagels, and spicy cakes with gingerbread and almond cream filling. *Open daily 11–5.*

Instead of returning on foot, you can catch the Museumboat from Blauwbrug on Waterlooplein to the central station or to a destination near your hotel. If you feel like a breath of fresh air, stroll along Nieuwe Herengracht, once known as the "Jewish Gentlemen's Canal." In Rembrandt's day, there were views of distant windjammers sailing into port, but today the canal is oddly deserted.

The Museum By crossing the bridge at the south side of the Leidseplein and
Quarter walking a short distance to the left on Stadshouderskade, you'll find three of the most distinguished museums in Holland—the Rijksmuseum, the Stedelijk Museum, and the Rijksmuseum
23 Vincent van Gogh. Of the three, the **Rijksmuseum,** easily recognized by its cluster of towers, is the most important, so be sure to allow adequate time to explore it. It was founded by Louis Bonaparte in 1808, but the current, rather lavish, building dates from 1885. The museum contains significant collections of furniture, textiles, ceramics, sculpture, and prints, as well as Italian, Flemish, and Spanish paintings, many of which are of the highest quality. But the museum's fame rests on its unrivaled collection of 16th- and 17th-century Dutch masters. Of Rembrandt's masterpieces, make a point of seeing *The Nightwatch,* concealed during World War II in caves in Maastricht. The painting was misnamed because of its dull layers of

varnish; in reality it depicts the Civil Guard in daylight. Also worth searching out are Jan Steen's family portraits, Frans Hals's drunken scenes, Van Ruysdael's romantic but menacing landscapes, and Vermeer's glimpses of everyday life bathed in his usual pale light. *Stadhouderskade 42, tel. 020/6732121. Admission: Fl. 7. Open Tues.–Sat. 10–5, Sun. 1–5.*

㉔ A few blocks down the road is the **Rijksmuseum Vincent van Gogh.** This museum contains the world's largest collection of the artist's works—200 paintings and 500 drawings—as well as works by some 50 other painters of the period. *Paulus Potterstraat 7, tel. 020/570-5200. Admission: Fl. 7. Open Mon.–Sat. 10–5, Sun. 1–5.*

㉕ Next door is the **Stedelijk Museum** (Municipal Museum), with its austere neoclassical facade designed to counterbalance the Rijksmuseum's neo-Gothic turrets. The museum has a stimulating collection of modern art and ever-changing displays of contemporary art. Before viewing the works of Cézanne, Chagall, Kandinsky, and Mondrian, check the list of temporary exhibitions in Room 1. Museum policy is to trace the development of the artist rather than merely to show a few masterpieces. Don't forget the museum's restaurant overlooking a garden filled with modern sculptures. *Paulus Potterstraat 13, tel. 020/ 5732911. Admission: Fl. 8. Open daily 11–5.*

㉖ Diagonally opposite the Stedelijk Museum, at the end of the broad Museumplein, is the **Concertgebouw,** home of the country's foremost orchestra, the world-renowned Concertgebouworkest. Many visiting orchestras also perform here. The building has two auditoriums, the smaller of which is used for chamber music and recitals. A block or two in the opposite direction is **Vondelpark,** an elongated rectangle of paths, lakes, and pleasant shady trees. A monument honors the 17th-century epic poet Joost van den Vondel, for whom the park is named. From Wednesday to Sunday during the summer, free concerts and plays are performed in the park.

The Jordaan One old part of Amsterdam that is certainly worth exploring is ㉗ the **Jordaan,** the area bordered by Herengracht, Lijnbaansgracht, Brouwersgracht, and Raadhuisstraat. The canals and side streets here are all named for flowers and plants. Indeed, at one time, when this was the French quarter of the city, the area was known as *le jardin* (the garden), a name that over the years has become Jordaan. The best time to explore this area is on a Sunday morning, when there are few cars and people about, or in the evening. This part of the town has attracted many artists and is something of a bohemian quarter, where rundown buildings are being renovated and converted into restaurants, antiques shops, boutiques, and galleries.

Time Out The Jordaan is the best part of Amsterdam for relaxing in a brown café, so named because of the rich wood furnishings and—some say—the centuries-old pipe-tobacco stains on the ceilings. You can while away a rainy afternoon chatting to friendly strangers over homemade meatballs or apple tarts. Spend an hour or three over a beer or coffee at either 't Doktorje (Rozenboomsteegweg 4) or De Egelantier (Egelantierstraat 72).

Maritime Quarter Another "see-worthy" district is the burgeoning **Maritime** ㉘ **Quarter.** To reach it, walk left from the Central Station along the Prins Hendrikkade and the Eastern Harbor, the hub of Holland's Golden Age. A growing permanent collection of restored vessels is moored at the **National Maritime Museum** (Scheepvaart Museum), a former naval complex at Kattenburgerplein 1. A short stroll farther down the Kattenburgergracht-Wittenburgergracht to the footbridge over the canal leads to the **Kromhout Museum** (Hoogte Kadijk 147). Many early steamships were built at this wharf, where models and motors are on display.

Shopping

Serious shoppers should buy the VVV's four excellent shopping guides to markets, art and antiques shops, boutiques, and department stores (Fl. 10).

Gift Ideas **Diamonds.** Since the 17th century, "Amsterdam cut" has been synonymous with perfection in the quality of diamonds. You can see this craftsmanship at any of the diamond-cutting houses. The cutters explain how the diamond's value depends on the four *c*'s—carat, cut, clarity, and color—before encouraging you to buy. There is a cluster of diamond houses on the Rokin. Alternatively, try **Van Moppes Diamonds** (Albert Cuypstraat 2–6, tel. 020/6761242; open daily 9–5).

Porcelain. The Dutch have been producing Delft, Makkum, and other fine porcelain for centuries. **Focke and Meltzer** stores have been selling it since 1823. The price range varies from affordable, newly painted tiles (Fl. 8) to expensive Delft blue-and-white pitchers. One store is situated near the Rijksmuseum (65–67 P. C. Hoofstraat, tel. 020/6231944).

Shopping Districts Amsterdam's chief shopping districts, which have largely been turned into pedestrianized areas, are the **Leidsestraat, Kalverstraat,** and **de Nieuwendijk,** on the other side of Dam Square. **Rokin,** somber and sedate, houses a cluster of renowned antiques shops selling 18th- and 19th-century furniture, antique jewelry, Art Deco lamps, and statuettes. By contrast, some of the **Nieuwe Spiegelstraat**'s old curiosity shops sell a more inexpensive range. **Haute couture** and other fine stores are at home on P.C. Hoofstraat, Van Baerlestraat, and Beethovenstraat. For trendy small boutiques and unusual crafts shops, locals browse through the Jordaan. When leaving Holland, remember that Schiphol Airport is Europe's best tax-free shopping center.

Department Stores **De Bijenkorf** (Damrak), the city's number-one department store, is excellent for contemporary fashions and furnishings. Running a close second is **Vroom and Dreesman** (Kalverstraat 201) with well-stocked departments carrying all manner of goods. The restaurants and cafeterias in these department stores are also worth trying.

Markets There is a lively open-air **flea market** on Waterlooplein around the Musiektheater (Mon.–Sat. 9:30–4). The **floating flower market** on the Singel is popular with locals and visitors alike. (Open Mon.–Sat. 9:30–5). An unusual Saturday **bird market** is held in the Noordermarkt. Philatelists will not want to miss the **stamp market** at Nieuwezijds Voorburgwal (Wed. and Sat. 1–4). If you are interested in old books, head for the **book market** at Oudemanhuispoort (Mon.–Sat.). For antiques, especially silver and toys, visit the Sunday **Nieuwe Markt** (New Market) during the summer. You can also try the **Antiekmarkt de Looier** (Elandsgracht 109. Open Sat.–Thurs. 11–5). During the summer, art lovers can buy etchings, drawings, and watercolors at the Sunday **art markets** on Thorbeckeplein and the Spui.

Dining

Amsterdammers are less creatures of habit than are the Dutch in general. Even so, set menus and early dinners are preferred by these health-conscious citizens. For travelers on a diet or budget, the blue-and-white "Tourist Menu" sign guarantees an economical (Fl. 20) yet imaginative set menu created by the head chef. For traditionalists, the "Nederlands Dis" soup tureen sign is a promise of regional recipes and seasonal ingredients. "You can eat in any language" is the city's proud boast, so when Dutch restaurants are closed, Indonesian, Chinese, and Turkish restaurants are often open. Between meals, you can follow your nose to the nearest herring cart or drop into a cozy brown café for coffee and an apple tart.

Breakfast tends to be hearty and substantial—several varieties of bread, butter, jam, ham, cheese, boiled eggs, and steaming coffee or tea. Dutch specialties for later meals include *erwtensoep*, a rich, thick pea soup with pieces of tangy sausage or pigs' knuckles, and *hutspot*, a meat, carrot, and potato stew; both are usually served during winter. *Haring* (herring) is particularly popular, especially the "new herring" caught between May and September and served in brine, garnished with onions. *Rodekool met rolpens* is red cabbage and rolled spiced meat with sliced apple. If Dutch food begins to pall, try an Indonesian restaurant, where the chief dish is *rijsttafel*, a huge bowl of steaming rice with 20 or more side dishes.

The indigenous Dutch liquor is potent and warming *jenever* (gin). Dutch liqueurs and beers are also popular.

Eating places range from snack bars, fast-food outlets, and modest local cafés to gourmet restaurants of international repute. Of special note are the "brown cafés," traditional pub-style eateries of great character that normally offer substantial snack meals.

Mealtimes The Dutch tend to eat dinner early, normally around 6 or 7 PM, so many restaurants close at about 10 PM and accept final orders at 9. In larger cities some "foreign" restaurants stay open until midnight.

Dress Jacket and tie are suggested for restaurants in the Very Expensive and Expensive categories. Elsewhere, casual dress is acceptable. In general, Holland is a somewhat formal country, so when in doubt, it's better to dress up.

Ratings Prices are per person including two courses, dessert, service, and sales tax but not drinks. For budget travelers, many restaurants offer a tourist menu at an officially controlled price, currently Fl. 20. Best bets are indicated by a star ★.

Category	Cost
Very Expensive	over Fl. 130
Expensive	Fl. 100–Fl. 130

Moderate	Fl. 50–Fl. 100
Inexpensive	under Fl. 50

Very Expensive **Excelsior.** Hôtel de l'Europe's renowned restaurant offers a varied menu of French cuisine that is based on local ingredients; try the sea bass in curry sauce and the smoked eel. The service is discreet and impeccable. *Nieuwe Doelenstraat 2–4, tel. 020/6234836. Reservations required. AE, DC, MC, V. Closed Sat. lunch.*

★ **De Trechter.** This is an intimate restaurant with some seven tables in a lime-green Parisian decor. The chef-patron chats with the guests, many of whom have booked weeks in advance. Adventurous diners choose the surprise menu. *Hobbemakade 62–63, tel. 020/6711263. Reservations advised. AE, DC, MC, V. Closed Sun. and Mon.*

Le Tout Court. This small, meticulously appointed restaurant features seasonal specialties (spring lamb, summer fruits, game during autumn and winter) personally prepared by owner-chef John Fagel, a member of Holland's first family of food. *Runstraat 13, tel. 020/6258637. Reservations required. AE, DC, MC, V. Closed Sun. and Mon. Dinner only.*

Expensive **Edo.** The Grand Hotel Krasnapolsky is home to a Dutch notion of Japanese cuisine. Artistic portions of raw fish and deep-fried tempura vegetables are served against a background of polished pine and equally polished service. You'll marvel at the way Dutch seafood lends itself to sushi preparation. *Sashimi* (raw fish) is prepared before your eyes. *Dam 9, tel. 020/5546096. Reservations required. AE, DC, MC, V.*

De Kersentuin. This superb restaurant, in the Garden Hotel, is known as one of the best in Holland. The dining room is elegant—you eat amid the greenery of a covered garden—and the menu has the flair of nouvelle cuisine. Try the salmon specialties. *Dijsselhofplantsoen 7, tel. 020/6642121. Reservations required. AE, DC, MC, V. Closed Sat. and Sun. lunch.*

Les Quatre Canetons. Pleasantly informal, this canalside restaurant is popular with local businesspeople. It serves mainly nouvelle cuisine and freshwater trout. *Prinsengracht 1111, tel. 020/6246307. Closed Sat. lunch and Sun. Reservations required. AE, DC, MC, V.*

★ **'t Swarte Schaep.** The Black Sheep is named after a proverbial 17th-century sheep that once roamed the area. With its creaking boards and array of copper pots, the interior is reminiscent of a ship's cabin. The Dutch chef uses seasonal ingredients to create classical French dishes with regional flourishes and a touch of nouvelle cuisine. Dinner orders are accepted until 11 PM—unusually late even for Amsterdam. *Korte Leidsedwarsstraat 24, tel. 020/6223021. Reservations required. AE, DC, MC, V.*

★ **d'Vijff Vlieghen.** Take a trip back in time to a warren of 17th-century charm. Each of the seven dining rooms is decorated in a different Renaissance style. The menu has a touch of nouvelle cuisine, more in presentation than in proportion; the game specialties are attractive and substantial. As befits an ex-tavern, the candlelight atmosphere is warm and relaxed. *Spuistraat 294, tel. 020/6248369. Reservations advised. AE, DC, MC, V. Dinner only.*

Moderate **De Orient.** Excellent Indonesian food is just minutes away from
★ major museums and the Concertgebouw. Complementing the

rijsttafel (rice with a dozen or more spicy side dishes) are excellent *loempia* (egg rolls) and soups. Every Wednesday night there is a rijsttafel buffet. *Van Baerlestraat 21, tel. 020/6734958. Reservations required. AE, DC, MC, V.*

Oesterbar. As its name suggests, the Oyster Bar specializes in seafood, some of which eyes you from the tank. The downstairs bistro offers relatively inexpensive dining, while upstairs, presentation and price are somewhat higher. Salmon and trout are the specialties, and the oysters themselves make a good, if expeosive, first course. *Leidseplein 10, tel. 020/6232988. Reservations advised. AE, DC.*

De Roode Leeuw. As a Nederlands Dis restaurant, the Red Lion guarantees traditional Dutch cuisine at its best. Depending on the season, you can sample smoked eel, Zeeland mussels, asparagus wrapped in ham, and various regional dishes. The reasonable wine list, attentive service, and friendly atmosphere live up to the Nederlands Dis tradition. *Damrak 93–4, tel. 020/6249683 and 020/6240396. Reservations advised. AE, DC, MC, V.*

Sea Palace. The Sea Palace is an appropriate establishment for a city built on canals—it's a huge, floating Chinese restaurant. The Cantonese menu is of only modest quality, but the surroundings make up for it. A special children's menu is also available. *Oosterdokskade (near the central station), tel. 020/6264777. Reservations accepted. No credit cards.*

Inexpensive   **Oud Holland.** This restaurant is in a convenient location for a night on the town—not far from the Leidseplein, yet just far enough from the red-light district. Oud Holland is one of the few Amsterdam restaurants to offer a tourist menu. A typical three-course meal is a game paté followed by pork in cream sherry sauce and an apple pancake for dessert. A children's menu is also available. The heated terrace opens at 5 PM for restaurant guests. *NZ Voorburgwal 105, tel. 020/6246848. Reservations accepted. AE, DC, MC, V.*

Pancake Bakery. Here is a chance to try a traditionally Dutch way of keeping eating costs down. The name of the game is pancakes—for every course including dessert, for which the topping can be ice cream, fruit, or liqueur. The Pancake Bakery is not far from Anne Frank Huis. *Prinsengracht 191, tel. 020/6251233. No reservations. No credit cards.*

★   **Speciaal.** Although set in the Jordaan area, this Indonesian restaurant is slightly off the beaten track. From the outside, the Speciaal looks very mundane, but inside, the soothing Indonesian prints, raffia work, and bamboo curtains create an intimate atmosphere. Along with the usual rijsttafel, chicken, fish, and egg dishes provide tasty variants on a sweet-and-sour theme. *Nieuwe Leliestraat 142, tel. 020/249706. Reservations accepted.*

Lodging

Accommodations are tight from Easter to summer, so early booking is advised if you wish to secure a popular hotel. The other snag is parking: Amsterdam is a pedestrian's paradise but a driver's nightmare. Since few hotels have parking lots, cars are best abandoned in a multistory parking ramp for the duration of your stay. Most tourists prefer to stay inside the concentric ring of canals. This area, the quiet museum quarter, is a convenient choice for the Rijksmuseum yet is near enough to the Vondelpark for light jogging. More atmospheric lodgings can be found in the historic canalside neighborhood with its gabled merchants' houses. Holland offers a wide range of accommodations, from the luxurious Golden Tulip hotel chain to traditional, small-town hotels and family-run guest houses. Budget travelers may prefer to stay in friendly bed-and-breakfast establishments; these are in short supply and need to be booked on the spot at local VVV offices.

Hotels   Dutch hotels are generally spotless, no matter how modest their facilities, and service is normally courteous and efficient. There are many moderate and inexpensive hotels, most of which are relatively small. English is spoken or understood by desk clerks almost everywhere. Hotels usually quote room prices for double occupancy, and rates include breakfast, service charges, and VAT.

To book hotels in advance, you can use the free **National Reservation Center** (Box 404, 2260 KA Leidschendam, tel. 070/3202500). Alternatively, for a small fee, VVV offices can usually make reservations at short notice. Bookings must be made in person, however.

Ratings   Prices are for two people sharing a double room. Best bets are indicated by a star ★.

Category	Cost
Very Expensive	Fl. 450–Fl. 600
Expensive	Fl. 300–Fl. 450
Moderate	Fl. 200–Fl. 300
Inexpensive	under Fl. 200

Very Expensive   **Amsterdam Hilton.** One of the first international chain hotels to open in Amsterdam, the Hilton is still one of the most gracious. In the southern part of the city, it overlooks the attractive Noorder Amstelkanal. All the rooms are luxuriously appointed. *Apollolaan 138, tel. 020/6780780. 274 rooms with bath. Facilities: casino. AE, DC, MC, V.*

Golden Tulip Barbizon Palace. The newest Golden Tulip Hotel in Amsterdam combines past and present with fantasy and flair. *Prins Hendrikkade 59–72, tel. 020/556–4564. 257 rooms with bath; 5 suites, 5 apartments (monthly). AE, DC, MC, V.*

Hôtel de l'Europe. The hotel hides its modern facilities behind a Renaissance-style facade. It has larger-than-average rooms, often decorated with old prints and Empire furniture. Apart from its world-renowned Excelsior restaurant, de l'Europe houses a sophisticated leisure complex and hotel swimming pool in Roman style. *Nieuwe Doelenstraat 2–4, tel. 020/6234836. 100 rooms with bath. Facilities: restaurant, pool, leisure complex. AE, DC, MC, V.*

★ **Sonesta.** Situated in the old port area, the Sonesta incorporates a striking domed church and its own brown café. Lobby-lounge service (drinks and snacks) in comfortable artistic surroundings make this a favorite spot to meet. Contemporary pictures and sculpture are also scattered throughout the bars and bedrooms. This hotel is now part of the Ramada chain. *Kattengat 1, tel. 020/212223. 425 rooms with bath. Facilities: restaurant, bar, health club, shopping complex. AE, DC, MC, V.*

Expensive **Golden Tulip Pulitzer.** The Pulitzer succeeds in making living in
★ the past a positive pleasure. This is one of Europe's most ambitious hotel restorations, using the shells of a row of 17th-cen-
tury merchants' houses. Inside, the refined atmosphere is
sustained by the modern art gallery, the lovingly restored
brickwork, oak beams, and split-level rooms—no two are alike.
The tranquil inner courtyards are equally adapted to contem-
plation and outdoor concerts. *Prinsengracht 315–331, tel. 020/
5235235. 250 rooms with bath. Facilities: restaurant, bar. AE,
DC, MC, V.*

★ **Grand Hotel Krasnapolsky.** This is one of the fine, Old World hotels in Amsterdam, dominated by its Winter Gardens restaurant and recently restored to its original 1818 luster. The
cosmopolitan atmosphere carries through all the rooms, with
decor ranging from Victorian to Art Deco. Each room is well
equipped, and there is a choice of restaurants—Edo (*see* Dining, above) and the Reflet d'Or. *Dam 9, tel. 020/5549111. 330
rooms with bath. Facilities: parking. AE, DC, MC, V.*

Moderate **Ambassade.** With its beautiful canalside location, its Louis XV-
★ style decoration, and its Oriental carpets, the Ambassade
seems more like a stately home than a hotel. Service is attentive and room prices include breakfast. For other meals, the
neighborhood has a good choice of restaurants for eating out.
*Herengracht 341, tel. 020/6262333. 11 rooms with bath. AE,
MC, V.*

Atlas Hotel. Renowned for its friendly atmosphere, this small
hotel has moderate-size rooms decorated in Art Nouveau style.
It's also very handy for Museumsplein, whose major museums are within easy walking distance. Ask for a room facing
Vondelpark. *Van Eeghenstraat 64, tel. 020/6766336. 22 rooms
with bath. Facilities: bar, restaurant. AE, DC, MC, V.*

Het Canal House. The American owners of this canalside hotel
also opt to put antiques rather than televisions in the rooms.
Spacious rooms overlook the canal or the illuminated garden. A
hearty Dutch breakfast comes with the room. *Keizergracht
148, tel. 020/6225182. 20 rooms with bath or shower. AE.*

Inexpensive **Agora.** Set beside the Singel flower market, this small hotel re-
★ flects the cheerful bustle. The rooms are light and spacious,
some decorated with period furniture; the best overlook the canal or the university. Recently refurbished, this 18th-century
house has a summery dining room. Considerate staff and a relaxed neighborhood ensure the hotel's popularity. Book well in
advance. *Singel 462, tel. 020/6272200. 14 rooms with bath or
shower. Facilities: dining room. No credit cards.*

★ **De Gouden Kettingh.** This 17th-century merchant's house is
called the Golden Necklace because an early mistress of the
house accused a servant of stealing one; when it was found in
the attic, the servant was hanged in Dam Square. Naturally,
her ghost is said to haunt the upper reaches of the house.
*Keizersgracht 270, tel. 020/6248287. 24 rooms, 20 with bath; 3
deluxe rooms. AE, DC, MC, V.*

Weichmann. Situated on the edge of the lively Jordaan area,
the Weichmann is popular for its quiet warmth and reasonable
prices. Although the modest bedrooms are modern, the old entrance hall and dining room are home to a shiny cannon and a
suit of armor. Family rooms are also available. Book out of season or well in advance. *Prinsengracht 328–330, tel. 020/*

*6263321. 35 rooms, most with bath or shower. Facilities: dining
room. No credit cards.*

The Arts

The arts flourish in tolerant and cosmopolitan Amsterdam. The
best sources of information about performances are the monthly publications *Amsterdam Times* and *What's On* (both in English) and the weekly *Amsterdam This Week;* the latter two can
be obtained from the VVV office, which can also help you secure tickets for the more popular events. Tickets must be
booked in person from 10 to 4. You can also book at the **Amsterdam Uit Buro,** Stadsschouwburg, Leidseplein 26, tel. 020/
2112111.

Classical Music Classical music is featured at the **Concertgebouw** (Concert-
gebouwplein 2–6), home of one of Europe's finest orchestras. A
smaller auditorium in the same building is used for chamber
music, recitals, and even jam sessions. While ticket prices for
international orchestras are fairly high, most concerts are good
value and the Wednesday lunchtime concerts are free. The box
office is open from 9:30 to 7; you can make telephone bookings
(020/6718345) from 10 to 3.

Opera and Ballet The Dutch national ballet and opera companies are housed in
the new **Muziektheater** on Waterlooplein. Guest companies
from foreign countries perform there during the three-week
Holland Festival in June.

Theater **Stalhouderij Theater** (1e Bloemdwarsstraat 4, tel. 020/
6262282). An international cast performs a wide range of English-language plays in a former stable in the Jordaan. For experimental theater and colorful cabaret in Dutch, catch the
shows at **Felix Meritis House** (Keizersgracht 324, tel. 020/
231311).

Film The largest concentration of movie theaters is on Leidseplein
and Reguliersbreestraat. Most foreign films are subtitled rather than dubbed, but to be sure—and to find out times—see
Amsterdam This Week.

Nightlife

Amsterdam has a wide variety of discos, bars, and exotic
shows, including some that surpass even the "hot spots" of such
cities as Hamburg; none, however, have the elegance of Paris.
The more respectable—and expensive—after-dark activities
in and around Leidseplein, Rembrandtsplein, and Thorbeckeplein; fleshier productions are on Oudezijds Achterburgwal
and near the Zeedijk. Names and locations change from year to
year, but most bars and clubs are open every night from 5 PM to
2 AM or 4 AM. It is wise to steer clear of the area around the central station at night. On weeknights, very few clubs charge admission, though the more lively ones sometimes ask for a "club
membership" fee of Fl. 20 or more. Drink prices are for the
most part not exorbitant.

Bars The **Bamboo Bar** (Lange Leidsedwarsstraat) is informal, expensive, relaxing, and typically international. It boasts good
jazz and blues around the longest bar in Amsterdam.

Jazz Clubs Set in a converted warehouse, the **BIMhuis** is currently the
most fashionable jazz club. Ticket holders can sit in the adjoin-

ing BIMcafé and enjoy a magical view across Oude Schans to the port (Oude Schans 173–7, tel. 020/6271255. Open Thurs.– Sat. from 9 PM). For jazz and vocals, try the discreet **Cab Kaye's Jazz Piano Bar** (Beulingstraat 9, tel. 020/6233594. Open Tues.– Sat. until 3 AM). If you long for good Dixieland jazz, go to **Joseph Lam Jazz Club** (Van Diemenstraat 8, tel. 020/6228086); it's only open on weekends.

Rock Clubs **Maloe Melo** (Lijnbaansgracht 160) caters to the slightly older-than-teenage crowd. A very trendy scene for teenagers and college-age music fans is **De Bios** (Leidseplein 12); it's open from 10 PM, and entrance is free.

Discos Mostly only hidden in cellars around the Leidseplein, the discos fill up after midnight. The **Cruise Inn** (Zeeburgerdijk 271, tel. 020/6927188) is the place to go for '50s and '60s music and dance. **Zorba The Buddha** (Oudezijds Voorburgwal 216, tel. 020/259642) is run by the religious Baghwan sect in the heart of the red-light district; despite or because of this, the young only seem interested in dancing. **Mazzo** (Rozengracht 114, tel. 020/267500) uses dramatic lighting and slick videos to attract student poseurs, would-be musicians, and artists.

Casinos Blackjack, roulette, and slot machines have come lately—but not lightly—to the thrifty Dutch. Now everyone wants to play. The newest and most elegant venue, **Holland Casino** (just off Leidseplein), opened in 1991 and is expected to draw even bigger crowds than its forerunner at the Amsterdam Hilton (Apollolaan 138–140, tel. 664–9911).

3 Athens

Arriving and Departing

By Plane Most visitors arrive by air at Helleniko Airport. All Olympic Airways flights, both international and domestic, use the Western terminal next to the ocean. All other flights arrive and depart from the Eastern terminal on the opposite side of the airport.

Between the Airport and Downtown A blue-and-yellow coach service connects the two air terminals, Syntagma Square, the bus and train stations, and Piraeus. The coaches run every 20 minutes from 6 AM until midnight (fare: 160 dr.) and every 90 minutes from midnight until 6 AM (fare: 200 dr.). A taxi to the center of Athens costs about 1,200 dr.

By Train Athens has two railway stations, side by side, not far from Omonia Square. International trains from the north arrive at, and depart from, Stathmos Larissis, and trains from the Peloponnese use the marvelously ornate and old-fashioned Stathmos Peloponnisos next door.

By Bus Greek buses arrive at the Athens bus station at 100 Kifissou. International buses drop their passengers off on the street, usually in the Omonia or Syntagma Square areas or at Stathmos Larissis.

By Car Whether you approach Athens from the Peloponnese or from the north, you enter by the National Road and then follow signs for the center. Leaving Athens, routes to the National Road are well marked; signs usually name Lamia for the north and Corinth or Patras for the southwest.

By Ship Except for cruise ships, few passenger ships from other countries call at Piraeus, the port of Athens, 10 kilometers (6 miles) from Athens' center. If you do dock at Piraeus, you can take the metro right into Omonia Square. The trip takes 20 minutes and costs 50 dr. Alternatively, you can take a taxi, which may well take longer due to traffic and will cost a great deal more, around 1,000 dr.

Getting Around

Many of the sights you'll want to see, and most of the hotels, cafés, and restaurants, are within a fairly small central area. It's easy to walk everywhere.

By Metro An electric (partially underground) railway is under construction. At present, it runs from Piraeus to Omonia Square and then on to Kifissia. It is not useful for getting around the central area. The standard fare is 50 dr. or 70 dr., depending on the distance. There are no special fares or day tickets for visitors, and there is, as yet, no public transport map.

By Bus The fare on blue buses and the roomier yellow trolley buses is 50 dr. You must have the exact change. Buses run from the center to all suburbs and suburban beaches until about midnight. For suburbs beyond central Kifissia, you have to change at Kifissia. Attica is well served by brown buses. Most buses, including those for Sounion, leave from the KTEL terminal, Platia Aigyptiou on Mavromateon, at the corner of Patission and Alexandras avenues.

By Taxi Taxis are plentiful except during rush hours and rainstorms. But they are often on strike. Also, drivers seem to lead a maverick life—those without occupants often refuse to pick up passengers, while those with occupants often stop to pick up more. Many drivers are unfamiliar with the city; some automatically deposit every American at the Hilton Hotel. There is a 330 dr. minimum and a basic charge of 48 dr. per kilometer; this increases to 82 dr. between midnight and 5 AM. There is a small charge for baggage. Some drivers overcharge foreigners, especially on trips from the airport or from Piraeus; insist that they turn on the meter as soon as you get in. The fare shown on obsolete meters in older taxis is not the one you will have to pay. The driver should consult a written scale, which will show the actual fare.

Important Addresses and Numbers

Tourist Information There are **Greek National Tourist Offices** at Karageorgi Servias 2, in the bank, tel. 01/322–2545; at East Helleniko Airport, tel. 01/970–2395; at Stadiou 4, tel. 01/322–1459; at Ermou 1, inside the General Bank building, tel. 01/325–2267; and at Piraeus, NTOG Building, Marina Zeus, tel. 01/413–5716.

Embassies **U.S.** (Vasilissis Sofias 91, tel. 01/721–2951); **Canadian** (Gennadiou 4, tel. 01/723–9511); **U.K.** (Ploutarchou 1, tel. 01/723–6211).

Emergencies **Police** Tourist Police (tel. 171); Traffic Police (tel. 01/523–0111); and City Police (tel. 100). **Ambulance** (tel. 166). **Doctors:** Top hotels usually have one on staff; any hotel will call one for you. You can also call your embassy. **Dentist:** Ask your hotel or embassy. **Pharmacies:** Most pharmacies in the central area have someone who speaks English and knows all the usual medical requirements. Try **Marinopoulois** (Kanari 23, tel. 01/361–3051).

English Bookstores **Pantelides** (Amerikas 11, tel. 01/364–5161); **Eleftheroudakis** (Nikis 4, tel. 01/770–8007).

Travel Agencies **American Express** (Ermou 2, tel. 01/324–4975); **Wagons-Lits Travel** (Stadiou 5, tel. 01/324–2281); **CHAT Tours** (Stadiou 4, tel. 01/322–2886); **Viking's Travel Bureau** (Filellinon 3, tel. 01/322–9383); **Thomas Cook** (Hellas Tours Ltd., 7 Stadiou St., tel. 01/92–35–358).

Guided Tours

Orientation Tours All tour operators offer a four-hour morning bus tour of Athens, including a guided tour of the Acropolis, for around 3,000 dr. Make reservations at your hotel or at a travel agency; besides those agents already mentioned, there are hundreds of others, many situated around Filellinon and Nikis streets off Syntagma Square.

Special-Interest Tours For those interested in folk dancing, there is a four-hour evening tour (May–Sept.) for around 3,500 dr. that begins with a son-et-lumière (sound-and-light-show) spectacle at the Acropolis and then goes on to a performance of Greek folk dances in the open-air theater nearby. Another evening tour offers a dinner show at a taverna in the Plaka area, after the son et lumière, for around 6,000 dr. Any travel agency can arrange these tours—and the excursions below—for you, but go first to **CHAT Tours** or **Viking Tours** (*see* Travel Agencies, above) for reliable and efficient service.

Excursions The choice is almost unlimited. A one-day tour to Delphi will cost up to 7,000 dr., with lunch included; a two-day tour to Corinth, Mycenae, Nauplio, and Epidaurus, around 14,000 dr., with meals and accommodations included. A full-day cruise from Piraeus, visiting three nearby islands—Aegina, Poros, and Ydra—costs around 6,000 dr., and a two-day cruise, including Mykonos and Delos, costs up to 30,000 dr., including accommodations in standard-class hotels. A three-day classical tour to Delphi and the breathtaking Meteora monasteries costs from 35,000 dr.

Personal Guides All the major tourist agencies can provide English-speaking guides for personally organized tours.

Exploring Athens

Athens is essentially a village that outgrew itself, spreading out from the original settlement at the foot of the Acropolis. Back in 1834, when it became the capital of modern Greece, the city had a population of 20,000. Now it houses more than a third of the Greek population—around 4 million—and 100,000 more join the masses every year. A modern concrete city has engulfed the old village and now sprawls for 388 square kilometers (150 square miles), covering almost all the surrounding plain from the sea to the encircling mountains.

The city is very crowded, very dusty, and overwhelmingly hot during the summer. It also has an appalling air-pollution problem, caused mainly by traffic fumes; in an attempt to lessen the congestion, it is forbidden to drive private cars in central Athens on alternate workdays. Despite the smog, heat, and dust, Athens is an experience not to be missed. It has a tangible vibrancy that makes it one of the most exciting cities in Europe, and the sprawling cement has failed to overwhelm the few striking and astonishing reminders of ancient Athens.

The central area of modern Athens is small, stretching from the Acropolis to Mount Lycabettos, with its small white church on top. The layout is simple: Three parallel streets—Stadiou, Venizelou, and Academias—link two main squares—Syntagma and Omonia. Do wander off this beaten tourist track to catch some of the real flavor of living Athens. Seeing the Athenian butchers in the central market near Monastiraki sleeping on their cold, marble slabs during the heat of the afternoon siesta may give you more of a feel for the city than seeing hundreds of fallen pillars.

Numbers in the margin correspond to points of interest on the Athens map.

The Historic Heart At the center of modern Athens is **Syntagma (Constitution)**
❶ **Square.** It has several leading hotels, airline and travel offices, and numerous cafés. Along one side of the square stands the
❷ **Parliament Building,** completed in 1838 as the royal palace for the new monarchy. In front of the palace, you can watch the changing of the vividly costumed **Evzone guard** at the Tomb of the Unknown Soldier. Amalias Avenue, leading out of Syntagma, will take you to the **National Gardens,** a large oasis in the vast sprawl of this largely concrete city.

Time Out There are several breakfast/lunch spots around Syntagma Square. **Brazilian,** at Voukourestiou 1B, one block from the square, is ideal for a quick coffee and snack (there are no tables or chairs). Just off the National Gardens, at Xenofontos 10, is **Diros,** efficiently serving good Greek food and steaks.

---

❸ Across the street, at the far end of the National Gardens, you will see the columns of the once huge **Temple of Olympian Zeus.** This famous temple was begun in the 6th century BC, and, when it was finally completed 700 years later, it exceeded in magnitude all other temples in Greece. It was destroyed during the invasion of the Goths in the 4th century, and today only the towering sun-browned columns remain. *Admission: 250 dr. Open Apr.–Oct., Tues.–Sun. 8:30–3.*

❹ To the right stands **Hadrian's Arch,** built at the same time by the Roman emperor. It consists of a Roman archway, with a Greek superstructure of Corinthian pilasters. Visiting heads of state are officially welcomed here; it is not open to the public.

❺ About three-quarters of a kilometer (a half mile) to the right, down Leoforos Olgas Avenue, you'll come to the marble **stadium** built for the first modern Olympic Games in 1896; it is a blindingly white, marble reconstruction of the ancient Olympic stadium of Athens and can seat 70,000 spectators. Greece hopes to be chosen to host the games in the centennial year, 1996.

❻ From Hadrian's Arch, take the avenue to the right, Dionysiou Areopagitou, a few blocks west to the **Theater of Dionysos,** built during the 6th century BC. Here the famous ancient dramas and comedies were originally performed in conjunction with bacchanalian feasts. *Tel. 01/323–6665. Admission: 300 dr. Open Apr.–Oct., Tues.–Sun. 8:30–3.*

❼ A little higher up, on the right, you'll see the massive back wall of the much better preserved **Theater of Herodes Atticus,** built by the Romans during the 2nd century AD. Here, on pine-scented summer evenings, the **Athens Festival** takes place. It includes opera, ballet, drama, and concerts (*see* The Arts, below). *Tel. 01/321–0219. Admission: 250 dr. Open Apr.–Oct., Mon.–Sat. 9–2:45, Sun. and holidays, 9–1:45.*

❽ Beyond the theater, a steep, zigzag path leads to the **Acropolis.** Though the Sacred Rock had been a center of worship for 5,000 years, the Athenians built this complex during the 5th century BC to commemorate the Greek naval victory at Salamis over the Persians. The first ruins you'll see are the **Propylaea,** the monumental gates that led worshippers from the temporal world into the spiritual world of the sanctuary; now only the columns of Pentelic marble remain. Above, to the right, stands the graceful **Temple of Wingless Victory** (or Athena Nike), so called because the sculptor depicted the goddess of victory without her wings in order to prevent her from flying away. The elegant and architecturally complex **Erechtheion temple,** most sacred of the shrines of the Acropolis and later turned into a harem by the Turks, has now emerged from extensive repair work. Dull, heavy copies of the infinitely more beautiful Caryatids (draped maidens) now support the roof. The Acropolis Museum houses five of the six originals, their faces much damaged by acid rain. The sixth is in the British Museum in London.

❾ The **Parthenon** dominates the Acropolis and indeed the Athens skyline. Designed by Ictinus, with Phidias as master sculptor, it is the largest Doric temple ever built and the most architec-

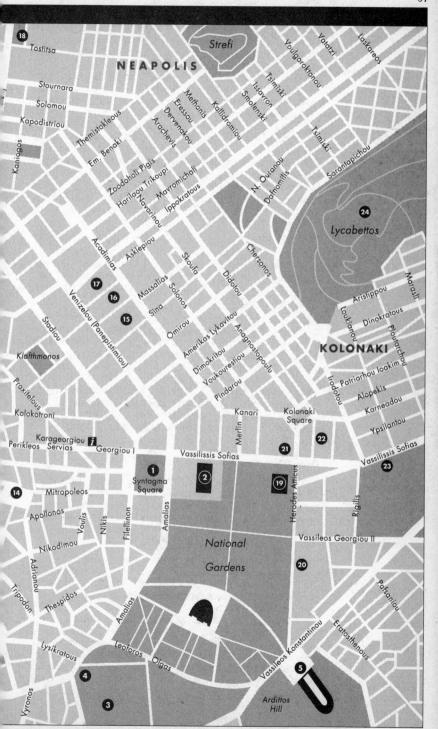

turally sophisticated. Even with hordes of tourists wandering around the ruins, you can still feel a sense of wonder. The temple was originally painted in vivid reds and blues, but time and neglect have given the marble pillars their golden-white shine, and the beauty of the building is all the more stark and striking. The British Museum houses the largest remaining part of the original 162-meter (523-foot) frieze (The Elgin Marbles). The building has 17 fluted columns along each side and 8 at the ends, and these lean slightly inward and bulge to cleverly counterbalance the natural optical distortion. The Parthenon has had a checkered history: It was made into a brothel by the Romans, a church by the Christians, and a mosque by the Turks. The Turks also stored gunpowder in the Propylaea, and when this was hit by a Venetian bombardment in 1687, a fire raged for two days and 28 columns fell, leaving the Parthenon in its present condition. *Tel. 01/321–0219. Admission: 800 dr., joint ticket to Acropolis and museum. Open weekdays 8–7, weekends and holidays 8:30–3.*

❿ The **Acropolis Museum,** just below the Parthenon, contains some superb sculptures from the Acropolis, including the Caryatids and a large collection of colored *kore* (statues of women in attendance to Athena). *Tel. 01/323–6665. Admission: 800 dr., joint ticket to the Acropolis. Open weekdays 8–7, weekends and holidays 8:30–3.*

On the rocky outcrop facing the Acropolis, St. Paul preached to the Athenians; the road leading down between it and the hill of Pnyx is called Agiou Pavlou (St. Paul). To the right stands the **⓫** **Agora,** which means "marketplace," the civic center and focal point of community life in ancient Athens. The sprawling confusion of stones, slabs, and foundations is dominated by the **⓬** best-preserved temple in Greece, the **Hephestaion** (often wrongly referred to as the Theseion), built during the 5th century BC. Nearby, the impressive Stoa of Attalus II, reconstructed by the American School of Classical Studies in Athens **⓭** with the help of the Rockefeller Foundation, houses the **Museum of the Agora Excavations.** *Tel. 01/321–0185. Admission: 400 dr. Open Tues.–Sun. 8:30–3.*

Next to the Agora you'll find the **Plaka,** almost all that's left of 19th-century Athens. During the 1950s and '60s, the area became garish with neon as nightclubs moved in and residents moved out. Renovation in recent years has restored the Plaka, and it is again lined with attractive houses and the vine-shaded courtyards of open-air tavernas and bars.

⓮ Below the Plaka, in Cathedral Square, stands a charming 12th-century Byzantine church known as the "Old" or **"Little Cathedral,"** nestled below the vast structure of the 19th-century **Cathedral of Athens.** From here, a short walk up Mitropoleos will take you back to Syntagma.

Time Out Visit the **De Profundis Tea Room** in an old mansion at Hatzimichali 1. This quiet café serves delicious homemade pastries. **Miltons,** at Adrianou 91, on the corner of Adrianou and Nikodimou in the Plaka, is ideal for a quiet, civilized lunch. Eat outside under white umbrellas and overhanging trees and watch the tourists amble by. The restaurant has a bright, clean look and serves a delightfully different—if expensive— *horiatiki* (Greek salad).

Downtown Athens

If you walk along Venizelou Avenue (also known as Pane-pistimiou Avenue) from the square, you will pass, on the right, three imposing buildings in Classical style: the **Academy,** the **Senate House of the University,** and the **National Library.** When you reach **Omonia Square,** a bedlam of touts and tourists, you are in the heart of downtown Athens.

Try to spare time to see the **National Archaeological Museum.** Despite being somewhat off the tourist route, a good 10-minute walk north of Omonia Square, it is well worth the detour. This is by far the most important museum in Athens. It houses one of the most exciting collections of antiquity in the world, including sensational archaeological finds made by Heinrich Schliemann at Mycenae, a 15th-century BC fresco from the Akrotiri ruins on Santorini, and the 6½-foot-tall bronze sculpture *Poseidon,* an original work of circa 750 BC, possibly by the sculptor Kalamis, which was found in the sea off Cape Artemision in 1928. *Tossitsa 1, off 28 Oktovriou, tel. 01/821-7717. Admission: 600 dr. Mon. 12:30-7, Tues.-Fri. 8-7, weekends and holidays 8:30-3.*

Alternatively, from Syntagma you can take Vassilissis Sofias Avenue along the edge of the National Gardens to reach the **Evzone Guards' barracks.** From here you have several options. If you continue farther along Vassilissis Sofias, it will eventually take you to the Hilton Hotel and the U.S. Embassy. Or, turn right onto Herodes Atticus, which leads to the **Presidential Palace,** a neo-Renaissance building now occupied by the present incumbent, Mr. Sartzetakis.

Opposite the Evzone Guards' barracks, on the corner of Vassilissis Sofias and Herodes Atticus, is the **Benaki Museum,** with an eclectic and interesting hodgepodge of objects from different countries and periods, ranging from ancient sculpture through Byzantine pieces, Ottoman ceramics, and Chinese jades to modern paintings. There is also a fabulous collection of genuine Greek national costumes, folk art, and embroidery. *Koumbari 1, tel. 01/361-1617. Admission: 200 dr. Open Wed.-Mon. 8:30-2.*

The **Museum of Cycladic Art** is up the next street to the right. The collection spans 5,000 years, with 230 exhibits of the Cycladic civilization (3,000-2,000 BC) in comparison with modern primitives. *Neofytou Douka 4, tel. 01/321-3018. Admission: 200 dr., free on Sat. Open Mon. and Wed.-Fri. 10-4, Sat. 10-3.*

A little farther along Vassilissis Sofias is the **Byzantine Museum,** housed in an 1840 mansion that was built by an eccentric French aristocrat. It has a unique collection of icons and the very beautiful 14th-century Byzantine embroidery of the body of Christ in gold, silver, yellow, and green. Sculptural fragments provide an excellent introduction to Byzantine architecture. *Vassilissis Sofias 22, tel. 01/721-1027. Admission: 400 dr. Open Tues.-Sun. 8:30-3.*

Kolonaki, the chic shopping district and one of the most fashionable residential areas, occupies the lower slopes of **Mount Lycabettos** and is only a 10-minute walk northeast of Syntagma; it's worth a stroll around if you enjoy window-shopping and people-watching. Three times the height of the Acropolis, Lycabettos can be reached by funicular railway from the top of Ploutarchou Street (the No. 23 bus from Kolonaki Square will drop you at the station, fare: 300 dr. round-trip). The view from the top—pollution permitting—is the finest in Athens. You can see all Athens, Attica, the harbor, and the islands of Aegina and Poros laid out before you.

Shopping

Gift Ideas Better tourist shops sell copies of traditional Greek jewelry, silver filigree, enamel, Skyrian pottery, onyx ashtrays and dishes, woven bags, attractive rugs (including *flokates*—shaggy wool rugs, often brightly colored), good leather items, and furs. Furs made from scraps are inexpensive. Some museums sell replicas of small items that are in their collections. The best handicrafts are sold in **National Welfare Organization shops** (Voukourestiou 24a and Ypatias 6) near the cathedral. Other shops sell dried fruit, packaged pistachios, and canned olives. For books in English, go to **Pantelides** (Amerikas 11) or **Eleftheroudakis** (Nikis 4). Most large hotels also maintain English-language bookstores, although these have a fairly limited selection.

Antiques Many shops, especially on **Pandrossou Street,** sell small antiques and icons. Keep in mind, however, that there are many fakes around, and remember that you must have permission to export genuine objects from the Greek, Roman, or Byzantine periods.

Shopping Areas The central shopping area lies between Syntagma and Omonia. The **Syntagma** area has good jewelers, shoe shops, and handicrafts and souvenir shops, especially along **Voukourestiou.** **Stadiou Street** is the best bet for men's clothing. Try **Ermou Street** and the fascinating small streets that lead off it for fabrics and housewares. Go to **Mitropoleos** for rugs and souvenirs. This is also the main furrier street, and most of the moderately priced fur shops are here, including Hydra, Maoum, Mitsakou, Samaras, and Voula. Ermou runs west to **Monastiraki,** a crowded market area popular with Athenians. Below the cathedral, **Pandrossou** has antiques, sandals (an especially good buy), and inexpensive souvenirs. **Kolonaki,** just beyond central Athens, has the best shops for gifts and shoes. Its boutiques include branches of such top French fashion houses as Dior (Kriezotou 7), Yves St. Laurent (Kriezotou 10), and Lanvin (Anagnostopoulou 3), with prices lower than those in Paris.

Department Stores The few that exist are neither large nor good. The best is **Lambropoulos** (Aeolou 99–101). **Marinopoulos** shops (Kanari 9, Kifissias 16, and elsewhere) specialize in toiletries and inexpensive casual clothing.

Flea Market The flea market, based on **Pandrossou** and **Ifestou streets,** operates on Sunday mornings and sells almost anything: secondhand clothes, daggers, cooking pots and pans, old books, guitars, *bouzouki* (stringed instruments), old furniture and carpets, and backgammon sets. However little it costs, you should haggle. Ifestou Street, where the coppersmiths have their shops, is more interesting on a weekday—and you can pick up copper wine jugs, candlesticks, cooking ware, etc., for next to nothing.

Dining

Greek cuisine cannot be compared to that of France, and few visitors would come to Greece for its food alone. You'll certainly be able to find a delicious and inexpensive meal, but don't look in hotel restaurants, where the menus usually consist of bland, unimaginative international fare (although it's only here that you will find a reasonably priced fixed menu). The principal elements of Greek cuisine are such vegetables as eggplants, tomatoes, and olives, fresh and inventively combined with lots of olive oil and such seasonings as lemon juice, garlic, basil, and oregano. While meat dishes are limited (mutton and poultry being the most common), fish is often the better choice, particularly on the coast. Your best bet is to look for tavernas and *estiatoria* (restaurants) and choose the one frequented by the most Greeks. The *estiatorio* serves oven-baked dishes, precooked and left to stand, while tavernas offer similar fare plus grilled meats and fish. The decor of both types of establishment may range from simple to sophisticated, with prices to match.

Be adventurous and go looking for the places that have at least half a dozen tables occupied by Athenians—they're discerning customers. Alternatively, if you would like a change of cuisine and don't object to higher prices, pick up a copy of the monthly English-language magazine, *The Athenian*, available at most bookshops and streetside kiosks. It lists all kinds of ethnic restaurants—from French to Lebanese to Chinese—with relevant addresses and telephone numbers.

Fast-food bars have sprung up all over Greece during recent years and serve *giros* (slices of grilled meat with tomato and onions in pita bread), *souvlaki* (shish kebab), pastries filled with a variety of stuffings (spinach, cheese, or meat), and the ubiquitous hamburgers and pizza.

Mealtimes Lunch in Greek restaurants is served from 12:30 until 3. Dinner begins at about 9 and is served until 1.

Precautions Tap water is safe to drink everywhere, but it is often heavily chlorinated. Excellent bottled mineral water, such as *Loutraki*, is available.

Dress You can dress informally for dinner, even at Expensive restaurants; in Athens, you may want to wear a jacket and tie at some of the top-price restaurants.

Ratings Prices are per person and include a first course, main course, and dessert (generally fruit and cheese). They do not include drinks or the 12%-15% service charge. Best bets are indicated by a star ★.

Category	Cost
Very Expensive	over 6,500 dr.
Expensive	3,000 dr.–6,500 dr.
Moderate	1,500 dr.–3,000 dr.
Inexpensive	under 1,500 dr.

Very Expensive **L'Abreuvoir.** This restaurant, outstanding among the many average French restaurants, is ideal for a romantic candlelight dinner. The classic French dishes are served on a terrace under the leaves of a mulberry tree. Frequented by wealthy Athenians and resident expatriates seeking a break from Greek cuisine, it has an elegant, dressed-up ambience. Specialties include spinach tart, steak *au poivre* (with pepper), and *entrecôte* (steak) *Provençale. Xenokratous 51, tel. 01/722–9061. Reservations advised. AE, DC, MC, V. Closed Mon.*

Bajazzo. This elegant wood-paneled restaurant, in a converted neoclassical mansion in fashionable Kolonaki, has a moving theater to entertain its guests. The food is exquisitely presented, and specialties include duck in mousseline sauce, salmon roulade, *bouzouki frivolitef* (squid with pine nuts and rice), and a Fisherman's Dream soup with clams, langoustines (crayfish), *moules* (mussels), and ouzo. *Ploutarchou 35, tel. 01/729–1420. Reservations advised. AE, DC, MC, V.*

Expensive **Aglamair.** The most civilized and expensive of the fish restaurants lining the picturesque Mikrolimano harbor, this is also one of the best in Athens. Practically on the water's edge, you can dine watching the lights shimmer across the bay. The decor is cheerful but sophisticated, with red tablecloths and green-and-black chairs. The menu includes lobster, shrimps, prawns, octopus, and squid. *Akti Koumoundourou 54, tel. 01/411–5511. Reservations advised. AE, DC, MC, V.*

Dionyssos. You may be able to get better food at better prices elsewhere in Athens, but the view of the Acropolis is unbeatable and the food is usually of a high standard. Try to go for dinner when there is a son-et-lumière performance on the Parthenon; the sight is unforgettable. The best view is from the terrace upstairs. House specialties include charcoalgrilled shrimps and veal mignonettes in oregano sauce. *Robertou Gali 43, tel. 01/923–3182. Reservations advised. AE, DC, MC, V.*

★ **Gerfinikas.** This cheerful and bustling restaurant, tucked away in a narrow alley off a street leading up to Kolonaki, has a loyal expense-account clientele. The two-tier dining room, with sun terrace on one side, has glass-fronted cases with inviting displays of Greek and Turkish specialties and seafood dishes. *Pinadrou 10, tel. 01/362–2719. Reservations advised. AE, DC, MC, V.*

Moderate **Dionyssos.** Located on top of Mount Lycabettos, this restaurant has a sweeping view of Athens and Piraeus, down to the sea. Take the funicular railway from the top of Ploutarchou Street, in Kolonaki. In addition to the restaurant, which serves Continental and Greek cuisine, there is a cafeteria and patisserie, open from the earliest to the latest cablecar run (check the time of the last one!). *Mount Lycabettos, tel. 01/722–6374. Reservations not necessary. AE, DC, V.*

Ideal. This typically old-style Athenian restaurant still displays the day's specialties in the front window, as it has done since 1922. The busy all-wood dining room is filled with Athenians of all ages, as well as students from the nearby university. It has an extensive menu featuring high-quality Greek and Continental dishes. *Venizelou 46, tel. 01/361–4604. Reservations not necessary. DC.*

★ **Kostoyannis.** If you're looking for authenticity, this is the place to go. One of the oldest and most popular tavernas in the area, located behind the Archaeological Museum, it has an impressively wide range of Greek dishes—including excellent shrimp and crab salads, stuffed mussels, rabbit *stifado* (a stew with onions), and fried brains. *Zaimi 37, tel. 01/821–2496. Reserva-*

tions advised in summer. AE, DC, MC, V. Dinner only. Closed Sun.

Xynus. A large, tumbledown taverna, with three rooms and a tree-covered patio, the Xynus is hidden in a narrow pebble-paved lane in the Plaka. The food is much more pleasing than the decor—exposed pipes and stoves and cretonne curtains—and is highly recommended by Athenians, who consider it one of the finest restaurants in the city. A trio of musicians wanders from room to room playing folk melodies. *Angelou Geronta 4, Plaka, tel. 01/322–1065. Reservations advised. AE, DC, MC, V. Dinner only. Closed Sun.*

Inexpensive **Delphi Restaurant.** Very popular with businessmen wanting a quick, cheap meal, this restaurant serves excellent Greek and international food and is always crowded. It may be a little touristy and service can be slow, but the food is worth the wait. The front part of the restaurant is rustic, while the back-room decor is more refined. *Nikis 13, tel. 01/323–4869. No reservations. AE, DC. Closed Sun.*

Eden. This macrobiotic restaurant, in a converted old Plaka villa, serves superb vegetable pies and spinach burgers in yogurt sauce—a delightful experience for those who are tired of seeing lamb roasted on a spit at every corner. You can sit outside at wrought-iron tables on a rooftop terrace. *Flessa 3, tel. 01/324–8858. Reservations not necessary. AE, DC. Closed Tues.*

O Platanos. Set in a picturesque corner of the Plaka, this is one of the oldest tavernas in the area. It has a shady garden for outdoor dining. There's no music, so prices are low. Although it's extremely friendly, not much English is spoken. *Diogenous 4, tel. 01/322–0666. Reservations not necessary. AE, DC, MC, V.*

Lodging

Since Athens is the starting point for so many travelers, its hotels are very full, and it's always advisable to reserve a room in advance. Which type of hotel you choose is really a matter of personal taste. Basically, the style of hotels in Athens can be divided into two neat brackets—traditional and modernistic—and these can be found both in the center of town, around Omonia and Syntagma Squares, near the U.S. Embassy, and farther out along the seacoast and near the airport. In the heat of the summer, it might be preferable to go for the fresh, clean lines of a more modern-style hotel, leaving the older hotels for winter visits. Hotels in the center of Athens can be so noisy that it's difficult to get a good night's sleep, while those out on the coast become more expensive, since you spend more money on taxis getting to and from town.

Greek hotels are classified as Deluxe, A, B, C, etc. (a star system is about to be introduced). These classifications do not always indicate price. A Deluxe hotel, for example, may charge less than some B-classified hotels. In this guide, hotels are classified according to price: Very Expensive, Expensive, Moderate, and Inexpensive. All Very Expensive and Expensive hotels have air-conditioning, so our listings in these categories mention only the absence of air-conditioning. If a Moderate or an Inexpensive hotel is air-conditioned, this is indicated. All have been built or completely renovated during the past 20 years, and all have private baths.

Prices quoted by hotels usually include service, local taxes, and VAT. Some may also include breakfast. Prices quoted are for double occupancy. Single occupancy is slightly less. The official price should be posted on the back of the door or inside a closet. Seaside hotels, especially those in the Very Expensive and Expensive categories, frequently insist that guests take half-board (lunch or dinner included in the price).

Ratings Prices quoted are for a double room in high season, including taxes and service, but not breakfast. Rates are the same throughout the country for each category. Best bets are indicated by a star ★.

Category	Cost
Very Expensive	over 25,000 dr.
Expensive	10,000 dr.–25,000 dr.
Moderate	6,000 dr.–9,000 dr.
Inexpensive	under 6,000 dr.

Very Expensive **Aphrodite Astir Palace.** Located in a coastal area 25 kilometers (16 miles) from Athens, this is actually a group of three hotels: Aphrodite, the newest and least expensive; Arion, the most exclusive; and Nafsika, the most chic and perhaps the most beautiful. The complex, on a pine-covered promontory, has its own beach, helicopter pad, and breathtaking views over Vouliagmeni Bay. This is Greece's most prestigious seaside hotel complex, and it is highly recommended. *Vouliagmeni, tel. 01/896–0211/0311. 570 rooms with bath. Facilities: restaurants, 3 outdoor pools, miniature golf, nightclub. AE, DC, MC, V.*

Athenaeum Inter-Continental. A large, modern hotel, the Athenaeum is not far from the Marriott and is convenient to the airport as well. *Syngrou 89, tel. 01/10562. 133 rooms with bath. Facilities: 5 restaurants, pool, shops. AE, DC, MC, V.*

★ **Athens Hilton.** Set in a commanding position on a hill near the U.S. Embassy, the Hilton is about a 10-minute walk from Syntagma Square. All rooms and suites have fine views and soundproof windows; some have balconies and black Carrara baths. On Monday evening in summer, there's a poolside barbecue. Lunch is served at the Galaxy on the roof (a piano bar by night), wines and appetizers at the new Kellari, and dinner at Ta Nissia, a Greek-style taverna. *Vassilissis Sofias 46, tel. 01/722–0201. 480 rooms with bath. Facilities: 2 restaurants, lounge, nighttime piano bar; outdoor pool with food and beverage service; shops. AE, DC, MC, V.*

★ **Grande Bretagne.** G.B., as it is known, is centrally located on Syntagma Square. An internationally famous landmark, this distinguished hotel was modernized a few years ago. Ask for an inside room to escape the noise of the traffic. The hotel houses the excellent G.B. Corner Restaurant. *Syntagma Square, tel. 01/323–0251/9. 400 rooms with bath. Facilities: 3 restaurants, rooftop garden. AE, DC, MC, V.*

Ledra Marriott. Between Athens center and the sea, this is a popular chain hotel known for comfort and service well above the standard. Its cafés and restaurants are fashionable meeting places. There's a very attractive Polynesian restaurant called Kona Kai, complete with waterfall; the Zephyros Café, which serves an outstanding Sunday buffet brunch; and a spectacular rooftop swimming pool with a snack area. *Syngrou 115, tel. 01/ 934–7711. 258 rooms with bath. Facilities: 4 restaurants, rooftop garden, outdoor pool, shops. AE, DC, MC, V.*

Expensive **Athens Chandris.** Located near the sea and the racecourse, the
★ Athens Chandris offers all the comfort, service, and facilities of a very expensive hotel, but at more reasonable prices. Visitors on combined flight-cruise tours stay here, and the individual traveler may feel a little overwhelmed and lost. The hotel runs a complimentary shuttle service to and from Syntagma. It has a fine Continental à la carte restaurant, the Four Seasons; a poolside snack bar; and a lounge. *Syngrou 385, tel. 01/941–4824. 386 rooms with bath. Facilities: restaurant, lounge, snack bar, rooftop garden, outdoor pool. AE, DC, MC, V.*

Divani Palace Acropolis. On a small street near the Acropolis and other ancient sites, this hotel seems to be gaining in popularity. It is also an ideal base from which to stroll and explore. The public areas are clean and attractive, and the upper-story bedrooms have excellent views. *Parthenos 19, tel. 01/922–2945. 242 rooms with bath. Facilities: restaurant, rooftop garden, outdoor pool. AE, DC, MC, V.*

★ **St. George Lycabettos Hotel.** Situated on the wooded slopes of Mount Lycabettos, this hotel has a splendid view. Getting there, however, involves a steep short walk or a ride up (remember, taxis are inexpensive). It is friendly and has, as its trump card, Le Grand Balcon, a two-tiered rooftop restaurant with excellent food and a marvelous panoramic view. It also has terraces with snack tables, a lower-level restaurant, an intimate, cozy grill room, and a very attractive coffee shop. *Kleomenous 2, tel. 01/729–0711/9. 149 rooms with bath. Facilities: restaurants, nightclub, outdoor pool, roof garden. AE, DC, MC, V.*

Moderate **Athens Gate Hotel.** This hotel looks across the busy Amalias Avenue to the Arch of Hadrian. Front rooms have the view, but also the traffic noise; back rooms are quiet and look out toward the Acropolis. The hotel is conveniently located between the center of town and the Acropolis. The restaurant is only mediocre, but it serves a good, American-style buffet breakfast. *Syngrou 10, tel. 01/923–8302/9. 106 rooms with bath. Facilities: restaurant, roof garden, air-conditioning. AE, DC, MC, V.*

Ilissia Hotel. This small, but rather shabby, friendly hotel is located near the Hilton, in an area where there are many good restaurants and night spots. Generally, it could use a good spring-cleaning, but the location makes up for its dowdy appearance. *Mihalakopoulou 25, tel. 01/724–4051. 90 rooms with bath. Facilities: restaurant, air-conditioning. AE, DC, MC, V.*

Inexpensive **Alkistis Hotel.** The market area, where the Alkistis is located, is full of life and color by day, but deserted at night. The hotel is pleasant and well run and was recently redecorated in glass and marble. The roof garden has a fine view of the Acropolis and seating for sunbathers. Try to get a room overlooking the Acropolis, if you can, as the other rooms have terraces over the street. *Platia Theatrou 18, tel. 01/321–9811/9. 120 rooms with bath. Facilities: restaurant, roof garden, outdoor pool. AE, DC, MC, V.*

Aphrodite Hotel. This is near Syntagma and perfectly comfortable. With all the facilities of other, more costly hotels, it offers excellent value for the money. Don't be put off by its cold-looking entrance. *Apollonos 21, tel. 01/323–4357/9. 84 rooms with bath. Facilities: bar, roof garden. AE, DC, MC, V.*

★ **Austria.** This small, unpretentious hotel is on Filopappou Hill, opposite the Acropolis, ideal as a base for wandering around the heart of ancient Athens. It has no restaurant and is at the top of the inexpensive category, but is well worth considering. *Mouson 7, tel. 01/923–5151. 40 rooms with bath. AE, DC, MC, V.*

The Arts

The **Athens Festival** runs from late June through September and includes concerts, recitals, opera, ballet, folk dancing, and drama. Performances are in various locations, including the open-air theater of Herodes Atticus at the foot of the Acropolis, nearby Philopappou Hill, and Mount Lycabettos. Tickets are available a few days before the performance from the festival box office in the arcade at Stadiou 4 (tel. 01/322–1459). Admission ranges from 600 dr. to 4,000 dr.

For those who are disappointed with the daytime view of the Acropolis, the **son-et-lumière** shows bring history to life. Performances are given nightly from April to October, in English, at 9:15 (the time is subject to change), and admission is 500 dr. The entrance is on Dion Areopagitou, opposite the Acropolis, and from your seat on the top of Philopappou Hill, you watch the changing lighting of the monuments.

During the winter, cultural activities are much less frequent and are rarely planned far in advance. Daily listings are published year-round in *The Athens News* and weekly listings in *This Week in Athens*, both available in hotels. **The Athenian** lists concerts, exhibitions, and showings of films in English.

Concerts Winter concerts are given at the **Pallas** by the State Orchestra and the Radio/TV Orchestra. Information and tickets are available from the theater box office on Voukourestiou, near Syntagma Square. Contact the **NTOG,** tel. 01/322–2545, for up-to-date information and additional details.

Opera The **Lyriki Skini Opera Company** has a winter season and a small—not very good—ballet season at the Olympia Theater, Akademias 59, tel. 01/361–2461. The best seats cost about 800 dr.

Films There are several cinemas that show foreign films, and *The Athens News* lists them in English. Try the **Elena Cinema** (Antifilon 47, tel. 01/778–9120) for new American films and the **Cinema Thission** (Pavlou 7, tel. 01/347–0980) for American and European classics.

Nightlife

Athens has an active nightlife, with hundreds of places offering some sort of entertainment, much of it distinctly Greek. One way to get a taste is to take an "Athens by Night" guided tour, which takes in a number of clubs. This can be arranged for you by any good travel agent (*see* Important Addresses, above), but try Viking Tours first. If you want to go on your own, try a *bouzoukia*, or a taverna with a floor show. Most are closed on Sunday. Tavernas with floor shows are concentrated in the Plaka area. Be forewarned that you will have to pay for an overpriced, second-rate meal at most places. The name, style, and quality of tavernas and bouzoukias change frequently. Ask your hotel for recommendations.

Tavernas **Palia Taverna Kritikou.** Here's a fun taverna where there's room for you to indulge in Greek dances to the amusement of the few Greek customers. *Mniskleous 24, tel. 01/322-2809. Reservations advised. AE, DC, V. Expensive.*

Psarra. The specialty in this taverna in one of the Plaka's most attractive squares is swordfish kebab. Customers are invited to play the guitar themselves and to join in the Greek dances. *Erehtheou 16, tel. 01/325-0285. Reservations advised. AE, DC, MC, V. Expensive.*

Bouzoukias **Athinaia.** Highly prized and priced, it's the real thing, where you'll find an orchestra, female vocalist, and lots of clanging of the *bouzouki*, an Oriental mandolin. *Leoforos Posidonos 63, tel. 01/942-3089. Reservations advised. AE, DC, MC, V. Very Expensive.*

Diogenes. Currently the "in" place with chic Greeks and very ritzy, it's also the most expensive. *Leoforos Syngrou 255, tel. 01/942-4267. Reservations required. AE. Very Expensive.*

4 Barcelona

Arriving and Departing

By Plane All international and domestic flights arrive at El Prat de Llobregat airport, 14 kilometers (8½ miles) south of Barcelona just off the main highway to Castelldefels and Sitges. For information on arrival and departure times, call the airport (tel. 93/401–3131 days, 93/401–3555 nights) or Iberia information (tel. 93/301–3993).

Between the Airport and Downtown The airport–city train leaves every 30 minutes between 6:30 AM and 11 PM and reaches the Barcelona Central (Sants) Station in 15 minutes. Taxis will then take you to your hotel. RENFE provides a bus service to the Central Station during the night hours. A cab from the airport to your hotel, including airport and luggage surcharges, will cost about 2,000 ptas.

By Train The main railroad station is Barcelona Central (or Sants) on the Plaça Països Catalans (tel. 93/490–9171). Almost all long-distance trains arrive and depart from here. Many also stop at the Passeig de Gràcia underground station at the junction of Aragó. This station is closer to the Plaça de Catalunya and Ramblas area than Central (Sants), but though tickets and information are available here, luggage carts and taxi ranks are not. The old Terminal (or França) Station on Avda. Marquès de l'Argentera was to reopen in 1992 after major renovations as Barcelona's main long-distance train station. The Central (Sants) station was simultaneously to be converted into a suburban train station. Check with tourist offices for current travel information and phone numbers. For RENFE information, call 93/490–0202 (24 hours).

By Bus Barcelona has no central bus station, but many buses operate from the old Estació Vilanova (or Norte) at the end of Avenida Vilanova. **Juliá,** Ronda Universitat 5, runs buses to Zaragoza and Montserrat; and **Alsina Graëlls,** Ronda Universitat 4, to Lérida and Andorra.

Getting Around

Modern Barcelona above the Plaça de Catalunya is mostly built on a grid system, though there's no helpful numbering system as in the United States. The Old Town from the Plaça de Catalunya to the port is a warren of narrow streets, however, and you'll need a good street map to get around. Most sightseeing can be done on foot—you won't have any other choice in the Gothic Quarter—but you'll need to use the metro or buses to link sightseeing areas.

By Metro The subway is the fastest way of getting around, as well as the easiest to use. You pay a flat fare, no matter how far you travel, or purchase a **targeta multiviatge,** good for 10 rides. Plans of the system are available from main metro stations or from branches of the Caixa savings bank.

By Bus City buses run from about 5:30 or 6 AM to 10:30 PM, though some stop earlier. Again, there's a flat-fare system though tickets cost a little more on weekends. Plans of the routes followed are displayed at bus stops. A reduced-rate targeta multiviatge, good for 10 rides, can be purchased at the transport kiosk on Plaça Catalunya.

By Taxi Taxis are black and yellow, and when available for hire show a "Libre" sign in the daytime and a green light at night. The meter starts at 245 ptas., and there are small supplements for luggage (60 ptas. per case), Sundays and fiestas, rides from a station or the port (75 ptas.), and for going to or from the bullring or a soccer match. The supplement to the airport is 175 ptas. There are cab stands all over town; cabs may also be flagged down on the street. Make sure the driver puts on his meter.

By Cable Car and Funicular Montjuïc Funicular is a cog railroad that runs from the junction of Avenida Paral-lel and Nou de la Rambla to the Miramar Amusement Park on Montjuïc. It runs only when the amusement park is open (weekends from noon to 9:15 PM, more often in summer). A cable car (*teleferic*) then runs from the amusement park up to Montjuïc Castle; same hours.

A **Transbordador Aeri Harbor Cable Car** runs from Miramar on Montjuïc across the harbor to the Torre de Jaume I on Barcelona *moll* (jetty), and on to the Torre de Sant Sebastià at the end of Passeig Nacional in Barceloneta. You can board at either stage. The cable car runs from 11:30 AM to 9:30 PM in summer, and only on Sunday in winter.

To reach Tibidabo summit, take either bus 58 or the Ferrocarrils de la Generalitat train from Plaça Catalunya to Avenida Tibidabo, then the *tramvía blau* (blue tram) to Peu del Funicular, and the Tibidabo Funicular from there to the Tibidabo Fairground. The funicular runs every half hour from 7:15 AM to 9:45 PM.

By Boat **Golondrinas** harbor boats operate short harbor trips from the Portal de la Pau near the Columbus Monument between 9 AM and 9:30 PM in summer, and on Sundays in winter.

Important Addresses and Numbers

Tourist Information The city's three main tourist offices are at the **Central** (Sants) train station (tel. 93/490–9171; open daily 8–8), the **Palacio de Congresos** (Avda. Maria Cristina, tel. 93/423–3101, ext. 8356; open 10–8 during holidays and business congresses), and in the **Ajuntament** (Plaça Sant Jaume, tel. 93/302–4200, ext. 433; open daily 9–8 during the summer months). In the summer there are tourist offices at **Palau de la Virreina** (Ramblas 99, tel. 93/301–7775; open daily 9:30–9).

Information on the province can be found at Gran Vía 658 (tel. 93/301–7443; open weekdays 9–7, Sat. 9–2) and at the airport (tel. 93/325–5829; open Mon.–Sat. 9:30–8, Sun. 9:30–3).

American Visitors' Bureau (Gran Vía 591 between Rambla de Catalunya and Balmes, 3rd floor, tel. 93/301–0150/0032).

Consulates **U.S.** (Vía Laietana 33, tel. 93/319–9550), **Canadian** (Vía Augusta 125, tel. 93/209–0634), **U.K.** (Diagonal 477, tel. 93/322–2151).

Emergencies **Police** (National Police, tel. 091; Municipal Police, tel. 092; Main Police [Policía Nacional] Station, Vía Laietana 43, tel. 93/301–6666). **Ambulance** (tel. 93/329–7766). **Doctor: Hospital Clínic** .(Casanova 143, tel. 93/323–1414); **Hospital Evangélico** (Alegre de Dalt 87, tel. 93/219–7100).

English Bookstores Several bookstalls on the Ramblas sell English guidebooks and novels. Also try **Librería Laie** (Pau Claris 85) or **Librería Francesca** (Passeig de Gràcia 91).

Travel Agencies **American Express** (Rosselló 257, on the corner of Passeig de Gràcia, tel. 93/217–0070), **Wagons-Lits** (Gran Vía 670, tel. 93/318–7975), **Iberia Airlines** (tel. 93/301–3993).

Guided Tours

Orientation Tours City sightseeing tours are run by **Juliá Tours** (Ronda Universitat 5, tel. 317–6454) and **Pullmantur** (Gran Vía Corts Catalanes 635, tel. 318–0241). Tours leave from the above terminals, though it may be possible to be picked up at your hotel. The content and price of tours are the same with both agencies. A morning sightseeing tour visits the Gothic Quarter and Montjuïc; an afternoon tour concentrates on Gaudí and the Picasso Museum. "Panorámica y Toros" (usually on Sundays only) takes in a bullfight and city drive; and various night tours include a flamenco show, dinner in a restaurant, and cabaret at La Scala.

Special-Interest and Walking Tours Consult any tourist office for details. Serious Gaudí enthusiasts should contact **Friends of Gaudí** (Avda. Pedralbes 7, tel. 204–5250) well ahead of their visit.

Excursions These are run by **Juliá Tours** and **Pullmantur** and are booked as above. Principal trips are a half-day tour to **Montserrat** to visit the monastery and shrine of the famous Black Virgin; a full-day trip to the **Costa Brava** resorts, including a boat cruise to Lloret de Mar; and a full-day trip to **Andorra** for tax-free shopping.

Personal Guides Ask at any tourist office, or contact the **Barcelona Tourist Guide Association** (tel. 93/345–4221).

Exploring Barcelona

Numbers in the margin correspond to points of interest on the Barcelona map.

Barcelona, capital of Catalonia and Spain's second-largest city, thrives on its business acumen and industrial muscle. Its hardworking citizens are almost militant in their use of their own language—with street names, museum exhibits, newspapers, radio programs, and movies all in Catalan. Their latest cause for rejoicing is the realization of their long-cherished goal to host the Olympic Games, and the city is currently in the throes of a massive building program in anticipation of the big event of 1992. This thriving metropolis also has a rich history and an abundance of sights. Few places can rival the narrow alleys of its Gothic Quarter for medieval atmosphere, the elegance and distinction of its Modernista Eixample area, or the fantasies of Gaudí's whimsical imagination.

It should take you two full days of sightseeing to complete the following tour. The first part covers the Gothic Quarter, the Picasso Museum, and the Ramblas. The second part takes you to Passeig de Gràcia, the Sagrada Familia, and Montjuïc.

Start on Plaça de la Seu, where on Sunday morning the citizens of Barcelona gather to dance the *Sardana*, a symbol of Catalan pride. Step inside the magnificent Gothic **Cathedral** built between 1298 and 1450, though the spire and Gothic facade were not added until 1892. Highlights are the beautifully carved **choir stalls,** Santa Eulalia's tomb in the crypt, the battle-

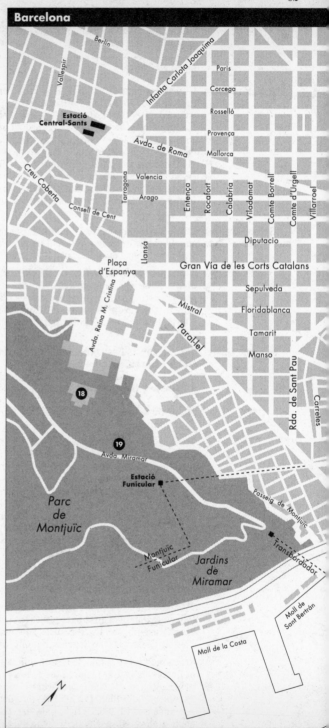

Barcelona

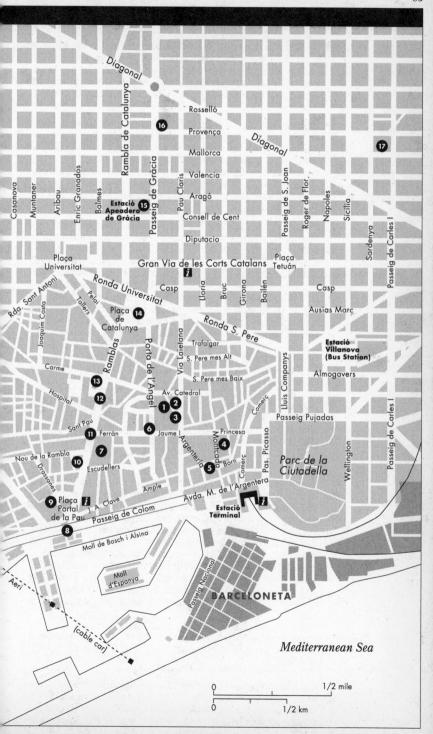

Diagonal

Rosselló

Provença

Diagonal

Mallorca

16

Valencia

Rambla de Catalunya

Pau Claris

Aragó

Passeig de Gràcia

Casanova

Muntaner

Aribau

Enric Granados

Balmes

Passeig de S. Joan

Roger de Flor.

Napoles

Sicilia

Sardenya

Passeig de Carles I

17

Consell de Cent

Estació
Apeadero
de Gràcia **15**

Diputacio

Plaça
Universitat

Gran Vía de les Corts Catalans

Plaça
Tetuán

Ronda Universitat

Casp

Lloria

Bruc

Girona

Bailén

Casp

Ronda S. Pere

Ausias Marc

Rda. Sant Antoni

Joaquim Costa

Pelai

Tallers

Plaça
de
Catalunya

14

Porta de l'Angel

Estació
Villanova
(Bus Station)

Ramblas

Carme

Trafalgar

S. Pere mes Alt

S. Pere mes Baix

Lluis Companys

Almogavers

Hospital

13

12

Av. Catedral

1 **2**

3

Comerç

Passeig Pujadas

Sant Pau

11

Ferràn

6

Jaume I

Argenteria

Princesa

Montcada

4

Pas. Picasso

Parc de la
Ciutadella

Wellington

Passeig de Carles I

Nou de la Rambla

7

10

Escudellers

Born

5

Comerç

Drassanes

Ample

Avda. M. de l'Argentera

9 Plaça
Portal
de la Pau

J. A. Clavé

Passeig de Colom

Estació
Terminal

8

Moll de Bosch i Alsina

Aeri

Moll
d'Espanya

Passeig Nacional

BARCELONETA

(cable car)

Mediterranean Sea

0   1/2 mile

0   1/2 km

scarred crucifix from Don Juan's galley in the **Lepanto Chapel,** and the cloisters. *Open 7:30–1:30 and 4–7:30.*

❷ Around the corner at Comtes de Barcelona 10 is the **Frederic Marès Museum,** where you can browse for hours among the miscellany of sculptor-collector Frederic Marès. On display is everything from polychrome crucifixes to hat pins, pipes, and walking sticks. *Admission free. Open Mon.–Sat. 9–2 and 4–7, Sun. 9–2.*

❸ The neighboring **Plaça del Rei** embodies the very essence of the Gothic Quarter. Legend has it that after Columbus's first voyage to America, the Catholic Kings received him in the **Saló de Tinell,** a magnificent banqueting hall built in 1362. Other ancient buildings around the square are the **Lieutenant's Palace;** the 14th-century **Chapel of St. Agatha,** built right into the Roman city wall; and the **Padellás Palace,** which houses the City History Museum.

❹ Cross Vía Laietana, walk down Princesa, and turn right into Montcada, where you come to one of Barcelona's most popular attractions, the **Picasso Museum.** Two 15th-century palaces provide a striking setting for the collections donated in 1963 and 1970, first by Picasso's secretary, then by the artist himself. The collection ranges from early childhood sketches done in Málaga to exhibition posters done in Paris shortly before his death. Of particular interest are his Blue Period pictures and his variations on Velázquez's *Las Meninas. Admission free. Open Tues.–Sun. 9:30–1:30 and 4:30–8, holidays 10–2.*

Time Out At the bottom of Montcada, on the left, is **La Pizza Nostra** (Arc de Sant Vicens 2, tel. 93/319–9058), an ideal spot for a cup of coffee, a slice of cheesecake, or a pizza and a glass of wine.

❺ **Santa María del Mar** is one of the loveliest Gothic churches in Barcelona. It was built between 1329 and 1383 in fulfillment of a vow made a century earlier by Jaume I to build a church for the Virgin of the Sailors. Its simple beauty is enhanced by a stunning rose window and magnificent soaring columns. *Open 8–1 and 4–7:30.*

❻ Continue up Carrer Argentería, cross Vía Laietana, and walk along Jaume I till you come to **Plaça Sant Jaume,** an impressive square built in the 1840s in the heart of the Gothic Quarter. The two imposing buildings facing each other across the square are very much older. The 15th-century **Ajuntament,** or City Hall, has an impressive black and gold mural (1928) by Josep María Sert (who also painted the murals for New York's Waldorf Astoria) and the famous **Saló de Cent** from which the Council of One Hundred ruled the city from 1372 to 1714. The **Palau de la Generalitat,** seat of the Catalan Regional Government, is a 15th-century palace open to the public on Sunday mornings only.

Time Out Among the best lunch spots in this area are **Agut d'Avignon** and **La Cuineta** (*see* Dining, below), and **Tinell** (Frenería 8, tel. 93/315–4604).

❼ Continue along the Carrer Ferrán, with its attractive 19th-century shops and numerous Modernista touches, to the **Plaça Reial.** Here in this splendid, if rather dilapidated, 19th-century square arcaded houses overlook the wrought-iron **Fountain of**

the Three Graces, and lampposts designed by a young Gaudí in 1879. Watch out for drug pushers here; the safest and most colorful time to come is on a Sunday morning when crowds gather at the stamp and coin stalls and listen to soap-box orators.

Time Out Nearby are two atmospheric restaurants, **Los Caracoles** and **Can Culleretes.**

⑧ Head to the bottom of Ramblas and take an elevator to the top of the **Columbus Monument** (open Mon.–Sat. 9:30–1:30 and 4:30–8:30, Sun. 11:30–7:30) for a breathtaking view over the city. Columbus faces out to sea, overlooking a replica of his own boat, the *Santa María.* Nearby you can board the cable car that crosses the harbor to Montjuïc.

⑨ Our next stop is the **Maritime Museum** (Plaça Portal de la Pau 1) housed in the 13th-century Atarazanas Reales, the old Royal Dockyards. The museum is packed with ships, figureheads, nautical paraphernalia, and several early navigation charts, including a map by Amerigo Vespucci, and the 1439 chart of Gabriel de Valseca from Mallorca, the oldest chart in Europe. *Admission: 150 ptas. Open Tues.–Sat. 10–2 and 4–7, Sun. 10–2.*

⑩ Turn back up the Ramblas to Nou de la Rambla. At No. 3 is Gaudí's **Palau Güell,** which houses the **Museum of Scenic Arts.** Gaudí built this mansion between 1885 and 1890 for his patron, Count Eusebi de Güell, and it's the only one of his houses that is readily open to the public. It makes an intriguing setting for the museum's collection of theatrical memorabilia. *Admission: 100 ptas. Open Mon.–Sat. 10–1 and 5–7.*

⑪ Back to the Ramblas and our next landmark, the **Gran Teatre del Liceu,** on the corner of Sant Pau. Built between 1845 and 1847, the Liceu claims to be the world's oldest opera house and is the only one in Spain. A fairly mundane facade conceals an exquisite interior with ornamental gilt and plush red velvet fittings. Anna Pavlova danced here in 1930, and Maria Callas sang here in 1959. *Admission: 100 ptas. Open for guided visits (some in English) Mon., Wed., Fri. at 11:30 and 12:15.*

⑫ This next stretch of the **Ramblas** is the most fascinating. The colorful paving stones on the Placa de la Boquería were designed by Joan Miró. Glance up at the swirling Modernista dragon and the Art Nouveau street lamps. Then take a look inside the bustling **Boquería Food Market** and the **Casa Antigua Figueras,** an old grocery store on the corner of Petxina, with a splendid mosaic facade.

⑬ The **Palau de la Virreina** was built by a viceroy from Peru in 1778. It's recently been converted into a major exhibition center, and you should check to see what's showing while you're in town. *Corner of Carme and Rambla de las Flores 99, tel. 93/ 301–7775. Open Tues.–Sat. 10–2 and 4:30–9, Sun. 10–2, Mon. 4:30–9. Last entrance 30 mins. before closing.*

On the next block is the 18th-century **Church of Betlem** (Bethlehem) and, opposite, the handsome ocher Baroque **Palau de Moja,** built in 1702.

⑭ The final stretch of the Ramblas brings us out onto the busy **Plaça de Catalunya,** the frantic business center and transport hub of the modern city. The first stage of the tour ends here.

You may want to head for the Corte Inglés department store across the square or for any of the stores on the nearby **Porta de l'Angel.** Alternatively, you can relax on the terrace of the ancient **Café Zurich** on the corner of Pelai, or stop at the colorful beer hall, the **Cervecería,** opposite the Hostal Continental.

Above the Plaça de Catalunya you come into modern Barcelona and an elegant area known as the **Eixample,** which was laid out in the late 19th century as part of the city's expansion scheme. Much of the building here was done at the height of the **Modernista** movement, a Spanish and mainly Barcelonian offshoot of Art Nouveau, whose leading exponents were the architects Antoní Gaudí, Domènech i Montaner, and Puig i Cadafalch. The principal thoroughfares of the Eixample are the Rambla de Catalunya and the Passeig de Gràcia, where some of the city's most elegant shops and cafés are found. Modernista houses are one of Barcelona's special drawing cards, so

⓯ walk up **Passeig de Gràcia** until you come to the **Manzana de la Discordía,** or Block of Discord, between Consell de Cent and Aragó. Its name is a pun on the word *manzana,* which means both "block" and "apple." The houses here are quite fantastic: The floral **Casa Lleó Morera** at No. 35 is by Domènech i Montaner. The pseudo-Gothic **Casa Amatller** at No. 41 is by Puig i Cadafalch. At No. 43 is Gaudí's **Casa Batlló.** Farther along the street on the right, on the corner

⓰ of Provença, is Gaudí's **Casa Milà** (paseo de Grazia 92), more often known as **La Pedrera.** Its remarkable curving stone facade with ornamental balconies actually ripples its way around the corner of the block.

Time Out — You can ponder the vagaries of Gaudí's work over a drink in **Amarcord,** a terrace café in the Pedrera building. If you're feeling a bit homesick, sip a cocktail or munch a deep-pan pizza in the **Chicago Pizza Pie Factory** at Provença 300. For a more sedate, old-world tearoom, head for the **Salón de Té Mauri** on the corner of Rambla de Catalunya and Provença.

Now take the metro at Diagonal directly to Barcelona's most

⓱ eccentric landmark, Gaudí's **Church of the Sagrada Familia** (Holy Family). Far from finished at his untimely death in 1926—the absentminded Gaudí was run over by a tram and died in a pauper's hospital—this striking creation will cause consternation or wonder, shrieks of protest or cries of rapture. In 1936 during the Civil War the citizens of Barcelona loved their crazy temple enough to spare it from the flames that engulfed all their other churches except the cathedral. An elevator takes visitors to the top of one of the towers for a magnificent view of the city. Gaudí is buried in the crypt. *Admission: 250 ptas. Open daily 9–8.*

Way across town to the south, the hill of **Montjuïc** was named for the Jewish community that once lived on its slopes. Montjuïc is home to a castle, an amusement park, several delightful gardens, a model Spanish village, an illuminated fountain, the recently rebuilt Mies van der Rohe Pavilion, and a cluster of museums—all of which could keep you busy for a day or more. This is to be the principal venue for the 1992 Olympics, having undergone major renovation and construction projects in preparation.

18 One of the leading attractions here is the recently restored **Museum of Catalan Art** in the Palau Nacional atop a long flight of steps. The collection of Romanesque and Gothic art treasures—medieval frescoes and altarpieces, mostly from small churches and chapels in the Pyrenees—is simply staggering. *Admission free. Open Tues.–Sun. 9:30–1:30.* The **Ceramics Museum** is in the same building (same hours and ticket).

19 Nearby is the **Miró Foundation,** a gift from the artist Joan Miró to his native city. One of Barcelona's most exciting contemporary galleries, it has several exhibition areas, many of them devoted to Miró's works. Miró himself now rests in the cemetery on the southern slopes of Montjuïc. *Admission: 300 ptas. Open Tues.–Sat. 11–7 (9:30 on Thurs.), Sun. 10:30–2:30.*

Shopping

Gift Ideas There are no special handicrafts associated with Barcelona, but you'll have no trouble finding typical Spanish goods anywhere in town. If you're into fashion and jewelry, then you've come to the right place, as Barcelona makes all the headlines on Spain's booming fashion front. **Xavier Roca i Coll,** Sant Pere mes Baix 24, just off Laietana, specializes in silver models of Barcelona's buildings.

Antiques Carrer de la Palla and Banys Nous in the Gothic Quarter are lined with antiques shops where you'll find old maps, books, paintings, and furniture. An **antiques market** is held every Thursday morning in Plaça Nova in front of the cathedral. The **Centre d'Antiquaris,** Passeig de Gràcia 57, has some 75 antiques stores. **Gothsland,** Consell de Cent 331, specializes in Modernista designs.

Boutiques The most fashionable boutiques are in the **Galerías** on Passeig de Gràcia and Rambla de Catalunya. Others are on Gran Vía between Balmes and Pau Claris; and on the Diagonal between Ganduxer and Passeig de Gràcia. **Adolfo Domínguez,** Spain's top designer, is at Passeig de Gràcia 89 and Valencia 245; **Loewe,** Spain's top leather store, is at Passeig de Gràcia 35 and Diagonal 570; **Joaquín Berao,** a top jewelry designer, is at Rosselló 277.

Shopping Districts Elegant shopping districts are the Passeig de Gràcia, Rambla de Catalunya, and the Diagonal. For more affordable, more old-fashioned, and typically Spanish-style shops, explore the area between Ramblas and Vía Laietana, especially around C. Ferran. The area around Plaça del Pi from Boquería to Portaferrisa and Canuda is recommended for young fashion stores and imaginative gift shops.

Department Stores **El Corte Inglés** is on the Plaça de Catalunya 14 (tel. 93/302–1212) and at Diagonal 617 (tel. 93/322–4011) near María Cristina metro. **Galerías Preciados** is at Porta de l'Angel 19 just off the Plaça de Catalunya; Diagonal 471 on the Plaça Francesc Macià; and Avenida Meridiana 352. All are open Monday to Saturday 10–8.

Food and Flea Markets The **Boquería** or **Sant Josep Market** on the Ramblas between Carme and Hospital is a superb, colorful food market, held every day except Sunday. **Els Encants,** Barcelona's fascinating Flea Market, is held every Monday, Wednesday, Friday, and Saturday at the end of Dos de Maig on the Plaça Glòries Catalanes. **Sant Antoni Market,** at the end of Ronda Sant

Antoní, is an old-fashioned food and clothes market, best on
Sundays when there's a secondhand **book market** with old post-
cards, press cuttings, lithographs, and prints. There's a **stamp
and coin market** in the Plaça Reial on Sunday mornings, and an
artists' market in the Placeta del Pi just off Ramblas and
Boquería on Saturday mornings.

Bullfighting

Barcelona has two bullrings, the **Arènes Monumental** on Gran
Vía and Carles I, and the smaller, rarely used, **Arènes las Are-
nas** on the Plaça d'Espanya. Bullfights are held on Sundays between March and October; check the newspaper for details.
The official ticket office, where there is no markup on tickets, is
at Muntaner 24 (tel. 93/253–3821) near Gran Vía. There's a
Bullfighting Museum at the Monumental ring, open March–October, daily 10–1 and 5:30–7; closed Nov.–Feb.

Dining

Visitors have a choice of restaurants, tapas bars, and cafés.
Restaurants are strictly for lunch and dinner; they do not serve
breakfast. Tapas bars are ideal for a glass of wine or beer accompanied by an array of savory tidbits *(tapas)*. Cafés, called
cafeterías, are basically coffee houses serving snacks, light
meals, tapas, pastries, and coffee, tea, and alcoholic drinks.
They also serve breakfast and are perfect for afternoon tea.

Mealtimes Mealtimes in Spain are much later than in any other European
country. Lunch begins between 1 and 3:30, with 2 being the
usual time, and 3 more normal on Sunday. Dinner is usually
available from 8:30 onward, but 10 PM is the usual time in the
larger cities and resorts. An important point to remember is
that lunch is the main meal, not dinner. Tapas bars are busiest
between noon and 2 and from 8 PM on. Cafés are usually open
from around 8 AM to midnight.

Precautions Tap water is said to be safe to drink. However, most Spaniards
drink bottled mineral water; ask for either *agua sin gas* (without bubbles) or *agua con gas* (with). A good paella should be
served only at lunchtime and should be prepared to order (usually 30 minutes); beware the all-too-cheap version.

Typical Dishes Paella—a mixture of saffron-flavored rice with seafood, chick-
en, and vegetables—is Spain's national dish. Gazpacho, a cold
soup made of crushed garlic, tomatoes, and olive oil and garnished with diced vegetables, is a traditional Andalusian dish
and is served mainly in summer. The Basque Country and Galicia are the gourmet regions of Spain, and both serve outstanding fish and seafood. Asturias is famous for its *fabadas* (bean
stews), cider, and dairy products; Extremadura for its hams
and sausages; and Castile for its roasts, especially *cochinillo*
(suckling pig), *cordero asado* (roast lamb), and *perdiz* (partridge). The best wines are those from the Rioja and Penedés
regions. Valdepeñas is a pleasant table wine, and most places
serve a perfectly acceptable house wine called *vino de la casa*.
Sherries from Jerez de la Frontera make fine aperitifs; ask for
a *fino* or a *manzanilla*; both are dry. In summer you can try
horchata, a sweet white drink made from ground nuts, or
granizados de limón or *de café*, lemon juice or coffee served
over crushed ice. *Un café solo* is a small, black, strong coffee,

and *café con leche* is coffee with cream, cappuccino-style; weak black American-style coffee is hard to come by.

Dress In Very Expensive and Expensive restaurants, jacket and tie are the norm. Elsewhere, casual dress is appropriate.

Ratings Spanish restaurants are officially classified from five forks down to one fork, with most places falling into the two- or three-fork category. In our rating system, prices are per person and include a first course, main course, and dessert, but not wine or tip. Sales tax (IVA) is often included in the menu price; check the menu for *IVA incluído* or *IVA no incluído*. When it's not included, an additional 6% (12% in the fancier restaurants) will be added to your bill. Most restaurants offer a fixed-price menu called a *menú del día*. This is usually the cheapest way of eating; *à la carte* dining is more expensive. Service charges are never added to your bill; leave around 10%, less in inexpensive restaurants and bars. Major centers such as Barcelona tend to be a bit more expensive. Best bets are indicated by a star ★.

Category	Cost
Very Expensive	over 6,500 ptas.
Expensive	4,300 ptas.–6,500 ptas.
Moderate	2,100 ptas.–4,300 ptas.
Inexpensive	850 ptas.–2,100 ptas.

Very Expensive **Eldorado Petit.** Luis Cruañas moved to Barcelona from the Costa Brava in 1984 and opened this restaurant, which rapidly became known as the best in Barcelona and one of the top
★ restaurants in Spain. The setting—a private villa with a delightful garden for summer dining—is simply beautiful, and so is the cuisine. *Dolors Monserdá 51, tel. 93/204–5153. Reservations required. AE, MC, V. Closed Sun. and 2 weeks in Aug.*

Expensive **Agut d'Avignon.** This venerable Barcelona institution takes a bit of finding; it's near the junction of Ferran and Avinyó in the Gothic Quarter. The ambience is rustic and it's a favorite with businesspeople and politicians from over the road in the Generalitat. The cuisine is traditional Catalan and game specialties are recommended in season. *Trinidad 3, tel. 93/302–6034. Reservations required. AE, DC, MC, V. Closed Holy Week.*

★ **Azulete.** This is one of Barcelona's most beautiful restaurants—its dining room is an old conservatory filled with flowers and plants. The highly imaginative cuisine is a mixture of Catalan, French, and Italian with an interesting blend of traditional and new dishes. *Vía Augusta 281, tel. 93/203–5943. Reservations required. AE, DC, MC, V. Closed Sat. lunch, Sun., and first 2 weeks of Aug.*

La Cuineta. This small intimate restaurant in a 17th-century house just off Plaça Sant Jaume specializes in Catalan *nouvelle cuisine*. The decor is smart but charming, the service professional; and it's popular with businesspeople at lunchtime. *Paradis 4, tel. 93/315–0111. Reservations accepted. AE, DC, MC, V. Closed Mon.*

Quo Vadis. Located just off the Ramblas, near the Boquería Market and Betlem Church, is an unimpressive facade camouflaging one of Barcelona's most respected restaurants. Its much-praised cuisine includes delicacies like *pot pourri de setas* (mushrooms), *lubina al hinojo* (sea bass in fennel), and *hígado de ganso con ciruelas* (goose liver with cherries). *Carmen 7, tel. 93/302-4072. Reservations advised. AE, DC, MC, V. Closed Sun.*

Moderate **Can Culleretes.** This picturesque old restaurant began life as a pastry shop in 1786, and it is one of the most atmospheric and reasonable finds in Barcelona. Located on an alleyway between Ferran and Boquería, its three dining rooms are decorated with photos of visiting celebrities. It serves real Catalan cooking and is very much a family concern; don't be put off by the prostitutes outside! *Quintana 5, tel. 93/317-6485. Reservations accepted. AE, MC, V. Closed Sun. evening and Mon.*

Los Caracoles. Just below the Plaça Reial is Barcelona's most famous restaurant, which caters to tourists but has real atmosphere. Its walls are hung thick with photos of bullfighters and visiting celebrities; its specialties are mussels, paella and, of course, snails (*caracoles*). Don't miss it, it's fun. *Escudellers 14, tel. 93/301-2041. Reservations accepted. AE, DC, MC, V.*

★ **Sete Portes.** With plenty of old-world charm, this delightful restaurant near the waterfront has been going strong since 1836. The cooking is Catalan, the portions enormous, and specialties are *paella de pescado* and *zarzuela sete portes* (seafood casserole). *Passeig Isabel II 14, tel. 93/319-3033. Reservations advised at weekends. AE, DC, MC, V. Open 1 PM–1 AM.*

★ **Sopeta Una.** Dining in this delightful small restaurant with old-fashioned decor and intimate atmosphere is more like eating in a private home. The menu is in Catalan, all the dishes are Catalan, and the atmosphere is very genteel and middle class. For dessert, try the traditional Catalan *música*—a plate of raisins, almonds, and dried fruit served with a glass of muscatel. It's near the Palau de la Música; don't be put off by the narrow street. *Verdaguer i Callis 6, tel. 93/319-6131. Reservations accepted. V. Closed Sun., and Mon. AM.*

Inexpensive ★ **Agut.** Simple, hearty Catalan fare awaits you in this unpretentious restaurant in the lower reaches of the Gothic Quarter. Founded in 1924, its popularity has never waned. There's plenty of wine to wash down the traditional home cooking, but you won't find frills like coffee or liqueurs. *Gignàs 16, tel. 93/315-1709. Reservations not necessary. No credit cards. Closed Sun. evening, Mon., and July.*

★ **Egipte.** This small, friendly restaurant hidden away in a very convenient location behind the Boquería Market—though it's far better known to locals than to visitors—is a real find. Its traditional Catalan home cooking, huge desserts, and swift personable service all contribute to its popularity and good value. *Jerusalem 12, tel. 93/317-7480. No reservations. No credit cards.*

Lodging

For a city of its size and importance, Barcelona has long been underendowed with hotels, but with the coming of the Olympics in 1992, the city's hotel industry is having to think afresh. New hotels are going up fast, international chains are vying for business, and existing hotels are undergoing extensive renovations. Hotels in the Ramblas and Gothic Quarter have plenty of old-world charm, but are less strong on creature comforts; those in the Eixample are mostly '50s or '60s buildings, often recently renovated; and the newest hotels are found out along the Diagonal or beyond, in the residential district of Sarriá. There are hotel reservation desks at the airport and Sants Central Station.

All hotels and hostels are listed with their rates in the annual *Guía de Hoteles* available from bookstores and kiosks for around 500 ptas., or you can see a copy in local tourist offices. Rates are always quoted per room, and not per person. Single occupancy of a double room costs 80% of the normal price. Breakfast is rarely included in the quoted room rate; always check. The quality of rooms, particularly in older properties, can be uneven; always ask to see your room *before* you sign the acceptance slip. If you want a private bathroom in a less expensive hotel, state your preference for shower or bathtub; the latter usually costs more though many hotels have both. Local tourist offices will privide you with a list of accommodations in their region, but they are not allowed to make reservations for you. In Madrid and Barcelona, hotel booking agencies are found at the airports and railroad stations.

Hotels and Hostels Hotels are officially classified from five stars (the highest) to one star, hostels from three stars to one star. Hostels are usually a family home converted to provide accommodations that often occupy only part of a building. If an R appears on the blue hotel or hostel plaque, the hotel is classified as a *Residencia*, and full dining services are not provided, though breakfast and cafeteria facilities may be available. A three-star hostel usually equates with a two-star hotel; two- and one-star hostels offer simple, basic accommodations. The main hotel chains are Husa, Iberotel Melia, Sol, and Tryp, and the state-run *paradores* (tourist hotels). Holiday Inn, InterContinental, and Trusthouse Forte also own some of the best hotels in Madrid, Barcelona, and Seville; only these and the paradores have any special character. The others mostly provide clean, comfortable accommodation in the two- to four-star range.

In many hotels rates vary according to the time of year. The hotel year is divided into *estación alta, media,* and *baja* (high, mid, and low season); high season covers the summer and usually Easter and Christmas periods, plus the major fiestas. IVA is rarely included in the quoted room rates, so be prepared for an additional 6%, or, in the case of luxury four- and five-star hotels, 12%, to be added to your bill. Service charges are never included.

Paradors There are about 80 state-owned-and-run paradors, many of which are located in magnificent medieval castles or convents or in places of great natural beauty. Most of these fall into the four-star category and are priced accordingly. All have restaurants that specialize in local regional cuisine and serve a full breakfast. The most popular paradors (Granada's San Francisco parador, for example) are booked far in advance, and many close for a month or two in winter (January or February) for renovations.

Ratings Prices are for two peopel in a double room and do not include breakfast. Best bets are indicated by a star ★.

Category	Cost
Very Expensive	over 19,000 ptas.
Expensive	12,000–19,000 ptas.
Moderate	7,000–12,000 ptas.
Inexpensive	4,200–7,000 ptas.

Very Expensive **Avenida Palace.** Right in the center of town, between the Rambla de Catalunya and Passeig de Gràcia, this hotel dates from 1952 but conveys a feeling of elegance and Old World style. Some rooms are rather plain, but most have been recently renovated and there's a superbly ornate lobby. *Gran Vía 605, tel. 93/301–9600. 211 rooms. AE, DC, MC, V.*

★ **Ritz.** Founded in 1919 by Caesar Ritz, this is still the grand old lady of Barcelona hotels. Extensive refurbishment has now restored it to its former splendor. The entrance lobby is awe-inspiring, the rooms spacious, and the service impeccable. *Gran Vía 668, tel. 93/318–5200. 314 rooms. AE, DC, MC, V.*

Melía Barcelona. This is a bit far out off the Diagonal, but if you like modern, luxurious hotels, this is the one for you. It's been dramatically refurbished with a spectacular waterfall and special executive floor ideal for businesspeople. *Avda Sarriá 50, tel. 93/410–6060. 314 rooms. AE, DC, MC, V.*

Expensive **Colón.** This cozy, older hotel has a unique charm and intimacy
★ reminiscent of an English country hotel, though some refurbishing would be very welcome. It's in an ideal location right in the heart of the Gothic Quarter, and the rooms on the front overlook the cathedral and square. It was a great favorite of Joan Miró. *Avda. Catedral 7, tel. 93/301–1404. 161 rooms. AE, DC, MC, V.*

★ **Condes de Barcelona.** As this is one of Barcelona's most popular hotels, rooms need to be booked well in advance. The decor is stunning, with marble floors and columns, an impressive staircase, and an outstanding bar area, but no restaurant. Guest rooms are on the small side. *Passeig de Gràcia 75, tel. 93/487–3737; for reservations, 93/215–7931. 100 rooms. AE, DC, MC, V.*

Regente. This smallish hotel on the corner of Valencia has a rooftop pool, plenty of style and charm, and a wonderful Modernista lobby. *Rambla de Catalunya 76, tel. 93/215–2570. 78 rooms. AE, DC, MC, V.*

Moderate **Gran Vía.** Architectural features are the special charm of this 19th-century mansion, close to the main tourist office. The original chapel has been preserved, you can have breakfast in a hall of mirrors, climb its Modernista staircase, and call from elaborate Belle Epoque phone booths. *Gran Vía 642, tel. 93/318–1900. 48 rooms. AE, DC, MC, V.*

★ **Oriente.** Barcelona's oldest hotel opened in 1843. Its public rooms are a delight—the ballroom and dining rooms have lost none of their 19th-century magnificence—though the bedrooms have undergone rather featureless renovation. It's located just below the Liceu and its terrace café is the perfect place for a drink. *Ramblas 45, tel. 93/302–2558. 142 rooms. AE, DC, MC, V.*

Rialto. In the heart of the Gothic Quarter, just two paces down from the Plaça Sant Jaume, this old 19th-century house has been renovated to high standards of comfort while preserving its charm. Here you're surrounded by sights, shops, and some of Barcelona's best restaurants. *Ferran 40, tel. 93/318–5212. 112 rooms. AE, DC, MC, V.*

Inexpensive **Continental.** Something of a legend among cost-conscious travelers, this comfortable hostel with canopied balconies stands at the top of Ramblas, just below Plaça Catalunya. The rooms are homey and comfortable, the staff is friendly, and the location's ideal. Buffet breakfasts are a plus. *Ramblas 136, tel. 93/301–2508. 30 rooms. V.*

★ **Urbis.** This family-run hostel on Barcelona's central parade is popular with businesspeople and Spanish families. Though generally comfortable, room standards can vary, so it's best to check first. Its location close to stores and only a short walk from most major sights is an advantage. *Passeig de Gràcia 23, tel. 93/317–2766. 61 rooms. AE, DC, MC, V.*

Bars and Cafés

Cafés and Tearooms **Zurich** (Plaça Catalunya 35), on the corner of Pelai, is one of the oldest and most traditional cafés, perfect for watching the world go by. **The Croissant Show** (Santa Anna 10 just off Ramblas), is a small coffee and pastry shop, ideal for a quick mid-morning or afternoon break. **Salón de Té Mauri,** on the corner of Rambla de Catalunya and Provença, and **Salón de Té Libre i Serra** (Ronda Sant Pere 3), are both traditional tearooms with a good selection of pastries.

Tapas Bars You'll find these all over town, but two of the most colorful are **Alt Heidelberg** (Ronda Universitat 5), with German beer on tap and German sausages, and the **Cervecería** at the top of Ramblas, opposite the Hostal Continental.

Cocktail Bars These places are both popular and plentiful everywhere, but the two best areas are the **Passeig del Born,** which is near the Picasso Museum and very fashionable with the affluent young, and the **Eixample,** near Passeig de Gràcia. A bar called **Dry Martini** (at Aribau 162), has more than 80 different gins; **Ideal Cocktail Bar,** on Aribau 89, has some good malt whiskeys. **El Paraigua,** on Plaça Sant Miquel, in the Gothic Quarter behind the city hall, serves cocktails in a stylish setting with classical music. **Boadas** (Tallers 1), on the corner of Ramblas, has been going strong for over 50 years.

Champagne Bars *Xampanyerías*, serving sparkling Catalan *cava*, are popular all over town and are something of a Barcelona specialty. Try **Brut** (Trompetas 3), in the Picasso Museum area; **La Cava del Palau** (Verdaguer i Callis 10), near the Palau de la Música; **La Folie** (Bailén 169), one of the best; or **La Xampanyería** (Provença 236), on the corner of Enric Granados.

Special Cafés **Els Quatre Gats** (Montsió 5, off Porta de l'Angel) is a reconstruction of the original café that opened in 1897, and a real Barcelona institution. Literary discussions, jazz, and classical music recitals take place in this café where Picasso held his first show, Albéniz and Granados played their piano compositions, and Ramón Casas painted two of its original murals. **Café de l'Opera** (Ramblas 74), right opposite the Liceu, is a long-standing Barcelona tradition, ideal for a coffee or drink at any time of day.

The Arts

To find out what's on in town, look in the daily papers or in the weekly *Guía del Ocio*, available from newsstands all over town. *Actes a la Ciutat* is a weekly list of cultural events published by the Ajuntament and available from its information office on Plaça Sant Jaume.

Concerts Catalans are great music lovers, and their main concert hall is **Palau de la Música** (Amadeo Vives 1, tel. 93/268–1000). The ticket office is open weekdays 11–1 and 5–8 and Saturday 5–8 only. Its Sunday morning concerts are a popular tradition. Tickets are reasonable and can usually be purchased just before the concert.

Opera The **Gran Teatre del Liceu** is one of the world's finest opera houses, considered by some second only to Milan's La Scala. The box office for advance bookings is on Sant Pau 1 (tel. 93/318–9277), open weekdays 8–3, Saturday 9–1. Tickets for same-day performances are on sale in the Ramblas entrance (tel. 93/301–6787) 11–1:30 and 4 PM onward. Tickets are inexpensive by New York or London standards.

Dance You can watch the traditional Catalan Sardana danced in front of the cathedral on Sunday mornings and often on Wednesday evenings, too.

Theater Most theater performances are in Catalan but look out for mime shows, especially if Els Joglars or La Claca, two famous Catalan troupes, are appearing.

Film Most foreign movies are dubbed into Spanish. Try the **Filmoteca** on Travessera de Gràcia 63, on the corner of Tusset, for original English-language films.

Nightlife

Cabaret **Belle Epoque** (Muntaner 246, tel. 93/209–7385) is a beautifully decorated music hall with the most sophisticated shows. **El Mediévolo** (Gran Vía 459, tel. 93/325–3480) has medieval feasts and entertainment; it's all geared to tourists but fun. **Scala Barcelona** (Passeig Sant Joan 47, tel. 93/232–6363) is the city's leading nightclub, with two shows nightly, the first with dinner.

Jazz Clubs Try **Abraxas Jazz Auditorium** (Gelabert 26); **La Cova del Drac** (Tuset 30, just off the Diagonal); and **Zeleste** (Almogávares 122).

Rock Check out **Zeleste** (Almogávares 122). Major concerts are usually held in sports stadiums; keep an eye out for posters.

Flamenco The best place is **El Patio Andaluz** (Aribau 242, tel. 93/209–3378). **El Cordobés** (Ramblas 35, tel. 93/317–5711) is aimed at tour groups but can be fun.

Casino The **Gran Casino de Barcelona** (tel. 93/893–3666), 42 kilometers (26 miles) south in Sant Pere de Ribes, near Sitges, also has a dance hall and some excellent international shows in a 19th-century atmosphere. Jacket and tie essential.

5   Berlin

Berlin is now a united metropolis—again the largest in continental Europe—and only two small sections of the wall have been left in place to remind visitors and residents alike of the hideous barrier that divided the city for nearly 40 years. Old habits die hard, however, and it will be a long time before Germans and even Berliners themselves can get accustomed to regarding Berlin as one entity with one identity. You'll still hear Berliners in the western, more prosperous half talking about "those over there" when referring to people in the still down-at-the-heels eastern part. All restrictions on travel within and beyond the city have, of course, disappeared, and the sense of newly won freedom hangs almost tangibly in the air. But there's still a strong feeling of passing from one world into another when crossing the scar that marks the line where the wall once stood. It's not just the very visible differences between the glitter of west Berlin and the relative shabbiness of the east. Somehow the historical heritage of a long-divided city permeates the place and penetrates the consciousness of every visitor. You'll almost certainly arrive in and depart from the western part of Berlin, but just as surely your steps will lead you into the east. On the way, ponder the miracle that made this easy access to a onetime fortress of communism possible.

Arriving and Departing

By Plane **Tegel Airport** is centrally located, only 7 kilometers (4 miles) from downtown. Airlines flying to Tegel include Pan Am, TWA, Air France, British Airways, Lufthansa, Euro-Berlin, and some charter specialists. Because of increased air traffic at Tegel following unification the former military airfield at **Tempelhof** (even closer to downtown) is being used more and more. East Berlin's **Schönefeld** airport is about 24 kilometers (15 miles) outside the downtown area. For information on arrival and departure times at Tegel, call 030/41011; for Schönefeld, call 02/672–4031.

Between the Airports and Downtown The No. 9 bus runs every ten minutes between Tegel airport and downtown. The journey takes 30 minutes and the fare is DM 2.70. A taxi fare will cost about DM 20. If you've rented a car at the airport, follow signs for the "Stadtautobahn" highway.

A shuttle bus leaves Schönefeld airport every 10–15 minutes for the nearby S-Bahn train station. S-Bahn trains leave every 20 minutes for the Friedrichstrasse station. The trip takes about 30 minutes, and you can get off at whatever stop is nearest your hotel. The fare by bus or subway is DM 2.70 and covers travel throughout Berlin. Taxis are usually available at the stops from Ostbahnhof onward. You can also take a taxi from the airport; the fare to your hotel will be about DM 30–DM 35, and the trip will take about 40 minutes. By car, follow the signs for "Stadtzentrum Berlin."

By Train There are six major rail routes to Berlin from the western half of the country (from Hamburg, Hannover, Cologne, Frankfurt, Munich, and Nürnberg), and the network is set to expand to make the rest of eastern Germany more accessible. Traveling time to and from Berlin is being progressively cut as the system in eastern Germany becomes modernized and streamlined to meet western standards. For the latest information on routes, tel. 030/19419 or 030/3110–2116, or enquire at the local main train station if you are in western Germany, where you will also get details of reduced fare rates. Three people or more can often travel at discounted group rates. The West Berlin terminus for all lines is the main train station (Bahnhof Zoo).

International trains headed directly for East Berlin arrive at Friedrichstrasse or the Ostbahnhof. Train information: tel. 02/ 49541 for international trains, 02/49531 for domestic services.

By Bus   Long-distance bus services link Berlin with numerous western German and other western European cities. For travel details, if you're in Berlin, call the main bus station (Messedam, tel. 030/301–8028), or if you're in western Germany, enquire at the local tourist office.

By Car   The eight former "transit corridor" roads linking the western part of Germany with Berlin have now been incorporated into the country-wide autobahn network, but they are ill prepared for the vast increase of motor traffic between east and west that has followed unification. Be prepared for large traffic jams, particularly during weekends. At the time of writing, speed restrictions of 100 kilometers (60 miles) an hour still apply, and you must carry your driver's license, car registration, and insurance documents. Seat belts must be worn at all times.

Expressways from eastern Germany lead to Berlin via Magdeburg, Leipzig, Rostock, Dresden, and Frankfurt-Oder. Road crossings also go to and from West Berlin. The downtown is marked "Stadtzentrum."

Getting Around

By Public   Berlin is surprisingly large, and only the center can comfort-
Transportation ably be explored on foot. Fortunately, the city is blessed with excellent public transportation, a combination of U-Bahn (subway) and S-Bahn (metropolitan train) lines, bus services, and even a ferry across the Wannsee lake. The eight U-Bahn lines alone have 116 stations. An all-night bus service (the buses are marked by the letter N next to their number) is also in operation. For DM 2.70 you can buy a ticket that covers travel on the entire system for 2 hours. A multiple ticket, valid for five trips, costs DM 11.50. Or, you can pay DM 9 for a 24-hour ticket that allows unlimited use (except on the Wannsee Lake ferries). Information can be obtained from the office of the city transport authority, the Berliner Verkehrsbetriebe (BVG) at Hardenbergplatz, in front of the Bahnhof Zoo, or by calling 030/216–5088.

Buses and streetcars in East Berlin are often crowded, and route maps, posted at each stop (marked H or HH), are not particularly clear to the uninitiated. The fare structure now covers both parts of Berlin, although cheap, subsidized tickets are still sold to East Berlin residents. Don't be tempted to buy one if you're traveling in East Berlin—the fine is quite heavy if unauthorized travelers are found in possession of tickets reserved for East Berliners. (It's difficult anyway, because East Berliners normally have to show their identity documents in order to take advantage of the special offer.) The fares in East Berlin are the same as those in the west.

By Taxi   Taxi meters start at DM 3.40 and the fare is DM 1.69 (DM 2.69 after midnight). Taxi drivers charge 50 pf for each piece of heavy luggage carried. A drive along the Kurfürstendamm will cost about DM 10. Taxis can be ordered by telephone: Call 030/6902, 030/216060, 030/240202; in East Berlin phone 02/3646, 02/365–4471, or 02/261026 for immediate or same-day reservations, 02/365–4176 for service during the coming week.

Important Addresses and Numbers

Tourist Information
The main tourist office, **Verkehrsamt Berlin,** is at the Europa Center (Budapesterstrasse, tel. 030/262–6031). It's open daily 7:30 AM–10:30 PM. There are other offices at the main hall of **Tegel airport** (tel. 030/4101–3145, open daily 8 AM–11 PM); the **Bahnhof Zoo,** (the main train station, tel. 030/313–9063, open daily 8 AM–11 PM); and at the former border crossing point **Dreilinden,** tel. 030/803–9057, open daily 8 AM–11 PM. Accommodations can be reserved at all offices, which also issue a free English-language information brochure, *Berlin Turns On.* Pretravel information on Berlin can be obtained by writing to the Verkehrsamt Berlin (Europa Center, D-1000 Berlin 30).

The main office of the **Reisebüro** (the former East German tourist office) in East Berlin is at Alexanderplatz 5 (tel. 02/215–4453 or 02/215–4497). It's open weekdays 8–8, Sat. 9–6. There's another branch at **Schönefeld Airport** (tel. 02/687–8248).

Consulates
U.S. (Clayallee 170, tel. 030/832–4087). **Canada** (Europa-Center, tel. 030/261–1161). **U.K.** (Uhlandstr. 7/8, tel. 030/309–5292).

Emergencies
Police (tel. 030/110). **Ambulance and emergency medical attention** (tel. 030/310–031). **Dentist** (tel. 030/1141). **Pharmacies:** for emergency pharmaceutical assistance, call 030/247033.

English Bookstores
Marga Schoeller (Knesebeckstrasse 33, tel. 030/881–1112); **Buchhandlung Kiepert** (Hardenbergstrasse 4–5, tel. 030/311–0090).

Guided Tours

By Bus
English-language bus tours of West and East Berlin are offered by a number of operators, the chief of which are **Severin & Kühn** (Kurfürstendamm 216, Charlottenburg, tel. 030/883–1015); **Berliner Bären Stadtrundfahrt** (Rankestrasse 35, corner of Kurfürstendamm, tel. 030/213–4077); **Reisebüro Berolina** (Meinekestr. 3, tel. 030/883–3131); and **Bus Verkehr Berlin (BVB,** Kurfürstendamm 225, tel. 030/882–2063). A two-hour tour of Berlin costs DM 22 and a four-hour tour of Berlin costs DM 49. There are also half-day tours to Potsdam and the Sans Soucis palace, favorite residence of Frederick the Great. Lunch is included in the DM 99 cost of the tour.

By Boat
Berlin is a city of waterways, and boat trips can be made on the Spree River and on the canals that connect the city's network of big lakes. For details, contact the city tourist office at the Europa Center, Budapesterstrasse, tel. 030/262–6031.

Exploring Berlin

Visiting Berlin is a bittersweet experience, as so many of the triumphs and tragedies of the past are tied up with the bustling present. The result can be either dispiriting or exhilarating. And by European standards, Berlin isn't that old: Cologne was more than 1,000 years old when Berlin was born from the fusion of two tiny settlements on islands in the Spree River. Although already a royal residence in the 15th century, Berlin really came into its own three centuries later, under the rule of King Friedrich II—Frederick the Great—whose liberal reforms and artistic patronage led the way as the city developed into a major cultural capital.

The events of the 20th century would have crushed the spirit of most other cities. Hitler destroyed the city's reputation for tolerance and plunged Berlin headlong into the war that led to the wholesale destruction of monuments and houses. And after World War II, Berlin was still to face the bitter division of the city and the construction of the infamous wall in 1961. But a storm of political events, beginning in 1989, brought the downfall of the Communist regime; the establishment of democracy in the east; and finally, in October 1990, the unification of Berlin and of all Germany. Now you can travel from one end of Berlin to the other and in and out of the long-isolated city as easily as you would in any other Western metropolis. You'll still notice the scars left by the infamous wall, however, and contrasts between the prosperous western half of the city and the run-down east are still very visible.

Numbers in the margin correspond to points of interest on the West Berlin map.

West Berlin The **Kurfürstendamm,** or Ku'damm as the Berliners call it, is one of Europe's busiest thoroughfares, throbbing with activity day and night. At its eastern end is the **Kaiser Wilhelm Gedächtniskirche** (Kaiser Wilhelm Memorial Church Tower). This landmark has come to symbolize not only West Berlin, but the futile destructiveness of war. The shell of the tower is all that remains of the church that was built at the end of the 19th century and dedicated to the memory of Kaiser Wilhelm. Inside is a historical exhibition of the devastation of World War II. *Admission free. Open Tues.–Sat. 10–6, Sun. 11–6.*

Cross Budapesterstrasse to enter the **Zoologischer Garten,** Berlin's zoo. It has the world's largest variety of individual types of fauna along with a fascinating aquarium. *Admission: DM 9 adults, DM 5 children. Open daily from 9–7 PM or to dusk in winter.*

The zoo is set in the 255-hectare (630-acre) **Tiergarten Park,** which has at last recovered from the war, when it was not only ripped apart by bombs and artillery, but was stripped of its wood by desperate, freezing Berliners in the bitter cold of 1945–46. In the northern section of the park is the **Englischer Garten** (English Garden), which borders the riverside **Bellevue Schloss,** a small palace built for Frederick the Great's brother: It is now the official Berlin residence of the German president.

The column in the center of a large traffic circle in the Tiergarten is the **Siegessäule** (Victory Column), erected in 1873 to commemorate four Prussian military campaigns against the French. The granite and sandstone monument originally stood in front of the Reichstag (parliament), which was burned by Hitler's men in 1933. Climb the 285 steps to its 65-meter (210-foot) summit and you'll rewarded with a fine view of both West Berlin and East Berlin. *Admission: DM 1.20 adults, 70 pf children. Open Tues.–Sun. 9–6, Mon. 1–6. Closed Nov. 1–Mar. 30.*

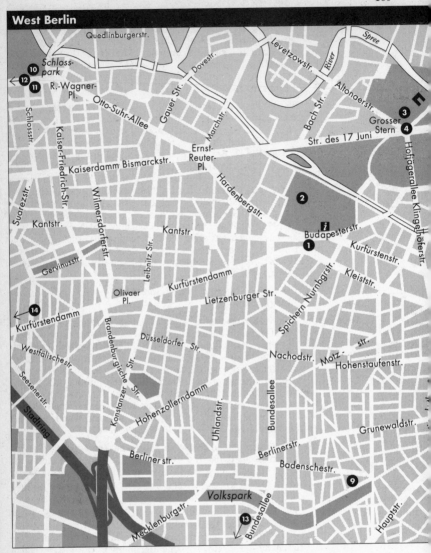

West Berlin

Ägyptisches
Museum, **11**

Brandenburger Tor, **6**

Checkpoint Charlie
Museum, **7**

Englischer Garten, **3**

Gemäldegalerie, **13**

Gipsformerei, **12**

Grunewald, **14**

Kaiser Wilhelm
Gedächtniskirche, **1**

Kreuzberg, **8**

Rathaus
Schöneberg, **9**

Schloss
Charlottenburg, **10**

Siegessäule (Victory
Column), **4**

Soviet Victory
Memorial, **5**

Zoologischer Garten, **2**

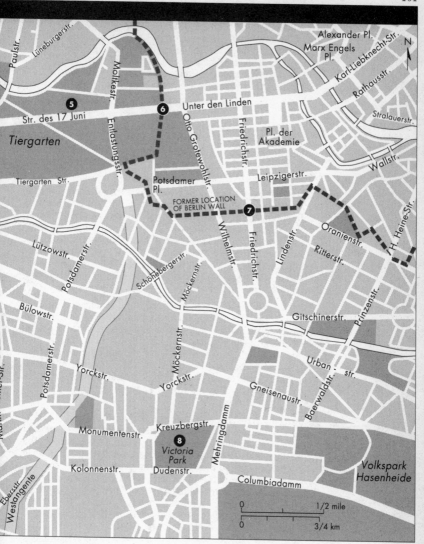

Paulstr.

Lüneburgerstr.

Moltkestr.

Alexander Pl.

Marx Engels Pl.

Karl-Liebknecht-Str.

Rathausstr.

Stralauerstr.

5

Str. des 17 Juni

Entlastungsstr.

Unter den Linden

Otto Grotewohlstr.

Friedrichstr.

Pl. der Akademie

6

N

Tiergarten

Wallstr.

Tiergarten Str.

Potsdamer Pl.

Leipzigerstr.

FORMER LOCATION OF BERLIN WALL

7

Wilhelmstr.

Friedrichstr.

Lindenstr.

Orantenstr.

Ritterstr.

H. Heine-Str.

Lützowstr.

Potsdamerstr.

Schönebergerstr.

Möckernstr.

Bülowstr.

Gitschinerstr.

Prinzenstr.

Potsdamerstr.

Yorckstr.

Möckernstr.

Urban - str.

Martin Luther-Str.

Yorckstr.

Gneisenaustr.

Baerwaldstr.

Monumentenstr.

Kreuzbergstr.

Mehringdamm

8

Victoria Park

Dudenstr.

Kolonnenstr.

Columbiadamm

Volkspark Hasenheide

Ebersstr.

Westtangente

0   1/2 mile

0   3/4 km

At the base of the Siegessäule, go east down the wide Strasse des 17 Juni (June 17th Street), named in memory of the day, in 1953, when 50,000 East Germans staged an uprising that was **⑤** put down by force. On the left, you'll pass the **Soviet Victory Memorial**, a semicircular colonnade topped with a statue of a Russian soldier and flanked by what are said to be the first Soviet tanks to have fought their way into Berlin in 1945.

⑥ Ahead of you is **Brandenburger Tor** (Brandenburg Gate), built in 1788 as a victory arch for triumphant Prussian armies. The horse-drawn chariot atop the arch was reerected after the war. The monumental gate was cut off from West Berlin by the wall, and it became a focal point of celebrations marking the unification of Berlin and of all Germany. It was here that German politicians formally sealed unification.

The wall that for so long isolated the Brandenburger Tor is no more, but the history of the hideous frontier fortification can be followed in the museum that arose at its most famous crossing point. Checkpoint Charlie, as it was known, disappeared along **⑦** with the wall, but the **Checkpoint Charlie Museum** is still there. You can walk to the museum by following Friedrichstrasse south for about a mile, but it's easier to call a cab. *Checkpoint Charlie Museum, Friedrichstr. 44, tel. 030/251–4569. Admission free. Open daily 9–9.*

Find the nearby Kochstrasse U-Bahn station and go two stops south on the U-6 line to Mehringdamm. Head for Kreuzberg- **⑧** strasse. Just on the left is the 62-meter (200-foot) **Kreuzberg**, West Berlin's highest natural hill. (There are higher hills made of the rubble gathered from the bombed-out ruins of the city when reconstruction began in 1945.) On the sheltered southern slopes of the Kreuzberg is a vineyard that produces some of Germany's rarest wines: They are served only at official Berlin functions.

Bordering Kreuzberg to the west is the Schöneberg district, where you'll find the seat of the city and state government of **⑨** Berlin, the **Rathaus Schöneberg** (City Hall). In the belfry of the Rathaus is a replica of the Liberty Bell, donated to Berliners in 1950 by the United States and rung every day at noon. In a room at the base of the tower are stored 17 million American signatures expressing solidarity with West Berlin, some, no doubt, inspired by President Kennedy's famous "Ich bin ein Berliner" speech, which he made here in 1963. *The tower is open to visitors Wed. and Sun. only, 10–4.*

Time Out   While at the Rathaus, go downstairs to the **Ratskeller Schöneberg**, an inexpensive place to get a good, filling set-price lunch. The atmosphere is busy and friendly.

Take the U-Bahn north one stop from Rathaus Schöneberg station and change to the U-7 line for eight stops, to Richard-Wagner-Platz station. From the station, walk left for about 465 **⑩** meters (500 yards) to the handsome **Schloss Charlottenburg** (Charlottenburg Palace). Built at the end of the 17th century by King Frederick I for his wife, Queen Sophie Charlotte, the palace was progressively enlarged for later royal residents. Frederick the Great's suite of rooms can be visited; in one glass cupboard, you'll see the coronation crown he inherited from his father—stripped of jewels by the ascetic son, who gave the most valuable diamonds and pearls to his wife. *Schloss Char-*

lottenburg, Luisenplatz, Charlottenburg. Admission: DM 6 adults, DM 2 children. Open Tues.–Sun. 10–5, Thurs. 10–8.

⑪ Opposite the palace is the **Ägyptisches Museum** (Egyptian Museum), home of perhaps the world's best-known portrait sculpture, the beautiful Nefertiti. The 3,300-year-old Egyptian queen is the centerpiece of a fascinating collection of Egyptology that includes one of the finest preserved mummies outside Cairo. *Ägyptisches Museum, Schlossstr. 70, Charlottenburg. Admission free. Open Mon.–Thurs. 9–5, weekends 10–5 PM. Closed Fri.*

If you like, you can take Nefertiti home with you. Behind **⑫** Schloss Charlottenburg is the **Gipsformerei** (State Museum Plaster Foundry), which will turn out a copy of any of a dozen masterpieces in stock. They're not cheap (portrait busts cost between DM 700 and DM 900), but how can you put a price on having Nefertiti on the mantelpiece? *Gipsformerei, Sophie-Charlotten-Str. 17/18, Charlottenburg. Open weekdays 9–4, (Wed. 9–6).*

Take U-Bahn line U-7 back toward Schöneberg until Fehrbelliner Platz, where you change to line U-2 southwest for five stops to Dahlem-Dorf station. This is the stop for West Berlin's **⑬** leading art museum, the **Gemäldegalerie,** in the district of Dahlem. The collection includes many works by the great European masters, with 26 Rembrandts and 14 by Rubens. Or is it 25 Rembrandts? *The Man in the Golden Hat,* until recently attributed to Rembrandt, has now been ascribed to one of the great Dutch master's pupils. Does it really matter? Maybe not to the public, which still sees it as a masterpiece, but it could affect the value of the painting by a million or two. *Gemäldegalerie, Arnimallee 23/27, Dahlem. Admission free. Open Tues.–Fri. 9–5, weekends 10–5.*

No visit to West Berlin is complete without an outing to the **⑭** city's outdoor playground, the **Grunewald** park. Bordering the Dahlem district to the west, the park is a vast green space, with meadows, woodlands, and lakes. There are a string of 60 lakes within Berlin's boundaries; some are kilometers long, others are no more than ponds. The total length of their shorelines—if stretched out in one long line—is 209.6 kilometers (130 miles), longer than Germany's Baltic Coast. There's even space for nudist beaches on the banks of the Wannsee lake, while in winter a downhill ski run and even a ski jump operate on the modest slopes of the Teufelsberg hill.

East Berlin The infamous wall is now gone, but the spirit of division remains in a city that was physically split for 28 years. The stately buildings of the city's past are not as overwhelmed by new high-rise construction as in West Berlin, but East Berlin's postwar architectural blunders are just as monumental in their own way. These will be obvious—along with the sad shabbiness of years of neglect—as you explore the side streets together with the main thoroughfares.

Numbers in the margin correspond to points of interest on the East Berlin map.

For a sense of déjà vu, enter the eastern part of Berlin at **⑮** **Checkpoint Charlie,** the most famous crossing point between the two Berlins during the Cold War and the setting of numerous spy novels and films. At this point both ends of Fried-

East Berlin

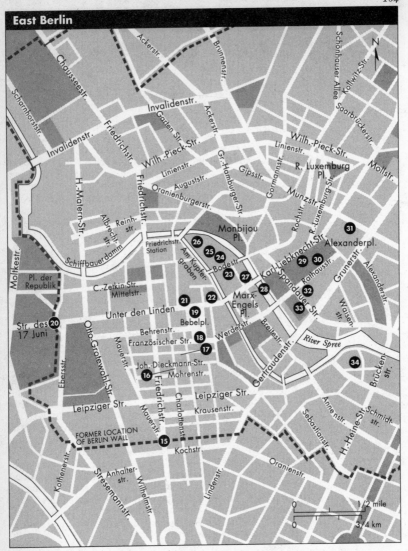

Altes Museum, **23**

Berliner Dom, **27**

Bodemuseum, **26**

Brandenburger Tor, **20**

Centrum department
store, **31**

Checkpoint Charlie, **15**

Deutsche
Staatsoper, **19**

Huguenot Museum, **17**

Humboldt
University, **21**

Marienkirche, **29**

Märkisches
Museum, **34**

Museum für Deutsche
Geschichte, **22**

Nationalgalerie, **24**

Nikolaikirche, **33**

Palast der
Republik, **28**

Pergamon Museum, **25**

Rathaus, **32**

Schauspielhaus, **16**

St. Hedwigs
Kathedrale, **18**

TV Tower, **30**

richstrasse—east and west—are lined with attractive new shops and trendy restaurants. Turn right onto Mohrenstrasse and you'll arrive at the Platz der Akadamie, with its beautifully

16 reconstructed **Schauspielhaus**—built in 1818, and now the city's main concert hall—and the twin **German** (on the south, undergoing restoration) and **French cathedrals**. In the latter,

17 you'll find the **Huguenot Museum**, which has some interesting collections of the history and art of the French Protestant Huguenots who took refuge in Germany after being expelled from Catholic France in 1685. *Platz der Akadamie. Open weekdays 10–5.*

Time Out The **Arkade Café** on the northwest corner of the plaza (Französischer Str. 25) is perfect for a light snack; some excellent pastry; and a beer, coffee, or tea.

Continue east along the Französischer Strasse and turn left into Hedwigskirchgasse to reach Bebelplatz. The peculiar

18 round shape of **St. Hedwigs Kathedrale** (St. Hedwig's Cathedral) calls to mind Rome's Pantheon. The tiny street named Hinter der Katholischen Kirche (Behind the Catholic Church) is a reminder that though Berlin was very much a Protestant city, St. Hedwig's was built (about 1747) for Catholics.

Walk north across Bebelplatz to Unter den Linden, the elegant central thoroughfare of old Berlin. On your right is the

19 **Deutsche Staatsoper,** the great opera house of Berlin, now with an entirely new interior. Just after Oberwallstrasse is the former crown prince's palace, the **Palais Unter den Linden,** now restored and used to house official government visitors.

Look back down the street to the western sector and you'll see

20 the monumental **Brandenburger Tor** (Brandenburg Gate), its chariot-and-horses sculpture now turned to face the east. Cross Unter den Linden and look into the courtyard of

21 **Humboldt University:** It was built as a palace for the brother of Friedrich II of Prussia but became a university in 1810, and today is one of Germany's largest universities. Marx and Engels were its two most famous students. Beyond the war memorial,

22 housed in a onetime arsenal (1695–1705) is the **Museum für Deutsche Geschichte** (Museum of German History), which traces events from 1789 to the present. *Unter den Linden 2. Open Mon.–Thurs. 9–7, weekends 10–5.*

Turning left along the Spree canal (along Am Zeughaus and Am Kupfergraben) will bring you to East Berlin's museum complex, at the northern end of what is known as **Museumsinsel** (Museum Island). The first of the Big Four that you'll encoun-

23 ter is the **Altes Museum** (entrance on Lustgarten), an austere neoclassical building just to the north of Marx-Engels-Platz. The collections here include postwar art from some of Germany's most prominent artists and numerous etchings and

24 drawings from the Old Masters. Next comes the **Nationalgalerie,** on Bodestrasse, which features 19th- and 20th-century

25 painting and sculpture. The **Pergamon Museum** on Am Kupfergraben, is one of Europe's greatest. Its name derives from the museum's principal exhibit and the city's number-one attraction, the **Pergamon Altar,** a monumental Greek temple dating from 180 BC that occupies an entire city block. Almost as impressive is the **Babylonian Processional Way.** The Pergamon Museum also houses vast Egyptian, early-Christian, and

Byzantine collections, plus a fine array of sculpture from the
(26) 12th to the 18th centuries. To the north is the **Bodemuseum**
(also on Am Kupfergraben, but with its entrance on Monbijou-
brücke), with an outstanding collection of early-Christian-Byz-
antine and Egyptian art, as well as special exhibits of Italian
Old Masters. *Museum complex open Wed.–Sun. 10–6; closed
Mon. and Tues. (except Pergamon Museum, whose Pergamon
Altar and architectural rooms remain open 9–6).*

From the museum complex, follow the Spree canal south to
(27) Unter den Linden and the vast and impressive **Berliner Dom**
(Berlin cathedral). The hideous modern building in bronze mir-
(28) rored glass opposite is the **Palast der Republik** (Palace of the
Republic), a postwar monument to socialist progress, also
housing restaurants, a theater, and a dance hall.

Time Out The cafeteria-style **Quick restaurant** in the Palast Hotel, although mobbed at noon, is a good spot for lunch or a snack (entrance on Karl-Liebknecht-Strasse).

Cross Spandauer Strasse diagonally for a closer look at the
(29) 13th-century **Marienkirche** (Church of St. Mary), especially
noting its late-Gothic *Dance of Death* fresco. You are now at the
(30) lower end of Alexanderplatz. Just ahead is the massive **TV tow-**
(31) **er,** a Berlin landmark. A focal point for shopping is the **Centrum
department store,** alongside the Hotel Stadt Berlin, at the very
top of the plaza.

(32) The area adjacent to the **Rathaus** (City Hall)—itself somewhat
of a marvel for its red-brick design and the frieze depicting
scenes from the city's history—has been handsomely rebuilt.
(33) **Nikolaikirche** (on Spandauer Strasse), dating from about 1200,
is Berlin's oldest building. It was heavily damaged in the war,
but has been beautifully restored and is now a museum. The
quarter surrounding the church is filled with delightful shops,
cafés, and restaurants. Wander back down Muhlendamm into
the area around the Breite Strasse—there are some lovely old
buildings here—and on over to the **Fischerinsel** area. The
throbbing heart of Old Berlin of 750 years ago, Fischerinsel retains a tangible medieval flavor.

Time Out The **Alt-Cöllner Schankstuben,** overlooking the Spree canal
(Friedrichsgracht 50), is as charming and friendly a café as
you'll find in East Berlin. On a sunny day, enjoy a glass of beer
at an outdoor table.

(34) Nearby is the **Märkisches Museum** (Museum of Cultural History), which has an amusing section devoted to automaphones—
"self-playing" musical instruments, demonstrated Sundays
10–12 and Wednesdays 3–4. Live bears—the city's symbol—
are in a pit next to the museum. *Am Köllnischen Park 5. Open
Wed.–Fri. 10–6, weekends 10–5.*

Shopping

Berlin is a city of alluring stores and boutiques. Despite its cosmopolitan gloss, prices are generally lower than in cities like
Munich and Hamburg.

Fine **porcelain** is still produced at the former Royal Prussian
Porcelain Factory, now called **Staatliche Porzellan Manufactur,**

or KPM. This delicate, handmade, hand-painted china is sold at KPM's store at Kurfürstendamm 26A (tel. 030/881–1802), but it may be more fun to visit the factory salesroom at Wegelystrasse 1. It also sells seconds at reduced prices. If you long to have the Egyptian Queen Nefertiti on your mantelpiece at home, try the **Gipsformerei der Staatlichen Museen Preussicher Kulturbesitz** (Sophie-Charlotte-Str. 17, tel. 030/321–7011, open weekdays 9–4). It sells plaster casts of this and other treasures from the city's museums.

Shopping Districts The liveliest and most famous shopping area in West Berlin is the **Kurfürstendamm** and its side streets, especially between **Breitscheidplatz** and **Oliver Platz**. The **Europa-Centre** at Breitscheidplatz encompasses more than 100 stores, cafés, and restaurants—this is not a place to bargain-hunt, though! Running east from Breitscheidplatz is **Tauenzientstrasse,** another shopping street. At the end of it is Berlin's most celebrated department store, **KaDeWe.** New and elegant malls include the **Gloria Galerie** (opposite the Wertheim department store on Ku' damm) and the **Uhland-Passage** (connecting Uhlandstrasse and Fasanenstrasse). In both, you'll find leading name stores as well as cafés and restaurants.

For trendier clothes, try the boutiques along **Bleibtreustrasse.** One of the more avant-garde fashion boutiques is **Durchbruch** (Schlutterstr. 54), around the corner. The name means "breakthrough," and the store lives up to its name by selling six different designers' outrageous styles. Less trendy and much less expensive is the mall, **Wilmersdorferstrasse,** where price-conscious Berliners do their shopping. It's packed on weekends.

East Berlin's chief shopping areas are along the Friedrichstrasse, Unter den Linden, and in the area around Alexanderplatz. The Palast and Grand hotels have small shopping malls. A number of smaller stores have sprung up in and around the Nikolai quarter; under the communist regime, all were supplied from the same central sources, but they make fun places to shop for trinkets.

Department Stores The classiest department store in Berlin is **KaDeWe**, the Kaufhaus des Western (Department Store of the West, as it's modestly known in English), at Wittenbergplatz. The biggest department store in Europe, the KaDeWe is a grand-scale emporium in modern guise. Be sure to check out the food department, which occupies the whole sixth floor. The other main department store downtown is **Wertheim** on Ku'damm. Neither as big nor as attractive as the KaDeWe, Wertheim nonetheless offers a large selection of fine wares.

East Berlin's **Centrum** department store, at the north end of Alexanderplatz, offered ridiculously cheap subsidized prices under the old regime, though style was somewhat lacking. Prices have changed, but its worth a visit for souvenirs and such East German specialties as wooden toys.

Antiques On Saturdays and Sundays from 10 to 5, the colorful and lively antiques and handicrafts fair on Strasse des 17 Juni swings into action. Don't expect to pick up any bargains—or to have the place to yourself. Not far from Wittenbergplatz is **Keithstrasse**, a street given over to antiques stores. There are also several small antiques stores in the converted subway cars of the **Nollendorf Flohmarkt.** Eisenacherstrasse, Fuggerstrasse,

Kalckreuthstrasse, Motzstrasse, and Nollendorfstrasse—all close to Nollendorfplatz—have many antiques stores of varying quality. Another good street for antiques is **Suarezstrasse,** between Kantstrasse and Bismarckstrasse.

In East Berlin, antiques are sold in the Metropol and Palast hotels in the Nikolai quarter and in the restored Husemannstrasse. Some private stores along the stretch of Friedichstrasse north of the Spree Bridge offer old books and prints.

Dining

Dining in Berlin can mean sophisticated nouvelle creations in upscale restaurants with linen tablecloths and hand-painted porcelain plates or hearty local specialties in atmospheric and inexpensive inns: The range is as vast as the city. Specialties include *Eisbein mit Sauerkraut,* knuckle of pork with pickled cabbage; *Rouladen,* rolled stuffed beef; *Spanferkel,* suckling pig; *Berliner Schüsselsülze,* potted meat in aspic; *Schlachteplatte,* mixed grill; *Hackepeter,* ground beef; and *Kartoffelpuffer,* fried potato cakes. *Bockwurst* is a chubby frankfurter that's served in a variety of ways and sold in restaurants and at Bockwurst stands all over the city. *Schlesisches Himmerlreich* is roast goose or pork served with potato dumplings in rich gravy. *Königsberger Klopse* consists of meatballs, herring, and capers—it tastes much better than it sounds.

East Germany's former ties to the Eastern Bloc persist in restaurants featuring the national cuisine of those other one-time socialist states, although such exotica as Japanese, Chinese, Indonesian, and French food is now appearing. Wines and spirits imported from those other countries can be quite good; try Hungarian, Yugoslav, and Bulgarian wines (the whites are lighter) and Polish and Russian vodkas.

It's hard to generalize about German food beyond saying that standards are high and portions are large. In fact, the range of dining experiences is vast: everything from highly priced nouvelle cuisine to hamburgers. As a visitor, you should search out local restaurants if atmosphere and regional specialties are your priority. *Kneipen*—the pub on the corner cum local café— in Berlin nearly always offer best value and atmosphere. But throughout the country you'll find *Gaststätten* and/or *Gasthöfe*—local inns—where atmosphere and regional specialties are always available. Likewise, just about every town will have a *Ratskeller,* a cellar restaurant in the town hall, where exposed beams, huge fireplaces, sturdy tables, and immense portions are the rule.

Germans like to nibble at roadside or market snack stalls, called *Imbisse.* Hot sausages, spicy meatballs *(Fleischpflanzerl),* Leberkas (in the south), and sauerkraut are the traditional favorites. But foods eaten on the hoof are creeping in, too: French fries, pizzas, gyros, and hamburgers. In eastern Germany, the old state-run self-service worker cafeterias may still be operating in some towns, but these are rapidly being replaced by commercial enterprises. For late breakfasts or good-value lunches, try the restaurants of the main department stores across the country: Hertie, Karstadt, Kaufhof.

The most famous German specialty is sausage. Nuremberg's sausage favorite is the *Nürnberger Bratwurst;* its fame is such that you'll find restaurants all over Germany serving it. Look for the "Bratwurststube" sign. Dumplings (*Knödel*) can also be found throughout the country, though their natural home is probably Bavaria; farther north, potatoes often take their place.

The natural accompaniment to German food is either beer or wine. Say "Helles" or Export if you want light beer; "Dunkles" if you want dark beer. Germany is a major wine-producing country, also, and much of it is of superlative quality. You will probably be happy with the house wine in most restaurants or with one of those earthenware pitchers of cold Moselle wine. If you want something more expensive, remember that all wines are graded in one of three basic categories: *Tafelwein* (table wine); *Qualitätswein* (fine wines); and *Qualitätswein mit Prädikat* (top-quality wines).

Mealtimes   Lunch is served from around 11:30 to around 2; dinner is generally from 6 until 9:30 PM. Big city hotels and popular restaurants serve later. Lunch tends to be the main meal, a fact reflected in the almost universal appearance of a lunchtime *Tageskarte*, or suggested menu; try it if you want maximum nourishment for minimum outlay. This doesn'tmean that dinner is a rushed or skimpy affair, however; the Germans have too high a regard for food for any meal to be underrated. Breakfast, served anytime from 6:30 to 10, is often a substantial meal, with cold meats, cheeses, rolls, and fruit. Many city hotels offer Sunday "brunch," and the custom is rapidly catching on.

Dress   Jacket and tie are recommended for restaurants in the Very Expensive and Expensive categories. Casual dress is appropriate elsewhere.

Ratings   Prices are per person and include a first course, main course, dessert, and tip and tax. Best bets are indicated by a star ★.

The following chart gives price ranges for restaurants in the western part of Germany. Food prices in the territory of former East Germany are still somewhat unstable, although in the bigger cities many of the better quality restaurants are already starting to mimic "western" rates. Generally speaking, the prevailing price structure in the eastern part of the country, except for restaurants in the priciest hotels, falls into the Inexpensive to Expensive categories listed below.

Category	Cost
Very Expensive	over DM 100
Expensive	DM 75–DM 100
Moderate	DM 50–DM 75
Inexpensive	DM 25–DM 50

West Berlin   **Alt-Luxembourg.** There are only nine tables at this popular
Expensive   restaurant in the Charlottenburg district, and you'll receive attentive service. Chef Kurt Wannebacher uses only fresh ingredients and announces his daily specials on the blackboard. If lobster lasagna is chalked up, look no further. *Pestalozzistr.*

70, tel. 030/323–8730. Reservations required. DC, V. Closed Sun., Mon., 3 weeks in Jan., 3 weeks in July.

★ **Bamberger Reiter.** Considered by Berliners to be the city's best restaurant, Bamberger Reiter is the pride of its chef, Franz Raneburger. He relies heavily on fresh market produce for his *neue deutsche Küche* (new German cuisine), so the menu changes from day to day. Fresh flowers, too, abound in his attractive, oak-beamed restaurant. *Regensburgerstr. 7, tel. 030/ 244282. Reservations required. DC, V. Dinner only. Closed Sun., Mon., Jan. 1–15, and Aug. 1–20.*

Frühsammer's Restaurant an der Rehwiese. From your table, you can watch chef Peter Frühsammer at work in his open kitchen. He's ready with advice on the daily menu: Salmon is always a treat here. The restaurant is located in the annex of a turn-of-the-century villa in the southern district of Zehlendorf (U-Bahn to Krumme Lanke and then bus No. 53 to Rehwiese). *Matterhornstr. 101, tel. 030/803–2720. Reservations required. MC, V. Closed Sun., Dinner only.*

Moderate **Alt-Nürnberg.** Step into the tavernlike interior and you could be in Bavaria: The waitresses even wear dirndls. The Bavarian colors of blue and white are everywhere, and such Bavarian culinary delights as *Schweinshaxe* (knuckle of pork) are well represented on the menu. If you prefer to eat in the Prussian style, the calves' liver *Berliner Art* is recommended. *Europa Center, tel. 030/261–4397. Reservations advised. AE, DC, MC, V.*

★ **Blockhaus Nikolskoe.** Prussian King Wilhelm III built this Russian-style wooden lodge for his daughter Charlotte, wife of Russia's Czar Nicholas I. It's located in the southwest of the city, on the eastern edge of Glienicke Park. In summer, you can eat on the open terrace overlooking the Havel River. In character with its history and appearance, the Blockhaus features game dishes. *Nikolskoer Weg, tel. 030/805–2914. Reservations advised. AE, DC, MC, V.*

Forsthaus Paulsborn. Game is the specialty in this former woodsman's home deep in the Grunewald Forest. You dine here as the forester did—from an oak table in a great dining room and under the baleful eye of hunting trophies on the wall. Apart from game, the menu extends to various German and international dishes. *Am Grunewaldsee, tel. 030/813–8010. Reservations advised on weekends. AE, DC, MC, V. Closed Mon., dinner in winter (Oct.–Mar.).*

Hecker's Deele. You could find yourself seated in one of the antique church pews that complete the oak-beamed interior of this restaurant that features Westphalian dishes. The *Westfälische Schlachtplatte* (a variety of meats) will set you up for a whole day's sightseeing—the Ku'damm is right outside. *Grolmannstr. 35, tel. 030/88901. No reservations. AE, DC, MC, V.*

Mundart Restaurant. Too many cooks don't spoil the broth (and certainly not the excellent fish soup) at this popular restaurant in the Kreuzberg district. Five chefs are at work in the spacious kitchen. Fortunately, they all agree on the day's specials, and you can follow their advice with impunity. *Muskauerstr. 33/34, tel. 030/612–2061. No reservations. No credit cards. Closed lunch, Mon., and Tues.*

Inexpensive **Alt-Berliner Weissbierstube.** A visit to the Berlin Museum (a permanent historical exhibition on Berlin) must include a stop at this pub-style restaurant in the museum building. There's a buffet packed with Berlin specialties, and a jazz band plays on

Sunday morning after 10. *Berlin Museum, Lindenstr. 14, tel. 030/251–0121. Reservations advised, particularly evenings. No credit cards. Closed Mon.*

Thürnagel. Also located in the Kreuzberg district, Thürnagel is a vegetarian restaurant where it's not only healthy to eat, but fun. The seitan in sherry sauce or the tempeh curry are good enough to convert a seasoned carnivore. *Gneisenaustr. 57, tel. 030/691–4800. Reservations advised. No credit cards. Dinner only.*

East Berlin
Very Expensive

Ermeler-Haus. The wine restaurant in a series of upstairs rooms reflects the elegance of this restored patrician house, which dates from 1567 (it was moved to its present location in 1969, however). The atmosphere is subdued, the wines are imported, and the service matches the international specialties. There's dancing on Saturday evening. *Märkisches Ufer 12, tel. 02/2755103. Reservations advised. No credit cards.*

Ganymed. Velvet draperies, oil paintings, and brass chandeliers adorn this particularly attractive restaurant, whose choice of dishes ranges from cold plates to cordon bleu, with even an Indonesian item or two thrown in. The front room has piano music in the evening. *Schiffbauerdamm 5, tel. 02/282–9540. Reservations required. No credit cards. Closed Mon. lunch.*

Expensive

Schwalbennest. This is a fairly new restaurant on the edge of the Nikolai quarter, overlooking the Marx-Engels-Forum. Both the food and service are variable, although on paper, at least, the choice is wide for both main dishes and wines. The grilled meats can be excellent, but note that no additional price is indicated on the menu for the flambéed dishes—ask about this, or you could be in for a surprise when the bill arrives! *Am Marstall, Rathausstr. at Marx-Engels-Forum, tel. 02/212–2869. Reservations required, even for lunch. No credit cards.*

Moderate

Ratskeller. This is actually two restaurants in one—a wine and a beer cellar, both vast, atmospheric, and extremely popular. The menus are limited, but offer good, solid Berlin fare. The beer cellar is guaranteed to be packed at main dining hours, and attempts at reservations may be ignored (locals simply line up and wait). *Rathausstr. 15–18, in basement of the City Hall, tel. 02/212–5301. Reservations advised. No credit cards.*

Sofia. Bulgarian and Russian specialties are the basis of the imaginative menu offered at this popular, central restaurant, a few paces from Potsdamer Platz. The Bulgarian wines are particularly recommended. *Leipziger Strasse 46, tel. 02/229–1533 or 02/229–1831. Reservations advised. No credit cards.*

Turmstuben. Not for the infirm or those who are afraid of heights, the Turmstuben restaurant is tucked away below the cupola of the Franzosicher Dom, the church that sits in classical splendor on one side of the beautiful Platz der Akademie. The restaurant, which runs a circular course around the base of the cupola, is approached by a long, winding staircase—fine for working up an appetite but certainly not recommended for the fainthearted. The reward at the top of the stairs is a table in one of Berlin's most original and attractive restaurants. The menu is as short as the stairway is long, but there's an impressive wine list. *Franzosischer Dom, Platz der Akademie, tel. 02/229–3969. Reservations strongly advised (the frustration of be-*

ing turned away after that climb could spoil anyone's day). No credit cards.

Inexpensive **Alt-Cöllner Schankstuben.** A charming and genuine old Berlin house is the setting for this conglomerate of no fewer than four tiny restaurants, all of which provide exceptionally friendly service. *Friedrichsgracht 50, 02/212–5972. No reservations. No credit cards.*

★ **Zur Letzten Instanz.** Established in 1525, this place combines the charming atmosphere of Old-World Berlin with a limited (but tasty) choice of dishes. Napoleon is said to have sat alongside the tiled stove in the front room. Mikhail Gorbachev enjoyed a beer here during a visit to Berlin in 1989. The emphasis here is on beer, both in the recipes and in the mug. Service can be erratic, though engagingly friendly. *Waisenstr. 14–16, tel. 02/212–5528. Reservations required for both lunch and dinner. No credit cards.*

Lodging

Berlin lost all its grand old luxury hotels in the bombing during World War II; though some were rebuilt, many of the best hotels today are modern. Although they lack little in service and comfort, you may find some short on atmosphere. For first-class or luxury accommodations, East Berlin is easily as good as West, because the East German government, eager for hard currency, built several elegant hotels—the Grand, Palast, Dom, and Metropol—which are up to the very best international standards and place in the very top price category. If you're seeking something more moderate, the better choice may be West Berlin, where there are large numbers of good-value pensions and small hotels, many of them in older buildings with some character. In East Berlin, however, the hostels run by the Evangelical Lutheran church offer outstanding value for your money.

The standard of German hotels is generally excellent. Prices can be high, but not disproportionately so in comparison to other northern European countries. You can expect courteous service; clean and comfortable rooms; and, in rural areas especially, considerable old-German atmosphere.

In addition to hotels proper, the country also has numerous *Gasthöfe* or *Gasthäuser* (country inns); pensions or *Fremdenheime* (guest houses); and, at the lowest end of the scale, *Zimmer*, meaning, quite simply, rooms, normally in private houses. Look for the sign "Zimmer frei" or "zu vermieten," meaning "for rent." A red sign reading "bestzt" means there are no vacancies.

There are no longer any restrictions on who can stay where in East Berlin, as there were in the past. In West Berlin, business conventions year-round and the influx of summer tourists means that you should make reservations well in advance. If you arrive without reservations, consult the board at Tegel Airport that shows hotels with vacancies or go to the tourist office. Lists of hotels are available from the German National Tourist Office and from all regional and local tourist offices. Tourist offices will also make reservations for you—they charge a nominal fee—but may have difficulty doing so after 4 PM in peak season and on weekends. A reservations service is also operated by the Deutsche Zentrale für Tourismus (DTZ)

(Beethovenstr. 69, Frankfurt/Main, tel. 069/75720). The reservation fee is DM 3 per person.

Most hotels have restaurants, but those describing themselves as *Garni* will provide breakfast only.

Tourist accommodations in eastern Germany are beginning to blossom under free enterprise after the straitjacket of state monopoly, although the choice and facilities are still far behind the western half of the country. At press time, the former state-owned Interhotel chain (34 hotels with several thousand rooms) was being broken up and numerous German and foreign companies were queuing to buy into the former monopoly. Other hotel groups are keen to build new properties in the region or to convert old buildings with the potential for atmospheric lodgings. But for now, accommodations remain tight at the top- and middle-quality levels. It cannot be too greatly stressed: If you want to stay in good hotels in eastern Germany, book well in advance. Hotel rooms in the cities are under pressure year-round because of the comings and goings of businesspeople involved in rebuilding the east's economy. Traditional inn accommodations have run down during the past 40 years, and those that survive are rather antiquated—still, you may well come across the odd gem.

The real boom in lodgings has been at the inexpensive end of the market, where thousands of beds are now available for the adventurous traveler. For just a few marks every village can now provide somewhere for the tourist to put his or her head and perhaps offer a simple but wholesome evening meal. Many guest houses have sprung up under the enterprising stewardship of housewives eager to supplement the family income. For a list of approved addresses, consult the local tourist office.

Rentals Apartments and hotel homes, most accommodating from two to eight guests, can be rented in Berlin. Rates are low, with reductions for longer stays. Charges for gas and electricity, and sometimes water, are usually added to the bill. There is normally an extra charge for linen, but not if you bring your own. Local and regional tourist offices have lists of apartments in their areas; otherwise write the **German Automobile Association** (ADAC), Am Westpark 8,8000 Munich 70, tel. 089/76760.

Youth Hostels Germany's youth hostels—*Jugendherberge*—are probably the most efficient, up-to-date, and proportionately most numerous of those in any country in Europe. There are more than 500 in all, many located in castles, adding a touch of romance to otherwise utilitarian accommodations. There's an age limit of 27 in Bavaria; elsewhere, there are no restrictions, though those under 20 take preference if space is limited. You'll need an International Youth Hostel card to stay in a German youth hostel; write **American Youth Hostels Association** (Box 37613, Washington, DC 20013) or **Canadian Hostelling Association** (333 River Rd., Ottawa, Ontario K1L 8H9). For full listings, write **Deutsches Jugendherbergswerk Hauptverband** (Bismarckstr. 8, D-4930 Detmold, tel. 05231/74010) or contact the German National Tourist Office.

The eastern part of Germany has a fairly extensive network of youth hostels throughout the countryside as well as in or near the major cities. Accommodations are good, but with the opening up of the region and the rise in the number of college-age tourists from the west, you'll need to book well in advance.

Rates are extremely reasonable The age limit is 30. Check with **Jugendtourist** (Alexanderplatz 5, 1026 Berlin) or local tourist offices.

Ratings Service charges and taxes are included in all quoted room rates. Similarly, breakfast is usually, but not always, included—large breakfasts are always extra—so check before you book in. Rates are often surprisingly flexible in German hotels, varying considerably according to demand. Major hotels in cities often have lower rates on weekends or other periods when business is quite. If you're lucky, you can find reductions of up to 60%. Likewise, rooms reserved after 10 PM will often carry a discount, on the basis that an occupied room at a reduced rate is better than an empty one. Although it's worthwhile to ask if your hotel will give you a reduction, don't count on finding rooms at lower rates late at night, especially in the summer. Prices are for two people in double room. Best bets are indicated by a star ★.

Category	Cost
Very Expensive	over DM 250
Expensive	DM 180–DM 250
Moderate	DM 120–DM 180
Inexpensive	under DM 120

West Berlin
Very Expensive **Bristol Hotel Kempinski.** Located in the heart of the city, this grand hotel has the best of Berlin's shopping on its doorstep. English-style furnishings give the "Kempi" an added touch of class. All the rooms and suites are luxuriously decorated and equipped, with marble bathrooms, air-conditioning, and cable TV. Children under 12 stay for free if they share their parents' room. *Kurfürstendamm 27, tel. 030/884340. 334 rooms with bath. Facilities: 3 restaurants, indoor pool, sauna, solarium, masseur, hairdresser, limousine service. AE, DC, MC, V.*

CC-City Castle Apartment Hotel. The CC (short for "Congress Center," which is nearby) is a fine fin de siècle Berlin mansion, commanding a corner on the Ku'damm (ask for one of the many quiet rooms at the back). *Kurfüstendamm 160, tel. 030/8918005. 39 rooms with bath. Facilities: restaurant, bar. AE, DC, MC, V.*

★ **InterContinental Berlin.** The "Diplomaten Suite" is expensive, but it is in a class of its own: It's as large as a suburban house and furnished in the Oriental style. The other rooms and suites are not so exotically furnished but still show individuality and exquisite taste. The lobby is worth a visit even if you're not tempted to stay overnight: It's a quarter the size of a football field, opulently furnished, and just the place for afternoon tea and pastries. *Budapesterstr. 2, tel. 030/26020. 600 rooms with bath. Facilities: 3 restaurants (including a rooftop garden), indoor pool, sauna, 24-hour room service, boutiques, Pan-Am check-in service. AE, DC, MC, V.*

Expensive **Berlin Excelsior Hotel.** Fixed rates that don't fluctuate with the seasons are offered by this modern, well-run establishment only five minutes from the Ku'damm. That means, however, that there are no special weekend offers (a usual feature of top German hotels). The comfortable rooms are furnished in

dark teak, and the helpful front-office staff will arrange sight-seeing tours and try to obtain hard-to-get theater and concert tickets. *Hardenbergerstr. 14, tel. 030/31993. 320 rooms with bath. Facilities: garden terrace, winter garden. AE, DC, MC, V.*

★ **Palace.** The rooms here are comfortable and adequately furnished, but can't quite match the scale of the palatial lobby. Ask for a room on the Budapesterstrasse: The view is memorable. Or even take a suite with a whirlpool bath. The Palace is part of Berlin's Europa Center, and guests have free use of the center's pool and sauna. The Palace is popular with Americans. *Europa Center, tel. 030/254970. 160 rooms with bath. Facilities: restaurant. AE, DC, MC, V.*

Schweizerhof Berlin. There's a rustic, Swiss look about most of the rooms in this centrally located hotel, but they have a high standard of comfort and facilities. Ask to be placed in the west wing, where the rooms are larger. Children stay for free if they are in their parents' room. The indoor pool is the largest of any Berlin hotel, and the hotel is opposite Tiergarten Park. *Budapesterstr. 21–31, tel. 030/26960. 430 rooms with bath. Facilities: sauna, solarium, fitness room, hairdresser, beauty salon. AE, DC, MC, V.*

Moderate **Casino Hotel.** The owner of the Casino is Bavarian, so his restaurant serves south German specialties. The hotel itself is a former Prussian military barracks but bears little evidence of its former role: The rooms are large and comfortable and well equipped. The hotel is located in the Charlottenburg district. *Königin-Elisabeth-Str. 47a, tel. 030/303090. 24 rooms with bath. AE, DC, MC, V.*

★ **Ravenna.** This small, friendly hotel is located in the Steglitz district, close to the Botanical Garden and the Dahlen Museum. All the rooms are well equipped, but suite 111B is a bargain: It includes a large living room and kitchen for the rate of only DM 200. *Grunewaldstr. 8–9, tel. 030/792–8031. 45 rooms with bath or shower. AE, DC, MC, V.*

Riehmers Hofgarten. Located in the interesting Kreuzberg district, this hotel, in a late-19th-century building, is a short walk from the Kreuzberg hill and has fast connections to the center of town. The high-ceiling rooms are elegantly furnished. *Yorckstr. 83, tel. 030/781011. 21 rooms with bath or shower. AE, DC, MC, V.*

Inexpensive **Econtel.** Families are well cared for at this hotel that's situated within walking distance of Charlottenburg Palace. Lone travelers also appreciate the touches in the single rooms, which come with a trouser press and hair dryer. *Sommeringstr. 24, tel. 030/344001. 205 rooms with bath or shower. Facilities: snack bar. MC.*

East Berlin **Dom.** The city's newest hotel (opened in 1990), the Dom is cen-
Very Expensive trally located. The rooms feature heated tubs; house facilities are equally plush. *Platz der Akademie, tel. 02/22040 or 02/220–4318. 366 rooms and suites, all with private bath. Facilities: pool, sauna, health club, bowling, squash, hairdresser, garage, car rental. AE, DC, MC, V.*

★ **Grand Hotel** This is Berlin's most expensive hotel. There's nothing of Eastern Europe here: Facilities range from the plush atrium lobby, four restaurants, winter garden, beer stube, bars, and a concert café to a swimming pool, sauna, and squash courts. *Friedrichstr. 158–164, corner Behrenstr., tel.*

02/20920. 336 rooms and suites with bath. Facilities: shopping arcade, hairdresser, theater-ticket office, car and yacht rental. AE, DC, MC, V.

★ **Metropol.** This is the businessperson's choice, not least for its excellent location opposite the Friedrichstrasse train station and the International Trade Center. The staff is particularly helpful and friendly. The best rooms are those in front, with a view toward the north. The main specialty restaurant (left of the lobby) is now one of the city's best and is full at noon (reservations advised); the other two restaurants are less memorable, except for their prices. The nightclub, in contrast, is excellent. *Friedrichstr. 150–153, tel. 02/22040. 336 rooms and apartments with bath. Facilities: pool, sauna, health club, shops; car, horse-drawn carriage, and yacht rental. AE, DC, MC, V.*

Palast. This is another of Berlin's mega-facility hotels. Ask for a room overlooking the Spree River; those on Alexanderplatz can be noisy if you like your windows open. The shopping arcade includes an antiques gallery and the main central theater-ticket office. *Karl-Liebknecht-Str. 5, tel. 02/2410. 583 rooms and suites with bath. Facilities: 6 restaurants, 4 bars, beer stube, nightclub, pool, sauna, health club, car rental. AE, DC, MC, V.*

Expensive **Stadt Berlin.** With its 40 stories (it's the city's largest hotel), the Stadt Berlin, at the top end of Alexanderplatz, competes with the nearby TV tower for the title City Landmark. The roof dining room, Panorama, features not only good food and service but stunning views as well; reservations are essential. *Alexanderplatz, tel. 02/2190. 997 rooms and apartments with bath. Facilities: 4 restaurants, beer garden, 3 bars, sauna, shops. AE, DC, MC, V.*

★ **Unter den Linden.** The class may be missing, but the location on what was once Berlin's most elegant boulevard couldn't be better. The restaurant is drab. *Unter den Linden 14, corner Friedrichstr., tel. 02/220–0311. 300 rooms and apartments with bath. Facilities: souvenir shop. AE, DC, MC, V.*

Moderate **Adria.** This hotel tends to be fully booked well in advance, attesting to its less expensive prices, rather than to any particular charm. The rooms in back are quieter, if you have any choice. *Friedrichstr. 134, tel. 02/280–5105. 67 rooms, 10 with bath. Facilities: restaurant, dance/bar, hairdresser. No credit cards.*

Newa. The Newa—an older hotel just a 10-minute streetcar ride from downtown—is popular, but, as with the Adria, this is mainly due to the price. The rooms in front can be noisy. *Invalidenstr. 115, tel. 02/282–5461. 57 rooms, some with bath. No credit cards.*

Inexpensive **Hospiz am Bahnhof Friedrichstrasse.** For reasons of both price and convenience, this Evangelical church-run hostel tends to be heavily booked months in advance. It appeals to families, so the public rooms are not always restful. *Albrechtstr. 8, tel. 02/282–5396. 110 rooms, some with bath. Facilities: restaurant. No credit cards.*

Hospiz Auguststrasse. Another church-run hostel, this one has comfortable rooms and a particularly friendly staff. It's about a 10-minute streetcar ride to the downtown sights. Only breakfast is served. *Auguststr. 82, tel. 02/282–5321. 70 rooms, some with bath. No credit cards.*

The Arts

Today's Berlin has a tough task in trying to live up to the
tation it gained from the film *Cabaret*, but if nightlife is a
toned down since the '20s, the arts still flourish. Apart from
many hotels that book seats, there are numerous ticket ag
cies, including **Europa-Center** (Tauentzienstrasse 9, tel. 0
261–7051); **Theaterkasse Centrum** (Meinekestrasse 25, tel. 030/
882–7611); and at any of the Top Ticket branches (in all major
stores, such as Hertie, Wertheim, and KaDeWe).

The Berlin Philharmonic performs in the **Philharmonie**
(Matthaikirchstrasse 1, tel. 030/254880). The **Deutsche Oper**
(Opera House, Bismarckstrasse 35), by the U-Bahn stop of the
same name, is the home of the opera and ballet companies.
Tickets are hard to obtain, but call 030/34381 for information.

West Berlin is still Germany's drag-show capital, as you'll see if
you go to **Chez Nous** (Marburgerstrasse 14). It's essential to
book (tel. 213–1810). The girls are for real next door (No. 15) at
the **Scotch Club 13**.

The quality of opera and classical concerts in East Berlin is impressively high. Tickets are available at the separate box offices, either in advance or an hour before the performance.
Tickets are also sold at the central tourist office of the
Reisebüro (Alexanderplatz 5), at the ticket offices in the Palast
and Grand hotels, or from your hotel service desk. Check the
monthly publication *Wohin in Berlin?*

Concerts **Schauspielhaus** (Platz der Akademie, tel. 02/227–2156); **Palast
der Republik** (Marx-Engels-Platz, tel. 02/238–2354).

Opera and Ballet **Deutsche Staatsoper** (Unter den Linden 7, tel. 02/200472);
Komische Oper (Behrenstr. 55–57, tel. 02/229–2555); **Metropol
Theater** (Friedrichstr. 101, tel. 02/208–2215).

Nightlife

Nightlife in West Berlin is no halfhearted affair. It starts late
(from 9 PM) and runs until breakfast. Almost 50 bars (*Kneipen*)
have live music of one kind or another, and there are numerous
small cabaret clubs and discos. The heart of this nocturnal
scene is the Kurfürstendamm, but some of the best bar discos
are to be found at Nollendorfplatz in Charlottenburg. Try the
Metropol (Nollendorfplatz 5, tel. 030/216–1020).

Berlin is a major center for jazz in Europe. If you're visiting in
the fall, call the tourist office for details of the annual international Jazz Fest. Throughout the year a variety of jazz groups
appear at the **Eierschale** (Egg Shell, Podbielskiallee 50, tel.
030/832–7097; evenings after 8:30).

The nightlife in the eatern half of the city is more modest than
in the western half—but the prices are less extravagant, too.
Music in the hotels is generally live; clubs have discos with DJs.
For nightclubs with music and atmosphere, try one of the fol-
lowing: **Club Metropol** (in the Metropol Hotel); **Panorama Bar**
(atop the Hotel Stadt Berlin); **Hafenbar** (Chauseestr. 20);
Checkpoint Null (Leipziger Strasse 55); **Jojo** (Wilhelm-Pieck-
Strasse 216).

Brussels

Arriving and Departing

By Plane All international flights arrive at Brussels's Zaventem Airport, about a 30-minute drive or a 16-minute train trip from the city center. **TWA** and **American** are major carriers that fly into Brussels from the United States. **Sabena** and **British Airways** dominate the short-haul London–Brussels route, but **Air Europe** is often cheaper and just as good. **British Midland** links Brussels with London City Airport.

Between the Airport and Downtown There is regular train service from the airport to the Gare du Nord (North Station) and the Gare Centrale (Central Station), which leaves every 20 minutes. The trip takes 16 minutes and costs BF200 (first-class round-trip) and BF140 (second-class round-trip); you can buy a ticket on the train for a BF30 surcharge. The first train from the airport runs at 5:24 AM and the last one leaves at 11:46 PM. A taxi to the city center takes about half an hour and costs about BF1,000. You can save up to 25% on the taxi fare by buying a voucher for the return trip at the same time.

By Train and Boat/Jetfoil From London, the train service connects with the Dover–Oostende ferry or jetfoil services. From Oostende, the train takes you to Brussels. The whole journey by jetfoil takes just under five hours, but is longer by boat. For reservations and times, contact **P & O Ferries** in London (tel. 071/734–4431). A one-way London–Brussels ticket costs £32, excluding the £5–£8 (depending on the season) jetfoil supplement.

There are three main stations in Brussels: the Gare du Nord, Gare Centrale, and Gare du Midi (South Station). There is also a Gare du Quartier Léopold on the east side of the city. The Gare Centrale is most convenient for the downtown area, which includes the Grand' Place. For train information, telephone 02/219–26–40 or inquire at any station.

By Bus and Hovercraft/Ferry From London, the Hoverspeed City Sprint bus connects with the Dover–Calais Hovercraft, and the bus then takes you on to Brussels. The journey takes 6½ hours; a one-way ticket costs £25. For reservations and times, contact **City Sprint** (tel. 081/554–7061). Other overnight services by **National Express-Eurolines** (tel. 071/730–0202) take the ferry; a one-way ticket costs £25.

By Car Follow signs marked "Brussel Centrum" or "Bruxelles Centre." Many of the approaches are via an outer ring road, a beltway surrounding the city, marked "ring." Exits for the city center are clearly marked. The same is true of the small ring within the city itself.

Getting Around

By Métro, Tram, and Bus The métro, trams (streetcars), and buses run as part of the same system. All three are clean and efficient, and a single ticket costs BF35. The best buy is a 10-trip ticket, which costs BF220, or a 24-hour card costing BF140. You need to stamp your ticket in the appropriate machine on the bus or tram; in the métro, your card is stamped as you pass through the automatic barrier. You can purchase these tickets in any métro station or at newsstands. Single tickets can be purchased on the bus. All services are few and far between after 10 PM.

Detailed maps of the Brussels public transportation network are available in most métro stations and at the Brussels tourist office in the Grand' Place (tel. 02/513–89–40).

By Taxi Taxis are expensive, but—as a small plus—the tip is included in the fare. To call a taxi, phone **Taxis Verts** (tel. 02/511–22–44) or **Taxis Oranges** (tel. 02/513–62–00) or catch one at a taxi stand (there are big stands on main squares and at all train stations). It is nearly impossible to pick up cruising taxis in Brussels. Hotels and restaurants will phone for taxis at your request. The price per kilometer is BF31, but airport taxis charge higher rates.

Important Addresses and Numbers

Tourist Information The main tourist office for **Brussels** is in the Hôtel de Ville on the Grand' Place (tel. 02/513–89–40), open Mon.–Sat. 9–6. The main tourist office for the rest of **Belgium** is near the Grand' Place (rue Marché-aux-Herbes 61, tel. 02/512–30–30) and has the same opening hours. There is a tourist office at **Waterloo** (chaussée de Bruxelles 149, tel. 02/354–99–10); it is open April–November 15, daily 9:30–6:30 and November 16–March, daily 10:30–5.

Embassies **U.S.** (blvd. du Régent 27, B–1000 Brussels, tel. 02/513–38–30). **Canadian** (2 ave. de Tervuren, B–1000 Brussels, tel. 02/735–60–40). **U.K.** (Britannia House, rue Joseph II 28, B–1040 Brussels, tel. 02/217–90–00).

Emergencies **Police** (tel. 101); **Accident** (tel. 100); **Ambulance** (tel. 02/649–11–22); **Doctor** (tel. 02/648–80–00 and 02/479–18–18); **Dentist** (tel. 02/426–10–26); **Pharmacy:** to find out which one is open on a particular night or on weekends, call 02/479–18–18.

English Bookstores **House of Paperbacks** (chaussée de Waterloo 813, Uccle, tel. 02/343–11–22) is open Tues.–Sat. 10–6, Sun. 10–1. **W. H. Smith** (blvd. Adolphe Max 71–75, tel. 02/219–50–34) is open Mon.–Sat. 9–6. **Librairie de Rome** (av. Louise 50b, tel. 02/511–79–37) is open Mon.–Sat. 8 AM–10 PM, Sun. 9–6; the bookshop sells U.S. and U.K. newspapers, periodicals, and paperbacks.

Travel Agencies **American Express** (pl. Louise 2, B–1000 Brussels, tel. 02/512–17–40). **Wagons-Lits** (rue Ravenstein 22, tel. 02/512–98–78, and other locations). **Thomas Cook** (Bureau de Change, 4 Grand' Place, tel. 02/513–28–44/5).

Guided Tours

The best of several available bus tours are those operated by **Brussels Sightseeing Line** (tel. 050/31–13–55), whose minibuses can negotiate the narrowest streets, and **Panavision** (tel. 02/218–36–30). Both services charge BF600 and pick up passengers at the tourist office in the town hall. Panavision also calls at major hotels. More original are the tours run by **Chatterbus,** rue des Thuyas 12. For reservations, call 02/673–18–35 weekdays after 7 PM and weekends. Tours include a minibus tour of the main sites (BF600) and a walking tour that includes a visit to a bistro (BF250). Tours are operated early June–September.

Special-Interest Bus Tours **ARAU** organizes thematic city bus tours (in English), including "Brussels 1900: Art Nouveau" and "Brussels 1930: Art Déco." The enthusiastic guides are all involved in working to protect the city's heritage. Tours begin in front of the post office and Bourse (stock exchange), rue Henri Maus; call 02/513–47–61 for times and bookings. The cost is around BF500 for a half-day tour.

Regional Tours **De Boeck Sightseeing Tours** (rue de la Colline 8, Grand' Place, tel. 02/513–77–44) visits Antwerp, the Ardennes, Bruges, Ghent, Ieper, and Waterloo.

Personal Guides Qualified guides for individual tours are available from the tourist center (tel. 02/513–89–40).

Exploring Brussels

At first sight, the capital of Belgium presents a somber, impersonal exterior, but a little exploration reveals a domestic, small-town atmosphere seeping through the institutional facade. Walk across the Grand' Place during a *son et lumière* (sound-and-light) show and your mood softens, or watch from a cozy bar, its tables stacked high with pancakes or covered with bottles of Duvel beer. Brussels is an odd mixture of the provincial and the international. Underneath the bureaucratic surface, the city is a subtle meeting of the Walloon and Flemish cultures. As the heart of the ancient Duchy of Brabant, Brussels retains its old sense of identity and civic pride. A stone's throw from the steel-and-glass towers, there are cobbled streets, canals where old barges still discharge their freight, and forgotten spots where the city's eventful and romantic past is plainly visible through its 20th-century veneer.

Numbers in the margin correspond to points of interest on the Brussels map.

The Grand' Place Begin in the **Grand' Place,** one of the most ornate market
❶ squares in Europe. There is a daily flower market and a colorful Sunday-morning bird market. On summer nights, the entire square is flooded with music and colored light. The Grand' Place also comes alive during local pageants, such as the *Mayboom;* the *Ommegang,* a splendid historical pageant (early July); and the biannual *Tapis de Fleurs,* when the entire square is covered by a carpet of flowers (mid-August, next in 1992).

❷ The bombardment of the city by Louis XIV's troops left only the **Hôtel de Ville** (town hall) intact. Civic-minded citizens started rebuilding the Grand' Place immediately, but the highlight of the square remains the Gothic town hall. The central tower, combining boldness and light, is topped by a statue of St-Michel, the patron saint of Brussels. Among the magnificent rooms are the Salle Gothique, with its beautiful paneling; the Salle Maximilienne, with its superb tapestries; and the Council Chamber, with a ceiling fresco of the *Assembly of the Gods* painted by Victor Janssens in the early 15th century. *Admission: BF50. Open Tues.–Fri. 9:30–5, Sun. 10–4.*

❸ Opposite the town hall is the **Maison du Roi** (King's House)— though no king ever lived there—a 16th-century palace housing the **City Museum.** The collection includes important ceramics and silverware—Brussels is famous for both—church sculpture, and statues removed from the facade of the town hall. *Grand' Place, tel. 02/511–27–42. Admission: BF50. Open Apr.–Sept., weekdays 10–5, weekends and holidays 10–noon; Oct.–Mar., weekdays 10–4, weekends and holidays 10–noon.*

Brussels

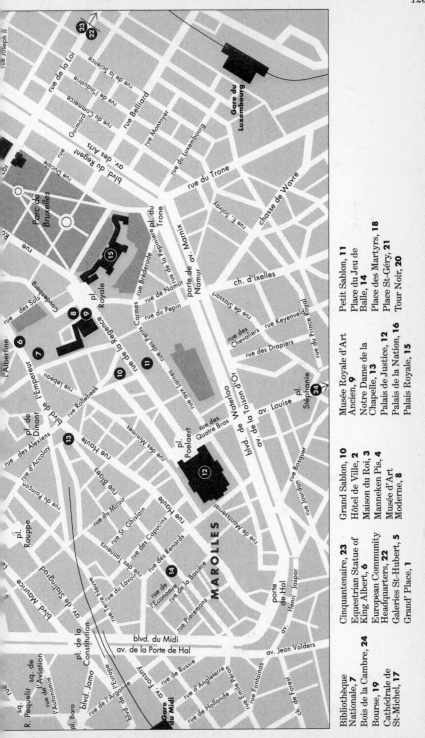

Time Out **La Rose Blanche** (Grand' Place 11, tel. 02/511–2754) is situated in a renovated three-story town house beside the town hall. Inside, brightly painted ceilings have been restored, but the minstrel's gallery, the creaking stairs, and the Chimay beer are original enough. Try a *fondue au parmesan* (cheese in batter) with a strong Chimay or a light *bière blanche.* A sweeter combination is coffee and a *dame blanche* (vanilla ice cream coated with hot chocolate sauce) or a *mousse au chocolat* (chocolate mousse). This is also the spot from which to view a son et lumière display on a summer's evening.

❹ Southwest of the town hall, on the corner of the rue de l'Etuve and rue du Chêne, stands the famous **Manneken Pis,** a fountain with a small bronze statue of a chubby little boy urinating. Made by Jerome Duquesnoy in 1619, the statue is known as "Brussels's Oldest Citizen" and is often dressed in costumes that are kept in the City Museum. He has quite a wardrobe! The present Manneken is a copy; the original was kidnapped by 18th-century French and English invaders (soldiers, not tourists!).

Leaving the Manneken, cross the Grand' Place in the direction of the Marché-aux-Herbes. If you are planning to visit the rest of Belgium, stop in at the regional tourist office (rue Marché-aux-Herbes 61).

❺ Opposite the tourist office, take the Petite rue des Bouchers, the main restaurant street in the heart of the tourist maelstrom. In Brussels fashion, each restaurant advertises its wares by means of large signs and carts packed with a selection of game and seafood. From here, explore the network of galleries called **Galeries St-Hubert,** which includes the Galerie de la Reine, Galerie du Roi, and Galerie des Princes, all built in 1847. Their harmonious glass-top design was the first of its kind in Europe; moreover, the galleries were designed by a 17 year old. Written on the central galleries is the motto "Omnibus Omnia" (Everything for Everyone), which is not altogether appropriate, given the designer prices.

Time Out **Le Vaudeville** is the most attractive bar in the galleries. Once a historic satirical theater, it is now an Art Deco bistro. In mirrored surroundings, this is the place to watch local trendies discuss art while eating *crêpes* (pancakes) filled with jam, ice cream, or liqueurs. At the back is the **Le Cocoon Club,** an equally fashionable discothèque (*see* Nightlife, below). *Galerie de la Reine 15, tel. 02/673–23–78. No credit cards. Inexpensive.*

❻❼ Head south along the rue Marché-aux-Herbes and the rue Madeleine until you come to the **equestrian statue of King Albert.** To the left of the statue is the Central Station and to the right, the **Bibliothèque Nationale** (National Library). Walk through the formal gardens next to the National Library and look back at the ornate clock, with moving figures, over the lower archway. Try to hear—and see—it at noon, when it strikes the hour.

Place Royale If you continue walking through the gardens, you will arrive at the **place Royale,** the site of the Coudenberg palace, where the sovereigns once lived. Here you have a superb view over the lower town. On the northwest corner of the square is the **Musée**
❽ **d'Art Moderne** (Museum of Modern Art), housed in an exciting

feat of modern architecture. On entry, a vertiginous descent into the depths reveals a sudden well of natural light. The paintings are displayed with the light and space they deserve. Although there are a few paintings by Matisse, Gauguin, Degas, and Dali, the surprise lies in the quality of Belgian modern art. See Magritte's luminous fantasies, James Ensor's masks and still lifes, and Spilliaert's coastal scenes. Do not miss Permeke's deeply brooding *Fiancés* or Delvaux's Surrealist works. *Pl. Royale 1, tel. 02/513–96–30. Admission free. Open Tues.–Sun. 10–1 and 2–5.*

9 Next door is the **Musée Royale d'Art Ancien** (Royal Museum of Ancient Art). Here the collection is of Flemish and Dutch paintings, ranging from magnificent 15th- and 16th-century works—Cranach, Matsys, and Brueghel the Elder, among them—to Rubens (several fine canvases), Van Dyck, and David. Do not miss Brueghel's dramatic *La Chute d'Icare* (The Fall of Icarus) or Hieronymous Bosch's *Le Dernier Jugement* (The Last Judgment), a malevolent portrait of humanity. *Pl. Royale. Admission free. Open Tues.–Sun. 10–1 and 2–5.*

As you stand in the place Royale facing back the way you came, the rue de la Régence runs on your left up to the Palais de Jus-
10 tice. The Sablon lies along this street, on the right. The **Grand Sablon,** the city's most sophisticated square, is alive with cafés, restaurants, and antiques shops. If you feel tired, have a drink or snack in Le Zavel (*see* Dining, below). Between the two bars lies the tempting Wittamer, the city's finest pastry shop. Toward the end of the square is the **church of Notre Dame du Sablon,** built in flamboyant Gothic style. Although much of the original workmanship was lost in restoration, it remains one of the city's best-loved churches. At night, the brilliant church windows illuminate the Grand Sablon and the Petit Sablon behind.

11 A small garden square, the **Petit Sablon** is surrounded by 48 statues representing Brussels's medieval guilds. Each craftsman carries an object that reveals his trade: The furniture maker holds a chair, for instance; the wine merchant, a goblet.

On the Petit Sablon is the **Musée Instrumental** (Museum of Musical Instruments). A huge collection of over 1,000 musical instruments is on display. Half of them are unique, and a few go back to the Bronze Age. The guide can often be persuaded to play one of the pianos. *Petit Sablon 17, tel. 02/512–08–48. Admission free. Open Tues., Thurs., and Sat. 2:30–4:30, Wed. 4–6, Sun. 10:30–12:30.*

Immediately behind the Petit Sablon is the **Palais d'Egmont,** at different times the residence of Christina of Sweden, Louis XV, and Voltaire. It is now used by the Belgian Ministry of Foreign Affairs for official meetings. If security allows, you can enter the Jardin d'Egmont, another small park, on this side. Come out of the entrance on rue du Grand Cerf and turn left toward the boulevard de Waterloo, a wide street full of bars and designer shops.

Time Out Among the bars on your right, **Le Nemrod** is the most typical. In summer, there is a sidewalk café. The interior is decorated like a Belgian hunting lodge, with lifelike deer and other stuffed animal heads on the walls. At the first chill, the

Nemrod's fireplace is surrounded by drinkers of Gueuze and Kriek beers.

Palais de Justice to the Black Tower
12

At the end of the rue de la Régence is the **Palais de Justice.** Often described as the ugliest building in Europe, the palais is designed to impress upon you the majesty of justice. It's located on the site of the former Gallows Hill. If you climb the more than 500 steps to the cupola, you will get an excellent view of the countryside around Brussels, weather permitting.

13

Down a rather steep hill from the Palais de Justice is the working-class **Marolles** district, where the artist Pieter Brueghel died in 1569. His imposing marble tomb is in **Notre Dame de la Chapelle,** his local church on rue Haute. From the church, head back to the Sablon via the cobbled rue Rollebeek. If you would rather see more of the authentic Marolles district, ignore the cluster of chic restaurants and designer shops on rue Rollebeek. Instead, from place de la Chapelle, take rue Blaes to the

14

flea market in **place du Jeu de Balle.** On the way, you will pass a number of rough Belgian bars and North African food shops. Until this century, bourgeois Belgians considered this labyrinth of small alleys a haven for thieves and political refugees. Although the Marolles continues to welcome immigrants and outsiders, it has lost its danger but kept its slightly raffish character. Before you leave, sample marinated herrings or *caricolles* (water snails) at one of the local bars.

15

Return via the Sablon to the place Royale. Directly ahead of you is the **Parc de Bruxelles** (Brussels Park) with the **Palais Royale** (Royal Palace) at the end closer to you. (The palace is usually open during August and a few days before and after. Dates vary from year to year.) You can walk through the park to the

16

Palais de la Nation (Palace of the Nation) at the opposite end, where the two houses of the Belgian Parliament meet. When Parliament is not sitting, you can visit the building. *Guided tours weekdays 10–noon and 2–5 (Sat. until 4).*

17

Surrounding the park are elegant turn-of-the-century houses. The prime minister's office is next to the Parliament building. A walk downhill (rue des Colonies) toward the downtown area and a short right-hand detour bring you to the **Cathédrale de St-Michel.** The cathedral's chief treasure is the beautiful stained-glass windows designed by Bernard van Orley, an early 16th-century painter at the royal court. In summer the great west window is floodlit from inside to reveal its glories.

Time Out

Situated between the cathedral and the galleries is **La Mort Subite** (Sudden Death) (rue Montagne-aux-Herbes-Potagères 7, tel. 02/513–13–18). Little known to outsiders, it is the city's most genuine beer hall. Locals sit on long benches and select drinks from the best beer list in Brussels. Choose a foamy *biere blanche* (white lager beer), a strong *trappiste* (brewed by monks), a *framboise* (made with raspberries), or a heady *kriek* (a cherry beer). Each has its own special glass. To accompany the beer, try the traditional *fromage 1900,* a pot of creamy white cheese, and crusty bread.

18

Continue downhill to the **place des Martyrs,** a dignified square over a mass grave for local patriots who died in the 1830 battle to expel the Dutch. This dilapidated square, where renovation is finally beginning, is at odds with the rue Neuve, the busy shopping street that runs along one side. Cross the rue Neuve and continue on to the boulevard Adolphe-Max. Turn left and **⑲** then right, in front of the imposing **Bourse** (stock exchange), to place Ste-Catherine.

⑳ The 13th-century **Tour Noir** (Black Tower) here is part of the city's first fortifications. Under the square runs the river Senne, channeled underground in the last century when the pollution of the canal basins and the stench from the open sewers became too great. As a result of its watery past, place Ste-Catherine still has the city's best seafood restaurants. If you **㉑** have enough energy, take the rue de la Vierge Noire to **place St-Géry,** the next square south. This whole area is undergoing exciting renovation as Bruxellois gradually realize the charms of the 17th-century buildings in this old port setting. Once an island, St-Géry has recently returned to its watery roots: The river Senne has been uncovered and the canalside houses, restored. Look at the **Vieux Marché St-Géry** (the Old Market), currently being converted into a galleried indoor garden and crafts center.

Parc du Cinquantenaire and Bois de la Cambre Another walk on the south side of the Parc de Bruxelles takes you from the Palais de la Nation down the rue de la Loi toward the Cinquantenaire (if the walk is too long for you, take the métro). On the way, you'll pass in front of the **European Communi- ㉒ ty Headquarters** at the Rond Point Schuman. The vast 13-story cruciform building houses the European Commission. The council offices are located nearby.

㉓ The **Cinquantenaire** is a huge, decorative archway, built in 1905 in a pleasant park. The buildings on either side of the archway house the **Royal Museums of Art and History.** Displays include Greek, Roman, and Egyptian artifacts and toys. Some galleries are closed on even dates, some on odd dates—check locally. *Parc du Cinquantenaire 10, tel. 02/733–96–10. Admission: BF5. Open weekdays 9:30–12:30 and 1:30–4:45, weekends 10–4:45.*

The new **Autoworld Museum,** also in the Cinquantenaire, has one of the world's most handsome collections of vintage cars. *Parc du Cinquantenaire 11, tel. 02/736–41–65. Admission: BF200. Open daily 10–6 (Nov.–Mar. until 5).*

㉔ South of the Palais de Justice is the **Bois de la Cambre,** a popular, rambling park on the edge of town. Take tram No. 93 or 94 from Sablon or place Stéphanie for a pleasant 10-minute ride along avenue Louise. Just before the bois is the former **Abbaye de la Cambre,** a 14th-century church with cloisters, an 18th-century courtyard, and a terraced park. The Bois de la Cambre is a good place for a family outing, with a lake, boat trips, pony rides, an outdoor roller-skating rink, and an inviting Swiss chalet bar and restaurant.

Beyond the bois is the **Boitsfort racecourse,** and eastward lies the **Forêt de Soignes,** 27 square kilometers (17 square miles) of forest, mostly beech trees, with walking and riding paths.

Waterloo No history buff can visit Brussels without making the pilgrimage to the site of the **Battle of Waterloo,** where Napoleon was finally defeated on June 18, 1815. It is easily reached from the city and lies 19 kilometers (12 miles) to the south of the Forêt de Soignes; take a bus from place Rouppe or a train from Gare Centrale to Waterloo station. In July and August, a red tourist train runs from Waterloo station to all the main sights (tel. 02/354–78–06).

Wellington's headquarters, now a museum, presents the complex battle through illuminated 3-D maps, scale models, and military memorabilia, including the general's personal belongings. *Admission: BF60. Open Apr.–mid-Nov., Tues.–Sun. 9:30–6:30; mid-Nov.–Mar., Tues.–Sun. 10:30–5.*

The **Battle Panorama Museum,** beside the battlefield, is a rotunda displaying a huge, naturalistic painting of one stage of the battle. *Admission: BF50. Open daily 9:30–6.*

Beside it is the pyramid-shape **Lion Monument,** erected by the Dutch. After climbing 226 steps, you'll find one of the bleakest views in the country before you. With a little imagination, you can quickly conjure up the desolation of the battlefield scene.

Time Out For a satisfying lunch of authentic Belgian cuisine, try the **Bivouac de l'Empereur,** an attractive 1720s farmhouse close to the Lion Monument. *Route de Lion 315, tel. 02/384–67–40. AE, DC, MC, V. Moderate.*

Musée du Caillou (Napoleon's Headquarters) is worth visiting to understand the French perspective of the battle. Tours of the site are led by multilingual guides. *Admission: BF60. Open Wed.–Mon. 9–5.*

If you are in Brussels around June 15, attend the reenactment of the battle. A thousand local citizens dress as French, Prussian, and English soldiers and realistically shoot one another with old muskets. Unlike the real battle, which ended in over 40,000 deaths, this one ends in a large buffet, a son et lumière show, and a fireworks display. Check the dates with the Brussels or Waterloo tourist office.

Shopping

Gift Ideas
Crystal The Val-St-Lambert mark is the only guarantee of hand-blown, hand-carved lead crystal tableware. You can buy it in many stores, including **Art and Selection** (Marché-aux-Herbes 83), near the Grand' Place. For cut-price porcelain and china, try the **Vaisselle au Kilo** (rue Bodenbroek 8, near the Sablon district), which is also open on Sunday.

Chocolates For "everyday" chocolate, try the Côte d'Or variety, available in any chocolate shop or larger store. For the delicious pralines—rich chocolates filled with every fruit, liqueur, or nut imaginable—try the brands made by Godiva, Neuhaus, or Leonidas. Although Godiva is better known abroad, Leonidas offers a better value for your money and is rated more highly by the Belgians. Leonidas shops are scattered throughout the city. The most exclusive pralines are handmade at the shops named Mary, Wittamer, or Nihoul.

Lace To avoid disappointment, ask the store assistant outright whether the lace is handmade Belgian or made in the Far East. As preparation, visit the **Lace Museum** (6 rue de la Violette, near the Grand' Place). **La Maison F. Rubbrecht,** on the Grand' Place, sells authentic, handmade Belgian lace. For a large choice of old and modern lace, try **Manufacture Belge de Dentelles** (Galerie de la Reine 6–8).

Shopping Districts For boutiques and stores, the main districts are in the **ville basse** (low town), the **Galeries St-Hubert** (luxury goods or gift items), **rue Neuve** (inexpensive clothes), and **City 2** and the **Anspach Center** (large covered shopping complexes). In City 2, **FNAC** is a cherished French institution: As well as being an outlet for books, records, cameras, and stereo equipment at the best prices in town, it is also a trendy cultural and exhibition center.

You'll find designer names and department stores (such as **Sarmalux**) in the **ville haute** (high town). **Avenue Louise** is its center, complete with covered galleries; **Galerie Louise;** and **Galerie de la Toison d'Or,** the appropriately named street of the Golden Fleece! To offset prices, many of these stores operate sales-tax refunds. The **place du Grand Sablon** is an equally expensive but more charming shopping district. This is the center for antiques, small art galleries, and designer shops. You'll also find **Wittamer** (12–13 Grand Sablon), Belgium's finest *patisserie* (pastry shop). Around the Sablon and its neighboring streets, **rue des Minimes** and **rue Lebeau,** it is possible to buy anything from Persian carpets and African primitives to 18th-century paintings and Art Nouveau.

Markets On Saturdays (9–6) and Sundays (9–2), the Sablon square is transformed into an **antiques market.** In early December it runs a traditional **European Christmas Market** with crafts from 12 countries. The **flower market** on the Grand' Place (Tues.–Sun. 8–6) is a colorful diversion. **Midi Market** is far more exotic (by Gare du Midi train station). On Sunday morning (5 AM–1 PM) the whole area becomes a colorful *souk* (bazaar) as the city's large North African community gathers to buy and sell exotic foods and household goods. The **Vieux Marché** (Old Market) in place du Jeu de Balle is a rough flea market worth visiting for the authentic atmosphere of the working-class Marolles district. The market is open daily 7–2. To make real finds, get there as early in the morning as you can.

Dining

Most Belgians take eating seriously and are discerning about fresh produce and innovative recipes. Regional cuisine is still clearly differentiated and traditions are maintained. At the top end of the scale, the *menus de dégustation* offer a chance to sample a large selection of the chef's finest dishes. Belgian specialties include *lapin à la bière* (rabbit in beer), *faisan à la brabanconne* (pheasant with chicory), *waterzooi* (a rich chicken or fish hotpot), and *carbonnades* (chunky stews). A Belgian peculiarity is that dogs are allowed into most restaurants.

Belgian snacks are equally appetizing. The waffle *(gaufre/ wafel)* has achieved world fame, but *couques* (sweet buns), *speculoos* (spicy gingerbread biscuits), and *pain d'amandes* (nutty after-dinner biscuits) are less well known. For lunch, cold cuts, rich pâtés, and *jambon d'Ardenne* (Ardenne ham) are popular, often accompanied by goat's cheese and rye or wholemeal bread.

Apart from hearty Belgian cuisine, Brussels is proud of its foreign restaurants: Chefs from at least 50 countries work in the city. The local *cuisine bruxelloise* is rich and, in the more expensive restaurants, an imaginative variant of French cuisine. The ambience tends to be formal, dignified, and old-fashioned in the more exclusive restaurants and cozy or jovial in the simpler brasseries or *estaminets*. Servings are plentiful everywhere. If you are interested in local gourmet restaurants, ask the tourist office on the Grand' Place for its booklet *Gourmet Restaurants* (BF50), updated annually. An independent jury presents awards for excellence: Look for restaurants displaying the iris symbol of quality.

Mealtimes Most hotels serve breakfast until 10. Belgians usually eat lunch between 1 and 3, some making it quite a long, lavish meal. However, the main meal of the day is dinner, which most Belgians eat betwen 7 and 10; peak dining time is about 8.

Dress Belgians tend to be fairly formal and dress conservatively when dining out in the evenings. Generally speaking, the more prestigious the restaurant, the more formal the dress. Younger Belgians favor stylish, casual dress in most restaurants.

Ratings Prices are per person and include a first course, main course, and dessert but no wine or tip. Best bets are indicated by a star ★.

Category	Cost
Very Expensive	over BF3,000
Expensive	BF2,000–BF3,000
Moderate	BF1,000–BF2,000
Inexpensive	under BF1,000

Very Expensive **Comme Chez Soi.** Pierre Wynants, the perfectionist owner-
★ chef, has decorated the restaurant in Art Nouveau style. Every detail is authentic, from the stained-glass panels to the carved mahogany woodwork and the artistic menus. The inventive French cuisine, excellent wine list, and attentive service complement the warm decor. The specialties include fillets of sole with a white wine mousseline and shrimps, saddle of young rabbit with lemon and basil, venison, and pheasant. This is one of the world's top restaurants and well deserves its three Michelin stars. *Pl. Rouppe, tel. 02/512–29–21. Reservations required. AE, DC. Closed Sun., Mon., July, and Christmas to New Year's.*

Écailler du Palais Royal. Situated on the fashionable Grand Sablon square, this dark, clubby restaurant makes a virtue of the gloom to protect its famous guests from prying eyes. Imaginative seafood dishes, such as the *ravioli de homard* (lobster ravioli), made the restaurant a society favorite from the start. *Rue Bodenbroek 18–20, tel. 02/512–87–51. Reservations required. AE, DC, MC, V. Closed Sun. and Aug.*

Maison du Cygne. With decor to match its classical cuisine, this restaurant is set in a grand 17th-century guild hall on the Grand' Place. Live piano music usually accompanies the evening meal. Typical French-Belgian dishes include *lotte aux blancs de poireaux*, a monkfish-and-leeks specialty. *Rue Charles Buyls 2, tel. 02/511–82–44. Reservations required. AE, DC, MC, V. Closed Sat. lunch, Sun.*

Expensive **La Charlotte aux Pommes.** This attractive restaurant has acquired a considerable following thanks to its light and inventive cuisine and attentive service. Ravioli stuffed with salmon is a specialty, and the lamb chops are terrific. The Place du Châtelain is Brussels' latest restaurant center, with several pleasant bistros, and, on Wednesday afternoon, a lively market. *Pl. du Châtelain 40, tel. 02/640–53–88. Reservations advised. AE, DC, MC, V. Closed Sat., Sun., Carnival week, and mid-Aug.– mid-Sept.*

★ **La Porte des Indes.** The city's finest Indian restaurant brings an exotic touch to the bustling avenue Louise business district. Gracious staff, dressed in traditional Indian attire, create a warm, sensitive atmosphere. The plant-filled lobby, wood carvings, soft music, and soothing blue-and-white decor provide a restful backdrop. The cuisine is surprisingly versatile, from a mild pilaf to a spicy *vindaloo* (chili-flavored curry). Exotic fruits complete the meal. If in doubt, ask for a "brass tray," which provides a chance to sample a range of specialties. *Av. Louise 455, tel. 02/647–86–51. Reservations advised. AE, DC, MC, V. Closed Sun.*

Ogenblik. This is a true bistro, with green-shaded lamps over marble-topped tables, sawdust on the floor, ample servings, and a great ambience. The long and imaginative menu changes frequently, but generally includes such specialties as *mille-feuille* of lobster and salmon and saddle or leg of lamb with fresh, young vegetables. *Galerie des Princes 1, tel. 02/511–61–51. No reservations after 8 PM. AE, DC, MC, V. Closed Sun.*

Moderate **Amadeus.** The restaurant occupies a cavernous studio that once belonged to the French sculptor Rodin. It is dramatically lit at night, when the courtyard, statues, and murals are seen at their best. Trendy diners can choose to have a drink, *blinis* (Russian-style pancakes), and caviar in the romantic Wine and Oyster Bar. The bohemian Amadeus restaurant offers spare ribs and unusual salads. Candlelight dinner is accompanied by the music of Mozart. Sunday brunch is a fashionable alternative. The check reflects the atmosphere, rather than the food and service, but it would be churlish to complain! *Rue Veydt 13, tel. 02/538–34–27. Reservations advised. AE, DC, MC, V. Wine and Oyster Bar closed Sun. and Mon.*

★ **Aux Armes de Bruxelles.** This restaurant is one of the few to escape the "tourist trap" label in this hectic little street. Inside, a lively atmosphere fills three rooms: The most popular section overlooks the street theater outside, but locals prefer the cozy rotunda. Service is fast and friendly, and portions are large. Specialties include *waterzooi de volaille* (a rich chicken stew) and *moules au vin blanc* (mussels in white wine). Order the *crêpe suzette* if you want to see your table engulfed by brandy flames! *Rue des Bouchers 13, tel. 02/511–21–18. Reservations advised. AE, DC, MC, V. Closed Mon. and June.*

La Quincaillerie. The name means "the hardware store"—and the character has been retained, with tables perched on the balcony and a zinc oyster bar downstairs. At BF875, the three-course *menu du patron* is a bargain. Excellent game dishes are nicely presented by a staff who, like the clientele, is young and pleasant. *Rue du Page 45, tel. 02/538–25–53. Reservations advised. AE, DC, MC, V.*

Inexpensive **La Grande Porte.** An old warren of interconnecting rooms provides a rustic setting for hearty and often rambunctious eating. Dressed in old bibs, the jovial waiters make no concessions to fashion or style; the genuine friendliness attracts Bruxellois from all backgrounds. Part of the appeal lies in the copious portions. The specialties include *carbonade à la flamande* (beef and onions stewed in beer); *ballekes à la marollienne* (spicy meatballs); steaks served with rice and/or french fries; and *salade folle* (mixed green salad with cold cuts), a meal in itself. *Rue Notre-Seigneur 9, tel. 02/539–21–32. Reservations advised. DC. Closed July.*

★ **Le Paradoxe.** This self-proclaimed "natural"-food restaurant serves unusual seafood and vegetarian dishes in a setting somewhat like an elegant greenhouse. Even the wines are "biologically approved" but taste none the worse for it! Specialties include samosas with rice, scampi with kiwi fruit, exotic vegetables in delicate sauces, and excellent homemade desserts. It is best to go on Friday or Saturday evening, when there is live music, ranging from Irish folk or flamenco to New Orleans jazz or Mozart. The Christmas and New Year's musical banquets are particularly good. *Chaussée d'Ixelles 329, tel. 02/649–89–81. AE, DC, MC, V. Reservations advised on musical evenings. Closed Sun. and 3 weeks in July–Aug.*

Le Zavel. Both a bar and a brasserie, the Zavel is a friendly, unpretentious spot on a pretentious square. Specialties include Belgian waterzooi and salad Liègoise (a warm bacon salad), *tagliatelle au pistou* (noodles with pine kernels), Russian *borscht* (beetroot soup), and *piroghi* (pancakes). The meal can be accompanied by wine or by Belgian beer. You can dine outside in summer. *Pl. du Grand Sablon, tel. 02/512–16–80. No credit cards.*

Lodging

You can trust Belgian hotels, almost without exception, to be clean and of a high standard. The more modern hotels can be very expensive, but there are smaller, well-appointed hotels, offering lodging at excellent rates. However, the moderate and inexpensive hotels are relatively disappointing in terms of charm and even value for the money, though not in terms of comfort and location.

The *Hotel Guide*, published every year by Tourist Information Brussels (TIB), provides the most reliable and up-to-date information on prices and services. In general, finding accommodations is not difficult. There has been a boom in hotel construction lately, adding several more hotels in all price categories. However, as a center of business and of the EC, Brussels has many more choices in the Very Expensive and Expensive ranges. The main hotel districts are in the ville basse, near the avenue Louise business district, near Zaventem Airport, and in Brussels's "Silicon Valley." Avoid the cheap hotel districts near Gare du Midi and Gare du Nord train stations. Hotels can be booked at the tourist office on the Grand' Place (tel. 02/513–89–40), and a deposit is required (deductible from the final hotel bill).

Pensions — Pensions offer a double room with bath or shower and full board from BF2,500 to BF3,500 in Brussels. These terms are often available for a minimum stay of three days.

Youth Hostels — For information about youth hostels, contact **Fédération Belge des Auberges de la Jeunesse** (tel. 02/215–31–00). In the United States: **American Youth Hostels, Inc.,** Box 37613, Washington, DC 20013. In the United Kingdom: **Camping and Caravan Club Ltd.,** 11 Lower Grosvenor Pl., London SW1, or **Youth Hostels Association International Travel Bureau,** 14 Southampton St., London WC2.

Ratings Hotel prices are inclusive and are usually listed in each room. All prices are for two people in a double room. Best bets are indicated by a star ★.

Category	Cost
Very Expensive	BF6,500–BF10,000
Expensive	BF4,500–BF6,500
Moderate	BF2,500–BF4,500
Inexpensive	under BF2,500

Very Expensive **Hilton International.** Renovated in 1989, the Hilton now justifies its high prices. This imposing 27-story tower has light, airy, modern rooms. The top-floor restaurant, Plein Ciel (lunch only), has a terrific view over the city. Centrally located, it is next to the main luxury shopping area and overlooks the quiet Parc d'Egmont. *Blvd. de Waterloo 38, tel. 02/513–88–77. 365 rooms with bath. Facilities: health club, sauna, 2 restaurants, coffee shop, bar, solarium. AE, DC, MC, V.*

★ **Royal Windsor.** This plush hotel is for those who rate a central location and old-fashioned charm above the latest high-tech business facilities. The hotel was refurbished in 1990, and all rooms are now decorated in blond oak paneling with marble bathrooms. The Windsor is renowned for its Quatre Saisons restaurant. Wood-paneled public rooms and an intimate bar make this one of the few quiet spots near the Grand' Place. At night, however, the hotel's Crocodile Club (*see* Nightlife, below) is considered the city's most sophisticated discotheque. Weekend rates are available. *Rue Duquesnoy 5, tel. 02/511–42–15. 300 rooms with bath. Facilities: restaurant, disco, parking, conference facilities, bar, garden. AE, DC, MC, V.*

SAS Royal Hotel. This brand-new hotel, a few minutes' walk through the Galerie de la Reine from Grand' Place, was built for business travelers. The rooms are decorated in different styles: Scandinavian, Oriental, Italian, and Art Deco. A portion of the city wall from 1134, discovered during the construction, forms part of the Atrium. A business service center and fully equipped conference rooms cater to businesspeople's needs, and the Sea Grill aspires to become one of the city's top seafood restaurants. Rooms for nonsmokers and for the disabled are available. *Rue du Fossé-aux-Loups 47, tel. 02/219–28–28. 281 rooms with bath. Facilities: 2 restaurants, valet parking, fitness center, in-room checkout, SAS airline checkin, Atrium coffee shop, bar. AE, DC, MC, V.*

Expensive **Amigo.** This world-famous, family-owned hotel, located off the Grand' Place, was built in the 1950s, but it has the charm of an older age. No one would guess that it was built on the site of the city prison. Each room is individually decorated, often in silk, velvet, and brocades. Prices vary wildly from BF5,350 to BF7,000 for a double room and far more for a penthouse suite with terrace. *Rue d'Amigo 1, tel. 02/511–59–10. 183 rooms with bath. Facilities: restaurant, bar, parking. AE, DC, MC, V.*

★ **Hotel Metropole.** Built at the turn of the century, this hotel was designed in Art Nouveau style: great columns towering over palms and a gilt-and-marble decor. Although many of the period features have been wantonly destroyed, they linger in the stylish café and the dining room. Some of the guest rooms have been decorated in Art Deco and Art Nouveau styles, so try to see more than one room. The hotel is centrally located. The candlelit restaurant offers a live orchestra—and a good set menu for around BF1,000. À la carte specialties include salmon in light curry and sole in apricot. The elegant café is worth visiting even if you are not staying here; brunch is also a popular choice. Weekend rates are available. *Pl. de Brouckère 31, tel. 02/217–23–00. 410 rooms with bath. Facilities: restaurant, bar, conference facilities, sauna, garden, sidewalk terrace. AE, DC, MC, V.*

Sofitel. Built in 1989, the Brussels Sofitel has an excellent location in the middle of the shopping district around avenue Louise. The rooms are decorated in the brown-and-beige tones typical of this upscale French chain. *Avenue de la Toison d'Or 40, tel. 02/514–22–00. 171 rooms with bath. Facilities: restaurant, bar. AE, DC, MC, V.*

Moderate **Alfa Louise.** Situated near the avenue Louise business and shopping district, this convenient hotel is tucked away down a quiet side street. The hotel is modern, the service is friendly, and the facilities are above average for a hotel in this price bracket. It is close to a number of good bars and restaurants, including the Amadeus (*see* Dining, above). Weekend rates are available. *Rue Blanche 4, tel. 02/537–92–10. 83 rooms, most with kitchenette and bath. Facilities: parking, bar, conference facilities, garden. AE, DC, MC, V.*

Arenberg. Recently renovated, this hotel enjoys a central location near the central station. The noted restaurant offers lunch for only BF450 and can cater to special dietary requirements. Weekend rates are available. *Rue d'Assaut 15, tel. 02/511–07–70. 156 rooms with bath. Facilities: restaurant, coffee shop, bar, secretarial service, garden. AC, DC, MC, V.*

Delta. This modern, rather anonymous-looking hotel is located within walking distance of the exclusive place Louise shopping district. The street itself is always busy, so ask for a room at the back. The hotel is comfortable, fairly convenient, but rather colorless. *Chaussée de Charleroi 17, tel. 02/539–01–60. 246 rooms with bath. Facilities: restaurant, bar, parking. AE, DC, MC, V.*

Inexpensive **Arlequin.** Owned and operated by a friendly young couple, this smallish hotel can be reached through an arcade that branches off the restaurant-packed Petite rue des Bouchers, a stone's throw from the Grand' Place. *Rue de la Fourche 17–19, tel. 02/514–16–15. 60 TV-equipped rooms with bath or shower. Facilities: breakfast room. AE, DC, MC, V.*

★ **Marie-José.** Each room is decorated in a different style, most with antiques, in this bargain hotel that is just a five-minute walk from the Parc de Bruxelles. The restaurant, Chez Callens, is moderately priced (a typical meal costs BF1,700) and great for seafood dishes. *Rue du Commerce 73, tel. 02/512–08–42. 17 rooms with bath or shower. Facilities: restaurant. AE, DC, MC, V.*

Sainte Catherine. This good, reasonably priced hotel is just a few blocks from the Grand' Place. Most rooms can accommodate families with two children. The decor leans toward the motelish. *Rue Joseph Plateau 2, tel. 02/513–76–20. 234 rooms with bath or shower. Facilities: coffee shop, bar. DC, MC, V.*

The Arts

The traditional performing arts—ballet, opera, theater—are well represented in Brussels. There is also a wide range of English-language entertainment, including movies and, on occasion, theater. The best way to find out what's going on is to buy a copy of the English-language weekly magazine *The Bulletin*. It's published every Thursday and sold at newsstands for BF70. For a fuller picture, see the Thursday *"Arts et Divertissements"* pull-out section in *Le Soir*, the French-language newspaper. It is often available from the Brussels tourist office.

Music Major classical music concerts are generally held at the **Palais des Beaux-Arts** (rue Ravenstein 23, tel. 02/512–50–45). Alternatively, there are many free Sunday morning concerts at various churches, including the Cathédrale de St-Michel and the Petite Église des Minimes (rue des Minimes 62).

Opera and Dance The national opera company, Compagnie Royale Belge de l'Opera, is based at the **Théâtre Royal de la Monnaie** (pl. de la Monnaie, tel. 02/218–12–02). The Monnaie is an attractive opera house, and its productions are of international quality. Tickets cost from BF500 to BF2,000 and are very hard to come by. Touring dance and opera companies often play at the **Cirque Royal** (rue de l'Enseignement 81, tel. 02/218–20–15).

Theater At Brussels's 30 theaters, actors perform in French, Flemish, and occasionally in English. The loveliest theater is the newly restored **Théâtre du Résidence Palace** (155 rue de la Loi, tel. 02/231–03–05). Avant-garde theater and ethnic music are performed at the cavernous **Halles de Schaerbeck** (rue Royale Ste-Marie 22a, tel. 02/218–00–31). Puppet theater is a Belgian experience not to be missed. In Brussels, visit the intimate **Théâtre Toone VII** (impasse Schuddeveld, petite rue des Bouchers 21, tel. 02/511–71–37). In this atmospheric medieval house, satirical plays are performed in a Bruxellois dialect.

Film Movies are mainly shown in their original language, so many are in English. **The Acropole** (Galeries de la Toison d'Or, tel. 02/511–43–28) and the multiscreen **Kinepolis** (av. du Centenaire 1, tel. 02/478–04–50) feature comfortable armchairs and first-run movies. For unusual movies or screen classics, visit the **Musée du Cinéma** (Cinema Museum) (9 rue Baron Horta, tel. 02/513–41–55). Five movies are shown daily, at only BF50 each.

Nightlife

Nightclubs These are not always distinguishable from striptease shows and lack the Parisian look, verve, and high kicks. **Show Point** (pl. Stéphanie 14, tel. 02/511–53–64) does its best.

Disco The **Crocodile Club** (rue Duquesnoy 5, tel. 02/511–42–15) at the Royal Windsor Hotel appeals to Eurocrats and visiting business executives. **Le Mirano** (Chaussée de Louvain 38, tel. 02/218–57–72) attracts a self-styled jet set (Saturdays only), while **L'Ecome des Nuits** (Galerie Louise 122 A, tel. 02/513–53–21) has an African atmosphere and is open Thursday–Sunday. **Le Cocoon Club** (Ancien Vaudeville, 14 rue de la Montagne, tel. 02/512–49–97) is a trendy spot just off the Galerie de la Reine. It is open on Fridays and Saturdays after 10:30 PM.

Bars The diversity is greater here than in many other European capitals. These are just a few of the best: **La Fleur en Papier Doré** (rue des Aléxiens 53, tel. 02/511–16–59) is a quiet bar that attracts an artistic audience to drink local beer and look at the ancient walls covered with surreal paintings and old etchings.

Falstaff (rue Henri Maus 25, tel. 02/511–98–77 or 02/511–87–89) is a famous Art Nouveau tavern that draws a mixed crowd.
Rick's Café (av. Louise 344, tel. 02/647–75–30) is as popular with homesick Americans as it is with the British expatriate community. It serves American and Tex/Mex food.
De Ultieme Hallucinatie (rue Royale 316, tel. 02/217–06–14) is another popular Art Nouveau bar and restaurant that serves imaginative cocktails, a full range of beers, and a short but appealing menu.
Le Wine Bar (rue des Pigeons 9, tel. 02/511–44–93) is set in 17th-century cellars and offers excellent (mainly French) wines, strong cheeses, and delicate pâtés.

Jazz Brussels lays claim to being Europe's jazz capital. Buy the monthly *Jazz Streets* magazine to find out details. The best-known venue is the smooth **Brussels Jazz Club** (Grand' Place 13, tel. 02/512–40–93), open every night except Wednesday and Sunday. While the Jazz Club attracts a sophisticated clientele, the **Bierodrome** (pl. Fernand Cocq 21, tel. 02/512–04–56) is a smoky rough-and-ready club in Ixelles, a lively part of the city. **La Samaritaine** (rue de la Samaritaine 16, tel. 02/511–33–95) is concealed in a rustic cellar between the Sablon and the Marolles districts. Except for weekend tickets at the Jazz Club, most entrance prices are low—from BF50 to BF500.

7 Budapest

Arriving and Departing

By Plane Hungary's international airport, the only commercial airport in the country, is about 22 kilometers (14 miles) southeast of the city. All **Malév** flights (except Paris flights) operate from the new terminal 2 (tel. 1577–831); other airlines use terminal 1 (tel. 1572–122). For same-day flight information, tel. 1577–155.

Between the Airport and Downtown Bus service to and from Erzsébet tér station, platform 1, leaves every half hour from 5 AM to 9 PM. The trip takes 30–40 minutes and costs either 40 Ft. or 50 Ft., depending on which terminal you use. A taxi ride to the center of Budapest should cost no more than 800 Ft. Avoid taxi drivers who offer their services before you are out of the arrivals lounge.

By Train There are three main train stations in Budapest: Keleti (East), Nyugati (West), and Déli (South). Trains from Vienna usually operate from the Keleti station, while those to the Balaton depart from the Déli.

By Bus Most buses to Budapest from the western region of Hungary, including those from Vienna, arrive at **Erzsébet tér** station.

By Car The main routes into Budapest are the M1 from Vienna (via Győr) and the M7 from the Balaton.

Getting Around

Budapest is best explored on foot. The maps provided by tourist offices are not very detailed, so arm yourself with one from any of the bookshops in Váci utca or from downtown stationery shops.

By Public Transportation The public transportation system—a metro (subway), buses, streetcars, and trolleybuses—is cheap, efficient, and simple to use but closes down around 11 PM. However, certain trams and buses run on a limited schedule all night. A day ticket *(napijegy)* costs 48 Ft. and allows unlimited travel on all services within the city limits. You can also buy tickets for single rides—blue for buses, costing 10 Ft., and yellow for streetcars, metro, and trolleybuses, costing 8 Ft.—from metro stations or tobacco shops. You can travel any distance on these tickets, but you can't change lines.

Bus, streetcar, and trolleybus tickets must be canceled on board—watch how other passengers do it. Don't get caught without a ticket: Spot checks are frequent, and you can be fined several hundred forints.

By Taxi Taxis are plentiful and a good value, but make sure that they have a meter that is working. The initial charge is 20 Ft., plus 20 Ft. per kilometer plus 6 Ft. per minute of waiting time. Note that these prices are only for **Volántaxi** and **Főtaxi** (run by the government). Private taxi services are more expensive. To call a taxi, tel. 1222–222 or 1666–666; to order one in advance, tel. 1188–188.

By Boat In summer a regular boat service links the north and south of the city, stopping at points on both banks, including Margitsziget (Margaret Island). From May to September boats leave from the quay at Vigadó tér on 1½-hour cruises between the Árpád and Petőfi bridges. The trip, organized by

MAHART, runs three times a day and costs around 200 Ft. (tel. 1181–223).

Important Addresses and Numbers

Tourist Information
Tourinform (Sütő utca 2 [Metro: Deák Tér], tel. 1179–800) is open daily 8–8. **IBUSZ Accommodation Office** (Petőfi tér 3, tel. 1185–707) is open 24 hours. **Budapest Tourist** (Roosevelt tér 5, tel. 1173–555).

Embassies
U.S. (Budapest V, Szabadság tér 12, tel. 1126–450). **Canadian** (Budapest II, Budakeszi út 32, tel. 1767–711). **U.K.** (Budapest V, Harmincad utca 6, tel. 1182–888).

Emergencies
Police (tel. 07); **Ambulance** (tel. 04); **Doctor:** Ask your hotel or embassy to recommend one. U.S. and Canadian visitors are advised to take out full medical insurance. U.K. visitors are covered for emergencies and essential treatment.

English Bookstores
Foreign-Language Book Store, Budapest V, Váci utca 32. Foreign publications—including those in English—can be bought at the reception desks of major hotels and at newsstands at major traffic centers.

Guided Tours

Orientation Tours
Three-hour bus tours of the city operate all year and cost about 800 Ft. Starting from Erzsébet tér, they take in parts of both Buda and Pest and offer a good introduction for further exploring on foot. Contact IBUSZ (*see* Important Addresses and Numbers, above).

Special-Interest Tours and Excursions
IBUSZ and Budapest Tourist organize a number of unusual tours, featuring trips to the Buda Hills or goulash parties, as well as visits to the National Gallery and Parliament and other traditional sights. These tour companies will provide personal guides on request. Also check at your hotel's Hostess Desk.

Excursions farther afield include day-long trips to the *Puszta* (the Great Plain), the Danube Bend, and Lake Balaton.

Exploring Budapest

Budapest, situated on both banks of the Danube, unites the colorful hills of Buda and the wide boulevards of Pest. Though it was the site of a Roman outpost in the 1st century, the actual creation of the city did not occur until 1873, when the towns of Obuda, Pest, and Buda were joined. The cultural, political, intellectual, and commercial heart of the nation beats here in Budapest; for the 20% of the nation's population who live in the capital, anywhere else is simply "the country."

Much of Budapest's real charm lies in unexpected glimpses into shadowy courtyards and in long vistas down sunlit cobbled streets. Although some 30,000 buildings were destroyed during World War II and in 1956, you'll find that a flavor of the past lingers on in the often crumbling architectural details of the structures and in the memories and lifestyles of the citizens.

The principal sights of the city fall roughly into three areas, which can be comfortably covered on foot. The hills of Budapest are best explored by public transportation.

Numbers in the margin correspond to points of interest on the Budapest map.

❶ ❷ Take a taxi or bus (No. 16 from **Erzsébet tér**) to **Dísz tér,** at the foot of **Várhegy** (Castle Hill), where the painstaking work of reconstruction has been in progress since World War II. Having made their final stand in the Royal Palace itself, the Nazis left behind them a blackened wasteland. Under the rubble, archaeologists discovered the medieval foundations of the palace of King Matthias Corvinus, who, in the 15th century, presided over one of the most splendid courts in Europe.

❸ The **Királyi Palota** (Palace), now a vast museum complex and cultural center, can be reached on foot from Dísz tér, or by funicular railway *(Sikló)* from Clark Adám tér. The northern wing of the building is devoted to the **Magyar Újkori Történeti Múzeum** (Museum of Modern Hungarian History) (open Tues.– Sun. 10–6). The central block houses the **Nemzeti Galléria** (National Gallery) (open Tues. 12–6, Wed. 12–8, Thurs.–Sun. 10–6), exhibiting a wide range of Hungarian fine art, from medieval paintings to modern sculpture. Names to look for are Munkácsy, a 19th-century Romantic painter, and Csontváry, an early Surrealist whom Picasso much admired. The southern block contains the **Budapesti Történeti Múzeum** (Budapest History Museum) (open Tues.–Sun. 10–6), with its permanent exhibition entitled "1,000 Years of Our Capital." Down in the cellars are the original medieval vaults of the palace, portraits of King Matthias and his second wife, Beatrice of Aragon, and many late-14th-century statues that probably adorned the Renaissance palace. *Palace Museums, 17 Dísz tér 1. Admission: 15 Ft., free on Sat.*

❹ The **Mátyás templom** (Matthias Church), northeast of Dísz tér, with its distinctive patterned roof, dates to the 13th century. The former mosque built by the occupying Turks was destroyed and reconstructed in the 19th century only to be bombed during World War II. Only the south porch is from the original structure. The Habsburg emperors were crowned kings of Hungary here, including Charles IV, in 1916. High mass is celebrated every Sunday at 10 AM with an orchestra and choir.

❺ The turn-of-the-century **Halászbástya** (Fishermen's Bastion) is on your left as you leave the church. It was built as a lookout tower to protect what was once a thriving fishing settlement. Its neo-Romanesque columns and arches provide frames for views over the city and river. Near the church, in Hess András tér, are remains of the oldest church on Castle Hill, built by Dominican friars in the 13th century. These have now been tastefully integrated into the modern structure of the Hilton hotel.

The town houses lining the streets of the Castle District are largely occupied by offices, restaurants, and diplomatic residences, but the house where Beethoven stayed in 1800 is now **❻** the **Zenetörténeti Múzeum** (Museum of Music History). *Táncsics Mihály utca 7. Admission: 15 Ft. Open Wed.–Sun. 10–6, Mon. 4–9.*

❼ The remains of a **medieval synagogue** are also in the neighborhood and open to the public. On display are a number of objects relating to the Jewish community, including religious inscriptions, frescoes, and tombstones dating to the 15th century.

Táncsics Mihály utca 26. Admission: 15 Ft. Open Apr.–Oct.,
Tues.–Fri. 10–4, weekends 10–6.

⑧ The **Hadtörténeti Múzeum** (War History Museum) is at the far
end of Castle Hill. The collection includes uniforms and regalia,
many belonging to the Hungarian generals who took part in the
abortive uprising against Austrian rule in 1848. Other exhibits
trace the military history of Hungary from the original Magyar
conquest in the 9th century through the period of Ottoman rule
and right to the middle of this century. *Tóth Árpád sétány 40.*
Admission: 15 Ft. Open Tues.–Sat. 9–5, Sun. 10–6.

Nearby stands a monument to Abdurrahman, the last pasha of
Buda, commander of the Turkish troops in Hungary, who died,
sword in hand, in 1686. For a good view of the Vérmezö (Blood
Meadow) and the surrounding Buda hills, stroll the length of
Tóth Árpád sétány, along the rampart that defended Castle
Hill to the west.

The Heart of Cross the **Széchenyi lánchíd** (Chain Bridge) from Clark Adám
the City tér to reach **Roosevelt tér** in Pest, with the 19th-century neo-
⑨ classical Academy of Sciences on your left. Pest fans out from
the **Belváros** (Inner City), which is bounded by the **Kiskörút**
(Little Circular Road). The **Nagykörút** (Grand Circular Road)
describes a wider semicircle from the Margaret Bridge to Petőfi Bridge. To your right, an elegant promenade, the **Korzó,**
runs south along the river.

Time Out The **Bécsi Kávéház** (Vienna Coffeehouse) in the Forum Hotel
serves the best coffee and cream pastries in town. *Apáczai*
Csere János utca 12–14. Moderate.

⑩ A square called **Vigadó tér** is dominated by the Danube view
and Vigadó concert hall, built in the Romantic style, where
Liszt, Brahms, and Bartók performed. Completely destroyed
during World War II, it has been rebuilt in its original style.
⑪ Another square, **Március 15 tér,** commemorates the 1848 struggle for independence from the Habsburgs with a statue of the
poet Petőfi Sándor, who died later in the uprising. Every
March 15, the square is packed with patriotic Hungarians. Be-
⑫ hind the square is the 12th-century **Belvárosi plébánia templom**
(Inner City Parish Church), the oldest in Pest. The church has
been redone in a variety of western architectural styles; even
Turkish influences, such as the Muslim prayer niche, remain.
Liszt, who lived only a few yards away, often played the organ
here.

Parallel to the Korzó, Pest's riverside promenade, lies Buda-
⑬ pest's most upscale shopping street, **Váci utca. Vörösmarty tér,**
a handsome square, is a welcome place in which to sit and relax
in the heart of the Inner City. Street musicians and sidewalk
cafés make it one of the liveliest places in Budapest.

Time Out **Gerbeaud,** an elegant pastry shop, was founded in 1857 and retains the old imperial style; it's a fashionable meeting place.
Try the chestnut puree with whipped cream while sitting on
the terrace overlooking the square. *Vörösmarty tér 7. Inex-*
pensive.

⑭ North of Roosevelt tér is the imposing neo-Gothic **Parliament**
(open for tours only), the riverfront's most striking landmark.
To its left sits an expressive statue of József Attila (1905–37),

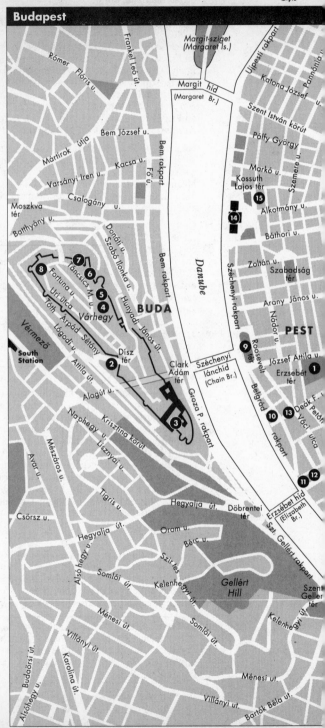

Budapest

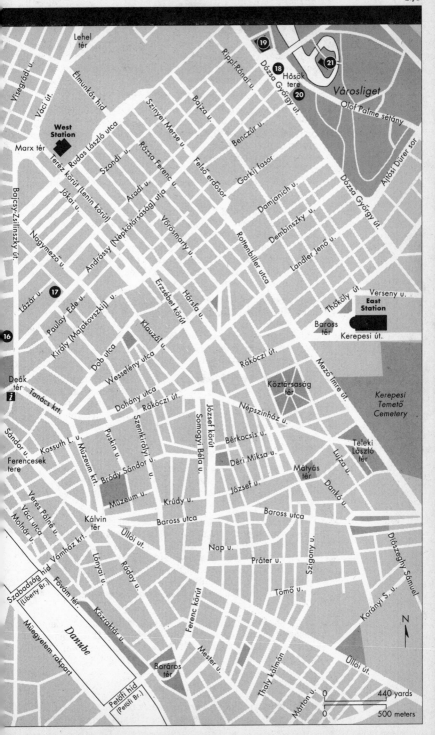

who, in spite of his early death, became known as one of Hungary's greatest poets.

⑮ Across from the Parliament is the **Néprajzi Múzeum** (Museum of Ethnography), with exhibits depicting folk traditions and such social customs as Hungarian costume and folklore. There is a particularly interesting collection from Oceania. *Kossuth Lajos tér 12. Admission: 10 Ft. Open Tues.–Sun. 10–6.*

⑯ Dark and massive, the 19th-century **Szt. István Bazilika** (St. Stephen's Basilica) is one of the chief landmarks of Pest. It was planned early in the 19th century as a neoclassical building, but was in the neo-Renaissance style by the time it was completed more than 50 years later. During World War II, the most precious documents from the Municipal Archives were placed in the cellar of the basilica—one of the few available bombproof sites.

Andrássy útja runs 3.2 kilometers (2 miles) from the basilica to
⑰ **Hősök tere** (Heroes' Square). On the left is the **State Opera House,** with its statues of the Muses in the second-floor corner niches. Completed in 1884, it was the crowning achievement of architect Miklós Ybl. It has been restored to its original ornate glory—particularly inside—and has been fortunate enough to be spared any attempts to modernize it.

Városliget Park In the center of Heroes' Square stands the 36.5-meter (118-
⑱ foot) **Millennium Monument,** begun in 1896 to commemorate the 1,000th anniversary of the Magyar Conquest. Prince Árpád and six other founders of the Magyar nation occupy the base of the monument, while between the columns on either side are Hungary's greatest rulers and princes.

⑲ The **Szépművészeti Múzeum** (Fine Arts Museum) stands on one side of the square. Egyptian, Greek, and Roman artifacts dominate an entire section of the museum, with an emphasis on rare ceramics. The works by the greatest of European painters have been chosen with great care, and almost every artist of renown is represented. *Admission: 15 Ft. Open Tues.–Sat. 10–6, Sun. 10–6.*

⑳ The **Műcsarnok** (Art Gallery), on the other side of the square, is the site of visiting exhibitions of fine arts, applied arts, and photography. *Admission: 15 Ft. Open Tues.–Sat. 10–6, Sun. 10–8.*

The **Városliget** (City Park) extends beyond the square; on the left as you enter it are the zoo, state circus, amusement park, and outdoor swimming pool of the Széchenyi mineral baths. On
㉑ the right is the **Mezőgazdasági Múzeum** (Agricultural Museum), housed in a number of buildings representing different styles of Hungarian architecture—again a part of the Millennium Exhibition of 1896. *Széchenyi sziget, Városliget XIV. Admission: 15 Ft. Open Tues.–Sat. 10–5, Sun. 10–6.*

On the shores of the artificial lake stands the statue of George Washington, erected in 1906 from donations by Hungarians living in the United States. The recently renamed **Olaf Palme sétány** (walk) is a pleasant route through the park.

Shopping

You'll find plenty of folk art and souvenir shops, foreign-language bookshops, and classical record shops in or around **Váci**

utca, but a visit to some of the smaller, more typically Hungarian shops on **Erzsébet** and **Teréz boulevards** (formerly Lenin Körút), and to the new **Skála-Coop** department store near the Nyugati train station may prove more interesting.

The **central market hall** at IX Vámhaz körút 1–3 and the **flea market** *(ecseri piac)* some way out on Nagykörösi utca 156 (take bus No. 58 from Boráros tér) stock antiques, clothes, lamps, and other Hungarian items.

Dining

There are plenty of good, affordably priced restaurants offering a variety of Hungarian dishes. Meats, rich sauces, and creamy desserts predominate, but the more health-concious will also find salads, even out of season. There are also self-service restaurants *(önkiszolgálá étterm)*, snack bars *(bistró* or *étel bár)*, buffets *(büfé,* cafés *(eszpresszó),* and bars *(drink-bár).* The pastry shops *(cukrászda)* are also worth a dry.

In almost all restaurants, an inexpensive fixed-price lunch, called a "menü," is available, usually for as little as 125 Ft. It includes soup or salad, an entrée, and a dessert.

Mealtimes Hungarians eat early—you risk off-hand service and cold food after 9 PM. Lunch—for many the main meal—is served noon–2. It is hard to find a sit-down meal between 2:30 and 4:30.

Dress Jacket and tie are appropriate for restaurants in the top price categories. At other restaurants, casual but neat dress is acceptable.

Ratings Prices are per person and include a first course, main course, and dessert, but no wine or tip. Prices in Budapest tend to be a good 30% higher then elsewhere in Hungary. Best bets are indicated by a star ★.

Category	Cost
Very Expensive	over 1,200 Ft.
Expensive	1,000–1,200 Ft.
Moderate	600–1,000 Ft.
Inexpensive	under 600 Ft.

Expensive **Alabárdos.** Castle Hill is the setting for this small, intimate res-
★ taurant with outstanding food, wine, and service. The setting is medieval, and soft guitar music helps to establish the Old World atmosphere. *I Országház utca 2, tel. 1560–851. Reservations required. AE, DC, MC, V. Dinner only. Closed Sun.*

Arany Hordó. True to its name (which means the Golden Barrel), this 14th-century building has a beer house on the ground floor. The cellar has a wine tavern, but the real attraction is the first-class restaurant on the second floor. The local specialty is *fogas,* a fish from Lake Balaton. There is gypsy music in the evening. *I Tárnok utca 16, tel. 1566–765. Reservations advised for restaurant. AE, DC, MC, V.*

Fortuna. Three medieval houses were reconstructed as a wood-furnished restaurant, nightclub, and tavern. The atmosphere is matched by the range of food, the distinguished wine list, and the draft beer. There is gypsy music in the evening. *I Hess András tér 4, tel. 1756–857. Reservations advised for dinner. AE, DC, MC, V.*

★ **Gundel.** Gundel is a famous restaurant in the City Park, where traditional meals are served in a warm, caring, though somewhat formal atmosphere. *Gundel palacsinta* (pancakes, with chocolate, walnuts, and cream) are flamed in rum at the table. There are outdoor tables in the summer and gypsy music in the evenings. It has a moderate section, the Bagolyvár. *XIV Állatkerti körút 2, tel. 1221–002. Reservations accepted. AE, DC, MC, V.*

Moderate **Kisbuda.** A small restaurant near the Buda end of the Margaret
★ Bridge, Kisbuda serves meat and fish specialties and a delicious variety of salads. Ask the waiter for the unlisted daily specials. In warm weather there are tables outside in a courtyard. A piano and violin duet play in the evening. *II Frankel L. utca 34, tel. 1152–244. Reservations advised in evenings. No credit cards. Closed Sun. dinner.*

Szeged. This is a traditional fish restaurant near the Szabadság Bridge and Gellért Hill. Folk art covers the walls, and there is gypsy music in the evening. The fish soup is fiery. *XI Bartók Béla út 1, tel. 1251–268. Reservations accepted. No credit cards.*

Tabáni Kakas. Situated just below Castle Hill, Tabáni Kakas is a popular restaurant with a friendly atmosphere. It specializes in large helpings of poultry dishes, particularly goose. A pianist plays and sings in the evening. *I Attila út 27, tel. 1757–165. No reservations. No credit cards.*

Inexpensive **Kaltenberg.** A beer hall in a brewery (which can be visited),
★ Kaltenberg serves solid Germanic food but offers a selection of surprisingly delicate desserts, including delicious raspberry strudel. *IX Kinizsi út 30–36, tel. 1189–792. Reservations accepted. AE, DC, MC, V.*

Márvány Menyasszony. Summer is the best time to appreciate this spacious restaurant in a back street near the Déli train station. It is popular with groups, probably because its long wooden tables and benches give way to space for dancing to gypsy music. *I Márvány utca 6, tel. 1756–165. Reservations accepted. No credit cards.*

Lodging

If you arrive in Budapest without a reservation, go to the IBUSZ travel office (open 24 hours) at Petőfi tér (tel. 1185–707) or to one of the tourist offices at any of the train stations or at the airport.

Hotels Establishments in the Inexpensive category seldom have private baths, but plumbing is adequate almost everywhere. Reservations should be made well in advance, especially in the less expensive establishments, which are still in short supply.

Rentals Apartments in Budapest are available. Rates and reservations can be obtained from tourist offices in Hungary and abroad. A Budapest apartment might cost 10,000 Ft. a week. Bookings can be made in Budapest at **IBUSZ** on Petőfi tér 3 (tel. 1185–707), which is open 24 hours a day, or through IBUSZ offices in the United States and Great Britain. (*see* Before You Go in Chapter 1).

Guest Houses Also called pensions, these offer simple accommodations in rooms with four beds. They are well suited to younger people on a budget, and there are separate bathrooms for men and women on each floor. Some offer simple breakfast facilities. Arrangements can be made through local tourist offices or travel agents abroad.

Ratings The following price categories are for a double room with bath and breakfast during the peak season. For single rooms with bath, count on about 80% of the double-room rate. Best bets are indicated by a star ★.

Category	Cost
Very Expensive	9,000–14,000
Expensive	7,000–9,000
Moderate	4,000–7,000
Inexpensive	1,500–4,000

During the off-season (in Budapest), September through March), rates can be considerably lower than those given above.

Very Expensive
★ **Atrium Hyatt.** This large luxury hotel in the Inner City has a good view over the Danube. Its range of services has made it a popular stop for businesspeople and those who don't mind being pampered. *V Roosevelt tér 2, tel. 1383–000, fax 1188–659. 356 rooms with bath. Facilities: 2 restaurants, bar, indoor pool, sauna, gym, conference rooms, and ballroom. AE, DC, MC, V.*

Duna Inter-Continental. The Duna makes the best of its location with a terrace café overlooking the river from the Danube Quay. Ask for a room facing west, across the river toward Gellért Hill in Buda. *V Apáczai Csere János utca 4, tel. 1175–122, fax 1184–973. 340 rooms with bath. Facilities: 3 restaurants, penthouse bar, nightclub, pool, squash. AE, DC, MC, V.*

Hilton. On Castle Hill in Buda, the Hilton offers an excellent view over the city. It incorporates the tower and other remains of a 13th-century church. Try your luck at the casino. *I Hess András tér 1–3, tel. 1751–000, fax 1560–285. 323 rooms with bath. Facilities: 3 restaurants, nightclub, casino. AE, DC, MC, V.*

Expensive
Béke Radisson. This traditional hotel near Nyugati train station has undergone a face-lift to give it modern comforts and easy access. Its nightclub, Orfeum, draws crowds. *VI Teréz körút 97, tel. 1323–300, fax 1533–380. 246 rooms with bath. Facilities: 2 restaurants, 2 bars, nightclub. AE, DC, MC, V.*

Buda-Penta. The new Buda-Penta is next door to Déli train station, close to Castle Hill and most of the sights in Buda. It houses the fashionable Horoszkóp nightclub and a pizzeria. *I Krisztina körút 41–43, tel. 1566–333, fax 1556–964. 399 rooms with bath. Facilities: indoor pool, sauna, gym. AE, DC, MC, V.*

★ **Gellért.** This traditional grand hotel overlooks the Danube from the Buda end of Szabadság Bridge. The rooms are all comfortable, and many have a good view of the historic Gellért district. *XI Gellért tér 1, tel. 1852–200, fax 1666–631. 235 rooms* *with bath. Facilities: thermal pools, terrace restaurant. AE, DC, MC, V.*

Grand Hotel Hungaria. Though Budapest's largest hotel is directly across from the Keleti station and near the metro on a busy boulevard, noise is kept firmly at bay with the triple-glazed windows in all rooms. *VII Rákóczi ut 90, tel. 1229–050, fax 1228–029. 528 rooms with bath. Facilities: 3 restaurants, nightclub, sauna, gym. AE, DC, MC, V.*

Moderate **Astoria.** This elegantly restored hotel reflects the atmosphere
★ of the turn of the century. Though located at a busy Pest intersection, it has been soundproofed and insulated from the 20th century. *V. Kossuth Lajos utca 19, tel. 1173–411, fax 1186–798. 198 rooms with bath or shower. Facilities: nightclub, café. AE, DC, MC, V.*

Erzsébet. This well-known hotel with a long tradition of good service was torn down and rebuilt between 1978 and 1985. Located in the center of the Inner City, it boasts a popular beer cellar (Janos Pince) among its attractions. *V Károly Mihály utca 11–15, tel. 1382–111, fax 1189–237. 123 rooms, mostly doubles with shower. Facilities: restaurant, beer hall. AE, DC, MC, V.*

Nemzeti. Another hotel that reflects the grand mood of the turn of the century, Nemzeti was completely restored in 1987 and offers all the modern comforts. It's cozy, with a central location in Pest. *VIII József krt. 4, tel. 1339–160, fax 1140–019. 76 rooms, mostly doubles with bath. Facilities: restaurant, brasserie. AE, DC, MC, V.*

★ **Panorama Hotels-Bungalows (Vörös Csillag).** Perched 310 meters (1,000 feet) above the Danube near the upper terminus of the cog-wheel railway, Vórós Csillag resembles a hunting lodge. Unless you have vertigo, you will admire the view of the entire city from the terrace. *XII Rege út 21, tel. 1750–522, fax 1750–412. 40 rooms with bath, 54 self-catering bungalows. Facilities: restaurant, bar terrace, pool, sauna. AE, DC, MC, V.*

Inexpensive **Citadella.** Comparatively basic, with four beds in some rooms and showers down the hall, the Citadella is nevertheless very popular, particularly with young people, who enjoy the lively communal atmosphere and the location—right inside the fortress. *XI Gellérthegy, tel. 1665–794. 40 rooms, none with bath. Facilities: restaurant, beer hall, nightclub. No credit cards.*

Wien. The Wien is located in the southwestern outskirts of the city, near the junction of the highways to Vienna and Balaton, making it popular and convenient for drivers. *XI Budaörsi út 88, tel. 1665–400. 110 rooms, most with bath. Facilities: restaurant, café, gas station, car repairs. AE, DC, MC, V.*

The Arts

Hotels and tourist offices will provide you with a copy of the monthly publication *Programme*, which contains details of all cultural events in the city. Tickets are available from your hotel desk, the **Central Booking Agency** (Vörösmarty tér, tel. 1176–222), or from **Budapest Tourist** (Roosevelt tér 5, tel. 1173–555).

There are two opera houses, for which dress can be informal. Concerts are given all year at the **Academy of Music** on Liszt F. tér, the **Vigadó** on Vigadó tér and at the **Old Academy of Music** on Vörösmarty út. Displays of Hungarian folk dancing are held at the **Cultural Center** on Corvin tér.

Nightlife

Budapest is a lively city by night. Establishments stay open late and Western European-style *drink-bárs* have sprung up all over the city.

Nightclubs Many of the nightclubs are attached to the luxury hotels. Beware of the inflated prices. Admission starts at 150 Ft. Drinks cost from 200 Ft. to 500 Ft.

Casanova offers music and dancing in an attractive building a few yards from the riverbank on the Buda side. *II Batthyány tér 4, tel. 1338–320. Open 10 PM–4 AM.*

Duna-bár Boat sails up and down the river with dancing and disco music on board. *Board at Quay 3, opposite the Forum Hotel, on the Pest side. Tel. 1170–803. Open 10 PM–3 AM.*

Pierrot is an elegant café in the Castle District with live piano music and good cocktails. *I Fortuna utca 14, tel. 1756–971. Open 5 PM–1 AM. No credit cards.*

Cabarets **Horoszkóp**, in the Buda-Penta Hotel, is the favorite among Budapest's younger set. Floor shows begin at 11 PM. *I Krisztina körút 41–43, tel. 1566–333. Open 10 PM–4 AM.*

Maxim's, in the Hotel Emke, currently offers three variety shows daily plus a "Crazy Cabaret" show. *VII Akácfa utca 3, tel. 1420–145. Open 8 PM–3 AM.*

Fortuna, opposite the Matthias Church on Castle Hill, is one of the city's most elegant night spots. It is located in the medieval hall of a 14th-century building. The program starts at 12:30 AM. *I Hess András tér, tel. 1557–451. Open 10 PM–4 AM.*

Discos The university colleges organize the best discos in town. Try the **ELTE Club** (Eötvös Loránd) in the Inner City, on the corner of Károlyi Mihály utca and Irányi utca. Admission and the price of drinks are reasonable. Bring some student I.D.

8 Copenhagen

Arriving and Departing

By Plane The main airport for both international and domestic flights is Copenhagen Airport, 10 kilometers (6 miles) from the center of town.

Between the Airport and Downtown There is frequent bus service to the city; the airport bus to the central station leaves every 15 minutes, and the trip takes about 25 minutes. You pay the 24-kr. fare on the bus. Public buses are half the price and run as often. Bus No. 32 or No. 32H takes you to Rådhus Pladsen, the city-hall square. A taxi ride takes 15 minutes and costs about 100 kr.

By Train Copenhagen's central station is the hub of the train networks. Express trains leave every hour, on the hour, from 6 AM to 10 PM for principal towns in Funen and Jutland. Find out more from **DSB Information** at the central station (tel. 33/14–17–01). You can make reservations at the central station (tel. 33/14–88–00) and most other stations and through travel agents. In Copenhagen, for those with Inter-Rail cards there is an Inter-Rail Center (open July–Sept. 17, 7 AM–midnight) at the central station that offers rest and a bath.

Getting Around

By Bus and Suburban Train The best bet for visitors is the **Copenhagen Card,** affording unlimited travel on buses and suburban trains (S-trains), admission to over 40 museums and sights around Zealand, and a reduction on the ferry crossing to Sweden. You can buy the card, which costs about 115 kr. (one day), 154 kr. (two days), or 198 kr. (three days), at tourist offices and hotels and from travel agents.

Buses and suburban trains operate on the same ticket system and divide Copenhagen and the surrounding areas into three zones. Tickets are validated on the time system: On the basic ticket, which costs 8 kr. for an hour, you can travel anywhere in the zone in which you started. You can obtain a discount by buying a packet of 10 basic tickets for 70 kr. Get zone information from the 24-hour information service: tel. 31/95–17–01 for buses, 33/14–17–01 for S-trains. Buses and S-trains run from 5 AM (6 AM on Sundays) to 12:30 AM.

By Car Copenhagen is a city for walkers, not drivers. The charm of its pedestrian streets is paid for by a complicated one-way road system and difficult parking. Leave your car in the garage: Attractions are relatively close together, and public transportation is excellent.

By Taxi Taxis are not cheap, but all are metered. The base charge is 12 kr., plus 8–10 kr. per kilometer. A cab is available when it displays the sign Fri (Free); it can be hailed or picked up at a taxi stand, or tel. 31/35–35–35.

By Bicycle More than half the 5 million Danes are said to ride bikes, which are popular with visitors as well. Bike rental costs 30–50 kr. a day, with a deposit of 100–200 kr. Contact **Danwheel-Rent-a-Bike** (Colbjørnsensgade 3, tel. 31/21–22–27); or **Urania Cykler** (Gammel Kongevej 1, tel. 31/21–80–88).

Important Addresses and Numbers

Tourist Information The main tourist information office is **Danmarks Turistråd** (Danish Tourist Board) (H. C. Andersens Boulevard 22, DK 1553 Copenhagen, tel. 33/11–13–25). Located opposite city hall, it is open May–Sept., weekdays 9–6, Sat. 9–2, Sun. 9–1; Oct.–Apr., weekdays 9–5, Sat. 9–noon, closed Sun. In summer there are also offices at Elsinore, Hillerød, Køge, Roskilde, Gilleleje, Hundersted, and Tisvildeleje. Youth information in Copenhagen is available at **Huset** (Rådhusstraede 13, tel. 33/15–65–18).

Embassies U.S. (Dag Hammarskjöldsallé 24, tel. 31/42–31–44). **Canada** (Kristen Benikowsgade 1, tel. 33/12–22–99). **U.K.** (Kastelsvej 40, tel. 31/26–46–00).

Emergencies **Police, Fire, Ambulance** (tel. 000). **Doctor** (tel. 33/12–00–41) (fees payable in cash only; night fees around 250 kr.). **Dentist: Dental Emergency Service,** Tandlægevagten, 14, Oslo Plads, near Østerport station (no telephone; emergencies only; cash only). **Pharmacies:** The following are open 24 hours in central Copenhagen: **Steno Apotek** (Vesterbrogade 6C, tel. 33/14–82–66); **Sønderbro Apotek** (Amagerbrogade 158 [Amager area], tel. 31/58–01–40); **Glostrup Apotek** (Hovedvegen 101 [Glostrup area], tel. 42/96–00–20).

English Bookstores English-language publications can be found at the central-station newsstand and in most bookstores around town. **Boghallen** (Rådhus Pladsen 37) has a particularly good selection.

Travel Agencies **American Express** (Dagmarhus, Amagertorv 18, tel. 33/12–23–01). **Tjæreborg Rejser** (Rådhus Pladsen 75, tel. 33/11–41–00) arranges charter flights and accommodations all over Europe.

Guided Tours

Orientation Tours Tours are a good way to get acquainted with Copenhagen. From May to September you can sail on the Öre Sound on board the *Isefjord,* Denmark's oldest schooner. The four-hour tours include lunch or dinner and leave from Amaliehavn (tel. 33/15–17–29). The "Harbor and Canal Tour" (by boat) leaves from Gammel Strand and the east side of Kongens Nytorv every half hour from 10 AM, while the following bus tours, monitored by the tourist office, leave from the Lur Blower Column in the Rådhus Pladsen: "City Tour" (May 15–Sept. 11, daily at 10; June 15–Aug., daily at 10, 12, 4); "Grand Tour of Copenhagen" (daily at 11, 1:30); "Royal Tour of Copenhagen" (June–Sept. 11, Tues., Thurs., and Sat. at 10); "City and Harbor Tour" (combined bus and boat; May–Sept. 11, daily 9:30, 1, 3). Tickets are available aboard the bus and boat or from travel agencies.

Special-Interest Tours The "Carlsberg Brewery Tour" meets at the Elephant Gate (Ny Carlsbervej 140) on weekdays at 11 and 2 or by arrangement for groups (tel. 31/21–12–21, ext. 1312). Tuborg Breweries also provides tours (Strandvejen 54, bus No. 6 or No. 23) weekdays at 10, 12:30, and 2:30 or by arrangement for groups (tel. 31/29–33–11, ext. 2212). The "Royal Copenhagen Porcelain" tour (Smallegade 45, tel. 31/86–48–48) is given on weekdays at 9, 10 and 11.

Walking Tours Two-hour guided walking tours, organized by the Copenhagen Tourist Information Center, operate all year (English-speaking guides are available in July and August only). The tourist office also has information about a taped cassette tour that you can take on your own. The "Guided Stroll" walking tour has English-speaking guides daily in July and August and on weekends from April to October (tel. 31/51–25–90).

Regional Tours The Danish Tourist Board has full details of excursions outside the city, including visits to castles (such as Hamlet's castle), the Viking Ship Museum, and Sweden.

Personal Guides The tourist information center can recommend multilingual guides for individual needs, while travel agents have details on hiring a limousine and guide.

Exploring Copenhagen

When Denmark ruled Norway and Sweden in the 15th century, Copenhagen was the capital of all three countries. Today it is still the liveliest Scandinavian capital, with about 1 million inhabitants. It's a city meant for walking, the first in Europe to recognize the value of pedestrian streets in fostering community spirit. As you stroll through the cobbled streets and squares, you'll find that Copenhagen combines the excitement and variety of big-city life with a small-town atmosphere. If there's such a thing as a cozy metropolis, you'll find it here.

Nor are you ever far from water, be it sea or canal. The city itself is built upon two main islands, Slotsholmen and Christianshavn, connected by drawbridges. Walk down Nyhavn Canal, an area formerly haunted by a fairly salty crew of sailors. Now it's gentrified, and the 18th-century houses lining it are filled with chic restaurants. You should linger, too, in the five main pedestrian streets collectively known as "Strøget," with shops, cellar galleries and crafts workshops, and street musicians and vendors by the dozen. In summer Copenhagen moves outside, and the best views of city life are from the sidewalk cafés in the shady squares.

Rådhus Pladsen *Numbers in the margin correspond to points of interest on the*
and Slotsholmen *Copenhagen map.*

The best place to start a stroll is the Rådhus Pladsen (City Hall Square), the hub of Copenhagen's commercial district. The ➊ mock-Renaissance building dominating it is the **Rådhus** (city hall), completed in 1905. A statue of Copenhagen's 12th-century founder, Bishop Absalon, sits atop the main entrance. Inside you can see the first World Clock, an astrological timepiece invented and built by Jens Olsen and put in motion in 1955. If you're feeling energetic, take a guided tour up the 350-foot tower for a panoramic view. *Rådhus Pladsen, tel. 33/15–38–00. Open weekdays 10–3. Tower tours: weekdays at 11 and 2, Sat. at 11.*

➋ On the right of Rådhus Pladsen is **Lur Blower's Column,** topped by two Vikings blowing an ancient trumpet called a *lur.* The artist took a good deal of artistic license—the lur dates from the Bronze Age, 1500 BC, while the Vikings lived a mere 1,000 years ago. The monument is a starting point for sightseeing tours of the city.

If you continue to the square's northeast corner and turn right, you will be in Frederiksberggade, the first of the five pedestri- ➌ an streets that make up the **Strøget,** Copenhagen's shopping district. Walk past the cafés and trendy boutiques to the double

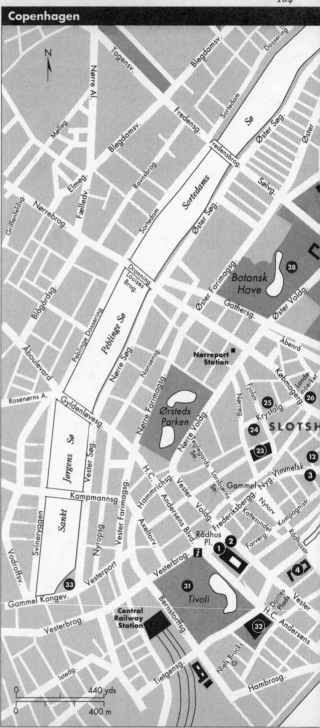

Copenhagen

Farimagsg.
Hammerskjölds Al.
Stockholmsg.
Kristianiag.
Østbaneg.
Langeliniebr.
Oslo Plads
Folke Bernadottes Al.
Forbindelsesv.
Langelinie

22

Yderhavn

Øster
Anlæg

30

29

Rigensg.

Grønningen

St. Kongensg.

21

*Churchill
Parken*

20

Esplanaden

Sølvg.

Fredericiag.

Bredg.

Amalieg.

19

27

*Kongens
Have*

Store Kongensg.

18

17

Dronningens Tværg.

Bredg.

15

16

Toldbg.

Kronprincesseg.

Adelg.

Borgerg.

Amalieg.

Sankt Annæ Plads

Vognmagerg.
Gammelmønt
Pilestræde

Gothersg.

Ny Østerg.

Kr. Berniko.

Bremerholm

Kongens
Nytorv

Nyhavn

Nyhavn

Canal

Inderhavn

HOLMEN

2

Østerg.

13

Højbro

14

Heibergsg.

Amagertorv

Læderstr.

Gammel Strand

Holmens

Hølbergsg.

Havnegade

Vindelbro

6

5

8

10

Børsg.

Chr.
IV's
Bro

CHRISTIANSHAVN

Tøjhusgade

9

7

Knippelsbro

Sankt Annæg.

11

Frederiksholms

Christians Brygge

Kanal

Voldg.

Blvd.

Langebro

Langerbrog.

Dronningensg.

Princessg.

Christianshavns Voldg.

Torveg.

Amager Blvd.

Stadsgraven

Torveg.

Vermlandsg.

square of **Gammel and Nytorv**, where, on April 16, golden apples (really gilded metal balls) dance on the water jets in the fountain to celebrate the queen's birthday.

❹ Turn down Rådhusstræde toward Frederiksholms Kanal. Here you'll find the entrance to the **National Museet** (National Museum), with extensive collections that chronicle Danish cultural history to modern times and display Egyptian, Greek, and Roman antiquities. Viking enthusiasts will want to see the Runic stones in the Danish cultural history section. *Frederiksholms Kanal 12, tel. 33/13–44–11. Admission free. Open June 16–Sept. 15, Tues.–Sun. 10–4; Sept. 16–June 15, Tues.–Fri. 11–3, weekends noon–4.*

❺ Cross Frederiksholms Kanal to Castle Island, dominated by the massive gray **Christiansborg Slot** (Christiansborg Castle). The complex, which contains the Folketinget (Parliament House) and the Royal Reception Chambers, is situated on the site of the city's first fortress, built by Bishop Absalon in 1167. While the castle that stands was being built at the turn of the century, the National Museum excavated the ruins beneath the site. *Ruins. Admission: 12 kr. adults, 5 kr. children. Open May–Oct., daily 9:30–3:30; closed Nov.–Apr., Mon. and Sat. Folketinget. Entrance free. Tours every hour on Sun., 10–4. Reception Rooms. Admission: 25 kr. adults, 10 kr. children. Open May–Oct., Tues.–Sun., English tours at 11, 1, and 3; Oct.–May, Tues.–Thurs., and Sun., English tours at 11 and 1.*

❻ Also on Castle Island, just north of the castle, is **Thorvaldsens Museum.** The 19th-century Danish sculptor Bertel Thorvaldsen, buried at the center of the museum, was greatly influenced by the statues and reliefs of classical antiquity. In addition to his own works, there is a collection of paintings and drawings by other artists illustrating the influence of Italy on Denmark's Golden Age artists. *Prins Jørgens Gård. Admission free. Open Tues.–Sun. 10–5.*

❼ Nearby, **Det Kongelige Bibliotek** (Royal Library) houses the country's largest collection of books, newspapers, and manuscripts. Look for early records of the Viking journeys to America and Greenland and the statue of the philosopher Søren Kierkegaard in the garden. *Christians Brygge 8. Admission free. Open weekdays 9–7, Sat. 10–7.*

❽ Close to the library is the **Teaterhistorisk Museum** (Theater History Museum), in the Royal Court Theater of 1766. You can see extensive exhibits in theater and ballet history, then wander around the boxes, stage, and dressing rooms to see where it all happened. *Christianborg Ridebane 18, tel. 33/11–51–76. Admission: 20 kr. adults, 10 kr. senior citizens and students, 5 kr. children. Open June–Sept., Wed. 2–4, Sun. noon–4.*

Also at this address are the **Royal Stables**, which display vehicles used by the Danish monarchy from 1776 to the present. *Admission: 5 kr. adults, 2 kr. children. Open Nov.–Apr., Sat.–Sun. 2–4; May–Oct., Fri.–Sun. 2–4.*

❾ Across the street that bears its name is **Tøjhuset Museum** (Royal Armory), with impressive displays of uniforms, weapons, and armor in an arched hall 200 yards long. *Tkjhusgade 3, tel. 33/11–60–37. Admission free. Open May–Sept., Tues.–Sat. 1–4, Sun. 10–4; Oct.–Apr., Tues.–Sat. 1–3, Sun. 11–4.*

10 A few steps from Tøjhuset is the old stock exchange, **Børsen,** believed to be the oldest still in use—although it functions only on special occasions. It was built by the 16th-century monarch King Christian IV, a scholar and warrior, and architect of much of the city. The king is said to have had a hand at twisting the tails of the four dragons that form the structure's distinctive green copper spire. With its steep roofs, tiny windows, and gables, the building is one of Copenhagen's treasures.

From Børsen, look east across the drawbridge (Knippelsbro) that connects Slotsholmen with Christianshavn, one of the old-
11 est parts of Copenhagen, to the green-and-gold spire of **Vor Frelser's Kirke** (Our Savior's Church). The Gothic structure was built in 1696. Local legend has it that the staircase encircling it was built curling the wrong way around, and that when its architect reached the top and saw what he had done, he jumped. The less impulsive will enjoy the spectacular view from the top. *Skt. Annægade, tel. 31/57–27–98. Admission: 10 kr. adults, 4 kr. children. Open Mar. 15–May, Mon.–Sat. 9–4:30, Sun. noon–3:30; June–Aug., Mon.–Sat. 9–4:30, Sun. noon–4:30; Sept.–Oct., Mon.–Sat. 9–3:30, Sun. noon–3:30. Nov.–Mar. 14, Mon.–Sat. 10–1:30, Sun. noon–1:30. Dec.–March 14, the tower is closed.*

12 Head back to Strøget, turning left along the Amagertov section. Toward the end and to the right (5 Niels Hemmingsens Gad) is the 18th-century **Helligånds Kirken** (Church of the Holy Ghost). The choir contains a marble font by the sculptor Thorvaldsen.

13 In Østergade, the easternmost of the streets that make up Strøget, you cannot miss the green spire of **Nikolaj Kirke** (Nikolaj Church). The building that currently stands was built in the 20th century; the previous structure, which dated to the 13th century, was destroyed by fire in 1728. Today the church's role is secular—it's an art gallery and an exhibition center.

Time Out **Café Nikolaj,** inside the old Nikolaj Kirke, is a good place to stop for a Danish pastry or a light meal. *Open Mon.–Sat. noon–5. Inexpensive.*

While Strøget is famous as a shopping area, and elegant stores abound, it's also where Copenhagen comes to stroll. Outside the posh displays of the fur and porcelain shops, the sidewalks have the festive aura of a street fair.

Around the **Kongens Nytorv** (the King's New Market) is the square mark-
Royal Palace ing the end of Strøget. The **Kongelige Teater** (Danish Royal
14 Theater), home of Danish opera and ballet as well as theater, sits on the south side. The Danish Royal Ballet remains one of the world's great companies, with a repertoire ranging from classical to modern. On the western side of the square you'll see the stately facade of the hotel D'Angleterre, the grande dame of Copenhagen hotels. When former president Reagan visited Denmark, he couldn't stay there for security reasons but asked for a tour of the place just the same.

The street leading southeast from Kongens Nytorv is **Nyhavn.** The recently gentrified canal was a longtime haunt of sailors. Now restaurants and boutiques outnumber the tattoo shops, but the area retains a genuine charm, with a fleet of old-time sailing ships and well-preserved 18th-century buildings. Hans

Christian Andersen lived at both Nos. 18 and 20. Nearer the harbor are old shipping warehouses, including two—Nyhavn 71 and the Admiral—that have been converted into comfortable hotels.

Turn left at the end of Nyhavn to see the harbor front and then make an immediate left onto Skt. Annæ Plads. Take the third
⑮ right onto Amaliegade. Continue straight ahead for **Amalienborg Palace,** the principal royal residence since 1784. When the royal family is in residence during the fall and winter, the Royal Guard and band march through the city at noon to change the palace guard. The palace interior is closed to the public.

Rest a moment on the palace's harbor side, amid the trees and
⑯ fountains of **Amaliehavn Gardens.** Across the square, it's just a
⑰ step to Bredgade and the **Marmorikirken** (Marble Church), a 19th-century Baroque church with a dome that looks several sizes too large for the building beneath it.

⑱ Bredgade is also home to the exotic onion domes of the **Russiske Ortodoxe Kirke** (Russian Orthodox Church). Farther on is the
⑲ **Kundindustrimuseet** (Museum of Decorative Art), with a large selection of European and Oriental handicrafts, as well as ceramics, silverware, and tapestry. *Bredgade 68, tel. 33/14–94– 52. Admission: 20 kr. July, Aug., Sun., and holidays; otherwise free. Open Tues.–Sun. 1–4.*

A little farther, turn right onto Esplanaden and you'll come to
⑳ **Frihedsmuseet** (Liberty Museum), situated in Churchill Parken. It gives an evocative picture of the heroic Danish Resistance movement during World War II, which managed to save 7,000 Jews from the Nazis by hiding them in homes and hospitals, then smuggling them across to Sweden. *Esplanaden, tel. 33/13–77–14. Admission free. Open Sept. 16– April, Tues.–Sat. 11–3, Sun. 11–4; May–Sept. 15, Tues.–Sat. 10–4, Sun. 10–5.*

At the park's entrance stands the English church, St. Alban's,
㉑ and, in the center, the **Kastellet** (Citadel), with two rings of moats. This was the city's main fortress in the 18th century, but, in a grim reversal during World War II, the Germans used it as the focal point of their occupation of Denmark. *Admission free. Open 6 AM to sunset.*

Continue on to the Langelinie, which on Sunday is thronged
㉒ with promenading Danes, and at last to **The Little Mermaid** (*Den Lille Havrue*), the 1913 statue commemorating Hans Christian Andersen's lovelorn creation, and the subject of hundreds of travel posters.

Around the Strøget From Langelinie, take the train or bus from Østerport station back to the center. Walk north from the Strøget on Nørregade un-
㉓ til you reach **Vor Frue Kirke** (The Church of Our Lady), Copenhagen's cathedral since 1924. The site itself has been a place of worship since the 13th century, when Bishop Absalon built a chapel here. The spare neoclassical facade was a 19th-century revamp, repairing damage incurred during Nelson's famous bombing of the city in 1801. Inside you can see Thorvaldsen's marble sculptures of Christ and the Apostles and Moses and David in bronze. *Nørregade, Frue Plads, tel. 33/15– 10–78. Open Mon.–Sat. 9–5, Sun. noon–5. Closed during mass.*

24 Head north up Fjolstraede until you come to the main **university** building, built in the 19th century on the site of the medieval bishops' palace. Past the university, turn right onto **25** Krystalgade. On the left is the **synagogue,** designed by the famous contemporary architect Gustav Friedrich Hetsch. Hetsch drew on the Doric and Egyptian styles to create the arklike structure.

26 Just across Købmagergade is the **Runde Tårn,** a round tower built as an observatory in 1642 by Christian IV. It is said that Peter the Great of Russia drove a horse and carriage up the 600 feet of the inner staircase. You'll have to walk, but the view is worth it. *Købmagergade, tel. 33/93–66–60. Admission: 10 kr. adults, 4 kr. children. Open Dec.–Mar., daily 10–4; Apr.–May and Sept.–Oct., daily 10–5; June–Aug. 10–8.*

Turn right at Runde Tårn onto Landemærket, then left onto Åbenrå. If your appetite for museums is not yet sated, turn right out of Åbenrå until you reach Gothersgade, where another right, onto **27** Øster Voldgade, will bring you to **Rosenborg Slot.** This Renaissance castle—built by Renaissance man Christian IV—houses the Crown Jewels, as well as a collection of costumes and royal memorabilia. Don't miss Christian IV's pearl-studded saddle. *Øster Voldgade 4A, tel. 33/15–32–86. Admission: 30 kr. adults, 5 kr. children. Open Apr.–May, daily 11–3; June–Aug. daily 10–4; Sept.–Oct. daily 11–3; Nov.–Mar., Tues. and Fri. 11–2, Sun. 10–3.*

The palace is surrounded by gardens, and just across Øster Voldgade is **Botansk Have,** Copenhagen's 25 acres of botanical gardens, with a rather spectacular Palm House containing tropical and subtropical plants. There's also an observatory and a geological museum. *Admission free. Open May–Aug., daily 8:30–6; Sept.–Apr., daily 8:30–4. Palm House open daily 10–3.*

29 Leave the gardens through the north exit to get to the **Statens Museum for Kunst** (National Art Gallery), where the official doorman greets you wearing a uniform with buckled shoes and a cocked hat. The collection ranges from modern Danish art to works by Rubens, Dürer, and the Impressionists. Particularly fine are the museum's 20 Matisses. *Sólvgade 48–50, tel. 33/91–21–26. Admission free. Open Tues.–Sun. 10–4:30.*

Time Out The subterranean **cafeteria** in the museum makes an excellent place to stop for lunch or coffee. Art posters deck the walls, and a cheerful staff serves hearty lunches. *Inexpensive.*

30 An adjacent building houses the **Hirschprung Collection** of 19th-century Danish art. The cozy museum features works from the Golden Age, an era characterized by images of the play of light and water, reminiscent of so much of the Danish countryside. *Stockholmsgade 20, tel. 31/42–03–36. Admission free. Open Wed.–Sun. 1–4. Oct.–Apr. also open Wed. 7–10 PM.*

From Stockholmsgade, turn right onto Sølvgade and then left onto Øster Søgade, just before the bridge. Continue along the canal (the street name will change from Øster Søgade to Nørre Søgade to Vester Søgade) until you reach the head of the harbor. Walk straight ahead and turn left onto Vesterbrogade.

31 On the right lies Copenhagen's best-known attraction, **Tivoli.** In the 1840s, the Danish architect Georg Carstensen persuaded King Christian VIII that an amusement park was the perfect opiate of the masses, preaching that "when people amuse themselves, they forget politics." In the comparatively short season, from May to September, about 4 million people come through the gates. Tivoli is more sophisticated than a mere funfair: It boasts a pantomime theater and open-air stage; elegant restaurants; and numerous classical, jazz, and rock concerts. On weekends there are elaborate fireworks displays and maneuvers by the Tivoli Guard, a youth version of the Queen's Royal Guard. Try to see Tivoli at least once by night, when the trees are illuminated along with the Chinese Pagoda and the main fountain. *Admission: 31 kr. adults, 20 kr. children. Open Apr. 24–Sept. 15, daily 10 AM–midnight.*

At the southern end of the gardens, on Hans Christian Andersens Boulevard, is the **Ny Carlsberg Glyptotek** (New Carlsberg Picture Hall). This elaborate neoclassical building houses a collection of works by Gauguin, Degas, and the Impressionists, as well as Egyptian, Greek, Roman, and French sculpture. *Dantes Plads 7, tel. 33/91–10–65. Admission: 15 kr. adults, children free; adults free on Wed. and Sun. Open Sept.–Apr., Tues.–Sat. noon–3, Sun. 10–4; May–Aug., Tues.–Sun. 10–4.*

Tucked between St. Jorgens Lake and the main arteries of Vesterbrogade and Gammel Kongsvej is the new **Tycho Brahe Planetarium**. The modern cylindrical building is filled with astronomy exhibitions and an Omnimax Theater, which takes visitors on a visual journey up through space and down under the seas. *Gammel Kongsvej 10, 1610 Kbh V, tel. 33/12–12–24. Admission: 40 kr. for exhibition and theater, noon–5; 50 kr. for exhibition and theater, 6–10 PM; exhibition only, 10 kr. Reservations advised for theater. (According to planetarium officials, the movie is not suitable for children under 4.) Open daily 10:30–9.*

Shopping

Gift Ideas While Copenhagen is a mecca for shoppers in search of impeccable designs and top-notch quality, budget shoppers may find bargains elusive. Several ideas for inexpensive gifts include simple table decorations—a porcelain candle holder or ashtray or the long-lasting candles, often handmade, for which Scandinavia is famous. Denmark also produces tasteful reproductions of Viking ornaments and jewelry, in bronze as well as silver and gold.

Specialty Shops Synonymous with shopping are Strøget's pedestrian streets. For glass, try **Holmegaard** at Østergade. Just off the street is Pistolstræde, a typical old courtyard that's been lovingly restored and filled with intriguing boutiques. **PosterLand** is the home of the largest collection of art prints and posters in northern Europe. There are such specialists as **Royal Copenhagen Porcelain,** which has a small museum attached, as does **Georg Jensen,** one of Denmark's most famous silversmiths.

Off the eastern end of Strøget on Ny Østergade, the **Pewter Center** has a large pewterware collection, and on Gammel Strand there's another pewter designer, **Selangor Designer,** founded in 1885. Back along Strøget, **Birger Christensen** will offer you a glass of sherry while you look at the furs, unless you decide to take your patronage to their competition, **A. C. Bang. FONA** is the place to buy Bang and Olufsen stereo systems, so renowned that they are in the permanent design collection of New York's Museum of Modern Art.

Dining

Food remains one of the great pleasures of a stay in Copenhagen, a city with over 2,000 restaurants. Danes take their food seriously, and Danish food, however simple, is excellent, with an emphasis on fresh ingredients and careful presentation. Fish and meat are both of top quality in this farming and fishing country, and both are staple ingredients of the famous smørrebrød. Some smørrebrød are huge meals in themselves: Innocent snackers can find themselves faced with a dauntingly large (but nonetheless delicious) mound of fish or meat, slathered with pickle relish, all atop *rugbrød* (rye bread) and *franskbrød* (wheat bread). Another specialty is *wiener brød* (a Danish pastry), an original far superior to anything that dares call itself "Danish pastry" elsewhere.

All Scandinavian countries have versions of the cold table, but Danes claim that theirs, *det store kolde bord*, is the original and the best. It's a celebration meal; the setting of the long table is a work of art—often with paper sculpture and silver platters—and the food itself is a minor miracle of design and decoration.

In hotels and restaurants the cold table is served at lunch only, though you will find a more limited version at hotel breakfasts—a good bet for budget travelers because you can eat as much as you like.

Liquid refreshment is top-notch. Denmark boasts more than 50 varieties of beer made by as many breweries; the best-known come from Carlsberg and Tuborg. Those who like harder stuff should try *snaps*, the famous aquavit traditionally drunk with cold food. Do as the locals do, and knock it back after some herring. The Danes have a saying about the herring-snaps combo: "The fish should be swimming."

Mealtimes The Danes start work early, which means they generally eat lunch at noon. Evening meals are also eaten early, but visitors can be certain of being able to eat and drink until 10 or 11.

Dress The Danes are a fairly casual lot, and few restaurants require a jacket and tie. Even in the most chic establishments, the tone is elegantly casual.

Ratings Meal prices vary little between town and country. While approximate gradings are given below, remember that careful ordering can get you a Moderate meal at a Very Expensive restaurant. Prices are per person and include a first course, main course, and dessert, plus taxes and tip, but not wine. Best bets are indicated by a star ★.

Category	Cost
Very Expensive	over 330 kr.
Expensive	180–330 kr.
Moderate	100–185 kr.
Inexpensive	under 100 kr.

Very Expensive **Den Gyldne Fortun-Fiskkaelderen.** The lime-and-white color scheme and dark wooden benches lend Copenhagen's number-one seafood restaurant an air of minimalist chic, while the menu remains classic, with such elegant dishes as turbot in puff pastry with lobster sauce. *Ved Stannden 18, tel. 33/12–20–11. Reservations advised. AE, DC, MC, V. Closed for lunch on weekends.*

Kong Hans Kaelder. Chef Daniel Letz's French-inspired cooking is superb, while the setting is subterranean and mysterious, with whitewashed arching ceilings, candles, and wooden carvings. *Vingårdsstræde 6, tel. 33/11–68–68. Reservations advised. AE, DC, MC, V. Dinner only. Closed Sun. and mid-July–mid-Aug.*

Pakhuskælderen. Cozily situated in the basement of the Nyhavn 71 hotel, with old Pomeranian beams along the ceilings, this is principally a grill house, serving fish as well as meat dishes, both French and Danish style. Look for store kolde bord at lunchtime. *Nyhavn 71, tel. 33/11–85–85. Reservations required. AE, DC, MC, V.*

★ **Skt. Gertrude's Kloster.** Chef Even Nielsen prepares international cuisine in this 700-year-old cloister. You feast on fish and meat specialties by the light of 1,200 candles, among vaulted spiral stairways and ecclesiastical antiques. *Hauser Plads 32, tel. 33/14–66–30. Reservations required. AE, DC, MC, V. Dinner only.*

Expensive ★ **L'Alsace.** The paintings of Danish surrealist Wilhelm Freddie deck bright, white walls at L'Alsace, and the food matches the understated elegance of the surroundings. Talented chef Franz Stockhammer's French repertoire includes a delicious rendition of quail, as well as some superb fresh-fruit tarts and cakes for dessert. Ask for a seat with a view of the old courtyard on Pistolstraede. *Ny Østergade 9, tel. 33/14–57–43. Reservations advised. AE, DC, MC, V. Closed Sun.*

La Brasserie. This is the place where Copenhagen's see-and-be-seen set goes to eat. Diners enjoy French-inspired food in charming bistro surroundings, under a giant illuminated clock suspended from the ceiling. *Hotel D'Angleterre, Kongens Nytorv 34, tel. 33/32–01–22. Reservations advised. AE, DC, MC, V. Closed Sun.*

Els. When it opened in 1853, the intimate Els was the place to be seen before the theater, and the painted muses on the walls still watch diners rush to make an eight o'clock curtain. The antique wooden columns and furniture complement Chef Ole Mathiesen's nouvelle Danish/French menu. The menu changes daily and incorporates game, fish, and market-fresh produce. *Stora Strandstæde 3, tel. 33/14–13–41. Reservations advised. AE, DC, MC, V. Closed Dec. 24–25 and 31, Jan. 1.*

Gilleje. Dining at Gilleje is like being in a scene from a Robert Louis Stevenson novel, since this 113-year-old restaurant is decorated with artifacts from old sea expeditions. Under hanging tortoise shells, diners can feast on Danish and international cuisines. Highlights include whiskey steak flambé and Indonesian rijsttafel, which has been on the menu for nearly half a century. *Nyhavn 10, tel. 33/12–58–58. Reservations advised. AE, DC, MC, V. Closed Sun. and July.*

Moderate ★ **Copenhagen Corner.** Diners get a great view of the Rådhus Pladsen here, and terrific smørrebrød besides. Plants hang from the ceiling; waiters hustle platters of herring, steak, and other Danish/French dishes; and businessmen clink glasses. In summer you can eat outside. *Rådhus Pladsen, tel. 33/91–45–45. Reservations advised. AE, DC, MC, V. Closed Dec. 24.*

Havfruen. A life-size wooden mermaid swings langorously from the ceiling in this snug fish restaurant in Nyhavn. Copenhagen natives love the maritime-bistro ambience and the French-inspired fish specialties. *Nyhavn 39, tel. 33/11–11–38. Reservations advised. DC, MC, V. Closed Sun.*

★ **Ida Davidsen.** A Copenhagen institution, this world-renowned lunch place has become synonymous with smørrebrød. The 56-inch menu came into existence at the beginning of the century—Ida is the fourth generation in the sandwich business. The oven in the back smokes fish and meat, while out front, a buffet displays heartbreakingly beautiful sandwiches, piled high with caviar, salmon, smoked duck, and other elegant ingredients. *Skt. Kongensgade 70, tel. 33/91–36–55. Reservations advised. DC, MC, V. Lunch only. Closed weekends and July.*

Peder Oxe. Located in an 18th-century square in the old center of town, the Peder Oxe is classically elegant, with whitewashed walls, wooden floors, an open fireplace, and crisp damask tablecloths. It's usually crowded with diners from every walk of life. All main courses include a self-service salad bar. *Gråbrøde Torv 11, tel. 33/11–00–77. Reservations accepted. DC, MC, V.*

Inexpensive **Café Asbæk.** Attached to a modern art gallery, this little establishment makes creative use of fresh ingredients. The menu changes every day, while the art on the walls changes with every new exhibition. The artist showing in the gallery designs the tablecloths and napkins as well! Try the desserts, made on the premises. *Ny Adelgade 8, tel. 33/12–24–16. Reservations accepted. AE, DC, MC, V. Lunch only.*

Green's. A vegetarian buffet by day and a restaurant by night, Green's serves healthy food with much emphasis on grains, natural sweeteners, and fresh fruit and vegetables. It's frequented by chic bohemians who welcome the classical music and friendly service of the youthful staff. *Grønnegade 12–14, tel. 33/15–16–90. Reservations accepted. MC, V. Closed Sun.*

Krasnapolsky. It's near the university, and there's a brooding youth at every table. Despite the trendy trappings, the food is light and inventive—market-fresh produce is used religiously. Not as healthy as the quiches and sandwiches, but equally delicious, are the cakes and tarts, made in-house. *Vestergade 10, tel. 33/32–88–00. Reservations accepted. No credit cards.*

Lodging

Copenhagen is well served by a wide range of hotels. Steer clear of those in the red-light district behind the train station, but otherwise you can expect your accommodations to be clean, comfortable, and well run. Most Danish hotels include a substantial breakfast in the room rate, but this isn't always the case with foreign chains: Inquire when making reservations. During summer reservations are always recommended, but if you should arrive without one, try the booking service at the *Vaerelseavivisning kiosk* (Rooms Service booth) in the central station. This service will also locate rooms in private homes, with rates starting at about 140 kr. for a single. Young travelers should head for "Use It" (Huset) at Rådhusstraede 13 (tel. 33/15–65–18); after hours, they can check the bulletin board outside for suggestions for accommodations.

Hotels Luxury hotels offer rooms of a high standard, and in a manor-house hotel you may find yourself sleeping in a four-poster bed. Less expensive accommodations, however, are uniformly clean and comfortable.

Inns A cheaper and charming alternative to hotels are the old stage-coach kro inns scattered throughout Denmark. You can save money by investing in a book of Inn Checks, valid at 66 inns. Each check costs 325–425 kr. per person or 495 kr. per couple and includes one overnight stay in a double room with bath, breakfast included.

Youth Hostels The 100 youth hostels in Denmark are excellent, and they're open to everyone regardless of age. If you have an International Youth Hostels Association card (obtainable before you leave home), the average rate is 60 kr. Without the card, there's a surcharge of 22 kr.

Rentals Many Danes rent out their summer homes, and a stay in one of these is another good way to see the countryside on your own terms. A simple house with room for four will cost from 1,000 kr. per week. Contact the Danish Tourist Board for details.

Ratings Prices are for two people in a double room and include service and taxes and usually breakfast. Best bets are indicated by a star ★.

Category	Cost
Very Expensive	over 1,100 kr.
Expensive	800–1,100 kr.
Moderate	670–800 kr.
Inexpensive	under 670 kr.

Very Expensive **D'Angleterre.** Clint Eastwood and Bruce Springsteen stay
★ here, as do NATO generals and various heads of state. Built in 1755, the place has recently undergone a $10 million renovation, but it retains an Old World, old-money aura. The rooms are done in pinks and blues, with overstuffed chairs and antique escritoires and armoires. There's a liberal use of brass, mahogany, and marble in the bathrooms, all of which are equipped with telephones. *Kongens Nytorv 34, tel. 33/12–00–95. 139 rooms with bath. Facilities: 2 restaurants, bar, barber, beauty salon. AE, DC, MC, V.*

Nyhavn 71. This cozy hotel started life in 1804 as a humble harbor warehouse, though its subsequent metamorphosis has won several design awards. Ask for a room overlooking the harbor—the quaint, porthole-style windows add to the charm. *Nyhavn 71, tel. 33/11–85–85. 82 rooms with bath. Facilities: restaurant, bar. AE, DC, MC, V.*

SAS Scandinavia. A modern, cloud-scraping tower, the Scandinavia is the city's tallest building. It's set midway between the airport and downtown, facing the old city moats. The prevalent atmosphere is of efficiency and functionality, tempered with expensive plush. *Amager Blvd. 70, tel. 33/11–23–24. 542 rooms with bath. Facilities: sauna, pool, restaurant, bar, coffee shop. AE, DC, MC, V.*

Expensive **Neptun.** Recently renovated and expanded, the centrally situated Neptun has been in business for nearly 150 years and shows no signs of flagging. The guest rooms are decorated with blond wood and are usually reserved by American visitors well in advance. *Skt. Annæ Plads 18, tel. 33/13-89-00. 192 rooms, 8 apartments, all with bath. Facilities: restaurant, café, conference rooms. AE, DC, MC, V. Closed Dec. 24-Jan. 2.*

★ **Savoy.** Tucked behind clothing stores on a busy shopping street, the Savoy is a hidden treasure, an oasis of peace and fin-de-siècle charm. The recently renovated rooms are decorated in cool blues and light woods, with Scandinavian-designed furniture and marble bathrooms. *Vesterbrogade 34, tel. 31/31-40-73. 65 rooms. Facilities: restaurant. AE, DC, MC, V.*

Webers. Webers is a modern hotel housed in a century-old building. Decorators have made liberal use of pastel tones and understated prints. Light sleepers should try for a room at the back, preferably overlooking the courtyard and its fountain. *Vesterbrogade 11b, tel. 31/31-14-32. 80 rooms with bath. Facilities: restaurant (breakfast only), lounge, bar, solarium. AE, DC, MC, V.*

Moderate **Ascot.** A charming old building in the city's downtown area, the Ascot features an elegant wrought-iron staircase and an excellent breakfast buffet. The rooms have cheerful blue bedspreads and cozy bathrooms. Many have been recently remodeled; a few have kitchenettes. *Studiestræde 57, tel. 33/12-60-00. 105 rooms, 10 apartments, all with bath. Facilities: restaurant (breakfast only), bar. AE, DC, MC, V.*

Copenhagen Admiral. A converted 18th-century granary, the Admiral has a massive and imposing exterior. Inside, sturdy wooden beams harmonize with an ultramodern decor. A few duplex suites are in the Expensive category. *Toldbrogade 24-28, tel. 33/11-82-82. 366 rooms with bath. Facilities: restaurant, bar, café, shop, sauna. AE, MC, V.*

Excelsior. Housed in a circa-1890 building, this hotel was renovated in 1989. The reception room, decorated in bright primary colors, resembles a postmodern playroom, but the bedrooms are slightly subtler, done in bold blue and white, with modern murals on the walls. The tranquil deck-garden in the back is lovely. *Colbjørnsgade 4, tel. 31/24-50-85. 59 rooms, 42 with bath. Facilities: restaurant (breakfast only), bar. AE, DC, MC, V. Closed two weeks at Christmas.*

Triton. Streamlined and modern, the Triton has a cosmopolitan clientele and a central location. The large rooms, in blond wood and warm tones, are equipped with every modern convenience, and many of the bathrooms have been recently updated with state-of-the-art fixtures. The buffet breakfast is exceptionally generous, as is the friendly staff. *Helgolandsgade 7-11, tel. 31/31-32-66. 123 rooms with bath. Facilities: restaurant (breakfast only), bar. AE, DC, MC, V.*

Inexpensive **Skovshoved.** A charming hotel about 8 kilometers (5 miles) from the center of town, the Skovshoved has as neighbors a few old fishing cottages beside the yacht harbor. Licensed since 1660, it has retained its Old World charm, though it is fully modernized. Individual rooms vary from spacious ones overlooking the sea to smaller rooms overlooking the courtyard. The restaurant provides gourmet dishes but ranks in the Expensive category. *Strandvejen 267, Charlottenlund, tel. 31/64-00-28. 20 rooms with bath. Facilities: conference room. AE, DC, MC, V.*

Viking. A comfortable, century-old former mansion close to Amalienborg Castle, Nyhavn, and the Little Mermaid, the Vi-

king is convenient to most sights and public transportation.
The rooms are surprisingly spacious. *Bredgade 65, tel. 33/12–
45–50. 90 rooms, 19 with bath. Facilities: restaurant (breakfast
only). AE, DC, MC, V.*

The Arts

Copenhagen This Week has good information on musical and
theatrical events, as well as on films and exhibitions. Concert
and festival information is available from the **Dansk Musik Information Center (DMIC,** Vimmelskaftet 48, tel. 33/11–20–86).
Copenhagen's main theater and concert season runs from September through May, and tickets can be obtained either directly from theaters and concert halls or from ticket agencies; ask
your hotel concierge for advice.

Music   **Tivoli Concert Hall** (Vesterbrogade 3, tel. 33/15–10–12), home
of the Zealand Symphony Orchestra, offers more than 150 concerts (many free of charge) each summer, featuring a host of
Danish and foreign soloists, conductors, and orchestras.

Theater, Opera,   The **Royal Theater** (Kongens Nytorv, tel. 33/14–10–02) regu-
and Ballet   larly holds performances alternating among theater, ballet,
and opera. For English-language theater, attend a performance at the **Mermaid Theater** (27 Skt. Peder Stræde, tel. 33/
11–43–03).

Film   Copenhagen natives are avid movie buffs, and since the Danes
rarely dub films or television imports, you can often see original American and British movies and TV shows.

Nightlife

Many of the city's restaurants, cafés, bars, and clubs stay open
after midnight, some as late as 5 AM. Copenhagen is famous for
jazz, but you'll find night spots catering to musical tastes ranging from bop to ballroom music. Younger tourists should make
for the **Minefield,** the district around the Nikolaj Kirke, which
has scores of trendy discos and dance spots, with admission
only the price of a beer. **Privé** (Ny Østergade 14) and **U-Matic**
(Vestergade 10) are particularly popular with the young set.

A few streets behind the railway station is Copenhagen's red-
light district, where sex shops share space with Indian gro-
cers. While the area is fairly well lighted and lively, women may
feel uncomfortable going there alone at night.

Nightclubs   Some of the most exclusive nightclubs are in the biggest hotels:
Fellini's in the SAS Royal (Hammerichsgade 1, tel. 33/14–14–
12), **After Eight** at SAS Scandinavia (Amager Blvd. 70, tel. 33/
11–23–24), and the **Penthouse** at the Sheraton (Vester Søgade
6, tel. 33/14–35–35).

Jazz   Copenhagen has a worldwide reputation for sophisticated jazz
clubs. These are a few of the best: **De Tre Musketerer** (Nikolaj
Plads 25); **Jazzhus Monmartre** (Nørregade 41), widely held to
be one of the best on the Continent; **Jazzhus Slukefter** (Tivoli);
La Fontaine (Kompagnistræde 11); and **Ben Webster's** (Vestergade 7).

9   Dublin

Arriving and Departing

By Plane All flights arrive at Dublin's Collinstown Airport, 10 kilometers (6 miles) north of town. For information on arrival and departure times, call individual airlines.

Between the Airport and Downtown Buses leave every 20 minutes from outside the Arrivals door for the central bus station in downtown Dublin. The ride takes about 30 minutes, depending on the traffic, and the fare is IR£2.50. A taxi ride into town will cost from IR£5 to IR£10, depending on the location of your hotel.

By Train There are three main stations. Heuston Station (at Kingsbridge) is the departure point for the south and southwest; Connolly Station (at Amiens Street), for Belfast, the east coast, and the west; Pearse Station (on Westland Row), for Bray and connections via Dun Laoghaire to the Liverpool/Holyhead ferries. Tel. 01/366222 for information.

By Bus The central bus station, Busaras, is at Store Street near the Custom House. Some buses terminate near Connolly Bridge. Tel. 01/734222 for information on city services (Dublin Bus); tel. 01/366111 for express buses and provincial services (Bus Eireann).

By Car The main access route from the north is N1; from the west, N4; from the south and southwest, N7; from the east coast, N11. On all routes there are clearly marked signs indicating the center of the city: "An Lar."

Getting Around

Dublin is small as capital cities go—the downtown area is positively compact—and the best way to see the city and soak in the full flavor is on foot.

By Train An electric train commuter service, DART (Dublin Area Rapid Transport), serves the suburbs out to Howth, on the north side of the city, and to Bray, County Wicklow, on the south side. Fares are about the same as for buses. Street-direction signs to DART stations read Staisiun/Station. The **Irish Rail** office is at 35 Lower Abbey Street; for rail inquiries, tel. 01/366222.

By Bus Most city buses originate in or pass through the area of O'Connell Street and O'Connell Bridge. If the destination board indicates "An Lar," that means that the bus is going to the city's central area. Timetables (45p) are available from the **Dublin Bus** office (59 Upper O'Connell St., tel. 01/720000) and give details of all routes, times of operation, and price codes. The minimum fare is 45p.

By Taxi Taxis do not cruise, but are located beside the central bus station, at train stations, at O'Connell Bridge, at St. Stephen's Green, and near major hotels. They are not of a uniform type or color. Make sure the meter is on. The initial charge is IR£2; the fare is displayed in the cab. A one-mile trip in city traffic costs about IR£3.50.

Important Addresses and Numbers

Tourist Information There is a tourist information office in the entrance hall of the **Irish Tourist Board** headquarters (Baggot Street Bridge, tel. 01/765871); open weekdays 9–5. More conveniently located is the office at 14 Upper O'Connell St., tel. 01/747733; open week-days 9–5:30, Saturday 9–1. There is also an office at the air-port, tel. 01/376387. From mid-June to September, there is an office at the Ferryport, Dun Laoghaire, tel. 01/806984.

Embassies **U.S.** (42 Elgin Rd., Ballsbridge, tel. 01/688–8777). **Canadian** (65 St. Stephen's Green, tel. 01/781988). **U.K.** (33 Merrion Rd., tel. 01/695211).

Emergencies **Police** (tel. 999), **Ambulance** (tel. 999), **Doctor** (tel. 01/537951 or 01/767273), **Dentist** (tel. 01/679–4311), **Pharmacy:** Hamilton Long (5 Upper O'Connell St., tel. 01/748456).

Travel Agencies **American Express** (116 Grafton St., tel. 01/772874). **Thomas Cook** (118 Grafton St., tel. 01/771721).

Guided Tours

Orientation Tours Both **Bus Eireann** (tel. 01/366111) and **Gray Line Sightseeing** (tel. 01/619666) offer bus tours of Dublin and its surrounding areas. Both also offer three- and four-hour tours of the main sights in the city center. During the summer **Dublin Bus** (tel. 01/734222) has a daily city-center tour using open-top buses in fine weather.

Special-Interest **Bus Eireann** has a "Traditional Irish Music Night" tour. **Ele-**
Tours **gant Ireland** (tel. 01/751665) organizes tours for groups inter-ested in architecture and the fine arts; these include visits with the owners of some of Ireland's stately homes and castles.

Walking Tours **Tour Guides Ireland** (tel. 01/794291) offers a selection of walk-ing tours, including "Literary Dublin," "Georgian Dublin," and "Pub Tours." The **Irish Tourist Board** has a "Tourist Trail" walk, which takes in the main sites of central Dublin and can be completed in about three hours. An accompanying booklet (75p) can be obtained from the office at 14 Upper O'Connell Street. Author and historian Eamonn MacThomas offers en-tertaining tours of Literary, Georgian, and Old Dublin; tours start at 2 PM on weekends at the Molly Malone statue in Grafton Street. Confirm the schedule with the Irish Tourist Board (tel. 01/747733).

Excursions **Bus Eireann** (tel. 01/366111) and **Gray Line Sightseeing** (tel. 01/) offer day-long tours into the surrounding countryside and longer tours elsewhere; price includes accommodations, break-fast, and admission costs. **CIE Tours International** offers vaca-tions lasting from one to 10 days that include touring by train or bus, accommodations, and main meals. Costs range from around IR£213 (IR£315, including round-trip airfare from Lon-don) to IR£345 (IR£484 from London) for an eight-day tour in July and August.

Exploring Dublin

Numbers in the margin correspond to points of interest on the Dublin map.

Dublin is a small city with a population of just over 1 million. For all that, it has a distinctly cosmopolitan air, one that com-plements happily the individuality of the city and the courtesy and friendliness of its inhabitants. Originally a Viking settle-ment, Dublin is situated on the banks of the river Liffey. The Liffey divides the city north and south, with the more lively and fashionable spots, such as the Grafton Street shopping area, to be found on the south side. Most of the city's historically interesting buildings date from the 18th century and, although many of its finer Georgian buildings disappeared in the overenthusiastic redevelopment of the '70s, enough remain, mainly south of the river, to recall the elegant Dublin of the past. The slums romanticized by writers Sean O'Casey and Brendan Behan have virtually been eradicated, but literary Dublin can still be recaptured by those who want to follow the footsteps of Leopold Bloom's progress, as described in James Joyce's *Ulysses.* And Trinity College, alma mater of Oliver Goldsmith, Jonathan Swift, and Samuel Beckett, among others, still provides a haven of tranquillity.

Dubliners are a talkative, self-confident people, eager to have visitors enjoy the pleasures of their city. You can meet a lively cross section of people in the city's numerous bars, probably the best places to sample the famous wit of the only city to have produced three winners of the Nobel Prize for Literature: William Butler Yeats, George Bernard Shaw, and Samuel Beckett.

O'Connell Street Begin your tour of Dublin at **O'Connell Bridge,** the city's most central landmark. Look closely and you will notice a strange ❶ feature: The bridge is wider than it is long. The north side of O'Connell Bridge is dominated by an elaborate memorial to Daniel O'Connell, "The Liberator," erected as a tribute to the great 19th-century orator's achievement in securing Catholic Emancipation in 1829. Today **O'Connell Street** is the city's main shopping area, though it seems decidedly parochial to anyone accustomed to Fifth Avenue or Rodeo Drive. Turn left just before the General Post Office and take a look at Henry Street. This pedestrians-only shopping area leads to the colorful **Moore Street Market,** where street vendors recall their most famous ancestor, Molly Malone, by singing their wares—mainly flowers—in the traditional Dublin style.

❷ The **General Post Office,** known as the GPO, occupies a special place in Irish history. It was from the portico of its handsome classical facade that Padraig Pearse read the Proclamation of the Republic on Easter Monday, 1916. You can still see the scars of bullets on its pillars from the fighting that ensued. The GPO remains the focal point for political rallies and demonstrations even today and is used as a viewing stand for VIPs during the annual St. Patrick's Day Parade.

❸ **The Gresham Hotel,** opposite the GPO, has played a part in Dublin's history since 1817, although, along with the entire O'Connell Street area, it is less fashionable now than it was during the last century. Just below the Gresham is the Irish Tourist Board information office; drop in for a free street map, shopping guides, and information on all aspects of Dublin tourism. Opposite is the main office of Bus Eireann, which can supply bus timetables and information on excursions.

❹ At the top of O'Connell Street is the **Rotunda,** the first maternity hospital in Europe, opened in 1755. Not much remains of the once-elegant Rotunda Assembly Rooms, a famous haunt of fashionable Dubliners until the middle of the last century. The **Gate Theater,** housed in an extension of the Rotunda Assembly Rooms, however, continues to attract crowds to its fine repertoire of classic Irish and European drama. The theater was founded by the late Micheál MacLiammoir in 1928.

⑤ Beyond the Rotunda, you will have a fine vista of **Parnell Square,** one of Dublin's earliest Georgian squares. You will notice immediately that the first-floor windows of these elegant brick-face buildings are much larger than the others and that it is easy to look in from street level. This is more than simply the result of the architect's desire to achieve perfect proportions on the facades: These rooms were designed as reception rooms, and fashionable hostesses liked passersby to be able to peer in and admire the distinguished guests at their luxurious, candle-lit receptions.

⑥ **Charlemont House,** whose impressive Palladian facade dominates the top of Parnell Square, now houses the **Hugh Lane Municipal Gallery of Modern Art.** Sir Hugh Lane, a nephew of Lady Gregory, who was Yeats's curious, high-minded aristocratic patron, was a keen collector of Impressionist paintings. The gallery also contains some interesting works by Irish artists, including Yeats's brother Jack. *Parnell Sq. Admission free. Open Tues.–Sat. 9:30–6, Sun. 11–5.*

The area surrounding Parnell Square is rich in literary associations and features in the work of Sean O'Casey, James Joyce, and Brendan Behan. Only devout literary pilgrims will care for the detour to Mountjoy Square, since this run-down area is in the middle of a rebuilding program.

⑦ Return to O'Connell Street, where a sign on the left will lead you to **St. Mary's Pro Cathedral,** the main Catholic church of Dublin. Try to catch the famous Palestrina Choir on Sunday at 11 AM. John McCormack is one of many famous voices to have **⑧** sung with this exquisite ensemble. The **Abbey Theatre,** a brick building dating from 1966, was given a much-needed new facade in 1991. It has some noteworthy portraits and mementos in the foyer. Seats are usually available at about IR£8.50, and with luck you may just have a wonderful evening. The luck element, unfortunately, must be stressed, since the Abbey has had both financial and artistic problems lately.

Time Out On Westmoreland Street is **Bewley's Coffee House** (there's another one nearby on Grafton Street), an institution that has been supplying Dubliners with coffee and buns since 1842. The aroma of coffee is irresistible, and the dark interior, with marble-top tables, original wood fittings, and stained-glass windows, evokes a more leisurely Dublin of the past. *12 Westmoreland St. and 78 Grafton St. Open Mon.–Sat. 9–5:30.*

Trinity and It is only a short walk across O'Connell Bridge to **Parliament**
Stephen's Green **House.** Today this stately early 18th-century building is no
⑨ more than a branch of the Bank of Ireland; originally, however, it housed the Irish Parliament. The original House of Lords, with its fine coffered ceiling and 1,233-piece Waterford glass chandelier, is open to the public during banking hours (weekdays 10–12:30 and 1:30–3). It's also worth taking a look at the main banking hall, whose judicial character—it was previously the Court of Requests—has been sensitively maintained.

⑩ Across the road is the facade of **Trinity College,** whose memorably atmospheric campus is a must for every visitor. Trinity College, Dublin (familiarly known as TCD) was founded by Elizabeth I in 1591 and offered a free education to Catholics—provided that they accepted the Protestant faith. As a legacy of this condition, right up until 1966, Catholics who wished to

172

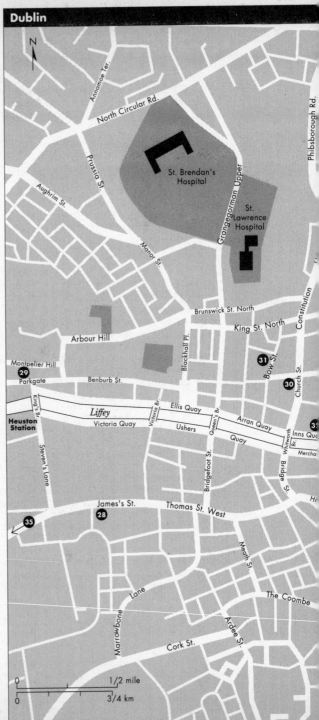

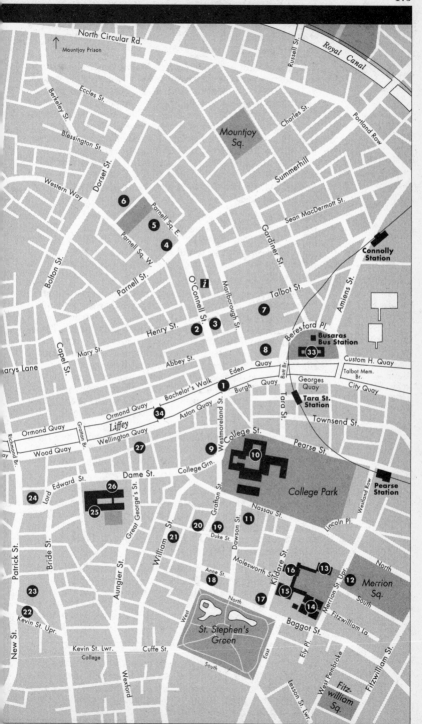

study at Trinity had to obtain a dispensation from their bishop or face excommunication. Today more than 70% of Trinity's students are Catholics, a clear indication of how far away those days seem to today's generation.

The facade, built between 1755 and 1759, consists of a magnificent portico with Corinthian columns. The design is repeated on the interior, so the view from outside the gates and from the quadrangle inside is the same. On the sweeping lawn in front of the facade are statues of two of the university's illustrious alumni—statesman Edward Burke and poet Oliver Goldsmith. Other famous students include the philosopher George Berkeley, who gave his name to the San Francisco area campus of the University of California; Jonathan Swift; Thomas Moore; Oscar Wilde; John Millington Synge; Henry Grattan; Wolfe Tone; Robert Emmet; Bram Stoker; Edward Carson; Douglas Hyde; and Samuel Beckett.

The 18th-century building on the left, just inside the entrance, is the chapel. There's an identical building opposite, the Examination Hall. The oldest buildings are the library in the far right-hand corner and a row of redbrick buildings known as the Rubrics, which contain student apartments; both date from 1712.

Ireland's largest collection of books and manuscripts is housed in **Trinity College Library.** There are more than 2½ million volumes gathering dust here; about half a mile of new shelving has to be added every year to keep pace with acquisitions. The library is entered through the library shop. Its principal treasure is the **Book of Kells,** a beautifully illuminated manuscript of the Gospels dating from the 8th century. Because of the beauty and the fame of the Book of Kells, at peak hours you may have to wait in line to enter the library; it's less busy early in the day. Apart from the many treasures it contains, the aptly named Long Room is impressive in itself, stretching for 65 meters (209 feet). Originally it had a flat plaster ceiling, but the perennial need for more shelving resulted in a decision to raise the level of the roof and add the barrel-vaulted ceiling and the gallery bookcases. *Admission: IR£1.50. Open weekdays 9:30–4:45, Sat. 9:30–12:45.*

A breath of fresh air will be welcome after the library, so, when you're done admiring the award-winning modern architecture of the New Library and the Arts Building, pass through the gate to the sports grounds—rugby fields on your left, cricket on your right. Leave Trinity by the Lincoln Place Gate—a handy "back door."

Shoppers will find a detour along Nassau Street in order here. As well as being well endowed with bookstores, it contains the **⑪ Kilkenny Design Workshops,** which, besides selling the best in contemporary Irish design for the home, also holds regular exhibits of exciting new work by Irish craftsmen. *Open Mon.–Sat. 9–5.*

Time Out The **Kilkenny Kitchen,** a self-service restaurant on the first floor of the Kilkenny Design Workshops, overlooking the playing fields of Trinity, is an excellent spot for a quick, inexpensive lunch in modern, design-conscious surroundings. The emphasis is on natural fresh foods and home baking. *Nassau St. Open Mon.–Sat. 9–5.*

12 Nassau Street will lead you into **Merrion Square,** past a distinctive corner house that was the home of Oscar Wilde's parents. Merrion Square is one of the most pleasant in Dublin. Its flower gardens are well worth a visit in the summer months. Note the brightly colored front doors and the intricate fan lights above them—a distinctive feature of Dublin's domestic architecture.

13 The **National Gallery** is the first in a series of important buildings on the west side of the square. It is one of Europe's most agreeable and compact galleries, with more than 2,000 works on view, including a major collection of Irish landscape painting, 17th-century French works, paintings from the Italian and Spanish schools, and a collection of Dutch masters. *Merrion Sq. Admission free. Open weekdays 10–5, Sat. 10–1, Sun. 2–5.*

14 Next door is **Leinster House,** seat of the Irish Parliament. This imposing 18th-century building has two facades: Its Merrion Square facade is designed in the style of a country house, while the other facade, in Kildare Street, is in the style of a town house. Visitors may be shown the house when the Dail (pronounced "Doyle"), the Irish Parliament, is not in session.

Time Out A half-block detour to your left, between Merrion Square and Stephen's Green, will bring you to the door of **Doheny & Nesbitt's,** an old Victorian-style bar whose traditional "snugs"—individual wood-paneled booths—are popular any time. Usually noisy and smoky, but always friendly, it is one of the few authentic pubs left in the city.

Stephen's Green, as it is always called by Dubliners, suffered more from the planning blight of the philistine '60s than did its neighbor, Merrion Square. An exception is the magnificent **Shelbourne Hotel,** which dominates the north side of the green. It is still as fashionable—and as expensive—as ever.

Time Out Budget-conscious visitors should put on their finery and try afternoon tea in the elegant splendor of the Shelbourne's **Lord Mayor's Room.** You can experience its old-fashioned luxury for around IR£7.50 (including sandwiches and cakes) per head.

Around the corner on Kildare Street, the town-house facade
15 of Leinster House is flanked by the **National Museum** and the
16 **National Library,** each featuring a massive colonnaded rotunda entrance built in 1890. The museum (Admission: free. Open Tues.–Sat. 10–5, Sun. 2–5) houses a remarkable collection of Irish treasures from 6000 BC to the present, including the Tara Brooch, the Ardagh Chalice, and the Cross of Cong. Every major figure in modern Irish literature, from James Joyce onward, studied in the National Library at some point. In addition to a comprehensive collection of Irish authors, it contains extensive newspaper archives. *Kildare St. Admission free, except for certain exhibits. Open Mon.–Thurs. 10–10, Fri. 10–5, Sat. 10–1.*

17 The **Genealogical Office**—the starting point for ancestor-tracing—also incorporates the **Heraldic Museum,** which features displays of flags, coins, stamps, silver, and family crests that highlight the uses and development of heraldry in Ireland. *2 Kildare St. Genealogical Office. Open weekdays 10–5. Heraldic Museum. Admission free. Open weekdays 10–12:30 and 2:30–4. Guided tours Mar.–Oct., cost IR£1.*

(18) The **Royal Irish Academy,** on Dawson Street, is the country's leading learned society; it has many important manuscripts in its unmodernized 18th-century library (open Mon.–Fri. 9:30–5:15). Just below the academy is **Mansion House,** the official residence of the Lord Mayor of Dublin. Its Round Room was the location of the first assembly of the Dail Eireann—the Irish Parliament—in January 1919. It is now used mainly for exhibitions.

(19) **Grafton Street,** which runs between Stephen's Green and Trinity College, is a magnet for shoppers. Check out **Brown Thomas,** Ireland's most elegant and old-fashioned department store; it has an extremely good selection of sporting goods and Waterford crystal—an odd combination. Many of the more stylish boutiques are just off the main pedestrians-only areas, so be **(20)** sure to poke around likely corners. Don't miss the **Powerscourt Town House,** an imaginative shopping arcade installed in and around the covered courtyard of an impressive 18th-century **(21)** building. Nearby is the **Civic Museum,** which contains drawings, models, maps of Dublin, and other civic memorabilia. *58 S. William St. Admission free. Open Tues.–Sat. 10–6, Sun. 11–4.*

(22) A short walk from Stephen's Green will bring you to one of the smaller and more unusual gems of old Dublin, **Archbishop Marsh's Library.** It was built in 1701, and access is through a tiny but charming cottage garden. Its interior has been unchanged for more than 300 years and still contains "cages" into which scholars who wanted to peruse rare books were locked. (The cages were to discourage students who, often impecunious, may have been tempted to make the books their own.) *St. Patrick's Close. Open Wed.–Fri. 10:30–12:30 and 2–4, Mon. 2–4, Sat. 10:30–12:30.*

(23) Opposite, on Patrick Street, is **St. Patrick's Cathedral.** Legend has it that St. Patrick baptized many converts at a well on the site of the cathedral in the 5th century. The building dates from 1190 and is mainly early English in style. At 93 meters (300 feet), it is the longest church in the country. Its history has not always been happy. In the 17th century, Oliver Cromwell, dour ruler of England and no friend of the Irish, had his troops stable their horses in the cathedral. It wasn't until the 19th century that restoration work to repair the damage was put in hand. St. Patrick's is the national cathedral of the Protestant Church of Ireland and has had many illustrious deans. The most famous was Jonathan Swift, author of *Gulliver's Travels,* who held office from 1713 to 1745. Swift's tomb is in the south aisle, and Dean Swift's corner at the top of the north transept contains his pulpit, his writing table and chair, his portrait, and his death mask. Memorials to many other celebrated figures from Ireland's past line the walls of St. Patrick's.

(24) St. Patrick's originally stood outside the walls of Dublin. Its close neighbor, **Christ Church Cathedral** (Christ Church Rd.), on the other hand, stood just within the walls and belonged to the See of Dublin. It is for this reason that the city has two cathedrals so close to each other. Christ Church was founded in 1172 by Strongbow, a Norman baron and conqueror of Dublin for the English crown, and it took 50 years to build. Strongbow himself is buried in the cathedral beneath an impressive effigy. The vast and sturdy **crypt** is Dublin's oldest surviving structure and should not be missed.

25 Signs in the Christ Church area will lead you to **Dublin Castle.** Guided tours of the lavishly furnished state apartments are offered every half hour and provide one of the most enjoyable sightseeing experiences in town. Only fragments of the original 13th-century building survive; the elegant castle you see today is essentially an 18th-century building. The state apartments were formerly the residence of the English viceroys—the monarch's representative in Ireland—and are now used by the president of Ireland to entertain visiting heads of state. The state apartments are closed when in official use, so phone first to check. *Off Lord Edward St., tel. 01/777129. Admission: IR£2.50. Open weekdays 10–12:15 and 2–5, weekends 2–5.*

26 Step into the **City Hall** on Dame Street to admire the combination of grand classical ornament and understated Georgian simplicity in its circular main hall. It also contains a good example of the kind of gently curving Georgian staircase that is a typical feature of most large town houses in Dublin.

Time Out A mosaic stag's head in the pavement of Dame Street marks the entrance to a narrow alley and a beautiful pub, **The Stag's Head** (1 Dame Court), dating from the early 19th century. Amid tall mirrors, stained-glass skylights, and mounted stags' heads, of course, you can enjoy a typical selection of lunchtime pub grub—smoked salmon sandwiches, hot meat dishes—and a pint of anything.

27 Between Dame Street and the river Liffey is a new semi-pedestrianized area known as **Temple Bar,** which should interest anyone who wants to discover "young Dublin." The area is chock-full of small, imaginative shops; innovative art galleries; and inexpensive restaurants.

28 The **Guinness Brewery,** founded by Arthur Guinness in 1759, dominates the area to the west of Christ Church, covering 60 acres. Guinness is proud of its brewery and invites visitors to attend a 30-minute film shown in a converted hops store next door to the brewery itself. After the film, you can sample the famous black beverage. *Guinness Museum and Visitors' Center, James's St. Admission free. Open weekdays 10–3.*

Phoenix Park and the Liffey

29 Across the Liffey is **Phoenix Park,** 7,122 square kilometers (1,760 acres) of green open space. Though the park is open to all, it has only two residents: the president of Ireland and the American ambassador. The park is dominated by a 64 meter-high (205-foot) obelisk, a tribute to the first duke of Wellington. Sunday is the best time to visit: A large open-air market is held from noon on the racecourse, while elsewhere games of cricket, soccer, polo, baseball, hurling—a combination of lacrosse, baseball, and field hockey—or Irish football will be in progress.

Returning to the city's central area along the north bank of the Liffey, you pass through a fairly run-down section that's scheduled for major redevelopment. A diversion up Church Street to **St. Michan's** will be relished by those with a macabre turn of mind. Open coffins in the vaults beneath the church reveal mummified bodies, some more than 900 years old. The sexton, who can be found at the church gate on weekdays, will guide you around the church and crypt.

③① **Irish Whiskey Corner** is just behind St. Michan's. A 90-year-old warehouse has been converted into a museum to introduce visitors to the pleasures of Irish whiskey. There's an audiovisual show and free tasting. Reservations are necessary. *Bow St., tel. 01/725566. Admission: IR£2.*

The Liffey has two of Dublin's most famous landmarks, both of them the work of 18th-century architect James Gandon and **③②** both among the city's finest buildings. The first is the **Four Courts,** surmounted by a massive copper-covered dome, giving it a distinctive profile. It is the seat of the High Court of Justice of Ireland. The building was completed between 1786 and 1802, then gutted in the Civil War of the '20s; it has since been painstakingly restored. You will recognize the same architect's hand **③③** in the **Custom House,** farther down the Liffey. Its graceful dome rises above a central portico, itself linked by arcades to the pavilions at either end. Behind this useful and elegant landmark is an altogether more workaday structure, the central bus station, known as Busaras.

Midway between Gandon's two masterpieces is the Metal **③④** Bridge, otherwise known as the **Halfpenny Bridge,** so called because, until early in this century, a toll of a half-penny was charged to cross it. The poet W. B. Yeats was one among many Dubliners who found this too high a price to pay—more a matter of principle than of finance—and so made the detour via O'Connell Bridge. Today no such high-minded concern need prevent you from marching out to the middle of the bridge to admire the view up and down the Liffey as it wends its way through the city.

③⑤ The **Royal Hospital Kilmainham** is a short ride by taxi or bus from the center; it's well worth the trip. The hospital is considered the most important 17th-century building in Ireland and has recently been renovated. It was completed in 1684 as a hospice—the original meaning of the term "hospital"—for veteran soldiers. Note especially the chapel with its magnificent Baroque ceiling. It also houses the **Irish Museum of Modern Art,** which opened in 1991. Parts of the old building, used as a national cultural center, are occasionally closed to the public. *District of Kilmainham, tel. 01/718666. Guided tours: Sun. noon–5 and holidays 2–5; cost £2. Exhibitions: open Tues.–Sat. 2–5.*

Devotees of James Joyce may wish to take the DART train south to **Sandycove,** about 8 kilometers (5 miles) out of the city center. It was here, in a Martello tower (a circular fortification built by the British as a defense against possible invasion by Napoleon at the beginning of the 19th century), that the maverick Irish genius lived for some months in 1904. It now houses the **Joyce Museum.** *Sandycove Coast. Admission: IR£1.20 adults, 60p children. Open Apr.–Oct., Mon.–Sat. 10–1 and 2–5, Sun. 2:30–6. Also by appointment, tel. 01/808571.*

Shopping

Although the rest of the country is well supplied with crafts shops, Dublin is the place to seek out more specialized items—antiques, traditional sportswear, haute couture, designer ceramics, books and prints, silverware and jewelry, and designer handknits.

Shopping Districts The most sophisticated shopping area is around **Grafton Street:** Its delis stock Irish whiskey marmalade, Irish lakeside wholegrain mustard, whole handmade cheeses, and sides of smoked salmon or trout. The new **St. Stephen's Green Center** contains 70 stores, large and small, in a vast Moorish-style glass-roof building on the Grafton Street corner. **Molesworth** and **Dawson Streets** are the places to browse for antiques; **Nassau** and **Dawson Streets,** for books; the smaller cross side streets for jewelry, art galleries, and old prints.

Department Stores The shops north of the river tend to be less expensive and less design-conscious; chain stores and lackluster department stores make up the bulk of them. The **ILAC Shopping Center,** on Henry Street, is worth a look, however. **Switzers** and **Brown Thomas** are Grafton Street's main department stores; the latter is Dublin's most elegantly decorated department store, with many international fashion labels on sale. **Arnotts,** on Henry Street, is Dublin's largest department store and has a good range of cut crystal. Visit **Kilkenny Design Workshops** on Nassau Street for the best selection of Irish designs for the home. Nearby, the **House of Ireland** has an abundance of traditional gifts and souvenirs.

Tweeds and Woolens Ready-made tweeds for men can be found at **Kevin and Howlin,** on Nassau Street, and at **Cleo Ltd.,** on Kildare Street. The **Blarney Woollen Mills,** on Nassau Street, has a good selection of tweed, linen, and woolen sweaters in all price ranges. The **Woolen Mills,** at Halfpenny Bridge, has a good selection of handknits and other woolen sweaters at competitive prices.

Dining

The restaurant scene in Dublin has improved beyond recognition in recent years. Though no one is ever likely to confuse the place with, say, Paris, the days of chewy boiled meats and soggy, tasteless vegetables are long gone. Food still tends to be substantial rather than subtle, but more and more restaurants are at last taking advantage of the magnificent livestock and fish that Ireland has in such abundance.

If your tastes run toward traditional Irish dishes, there are still a few old-fashioned restaurants serving substantial portions of excellent, if plain, home cooking. Look for boiled bacon and cabbage, Irish stew, and *colcannon* (cooked potatoes diced and fried in butter with onions and either cabbage or leeks and covered in thick cream just before serving). The best bet for daytime meals is "pub grub"—a choice of soup and soda bread, two or three hot dishes of the day, salad platters, or sandwiches. Most bars serve food, and a growing number offer coffee and tea as an alternative to alcohol. Guinness, a dark beer, or "stout," brewed with malt, is the Irish national drink, consumed in vast quantities. Even if you never go out for a drink at home, you should visit at least one or two pubs in Ireland. The pub is one of the pillars of Irish society, worth visiting as much for entertainment and conversation as for drinking.

Mealtimes Breakfast is served between 8 and 10—earlier by special request only—and is a substantial meal of cereal, bacon, eggs, sausage, and toast. Lunch is eaten between 12:30 and 2. Having enjoyed a hearty breakfast, however, most visitors tend to have a light lunch and to eat their main meal in the evening. The old tradition of "high tea" taken around 5, followed by a light snack before bed, is still encountered in many Irish homes, including many bed-and-breakfasts. Elsewhere, however, it is generally assumed that you'll be eating between 7 and 9:30 and that this will be your main meal of the day.

Dress   A jacket and tie or upscale casual dress are suggested for expensive restaurants. Otherwise casual dress is acceptable.

Ratings   Prices are per person and include a first course, a main course, and dessert, but no wine or tip. Sales tax at 10% is included in all Irish restaurant bills. Some places, usually the more expensive establishments, add a 12% or 15% service charge, in which case no tip is necessary; elsewhere a tip of 10% is adequate. The most highly recommended restaurants are indicated by a star ★.

Category	Cost
Very Expensive	over IR£28
Moderate	IR£16–IR£28
Inexpensive	under IR£16

Expensive   **Ernie's.** This luxurious place is built around a small floodlit courtyard shaded by an imposing mulberry tree. The rustic interior's granite walls and wood beams are adorned by paintings of Kerry, where, for generations, owner-chef Ernie Evans's family ran the famous Glenbeigh Hotel. Ernie serves generous portions of the very best seafood—try scallops Mornay or prawns in garlic butter—and steaks. *Mulberry Gardens, Donnybrook, tel. 01/693300. Reservations advised. AE, DC, MC, V. Dinner only. Closed Sun., Mon.*

★   **Le Coq Hardi.** Award-winning owner-chef John Howard is noted for his wine cellar and for such specialties as Coq Hardi smokies—smoked haddock baked in tomato, cream, and cheese—and (in season) roast loin of venison with fresh cranberries and port wine. The seriousness of the cooking is complemented by the polished wood and brass and the gleaming mirrors of the sumptuous interior. *35 Pembroke Rd., Ballsbridge, tel. 01/689070. Reservations required. AE, DC, MC, V. Closed weekends, lunch, and holidays.*

★   **King Sitric.** This quayside restaurant in the fishing village-cum-suburb of Howth is a 20-minute ride north of Dublin by DART or cab. It's worth the journey to taste the succulent selection of locally caught seafood; try wild Irish salmon steaks with Hollandaise sauce, or *goujons* of turbot with saffron. You eat in the quietly elegant Georgian dining room of the former harbormaster's house under the supervision of owner-chef Aidan MacManus. *East Pier, Howth, tel. 01/325235. Reservations advised. AE, DC, MC, V. Closed Sun., Sat. lunch, holidays, Dec. 24–Jan. 1, and the week preceding Easter.*

Oisin's Irish Restaurant. Situated on the first floor of a Victorian terrace, this intimate and relaxing place features modern Irish art on the walls, pottery on the polished tables, and a piano player performing old airs. Traditional Irish cuisine is enhanced by up-to-date sauces and garnishes. The six-course dinner menu includes appetizer-size portions of such traditional dishes as Dublin coddle (bacon, sausages, onions, and carrots boiled together) or a chowder made with cockles and mussels. Baked ham and spiced beef, as well as Irish stew, are among the main-course offerings. *31 Upper Camden St., tel. 01/753433. Reservations advised. No credit cards. Dinner only. Closed Sun.–Mon., Christmas week, and Easter week.*

Patrick Guilbaud. This is an authentic, rather formal, French restaurant with a consistently good reputation, decked out in a refreshing combination of pink, white, and green with hanging plants. The emphasis is firmly on traditional bourgeois cuisine; the Gallic connection is reinforced by the all-French staff. *46 James Pl., tel. 01/764192. Reservations advised. AE, DC, MC, V. Closed Sun. and holidays.*

Whites on the Green. A sophisticated spot with soothing cream-and-white decor, this place will appeal to those who appreciate delicate and subtle nouvelle cuisine. Typical dishes include medallions of veal gratiné with a parsley mousse and roast mallard with honey and juniper berries. *119 St. Stephen's Green, tel. 01/751975. Reservations required. AE, DC, MC, V. Closed weekends lunch.*

Moderate
★

Beefeaters. The clientele here has long been loyal to this restaurant's type of hearty meat dishes. Specialties are fillets, sirloins, and T-bones of prime Irish beef, prepared in 15 different ways. Try Gaelic steak, with a sauce of Irish whiskey, onions, mushrooms, and cream, or Surf 'n' Turf, an eight-ounce fillet accompanied by Dublin Bay prawns. The restaurant is located in the labyrinthine basement of two Georgian town houses and is furnished with wood-top tables and burgundy drapes and carpets. *99–100 Lower Baggot St., tel. 01/760784. Reservations advised. AE, DC, MC, V. Closed weekends lunch.*

Café Klara. This is the in-place to see and be seen, a bustling brasserie in one of Dublin's finest rooms, originally a ballroom. It's just opposite the Mansion House, a stone's throw from St. Stephen's Green. Frankly, the food is variable and the service is erratic, but the atmosphere is great. The menu offers traditional French and *cuisine moderne*, with choices ranging from warm pigeon salad to hearty chicken stew. *35 Dawson St., tel. 01/778611. Weekend reservations advised. MC, V. Closed Dec. 25–26.*

Dobbin's Wine Bistro. Though Dobbin's aims at a French identity, with its red-and-white gingham tablecloths and sawdust-strewn slate floor, the cooking here is international and imaginative, with an emphasis on fresh Irish produce. Specialties are phyllo pastry with pepper and seafood filling, paupiettes of salmon and sole with spinach and dill sauce, and Szechuan boned crispy duckling with fresh peaches. *Stephen's La., tel. 01/764670. Reservations advised. AE, DC, MC, V. Closed Sun.*

Inexpensive

Bad Ass Café. Definitely one of Dublin's loudest restaurants, this barnlike place, situated in the trendy Temple Bar area, between the Central Bank and the Halfpenny Bridge, is always a fun place to eat. American-style fast food—burgers, chili, and pizzas—and the pounding rock music attract a lively crowd, both the young and the young at heart. Look out for the old-fashioned cash shuttles whizzing around the ceiling! *9–11 Crown Alley, tel. 01/712596. AE, MC, V. Closed Jan. 1, Good Friday, and Dec. 25–26.*

Corncucopia Wholefoods. This vegetarian restaurant above a health-food shop provides good value for the money. The seating consists of bar stools at high, narrow glass-top tables. It's popular with student types from nearby Trinity College. The menu includes red lentil soup, avocado quiche, vegetarian spring roll, and vegetarian curry—all of them regular favorites. *19 Wicklow St., tel. 01/777583. No reservations. No credit cards. Closed Sun.*

Da Vicenza. Watching the pizza dough being kneaded, rolled, topped off, and thrust into the brick oven will probably influence your menu choice here. The pizzas are indeed excellent, but the restaurant also offers interesting pasta combinations, and fish and steak. Dark blue blinds and drapery against natural stone and wood are the background for a venue that is popular with all age groups. *133 Upper Leeson St., tel. 01/609906. Reservations advised. AE, DC, MC, V.*

Pasta Pasta. This small, bright, and unpretentiously pretty Italian eatery serves combinations of pasta shapes and sauces plus a few Italian specials—medallions of pork *à la funghi, escalope milanesa*—against a background of muted jazz-rock. It's an excellent value. *27 Exchequer St., tel. 01/679–2565. Reservations advised for groups over 6 and on weekends. MC, V. Closed Sun.*

Pub Food All the pubs listed here serve food at lunchtime; some also have food in the early evening. They form an important part of the dining scene in Dublin and make a pleasant and informal alternative to a restaurant meal. In general, a one-course meal should not cost much more than IR£4–IR£5, but a full meal will put you in the lower range of the Moderate category. In general, credit cards are not accepted.

Barry Fitzgerald's. Salads and a freshly cooked house special are available in the upstairs bar at lunch on weekdays. Pre-theater dinners are served in the early evening. *90 Marlboro St., tel. 01/774082.*

Davy Byrne's. James Joyce immortalized Davy Byrne's in his sprawling novel *Ulysses.* Nowadays it's more akin to a cocktail bar than a Dublin pub, but it's good for fresh and smoked salmon, salads, and a hot daily special. Food is available at lunchtime and in the early evening. *21 Duke St., tel. 01/711298.*

Kitty O'Shea's. Kitty O'Shea's cleverly, if a little artificially, recreates the atmosphere of old Dublin. *23–25 Grand Canal St., tel. 01/609965. Reservations accepted for lunch and Sun. brunch.*

Lord Edward Bar. With its Old World ambience, the Lord Edward Bar serves a wide range of salads and a hot dish of the day at lunchtime only. *23 Christ Church Pl., tel. 01/542158.*

Old Stand. Located conveniently close to Grafton Street, the Old Stand offers grilled food, including steaks. *37 Exchequer St., tel. 01/770821.*

Lodging

Although only one major hotel has opened in Dublin in the past few years, considerable investment in redevelopment, updating of facilities, and refurbishing of some of the older establishments is taking place. As in most major cities, there is a shortage of mid-range accommodations. For value-for-the-money, try one of the registered guest houses; in most respects they are indistinguishable from small hotels. Most economical of all is the bed-and-breakfast. Both guest houses and B&Bs tend to be located in suburban areas—generally a 10-minute bus ride from the center of the city. This is not in itself a great drawback, and savings can be significant.

The Irish Tourist Board (14 Upper O'Connell St.) publishes a comprehensive booklet, *Guest Accommodation* (IR£2), official grading system and a detailed price list of all approved accommodations, including hotels, guesthouses, farmhouses, B&Bs, and hostels. No hotel may exceed this price without special authorization from the ITB; prices must also be displayed in every room. Don't hesitate to complain either to the manager or to the ITB, or both, if prices exceed this maximum. The office can usually help if you find yourself without reservations.

In general, hotels charge per person. In most cases (but not all, especially in more expensive places), the price includes a full breakfast. In Moderate and Inexpensive hotels, be sure to specify whether you want a private bath or shower; the latter is cheaper. Off-season (October–May) prices are reduced by as much as 25%.

Guest Houses Some smaller hotels are graded as guest houses. To qualify, they must have at least five bedrooms. A few may have restaurants; those that do not will often provide evening meals by arrangement. Few will have a bar. Otherwise these rooms can be as comfortable as those of a regular hotel, and in major cities they offer very good value for the money, compared with the inexpensive hotels.

Bed-and-Breakfasts Bed-and-breakfast means just that. The bed can vary from a four-poster in the wing of a castle to a feather bed in a whitewashed farmhouse or the spare bedroom of a modern cottage. Rates are generally around IR£12 per person, though these can vary significantly. Although many larger B&Bs offer rooms with bath and shower, in the majority you'll have to use the bathroom in the hall and, in many cases, pay 50p–IR£1 extra for the privilege.

Ratings There is a VAT of 10% on hotel charges, which should be included in the quoted price. A service charge of 12–15% is also included and listed separately in the bills of top-grade hotels; elsewhere, check to see if the service is included. If it's not, a tip of between 10% and 15% is customary—if you think the service is worth it.

Prices are for two people in a double room, based on high season (June to September) rates. Best bets are indicated by a star ★.

Category	Cost
Very Expensive	IR£120 and up
Expensive	IR£80–IR£120
Moderate	IR£60–IR£80
Inexpensive	under IR£60

Very Expensive **Berkeley Court.** The most quietly elegant of Dublin's large modern hotels, Berkeley Court is located in Ballsbridge—a leafy suburb about a 10-minute cab ride from the center of town. Its new conservatory gives freshness and spaciousness to the atmosphere of the public rooms; among the other new features are five luxury suites, each with its own Jacuzzi. *Lansdowne Rd., Ballsbridge, Dublin 4, tel. 01/601711. 262 rooms with bath. Facilities: parking. AE, DC, MC, V.*

★ **Shelbourne.** The Shelbourne is one of Europe's grand old hotels whose guestbook contains names ranging from the Dalai Lama and Princess Grace to Laurel and Hardy, Richard Burton, and Peter O'Toole. The blazing open fire in its bustling marble lobby, flanked by two huge rose brocade sofas, is proof that the Shelbourne has not lost the sense of grandeur of its past. Between 1986 and 1988, IR£7 million was lavished on major refurbishment, which included restoring many original Georgian features and emphasizing them with luxurious drapes and a prominently displayed collection of fine antiques and heirlooms. A supplement is charged for rooms overlooking the leafy but busy green; the back bedrooms without views are far quieter, however. *27 Stephen's Green, tel. 01/766471. 165 rooms with bath. Facilities: bar, restaurant, coffee shop, sporting facilities available by arrangement. AE, DC, MC, V.*

Conrad. Dublin's newest luxury hotel (opened October 1989) and a subsidiary of Hilton Hotels, the Conrad is firmly aimed at the international business executive. The seven-story redbrick and smoked-glass building is well located just off Stephen's Green. The spacious rooms are decorated in pastel shades of green and brown, the bathrooms fitted in Spanish marble. Alfie Byrne's, the main bar, attempts to re-create the traditional Irish pub atmosphere in spite of its high-powered clientele. *Earlsfort Terrace, tel. 01/765424. 192 rooms with bath. Facilities: restaurant, 2 bars, coffee shop, sauna, gym, sporting facilities available by arrangement, parking. AE, DC, MC, V.*

Expensive　**Burlington.** Dublin's largest hotel is popular with American tour groups and Irish and European business travelers. It is about five minutes by car from the city's central area. At night the Burlington's disco and Irish cabaret turn it into a lively spot for overseas visitors. Bedrooms are the usual modern plush in neutral tones. *Upper Leeson St., tel. 01/605222. 472 rooms with bath. Facilities: restaurants, bars, disco, and cabaret. AE, DC, MC, V.*

Buswell's. You'll either love or hate Buswell's. The hotel is located just across the street from the Dail, and its bars and conference rooms are dominated by the frantic bustle of politicians and lobbyists. Curiously, Buswell's also has a loyal provincial clientele, who seem blissfully blind to the clashing patterns of carpets, drapes, and wallpaper; the smallness of the bedrooms; and the grim food. The central location (between Stephen's Green and Grafton Street) and charming Georgian facade are a potent attraction for many independent American travelers, too. *Molesworth St., tel. 01/764013. 67 rooms with bath. AE, DC, MC, V.*

★　**Gresham.** With a prime central location opposite the historic General Post Office, this place has played a part in Dublin's history since 1817. The interior has a predominantly '30s character, with an emphasis on comfort rather than upscale chic. Bedrooms are reached via long windowless corridors, and the monumentally solid plumbing arrangements give character to the bland modern-repro style of the newly decorated rooms. The hotel feels much bigger than it actually is, and the lobby, decked out with "Gresham (royal) Blue" carpet and gold brocade armchairs, exudes a sense of history. *Higher O'Connell St., tel. 01/746881. 198 rooms with bath. AE, DC, MC, V.*

Jury's. This lively and fashionable spot has more atmosphere than most comparable modern hotels. It's a short cab ride from the center of town. Bedrooms are relatively spacious, standard modern plush, and each comes with a picture-window view of town. Exclusive facilities for businessmen are provided in the

100-room Towers annex. *Ballsbridge, Dublin 4, tel. 01/605000. 300 rooms with bath. Facilities: indoor/outdoor pool, Jacuzzi, 2 bars, 3 restaurants, cabaret May–Oct. AE, DC, MC, V.*

Moderate
★ **Ariel Guest House.** This is Dublin's leading guest house, just a block away from the elegant Berkeley Court and a 10-minute walk from Stephen's Green. The lobby lounge and restaurant of this Victorian villa are furnished with leather and mahogany heirlooms. Some prefer the spacious modern rooms in the quiet back annex. This is a good bet if you're in town for a leisurely, relaxing holiday. *52 Lansdowne Rd., tel. 01/685512. 15 rooms with bath. Facilities: restaurant (wine license only), lounge, parking. AE, MC, V. Closed Dec. 21–Jan. 31.*

Ashling. This family-run hotel sits on the edge of the river Liffey, close to Heuston Station. Some may find that the Ashling's relentlessly bright modern decor verges on the garish. It has a faithful following, however, not least because of its proximity to Phoenix Park and its friendly staff. The center of town is a brisk 10–15 minute walk away, taking in many famed landmarks en route. *Parkgate St., Kingsbridge, tel. 01/772324. 56 rooms with bath. AE, DC, MC, V.*

Clarence. You'll find the Clarence either charmingly old-fashioned or just plain dowdy; it's all a matter of taste. Most of its Edwardian interior is dominated by oak-paneled walls and solid leather sofas and chairs. The restaurant and lobby have been prettified by fake Art Deco drapes and cane chairs. The bedrooms are small and functional: no frills here. Its central Liffey-side location is relentlessly urban. Beware of early-morning traffic noise in the front bedrooms. It remains an excellent place to meet a cross section of Dubliners and mildly eccentric provincials. *6–7 Wellington Quay, tel. 01/776178. 67 rooms with bath. Facilities: restaurant. AE, DC, MC, V.*

Leeson Court. Two 18th-century terraced houses have been combined to form this recently opened hotel, which is close to St. Stephen's Green. The small bedrooms are all cheerfully decorated in matching colors, with thick carpeting and stained-wood furnishings. The tiled bathrooms are surprisingly spacious. In spite of double-glazing, there is some daytime traffic noise. The conservatory at the back of the hotel faces a pleasant patio and beer garden. The basement nightclub is fully soundproofed from the rest of the building. *26–27 Lower Leeson St., Dublin 2, tel. 01/763380. 20 rooms. Facilities: bar, nightclub, restaurant. AE, DC, MC, V.*

Inexpensive
Abrae Court Guest House. This is a typical, large early-Victorian house in the highly respectable suburb of Rathgar. It's a 10-minute bus ride to the center of Dublin. There are six bedrooms in the main house; the rest are in a carefully designed period-style annex with ornate stucco ceilings. All are furnished with Irish carpets and handcrafted Irish furniture. The restaurant is open for evening meals. *9 Zion Rd., Rathgar, tel. 01/979944. 14 rooms with bath. Facilities: restaurant (wine license only). AE, DC, MC, V.*

Kilronan House. This guest house, a five-minute walk from St. Stephen's Green, is a favorite with vacationers. The large, late-19th-century terraced house is well-converted, and the decor and furnishings are updated each year by the Murray family, who have run the place for the past 30 years. The bedrooms are pleasantly furnished with plush carpeting and pastel colored walls. *70 Adelaide Rd., Dublin 2, tel. 01/755266. 12 rooms. Closed Dec.23–Jan. 1. No credit cards.*

★ **Maples House.** According to the ITB's complex grading system, Maples House is a guest house; to the rest of the world, however, it is definitely a small hotel. The lobby of this Edwardian house is decked out with oil paintings, Waterford crystal chandeliers, and a discreetly modern carpet, and is dominated by a vast mirror-topped Victorian rococo sideboard that sets the tone for the ornate decor of the public rooms. The bedrooms are small but adequate, lacking the rococo splendor of the rest of the building. *Iona Rd., Glasnevin, tel. 01/303049. 21 rooms with bath. Facilities: grill restaurant and bar. AE, DC, MC, V. Closed Dec. 25, 26.*

Mount Herbert Guest House. Located close to the swank luxury hotels in the tree-lined inner suburb of Ballsbridge, a 10-minute bus ride from Dublin's center of town, the Mount Herbert is popular with budget-minded American visitors in the high season. Bedrooms are small, but all have 10-channel TV and hair dryers. There is no bar on the premises, but there are plenty to choose from nearby. *7 Herbert Rd., Ballsbridge, tel. 01/684321. 88 rooms, 77 with bath. Facilities: restaurant (wine license only). AE, DC, MC, V.*

The Arts

The fortnightly magazine *In Dublin* contains comprehensive details of upcoming events, including ticket availability. In peak season, consult the free ITB leaflet *Events of the Week*.

Theaters Ireland has a rich theatrical tradition. The **Abbey Theatre,** Marlborough Street, is the home of Ireland's national theater company, its name forever associated with J. M. Synge, William Butler Yeats, and Sean O'Casey. The **Peacock Theatre** is the Abbey's more experimental small stage. The **Gate Theatre,** Parnell Square, is an intimate spot for modern drama and plays by Irish writers. The **Gaiety Theatre,** South King Street, features musical comedy, opera, drama, and revues. The **Olympia Theatre,** Dame Street, has seasons of comedy, vaudeville, and ballet. The **Project Arts Centre,** East Essex Street, is an established fringe theater. The new **National Concert Hall,** in Earlsfort Terrace, just off Stephen's Green, is the place to go for classical concerts.

Nightlife

Dublin does not have sophisticated nightclubs in the international sense. Instead, there is a choice of discos (often billed as nightclubs) and cabarets, catering mainly to visitors. There is also a very animated bar-pub scene—some places with live music and folksinging. No visit to this genial city will be complete without spending at least one evening exploring them.

Discos New Annabels (Mespil Rd., tel. 01/605222) is a popular late-evening spot; so is **The Pink Elephant** (S. Frederick St., tel. 01/775876).

Cabarets The following all offer Irish cabaret, designed to give visitors a taste of Irish entertainment: **Braemor Rooms** (Churchtown, tel. 01/988664); **Burlington Hotel** (Upper Leeson St., tel. 01/605222, open Apr.–Oct.); **Jury's Hotel** (Ballsbridge, tel. 01/605000, open Apr.–mid Oct.); **Abbey Tavern** (Howth, Co. Dublin, tel. 01/390307).

Pubs Check advertisements in evening papers for "sessions" of folk, ballad, Irish traditional, or jazz music. The **Brazen Head** (20 Lower Bridge St., tel. 01/779549)—Dublin's oldest pub, dating from 1688—and **O'Donoghue's** (15 Merrion Row, tel. 01/607194) feature some form of musical entertainment on most nights. Several of Dublin's centrally located pubs are noted for their character and ambience; they're usually at their liveliest from 5 to 7 PM and again from 10. The **Bailey** (2 Duke St.) is mentioned in *Ulysses* (under its original name, Burton's) and retains something of its Edwardian character, while **William Ryan's** (28 Parkgate St.) is a beautifully preserved Victorian gem. **Henry Grattan** (47–48 Lower Baggot St.) is popular with the business and sporting crowd; **O'Neill's Lounge Bar** (37 Pearse St.) is always busy with students and faculty from nearby Trinity College; and the **Palace Bar** (21 Fleet St.) is a journalists' haunt. You can eavesdrop on Dublin's social elite and their hangers-on at the expensive **Horseshoe Bar** in the Shelbourne Hotel or bask in the theatrical atmosphere of **Neary's** (Chatham St.)

10 Florence

Arriving and Departing

By Plane The nearest, medium-size airport is the Galileo Galilei Airport at Pisa (tel. 050/28088), connected with Florence by train direct from the airport to the Santa Maria Novella Station. Service is hourly throughout the day and takes about 60 minutes. Some domestic and a few European flights use Florence's Peretola Airport (tel. 055/373498), connected by bus to the downtown area.

By Train The main train station is Santa Maria Novella Station, abbreviated SMN on signs. There is an Azienda Transporti Autolinee Fiorentina (ATAF) city bus information booth across the street from the station (and also at Piazza Duomo 57/r). Inside the station is an Informazione Turistiche Alberghiere (ITA) hotel association booth, where you can get hotel information and bookings.

By Bus The SITA bus terminal is on Via Santa Caterina di Siena, near Santa Maria Novella train station. The CAP bus terminal is at Via Nazionale 13, also near the station.

By Car The north–south access route to Florence is the Autostrada del Sole (A1) from Milan or Rome. The Florence–Mare autostrada (A11) links Florence with the Tyrrhenian coast, Pisa, and the A12 coastal autostrada.

Getting Around

On Foot You can see most of Florence's major sights on foot, as they are packed into a relatively small area in the city center. It's best not to plan to use a car in Florence; most of the center is off-limits and ATAF buses will take you where you want to go. Wear comfortable shoes and wander to your heart's content. It is easy to find your way around in Florence. There are so many landmarks that you cannot get lost for long. The system of street numbers is unusual, with commercial addresses written with a red "r" and residential addresses in blue (32/r might be next to or even a block away from 32 blue).

By Bus ATAF city buses run from about 5:15 AM to 1 AM. Buy tickets before you board the bus; they are on sale singly or in books of five at many tobacco shops and newsstands. The cost is 700 lire for a ticket good for 70 minutes on all lines, 1,000 lire for 120 minutes. An all-day ticket (*turistico*) costs 4,000 lire.

By Taxi Taxis wait at stands. Use only authorized cabs, which are white with a yellow stripe or rectangle on the door. The meter starts at 2,500 lire. To call a taxi, tel. 055/4798 or 055/4390.

By Bicycle You can rent a bicycle at **Ciao e Basta,** on Via Alamanni, on the stairway side of the train station; at **Costa del Magnoli 24,** tel. 055/234-2726; and at city concessions in several locations, including Piazza della Stazione, Piazza Pitti, and Fortezza da Basso.

By Moped For a moped, go to **Program** (Borgo Ognissanti 135/r, tel. 055/282916), **Excelsior** (Via della Scala 48/r, tel. 055/293186), or to **Ciao e Basta** (*see* By Bicycle, above).

Important Addresses and Numbers

Tourist Information The municipal tourist office is at Via Cavour 1/r (tel. 055/276–0382; open 8:30–7). The **Azienda Promozione Turistica (APT)** tourist board has its headquarters and an information office at Via Manzoni 16 (tel. 055/247–8141; open Mon.–Sat. 8:30–1:30).

Consulates U.S. (Lungarno Vespucci 38, tel. 055/298276). U.K. (Lungarno Corsini 2, tel. 055/284133).

Emergencies **Police** (tel. 113). **Ambulance** (tel. 055/212222). **Doctor:** Call your consulate for recommendations, or call the **Tourist Medical Service** (tel. 055/475411), associated with IAMAT, for English-speaking medical assistance 24 hours a day. **Pharmacies:** There are 24-hour pharmacies at Via Calzaiuoli 7/r (tel. 055/263490); Piazza San Giovanni 20/r (tel. 055/284013); and at the train station (tel. 055/263435).

English Bookstores You'll find English-language magazines and paperbacks on the newsstands in Piazza della Repubblica. **The Paperback Exchange** (Via Fiesolana 31/r, tel. 055/247–8154), in the Santa Croce area, has new and used paperbacks for sale. **The BM Bookshop** (Borgo Ognissanti 4/r, tel. 055/294575) has a good selection of English-language books.

Travel Agencies **American Express** (Via Guicciardini 49/r, tel. 055/278751). **CIT** (Via Cavour 54/r, tel. 055/294306). **Wagons-Lits** (Via del Giglio 27/r, tel. 055/218851).

Guided Tours

Orientation Tours **American Express** (tel. 055/278751), **CIT** (tel. 055/294306), and **SITA** (tel. 055/214721) offer three-hour tours in air-conditioned buses. Two tours cover most of the important sights: The morning itinerary gives you a look at the outside of the cathedral, baptistry, and bell tower, takes you to the Accademia to see Michelangelo's *David*, to Piazzale Michelangelo for the view, and then to the Pitti Palace to visit the Palatine Gallery; the afternoon tour includes Piazza della Signoria, a visit to the Uffizi Gallery and to Santa Croce, and an excursion to Fiesole. The cost is 40,000–45,000 lire for a three-hour tour, including entrance fees, and can be booked through travel agents.

Personal Guides **American Express** (tel. 055/278751) can arrange for limousine or minitours and personal guide services. **Europedrive** (Via Bisenzio 35, te. 055/437–6862) will provide cars with English-speaking drivers.

Special-Interest Tours Inquire at travel agents or at **Agriturist** (Piazza San Firenze 3, tel. 055/287838) for visits to villa gardens around Florence from April to June, or for visits to farm estates during September and October.

Excursions Operators offer a half-day excursion to Pisa, usually in the afternoon, and a full-day excursion to Siena and San Gimignano, costing about 30,000 lire and 45,000 lire, respectively. Pick up a timetable at ATAF information offices near the train station, at Piazza Duomo 57/r (tel. 055/580528), or at the APT Tourist Office (*see* Tourist Information in Important Addresses and Numbers).

Both ATAF and tourist information offices offer a free booklet containing information on interesting excursions in the vicinity of Florence, complete with timetables of local bus and train services.

Exploring Florence

Founded by Julius Caesar, Florence has the familiar grid pattern common to all Roman colonies. Except for the major monuments, which are appropriately imposing, the buildings are low and unpretentious. It is a small, compact city of ocher and gray stone and pale plaster; its narrow streets open unexpectedly into spacious squares populated by strollers and pigeons. At its best, it has a gracious and elegant air, though it can at times be a nightmare of mass tourism. Plan, if you can, to visit Florence in late fall, early spring, or even in winter, to avoid the crowds.

A visit to Florence is a visit to the living museum of Italian Renaissance. The Renaissance began right here in Florence, and the city bears witness to the proud spirit and unparalleled genius of its artists and artisans. In fact, there is so much to see that it is best to savor a small part rather than attempt to absorb it all in a muddled vision.

Numbers in the margin correspond to points of interest on the Florence map.

Piazza del Duomo and the Piazza della Signoria The best place to begin a tour of Florence is **Piazza del Duomo,** where the cathedral, bell tower, and baptistry stand in the rather cramped square. The lofty **cathedral of Santa Maria del**
❶ **Fiore** is one of the longest in the world. Begun by master sculptor and architect Arnolfo di Cambio in 1296, its construction took 140 years to complete. Gothic architecture predominates; the facade was added in the 1870s but is based on Tuscan Gothic models. Inside, the church is cool and austere, a fine example of the architecture of the period. Among the sparse decorations, take a good look at the frescoes of equestrian monuments on the left wall; the one on the right is by Paolo Uccello, the one on the left by Andrea del Castagno. The dome frescoes by Vasari have been hidden by the scaffolding put up some years ago in order to study a plan for restoring the dome itself, Brunelleschi's greatest architectural and technical achievement. It was also the inspiration of such later domes as Michelangelo's dome for St. Peter's in Rome and even the Capitol in Washington. You can climb to the cupola gallery, 463 fatiguing steps up between the two skins of the double dome for a fine view of Florence and the surrounding hills. *Dome entrance is in the left aisle of cathedral. Admission: 4,000 lire. Open Mon.–Sat. 10–5. Cathedral open Mon.–Sat. 10–5, Sun. 2:30–5.*

❷ Next to the cathedral is Giotto's 14th-century **bell tower,** richly decorated with colored marble and fine sculptures (the originals are in the Museo dell'Opera del Duomo). The 414-step climb to the top is less strenuous than that to the cupola. *Piazza del Duomo. Admission: 4,000 lire. Open Mar.–Oct., daily 9–7; Nov.–Feb., daily 9–5.*

❸ In front of the cathedral is the **baptistry,** one of the city's oldest and most beloved edifices, where, since the 11th century, Florentines have baptized their children. A gleaming copy of the most famous of the baptistry's three portals has been installed facing the cathedral, where Ghiberti's doors (dubbed "The Gate of Paradise" by Michelangelo) stood. The originals have
❹ been removed to the **Museo dell'Opera del Duomo** (Cathedral

Accademia Gallery, **9**
Baptistry, **3**
Bell Tower, **2**
Boboli Gardens, **20**
Casa Guidi, **21**
Cathedral of Santa Maria del Fiore (Duomo), **1**
Church of San Lorenzo, **13**
Loggia del Mercato Nuovo, **7**
Medici Chapels, **14**
Museo Archeologico, **10**
Museo dell'Opera del Duomo, **4**
Museo Nazionale, **16**
Museo di San Marco, **11**
Orsanmichele, **5**
Palazzo Medici Riccardi, **12**
Palazzo Pitti, **19**
Palazzo Vecchio, **6**
Ponte Vecchio, **18**
Santa Croce, **17**
Santa Maria del Carmine, **23**
Santa Maria Novella, **15**
Santo Spirito, **22**
Uffizi Gallery, **8**

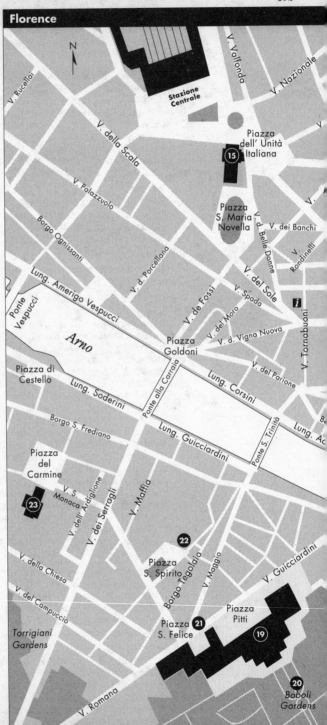

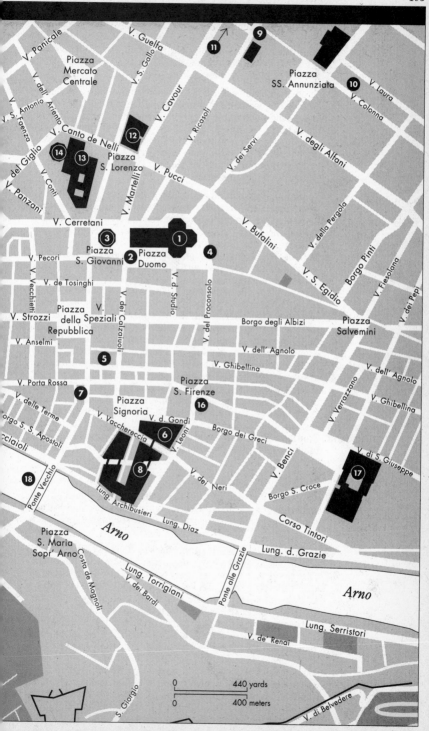

Museum). The museum contains some superb sculptures by Donatello and Luca della Robbia—especially their *cantorie*, or choir decorations—as well as an unfinished *Pietà* by Michelangelo, which was intended for his own tomb. *Piazza del Duomo 9, tel. 055/230-2885. Admission: 4,000 lire. Open Mar.–Oct., Mon.–Sat. 9–8; Nov.–Feb., Mon.–Sat. 9–6.*

❺ Stroll down fashionable Via Calzaiuoli to the church of **Orsanmichele,** for centuries an odd combination of first-floor church and second-floor wheat granary. The statues in the niches on the exterior constitute an anthology of the work of eminent Renaissance sculptors, including Donatello, Ghiberti, and Verrocchio, while the tabernacle inside is an extraordinary piece by Andrea Orcagna. In 1991 parts of the building may still be under wraps for restoration.

Continuing another two blocks along Via Calzaiuoli you'll come upon **Piazza della Signoria,** the heart of Florence, and the city's largest square. During the long and controversial process of replacing the paving stones over the past few years, well-preserved remnants of Roman and medieval Florence came to light and were thoroughly examined and photographed before being buried again and covered with the new paving. In the center of the square a slab marks the spot where in 1497 Savonarola—the Ayatollah Khomeini of the Middle Ages—induced the Florentines to burn their pictures, books, musical instruments, and other worldly objects—and where a year later he was hanged and then burned at the stake as a heretic. The square, the **Neptune Fountain** by Ammanati, and the surrounding cafés are popular gathering places for Florentines and for tourists who come to admire the massive **Palazzo della Signoria,** better **❻** known as the **Palazzo Vecchio,** the copy of Michelangelo's *David* on its steps, and the frescoes and artworks in its impressive salons. *Piazza della Signoria, tel. 055/2768465. Admission: 4,000 lire; Sun. free. Open weekdays 9–7, Sun. 8–1; closed Sat.*

Time Out Stop in at **Rivoire,** a Florentine institution, for some of its delectable ice cream and/or chocolate goodies. *Piazza della Signoria 5/r.*

❼ If you'd like to do a little shopping, make a brief detour off Piazza della Signoria to the **Loggia del Mercato Nuovo** on Via Calimala. It's crammed with souvenirs and straw and leather goods at reasonable prices; bargaining is acceptable here. *Open Mon.–Sat. 8–7 (closed Mon. AM).*

❽ If time is limited, this is your chance to visit the **Uffizi Gallery,** which houses Italy's most important collection of paintings. (Try to see it at a more leisurely pace, though—it's too good to rush through!) The Uffizi Palace was built to house the administrative offices of the Medicis, onetime rulers of the city. Later their fabulous art collection was arranged in the Uffizi Gallery on the top floor, which was opened to the public in the 17th century—making this the world's first public gallery of modern times. The emphasis is on Italian art of the Gothic and Renaissance periods. Make sure you see the works by Giotto, and look for the Botticellis in Rooms X–XIV, Michelangelo's *Holy Family* in Room XXV, and the works by Raphael next door. In addition to its art treasures, the gallery offers a magnificent close-up view of Palazzo Vecchio's tower from the little coffee bar at the end of the corridor. *Loggiato Uffizi 6, tel. 055/*

218341. Admission: 10,000 lire. Open Tues.–Sat. 9–7, Sun. 9–1.

Accademia, San Marco, San Lorenzo, Santa Maria Novella

⑨

Start at the **Accademia Gallery**, and try to be first in line at opening time so you can get the full impact of Michelangelo's *David* without having to fight your way through the crowds. Skip the works in the exhibition halls leading to the *David;* they are of minor importance and you'll gain a length on the tour groups. Michelangelo's statue is a tour de force of artistic conception and technical ability, for he was using a piece of stone that had already been worked on by a lesser sculptor. Take time to see the forceful *Slaves*, also by Michelangelo; the rough-hewn, unfinished surfaces contrast dramatically with the highly polished, meticulously carved *David*. Michelangelo left the *Slaves* "unfinished" as a symbolic gesture, to accentuate the figures' struggle to escape the bondage of stone. *Via Ricasoli 60, tel. 055/214375. Admission: 10,000 lire. Open Tues.–Sat. 9–2, Sun. 9–1.*

⑩

You can make a detour down Via Cesare Battisti to Piazza Santissima Annunziata to see the arcade of the **Ospedale degli Innocenti** (Hospital of the Innocents) by Brunelleschi, with charming roundels by Andrea della Robbia, and the **Museo Archeologico** (Archaeological Museum) on Via della Colonna, under the arch. It has some fine Etruscan and Roman antiquities, and a pretty garden. *Via della Colonna 36, tel. 055/247-8641. Admission: 6,000 lire. Open Tues.–Sat. 9–2, Sun. 9–1.*

⑪

Retrace your steps to Piazza San Marco and the **Museo di San Marco,** housed in a 15th-century Dominican monastery. The unfortunate Savonarola meditated on the sins of the Florentines here, and Fra Angelico decorated many of the austere cells and corridors with his brilliantly colored frescoes of religious subjects. (Look for his masterpiece, *The Annunciation*.) Together with many of his paintings arranged on the ground floor, just off the little cloister, they form an interesting collection. *Piazza San Marco 1, tel. 055/210741. Admission: 6,000 lire. Open Tues.–Sat. 9–2, Sun. 9–1.*

⑫
⑬

Lined with shops, Via Cavour leads to **Palazzo Medici Riccardi,** a massive Renaissance mansion (*see* Off the Beaten Track, below). Turn left here to the elegant **Church of San Lorenzo,** with its Old Sacristy designed by Brunelleschi, and two pulpits by Donatello. Rounding the left flank of the church, you'll find yourself in the midst of the sprawling **San Lorenzo Market,** dealing in everything and anything, including some interesting leather items. *Piazza San Lorenzo, Via dell'Ariento. Open Tues.–Sat. 8–7.*

Time Out

On Via Sant'Antonio near the big covered food market, **Palla d'Oro** is a favorite with market workers for a quick sandwich or plate of pasta, which they usually eat standing at the counter. You can sit at the tables in the back for an extra charge. It's impossibly crowded between 1 and 1:30. *Via Sant'Antonino 45/r. Closed Sun.*

⑭

Enter the **Medici Chapels** from Piazza Madonna degli Aldobrandini, behind San Lorenzo. These remarkable chapels contain the tombs of practically every member of the Medici family, and there were a lot of them, for they guided Florence's destiny from the 15th century to 1737. Cosimo I, a Medici whose acumen made him the richest man in Europe, is buried in the crypt of the Chapel of the Princes, and Donatello's tomb is next to that of his patron. The chapel upstairs is decorated in an eye-dazzling array of colored marble. In Michelangelo's New Sacristy, his tombs of Giuliano and Lorenzo Medici bear the justly famed statues of *Dawn* and *Dusk*, and *Night* and *Day*. *Piazza Madonna degli Aldobrandini, tel. 055/213206. Admission: 8,000 lire. Open Tues.–Sat. 9–2, Sun. 9–1.*

Time Out **Baldini** is an unpretentious trattoria, low on atmosphere but offering a good range of antipasti and delicious *fazzoletti*, pasta filled with ricotta and spinach. *Via Panzani 57. Closed Wed.*

⑮ You can take either Via Panzani or Via del Melarancio to the large square next to the massive church of **Santa Maria Novella,** a handsome building in the Tuscan version of Gothic style. See it from the other end of Piazza Santa Maria Novella for the best view of its facade. Inside are some famous paintings, especially Masaccio's *Trinity*, a Giotto crucifix in the sacristy, and Ghirlandaio's frescoes in the apse. *Piazza Santa Maria Novella, tel. 055/210113. Open Mon.–Sat. 7–11:30 and 3:30–6, Sun. 7–11:30 and 3:30–5.*

Next door to the church is the entrance to the **cloisters,** worth a visit for their serene atmosphere and the restored Paolo Uccello frescoes. *Piazza Santa Maria Novella 19, tel. 055/282187. Admission: 3,000 lire. Open Mon.–Thurs., Sat. 9–2, Sun. 8–1.*

⑯ Only a few blocks behind Piazza della Signoria is the **Bargello,** a fortresslike palace that served as residence of Florence's chief magistrate in medieval times, and later as a prison. Don't be put off by its grim look, for it now houses Florence's **Museo Nazionale** (National Museum), a treasure house of Italian Renaissance sculpture. In a historically and visually interesting setting, it displays masterpieces by Donatello, Verrocchio, Michelangelo, and many other major sculptors. This museum is on a par with the Uffizi, so don't shortchange yourself on time. *Via del Proconsolo 4, tel. 055/210801. Admission: 6,000 lire. Open Tues.–Sat. 9–2, Sun. 9–1.*

Time Out From Piazza San Firenze follow Via degli Anguillara or Borgo dei Greci toward Piazza Santa Croce. Don't miss the chance to taste what's held by many to be the best ice cream in Florence at **Vivoli,** on a little side street, the second left off Via degli Anguillara as you head toward Santa Croce. *Via Isole delle Stinche 7/r. Closed Mon.*

⑰ The mighty church of **Santa Croce** was begun in 1294; inside, Giotto's frescoes brighten two chapels and monumental tombs of Michelangelo, Galileo, Machiavelli, and other Renaissance luminaries line the walls. In the adjacent museum, you can see what remains of a Giotto crucifix, irreparably damaged by a flood in 1966, when water rose to 16 feet in parts of the church. The **Pazzi Chapel** in the cloister is an architectural gem by Brunelleschi. *Piazza Santa Croce, tel. 055/244619. Church open Mon.–Sat. 7–12:30 and 3–6:30, Sun. 3–6. Opera di Santa Croce (Museum and Pazzi Chapel), tel. 055/244619. Admission: 2,000 lire. Open Mar.–Sept., Thurs.–Tues. 10–12:30 and 2:30–6:30; Oct.–Feb., Thurs.–Tues. 10–12:30 and 3–5.*

The monastery of Santa Croce harbors a leather-working school and showroom, with entrances at Via San Giuseppe 5/r and Piazza Santa Croce 16. The entire Santa Croce area is known for its leather factories and inconspicuous shops selling gold and silver jewelry at prices much lower than those of the elegant jewelers near Ponte Vecchio.

Time Out You have several eating options here. For ice cream, the **bar** on Piazza Santa Croce has a tempting selection. If it's a snack you're after, the **Fiaschetteria** (Via dei Neri 17/r) makes sandwiches to order and has a choice of antipasti and a hot dish or two. **Da Marco,** between Santa Croce and the Arno, is a typical trattoria, where you can either eat downstairs or outdoors. (Via dei Benci 13/r. Closed Mon.)

⑱ Now head for **Ponte Vecchio,** Florence's oldest bridge. It seems to be just another street lined with goldsmiths' shops until you get to the middle and catch a glimpse of the Arno flowing below. Spared during World War II by the retreating Germans (who blew up every other bridge in the city), it also survived the 1966 flood. It leads into the **Oltrarno district,** which has its own charm and still preserves much of the atmosphere of oldtime Florence, full of fascinating craft workshops.

⑲ But for the moment you should head straight down Via Guicciardini to **Palazzo Pitti,** a 15th-century extravaganza that the Medicis acquired from the Pitti family shortly after the latter had gone deeply into debt to build it. Its long facade on the immense piazza was designed by Brunelleschi: Solid and severe, it looks like a Roman aqueduct turned into a palace. The palace houses several museums: One displays the fabulous Medici collection of objects in silver and gold; another is the **Gallery of Modern Art.** The most famous museum, though, is the **Palatine Gallery,** with an extraordinary collection of paintings, many hung frame-to-frame in a clear case of artistic overkill. Some are high up in dark corners, so try to go on a bright day. *Piazza Pitti, tel. 055/210323. Gallery of Modern Art. Admission: 4,000 lire. Palatine Gallery. Admission: 8,000 lire (includes state apartments). Silver Museum. Admission: 6,000 lire (includes admission to the Porcelain Museum and Historical Costume Gallery). All open Tues.–Sat. 9–2, Sun. 9–1.*

⑳ Take time for a refreshing stroll in the **Boboli Gardens** behind Palazzo Pitti, a typical Italian garden laid out in 1550 for Cosimo Medici's wife, Eleanor of Toledo. *Piazza dei Pitti, tel. 055/213440. Admission free. Open Apr., May, and Sept., daily 9–6:30; June–Aug., 9–7:30; Oct. and Mar.–Apr., 9–5:30; Nov.–Feb., 9–4:30.*

㉑ In the far corner of Piazza dei Pitti, poets Elizabeth Barrett and Robert Browning lived at No. 9 **Casa Guidi,** facing the smaller Piazza San Felice. *Piazza San Felice 8, tel. 055/284393. Admission free. Open by appointment.*

Time Out From Piazza San Felice it's not far to the **Caffè Notte,** a wine and sandwich shop featuring a different salad every day (corner of Via della Caldaia and Via della Chiesa). For more substantial sustenance, go to the **Cantinone del Gallo Nero,** an atmospheric wine cellar where Chianti is king and locals lunch on soups, pastas, and salads (Via Santo Spirito 6/r. Closed Mon.). In front of the church of Santo Spirito, **Borgo Antico** is an attractive, small place for pizza and other lunch fare. (Piazza Santo Spirito 6/r. Closed Sun.).

㉒ The church of **Santo Spirito** is important as one of Brunelleschi's finest architectural creations, and it contains some superb paintings, including a Filippino Lippi *Madonna*. Santo Spirito is the hub of a colorful neighborhood of artisans and intellectuals. An **outdoor market** enlivens the square every morning except Sunday; in the afternoon, pigeons, pet owners, and pensioners take over. The area is definitely on an upward trend, with new cafés, restaurants, and upscale shops opening every day.

㉓ Walk down Via Sant'Agostino and Via Santa Monaca to the church of **Santa Maria del Carmine,** of no architectural interest but of immense significance in the history of Renaissance art. It contains the celebrated frescoes painted by Masaccio in the **Brancacci Chapel,** unveiled not long ago after a lengthy and meticulous restoration. The chapel was a classroom for such artistic giants as Botticelli, Leonardo da Vinci, Michelangelo, and Raphael, since they all came to study Masaccio's realistic use of light and perspective and his creation of space and depth. *Piazza del Carmine, tel. 055/218331. Admission: 5,000 lire. Open Mon.–Sat. 10–5, Sun. 1–5.*

Time Out The small trattoria on the square has a friendly atmosphere and is a delightful spot where you can eat outdoors and enjoy the view. *Piazza del Carmine 18/r. Closed Sat. evening and Sun.*

Shopping

Florence offers top quality for your money in leather goods, linens and upholstery fabrics, gold and silver jewelry, and cameos. Straw goods, gilded wooden trays and frames, handprinted paper desk accessories, and ceramic objects make good inexpensive gifts. Many shops offer fine old prints.

Shopping Districts The most fashionable streets in Florence are **Via Tornabuoni** and **Via della Vigna Nuova.** Goldsmiths and jewelry shops can be found on and around **Ponte Vecchio** and in the **Santa Croce area,** where there is also a high concentration of leather shops.

Antiques Most of Florence's many antiques dealers are located in **Borgo San Jacopo** and **Borgo Ognissanti,** but you'll find plenty of small shops throughout the center of town.

Department Stores **Principe,** in Piazza Strozzi, is a quality apparel store incorporating several designer boutiques. At the other end of the price range, **UPIM,** in Piazza della Repubblica and various other locations, has inexpensive goods of all types.

Markets The big food market at **Piazza del Mercato Centrale** is open in the morning (Mon.–Sat.) and is worth a visit. The **San Lorenzo market** on Piazza San Lorenzo and Via dell'Ariento is a fine place to browse for buys in leather goods and souvenirs (open Tues. and Sat. 8–7; also Sun. in summer). The **Mercato del Porcellino,** Piazza del Mercato Nuovo, takes its name from the famous bronze statue of a boar at one side, and is packed with stalls selling souvenirs and straw goods (open Tues.–Sat. 8–7; closed Sun. and Mon. morning in winter). There's a colorful neighborhood market at **Sant'Ambrogio,** Piazza Ghiberti (open Mon.–Sat. morning), and a permanent flea market at **Piazza Ciompi** (open Mon.–Sat. 9–1 and 4–7, Sun. 9–1 in summer).

Dining

Generally speaking, a *ristorante* pays more attention to decor, service, and menu than does a *trattoria*, which is simpler and often family-run. An *osteria* used to be a lowly tavern, though now the term may be used to designate a chic and expensive eatery. A *travola calda* offers hot dishes and snacks, with seating. A *rosticceria* has the same, to take out.

The menu is always posted in the window or just inside the door of an eating establishment. Check to see what is offered, and note the charges for *coperto* (cover) and *servizio* (service), which will increase your check. A *menu turistico* includes taxes and service, but beverages are extra.

Mealtimes Mealtimes in Florence are 12:30–2 and 7:30–9 or later. Many Moderate and Inexpensive places are small, and you may have to share a table. Reservations are always advisable; to find a table at inexpensive places, get there early. Practically all restaurants close one day a week; some close for winter or summer vacation.

Precautions Tap water is safe in large cities unless noted *Non Potabile*. Bottled mineral water is available everywhere, *gassata* (with bubbles) or *non gassata* (without). If you prefer tap water, ask for *acqua semplice.*

Dress Except for restaurants in the Very Expensive and occasionally in the Expensive categories, where jacket and tie are advisable, casual attire is acceptable.

Ratings Prices are per person and include first course, main course, dessert or fruit, and house wine, where available. Best bets are indicated by a ★.

Category	Cost
Very Expensive	over 100,000 lire
Expensive	60,000–100,000 lire
Moderate	40,000–60,000
Inexpensive	under 40,000 lire

Very Expensive **Cestello.** The restaurant of the hotel Excelsior has a lovely setting, whether you dine on the rooftop terrace overlooking the Arno in the summer, or in a ritzy salon with coffered ceiling, pink linen tablecloths, and antique paintings in the winter. The menu features such deliciously visual delights as *linguine con rughetta e scampi* (flat spaghetti with chicory and shrimps) and *tagliata di manzo con mosaico di insalatine* (sliced beef on a bed of salad greens arranged in a mosaic pattern). *Piazza Ognissanti 3, tel. 055/264201. Reservations advised in summer. AE, DC, MC, V.*

★ **Enoteca Pinchiorri.** In the beautiful Renaissance palace and its charming garden courtyard that was home to Giovanni da Verrazzano (a 15th-century Florentine navigator), husband-and-wife team Giorgio Pinchiorri and Annie Feolde have created an exceptional restaurant that ranks as one of Italy's best. Guests can enjoy Annie's rediscoveries of traditional Tuscan dishes, or her own brand of imaginatively creative nouvelle cuisine, while Giorgio oversees the extraordinary wine cellar. There is a moderately priced luncheon menu. *Via Ghibellina 87, tel. 055/ 242757. Reservations well in advance are advised at all times. AE, DC, V. Closed Sun., Mon. lunch, Aug.*

Expensive   **Cammillo.** This is a classic Florentine eating place, with terracotta tiles on the floor and several brick-vaulted rooms where guests enjoy such regional and international specialties as chicken livers with sage and beans or porcini mushrooms *alla parmigiana*, with a touch of truffle. The excellent house wine and olive oil are made by the owners. *Borgo San Jacopo 57/r, tel. 055/212427. Reservations advised; required for dinner. AE, DC, MC, V. Closed Wed., Thurs.; 3 weeks in Aug.; 3 weeks in Dec.*

★   **Da Noi.** Located near Santa Croce, Da Noi has a reputation as one of Florence's best for creative cuisine and a relaxed atmosphere. It's small, seating only 28 in a dining room whose dark antique sideboards contrast with rustic white walls. The cooking reflects French influences; among the specialties are crêpes with a sauce of peppers, and warm squab salad. *Via Fiesolana 46/r, tel. 055/242917. Reservations required; call 3 days ahead. No credit cards. Closed Sun., Mon., Aug.*

★   **Sabatini.** One of Florence's finest for many years, Sabatini upholds the tradition very well. Classic Florentine decor, with dark wood-paneled walls, terra-cotta floors, and white linen tablecloths, is brightened by the paintings on the walls and by a cordial welcome. Specialties on the menu, which offers both Tuscan and international cuisines, are *panzerotti alla Sabatini* (creamy, cheese-filled crêpes) and baked spinach with a chicken liver sauce. *Via Panzani 9/a, tel. 055/211559. Reservations advised. AE, DC, MC, V. Closed Mon.*

★   **Terrazza Brunelleschi.** The rooftop restaurant of the hotel Baglioni has the best view in town. The dining room, decorated in creamy tones and with a floral carpet, has big picture windows; the summer-dining terrace is charming, with tables under arbors and turrets for guests to climb to get an even better view. The menu offers such traditional Tuscan dishes as *minestra di fagioli* (bean soup) and other more innovative choices, such as a pâté of peppers and tomato. *Hotel Baglioni, Piazza Unità Italiana 6, tel. 055/215642. Reservations advised, especially in summer. AE, DC, MC, V.*

Moderate   **Buca Mario.** Visitors can expect to share a table at this characteristically unadorned *buca* (downstairs trattoria), whose menu includes such hearty down-to-earth Tuscan food as homemade *pappardelle* (noodles) and *stracotto* (beef stew with beans). It's near Santa Maria Novella. *Piazza Ottaviani 16/r, tel. 055/214179. Reservations advised in evening. AE, DC, MC, V. Closed, Wed. and Aug.*

Il Fagioli. This typical Florentine trattoria near Santa Croce has a simple decor and a menu in which such local dishes as *ribollita* (a sort of minestrone) and *involtini* (meat roll) predominate. The antipasti are always tempting here, but you're expected to have a two-course meal. *Corso Tintori 47/r, tel. 055/244285. Dress: informal. Reservations advised. No credit cards. Closed weekends, Aug., and Christmas Day.*

Leo. Located in the Santa Croce area, Leo serves tourists (especially at lunch) and locals in an attractive setting of vaulted ceilings and dark Tuscan-style wooden chairs. Order the daily specials here and the *crostini Pier Capponi* (toast rounds with a savory topping) and *Lombatina alla Leo* (veal chop with mushrooms, asparagus, and truffle). *Via Torta 7/r, tel. 055/ 210829. Dinner reservations advised. AE, DC, MC, V. Closed Mon. and mid-July–mid-Aug.*

Mario da Ganino. Highly informal, rustic, and cheerful, this trattoria greets you with a taste of mortadella, and offers homemade pastas and *gnudoni* (ravioli without pasta), plus a heavenly cheesecake for dessert. There are plenty of other taste-tempters on the menu. It's tiny, seating only 35, double that in summer at outdoor tables. *Piazza dei Cimatori 4/r, tel. 055/214125. Reservations advised. AE, DC. Closed Sun. and Aug. 15–25.*

Inexpensive
★
Angiolino. You won't regret taking a meal at this bustling little trattoria, which has a real charcoal grill and an old wood-burning stove to keep its customers warm on nippy days. Glowing with authentic atmosphere, Angiolino offers such Tuscan specialties as *ribollita* (minestrone) and juicy *bistecca alla fiorentina* (T-bone steak basted in olive oil and black pepper). The bistecca will push the bill up into the Moderate range. *Via Santo Spirito 36/r, tel. 055/298976. Reservations advised in the evening. No credit cards. Closed Sun. dinner, Mon., and last 3 weeks in July.*

Caminetto. Try the *maccheroni alla Maremmana* (pasta with sausages, tomato, and black olive) or *pappa al pomodoro* (tomato and bread soup) in the typically rustic setting of Caminetto. It's very handy for a quick lunch before or after visiting the cathedral. *Via dello Studio 34/r, tel. 055/296274. Dinner reservations advised. No credit cards. Closed Tues., Wed., and July.*

Lodging

What with mass tourism and trade fairs, rooms are at a premium in Florence for most of the year. Make reservations well in advance. If you arrive without a reservation, the ITA office in the railway station (open 8:20 AM–9 PM) can help you, but there may be a long line. Now that most traffic is banned in the downtown area, hotel rooms are quieter. Local traffic and motorcycles can still be bothersome, however, so check the decibel level before you settle in.

Florence offers a good choice of accommodations. Room rates are on a par with other European capitals, and porters, room service, and in-house cleaning and laundering are disappearing in Moderate and Inexpensive hotels. Taxes and service are included in the room rate. Breakfast is an extra charge, and you can decline to take breakfast in the hotel, though the desk may not be happy about it; make this clear when booking or checking in. Air-conditioning also may be an extra charge. In older hotels, room quality may be uneven; if you don't like the room you're given, ask for another. Specify if you care about having either a bath or shower, as not all rooms have both. In Moderate and Inexpensive places, showers may be the drain-in-the-floor type guaranteed to flood the bathroom.

Hostels Italian hotels are officially classified from five-star (deluxe) to one-star (guest houses and small inns). Prices are established officially and a rate card on the back of the door of your room or inside the closet door tells you exactly what you will pay for that particular room. Any variations should be cause for complaint and should be reported to the local tourist office. CIGA, Jolly, Space, Atahotels, and Italhotels are among the reliable chains or groups operating in Italy, with CIGA among the most luxurious. Sheraton hotels are making an impact in Italy in a big way, though most, located in Rome, Florence, Bari, Padua, and Catania, tend to be geared toward convention and business travel. There are a few Relais et Châteaux member hotels that are noted for individual atmosphere, personal service, and luxury; they are also expensive. The AGIP chain is found mostly on main highways.

Good-value accommodations can be found at one-star hotels and *locande* (inns). Rooms are usually spotlessly clean but basic, with shower and toilets down the hall.

Rentals More and more people are discovering the attractions of renting a house, cottage, or apartment in the Italian countryside. These are ideal for families or for groups of up to eight people looking for a bargain—or just independence. Availability is subject to change, so it is best to ask your travel agent or the nearest branch of ENIT, the Italian tourist board, about rentals.

Ratings The following price categories are for two people in a double room. Best bets are indicated by a star ★.

Category	Cost
Very Expensive	over 400,000 lire
Expensive	200,000–400,000 lire
Moderate	130,000–180,000 lire
Inexpensive	under 110,000 lire

Very Expensive **Excelsior.** One of the flagships of the CIGA chain, the Excelsior
★ provides consistently superlative service and is lavishly appointed with old prints, bouquets of flowers, pink marble, and carpets so deep you could lose a shoe in them. The hotel occupies a former patrician palace on the Arno, and many rooms have river views (some with Tuscan antiques scattered around as well). The Cestello restaurant (*see* Dining, above) is excellent. *Piazza Ognissanti 3, tel. 055/264201, fax 055/210278. 205 rooms with bath. Facilities: garage. AE, DC, MC, V.*

Regency. One of the Ottaviani family's small, select hotels, the Regency has the intimate and highly refined atmosphere of a private villa, luxuriously furnished with antiques and decorated with great style. Just outside the historic center of the city, it has a charming garden and the pleasant Le Jardin restaurant. *Piazza Massimo d'Azeglio 3, tel. 055/245247, fax 055/234-2937. 31 rooms with bath. Facilities: garage. AE, DC, MC, V.*

Villa Cora. Located in a residential area on a hill overlooking the Oltrano section of Florence and across the Arno to the Duomo and Bell Tower, the Villa Cora is a converted private villa. Furnishings are exquisite and the atmosphere is quietly elegant. There are gardens in which to stroll, a pool in which to wallow, and a formal but charming restaurant in which to dine. There is a Mercedes shuttle service between the hotel and the center of Florence. *Viale Machiavelli 18, tel. 055/229–8451, fax 055/229086. 48 rooms with bath. AE, DC, V.*

Expensive **Baglioni.** Spacious, elegant, and very grand, Baglioni has well-
★ proportioned rooms tastefully decorated in antique Florentine style. Many rooms have leaded glass windows, and some have views of Santa Maria Novella. The hotel also has a charming roof terrace, and the splendid Terrazza Brunelleschi restaurant (*see* Dining, above), which has the best view in all Florence (the food is memorable, too). *Piazza Unità d'Italia 6, tel. 055/218441, fax 055/215695. 197 rooms with bath. Facilities: garage. AE, DC, MC, V.*

Bernini Palace. The atmosphere here is one of austere yet elegant simplicity. Rooms are not ostentatious but are, rather, well-furnished in pastel fabrics and mahogany furniture. Entirely air-conditioned and double-glazed, the Bernini has a quiet, tranquil feel, yet is only a few steps from the frenetically busy Piazza della Signoria. There is no restaurant, but breakfast is served in a historic salon. *Piazza San Firenze 29, tel. 055/278621, fax 055/219653. 86 rooms with bath. AE, DC, MC, V.*

Grand Hotel Minerva. A modern building with views of one of the city's beautiful squares, the Minerva will suit travelers who care more for efficiency than atmosphere. The nicest rooms overlook the garden, and the rooftop pool provides a refreshing diversion. *Piazza Santa Maria Novella 16, tel. 055/284555, fax 055/268281. 96 rooms with bath. Facilities: restaurant, pool. AE, DC, MC, V.*

★ **Monna Lisa.** This place is the closest you may come to living in an aristocratic palace in the heart of Florence. American visitors in particular are fond of its smallish but homey bedrooms and sumptuously comfortable sitting rooms. Ask for a room on the quiet 17th-century courtyard, especially the one with the delightful balcony. A lavish buffet breakfast is included in the price. Make reservations months in advance to be assured of a room at this very special hotel. *Borgo Pinti 27, tel. 055/247–9751, fax 055/247–9755. 20 rooms with bath. Facilities: garden, bar, parking. AE, DC, MC, V.*

Moderate **Calzaiuoli.** Although there's an elegant entrance on the pedestrians-only shopping street connecting the cathedral with Piazza della Signoria, don't expect distinctive decor once you're inside (it's actually anemic modern). Still, you couldn't ask for anything more central. *Via dei Calzaiuoli 6, tel. 055/212456. 41 rooms with bath. Facilities: bar. AE, DC, MC, V.*

★ **Loggiato dei Serviti.** You'll find the Loggiato dei Serviti tucked under an arcade in one of the city's quietest and most attractive squares. Vaulted ceilings and tasteful furnishings (some of them antiques) go far to make this hotel a real find for those who want to get the genuine Florentine feel and who will appreciate the 19th-century town house surroundings while enjoying modern creature comforts. There is no restaurant. *Piazza Santissima Annunziata 3, tel. 055/289592, fax 055/289595. 29 rooms with bath. AE, DC, MC, V.*

Porta Rossa. This period piece is only a few steps from the Porcellino straw market and the city's major sights. The authentic Art Nouveau lobby gives a clue to the age of this establishment, as do the worn carpets and creaky plumbing. But it exudes atmosphere; most of the rooms are spacious and comfortable in an old-fashioned way, and a lot of discerning people love it. There is no restaurant. *Via di Porta Rossa 19, tel. 055/*

287551, fax 055/282179. 71 rooms, most with bath. AE, DC, MC, V.

Inexpensive **Liana.** Located in a residential neighborhood, this small hotel is within walking distance of most sights. It's a dignified 19th-century town house with pleasant rooms overlooking the garden and bright new baths. *Via Vittorio Alfieri 18, tel. 055/ 245303., fax 055/234–4596. 18 rooms, 14 with bath. Facilities: parking lot, garden. AE, MC, V.*

Palazzo Vecchio. The Vecchio presents a fine example of minimal decor in an otherwise attractive 19th-century building close to the train station. Spacious rooms can accommodate extra beds. *Via Cennini 4, tel. 055/212182. 18 rooms, 16 with bath. Facilities: parking lot. AE, DC, MC, V.*

The Arts

For a list of events, pick up a *Florence Concierge Information* booklet from your hotel desk, or the monthly information bulletin published by the **Comune Aperto** city information office (Via Cavour 1/r).

Music and Ballet Most major musical events are staged at the **Teatro Comunale** (Corso Italia 16, tel. 055/277–9236). The box office (closed Monday) is open from 9 to 1, and a half-hour before performances. It's best to order your tickets by mail, however, as they're difficult to come by at the last minute. You can also order concert and ballet tickets through **Universalturismo** (Via degli Speziali 7/r, tel. 055/217241). **Amici della Musica** (Friends of Music) puts on a series of concerts at the **Teatro della Pergola** (box office, Via della Pergola 10a/r, tel. 055/247–9651). For program information, contact the Amici della Musica directly at Via Sirtori 49 (tel. 055/608420).

Film English-language films are shown at the **Cinema Astro,** on Piazza San Simone near Santa Croce. There are two shows every evening, Tuesday through Sunday. It closes in July.

Nightlife

Piano Bars Many of the top hotels have piano bars; that of the **Plaza Lucchesi** (Lungarno della Zecca Vecchia 38, tel. 055/264141) is particularly spacious and pleasant. The terrace of the hotel **Baglioni** *(see* Lodging, above) has no music but has one of the best views in Florence, candlelit tables, and a wonderful atmosphere. **Loggia Tornaquinci** (Via Tornabuoni 6, tel. 055/219148) is a sophisticated cocktail lounge with yet another soul-stirring view. **Caffé Pitti** (Piazza Pitti 9, tel. 055/296241) is a social center for a young international crowd.

Nightclubs **The River Club** (Lungarno Corsini 8, tel. 055/282465) has winter-garden decor and a large dance floor (closed Sun.). **Central Park** (Via Fosso Macinante 13, tel. 055/356723), in the Cascine park, is open all year.

Discos **Jackie O** (Via dell'Erta Canina 24a, tel. 055/234–2442) is a glittering Art Deco disco with lots of mirrors and marble and a trendy clientele (closed Wed.). **Space Electronic** (Via Palazzuolo 37, tel. 055/295082) is exactly what its name implies: ultramodern and psychedelic (closed Mon., except from Mar. to Sept., when it's open every night). **Yab Yum** (Via Sassetti 5/r, tel. 055/282018) is another futuristic-style disco popular with the young international set. It's closed Monday.

11 Geneva

Arriving and Departing

By Plane Cointrin (tel. 022/7177111), Geneva's airport, is served by several airlines that fly directly to the city from New York, Toronto, or London. Check with individual airlines for their schedules.

Between the Airport and Downtown Cointrin has a direct rail link with Cornavin, the city's main train station, which is located in the center of town. Trains run about every 10 minutes from 5:30 AM to midnight. The trip takes about six minutes, and the fare is 4.50 Fr. for second class.

There is regular city bus service from the airport to the center of Geneva. The bus takes about 20 minutes, and the fare is 1.80 Fr. Some hotels have their own bus service.

Taxis, though plentiful, are very expensive, charging at least 20 Fr. to the city center.

By Train All services—domestic and international—use Cornavin Station in the center of the city. For information, dial 022/7152111.

By Bus Buses generally arrive at and depart from the bus station at place Dorcière, behind the English church, in the city center.

By Car Since Geneva sits on France's doorstep, entry from France, just a few minutes away, is the most accessible. Or enter from the north, via Lausanne.

Getting Around

By Bus and Streetcar There are scheduled services by local buses and trains every few minutes on all routes. Before you board, you must buy your ticket from the machines at the stops (they have English instructions). Save money and buy a ticket covering unlimited travel all day for 8 Fr. If you have a **Swiss Pass,** you can travel free.

By Taxi Taxis are extremely expensive; use them only if there's no alternative. There is a 5 Fr. minimum charge per passenger just to get into the cab.

Guided Tours

Orientation Tours Bus tours around Geneva are operated by **Key Tours** (tel. 022/7314140). They leave from the bus station in place Dorcière, behind the English church, at 10 and 2. These tours, which involve some walking in the Old Town, last about two hours and cost 20 Fr.

Special-Interest Tours The United Nations organizes tours around the Palais des Nations. Take bus No. 8 or F past Nations to the Appia stop. Enter by the Pregny Gate in the avenue de la Paix. Tours, lasting about an hour, are given regularly from September to June, 10–noon and 2–4; July and August, 9–noon and 2–6. They cost 7 Fr.

The tourist office will provide you with an audio-guided tour (in English) of the Old Town that covers 26 points of interest, complete with map, cassette, and player; rental: 7 Fr. A refundable deposit of 50 Fr. is required.

Excursions There are bus excursions from Geneva to Lausanne, Montreux, the Mont Blanc area, the Jura, and the Bernese Oberland. They vary considerably according to the weather and time of year, so inquire locally.

Boat excursions vary for the same reasons. When the weather is good, take one of the delightful day-long trips that stop at some of the waterside villages on the vineyard-fringed lake; some trips also pass by or stop at the 13th-century Château de Chillon, inspiration of Byron's *The Prisoner of Chillon.* Full details are available from **Mouettes Genevoises** (tel. 022/7322944), **Swiss Boat** (tel. 022/7324747), **Compagnie de Navigation** (tel. 022/212521), or from the tourist office.

Tourist Information

Cornavin Station (tel. 022/7385200). Open July–Sept., daily 8 AM–10 PM; Oct.–June, Mon.–Sat. 9–6, Sun. 4–8. **Thomas Cook** (64 Rue de Lausanne, tel. 022/7324555).

Exploring Geneva

Draped at the foot of the Juras and the Alps on the westernmost tip of Lake Geneva (or Lac Léman, as the natives know it), Geneva is the most cosmopolitan and graceful of Swiss cities and the stronghold of the French-speaking territory. Just a stone's throw from the French border and 160 kilometers (100 miles) or so from Lyon, its grand mansarded mansions stand guard beside the river Rhône, where yachts bob, gulls dive, and Rolls-Royces purr beside manicured promenades. The combination of Swiss efficiency and French savoir faire gives the city a chic polish, and the infusion of international blood from the United Nations adds a heterogeneity that is rare for a population of only 160,000.

Headquarters of the World Health Organization and the International Red Cross, Geneva has always been a city of humanity and enlightenment, offering refuge to writers Voltaire, Hugo, Dumas, Balzac, and Stendhal, as well as to religious reformers Calvin and Knox. Byron, Shelley, Wagner, and Liszt all fled from scandals to Geneva's sheltering arms.

A Roman seat for 500 years (from 120 BC), then home to early Burgundians, Geneva flourished under bishop-princes into the 11th century, fending off the greedy dukes of Savoy in conflicts that lasted into the 17th century. Under the guiding fervor of Calvin, Geneva rejected Catholicism and became a stronghold of Protestant reforms. In 1798 it fell to the French, but joined the Swiss Confederation as a canton in 1815, shortly after Napoleon's defeat. The French accent remains nonetheless.

Numbers in the margin correspond to points of interest on the Geneva map.

Start your walk from Gare de Cornavin (Cornavin Station) and
❶ head down the rue du Mont-Blanc to the **Pont du Mont-Blanc,** which spans the last gasp of the Rhône as it pours into the open waters of Lac Léman. From the middle of the bridge (if it's clear) you can see the snowy peak of Mont Blanc itself, and from March to October you'll have a fine view of the **Jet D'Eau,** Europe's highest fountain, gushing 132 meters (425 feet) into the air.

Back at the foot of the bridge, turn right onto quai du Mont-
❷ Blanc to reach the **Monument Brunswick,** the high-Victorian

tomb of a duke of Brunswick who left his fortune to Geneva in 1873. Just north are the city's grandest hotels, overlooking a manicured garden walk and the embarkation points for excursion boats. If you continue north a considerable distance through elegant parks and turn inland on the avenue de la Paix, ❸ you'll reach the enormous **International Complex,** where the Palais de Nations houses the European seat of the United Nations. (You can also reach it by taking bus No. 8 or F from the train station. For guided tour information, *see* Special-Interest Tours.)

Or turn left from the Pont du Mont-Blanc and walk down the ❹ elegant quai des Bergues. In the center of the Rhône is **Ile J.J. Rousseau** (Rousseau Island), with a statue of the Swiss-born ❺ philosopher. Turn left onto the **Pont de l'Ile,** where the tall Tour de l'Ile, once a medieval prison, houses the tourist office. Turn left again and cross the place Bel-Air, the center of the business and banking district, and follow the rue de la Corraterie to the ❻ **place Neuve.** Here you'll see the **Grand Théâtre,** which hosts opera, ballet, and sometimes the Orchestre de la Suisse Romande (it also performs at nearby Victoria Hall), and the **Conservatoire de Musique.** Also at this address is the **Musée Rath,** with top-notch temporary exhibitions. *Tel. 022/285616. Admission: 5 Fr. Open Tues.–Sun. 10–noon and 2–6; also Wed. evening 8–10.*

Above the ancient ramparts on your left are some of the wealthiest old homes in Geneva. Enter the gated park before you, the promenade des Bastions, site of the university, and keep left ❼ until you see the famous **Monument de la Réformation,** which pays homage to such Protestant pioneers as Bèze, Calvin, Farel, and Knox. Passing the uphill ramp and continuing to the farther rear gate, take the park exit just beyond the monument and turn left on the rue St-Leger, passing through the ivy-covered arch and winding up in the **Vieille Ville,** or Old Town.

When you reach the ancient place du Bourg-de-Four, once a Roman forum, you can turn right on rue des Chaudronniers and ❽ head for the **Musée d'Art et Histoire,** with its fine collection of paintings, sculpture, and archaeological relics. *2 rue Charles-Galland, tel. 022/290011. Admission free. Open Tues.–Sun. 10–5.*

❾ Just beyond are the spiraling cupolas of the **Russian church** and ❿ the **Bauer Collection** of Oriental arts. *8 rue Munier-Romilly, tel. 022/461729. Admission: 5 Fr. Open Tues.–Sun. 2–6.*

Alternatively, from the place du Bourg-de-Four, head left up ⓫ any number of narrow streets and stairs toward the **Cathédrale St-Pierre,** with its schizophrenic mix of Classical and Gothic styles. Under its nave (entrance outside) is concealed one of the biggest archaeological digs in Europe, a massive excavation of the cathedral's early Christian roots, now restored as a stunning maze of backlit walkways over mosaics, baptisteries, and ancient foundations. *Admission: 5 Fr. Open Tues.–Sun. 10–1 and 2–6.*

⓬ Opposite the cathedral is the 16th-century **Hôtel de Ville,** where in 1864, in the Alabama Hall, the Geneva Convention was signed by 16 countries, laying the foundations for the International Red Cross. *Individual visits by request. Guided group tours by advance arrangement, tel. 022/272209.*

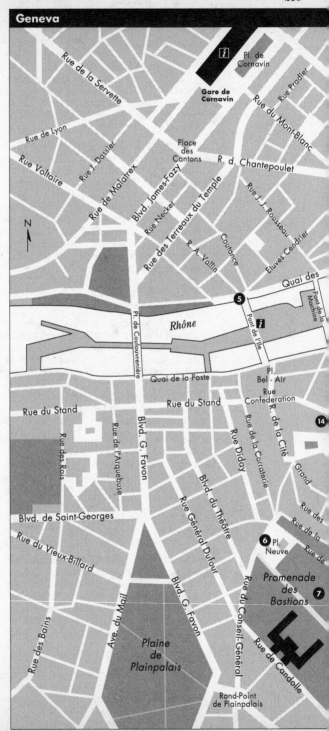

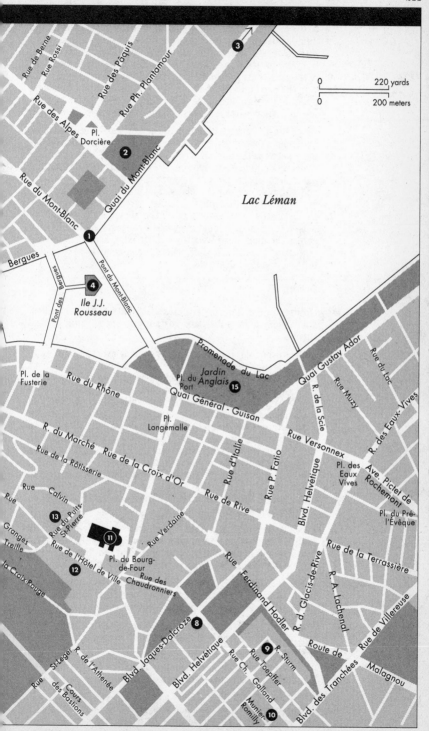

Rue de Berne

Rue Rossi

Rue des Pâquis

Rue Ph. Plantamour

3

Rue des Alpes

Pl. Dorcière

2

Rue du Mont-Blanc

Quai du Mont-Blanc

Lac Léman

220 yards

200 meters

1

Bergues

Pont des Bergues

Pont du Mont-Blanc

4

Ile J.J. Rousseau

Pl. de la Fusterie

Rue du Rhône

Promenade du Lac

Pl. du Port

Jardin Anglais **15**

Quai Général - Guisan

Quai Gustav Ador

R. de la Scie

Rue Muzy

Rue du Lac

R. des Eaux-Vives

R. du Marché

Rue de la Croix d'Or

Pl. Longemalle

Rue Versonnex

Rue de la Rôtisserie

Rue d'Italie

Rue P. Fatio

Blvd. Helvétique

Pl. des Eaux Vives

Ave. Pictet de Rochemont

Rue

Calvin

Rue de Rive

Pl. du Pré-l'Évêque

Rue

Rue du Puits-St-Pierre

13

Granges

Treille

11

Rue Verdaine

Rue de la Terrassière

R. d. Glacis-de-Rive

R.-A.-Lachenal

la Croix-Rouge

Rue de l'Hôtel de Ville

12

Pl. du Bourg-de-Four

Rue des Chaudronniers

Rue Ferdinand Hodler

Rue de Villereuse

8

Rue Jaques-Dalcroze

Blvd. Helvétique

Rue Ch. Galland

Rue Toepffer

R. Sturm

9

Route de

Blvd. des Tranchées

Malagnou

St-Léger

R. de l'Athénée

Rue

Cours des Bastions

Munier-Romilly

10

The winding, cobbled streets leading from the cathedral down to the modern city are lined with antiques shops, galleries, and unique but often expensive boutiques. The medieval Grand Rue is the oldest in Geneva, the rue de l'Hôtel de Ville features lovely 17th-century homes, and the rue Calvin has noble mansions of the 18th century (No. 11 is on the site of Calvin's house). No. **⑬** 6 on the rue du Puits-St-Pierre is the **Maison Tavel,** the oldest building in town and home of an intimate re-creation of daily life and urban history. *Admission free. Open Tues.–Sun. 10–5.*

Down the hill, plunge back into the new city and one of the most luxurious shopping districts in Europe, which stretches temptingly between the quai Général-Guisan, rue du Rhône, rue de la Croix d'Or, and rue du Marché. It's tough enough to resist top name *prêt-à-porter* (ready-to-wear clothing), dazzling jewelry and watches, luscious chocolates, and luxurious furs and leathers, but the glittering boutiques of the new three-story **⑭ Confédération Centre**—where all the above are concentrated with a vengeance—could melt the strongest resolve. Escape across the quai, head back toward the lake, and come to your **⑮** senses in the **Jardin Anglais,** where the famous floral clock will tell you that it's time to stop.

Dining

Options range from luxury establishments to modest cafés, *stübli* (cozy little pubs), and restaurants specializing in local cuisine.

Because the Swiss are so good at preparing everyone else's cuisine, it is sometimes said that they have none of their own, but there definitely is a distinct and characteristic Swiss cuisine. Switzerland is the home of great cheeses—Gruyère, Emmentaler, Appenzeller, and Vacherin—which form the basis of many dishes. *Raclette* is cheese melted over a fire and served with potatoes and pickles, *Rösti* are hash brown potatoes, and *fondue* is a bubbling pot of melted cheeses flavored with garlic and kirsch, into which you dip chunks of bread. Other Swiss specialties to look for are *geschnetzeltes Kalbfleisch* (veal bits in cream sauce), *polenta* (cornmeal mush) in the Italian region, and fine game in autumn. A wide variety of Swiss sausages make both filling and inexpensive meals, and in every region the breads are varied and superb.

Perch fresh from Lac Léman, cream-sauced *omble chevalier* (a kind of salmon trout), Lyonnaise *cardon* (a celerylike vegetable often served in casseroles), pigs' feet, and the famous cheese fondue are specialties of this most French of Swiss cities.

Mealtimes At home, the main Swiss meal of the day is lunch, with a snack in the evening. Restaurants, however, are open at midday and during the evening; often limited menus are offered all day.

Watch for *Tagesteller* (fixed-price lunch menus), which enable you to experience the best restaurants without paying high à la carte rates.

Dress Jacket and tie are suggested for restaurants in the Very Expensive and Expensive categories; casual dress is acceptable elsewhere.

Ratings Prices are per person, without wine or coffee, but including tip and taxes. Best bets are indicated by a star ★.

Category	Cost
Very Expensive	over 80 Fr.
Expensive	50 Fr.–80 Fr.
Moderate	30 Fr.–50 Fr.
Inexpensive	under 30 Fr.

Very Expensive **Le Béarn.** A gastronomic mecca whose reputation carries well
★ past Geneva's boundaries, this relatively unpretentious place
is discreetly tucked into a tiny basement room. Chef Goddard's
innovative *cuisine du marché* includes such specialties as ravioli stuffed with Scotch salmon and *fin de claire* oysters, as well as
a spectacular soufflé of fresh truffles. The business lunch special, averaging under 60 Fr., offers extraordinary savings—
but reserve well in advance. *4 quai de la Poste, tel. 022/210028.
Reservations required. AE, DC, MC, V.*

Les Continents. It's often a shock to find exceptional restaurants in modern business hotels, but this one—at the base of
the Inter-Continental's 18 stories—serves contemporary
French cuisine at its very best. Because it's located in the
United Nations and embassy district, *tout le monde* gathers
here. 7–9 ch. du Petit-Saconnex, tel. 022/7346091. Reservations required. AE, DC, MC, V.

Expensive **Brasserie Lipp.** Oddly out of context on the third floor of a glitzy
★ new shopping center, this clever variation on its Parisian counterpart serves upscale brasserie fare (oysters, foie gras), as
well as earthy classics to mobs of glossy, lively internationals. Diners go dressy-casual, usually with furs. *Confédération
Centre, tel. 022/293122. Reservations advised. AE, DC, MC,
V.*

Restaurant et Brasserie Lyrique. Across the place Neuve from
the Grand Théâtre, this grand old bentwood-and-tile café and
its plush, pillared dining hall share several menu items (you pay
about 20% more for the full restaurant experience), including
hot entrée salads and classic grilled meats. The last seating is
after the opera. *12 blvd. du Théâtre, tel. 022/280095. Reservations required. AE, DC, MC, V.*

Moderate **Les Armures.** When exploring the Old Town, it's worth veering
off the place du Bourg-de-Four to lunch here, by the Hôtel de
Ville: The ambience is warm and lively, the setting historic
(medieval armor and arms), and local dishes are unusually well
prepared. Daily lunch specials are generous and cheap. This
claims to be the oldest restaurant in Geneva. *1 rue du Puits-St-
Pierre, tel. 022/283442. Reservations advised. AE, DC, MC, V.*

Chez Bouby. This bistro has been stripped, scrubbed, and renovated to *look* old. Chez Bouby hops at all hours; good, plain
food, with an emphasis on *abats* or innards (tripe, andouillette,
sweetbreads), is served until 1 AM. Open wine specials. *1 rue
Grenus, tel. 022/7310927. Reservations not necessary; there's
often a line. MC, V.*

Café du Centre. There's a restaurant upstairs, but the action's
in the slightly grubby, downscale diner on the ground floor,
where crowds of students, businessmen, chic couples, and
marginals all let their hair down and dig into impeccably fresh,
plain seafood. Skip the meat standards, watch for fixed-price
fish menus, stretch out your legs in a booth, and relax: Most

people linger long after their meal. *5 place du Molard, tel. 022/ 218586. No reservations. AE, DC, MC, V.*

Inexpensive **Buffet de la Gare.** It's the real thing, with wooden benches, mesh curtains, and locals dining and drinking at all hours. The noisy open kitchen, bustling waiters, and incongruous cocktail piano give a sausage, schnitzel, or omelet a festive touch. There are generous portions and daily wine specials. One isolated wing attracts unsavory young characters, so stick to the cheery main room off the "restaurant français." *Gare Cornavin, tel. 022/7324306. No reservations. AE, DC, MC, V.*

★ **Le Café du Grütli.** This is a high-tech, high-style student canteen in the postmodernized Maison Grütli, where Geneva offers creative space to its painters, sculptors, photographers, and filmmakers. The light nouvelle lunches and late snacks are as hip as the clientele. *Maison Grütli, rue Général-Dufour 16, tel. 022/294495. Reservations advised. No credit cards.*

Lodging

Switzerland's accommodations cover a broad range, from the most luxurious hotels to the more economical rooms in private homes. Pick up the *Schweizer Hotelführer (Swiss Hotel Guide)* from the SNTO before you leave home. The guide is free and lists all the members of the Swiss Hotel Association (comprising nearly 90% of the nation's accommodations); it tells you everything you'll want to know.

Most hotel rooms today have private bath and shower; those that don't are usually considerably cheaper. Single rooms are generally about two-thirds the price of doubles, but this can vary considerably. Remember that the no-nonsense Swiss sleep in separate beds or, at best, a double with separate bedding. If you prefer more sociable arrangements, ask for the rare "matrimonial" or "French" bed. Service charges and taxes are included in the price quoted and the bill you pay. Breakfast is included unless there is a clear notice to the contrary. In resorts especially, half pension (choice of a noon or evening meal) may be included in the room price. If you choose to eat à la carte or elsewhere, the management will generally reduce your price. Give them plenty of notice, however.

All major towns and train stations have hotel-finding services, which sometimes charge a small fee. Local tourist offices will also help.

Hotels Hotels are graded from one star (the lowest) to five stars. Always confirm what you are paying before you register, and check the posted price when you get to your room. Major credit cards are generally accepted, but, again, make sure beforehand.

Two important hotel chains are the Romantik Hotels and Restaurants and Relais & Châteaux, with premises that are generally either in historic houses or houses that have some special character. Another chain that has a good reputation is Best Western, affiliated with the familar American chain. The Check-In E and G Hotels is a voluntary group of small hotels, boardinghouses, and mountain lodges that offer accommodations at reasonable prices. Details are available from the SNTO, which also offers pamphlets recommending family ho-

tels and a list of hotels and restaurants that cater specifically to
Jewish travelers.

Rentals Rentals are available from the **Swiss Touring Club** (rue Pierre
Fatio 9, CH-1211 Geneva 3) or from **Uto-Ring AG** (Beetho-
venstr. 24, 8002 Zürich). In the United States, write to
Interhome (36 Carlos Dr., Fairfield, NJ 07006). In Britain, con-
tact **Interhome** (383 Richmond Rd., Twickenham, Middlesex
TW1 2EF).

Ratings Prices are for two people in a double room with bath or shower,
including taxes, service charges, and breakfast. Best bets are
indicated by a star ★.

Category	Cost
Very Expensive	over 400 Fr.
Expensive	250 Fr.–400 Fr.
Moderate	120 Fr.–250 Fr.
Inexpensive	under 120 Fr.

Very Expensive **Les Armures.** In the heart of the Vieille Ville, this archaeologi-
★ cal treasure, restored to its 17th-century splendor, offsets its
charming original stonework, frescoes, and stenciled beams
with impeccable modern comforts. Its popular restaurant—
the oldest in Geneva—serves Swiss specialties. *1 rue du Puits-
St-Pierre, tel. 022/289172. 28 rooms with bath. Facilities: restaurant, bar. AE, DC, MC, V.*

Beau Rivage. Hushed, genteel, and a trifle creaky, this grand
old Victorian palace has had much of its original 1865 decor
restored: It's all velvet, parquet, and frescoed splendor. Its
highly rated restaurant, Le Chat Botté, has a terrace with
magnificent views across the lake. *13 quai du Mont-Blanc, tel.
022/7310221. 115 rooms with bath. Facilities: 2 restaurants,
terrace café, bar. AE, DC, MC, V.*

Expensive **La Cigogne.** Offbeat and fantastical, every room here show-
cases varied decorative styles and sometimes questionable
tastes. You can enjoy antiques, some working fireplaces, and
lovely slate-roof-and-chimney views while being in the heart of
the luxury shopping area. *17 pl. Longemalle, tel. 022/214242.
50 rooms with bath. Facilities: restaurant, bar. AE, DC, MC,
V.*

★ **Metropole.** Built in 1855, then lent to the city of Geneva to
house Red Cross archives for prisoners of war, now lovingly
renovated by its management of 24 years, the Metropole has as
much riverside splendor as its Right Bank sisters—for a lower
price. There's a relaxed, unfussy ambience, with leather and
hunting prints, and the sleek restaurant L'Arlequin has earned
gastronomic kudos. The riverside rooms are noisier, but the
view merits the inconvenience; ask for the quieter third or
fourth floors. It's seconds from the best shopping and minutes
from the Old Town. *34 quai Général-Guisan, tel. 022/211344.
140 rooms with bath. Facilities: restaurant, bar, café. AE, DC,
MC, V.*

Moderate **Strasbourg-Univers.** A stylish oasis in the slightly sleazy train-
station neighborhood, this just-renovated spot offers sleek de-
cor, convenience, and four-star quality for a three-star price.
The new look is marble and faux exotic wood; a few older, less

flashy rooms were redone eight years ago but don't show the wear. *10 rue Pradier, tel. 022/7322562. 58 rooms with bath or shower. AE, DC, MC, V.*

★ **Touring-Balance.** The lower floors are tired but gracious, with French doors and chic new paint; ask to stay in the slick, solid high-tech rooms on the higher floors. There are gallery-quality lithos in every room. This place shares La Cigogne's great location. The single rooms without bath are the best deal in town at 80 Fr. *13 pl. Longemalle, tel. 022/287122. 64 rooms with bath. Facilities: restaurant, café. AE, DC, MC, V.*

Inexpensive **De la Cloche.** This once luxurious walk-up flat has a tidy, taste-
★ ful new decor and a quiet courtyard setting. Good-size rooms share a bath down the hall. The price may be the lowest in town. *6 rue de la Cloche, tel. 022/7329481. 8 rooms without shower. Breakfast only.*

Des Tourelles. Once worthy of a czar, now host to backpacking bolshevists, this fading Victorian vision offers enormous bay-windowed corner rooms, many with marble fireplaces, French doors, and views over the Rhône. The furnishings are sparse and strictly functional, but the staff is young and friendly. Bring earplugs: The location is extremely noisy, over roaring bridge traffic. *2 blvd. James-Fazy, tel. 022/7324423. 25 rooms, some with shower. Breakfast only. AE, DC, MC, V.*

12 Lisbon

Arriving and Departing

By Plane Lisbon's Portela Airport is only about 20 minutes from the city by car or taxi. The airport is small, but has been recently modernized; for information, tel. 01/802060.

Between the Airport and Downtown There is a special bus service from the airport into the city center called the *Linha Verde* (Green Line), but taxis here are so much cheaper than in other European capitals that visitors would be wise to take a taxi straight to their destination. The cost into Lisbon is about 700$00, and to Estoril or Sintra, 4,000$00. There are no trains or subways between the airport and the city. Car-rental firms at the airport will provide free maps.

By Train International trains from Paris and Madrid arrive at Santa Apolonia Station (tel. 01/876025), in the center of the city. There is a tourist office at the station and plenty of taxis and porters, but car-rental firms do not have offices there.

Getting Around

Lisbon is a hilly city, and the sidewalks are paved with cobblestones, so walking can be tiring, even when you're wearing comfortable shoes. Fortunately, Lisbon's tram service is one of the best in Europe and buses go all over the city. A **Tourist Pass** for unlimited rides on the tram or bus costs 1,355$00 for a week or 940$00 for four days; it can be purchased at the Cais do Sodré Station and other terminals. Books of 20 discount tickets are also available.

By Tram and Bus Buses and trams operate from 4 AM to 2 AM. Try tram routes 13, 24, 28, 29, and 30 for an inexpensive tour of the city; buses nos. 52, 53, and 54 cross the Tagus bridge. Many of the buses are double-deckers, affording an exceptional view of the city's architecture, which includes a remarkable number of Art Nouveau buildings.

By Subway The subway, called the Metropolitano, operates from 6:30 AM to 1 AM; it is modern and efficient but covers a limited route—watch out for pickpockets!

By Taxi Taxis are easily recognizable by a lighted sign on green roofs. There are ranks in the main squares, but it is easy to hail a cruising vehicle. Taxis take up to four passengers at no extra charge. Rates start at 130$00.

Important Addresses and Numbers

Tourist Information The main Lisbon tourist office (tel. 01/3463643) is located in the Palacio Foz, Praça dos Restauradores, at the Baixa end of the Avenida da Liberdade, the main artery of the city; open Mon.–Sat. 9–8, Sun. 10–6. The tourist office at Lisbon airport (tel. 01/893689) is open daily 9 –midnight, and the office at Avenida António Augusto Aguiar 86 (tel. 01/575086) is open daily 9–6.

Embassies U.S. (Avenida Forças Armadas, tel. 01/726–6600). **Canadian** (Avenida da Liberdade 144-3, tel. 01/3474892). **U.K.** (Rua S. Domingos à Lapa 37, tel. 01/661191).

Emergencies SOS Emergencies (tel. 115). Police (tel. 01/3466141). **Ambulance** (tel. 01/301–7777). **Fire Brigade** (tel. 01/342–2222). **Doc-**

tor: British Hospital (Rua Saraiva de Carvalho 49, tel. 01/602020; night: 01/603785). You can also contact native English-speaking doctors at tel. 01/554113 (Lisbon) and tel. 01/2845317 (Cascais). **Pharmacies:** open weekdays 9–1, 3–7, Saturday 9–1; consult notice on door for nearest one open on weekends or after hours.

Travel Agencies	**American Express Star** (Avenida Sidonio Pais 4, tel. 01/539871). **Wagons-Lits** (Avenida da Liberdade 103, tel. 01/3465344). **Viagens Rawes** (Travessa do Corpo Santo 15, tel. 01/3474089).

Guided Tours

Orientation Tours and Excursions	Various companies organize half-day tours of Lisbon and environs and also full-day trips to more distant places of interest. Those listed below are reliable and offer similar trips and prices. Reservations can be made through any travel agent or hotel. A half-day tour of Lisbon will cost about 4,000$00. A full-day trip north to Obidos, Nazaré, and Fatima will run about 10,000$00. A full day east on the "Roman Route" to Evora and Monsaraz will cost about 9,000$00. Companies are **Gray Line Tours** (Ave. Fontes Pereira de Melo 14–12, tel. 01/577523); **Capristanos** (Ave. Duque de Loulé 47, tel. 01/543580); **Citirama** (Ave. Praia da Vitoria, 12-b, tel. 01/575564); and **Tip Tours** (Ave. Costa Pinto 91–A, 2750 Cascais, tel. 01/283821).
Personal Guides	You can arrange to have the services of a personal guide by contacting the main Lisbon tourist office (*see* Important Addresses and Numbers, above). Beware of unauthorized guides who will approach you at some of the most popular attractions. These people usually are more concerned with "guiding" you to a particular shop or restaurant.

Exploring Lisbon

North of the river Tagus estuary, spread out over a string of hills, Portugal's capital presents unending treats for the eye. Its wide boulevards are bordered by black-and-white mosaic sidewalks made up of tiny cobblestones called *calçada*. Modern, pastel-colored apartment blocks vie for attention with Art Nouveau houses faced with decorative tiles. Winding, hilly streets provide scores of *miradouros*, natural vantage points that offer spectacular views of the bay.

Lisbon is not a city that is easily explored on foot. The steep inclines of many streets present a tough challenge to the casual tourist, and visitors are often surprised to find that, because of the hills, places that appear to be close to one another on a map are actually on different levels. Yet the effort is worthwhile—judicious use of cable cars and the majestic city-center elevator make walking tours a treat even on the hottest summer day.

With a population of around 1 million, Lisbon is a small capital by European standards. Its center stretches north from the spacious Praça do Comércio, one of the largest riverside squares in Europe, to the Rossio, a smaller square lined by shops and sidewalk cafés. This district is known as the Baixa (Low District), and it is one of the earliest examples of town planning on a large scale. The grid of parallel streets between the two squares was built after an earthquake and tidal wave destroyed much of the city in 1755.

The Alfama, the old Moorish quarter that survived the earthquake, lies just to the east of the Baixa, while Belém, where many of the royal palaces and museums are situated, is about 3.2 kilometers (2 miles) to the west.

Numbers in the margin correspond to points of interest on the Lisbon map.

Castelo de São Jorge and the Alfama
The Moors, who imposed their rule on most of the southern Iberian Peninsula during the 8th century, left their mark on Lisbon in many ways. The most visible examples are undoubtedly the imposing castle, set on one of the city's highest hills, and the Alfama, a district of narrow, twisting streets that wind their way up toward the castle. The best way to tour this area of Lisbon is to take a taxi—they're plentiful and cheap—to the castle and walk down; otherwise you'll have little energy left for sightseeing.

① Although the **Castelo de São Jorge** (St. George's Castle) is Moorish in construction, it stands on the site of a fortification used by the Visigoths in the 5th century. Today its idyllic atmosphere is shattered only by the shrieks of the many peacocks that strut through the grounds, a well-tended area that is also home to swans, turkeys, ducks, ravens, and other birds. The castle walls enclose an Arabian palace that formed the residence of the kings of Portugal until the 16th century; there is also a small village lived in by artists and craftspeople. Panoramic views of Lisbon can be seen from the castle walls, but visitors should take care, since the uneven, slippery surfaces have barely been touched for centuries. *Admission free. Open daily 8:30–6.*

② After leaving the castle by its impressive gate, wander down through the warren of streets that make up the **Alfama.** This jumble of whitewashed houses, with their flower-laden balconies and red-tile roofs, managed to survive devastating earthquakes because it rests on foundations of dense bedrock.

③ The Alfama district is a notorious place for getting lost in, but if you can find your way to the Largo Rodrigues de Freitas, a street to the east of the castle, then take a look at the **Museu Marionetta** (Puppet Museum) at No. 19A (Admission: 200$00. Open Tues.–Sun. 11–5). From there head south along the Rua de São Tome to the Largo das Portas do Sol, where you'll find **④** the **Museu de Artes Decorativas** (Museum of Decorative Arts) in the Fundação Ricardo Espirito Santo (Admission: 500$00. Open Tues.–Sat. 10–5). More than 20 workshops teach rare handicrafts—bookbinding, ormulu, carving, and cabinetmaking.

⑤ Head southwest past the Largo de Santa Luzia along the Rua do Limoeiro, which eventually becomes the Rua Augusto Rosa. This route takes you past the **Sé** (cathedral), which is also worth a visit. Built in the 12th century, the Sé has an austere Romanesque interior; its extremely thick walls bear witness to the fact that it also served as a fortress. *Sé. Largo da Sé. Open daily 8:30–6.*

Continue northwest from the cathedral along the Rua de Santo António da Sé, turn left along the Rua da Conceiçao, then right and north up the Rua Augusta. A 10-minute stroll along this street takes you through the **Baixa,** which is also one of Lisbon's main shopping and banking districts. Semipedes-

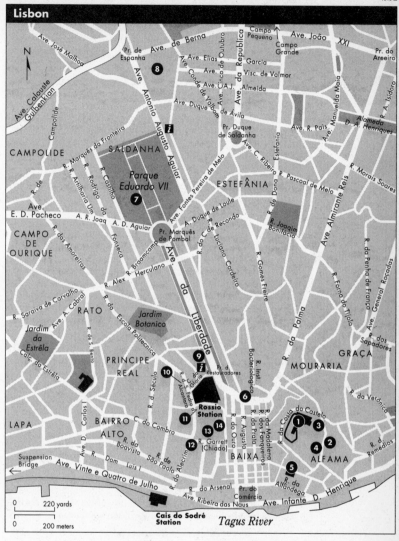

Lisbon

Alfama, **2**

Ascensor de Santa Justa, **14**

Castelo de São Jorge, **1**

Elevador da Gloria, **9**

Gulbenkian Foundation, **8**

Igreja do Carmo, **13**

Igreja de São Roque, **11**

Instituto do Vinho do Porto, **10**

Largo do Chiado, **12**

Museu des Artes Decorativas, **4**

Museu Marionetta, **3**

Parque Eduardo VII, **7**

Rossio Square, **6**

Sé, **5**

trianized, this old-fashioned area boasts a small crafts market, some of the best shoe shops in Europe, and a host of delicatessens selling anything from game birds to *queijo da serra*—a delicious mountain cheese from the Serra da Estrela range north of Lisbon.

Avenida da Liberdade

6 Rua Augusta leads into the **Rossio,** Lisbon's principal square, which in turn opens on its northwestern end into the Praça dos Restauradores. This can be considered the beginning of modern Lisbon, for here the broad, tree-lined **Avenida da Liberdade** (sometimes known as the Portuguese Champs-Élysées) begins its northwesterly ascent, ending more than 1.6 kilo-

7 meters (1 mile) away at the **Parque Eduardo VII** (Edward VII Park).

A leisurely stroll from the Praça dos Restauradores to the park takes about 45 minutes. As you make your way up the Liberdade, you'll find several cafés at its southern end serving coffee and cool drinks, notably the open-air *esplanada* (café), which faces the main post office on the right. You'll also pass through a pleasant mixture of ornate 19th-century architecture and Art Deco buildings from the '30s—a marked contrast to the cool, green atmosphere of the park itself. Rare flowers, trees, and shrubs thrive in the *estufa fria* (cold greenhouse) and the *estufa quente* (hot greenhouse). *Parque Eduardo VII. Admission: 57$00. Open winter, daily 9–5; summer, daily 9–6.*

Turn right from the park and head north along the Avenida António Augusto de Aguiar. A 15-minute walk will bring you to the busy Praça de Espanha, to the right of which, in the Parque

8 de Palhava, is the renowned **Gulbenkian Foundation,** a cultural trust. The foundation's art center houses treasures that were collected by Armenian oil magnate Calouste Gulbenkian and donated to the people of Portugal. The collection includes superb examples of Greek and Roman coins, Persian carpets, Chinese porcelain, and paintings by such Old Masters as Rembrandt and Rubens. *Museu de Calouste Gulbenkian. Admission: 250$00. Open 10–5. Closed Mon. and public holidays.*

The complex also houses two concert halls where music and ballet festivals are held during the winter and spring. Modestly priced tickets are available at the box office (tel. 01/774167) thanks to subsidies from the Gulbenkian Foundation.

Bairro Alto Lisbon's **Bairro Alto** (High District) is largely made up of 18th- and 19th-century buildings that house an intriguing mixture of restaurants, theaters, nightclubs, churches, bars, and antiques shops. The best way to start a tour of this area is via the

9 **Elevador da Gloria** (funicular railway), located on the western side of Avenida da Liberdade by the Praça dos Restauradores. The trip takes about a minute and drops passengers at the São Pedro de Alcântara miradouro, a viewpoint that looks toward the castle and the Alfama (Cost: 25$00. Open 5 AM–midnight).

10 Across the street from the miradouro is the **Instituto do Vinho do Porto** (Port Wine Institute), where, in its cozy, clublike lounge, visitors can sample from more than 100 brands of Portugal's most famous beverage—from the extra-dry white varieties to the older, ruby-red vintages. *Rua S. Pedro de Alcântara 45, tel. 01/3423307. Admission free. Prices of tastings vary. Open Mon.–Sat. 9–6.*

From the institute, turn right and walk down Rua da Miseri-córdia (also called Rua S. Pedro Alcântara). On your left is the **⑪** Largo Trinidade Coelho, site of the highly decorative **Igreja de São Roque** (Church of São Roque). The church (open daily 8:30–6) is best known for the flamboyant 15th-century **Capel de São João Baptista** (Chapel of St. John the Baptist), but it is nonetheless a showpiece in its own right. The precious stones that adorn its walls were imported from Italy. Adjoining the church is the **Museu de Arte Sacra** (Museum of Sacred Art). *Admission: 250$00. Open Tues.–Sun. 10–5.*

Continue south down Rua da Misericórdia until you reach the **⑫** **Largo do Chiado** on your left. The Chiado, once Lisbon's chic shopping district, was badly damaged by a fire in August 1988, but it still houses some of the city's most fashionable department stores. An ambitious building program has restored much of the area's former glory.

Time Out   The Chiado's wood-paneled coffee shops attract tourists and lo-cal bohemian-types alike; the most popular of these is the **Brasileira**, which features a life-size statue of Fernando Pessoa, Portugal's national poet, at one of the sidewalk tables. *Rua Garrett 120, tel. 01/3469541. Closed Sun. Inexpensive.*

North of the Chiado, on the Largo do Carmo, lies the partially **⑬** ruined **Igreja do Carmo** (Carmo Church), one of the few older structures in the area to have survived the 1755 earthquake. Today open-air orchestral concerts are held beneath its majes-tic archways during the summer, and its sacristy houses an **ar-chaeological museum**. *Museu Arqueologico. Largo do Carmo. Admission: 250$00. Open Mon.–Sat. 10–1 and 2–5.*

Return directly to the Praça dos Restauradores via the nearby **⑭** **Ascensor de Santa Justa** (the Santa Justa elevator), which is en-closed in a Gothic tower created by Raul Mesnier, the Portu-guese protégé of Gustave Eiffel. (Cost: 28$00. Open 5 AM– midnight.)

An alternative, though somewhat macabre, route can be taken through the fire ruins. A temporary covered walkway has been built through parts of Rua Garrett and Rua do Carmo, and here visitors can see the disastrous effects of the 1988 fire on what was once the heart of sophisticated Lisbon.

Numbers in the margin correspond to points of interest on the Belém map.

Belém   To see the best examples of that uniquely Portuguese, late-Gothic architecture known as Manueline, head for Belém at the far southwestern edge of Lisbon. If you are traveling in a group of three or four, taxis are the cheapest means of transportation; otherwise take a No. 15, 16, or 77 tram from the Praça do Comércio for a more scenic, if bumpier, journey.

⑮ Trams Nos. 15 and 16 stop directly outside the **Mosteiro dos Jerónimos**, Belém's Hieronymite monastery, located in the Praça do Império. This impressive structure was conceived and planned by King Manuel I at the beginning of the 16th century to honor the discoveries of such great explorers as Vasco da Gama, who is buried here. Construction of the monastery be-gan in 1502, largely financed by treasures brought back from the so-called *descobrimentos*—the "discoveries" made by the

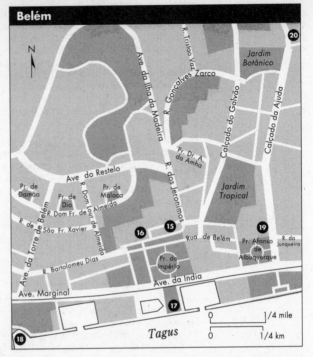

Portuguese in Africa, Asia, and South America. Don't miss the stunning double cloister with its arches and pillars heavily sculpted with marine motifs. *Church free. Closed 12–2. Admission to cloisters: 400$00. Open Oct.–Apr., daily 10–5; May.–Sept., daily 10–6:30.*

16 The **Museu de Marinha** (Maritime Museum) is located at the other end of the monastery. Its huge collection reflects Portugal's long seafaring tradition, and exhibitions range from early maps and navigational instruments to entire ships, including the sleek caravels that took Portuguese explorers and traders around the globe. *Admission: 200$00, free Wed. Open Tues.–Sun. 10–5.*

Time Out There are a number of small restaurants and cafés close to the monastery on Rua de Belém. Stop for coffee at the **Fabrica dos Pasteis de Belém** (the Belém Pastry Factory) to sample the delicious custard pastries served hot with cinnamon and powdered sugar.

17 Across from the monastery at the water's edge stands the **Monumento dos Descobrimentos** (Monument to the Discoveries). Built in 1960, this modern tribute to the seafaring explorers stands on what was the departure point of many of their voyages. An interesting mosaic lies at the foot of the monument, surrounded by an intricate wave pattern composed of black-and-white cobblestones. *Admission for elevator: 150$00. Open Tues.–Sun. 10–5.*

A 15-minute walk west of the monument brings you to the
Torre de Belém (the Belém Tower), another fine example of
Manueline architecture with openwork balconies, loggia, and
domed turrets. Although it was built in the 16th century on an
island in the middle of the river Tagus, today the tower stands
near the north bank—the river's course has changed over the
centuries. *Torre de Belém. Ave. de India. Admission: 200$00.
Open Tues.–Sun., 10–6:30 summer, 5 winter.*

Away from the Tagus and southeast of the monastery, on the
Praça Afonso de Albuquerque, is the **Museu Nacional do
Coches** (National Coach Museum), which houses one of the
largest collections of coaches in the world. The oldest vehicle on
display was made for Philip II of Spain in the late 16th century,
but the most stunning exhibits are three golden Baroque
coaches, created in Rome for King John V in 1716. *Admission:
250$00. Open Tues.–Sun. 10–5:30. Free Sun.*

Head north of the coach museum on Calçada da Ajuda to the
Palácio da Ajuda (Ajuda Palace). Once a royal residence, this
impressive building now contains a collection of 18th- and 19th-
century paintings, furniture, and tapestries. *Admission:
200$00. Guided tours arranged on request. Open daily 10–5.
Closed Wed.*

Shopping

Gift Ideas
Leather Goods Fine leather handbags and luggage are sold at **Galeão,** Rua
Augusto 190, and at **Casa Canada,** 232 Rua Augusto. Shoe
stores abound in Lisbon, but they may have a limited selection
of large sizes (the Portuguese have relatively small feet); however, the better shops can make shoes to measure on short notice. Leather gloves can be purchased at a variety of specialty
shops on Rua do Carmo and Rua do Ouro.

Handicrafts **Viúva Lamego,** Largo do Intendente 25, has the largest selection of tiles and pottery, while **Fabrica Sant'Anna,** Rua do
Alecrim 95, Chiado, sells wonderful handpainted ceramics and
tiles based on antique patterns. For embroidered goods and
baskets, try **Casa Regional da Ilha Verde,** Rua Paiva de
Andrade 4, or **Tito Cunha** at Rua do Ouro, 286. **Casa Quintão,**
Rua Ivens 30, probably has the largest selection of *arraiolos*
rugs, the traditional, hand-embroidered Portuguese carpets,
in town. For fine porcelain, visit **Vista Alegre** in the Largo do
Chiado.

Jewelry and **Antonio da Silva,** Praça Luis de Camoes 40, at the top of the
Antiques Chiado, specializes in antique silver and jewelry, as does
Barreto e Goncalves, Rua das Portas De Santo Antão 17. Most
of the antique shops are along the Rua Escola Politecnica, the
Rua de São Bento, and the Rua de Santa Marta.

Look for characteristic Portuguese gold- and silver-filigree
work at **Sarmento,** Rua do Ouro 251.

Shopping Districts Fire destroyed much of Lisbon's choicest shopping street in
1988; however, an extensive reconstruction project is well un-
der way. Another important shopping area is in the **Baixa**
quarter between the Rossio and the Tagus River. The blue-
and-pink towers of the **Amoreiras,** a huge modern shopping center located on Avenida Engeneiro Duarte Pacheco, dominate
the Lisbon skyline.

Flea Markets A **Feira da Ladra** (flea market) is held on Tuesday and Saturday in the Largo de Santa Clara behind the Church of São Vicente, near the Alfama district.

Dining

Eating is taken quite seriously in Portugal, and, not surprisingly, seafood is a staple. Freshly caught lobster, crab, shrimp, tuna, sole, and squid are prepared in innumberable ways, but if you want to sample a little bit of everything, try *caldeirada*, a piquant stew made with whatever is freshest from the sea. In the Algarve, *cataplana* is a must—a mouth-watering mixture of clams, ham, tomatoes, onions, garlic, and herbs, named for the dish in which it is cooked. There are some excellent local wines, and in modest restaurants even the *vinho da casa* (house wine) is usually very good. Water is generally safe, but visitors may want to drink bottled water—*sem gas* for still, *com gas* for fizzy—from one of the many excellent Portuguese spas.

Mealtimes Lunch usually begins around 1 PM; dinner is served at about 8 PM.

Dress Jacket and tie are generally advised for restaurants in the Expensive category. Otherwise casual dress is acceptable.

Ratings Prices are per person, without alcohol. Taxes and service are usually included, but a tip of 5–10% is always appreciated. All restaurants must post a menu with current prices in a window facing the street. Best bets are indicated by a star ★.

Category	Cost
Expensive	over 5,000$00
Moderate	2,500$00–5,000$00
Inexpensive	under 2,500$00

Expensive **António Clara.** Housed in an attractive Art Nouveau building, this restaurant serves French and international dishes with a flourish in an elegant room with a decorated ceiling, heavy draperies, and huge chandelier. *Ave. República 38, tel. 01/766380. Reservations advised. AE, DC, MC, V. Closed Sun.*

★ **Aviz.** One of the best and classiest restaurants in Lisbon, Aviz has a Belle Époque decor—even the rest rooms are impressive—and an excellent French and international menu. *Rua Serpa Pinto 12, tel. 01/3428391. Reservations required. AE, DC, MC, V. Closed Sat. lunch and Sun.*

Casa da Comida. Imaginative French and Portuguese fare is served in a former private house surrounding a flower-filled patio. *Travessa das Amoreiras 1, tel. 01/685376. Reservations advised. AE, DC, MC, V. Closed Sat. lunch and Sun.*

Gambrinus. One of Lisbon's older restaurants, Gambrinus is noted for its fish and shellfish. Entered through an inconspicuous door on a busy street, the restaurant has numerous small dining rooms. *Rua Portas S. Antão 23, tel. 01/3421466. Reservations advised. AE, DC, MC, V.*

Michel's. Innovative French cooking is served in an intimate atmosphere in this attractive restaurant in the village within the walls of St. George's Castle. *Largo S. Cruz do Castelo 5, tel. 01/864338. AE, DC, MC, V. Closed Sun.*

O Terraco. On the top of the Tivoli hotel, The Terrace offers a panoramic view of Lisbon. The food is excellent, especially from the grill, and the service is quietly attentive. *Ave. da Liberdade 185, tel. 01/530181. AE, DC, MC, V.*

Tagide. Delicious food and wine are served in this fine old house with antique tiles, overlooking the Baixa and river Tagus. *Largo Academia das Belas Artes 18, tel. 01/3460570. AE, DC, MC, V. Closed Sat. and Sun.*

★ **Tavares.** Superb food, an excellent wine list, and a handsome Edwardian dining room have made this one of Lisbon's most famous restaurants. *Rua Misericórdia 37, tel. 01/342–1112. Reservations advised. AE, DC, MC, V. Closed Sat. and Sun. lunch.*

Moderate **Alcantara.** Newest in-place. Fun and smart. Modernistic decor. Good food. Dinner only. *Rua Maria Luisa Holstein 15, tel. 3637176. Reservations necessary. Closed Tues.*

Comida de Santo. The Brazilian-style food is excellent, and is served in an attractive, bohemian atmosphere. Lively Brazilian music ensures that this restaurant is packed during later hours. *Rua Engenheiro Miguel Pais 39, tel. 01/396–3339. Reservations not necessary. AE, DC, MC, V.*

O Paco. Good steaks, regional food, and folkloric decor attract a literary crowd to this restaurant opposite the Gulbenkian Foundation. *Ave. Berna 44, tel. 01/797–0642. AE, DC, MC, V. Closed Mon.*

Pap' Acorda. This very popular restaurant in the Bairro Alto is housed in a converted bakery. It offers good food and service in a pleasant garden atmosphere. *Rua da Atalaia 57, tel. 01/3464811. Reservations advised. AE, DC, MC, V. Closed Sat. lunch and Sun.*

Solmar. This restaurant near the Rossio, Lisbon's main square, is best known for its seafood and shellfish, but try the wild boar or venison in season. *Rua Portas de S. Antão 108, tel. 01/346–0010. AE, DC, MC, V.*

Inexpensive **A Quinta.** A menu of Portuguese, Russian, and Hungarian dishes is available at this country-style restaurant overlooking the Baixa and the Tagus from next to the top of the Santa Justa elevator. *Carmo Sq., tel. 01/346–5588. AE, DC, MC, V. Closed Sat. and Sun. dinner.*

Bonjardim. Known locally as *Rei dos Frangos* (the King of Chickens), the Bonjardim specializes in the spit-roasted variety. Just off the Restauradores, it gets very crowded at peak hours. *Travesssa S. Antão 11, tel. 01/342–4389. AE, DC, MC, V.*

Cervejaria Trindade. You get good value for your money at this large restaurant, which has a garden and a cave-style wine cellar. *Rua Nova da Trindade 20, tel. 01/342–3506. AE, DC, MC, V.*

Chimarrão. A lively, attractive restaurant near the Roma metro stop, Chimarrão features authentic Brazilian dishes, an extensive salad bar, and a large selection of grilled meats. *Avenida Roma 90 D, tel. 01/800784. MC, V.*

Lodging

Lisbon has a good array of hotels in all price-categories, from major international chain hotels to charming little family-run establishments. During peak season, however, reservations should be made well in advance. Portugal offers the lowest rates in Europe for accommodations. Hotels are graded from one up to five stars, as are the smaller inns called *estalagems*, which usually provide breakfast only. *Pensions* go up to four stars and often include meals.

Tourist offices can help visitors with hotel or other reservations and will provide lists of the local hostelries without charge. Few international chains have hotels in Portugal. Almost all bathrooms have showers over the tubs.

Aparthotels, with double rooms, bath, and kitchenette, are to be found in the main resorts and are good value. Villas can be rented by the week or longer in the Algarve from various agents. One of the best-run complexes is Luz Bay Club, at Praia da Luz near Lagos, where all the well-designed villas have daily maid service.

Ratings Prices are for two people in a double room, based on high-season rates. Best bets are indicated by a star ★.

Category	All Areas
Very Expensive	over 35,000$00
Expensive	20,000$00–35,000$00
Moderate	13,000$00–20,000$00
Inexpensive	under 13,000$00

Very Expensive **Meridian Lisboa.** The rooms in Lisbon's newest luxury hotel are a bit on the small side, but they are soundproofed and attractively decorated; the front ones overlook the park. *Rua Castilho 149, tel. 01/690900, fax 01/693231. 331 rooms with bath. Facilities: health club with sauna, shops, garage. AE, DC, MC, V.*

★ **Ritz Lisboa.** One of the finest hotels in Europe, this Intercontinental is renowned for its excellent service. The large, handsomely decorated guest rooms all have terraces, and the elegantly appointed public rooms feature tapestries, antique reproductions, and fine paintings. The best rooms are in the front overlooking Parque Eduardo VII. There's convenient dining at the outstanding restaurant and grill. *Rua Rodrigo da Fonseca 88, tel. 01/692020, fax 01/691783. 304 rooms with bath. Facilities: shops, garage. AE, DC, MC, V.*

Expensive **Lisboa Sheraton.** This is a typical Sheraton hotel with a huge reception area and medium-size rooms. The deluxe rooms in the Towers section, which has a separate reception desk in the lobby and a private lounge, are about the same size but are more luxuriously appointed. The hotel is centrally located and is just across the street from a large shopping center. Parking is difficult. *Rua Latino Coelho 1, tel. 01/575757, fax 01/575073. 384 rooms with bath. AE, DC, MC, V. Facilities: pool, health club and sauna. AE, DC, MC, V.*

★ **Tivoli Lisboa.** Located on a main thoroughfare, this comfortable, well-run establishment has a large public area furnished with inviting armchairs and sofas. The guest rooms are all pleasant, but the ones in the rear are quieter. There's also a good restaurant, and the grill on the top floor has wonderful views of the city and the Tagus. *Ave. da Liberdade 185, tel. 01/530181, fax 01/579461. 344 rooms with bath. Facilities: outdoor pool, tennis courts, shops, garage. AE, DC, MC, V.*

Moderate **Florida.** This centrally located hotel has a pleasant atmosphere and is popular with Americans. *Rua Duque de Palmela 32, tel. 01/576145, fax 01/543584. 112 rooms with bath. AE, DC, MC, V.*

Lisboa Penta. The city's largest hotel, the Penta is located about midway between the airport and the city center, next to the U.S. Embassy and close to the Gulbenkian Foundation (shuttle-bus service to the center of the city is available). The rooms are rather small, but each one has a terrace. *Ave. dos Combatantes, tel. 01/726-4554, fax 01/726-4418. 592 rooms with bath. Facilities: outdoor pool, health club and solarium, squash courts, shops, garage. AE, DC, MC, V.*

★ **Novotel Lisboa.** There's an attentive staff and a quiet, welcoming atmosphere at this pleasant, modern hotel near the U.S. Embassy. The public rooms are spacious and the guest rooms attractive. *Ave. Jose Malhoa, tel. 01/726-6022, fax 01/726-6496. 246 rooms with bath. Facilities: pool, garage. AE, MC, V.*

York House. A former 17th-century convent, this residencia is set in a shady garden, up a long flight of steps, near the **Museu de Arte Antiga** (Museum of Ancient Art). It has a good restaurant, and full or half board is available. Book well in advance: This atmospheric place is small and has a loyal following. *Rua das Janelas Verdes 32, tel. 01/396-2435, fax 01/672793. 54 rooms with bath. AE, DC, MC, V.*

Inexpensive **Eduardo VII.** An elegant old hotel, the Eduardo is well situated
★ in the center of the city. The best rooms are in the front, but the ones in the rear are quieter. The top-floor restaurant has a marvelous view of the city and the Tagus. *Ave. Fontes Pereira de Melo 5, tel. 01/530141, fax 01/533879. 130 rooms with bath. AE, DC, MC, V.*

Fenix. Located at the top of Avenida da Liberdade, this hotel has largish guest rooms and a pleasant first-floor lounge. Its restaurant serves good Portuguese food. *Praça Marquês de Pombal 8, tel. 01/535121. 113 rooms with bath. AE, DC, MC, V.*

Flamingo. Another good value near the top of the Avenida da Liberdade, this hotel has a friendly staff and pleasant guest rooms, though the ones in the front tend to be noisy. There's a pay parking lot right next door, which is a bonus in this busy area. *Rua Castilho 41, tel. 01/532191, fax 01/3521216. 39 rooms with bath. AE, DC, MC, V.*

★ **Senhora do Monte.** The rooms in this unpretentious little hotel, located in the oldest part of town near St. George's Castle, have terraces that offer some of the loveliest views of Lisbon, especially at night when the castle and Carmo ruins in the middle distance are softly illuminated. The top-floor grill has a picture window. The surrounding neighborhood is quiet, and parking is available. *Calçada do Monte 39, tel. 01/866002, fax 01/877783. 28 rooms with bath. AE, DC, MC, V.*

The Arts

Two local supplements provide listings of music, theater, ballet, film, and other entertainment in Lisbon: *Sete*, published on Wednesdays, and *Sabado*, published on Fridays.

Plays are performed in Portuguese at the **Teatro Nacional de D. Maria II** (Praça Dom Pedro IV, tel. 01/371078) year-round except in July, and there are revues at small theaters in the Parque Mayer. Classical music, opera, and ballet are presented in the beautiful **Teatro Nacional de Opera de São Carlos** (Rua Serpa Pinto 99, tel. 01/395914). Classical music and ballet are also staged from autumn to summer by the **Fundação Calouste Gulbenkian** (Ave. Berna 45, tel. 01/793–5131). Of particular interest is the annual Early Music and Baroque Festival held in churches and museums around Lisbon every spring; for details contact the Gulbenkian Foundation. The **Nova Filarmonica,** a recently established national orchestra, performs concerts around the country throughout the year; consult local papers for details.

Nightlife

The most popular night spots in Lisbon are the **adegas tipicas** (wine cellars), where customers dine on Portuguese specialties, drink wine, and listen to *fado,* those haunting songs unique to Portugal. Most of these establishments are scattered throughout the Alfama and Bairro Alto districts. Try the **Senhor Vinho** (Rua Meio a Lapa 18, tel. 01/672681; closed Sun.), **Lisboa à Noite** (Rua das Gaveas 69, tel. 01/3468557; closed Sun.), or the **Machado** (Rua do Norte 91, tel. 01/346–0095; closed Mon.). The singing starts at 10 PM, and reservations are advised. Lisbon's top spot for live jazz is **The Hot Clube** (Praça da Liberdade 39, tel. 01/346–7369).

Discos New discos open and close with frequency in Lisbon, and many have high cover charges. Among the more respectable ones are **Ad Lib** (Rua Barata Salgueiro 28–7, tel. 01/561717), **Banana Power** (Rua Cascais 51, tel. 01/3631815), **Stones** (Rua do Olival 1, tel. 01/664545), and **Alcantara-Mar** (Rua da Cozinha Económica 11, tel. 01/636432). The current sensation is **Kremlin** (Escadinhas da Praia 5, tel. 01/608768).

13 London

Arriving and Departing

By Plane International flights to London arrive at either Heathrow Airport, 19.4 kilometers (12 miles) west of London, or at Gatwick Airport, 40.3 kilometers (25 miles) south of the capital. Most— but not all—flights from the United States go to Heathrow, while Gatwick generally serves European destinations, often with charter flights.

Between the Airport and Downtown The Piccadilly Line serves Heathrow (all terminals) with a direct Underground (subway) link. The 40-minute ride costs £2.30 at press time. Three special buses also serve Heathrow: A1 leaves every 30 minutes for Victoria Station; A2 goes to Euston Station every 20 minutes and takes 80 minutes; night bus N97 runs hourly from midnight to 5 AM into central London. The one-way cost is £4.

From Gatwick, the quickest way to London is the nonstop rail Gatwick Express, costing (at press time) £6.30 one-way and taking 30 minutes to reach Victoria Station. Regular bus services are provided by Greenline Coaches, including the Flightline 777 to Victoria Station. This takes about 70 minutes and costs £5 one-way.

Cars and taxis drive into London on the M4; the trip can take more than an hour, depending on traffic. The taxi fare is about £25. If you are driving from Gatwick, take M23 and then A23 to central London. The taxi fare is about £35.

By Train London is served by no fewer than 15 train stations, so be absolutely certain of the station for your departure or arrival. All have Underground stations either in the train station or within a few minutes' walk from it, and most are served by several bus routes. British Rail controls all major services. The principal routes that connect London to other major towns and cities are on an InterCity network; unlike its European counterparts, British Rail makes no extra charge for the use of this express service network.

Seats can be reserved only by phone with a credit card. You can, of course, apply in person to any British Rail Travel Centre or directly to the station from which you depart. Below is a list of the major London rail stations and the areas they serve.

Charing Cross (tel. 071/928–5100) serves southeast England, including Canterbury, Margate, Dover/Folkestone.
Euston/St. Pancras (tel. 071/387–7070) serves East Anglia, Essex, the Northeast, the Northwest, and North Wales, including Coventry, Stratford-upon-Avon, Birmingham, Manchester, Liverpool, Windermere, Glasgow, and Inverness.
King's Cross (tel. 071/278–2477) serves the east Midlands; the Northeast, including York, Leeds, and Newcastle; and north and east Scotland, including Edinburgh and Aberdeen.
Liverpool Street (tel. 071/928–5100) serves Essex and East Anglia.
Paddington (tel. 071/262–6767) serves the south Midlands, west and south Wales, and the west country, including Reading, Bath, Bristol, Oxford, Cardiff, Swansea, Exeter, Plymouth, and Penzance.
Victoria (tel. 071/928–5100) serves southern England, including Gatwick Airport, Brighton, Dover/Folkestone (from May), and the south coast.
Waterloo (tel. 071/928-5100) serves the southwestern Unit-

ed Kingdom, including Salisbury, Bournemouth, Portsmouth, Southampton, Isle of Wight, Jersey, and Guernsey.

Fares There is a wide, bewildering range of "savers" and other ticket bargains. Unfortunately, ticket clerks cannot always be relied on to know which type best suits your needs, so be sure to ask at the information office first. **Cheap Day Returns** are best if you're returning to London the same day, and many family and other discount railcards are available. You can hear a recorded summary of timetable and fare information to many InterCity destinations by dialing the appropriate "dial and listen" numbers listed under British Rail in the telephone book.

By Bus The **National Express** coach service has routes to over 1,000 major towns and cities in the United Kingdom. It's considerably cheaper than the train, although the trips usually take longer. National Express offers two types of service: an ordinary service, which makes frequent stops for refreshment breaks, and a Rapide service, which has hostess and refreshment facilities on board. Day returns are available on both, but booking is advised on the Rapide service. National Express coaches leave Victoria Coach Station (Buckingham Palace Rd.) at regular intervals, depending on the destination. For travel information, dial 071/730–0202.

In addition to National Express, **Greenline** operates bus services within a 50–60 kilometer (30–40 mile) radius of London. A **Golden Rover** ticket, which allows unlimited travel, is available. Contact Greenline for more information, tel. 071/668–7261.

Getting Around

By Underground Known as "the tube," London's extensive Underground system is by far the most widely used form of city transportation. Trains run both beneath and above ground out into the suburbs, and all stations are clearly marked with the London Underground circular symbol. (A "subway" sign refers to an under-the-street crossing.) Trains are all one class; smoking is *not* allowed on board or in the stations.

There are nine basic lines—all named—plus the East London line, which runs from Shoreditch and Whitechapel across the Thames south to New Cross, and the Docklands Light Railway, which is the best way to travel around the Isle of Dogs in London's East End. The trains on the light railway are computer operated and run from Tower Gateway to Island Gardens. The Central, District, Northern, Metropolitan, and Piccadilly lines all have branches, so be sure to note which branch is needed for your particular distination. Electronic platform signs tell you the final stop and route of the next train, and some signs also indicate how many minutes you'll have to wait for the train to arrive.

From Monday to Saturday, trains begin running around 5:30 AM; the last services leave central London between midnight and 12:30 AM. On Sundays, trains start two hours later and finish about an hour earlier. The frequency of trains depends on the route and the time of day, but normally you should not have to wait more than 10 minutes in central areas.

A pocket map of the entire tube network is available free from most Underground ticket counters. There should also be a

London Underground

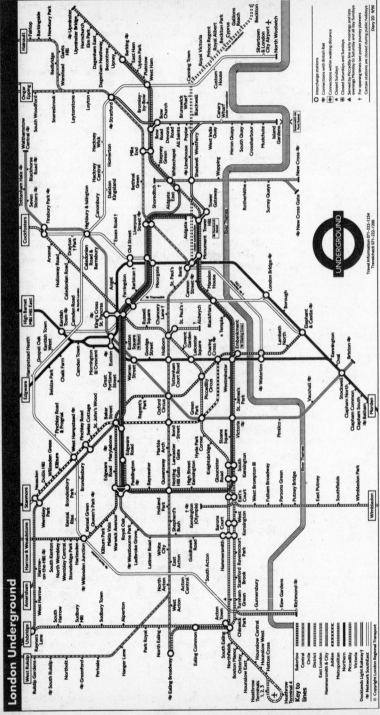

large map on the wall of each platform—though often these are defaced beyond recognition.

Fares   For both buses and tube fares, London is divided into six concentric zones; the fare goes up the farther afield you travel. Ask at Underground ticket counters for the London Regional Transport (LRT) booklet "Tickets," which gives details of all the various ticket options and bargains for the tube; after some experimenting, you'll soon know which ticket best serves your particular needs. Till then, here is a brief summary of the major ticket categories, but note that these prices are subject to increases.

Singles and Returns. For one trip between any two stations, you can buy an ordinary single for travel anytime on the day of issue; if you're coming back on the same route the same day, then an ordinary return costs twice the single fare. Singles vary in price from 70p in the central zone to £2.10 for a six-zone journey—not a good option for the sightseer who wants to make several journeys.

Cheap Day Return. Issued weekdays after 9:30 AM and anytime on weekends, these are basically good for one return journey within the six zones.

One-Day Off-Peak Travelcards. These allow unrestricted travel on the tube, most buses, and British Rail trains in the Greater London zones and are valid weekdays after 9:30 AM, weekends, and all public holidays. They cannot be used on airbuses, night buses, Route 128, for special services, or on tours and excursions. The price is £2.60.

Visitor's Travelcard. These are the best bet for visitors, but they must be bought before leaving home and are available both in the United States and Canada. They are valid for periods of one, three, four, or seven days ($6, $18, $23, $40) and can be used on the tube and virtually all buses and British Rail services in London. This card also includes a set of money-saving discounts to many of London's top attractions. Apply to travel agents or to BritRail Travel International.

For more information, there are **LRT Travel Information Centres** at the following tube stations: Euston, *open Sat.–Thurs. 7:15–6, Fri. to 7:30;* King's Cross, *open Sat.–Thurs. 8:15–6, Fri. to 7:30;* Oxford Circus, *open Mon.–Sat. 8:15–6;* Piccadilly Circus, *open Mon.–Sun. 8:15–6;* Victoria, *open Mon.–Sun. 8:15–9:30;* and Heathrow, *open Mon.–Sun. (to 9 or 10 PM in Terminals 1 and 2).* For information on all London bus and tube times, fares, etc., dial 071/222–1234; the line is operated 24 hours.

By Bus   London's bus system now consists of the bright red double- and single-deckers, plus, in the outer zones, other buses of various colors. Destinations are displayed on the front and back, with the bus number on the front, back, and side. By no means do all buses run the full length of their route at all times, so always check the termination point before boarding, preferably with the conductor or driver. Many buses are still operated with a conductor whom you pay after finding a seat, but there is now a move to one-man buses, in which you pay the driver upon boarding.

Buses stop only at clearly indicated stops. Main stops—at which the bus *should* stop automatically—have a plain white background with a red LRT symbol on it. There are also request stops with red signs, a white symbol, and the word "Request" added; at these you must hail the bus to make it stop. Smoking is not allowed on the lower deck of a double-decker and is discouraged on the top deck, except at the back. Although you can see much of the town from a bus, *don't* take one if you want to get anywhere in a hurry; traffic often slows travel to a crawl, and during peak times you may find yourself waiting at least 20 minutes for a bus and not being able to get on it once it arrives. If you intend to go by bus, ask at a Travel Information Centre for a free London Wide Bus Map.

Fares Single fares start at 40p for short distances (60p in the central zone). Travelcards are good for tube, bus, and British Rail trains in the Greater London Zones. There are also a number of bus passes available for daily, weekly, and monthly use, and prices vary according to zones. A photograph is required for weekly or monthly bus passes; this also applies to children and older children who may need a child-rate photocard to avoid paying the adult rate.

By Taxi London's black taxis are famous for their comfort and for the ability of their drivers to remember the mazelike pattern of the capital's streets. Hotels and main tourist areas have ranks (stands) where you wait your turn to take one of the taxis that drive up. You can also hail a taxi if the flag is up or the yellow "for hire" sign is lighted. Fares start at £1 and increase by units of 20p per 340 yards or 1 minute and 12 seconds. A surcharge of 60p is added in the evenings until midnight, on Sundays, and on holidays.

By Car The best advice is to avoid driving in London because of the illogical street patterns and the chronic parking shortage. A constantly changing system of one-way streets adds to the confusion.

Things are a lot easier outside the rush hours (8 AM–10 AM and 4 PM–6 PM), and if you drive through central London in the early hours of the morning, you'll see that the traffic-choked arteries of daytime (such as the Strand and Oxford Street) are convenient ways to cross London.

By Boat The **Thamesline Riverbus** operates between Chelsea and Greenwich, with seven stops between. For information, tel. 081/897–0311.

Important Addresses and Numbers

Tourist Information The main **London Tourist Information Centre** at Victoria Station Forecourt provides details about London and the rest of Britain, including general information; tickets for tube and bus; theater, concert, and tour bookings; and accommodations. Telephone information service: 071/730–3488. Open Apr.–Oct., daily 9–8:30; rest of the year, Mon.–Sat. 9–7, Sun. 9–5.

Other information centers are located in **Harrods** (Brompton Rd., SW1 7XL) and **Selfridges** (Oxford St., W1A 2LR) and are open store hours only; at **Tower of London** (West Gate, EC3W 4AB), open summer months only; and **Heathrow Airport** (Terminals 1, 2, and 3). The **City of London Information Centre** (St. Paul's Churchyard, EC4M 8BX, tel. 071/606–3030) has information on sights and events in the City. Open May–Oct., daily 9:30–5; Nov.–Apr., weekdays 9:30–5, Sat. 9:30–12:30.

The **British Travel Centre** (12 Regent St., SW1Y 4PQ, tel. 071/
730–3400) provides details about travel, accommodations, and
entertainment for the whole of Britain. Open weekdays 9–6:30
and weekends 10–4.

Embassies and   **American Embassy** (24 Grosvenor Sq., W1A, 1AE, tel. 071/
Consulates   499–9000). Located inside the embassy is the **American Aid Society,** a charity set up to help Americans in distress. Dial the
embassy number and ask for extension 570 or 571.

Canadian High Commission (Canada House, Trafalgar Sq.,
London SW1 Y 5BJ, tel. 071/629–9492).

Emergencies   For police, fire brigade, or ambulance, dial 999.

The following **hospitals** have 24-hour emergency rooms: **Guys**
(St. Thomas St., SE1, tel. 071/955–5000); **Royal Free** (Pond St.,
Hampstead, NW3, tel. 071/794–0500); **St. Bartholomew's**
(West Smithfield, EC1, tel. 071/601–8888); **St. Thomas's** (Lam-
beth Palace Rd., SE1, tel. 071/928–9292); **University College**
(Gower St., W1, tel. 071/387–9300); **Westminster** (Dean Ryle
St., Horseferry Rd., SW1, tel. 071/828–9811, adults only).

Pharmacies   Chemists (drugstores) with late opening hours include **Bliss
Chemist** (50–56 Willesden Lane, NW6, tel. 071/624–8000, open
daily 9 AM–midnight, also the branch at 5 Marble Arch, W1, tel.
071/723–6116, open daily 9 AM–midnight) and **Boots** (44 Piccadilly Circus, W1, tel. 071/734–6126, open Mon.–Sat. 8:30–8,
also the branches at 439 Oxford St., W1, tel. 071/409–2857,
open Thurs. 8:30–7, and 114 Queensway, W2, tel. 071/229–
4819, open Mon.–Sat. 9–10, Sun. 10–10).

Travel Agencies   **American Express** (6 Haymarket, SW1, tel. 071/930–4411, and
at 89 Mount St., W1, tel. 071/499–4436). **Hogg Robinson Travel/
Diners Club** (176 Tottenham Court Rd., W1, tel. 071/636–
8244). **Thomas Cook** (45 Berkeley St., Piccadilly W1, tel. 071/
499–4000).

Credit Cards   Should your credit cards be lost or stolen, here are some numbers to dial for assistance: **Access (MasterCard)** (tel. 0702/
352244 or 352255); **American Express** (tel. 071/222–9633, 24
hours, or 0273/696933 8–6 only for credit cards, tel. 0800/
521313 for traveler's checks); **Barclaycard (Visa)** (tel. 0604/
230230); **Diners Club** (tel. 0252/516261).

Guided Tours

Orientation Tours   **London Regional Transport's** official guided sightseeing tours
By Bus   (tel. 071/227–3456) offer passengers a good introduction to the
city from double-decker buses (seating capacity 64–72). Tours
run daily every half hour 10–5, from Marble Arch (top of Park
Lane near Speakers' Corner), Victoria Station, and Piccadilly
Circus (Haymarket). The route covers roughly 18–20 miles and
lasts 1½ hours; no stops are included. Tickets can be bought
from the driver, any London Transport Travel Information
Centre (ticket price reduced), or in advance from the London
Tourist Information Centre at Victoria. Other agencies offering half- and full-day bus tours include **Evan Evans** (tel. 071/
930–2377), **Frames Rickards** (tel. 071/837–3111), and **London
Tour Company** (tel. 071/734–3502). These tours have a smaller
seating capacity of approximately 50 passengers and include
stops at places of special interest, such as St. Paul's Cathedral
and Westminster Abbey. Prices and pick-up points vary ac-

cording to the sights visited, but many pick-up points are at major hotels.

By River From April to October, boats cruise up and down the Thames, offering a different view of the London skyline. Most leave from Westminster Pier (tel. 071/930–4721), Charing Cross Pier (Victoria Embankment, tel. 071/839–3572), and Tower Pier (tel. 071/488–0344). Downstream routes go to the Tower of London, Greenwich, and Thames Barrier; upstream destinations include Kew, Richmond, and Hampton Court. Most of the launches seat between 100 and 250 passengers, have a public-address system, and provide a running commentary on passing points of interest. Depending upon the destination, river trips may last from one to four hours. For more information, call **Catamaran Cruises,** tel. 071/839–2349, or **Tidal Cruises,** tel. 071/928–9009.

By Canal During summer, narrow boats and barges cruise London's two canals, the Grand Union and Regent's Canal; most vessels (seating about 60) operate on the latter, which runs between Little Venice in the west (the nearest tube is Warwick Ave. on the Bakerloo Line) and Camden Lock (about 200 yards north of Camden Town tube station). **Jason's Canal Cruises** (tel. 071/286–3428) operates one-way and round-trip narrow boat cruises on this route. During April, May, and September, there are two cruises per day; from June to August there are four. Trips last 1½ hours.

Canal Cruises (tel. 071/485–4433) also offers cruises from March to October on the *Jenny Wren* and all year on the cruising restaurant *My Fair Lady*.

Walking Tours One of the best ways to get to know London is on foot, and there are many guided walking tours from which to choose. **London Walks** (tel. 081/441–8906), **City Walks** (tel. 071/937–4281), and **Citisights** (tel. 081/806–4325) are just a few of the better-known firms, but your best bet is to peruse a variety of leaflets at the London Tourist Information Centre at Victoria Station. The duration of the walks varies (usually 1–3 hours), and you can generally find one to suit even the most specific of interests— Shakespeare's London, say, or a Jack the Ripper tour. Prices are around £4 for adults.

If you'd rather explore on your own, then the City of London Corporation has laid out a **Heritage Walk** that leads through Bank, Leadenhall, and Monument; follow the trail by the directional stars set into the sidewalks. A map of this walk can be found in *A Visitor's Guide to the City of London*, available from the City Information Centre across from St. Paul's Cathedral. Another option is to follow the **Silver Jubilee Walkway,** created in 1977 in honor of the 25th anniversary of the reign of the present queen. The entire route covers 16 kilometers (10 miles) and is marked by a series of silver crowns set into the sidewalks; Parliament Square makes a good starting point. Several books are available from the British Travel Centre (12 Regent St., SW1Y 4PQ) that also list a number of different walks to follow.

Excursions **LRT, Evan Evans, and Frames Rickards** (*see* Orientation Tours, above) all offer day excursions (some combine bus and boat) to places of interest within easy reach of London, such as Windsor, Hampton Court, Oxford, Stratford, and Bath. Prices vary and may include lunch and admission prices or admission only.

Personal Guides With 30 years' experience of providing a customized sightseeing service, **British Tours** (tel. 071/629–5267) will pick you up
from your hotel and take you anywhere in the United Kingdom.
Tour prices include car and driver-guide expenses and range
from £70 for two people in a medium-size car going on a three-
hour tour of London to £230 for one to four people in a large car
taking in Bath and Stonehenge (10 hours). A good choice of
tours, for one to six people, is available all year. Details of similar private operators can be found at the London Tourist Information Centre in Victoria Station or at the British Travel
Centre.

Exploring London

Traditionally London has been divided between the City, to the
east, where its banking and commercial interests lie, and Westminster to the west, the seat of the royal court and of government. Today the distinction between the two holds good, and
even the briefest exploration will demonstrate that each enjoys
a quite distinct atmosphere. It is also in these two areas that
you will find most of the grand buildings that have played a central role in British history: the Tower of London and St. Paul's
Cathedral, Westminster Abbey and the Houses of Parliament,
Buckingham Palace, and the older royal palace of St. James's.

These sites are natural magnets for visitors to London, as the
crowds of people and the ubiquitous tourist coaches demonstrate. But visitors who restrict their sightseeing to these
well-known tourist areas miss much of the best the city has to
offer. Within a few minutes' walk of Buckingham Palace, for instance, lie St. James's and Mayfair, two neighboring quarters
of elegant town houses built for the nobility in the 17th and early 18th centuries and now full of stylish shops patronized by an
international, jet-setting clientele. The same lesson applies to
the City, where, tucked away in quiet corners, stand many
of the churches Christopher Wren built to replace those destroyed during the Great Fire of 1666.

Other parts of London worth exploring include Covent Garden,
where a former fruit and flower market has been converted into
a lively shopping and entertainment center with a bazaar
where craftspeople sell their own wares. The atmosphere here
is informal, and you can stroll for hours enjoying the friendly
bustle of the streets. Hyde Park and Kensington Gardens, by
contrast, offer a great swathe of green parkland across the city
center, preserved by past kings and queens for their own hunting and relaxation. A walk across Hyde Park will bring you to
the museum district of South Kensington, with four major national collections: the Natural History Museum, the Science
Museum, the Geological Museum, and the Victoria and Albert
Museum, which specializes in costume and the fine and applied
arts.

The south side of the river Thames has its treats as well. A
short stroll across Waterloo Bridge brings you to the South
Bank Arts Complex, which includes the National Theatre, the
Royal Festival Hall, the Hayward Gallery (with changing exhibitions of international art), the National Film Theatre, and
the recently opened Museum of the Moving Image (MOMI)—a
must for movie buffs. The views from here are stunning—to
the west are the Houses of Parliament and Big Ben, to the east

the dome of St. Paul's is just visible on London's changing sky-line.

The key to London is thus a simple one. Explore for yourself off the beaten track. Use your feet, and when you're tired, take to the bus or the Underground. And look around you, for London's centuries of history and its vibrant daily life are revealed as much in the individual streets and houses of the city as in its grand national monuments and galleries.

Numbers in the margin correspond to points of interest on the London map.

Westminster **Westminster** is the royal backyard—the traditional center of the royal court and of government. Here, within a kilometer or so of each other, are virtually all London's most celebrated buildings (St. Paul's Cathedral and the Tower of London excepted), and there is a strong feeling of history all around you. Generations of kings and queens and their offspring have lived here since the end of the 11th century, in no less than four palaces, three of which (Buckingham, St. James's, and Westminster) still stand.

① Start at **Trafalgar Square,** which is on the site of the former Royal Mews. Both the square's name and its present appearance date from about 1830. A statue of Lord Nelson, victor over the French in 1805 at the Battle of Trafalgar, at which he lost his life, stands atop a column. Lions guard the base of the column, which is decorated with four bronze panels depicting naval battles against France and cast from French cannons captured by Nelson. The bronze equestrian statue on the south side of the square is of the unhappy Charles I; he is looking down Whitehall toward the spot where he was executed in 1649.

② In the **National Gallery,** which occupies the long neoclassical building on the north side of the square, is a comprehensive collection of paintings, with works from virtually every famous artist and school from the 14th to the 19th century. The gallery is especially strong on Flemish and Dutch masters, Rubens and Rembrandt among them, and on Italian Renaissance works. The recently completed Sainsbury Wing houses the early Renaissance collection. *Trafalgar Sq., tel. 071/839–3321; 071/839–3526 (recorded information). Admission free. Open Mon.–Sat. 10–6, Sun. 2–6; June–Aug., Wed. until 8.*

③ Around the corner, at the foot of Charing Cross Road, is a second major art collection, the **National Portrait Gallery,** which contains portraits of well-known (and not so well-known) Britons, including monarchs, statesmen, and writers. *2 St. Martin's Pl., tel. 071/930–1552. Admission free. Open weekdays 10–5, Sat. 10–6, Sun. 2–6.*

④ The Gallery's entrance is opposite the distinctive neoclassical church of **St. Martin-in-the-Fields,** built in about 1730. Regular lunchtime music recitals are held here.

Time Out Both the **National Gallery Restaurant** and **Field's Restaurant** in the crypt of St. Martin's serve light lunches and offer a good selection of salads, sandwiches, and pastries.

⑤ **Admiralty Arch** guards the entrance to **The Mall,** the great ceremonial way that leads alongside **St. James's Park** to Buckingham Palace. The Mall takes its name from a game called "pell mell," a version of croquet that society people, including Charles II and his courtiers, used to play here in the late 1600s. The park, one of central London's smallest and most attractive, with superbly maintained flowerbeds, was developed by successive monarchs, most recently by George IV in the 1820s, having originally been used for hunting by Henry VIII. Join office workers relaxing with a lunchtime sandwich, or stroll here on a summer's evening when the illuminated fountains play and Westminster Abbey and the Houses of Parliament beyond the trees are floodlit.

On the other side of the Mall, you'll pass along the foot of the imposing **Carlton House Terrace,** built in 1827–32 by John Nash. A right turn up Marlborough Road brings you to the complex of royal and government buildings known collectively as **St. James's Palace.** Although the earliest parts of this lovely brick building date from the 1530s, it had a relatively short career as the center of royal affairs, from the destruction of Whitehall Palace in 1698 until 1837, when Victoria became queen and moved the royal household down the road to Buckingham Palace. A number of royal functionaries have offices here, however, and various court functions are held in the state rooms. Foreign ambassadors are still accredited to the "Court of St. James's."

At the end of Marlborough Road, beyond the open-sided **Friary Court,** turn left along **Cleveland Row,** and walk past **York House,** the London home of the duke and duchess of Kent. Another left turn into **Stable Yard Road** takes you to **Lancaster House,** built for the duke of York by Nash in the 1820s and used today for government receptions and conferences. On the other side of Stable Yard is **Clarence House,** so called because it was designed and built by Nash in 1825 for the duke of Clarence, who later became King William IV. It was restored in 1949 and is now the home of the Queen Mother. Inside the palace is the **Chapel Royal,** said to have been designed for Henry VIII by the painter Holbein; it was heavily redecorated in the mid-19th century. The ceiling still has the initials H and A, intertwined, standing for Henry VIII and his second wife, Anne Boleyn, the mother of Elizabeth I and the first of his wives to lose her head. The public can attend Sunday morning services here between the first week of October and Good Friday.

Buckingham Palace, at the end of the Mall, is the London home of the queen and the administrative hub of the entire royal family. When the queen is in residence (on weekdays except in January, August, September, and part of June), the royal standard flies over the east front. Inside there are dozens of splendid state rooms used on such formal occasions as banquets for visiting heads of state. The private apartments of Queen Elizabeth and Prince Philip are in the north wing. Behind the palace lie some 40 acres of private gardens, a haven for wildlife in the midst of the capital.

The ceremony of the **Changing of the Guard** takes place in front of the palace at 11:30 daily, April through July, and on alternate days during the rest of the year. It's advisable to arrive early; the Queen Victoria Memorial in the middle of the traffic round-about provides a grandstand view.

London

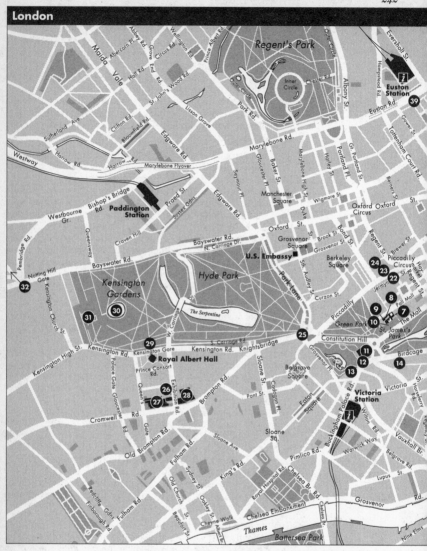

Admiralty Arch, **5**
Albert Memorial, **29**
Bank of England, **45**
Banqueting House, **20**
Barbican, **42**
British Museum, **38**
Buckingham Palace, **11**
Cabinet War Rooms, **15**

Carlton House Terrace, **6**
Cenotaph, **19**
Clarence House, **10**
Covent Garden, **33**
Guildhall, **43**
Horse Guards Parade, **21**
Hyde Park Corner, **25**
Jewish Museum, **39**
Kensington Palace, **31**
Lancaster House, **9**

Leadenhall Market, **48**
Lloyd's of London, **49**
London Transport Museum, **35**
Mansion House, **47**
Museum of London, **41**
Museum of Mankind, **24**
National Gallery, **2**

National Portrait Gallery, **3**
Natural History Museum, **27**
Palace of Westminster, **17**
Parliament Square, **16**
Portobello Road, **32**
Queen's Gallery, **12**
Round Pond, **30**
Royal Academy, **23**

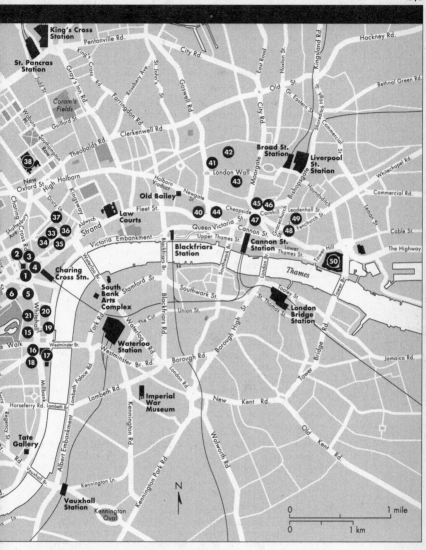

Buckingham Palace is not open to the public. The former chapel, bombed during World War II and rebuilt in 1961, has been
(12) converted into the **Queen's Gallery,** however, where regular exhibitions are drawn from the vast royal art collections. *Buckingham Palace Rd., tel. 071/799–2331. Admission: £2 adults, £1 children, £1.50 senior citizens. Open Tues.–Sat. 10:30–4:30, Sun. 2–4:30; closed between exhibitions.*

Just along Buckingham Palace Road from the Queen's Gallery
(13) is the **Royal Mews,** where some of the queen's horses are stabled and the elaborately gilded state coaches are on view. *Tel. 071/930–4832. Admission: £1.30 adults, 70p children, £1 senior citizens. Open Wed. and Thurs. 2–4; closed during state occasions involving royal carriage processions and during Royal Ascot week (June).*

Birdcage Walk, so called because it was once the site of the royal aviaries, runs along the south side of St. James's Park, past the
(14) **Wellington Barracks.** These are the regimental headquarters of the Guards Division, the elite troops that traditionally guard the sovereign and mount the guard at Buckingham Palace. The **Guards Museum** relates the history of the Guards from the 1660s to the present; paintings of battle scenes, uniforms, and a cat o'nine tails are among the items on display. *Tel. 071/930–4466, ext. 3271. Admission: £2 adults, £1 children under 16 and senior citizens. Open Sat.–Thurs. 10–4.*

(15) The **Cabinet War Rooms,** between the Foreign Office and the Home Office, are the underground offices used by the British High Command during World War II. Among the rooms on display are the Prime Minister's Room, from which Winston Churchill made many of his inspiring wartime broadcasts, and the Transatlantic Telephone Room, from which he spoke directly to President Roosevelt in the White House. *Clive Steps, King Charles St., tel. 071/930–6961 or 071/735–8922. Admission: £3.50 adults, £1.75 children under 16, £2.30 senior citizens. Open daily 10–5:15.*

(16) **Parliament Square** is flanked, on the river side, by the Palace of Westminster. Among the statues of statesmen long since dead are those of Churchill, Abraham Lincoln, and Oliver Cromwell, the Lord Protector of England during the country's sole, brief republican period (1648–60).

(17) The **Palace of Westminster** was the monarch's main residence from the 11th century until 1512, when the court moved to the newly built Whitehall Palace. The only part of the original building to have survived, however, is **Westminster Hall,** which has a fine hammer-beam roof. The rest was destroyed in a disastrous fire in 1834 and was rebuilt in the newly popular mock-medieval Gothic style with ornate interior decorations. The architect, Augustus Pugin, provided many delightful touches, such as Gothic umbrella stands. In addition to Westminster Hall, which is used only on rare ceremonial occasions, the palace contains the debating chambers and committee rooms of the two Houses of Parliament—the Commons (whose members are elected) and the Lords (whose members are appointed or inherit their seats). There are no tours of the palace, but the public is admitted to the Public Gallery of each House; expect to wait in line for several hours (the line for the Lords is generally much shorter than that for the Commons).

The most famous features of the palace are its towers. At the south end is the 104-meter (336-foot) **Victoria Tower.** At the other end is **St. Stephen's Tower,** better known, but inaccurately so, as Big Ben. That name properly belongs to the 13-ton bell in the tower on which the hours are struck; Big Ben himself was Sir Benjamin Hall, commissioner of works when the bell was installed in the 1850s. A light shines from the top of the tower during a night sitting of Parliament.

⑱ **Westminster Abbey** is the most ancient of London's great churches and the most important, for it is here that Britain's monarchs are crowned. It is unusual for a church of this size and national importance not to be a cathedral. The abbey dates largely from the 13th and 14th centuries, although **Henry VII's Chapel,** an exquisite example of the heavily decorated late Gothic style, was not built until the early 1600s, and the twin towers over the west entrance are an 18th-century addition. There is much to see inside, including the memorial to Winston Churchill; the tomb of the Unknown Warrior, a nameless World War I soldier buried in earth brought with his corpse from France; and Poets' Corner, where some of the country's finest writers are commemorated. Behind the high altar are the royal tombs, including those of Queen Elizabeth I, Mary Queen of Scots, and Henry V. In the Chapel of Edward the Confessor stands the Coronation Chair. Among the royal weddings that have taken place here are those of the present queen and most recently, in 1986, the duke and duchess of York.

It is all too easy to forget, swamped by the crowds trying to see the abbey's sights, that this is a place of worship. Early morning is a good moment to catch something of the building's atmosphere. Better still, take time to attend a service. *Broad Sanctuary, tel. 071/222–5152. Admission to the nave is free, to Poets' Corner and Royal Chapels, £2.60 adults, £1.30 students and senior citizens, £60p children (Royal Chapels, free Wed. 6–7:45 PM). Open weekdays 9–4, Sat. 9–2 and 3:45–5; Sun. all day for services only; museum and cloisters open Sun.; closed weekdays to visitors during services; Royal Chapels closed Sun. No photography except Mon. evening.*

The Norman **Undercroft,** off the original monastic cloisters, houses a small museum with exhibits on the abbey's history. In the **Pyx Chamber** next door are fine examples of silver vessels and other treasures. The nearby **Chapter House** was where the English Parliament first met. *Tel. 071/222–5152. Joint admission: £1.60 adults, 80p students and senior citizens, 40p children. Open daily 10:30–1:45.*

⑲ From Parliament Square, walk up **Parliament Street** and **Whitehall** (this is a single street—its name changes), past government offices, toward Trafalgar Square. The **Cenotaph,** in the middle of the road, is the national memorial to the dead of both world wars. On the left is the entrance to **Downing Street,** an unassuming row of 18th-century houses. The prime minister's office is at No. 10 (he has a private apartment on the top floor). The chancellor of the exchequer, the finance minister, occupies No. 11.

⑳ On the right side of Whitehall is the **Banqueting House,** built by the architect Inigo Jones in 1625 for court entertainments. This is the only part of Whitehall Palace, the monarch's principal residence in the 16th and 17th centuries, that was not burned down in 1698. It has a magnificent ceiling by Rubens, and outside there is an inscription that marks the window through which King Charles I stepped to his execution. *Tel. 071/930-4179. Admission: £2 adults, £1.50 students and senior citizens, £1.35 children. Open Tues.–Sat. 10–5, Sun. 2–5.*

㉑ Opposite is the entrance to **Horse Guards Parade,** the former tilt yard of Whitehall Palace. This is the site of the annual ceremony of Trooping the Colour, when the queen takes the salute in the great military parade that marks her official birthday on the second Saturday in June (her real one is on April 21). There is also a daily guard-changing ceremony outside the guard house, at 11 AM (10 on Sunday).

St. James's and Mayfair After such a concentrated dose of grand, historical buildings, it's time to explore two of London's elegant shopping areas. Start by walking west from Piccadilly Circus along **Piccadilly,** which contains a mixture of airline offices, shops (including **Hatchards,** the booksellers, and **Fortnum and Mason,** the queen's grocer), and academic societies.

㉒ **St. James's Church** was designed by the 17th-century architect Christopher Wren and contains beautiful wood carvings by Grinling Gibbons.

Time Out **The Wren** at St. James's is a friendly café in the church precincts. Coffee, pastries, and light lunches are served.

Jermyn Street, south of Piccadilly, is famous for upscale shops selling costly shirts, ties, and sweaters. **Paxton & Whitfield** sells an extraordinary variety of cheeses. Shops along **Duke Street** and **Bury Street** specialize in paintings, the former in Old Masters, the latter in early English watercolors. Don't be put off by the exclusive appearance of these establishments—anyone is free to enter, and there is no obligation to buy. **King Street** is home to **Christie's,** the fine art auctioneer, and to **Spink and Son,** renowned for Oriental art.

On the north side of Piccadilly, **Burlington House** contains the offices of many learned societies and the headquarters of the **㉓** **Royal Academy.** The RA, as it is generally known, stages major visiting art exhibitions. The best known is the Summer Exhibition (May–Aug.), featuring works by living British artists.

Burlington Arcade, beside the RA, is a covered walkway with tiny shops selling primarily jewelry and craft goods, such as woolens. Built in 1819, it was the first shopping precinct in the country, and it retains something of its original atmosphere. A uniformed beadle is on duty to ensure that no one runs, whistles, or sings here.

㉔ The **Museum of Mankind,** behind the RA, contains the British Museum's ethnographic collection. There are displays on the South Seas, the Arctic, and other regions of the world. *6 Burlington Gardens, tel. 071/437-2224. Admission free. Open Mon.–Sat. 10–5, Sun. 2:30–6.*

There are three special shopping streets in this section of Mayfair, each with its own specialties. **Savile Row** is the home of gentlemen's tailors. Nearby **Cork Street** has many dealers in modern and classical art. **Bond Street** (divided into two parts, Old and New, though both are some 300 years old) is the classiest shopping street in London, the home of haute couture, with such famous names as **Gucci, Hermès,** and **St. Laurent,** and costly jewelry from such shops as **Asprey, Tiffany,** and **Cartier.**

Some of the original 18th-century houses survive on the west side of **Berkeley Square.** Farther along is **Curzon Street,** which runs along the northern edge of **Shepherd Market,** a maze of narrow streets full of antiques shops, restaurants, and pubs that retain something of a village atmosphere.

Time Out *L'Artiste Musclé* is a popular bistro serving French food; the *boeuf bourguignonne* is very tasty. *1 Shepherd Market.*

Hyde Park and Beyond A great expanse of green parkland begins at **Hyde Park Corner** and cuts right across the center of London. **Hyde Park,** which ㉕ covers about 137 hectares (340 acres), was originally a royal hunting ground, while **Kensington Gardens,** which adjoins it to the west, started life as part of the royal Kensington Palace. These two parks contain many fine trees and are a haven for wildlife. The sandy track that runs along the south edge of the parks has been a fashionable riding trail for centuries. Though it's called **Rotten Row,** there's nothing rotten about it. The name derives from *route du roi* ("the King's Way")—the route William III and Queen Mary took from their home at Kensington Palace to the court at St. James's. There is boating and swimming in the **Serpentine,** the S-shaped lake formed by damming a stream that used to flow here. Refreshments can be had at the Serpentine bars, buffet, and restaurant complex, and the **Serpentine Gallery** holds temporary exhibitions of modern art (tel. 071/402–6075).

Leave the park at **Exhibition Road** and visit three of London's ㉖ major museums. The **Science Museum** is the leading national collection of science and technology, with extensive hands-on exhibits on outer space, astronomy, computers, transportation, and medicine. *Tel. 071/938–8111; 071/938–8123 (recorded information). Admission: £2 adults, £1.50 children under 15 and senior citizens. Open Mon.–Sat. 10–6, Sun. 11–6.*

㉗ The **Natural History Museum** is housed in an ornate late-Victorian building with striking modern additions. As in the Science Museum, its displays on topics such as human biology and evolution are designed to challenge visitors to think for themselves. *Cromwell Rd., tel. 071/938–9123; 042/692–7654 (recorded information). Admission: £2.50 adults, £1.25 children under 15 and senior citizens; free weekdays 4:30–6. Open Mon.–Sat. 10–6, Sun. 2:30–6.*

㉘ The **Victoria and Albert Museum** (or V & A) originated in the 19th century as a museum of decorative art and has extensive collections of costumes, paintings, jewelry, and crafts from every part of the globe. The collections from India, China, and the Islamic world are especially strong. *Cromwell Rd., tel. 071/938–8500; 071/938–8441 (recorded information). Voluntary contribution for admission. Open Mon.–Sat. 10–5:50, Sun. 2:30–5:50.*

Time Out The **V & A restaurant** is just the place to recuperate after visiting the museum. You can enjoy morning coffee, hot lunchtime dishes, or afternoon tea.

㉙ Back in Kensington Gardens, the **Albert Memorial** commemorates Queen Victoria's much-loved husband, Prince Albert, who died in 1861 at the age of 42. The monument, itself the epitome of high Victorian taste, commemorates the many socially uplifting projects of the prince, among them the Great Exhibition of 1851, whose catalog he is holding. The Memorial, which has been badly eroded by pollution, is currently being restored.

From the **Flower Walk,** behind the Albert Memorial, carefully planted so that flowers are in bloom virtually throughout the
❸⓪ year, strike out across Kensington Gardens to the **Round Pond,** a favorite place for children to sail toy boats.

❸① **Kensington Palace,** across from the Round Pond, has been a royal home since the late 17th century—and is one still, for the prince and princess of Wales and Princess Margaret. From the outside it looks less like a palace than a country house, which it was until William III bought it in 1689. Inside, however, are state rooms on a grand scale, mostly created in the early 18th century. Such distinguished architects as Wren, Hawksmoor, Vanbrugh, and William Kent were all employed here. Queen Victoria lived at Kensington Palace as a child, and several rooms are furnished as they were during her time. The public part of the palace also contains an exhibition of court dress. *Tel. 071/937–9561. Admission: £3.50 adults, £2.60 students and senior citizens, £2.30 children. Open Mon.–Sat. 9–5, Sun. 1–5.*

North of Kensington Gardens are two lively districts, **Bayswater** and **Notting Hill,** both full of restaurants and cafés where young people gather. The best-known attraction in this area is
❸② **Portobello Road,** where the lively antiques and bric-a-brac market is held each Saturday (arrive early in the morning for the best bargains). The street is also full of regular antiques shops that are open most weekdays.

Time Out   **Geales** (2 Farmer St.) is a superior Notting Hill fish-and-chips restaurant, popular with locals and visitors alike.

Covent Garden   You could easily spend a half day exploring the block of streets
❸③ north of the Strand known as **Covent Garden.** The heart of the area is a former wholesale fruit and vegetable market, established in 1656. The market moved to more modern and accessible premises only in 1974. The Victorian **Market Building** is now a vibrant shopping center, with numerous boutiques, crafts shops, and health-food bars. On the south side of the market building is the lively and much less formal **Jubilee open-air market,** where artists and craftspeople sell their wares at stalls.

The atmosphere in Covent Garden is friendly and informal. Look for the open-air entertainers performing under the porti
❸④ co of **St. Paul's Church**—you can enjoy an excellent show for the price of a few coins thrown in the hat that's passed among the onlookers. The church, entered from Bedford Street, is known as the Actors' Church, and inside are numerous memorials to theater people. The **Royal Opera House** and the **Theatre Royal Drury Lane,** two of London's oldest theaters, are close by.

Time Out   There's a good selection of eating places in and around the Market Building. **Crank's,** at No. 11, serves delicious quiches, salads, and cakes. The **Calabash,** in the basement of the Africa

Center at 38 King Street, serves authentic African dishes at reasonable prices.

For interesting specialty shops, head north of the Market Building. Shops on **Long Acre** sell maps, art books, and glass; shops on **Neal Street** sell clothes, pottery, jewelry, and goods from the Far East.

㉟ The collection of vehicles at the **London Transport Museum** includes a steam locomotive, a tram, a subway car, and an Underground train simulator. Visitors are encouraged to operate many of the vehicles. The shop sells T-shirts, books, souvenirs, and current and historic London Transport posters. *The Piazza (southeast corner), tel. 071/379-6344. Admission: £2.60 adults, £1.20 children 5-16 and senior citizens, children under 5 free. Open daily 10-5:15.*

㊱ The **Theatre Museum** contains a comprehensive collection of material on the history of the English theater—not merely the classic drama but also opera, music hall, pantomime, and musical comedy. Scripts, playbills, costumes, and props are displayed; there is even a re-creation of a dressing room filled with memorabilia of former stars. *Russell St., tel. 071/836-7891. Admission: £2.50 adults, £1.50 children under 14, students, and senior citizens. Open Tues.–Sun. 11-7.*

㊲ On **Bow Street** is the **Royal Opera House,** home of the Royal Ballet and the Royal Opera Company. The plush interior captures the richness of Victorian England.

Bloomsbury **Bloomsbury** is a semiresidential district to the north of Covent Garden that contains some spacious and elegant 17th- and 18th-century squares. It could claim to be the intellectual center of London, since both the British Museum and the University of London are found here. The area also gave its name to the Bloomsbury Group, a clique of writers and painters who thrived here in the early 20th century. The antiquarian and specialist bookshops, publishing houses, restaurants, and pubs frequented by the local literati add to the academic-cum-bohemian ambience of the area.

㊳ The **British Museum** houses a vast and priceless collection of treasures, including Egyptian, Greek, and Roman antiquities; Renaissance jewelry; pottery; coins; glass; and drawings from virtually every European school since the 15th century. It's best to pick out one section that particularly interests you—to try to see everything would be an overwhelming and exhausting task. Some of the highlights are the **Elgin Marbles,** sculptures that formerly decorated the Parthenon in Athens; the **Rosetta Stone,** which helped archaeologists to interpret Egyptian script; a copy of the **Magna Carta,** the charter signed by King John in 1215 to which is ascribed the origins of English liberty; and the **Mildenhall treasure,** a cache of Roman silver found in East Anglia in 1842. *Great Russell St., tel. 071/636-1555; 071/580-1788 (recorded information). Admission free; guided tours of museum's highlights, £5. Open Mon.–Sat. 10-5, Sun. 2:30-6.*

㊴ The **Jewish Museum** has a small but interesting collection of antiquities illustrating Judaism, Jewish life, and history. There are also audiovisual programs on Jewish festivals and ceremonies. *Woburn House, Upper Woburn Pl., tel. 071/388-4525.*

Admission free. Open Tues.–Thurs. (and Fri. in summer) 10–4, Sun. (and Fri. in winter) 10–12:45.

The City   The **City**, the traditional commercial center of London, is the most ancient part of the capital, having been the site of the great Roman city of Londinium. Since those days, the City has been built and rebuilt several times. The wooden buildings of the medieval City were destroyed in the Great Fire of 1666. There were further waves of reconstruction in the 19th century, and then again after World War II, to repair the devastation wrought by air attacks. The 1980s have seen the construction of many mammoth office developments, some undistinguished, others incorporating adventurous and exciting ideas.

Throughout all these changes, the City has retained its unique identity and character. The lord mayor and Corporation of London are still responsible for the government of the City, as they have been for many centuries. Commerce remains the lifeblood of the City, which is a world financial center rivaled only by New York, Tokyo, and Zurich. The biggest change has been in the City's population. Until the first half of the 19th century, many of the merchants and traders who worked in the City lived there, too. Today, despite its huge daytime population, scarcely 8,000 people live in the 274 hectares (677 acres) of the City. Try, therefore, to explore the City on a weekday morning or afternoon. On weekends its streets are deserted, and many of the shops and restaurants, even some of the churches, are closed.

40   Following the Great Fire, **St. Paul's Cathedral** was rebuilt by Sir Christopher Wren, the architect who was also responsible for designing 50 City parish churches to replace those lost in the Great Fire. St. Paul's is Wren's greatest work. Fittingly, he is buried in the crypt, under the simple epitaph composed by his son: "Reader, if you seek his monument, look around you." The cathedral has been the site of many famous state occasions, including the funeral of Winston Churchill in 1965 and the marriage of the prince and princess of Wales in 1981. There is much fine painting and craftsmanship—the choir stalls are by the great 17th-century wood carver Grinling Gibbons—but overall the atmosphere is somewhat austere and remote. The cathedral contains many monuments and tombs. Among those commemorated are George Washington; the essayist and lexicographer Samuel Johnson; and two military heroes—Nelson, victor over the French at Trafalgar in 1805, and Wellington, who defeated the French on land at Waterloo 10 years later. In the ambulatory (the area behind the high altar) is the American Chapel, a memorial to the 28,000 U.S. citizens stationed in Britain during World War II who lost their lives while on active service.

The greatest architectural glory of the cathedral is the dome. This consists of three distinct elements: an outer, timber-framed dome covered with lead; an interior dome built of brick and decorated with frescoes of the life of St. Paul by the 18th-century artist Sir James Thornhill; and, in between, a brick cone that supports and strengthens both. There is a good view of the church from the **Whispering Gallery**, high up in the inner dome. The gallery is so called because of its remarkable acoustics, whereby words whispered on one side can be clearly heard on the other, 35 meters (112 feet) away. Above this gallery are two others, both external, from which there are fine views over the City and beyond. *Tel. 071/248–2705. Admission to cathedral free (donation requested); Ambulatory (American Chapel): 70p adults, children free; to Crypt and Treasury: £1.20 adults, 60p children; to galleries: £2 adults, £1 children. Tours of the cathedral weekdays at 11, 11:30, 2, and 2:30, £4 adults, £1.80 children. Cathedral open Mon.–Sat. 7:30–6, Sun. 8–6; the Ambulatory, Crypt, and Galleries weekdays 10–4:15, Sat. 11–4:15.*

Time Out | **Balls Brothers Wine Bar** (2 Old Change Court, St. Paul's Churchyard) is a good place for a bite and a drink. Freshly made soup and grilled steak in a French bread sandwich are two specialties. Try to arrive early to beat the crowds of lunchtime City workers. Like much of the City, however, Balls Brothers is closed on weekends.

A short walk north of the cathedral, to **London Wall,** so called because it follows the line of the wall that surrounded the Roman settlement, brings you to the **Museum of London.** Its displays enable you to get a real sense of what it was like to live in London at different periods of history, from Roman times to the present day. Among the highlights are the Lord Mayor's Ceremonial Coach, an imaginative reconstruction of the Great Fire, and the Cheapside Hoard, jewelry hidden during an outbreak of plague in the 17th century and never recovered by its owner. A new gallery devoted to the 18th century was opened in 1989. The 20th-century exhibits include a Woolworth's counter and elevators from Selfridges; both stores were founded by Americans and had an immense impact on the life of Londoners. *London Wall, tel. 071/600–3699. Admission free. Open Tues.–Sat. 10–6, Sun. 2–6.*

The **Barbican** is a vast residential complex and arts center built by the City of London. It takes its name from the watchtower that stood here during the Middle Ages, just outside the City walls. The arts center contains a concert hall, where the London Symphony Orchestra is based, two theaters, an art gallery, a cinema, and several cafés and restaurants. The theaters are the London home of the Royal Shakespeare Company.

On the south side of London Wall stands **Guildhall,** the much reconstructed home of the Corporation of London; the lord mayor of London is elected here each year with ancient ceremony. *King St., tel. 071/606–3030. Admission free. Open weekdays 10–5.*

Now walk south to **Cheapside.** This was the chief marketplace of medieval London (the word *ceap* meant "market"), as the street names hereabouts indicate: Milk Street, Ironmonger Lane, etc. Despite rebuilding, many of the streets still run on the medieval pattern. The church of **St. Mary-le-Bow** in Cheapside was rebuilt by Christopher Wren after the Great Fire; it was built again after being bombed during World War II. It is said that to be a true Cockney, you must be born within the sound of Bow bells.

A short walk east along Cheapside brings you to a seven-way intersection. The **Bank of England,** which regulates much of Britain's financial life, is the large windowless building on the left. At the northern side of the intersection, at right angles to the bank, is the **Royal Exchange,** originally built in the 1560s as a trading hall for merchants. The present building, opened in

1844 and the third on the site, is now occupied by the **London International Financial Futures Exchange.** You can watch the hectic trading from the Visitors' Gallery. *Tel. 071/623–0444. Admission free. Visitors' Gallery open weekdays 11:30–1:45.*

47 The third major building at this intersection, on its south side, is the **Mansion House,** the official residence of the lord mayor of London.

48 Continue east along **Cornhill,** site of a Roman basilica and of a medieval grain market. Turn right into Gracechurch Street and then left into **Leadenhall Market.** There has been a market here since the 14th century; the present building dates from 1881.

49 Just behind the market is one of the most striking pieces of contemporary City architecture: the headquarters of **Lloyd's of London,** built by the modernist architect Richard Rogers. Its main feature is a 62-meter-high (200-foot-high) barrel vault made of sparkling glass. The underwriters of Lloyd's provide insurance for everything imaginable, from oil rigs to a pianist's fingers. An exhibit traces the history of Lloyd's from the 17th century. *1 Lime St., tel. 071/623–7100, ext. 6210 or 5786. Admission free. Open weekdays 10–2:30.*

Time Out Lloyd's started life in a coffeehouse, and so **Lloyd's Coffee House,** at the foot of the modern building, is an apt place for coffee and pastries, a full lunch, or afternoon tea.

50 From here it's a short walk east to the **Tower of London,** one of London's most famous sights and one of its most crowded, too. Come as early in the day as possible and head for the Crown Jewels so you can see them before the crowds arrive.

The tower served the monarchs of medieval England as both fortress and palace. Every British sovereign from William the Conqueror in the 11th century to Henry VIII in the 16th lived here, and it remains a royal palace, in name at least. The **History Gallery,** south of the White Tower, is a walk-through display designed to answer questions about the inhabitants of the tower and its evolution over the centuries.

The **White Tower** is the oldest and also the most conspicuous building in the entire complex. Inside, the **Chapel of St. John** is one of the few unaltered parts. A structure of great simplicity, it is almost entirely lacking in ornamentation. The **Royal Armories,** England's national collection of arms and armor, occupies the rest of the White Tower. Armor of the 16th and 17th centuries forms the centerpiece of the displays, including pieces belonging to Henry VIII and Charles I.

Among other buildings worth seeing is the **Bloody Tower.** This name has been traced back only to 1571; it was originally known as the Garden Tower. Sir Walter Raleigh was held prisoner here, in relatively comfortable circumstances, between 1603 and 1616, during which time he wrote his *History of the World;* his rooms are furnished much as they were during his imprisonment. The little princes in the tower—the boy king Edward V and his brother Richard, duke of York, supposedly murdered on the orders of Gloucester, later crowned Richard III—certainly lived in the Bloody Tower, and may well have died here, too. Another bloody death is alleged to have occurred in the **Wakefield Tower,** when Henry VI was murdered in 1471 during

England's medieval civil war, the Wars of the Roses. It was a rare honor to be beheaded in private inside the tower; most people were executed outside, on **Tower Hill,** where the crowds could get a much better view. Important prisoners were held in the **Beauchamp Tower;** the walls are covered with graffiti and inscriptions carved by prisoners.

The **Crown Jewels,** housed in the **Jewel House,** are a breathtakingly beautiful collection of regalia, precious stones, gold, and silver. The Royal Scepter contains the largest cut diamond in the world. The Imperial State Crown, made for the 1838 coronation of Queen Victoria, contains some 3,000 precious stones, largely diamonds and pearls. Look for the ravens whose presence at the tower is traditional. It is said that if they leave, the tower will fall and England will lose her greatness. *Tower Hill, tel. 071/709–0765. Admission: £5.90 adults, £4.50 students and senior citizens, £3.70 children under 16, family ticket £17. Reduced admission charges apply during Feb. when the Jewel House is closed. Small additional admission charge to the Fusiliers Museum only. Open Mar.–Oct., Mon.–Sat. 9:30–5, Sun. 2–5; Nov.–Feb., Mon.–Sat. 9:30–4.*

Yeoman Warder guides conduct tours daily from the Middle Tower, no charge, but a tip is always appreciated. Subject to weather and availability of guides, tours are conducted about every 30 minutes until 3:30 in summer, 2:30 in winter.

Shopping

Shopping is one of London's great pleasures. Different areas retain their traditional specialties, as described below, but part of the fun is to seek out the small crafts, antiques, and gift stores that have sprung up all over the city during the past few years.

Shopping Districts **Chelsea** is a mecca for those in search of up-to-the-minute fashions, antiques, and classy home furnishings. A Saturday stroll along the **King's Road** will reveal some of the weirder fashion trends among London's youngsters.

Covent Garden is the home of crafts shops and trendy boutiques. Antiques are the main draw in **Kensington,** especially along **Kensington Church Street.** There are some good clothes stores on **Kensington High Street.**

The great Edwardian bulk of Harrods dominates **Knightsbridge,** but don't neglect the boutiques and art galleries on other shopping streets in the area, such as **Sloane Street, Beauchamp Place,** and **Walton Street.**

In **Mayfair,** the area between **Piccadilly** and **Oxford Street,** the emphasis is on traditional British clothing for men and women. **South Molton Street** adds a modern, raffish, and pricey accent. Go to **Bond Street** for designer-label fashions and world-famous jewelry. Both quality and prices are tops here.

Noisy, crowded **Oxford Street** is to be endured rather than enjoyed. **Selfridges, Marks and Spencer,** and **John Lewis** are all good department stores here, and little **St. Christopher's Place,** almost opposite Bond Street tube, adds a chic touch.

There are still a number of classy stores along **Piccadilly,** including **Simpsons** (clothes), **Hatchards** (books), and **Fortnum and Mason** (foodstuffs, fashions). Several elegant shopping arcades lead off Piccadilly, the best-known of which is the **Burlington Arcade.**

China, clothes, fabrics, and good department stores help to make **Regent Street** an appealing alternative to neighboring Oxford Street. The crowds are almost as thick, but the presence of **Liberty**—the city's most appealing department store, still with its original emphasis on Oriental goods—compensates somewhat.

Though his suits may be made in Savile Row, the English gentleman comes to **St. James's** for the rest of his outfit, which includes shoes, shirts, silk ties, hats, and all manner of accessories. The prices mirror the quality.

Markets Street markets are one aspect of London life not to be missed. Here are some of the more interesting markets:

Bermondsey. Arrive as early as possible for the best treasure—or junk. *Tower Bridge Rd., SE1. Open Fri. 4:30 AM–noon. Take the tube to London Bridge and walk or take the No. 15 or 25 bus to Aldgate and then a No. 42 bus over Tower Bridge to Bermondsey Square.*

Camden Lock. This is just the place for an unusual and inexpensive gift; it's also a picturesque place to wander around. There's an open-air antiques market on weekends, but it gets horribly crowded. *Chalk Farm Rd., NW1. Open Tues.–Sun. 9:30–5:30. Take the tube or the No. 24 or 29 bus to Camden Town.*

Camden Passage. The rows of little antiques shops are a good hunting ground for silverware and jewelry. Saturday is the day for stalls; shops are open the rest of the week. *Islington, N1. Open Wed.–Sat. 8:30–3. Take the tube or No. 19 or 38 bus to the Angel.*

Petticoat Lane. Look for good-quality, budget-priced leather goods, dazzling knitwear, and bargain-price fashions, plus cameras, videos, and stereos at budget prices. *Middlesex St., E1. Open Sun. 9–2. Take the tube to Liverpool Street, Aldgate, or Aldgate East.*

Portobello Market. Saturday is the best day to search the stalls for not-quite-bargain-priced silverware, curios, porcelain, and jewelry. It's always crowded, with an authentic hustle-and-bustle atmosphere, and firmly on the tourist route. *Portobello Rd., W11. Open Fri. 5–3, Sat. 8–5. Take the tube or No. 52 bus to Notting Hill Gate or Ladbroke Grove or No. 15 bus to Kensington Park Road.*

Dining

Until relatively recently, British food was condemned the world over for its plainness and mediocrity. But nowadays the problem is not so much bad food as expensive food. The best of traditional British cooking is solid and straightforward and dependent on top-quality, fresh materials, such as succulent spring beef and seasonal vegetables. The worst consists of heavy, starchy foods, overboiled and deep-fat fried, and vegetables boiled to within an inch of their lives.

Mealtimes These vary somewhat, depending on the region of the country you are visiting. But in general, breakfast is served between 7:30 and 9 and lunch between noon and 2. Tea—an essential and respected part of British tradition and often a meal in itself—is served between 7:30 and 9:30, sometimes earlier, but rarely later. High tea, at about 6, replaces dinner in some areas, and in large cities, after-theater suppers are often available.

Dress Jacket and tie are suggested for the more formal restaurants in the top-price categories, but, in general, casual chic or informal dress is acceptable in most establishments.

Ratings Prices are per person and include a first course, a main course, and dessert, but not wine or service. Best bets are indicated by a star ★.

Category	Cost
Very Expensive	over £40
Expensive	£30–£40
Moderate	£15–£30
Inexpensive	under £15

Bloomsbury
Expensive

The White Tower. The most upscale Greek restaurant in town has barely changed since it first opened in 1939. There are portraits on the walls, glass partitions between the tables, and an entertainingly rhapsodic menu. Dishes range from the traditional—*taramasalata*—to the more creative—roast duckling with crushed wheat. *1 Percy St., tel. 071/636–8141. Reservations required. AE, DC, MC, V. Closed weekends, 3 weeks in Aug., 1 week at Christmas, holidays.*

Inexpensive

The Agra. This Indian restaurant is popular with media folk for its good value and wide choice of meat and vegetarian curries. Overhead fans, low lighting, and attentive waiters add a touch of class. *135–137 Whitfield St., tel. 071/387–8833. Reservations advised for dinner. AE, DC, MC, V. Closed Dec. 25.*

The North Sea Fish Restaurant. Only freshly caught fish is served in this popular haunt. It's a bit tricky to find—three blocks south of St. Pancras station, down Judd Street. Recommended are the seafood platter and Dover sole. You can eat in or take out. *7–8 Leigh St., tel. 071/387–5892. Reservations advised. AE, DC, MC, V. Closed Sun., holidays, 10 days at Christmas.*

Chelsea
Very Expensive

La Tante Claire. This spot is justly famous for its superb haute cuisine: hot foie gras on shredded potatoes with a sweet wine and shallot sauce and pig's trotter studded with mousse of white meat with sweetbreads and wild mushrooms. *68 Royal Hospital Rd., tel. 071/352–6045. Reservations 3–4 weeks in advance. AE, DC, MC, V. Closed weekends, 10 days at Easter and Christmas, 3 weeks in Aug.–Sept.*

Expensive
★

English House. This charming place is decorated in chintz with antiques and cream linen tablecloths. Authentically historic English recipes include oak-smoked pigeon breasts with rhubarb and ginger preserve and hot toffee and apple tart. *3 Milner St., tel. 071/584–3002. Reservations required for dinner. AE, DC, MC, V. Closed Dec. 25, Good Friday.*

Moderate

Gavvers. This is the down-market branch of the Gavroche empire, located two blocks below Sloane Square. The set menus at £15 for lunch and £27 for dinner offer simpler versions of the Roux brothers' classic French dishes. The place is rather cramped and noisy but full of character. *61–63 Lower Sloane*

St., tel. 071/730–4772. Reservations essential. AE, DC, MC, V. Closed Sat. lunch, Sun.

Inexpensive **Henry J. Bean's.** Hamburgers and Tex-Mex food are served to American oldies music. There's American-bar decor: The walls are covered with newspapers and other ephemera. *195–197 King's Rd., tel. 071/352–9255. No reservations. No credit cards. Closed Dec. 25, 26, 31.*

The City **Bill Bentley's.** Once a wine merchant's vault with bare walls
Expensive and arched ceiling, this atmospheric spot is recommended for the seafood platters and Bill Bentley's special oysters. There are two other branches, at Beauchamp Place and Baker Street. *Swedeland Ct., 202 Bishopsgate, tel. 071/283–1763. Reservations required. AE, DC, MC, V. Open weekdays for lunch only.*

★ **Le Poulbot.** Here you'll find one of the best fixed-price lunches in the entire city, with a classic French menu that offers new specialties daily. Top-class, well-balanced food is served in an intimate red-plush setting. There is a good choice of dishes for each course and an aperitif is included in the price. Try the moderately priced brasserie upstairs, too. *45 Cheapside, tel. 071/236–4379. Reservations 2–3 days in advance. AE, DC, MC, V. Open weekdays for lunch only.*

Moderate **Sweetings.** City gents stand in line to lunch at this tiny, basic Victorian restaurant close to the remains of a Roman temple. The service is Old World courteous; the fish, cheese, and puddings are comforting and well prepared. *39 Queen Victoria St., tel. 071/248–3062. No reservations. No credit cards. Open weekdays for lunch only; closed Christmas, holidays.*

Covent Garden **The Savoy Grill.** Continuing to attract more than its fair share
Very Expensive of literary and artistic names, as well as the odd tycoon, this
★ paneled French-English place guarantees top-notch cooking. Order an omelet Arnold Bennett (seafood is the extra ingredient) or a fillet of pork with fresh cranberries. It is especially good for such traditional English specialties as jugged hare (rabbit stew). Playgoers can split their theatre menu—part before the show, the rest after. *Strand, tel. 071/836–4343. Reservations advised for lunch and for Thurs.–Sat. dinner. AE, DC, MC, V. Closed Sat. lunch, Sun., and Aug.*

Expensive **Rules.** This is a London institution with a splendid Edwardian atmosphere; it features good roast beef, lamb, and Dover sole, as well as game in season. Try the homemade whiskey-and-ginger ice cream for dessert. Service can be very slow. *35 Maiden La., tel. 071/836–5314. Reservations at least 1 day in advance. AE, DC, MC, V. Closed Sun., Dec. 25.*

Moderate **Bertorelli's.** Opposite the stage door of the Royal Opera House,
★ Bertorelli's is a favorite with opera goers. Chic, postmodern decor complements the traditional Italian food—try the hot mushroom and garlic salad and whatever is the fresh fish of the day. *44a Floral St., tel. 071/836–3969. Reservations advised. AE, DC, MC, V. Closed Sun., Dec. 25.*

Frère Jacques. This airy, light spot—a combination wine bar and brasserie—specializes in the best seafood in the area. The oysters are excellent here and the shellfish platter, a joy. *38 Long Acre, tel. 071/836–7823. Reservations advised. AE, DC, MC, V. Open daily.*

★ **Joe Allen.** This basement restaurant behind the Strand Palace Hotel follows the style of its New York counterpart. It's a great place to spot stage or screen stars. The barbecued ribs and Caesar's salad are a real treat. There's a pianist after 9 PM, if you can hear through the surrounding decibels. *13 Exeter St., tel. 071/836–0651. Reservations required. No credit cards. Closed Christmas.*

Inexpensive **Food for Thought.** This is a simple downstairs vegetarian restaurant, with seats for only 50, so there's almost always a waiting line. The menu—stir fries, casseroles, salads, and dessert—changes daily, and each dish is freshly made. No alcohol is served here. *31 Neal St., tel. 071/836–0239. No reservations. No credit cards. Closed Sun., Sat. after 4:30 PM, weekdays after 8 PM, 2 weeks at Christmas, holidays.*

Kensington **Bombay Brasserie.** Here's one of London's most fashionable
Moderate and stylish Indian restaurants. The fine menu, drawn from different regions, includes *Bombay thali* (small bowls of vegetables or meat), Kashmiri lamb, and Goan fish curry. The Sunday lunch buffet is particularly popular. Try for a table in the conservatory. *Courtfield Close, Courtfield Rd., tel. 071/370–4040. Reservations required for dinner. AE, DC, MC, V. Closed Christmas.*

★ **Lou Pescadou.** A boating theme predominates at this Provençal restaurant—there are pictures of boats, boats as lamps, and so on. Fish is the specialty: Try the *petite bouillabaisse* (fish soup) or red mullet poached in tarragon sauce. *241 Old Brompton Rd., tel: 071/370–1057. No reservations. AE, DC, MC, V. Closed Aug., Dec. 25.*

Tui. This stylish, modern Thai spot is just around the corner from the Victoria and Albert Museum. Wake your taste buds up with a crab claw-and-prawn hot pot or a spicy beef curry. *19 Exhibition Rd., tel. 071/584–8359. Reservations advised. AE, DC, MC, V. Closed holidays.*

Knightsbridge **Bibendum.** Upstairs in the renovated 1911 Michelin building,
Very Expensive this excellent restaurant has been the flavor of the month for
★ some time now. The decor has a feel of the period without going over the top, though having two big stained-glass windows featuring the tire man helps. From the scallops in a citrus sauce to the passion-fruit *bavarois*, all the dishes taste exactly as they should. *81 Fulham Rd., tel. 071/581–5817. Reservations required. MC, V. Closed Christmas and holidays.*

Waltons. Formal and sumptuous, this Anglo-French restaurant with soft lighting and miles of mirrors has an imaginative, constantly changing menu. The seafood sausage and the roast duck are a must. *121 Walton St., tel. 071/584–0204. Reservations required. AE, DC, MC, V. Closed Dec. 25, 26, and Easter.*

Expensive **Ménage à Trois.** Appetizers and desserts only are served at this
★ stylish restaurant. Recommended are the terrine of leeks and duck confit served with grilled foie gras and, to top it off, the chocoholics anonymous—six chocolate puddings on one plate! *15 Beauchamp Pl., tel. 071/589–4252. Reservations required for dinner. AE, DC, MC, V. Closed Sat. and Sun. lunch, Christmas, and Easter.*

Moderate **Grill St. Quentin.** This is a popular French spot just five blocks west of Harrods. Choose from a selection of fresh meat from Scotland or fish, which is then cooked on an open grill. The set lunch at £12 is excellent value for shoppers. *2 Yeoman's Row, tel. 071/583–8377. Reservations advised. AE, DC, MC, V. Closed Sun.*

Inexpensive **Stockpot.** Speedy service is the mark of this large, jolly restaurant full of young people. The food is filling and wholesome; try the homemade soups, the Lancashire hot pot, or the apple crumble. Breakfast is also served Monday–Saturday. *6 Basil St., tel. 071/589–8627. Reservations accepted. No credit cards. Closed Dec. 25, New Year's Day.*

Mayfair **Chez Nico.** Those with refined palates and very deep pockets
Very Expensive should not miss Nico Ladenis's exquisite gastronomy. He is one
★ of the world's great chefs, and is famous for knowing it. Nowhere is food taken more seriously; the menu is in French (untranslated); vegetarians and children are not welcome. *35 Great Portland St., W1, tel. 071/436–3846. Jacket and tie required. Reservations required in advance. MC, V. Closed weekends, public holidays, 3 weeks in Aug.*

★ **Le Gavroche.** Generally regarded as London's finest restaurant, Le Gavroche has excellent service, discreetly sumptuous decor, and lavish haute cuisine—duck with foie gras, lobster and champagne mousse. It's near the U.S. embassy. *43 Upper Brook St., tel. 071/408–0881. Reserve at least 1 week in advance. AE, DC, MC, V. Closed weekends, 10 days at Christmas, holidays.*

Expensive **Langan's Brasserie.** Langan's is as much a haunt of tourists as of celebrities these days. If you do manage to get in, you'll be impressed by the modern art on the walls, the vast menu, the frank service (the waiters sometimes advise against certain dishes), and the top-quality food. Try the spinach soufflé with anchovy sauce and the stuffed artichokes with hollandaise sauce. *Stratton St., tel. 071/493–6437. Reservations required far in advance. AE, DC, MC, V. Closed Sat. lunch, Sun., holidays.*

Moderate **Pizzeria Condotti.** Run by the cartoonist Enzo Apicella, this spot has walls lined with cartoons and modern paintings. The pizzas are first-class, if calorie laden; the figure conscious can choose salads instead—such as the *insalata Condotti* (mixed salad with mozzarella and avocado). *4 Mill St., tel. 071/499–1308. No reservations. AE, DC, MC, V. Closed Sun., holidays, Dec. 25, 26.*

Inexpensive **The Chicago Pizza Pie Factory.** Huge pizzas with salad and garlic bread are served at reasonable prices in this bright basement spot. The choice of toppings is somewhat limited, but try the American sausage and mushroom version. There's also a cocktail bar, rock music, and videos. *17 Hanover Sq., tel. 071/629–2669. Reservations advised for lunch. No credit cards. Closed Dec. 25, 26.*

Justin de Blank's. This attractive, upscale, self-service spot is ideal for a break from Oxford Street shopping. The food is all homemade. Favorites include the crab-and-cucumber mousse, fruit brûlé, and chocolate roulade. Other branches include the British Museum cafeteria and the General Trading Company, off Sloane Square. *54 Duke St., tel. 071/629–3174. MC, V. Closed after 9 PM, Sat. dinner, Sun., holidays.*

Notting Hill Gate **Clarke's.** There's no choice of dishes at dinner (and only a lim-
Expensive ited choice at lunch); chef Sally Clarke plans the meal according to what is fresh in the market each day, using the freshest herbs and the best olive oils. It's fine cuisine. *124 Kensington Church St., tel. 071/221–9225. Reservations advised. MC, V.*

Closed weekends, 10 days at Christmas, Easter, 3 weeks in Aug.

Moderate ★ **L'Artiste Assoiffé.** The parrots Stanley and Sally will amuse you in the bar of this eccentric Victorian house before you escape to eat in the can-can room or the merry-go-round room to the accompaniment of operatic music. Pop stars, actors, and royals come here for the unique atmosphere and the French food: fillet of steak caramelized with Dijon mustard and spinach pancakes with nuts and cheese. It's open for lunch on Saturdays only. *122 Kensington Park Rd., tel. 071/727–4714. Reservations required. AE, DC, MC, V. Closed Sun., holidays; no lunch weekdays.*

Inexpensive **Hollands.** London's only Filipino wine bar, this is a relaxed and friendly place with a bar downstairs and a restaurant area and rooftop conservatory (lovely in summer) upstairs. The food is angelicized Filipino (stirfried squid with ginger) or wine bar staples (steak, taramosalata). *6 Portland Rd., W11, tel. 071/ 229–3130. Dress: casual. Reservations advised for restaurant. AE, MC, V. Closed Christmas.*

Soho *Expensive* **Alastair Little.** A favorite among table-hopping media types, chef Alastair serves nouvelle British designer and international food. Try especially the soups and fish—steamed sea bass and Lyons *onglet*. The decor is functional and space at a premium. *49 Frith St., tel. 071/734–5183. Reservations advised. No credit cards. Closed Sat. lunch, Sun., Christmas, Easter.*
La Bastide. An elegant restaurant where heavy velvet drapes and linen napery set off generous and hearty regional French cuisine—whether the region is Burgundy (*coq au vin*, frogs' legs) or Brittany (crepes, seafood). Wines and cheeses are always excellent. *50 Greek St., W1, tel. 071/734–3300. Jacket and tie advised. Reservations advised. AE, DC, MC, V. Closed Sat., Sun. lunch, Sun. dinner, national holidays.*

Moderate ★ **Chiang Mai.** The interior is modeled on a traditional Thai stilt house. The food is delicious and spicy, all easy to order from an English menu. Try a *Tom Yum* (hot-and-sour soup) or a *Pad Kra Prow* (beef, pork, or chicken with fresh Thai basil and chili). *48 Frith St., tel. 071/437–7444. Reservations advised. AE, MC, V. Closed Sun. and holidays.*
Manzi's. Just off Leicester Square, this is one of London's oldest and most traditional fish restaurants. The downstairs restaurant is the more lively and atmospheric; the decor is kitsch Moulin Rouge murals and monstrous plastic lobsters. *1–2 Leicester St., tel. 071/734–0224. Reservations advised. AE, DC, MC, V. Closed Sun. lunch, Dec. 25, 26.*

Inexpensive **Crank's.** One restaurant of a popular vegetarian chain (other branches are at Covent Garden, Great Newport Street, Tottenham Street, and Barrett Street), Crank's has a nutritious and tasty menu. Lunch is self-service, dinner candlelit waiter-service (many branches, though not this one, close at 8 PM). *8 Marshall St., tel. 071/437–9431. Reservations advised for dinner. AE, DC, MC, V. Closed Sun., Dec. 25.*
Poon's. A popular Chinese restaurant (there are long lines in the evening), Poon's specializes in wind-dried meats. There are two other Poon's, but this one is the cheapest and most authentic. *4 Leicester St., tel. 071/437–1528. Reservations required. Closed Sun., Dec. 25, 26.*

St. James's
Very Expensive

Suntory. Frequented by ministers and officials from the Japanese embassy, this is a gracious place to appreciate the delicacy of Japanese cuisine. There's a *teppanyaki* bar, where fresh meat or fish is cooked in front of you. The main dining room is where you can choose from an extensive menu of exotic dishes. There are also private *tatami* rooms, where seating is on the floor. *72 St. James's St., tel. 071/409–0201. Reservations required. AE, DC, MC, V. Closed Sun., holidays.*

Wilton's. Traditional British fare—turtle soup, sausage and mashed potatoes, partridge, Stilton—is served here in Edwardian surroundings. Each day has its own specialty. The oysters are London's best—all the seafood arrives fresh several times a day. *55 Jermyn St., tel. 071/629–9955. Reservations advised 2 days in advance. AE, DC, MC, V. Closed Sat. lunch, Sun., holidays, 1st 2 weeks in Aug., Christmas.*

Expensive

Le Caprice. The cool and elegant decor here matches the often well-known clientele exactly. The international menu should appeal to all tastes, with dishes from North Africa, France, and the Far East. Finish with a mousse of dark and white chocolate. *Arlington House, Arlington St., tel. 071/629–2239. Reservations required. AE, DC, MC, V. Closed 10 days at Christmas.*

Lodging

Britain offers a wide variety of accommodations, ranging from enormous, top-quality, top-price hotels to simple, intimate guest houses.

Hotels

British hotels vary greatly, and there is no official system of classification. Most have rooms with private bathrooms, although there are still some—usually older hotels—that offer rooms with only wash basins; in this case, showers and bathtubs (and toilets) are usually just down the hall. Many also have "good" and "bad" wings. Be sure to check before you take the room. Generally, British hotel prices include breakfast—often little more than tea and toast. A hotel that includes a traditional English breakfast in its rates is usually a good bet. Hotel prices in London are significantly higher than in the rest of the country, and often the quality is not as good. Tourist information centers all over the country will reserve rooms for you, usually for a small fee. A great many hotels offer special weekend and off-season bargain packages. For extra thrills (or chills), the British Tourist Authority can recommend overnight accommodations in one of Britain's "haunted" hotels.

Bed-and-Breakfast

These small, simple establishments are a special British tradition. They offer modest, inexpensive accommodations, usually in a family home. Few have private bathrooms, and most offer no meals other than breakfast. Guest houses are a slightly larger, somewhat more luxurious, version. Both provide the visitor with an excellent glimpse of everyday British life that's seldom seen in large city hotels.

Holiday Cottages

Furnished apartments, houses, cottages, and trailers are available for weekly rental in all areas of the country. These vary from quaint, cleverly converted farmhouses to brand-new buildings set in scenic surroundings. For families and large groups, they offer the best value-for-money accommodations. Lists of rental properties are available free of charge from the

British Tourist Authority. Discounts of up to 50% apply during the off-season (October to March).

Stately Homes It is possible to stay as a paying guest in a number of famous stately homes scattered throughout the countryside. Styles range from Jacobean castles and manors to Regency houses. The equally stately prices usually include both meals and lodging. Reservations are essential. For details, contact the **British Travel Centre** (tel. 071/730–3400) or write to the **British Tourist Authority** (Thames Tower, Blacks Road, London W6 9EL).

University Housing In larger cities and in some towns, certain universities offer their residence halls to paying vacationers. The facilities available are usually compact sleeping units, and they can be rented on a nightly basis. For information, contact the **British University Accommodation Consortium** (Box 486, University Park, Nottingham NG7 2RD, tel. 0602/504571).

Youth Hostels There are more than 350 youth hostels throughout England, Wales, and Scotland. They range from very basic to very good. Many are located in remote and beautiful areas; others can be found on the outskirts of large cities. Despite the name, there is no age restriction. The accommodations are inexpensive and generally reliable and usually include cooking facilities. For additional information, contact the **YHA Headquarters** (Trevelyan House, 8 St. Stephen's Hill, St. Albans, Hertfordshire AL1 2DY, tel. 0727/55215).

Ratings Prices are for two people in a double room and include all taxes. Best bets are indicated by a star ★.

Category	Cost
Very Expensive	over £200
Expensive	£95–£200
Moderate	£50–£95
Inexpensive	under £50

Bayswater
Very Expensive
★

Whites. This cream-faced Victorian "country mansion" has a wrought-iron portico and a view of Kensington Gardens, especially grand when floodlit at night. Thick carpets, gilded glass, marble balustrades, swagged silk draperies, and Louis XV-style furniture all help to give a sense of deep luxury. Some of the bedrooms have balconies, seating areas, and personal safes. Colors are muted: powder blue, old rose, and pale green. *90–92 Lancaster Gate, W2 3NR, tel. 071/262–2711. 54 rooms with bath. Facilities: restaurant, lounge, valet service, free in-house movies. AE, DC, MC, V.*

Expensive

Abbey Court. A short walk from Kensington Gardens brings you to this luxury bed-and-breakfast establishment in a historic 1850 building. Each bedroom is individually designed with 19th-century French furniture, Venetian mirrors, and oil portraits; some have four-poster beds. *20 Pembridge Gardens, W2 4DU, tel. 071/221–7518. 22 rooms with bath. Facilities: Jacuzzis, garden. AE, DC, MC, V.*

Portobello. A faithful core of visitors return again and again to this tiny hotel in a Victorian terrace near the Portobello Road antiques market. Some rooms are tiny, but the suites have sitting rooms attached, and the atmosphere is relaxed and informal. *22 Stanley Gardens, W11 2NG, tel. 071/727–2777. 25 rooms with bath or shower. Facilities: restaurant, 24-hour bar. AE, DC, MC, V. Closed 10 days at Christmas.*

Moderate ★ **Camelot.** This affordable hotel, recently refurbished and extended, has beautifully decorated rooms. The breakfast room has a large open fireplace with wooden trestle tables and a polished wood floor. *45–47 Norfolk Sq., W2 1RX, tel. 071/723–9118. 43 rooms, 33 with bath or shower. Facilities: lounge, free in-house videos. MC, V.*

Edward Lear. The former home of Edward Lear, the artist and writer of nonsense verse, this hotel has an imposing entrance leading to a black-and-white tiled lobby. Ask for one of the quieter rooms to the rear. The breakfast room has huge French windows. *28–30 Seymour St., W1H 5WD, tel. 071/402–5401. 32 rooms, 12 with bath or shower. V.*

Inexpensive **Norfolk Court.** Though small, this is a modest, pleasant Regency hotel near Paddington Station. Some rooms have French windows and balconies overlooking the square. *20 Norfolk Sq., W2 1RS, tel. 071/723–4963. 28 rooms, 9 with bath. MC.*

Bloomsbury
Expensive ★ **Grafton.** This hotel features an Edwardian drawing room with red-plush armchairs, classical columns, and an open fireplace. The refurbished bedrooms are modern, especially in the new executive wing. The Grafton's location makes it convenient for Euston and King's Cross stations. *130 Tottenham Court Rd., W1P 9HP, tel. 071/388–4131. 236 rooms with bath or shower. Facilities: restaurant, bar, lounge, laundry, free in-house movies. AE, DC, MC, V.*

Moderate **Academy.** Convenient to the British Museum and area shops, the Academy is in a Georgian building and has a bar, library/lounge, and patio garden. *17–21 Gower St., WC1E 6HG, tel. 071/631–4115. 32 rooms, 24 with bath. AE, DC, MC, V.*

Morgan. This charming family-run hotel in an 18th-century terrace house has rooms that are small and comfortably furnished, but friendly and cheerful. The tiny paneled breakfast room is straight out of a doll's house. The back rooms overlook the British Museum. *24 Bloomsbury St., WC1B 3QJ, tel. 071/636–3735. 14 rooms with shower. No credit cards.*

Inexpensive **Gower House.** This is an adequate, simple hotel with reasonable rates. The rooms are on the small side, but are well kept. Centrally located for sightseeing. *57 Gower St., WC1E 6HJ, tel. 071/636–4685. 16 rooms, 3 with bath. MC, V.*

Chelsea and Kensington
Very Expensive ★ **Blakes.** Patronized by musicians and film stars, this hotel is one of the most exotic in town. Its Victorian exterior contrasts with the 1980s ultrachic interior, with an arty mix of Biedermeier, leather, and bamboo furniture; rich fabrics; four-poster beds; and Oriental enameled screens. The bedrooms have individual designs ranging from swaths of black moiré silk to a more severe plain gray. *33 Roland Gardens, SW7 3PF, tel. 071/370–6701. 52 rooms with bath. Facilities: restaurant, bar, satellite TV. AE, DC, MC, V.*

Expensive **London Tara.** This vast, fully air-conditioned, functional international hotel, close to Kensington High Street, has a cordial atmosphere and light and colorful rooms. *Scarsdale Pl., W8 5SR, tel. 071/937–7211. 831 rooms with bath; 10 converted for the disabled. Facilities: 3 restaurants, lounge, bars, in-house movies. AE, DC, MC, V.*

Inexpensive **Abbey House.** Standards are high and the rooms unusually spacious in this hotel in a fine residential block near Kensington Palace and Gardens. *11 Vicarage Gate, W8 4AG, tel. 071/727–2594. 15 rooms, none with bath. Facilities: orthopedic beds. No credit cards.*

Vicarage Hotel. This genteel establishment, run by the same husband-wife team for the past 25 years, has high standards of cleanliness throughout. Bedrooms are traditional and comfortable with solid English furniture. It attracts many repeat visitors from the United States and welcomes single travelers. *10 Vicarage Gate, W8 4AG, tel. 071/229–4030. 20 rooms, none with bath. Facilities: small TV lounge. No credit cards.*

Knightsbridge and Victoria **Cadogan.** This turreted Edwardian building has changed hands and is now owned by the prestigious Historic House Hotels group, which runs Middlethorpe Hall in York. Cadogan is slated for refurbishing in 1992. The front part of the hotel was once the home of Lily Langtry, the actress who was Edward VII's mistress while he was prince of Wales. *75 Sloane St., SW1X 9SG, tel. 071/235–7141. 69 rooms with bath. Facilities: restaurant, bar, lounge. AE, DC, MC, V.*

Very Expensive

Goring. Around the corner from Buckingham Palace and often used by visiting VIPs, this hotel was built in 1910 and is now run by the third generation of Gorings. The atmosphere remains opulently Edwardian: marble fixtures in the bathrooms, with brass trim and the original fitted closets in some of the bedrooms. *17 Beeston Pl., Grosvenor Gardens, SW1W 0JW, tel. 071/834–8211. 90 rooms with bath. Facilities: restaurant, bar, lounge. AE, DC, MC, V.*

Hyde Park Hotel. During the 1920s, this was the favored accommodation of Rudolph Valentino and of sultans and maharajahs, who would book entire floors. The decor is high Victorian, with sumptuous green-veined marble, gold-topped columns, potted palms, and sparkling chandeliers. The bedrooms are furnished in the best of English taste: Edwardian darkwood furniture and pretty arrangements of fresh flowers. It's well placed for shopping and Hyde Park; some rooms overlook the park. *66 Knightsbridge, SW1Y 7LA, tel. 071/235–2000. 186 rooms with bath. Facilities: 2 restaurants, bar, hairdresser, satellite TV, in-house movies, coffee shop. AE, DC, MC, V.*

St. James Court. This elegant 1900 apartment block has been converted into a stylish hotel with a stately courtyard adorned by a fountain and a terra-cotta frieze portraying Shakespearean scenes. The reception area is grand, all marble and wood with lots of greenery. The bedrooms are appealingly decorated in different color schemes; the bathrooms are well equipped. One restaurant serves Mediterranean cuisine; the other, Chinese. *Buckingham Gate, SW1E 6AF, tel. 071/834–6655. 390 rooms with bath. Facilities: 2 restaurants, coffee shop, fitness center with sauna, spa pools, satellite TV. AE, DC, MC, V.*

Expensive ★ **Basil Street.** Women guests here are granted automatic membership in the ladies' organization called "Parrot Club." Family-run for some 75 years, this is a gracious Edwardian hotel on a quiet street. The rooms are filled with antiques. The Gallery is a writing area, with desks in the window alcoves, unusual paintings on glass, polished wooden floors, and fine Oriental carpets. *Basil St., SW3 1AH. tel. 071/581–3311. 96 rooms, 72 with bath. Facilities: 2 restaurants, wine bar, lounge, ladies' club. AE, DC, MC, V.*

★ **Knightsbridge Green.** There are more suites than bedrooms at this recently refurbished 18th-century hotel just two minutes' walk from Harrods. The style of the second floor is French with white furniture; the third is English, in beech. Breakfast is served in your room—there's no restaurant. *159 Knightsbridge, SW1X 7PD, tel. 071/584–6274. 22 rooms/suites with bath. Facilities: club room. AE, MC, V. Closed 5 days at Christmas.*

Stakis St. Ermins. Convenient for Westminster Abbey, this is a Victorian hotel with high ceilings, a fine curved stairwell, and roomy bedrooms brightened by floral fabrics. Most of the guests are businesspeople. *Caxton St., SW1H 0QW, tel. 071/222–7888. 290 rooms with bath or shower. Facilities: 2 restaurants, bar, coffee lounge, satellite TV, in-house movies. AE, DC, MC, V.*

Moderate **Claverley.** Located on a quiet, tree-lined street, the Claverley offers friendly, attractive surroundings, some four-poster beds, and the wealthy world of Knightsbridge shopping, just around the corner. *13–14 Beaufort Gdns., SW3 1PS, tel. 071/589–8541. 36 rooms, all with bath. AE, V.*

Ebury Court. This small, old-fashioned, country house–style hotel is near Victoria Station. The rooms are small, with chintz and antique furniture to give them extra character. You must buy temporary membership for use of the bar and lounge. *26 Ebury St., SW1W 0LU, tel. 071/730–8147. 42 rooms, 18 with bath. Facilities: restaurant, club with bar and lounge (membership fee payable). DC, MC, V.*

West End **Brown's.** Close to Bond Street, Brown's is like a country house
Very Expensive in the middle of town, with wood paneling, grandfather clocks, and large fireplaces. The elegant furnishings of the bedrooms include brass chandeliers and matching olive carpets, velour armchairs, and sweeping curtains. *34 Albemarle St., W1A 4SW, tel. 071/493–6020. 133 rooms with bath. Facilities: restaurant, lounge, writing room, cocktail bar. AE, DC, MC, V.*

★ **Claridges.** This legendary hotel has one of the world's classiest guest lists. The liveried staff are friendly, not at all condescending, and the rooms are luxurious. The hotel was founded in 1812, but present decor is either 1930s Art Deco or country-house style. Have a drink in the lounge and hear the orchestra, or retreat to the peaceful reading room. The rooms are spacious, the staircase and elevator are grand. *Brook St., W1A 2JQ, tel. 071/629–8860. 200 rooms with bath. Facilities: 2 restaurants, lounge (with orchestra), hairdresser, valet, AE, DC, MC, V.*

Duke's. This small Edwardian hotel is situated in a cul-de-sac in St. James's and enjoys a distinct Old World character, helped by the portraits of dukes adorning the walls. The top-floor bedrooms are the most spacious. *35 St. James's Pl., SW1A 1NY, tel. 071/491–4840. 62 rooms with bath. Facilities: restaurant, bar. AE, DC, MC, V.*

Hampshire. This luxury hotel is right on Leicester Square, and you can't get more central than that. The surroundings may be a bit squalid, but the interior is lavishly furnished and the service is excellent. The decorations give an air of a wealthy country house, mixing handwoven Thai carpets with deep armchairs. It was once the Dental Hospital, but of the original building, only the facade is left. *31 Leicester Sq., WC2 7LH, tel.*

071/839–9399. 124 rooms with bath. Facilities: restaurant, satellite TV. AE, DC, MC, V.

Inn on the Park. Once one of Howard Hughes's hideaways, this opulent hotel, with its polished marble entrance hall, is close to Hyde Park. The strikingly decorated rooms have gigantic beds and plenty of extras, such as guest bathrobes and phone extensions in the bathrooms. *Hamilton Pl., Park Lane, W1A 1AZ, tel. 071/499–0888. 228 rooms with bath. Facilities: 2 restaurants, coffee shop, bar, lounge, shopping arcade, free in-house movies, garden. AE, DC, MC, V.*

★ **Savoy.** This grand, historic late-Victorian hotel has been the byword for luxury for just over a century. The best rooms, with antiques and cream plasterwork, overlook the Thames; others are in 1920s style with the original splendid bathroom fittings. *Strand, WC2R 0EU, tel. 071/836–4343. 202 rooms with bath. Facilities: 3 restaurants, 2 bars, grill room, coffee shop, florist, theater-ticket desk, free in-house movies. AE, DC, MC, V.*

Expensive **Chesterfield.** This former town house of the earls of Chesterfield is very popular with U.S. visitors, who are often return guests. It is deep in the heart of Mayfair, with welcoming, paneled public rooms; a good restaurant; spacious bedrooms; and an outstandingly helpful staff. *35 Charles St., W1X 8LX, tel. 071/491–2622. 113 rooms, all with bath. Facilities: restaurant, in-house movies. AE, DC, MC, V.*

Clifton-Ford. This is one of central London's most peaceful hotels, situated in a modern building on an 18th-century street north of Oxford Street. The hotel has recently been refurbished, with some larger suites now available. *47 Welbeck St., W1M 8DN, tel. 071/486–6600. 211 rooms with bath. Facilities: restaurant, bar, laundry, free in-house movies. AE, DC, MC, V.*

Pastoria. Though located just off busy Leicester Square, the Pastoria stands on a surprisingly quiet street. The limed oak bedrooms have light pink walls and navy blue carpets. *3–6 St. Martin's St., WC2H 7HL, tel. 071/930–8641. 58 rooms with bath. Facilities: restaurant, bar, coffee shop. AE, DC, MC, V.*

Moderate **Bryanston Court.** Three 18th-century houses have been converted into a traditional English family-run hotel with open fires and comfortable armchairs; the bedrooms are more contemporary. *56–60 Great Cumberland Pl., W1H 7FD, tel. 071/262–3141. 56 rooms with bath or shower. Facilities: restaurant, bar, lounge, satellite TV. AE, DC, MC, V.*

The Arts

For a list of events in the London arts scene, visit a newsstand or bookstore to pick up the weekly magazine: *Time Out*. The city's evening paper, the *Evening Standard*, carries listings, as do the major Sunday papers; the daily *Independent* and *Guardian*; and, on Friday, *The Times*. Additional information on any aspect of the arts in the capital is available from **Greater London Arts,** 9 White Lion St., tel. 071/837–8808; open weekdays 9:30–5:30.

Theater London's theater life can broadly be divided into three categories: the government-subsidized national companies; the commercial, or "West End," theaters; and the fringe.

The main national companies are the **National Theatre** (NT) and the **Royal Shakespeare Company** (RSC). Each has its own custom-designed facilities, in the South Bank arts complex and in the Barbican Arts Centre, respectively. Each presents a variety of plays by writers of all nationalities, ranging from the classics of Shakespeare and his contemporaries to specially commissioned modern works. Box office: NT, tel. 071/928–2252; RSC, tel. 071/638–8891.

The West End theaters largely stage musicals, comedies, whodunits, and revivals of lighter plays of the 19th and 20th centuries, often starring television celebrities. Occasionally there are more serious productions, including successful productions transferred from the subsidized theaters, such as RSC's *Les Liaisons Dangereuses* and *Les Misérables*.

The dozen or so established fringe theaters, scattered around central London and the immediate outskirts, frequently present some of London's most intriguing productions, if you're prepared to overlook occasional rough acting and uncomfortable seating.

Most theaters have an evening performance at 7:30 or 8 daily, except Sunday, and a matinee twice a week (Wednesday or Thursday and Saturday). Expect to pay from £6 for a seat in the upper balcony to £20 for a good seat in the stalls (orchestra) or dress circle (mezzanine)—more for musicals. Tickets may be booked in person at the theater box office; over the phone by credit card; or through ticket agents, such as **Keith Prowse** (tel. 081/741–9999, or look in the phone book under *Keith* for the nearest office). In addition, the ticket booth in Leicester Square sells half-price tickets on the day of performance for about 45 theaters; there is a small service charge. Beware of unscrupulous ticket agents who sell tickets at four or five times their box-office price (a small service charge is legitimate) and scalpers, who stand outside theaters offering tickets for the next performance; they've been known to charge £200 for a sought-after show.

Concerts   Ticket prices for symphony orchestra concerts are still relatively moderate—between £5 and £15, although you can expect to pay more to hear big-name artists on tour. If you can't book in advance, arrive half an hour before the performance for a chance at returns.

The London Symphony Orchestra is in residence at the **Barbican Arts Centre** (tel. 071/628–8795), although other top symphony and chamber orchestras also perform here. The **South Bank arts complex** (tel. 071/928–8800), which includes the **Royal Festival Hall** and the **Queen Elizabeth Hall,** is another major venue for choral, symphony, and chamber concerts. For less expensive concert going, try the **Royal Albert Hall** (tel. 071/589–8212) during the summer Promenade season; special tickets for standing room are available at the hall on the night of performance. **The Wigmore Hall** (tel. 071/935–2141) is a small auditorium, ideal for recitals. Inexpensive lunchtime concerts take place all over the city in smaller halls and churches, often featuring string quartets, singers, jazz ensembles, and gospel choirs. **St. John's, Smith Square** (tel. 071/222–1061), a converted Queen Anne church, is one of the more popular venues. It has a handy crypt cafeteria.

Opera   The **Royal Opera House** ranks alongside the New York Met in cost. Prices range from £8.50 (in the upper balconies, from which only a tiny portion of the stage is visible) to £392 for a box in the Grand Tier. Bookings are best made at the box office (tel. 071/240–1066). The **Coliseum** (tel. 071/836–3161) is the home of the English National Opera Company; productions are staged in English and are often a good deal more exciting than those at the Royal Opera House. The prices, which range from £36 to £37.50, are much cheaper, too.

Ballet The Royal Opera House also hosts the **Royal Ballet.** The prices are slightly more reasonable than for the opera, but be sure to book well ahead. The **English National Ballet** and visiting companies perform at the Coliseum from time to time, especially during the summer. **Sadler's Wells Theatre** (tel. 071/278–8916) hosts regional ballet and international modern dance troupes. Prices here are reasonable.

Film Most West End cinemas are in the area around Leicester Square and Piccadilly Circus. Tickets run from £4 to £7.50. Matinees and Monday evenings are cheaper. Cinema clubs screen a wide range of films: classics, Continental, underground, rare, or underestimated masterpieces. A temporary membership fee is usually about £1. One of the best-value clubs is the **National Film Theatre** (tel. 071/928–3232), part of the South Bank arts complex.

Nightlife

London's night spots are legion, and there is only space here to list a few of the best known. For up-to-the-minute listings, buy *Time Out.*

Jazz **Bas Clef** (85 Coronet St., tel. 071/729–2476), situated in an out-of-the-way warehouse on the northern edge of the City, (the nearest tube is Old Street), offers some of the best live jazz in town and a gourmet Anglo-French menu. **Ronnie Scott's** (47 Frith St., tel. 071/439–0747) is the legendary Soho jazz club where a host of international performers have played.

Nightclubs **Legends** (29 Old Burlington St., tel. 071/437–9933) has an impressive high-tech interior; a large choice of cocktails is served at the upstairs bar, while the downstairs area is graced with a large cool dance floor and central bar. Glitzy **Stringfellows** (16 Upper St. Martin's Lane, tel. 071/240–5534) has an Art Deco upstairs restaurant, mirrored walls, and a dazzling light show in the downstairs dance floor. **The Limelight** (136 Shaftesbury Ave., tel. 071/434–0572) is one of London's most fashionable night spots, with lots of one-nighter shows and special events. Liveliest on the weekend.

Casinos By law, you must apply in person for membership in a gaming house; in many cases, clubs prefer an applicant's membership to be proposed by an existing member. Approval usually takes about two days.

Crockford's (30 Curzon St., tel. 071/493–7771) is a civilized and unflashy 150-year-old club with a large international clientele; American roulette, punto banco, and blackjack are played. **Sportsman Club** (3 Tottenham Court Rd., tel. 071/637–5464) is one of the few gaming houses in London to have a dice table as well as punto banco, American roulette, and blackjack.

Disco **Camden Palace** (1A Camden High St., tel. 071/387–0428) is perennially popular with both London and visiting youth. This multitier dance hall features different theme nights, three bars, and a colorful light show. American-style food is served. The **Hippodrome** (Cranbourn St., tel. 071/437–4311) is a hugely popular and lavish disco with an exciting sound-and-laser light system, live bands and dancing acts, video screen, bars, and restaurant.

Rock **Dingwalls** (Camden Lock, Chalk Farm Rd., tel. 071/267–4967) is a very popular dance venue where a good selection of live bands play everything from rock to jazz every night of the week.

The Rock Garden (67 The Piazza, Covent Garden, tel. 071/240–3961) is famous for encouraging younger talent; Talking Heads, U2, and The Smiths are among those who played here while still virtually unknown. Music is in the standing-room-only basement, so eat first in the American restaurant upstairs.

The Marquee (105 Charing Cross Rd., tel. 071/437–6603), Soho's original rock club, is now in new premises; at least two live bands perform every night.

Cabaret The best comedy in town can be found in the small, crowded basement of the **Comedy Store** (28A Leicester Sq., tel. 071/839–6665). There are two shows, at 8 and midnight on Friday and Saturday, other evenings the show starts at 8:30 PM. **Madame Jo Jo's** (8 Brewer St., tel. 071/734–2473) offers possibly the most fun-filled evenings of any London cabaret. The place is new, luxurious, and civilized. There are two shows, at 12:15 and 1:15 AM, and the food and drinks are reasonably priced.

14 Madrid

Arriving and Departing

By Plane All international and domestic flights arrive at Madrid's Barajas Airport (tel. 91/205–8343/8344/8345), 16 kilometers (10 miles) northeast of town just off the N-II Barcelona highway. For information on arrival and departure times, call **Inforiberia** (tel. 91/411–2545) or the airline concerned.

Between the Airport and Downtown Buses leave the national and international terminals every 15 minutes from 5:40 AM to 2 AM for the downtown terminal at Plaza de Colón just off the Paseo de la Castellana. The ride takes about 20 minutes and the fare at press time was 200 ptas. Most city hotels are then only a short ride away. The fastest and most expensive route into town (up to 1,500 ptas. plus tip) is by taxi. Pay what is on the meter plus 200 ptas. surcharge and 35 ptas. for each suitcase. By car, take the N-II, which becomes Avda. de América, into town, then head straight into Calle María de Molina and left on either Calle Serrano or the Castellana.

By Train Madrid has three railroad stations. Chamartín, in the northern suburbs beyond the Plaza de Castilla, is the main station, with trains to France, the north, and the northeast (including Barcelona). Most trains to Valencia, Alicante, and Andalusia now leave from here, too, but stop at Atocha station, at the southern end of Paseo del Prado on the Glorieta del Emperador Carlos V. Also departing from Atocha, where a new station was built in 1989, are trains to Toledo, Granada, Extremadura, and Lisbon. The old Atocha station, designed by Eiffel and refurbished in 1990, was to inaugurate a new high-speed rail service to Seville by 1992. Norte (or Príncipe Pío), on Paseo de la Florida, in the west of town below the Plaza de España, is the departure point for Ávila, Segovia, El Escorial, Salamanca, Santiago, La Coruña, and all destinations in Galicia.

For all train information, tel. 91/429–0202, or go to the RENFE office on Calle de Alcalá 44, open weekdays 9–3 and 5–7. There's another RENFE office at Barajas Airport in the International Arrivals Hall, or you can purchase tickets at any of the three main stations, or from travel agents displaying the blue and yellow RENFE sign.

By Bus Madrid has no central bus station. The two main bus stations are the Estación del Sur (Canarias 17, tel. 91/468–4200), nearest metro Palos de la Frontera, for buses to Toledo, La Mancha, Alicante, and Andalusia (and due to move shortly, so double-check its location); and Auto-Rés (Plaza Conde de Casal 6, tel. 91/551–7200), nearest metro Conde de Casal, for buses to Extremadura, Cuenca, Salamanca, Valladolid, Valencia, and Zamora. Auto-Rés has a central ticket and information office at Salud 19 near the Hotel Arosa, just off Gran Vía. Buses to other destinations leave from various points, so check with the tourist office. For Ávila, Segovia, and La Granja, Empresa La Sepulvedana (tel. 91/230–4800) leaves from Paseo de la Florida 11, metro Norte, and to El Escorial and Valley of the Fallen. Empresa Herranz (tel. 91/890–4100) leaves from Isaac Peral 10, metro Moncloa. La Veloz (Sanchez Bustillo 7, tel. 91/409–7602) serves Chinchón.

By Car The main roads are north–south, the Paseo de la Castellana and Paseo del Prado; and east–west, Calle de Alcalá, Gran Vía, and Calle de la Princesa. The M30 ring road circles Madrid to the east and south. For Burgos and France, drive north up the Castellana and follow the signs for the N–I. For Barcelona, head up the Castellana to Plaza Dr. Marañón, then right onto María de Molina and the N–II; for Andalusia and Toledo, head south down Paseo del Prado, then follow the signs to the N–IV and N401, respectively. For Segovia, Àvila, and El Escorial, head west along Princesa to Avenida Puerta de Hierro and onto the N–VI La Coruña road.

Getting Around

Madrid is a fairly compact city and most of the main sights can be visited on foot. But if you're staying in one of the modern hotels in the north of town off the Castellana, you may well need to use the bus or subway (metro). As a rough guide, the walk from the Prado to the Royal Palace at a comfortable sight-seeing pace but without stopping takes around 30 minutes; from Plaza del Callao on Gran Vía to the Plaza Mayor, it takes about 15 minutes.

By Metro The subway offers the simplest and quickest means of transport and is open from 6 AM to 1:30 AM. Metro maps are available from ticket offices, hotels, and tourist offices. Fares are 90 ptas. a ride. Savings can be made by buying a *taco* of 10 tickets for 410 ptas., or a tourist card called **Metrotour** that is good for unlimited travel for three or five days. Keep some change (5, 25, and 50 ptas.) handy for the ticket machines, especially after 10 PM.

By Bus City buses are red and run from 6 AM to midnight (though check, as some stop earlier). Again there is a flat-fare system, with each ride costing 90 ptas. The smaller, yellow microbuses also cost 90 ptas. and are slightly faster. Route plans are displayed at bus stops *(paradas)*, and a map of the entire system is available from EMT (Empresa Municipal de Transportes) booths on Plaza de la Cibeles, Callao, or Puerta del Sol. Savings can be made by buying a **Bonobus** (410 ptas.), good for 10 rides, from EMT booths or any branch of the Caja de Ahorros de Madrid.

By Taxi Madrid has more than 18,000 taxis, and fares are low by New York or London standards. The meter starts at 105 ptas. and each additional kilometer costs 45 ptas. The average city ride costs 400–500 ptas., and there is a surcharge of 65 ptas. between 11 PM and 6 AM. A supplemental fare of 75 ptas. applies to trips to the bullring or soccer matches, and there is a charge of 35 ptas. per suitcase. Cabs available for hire display a "Libre" sign during the day and a green light at night. They hold four passengers. Make sure the driver puts his meter on when you start your ride, and tip up to 10% of the fare.

Important Addresses and Numbers

Tourist Information The main Madrid tourist office (tel. 91/541–2325) is on the ground floor of the Torre de Madrid in Plaza de España, near the beginning of Calle Princesa, and is open weekdays 9–7, Saturdays 10–2. Another Madrid Provincial Tourist Office (Duque de Medinacelli 2, tel. 91/429–4951) is conveniently located on a small street across from the Palace Hotel. The municipal tourist office is at Plaza Mayor 3 (tel. 91/266–5477) and is open weekdays 10–1:30 and 4–7, Saturdays 10–1:30. A third office is in the International Arrivals Hall of Barajas Airport (tel. 91/205–8656) and is open weekdays 8–8, Saturdays 8–1.

Embassies **U.S.** (Serrano 75, tel. 91/577–4000), **Canadian** (Núñez de Balboa 35, tel. 91/431–4300), **U.K.** (Fernando el Santo 16, tel. 91/319–0200).

Emergencies **Police** (National Police, tel. 091; Municipal Police, tel. 092; Main Police [Policía Nacional] Station, Puerta del Sol 7, tel. 91/522–0435). To report lost passports, go to Los Madrazos 9 just off the top of Paseo del Prado. **Ambulance:** Municipal Ambulance Service (tel. 91/230–7145); Red Cross (tel. 91/734–4794). **Doctor:** Your hotel reception will contact the nearest doctor for you. Emergency clinics: **Hospital 12 de Octubre** (Avda. Córdoba, tel. 91/390–8000) and **La Paz Ciudad Sanitaria** (Paseo de la Castellana 261, tel. 91/734–3200). English-speaking doctors and dentists are available at Plaza Marques de Salamanca 9 (tel. 91/431–2229 and 91/435–1595). **Pharmacies:** A list of pharmacies open 24 hours *(farmacias de guardia)* is published daily in *El País.* Hotel receptions usually have a copy. **Company** (Puerta del Sol 14) has English-speaking pharmacists. It does not stock American medicines but will recognize many American brand names.

English Bookstores **Booksellers S.A.** (José Abascal 48, tel. 91/442–8104) and **Turner's English Bookshop** (Génova 3, tel. 91/308–0709).

Travel Agencies **American Express** (Plaza de las Cortes 2, tel. 91/429–5972), **Marsans** (Gran Vía 59, tel. 91/542–9602), **Wagons-Lits** (Alcalá 23, tel. 91/522–4334).

Airlines **Iberia** (Velázquez 130, tel. 91/585–8585; for flight information, call Inforiberia, tel. 91/411–2545), **British Airways** (Serrano 60, 5th floor, tel. 91/431–7575 and Princesa 1 in the Torre de Madrid, tel. 91/431–1830), and **TWA** (Plaza de Colón 2, tel. 91/410–6007).

Guided Tours

Orientation Tours City sightseeing tours are run by **Juliá Tours** (Gran Vía 68, tel. 91/248–9605), **Pullmantur** (Plaza de Oriente 8, tel. 91/541–1807), and **Trapsatur** (San Bernardo 23, tel. 91/248–3002). All three run the same tours, mostly in 48-seat buses and conducted in Spanish and English. Book tours directly with the offices above, through any travel agent, or through your hotel. Departure points are from the addresses above, though in many cases you can be picked up at your hotel. "Madrid Artístico" is a morning tour of the city with visits to the Royal Palace and Prado Museum, entrances included. The "Madrid Panorámico" tour includes the University City, Casa del Campo park, and the northern reaches of the Castellana. This is a half-day tour, usually in the afternoon, and makes an ideal orientation for the first-time visitor. Also offered are "Madrid de Noche," a night tour combining a drive round the illuminations, dinner in a restaurant, flamenco show, and cabaret at La Scala nightclub; and "Panorámica y Toros," on bullfight days only (usually Sunday), a panoramic drive and visit to a bullfight.

Walking and Special-Interest Tours Spanish-speaking people can take advantage of a hugely popular selection of tours recently launched by the **Ayuntamiento** (city hall) under the title "Conozcamos Madrid." Walking tours are held most mornings and afternoons in spring and summer, and visit many of the capital's hidden corners, as well as the major sights. Special-interest tours include "Madrid's Railroads," "Medicine in Madrid," "Goya's Madrid," and "Commerce and Finance in Madrid." Some tours are by bus, others on foot. Schedules are listed in the "Conozcamos Madrid" leaflet available from the municipal tourist office.

Excursions **Juliá Tours, Pullmantur,** and **Trapsatur** run full- or half-day trips to El Escorial, Avila, Segovia, Toledo, and Aranjuez, and in summer to Cuenca and Salamanca. The "Tren de la Fresa" (Strawberry Train) is a popular excursion on summer weekends; a 19th-century train carries passengers from the old Delicias Station to Aranjuez and back. Tickets can be obtained from RENFE offices, travel agents, and the Delicias Station (Paseo de las Delicias 61). Other one- or two-day excursions by train to such places as Avila, Cuenca, or Salamanca are available on weekends in summer. Contact RENFE for details.

Personal Guides Contact any of the tourist offices or the **Association of Madrid Guides** (Ferraz 82, tel. 91/542–1214 or 91/541–1221) for details.

Exploring Madrid

Numbers in the margin correspond to points of interest on the Madrid map.

You can walk the following route in a day, or even half a day if you stop only to visit the Prado and Royal Palace. Two days should give you time for browsing. Begin in the Plaza Atocha, more properly known as the Glorieta del Emperador Carlos V, at the bottom of the Paseo del Prado, and check out what's showing in the **Reina Sofía Arts Center** opened by Queen Sofía in 1986. This converted hospital, home of art and sculpture exhibitions and symbol of Madrid's new cultural pride, aims to become one of Europe's most dynamic venues—a Madrileño rival to Paris's Pompidou Center. The main entrance is on Calle de Santa Isabel 52. *Admission: 400 ptas. Open daily except Tues. 10 AM–9 PM.*

Walk up Paseo del Prado to Madrid's number-one sight, the famous **Prado Museum,** one of the world's most important art galleries. Plan on spending at least 1½ hours here, though it will take at least two full days to view its treasures properly. Brace yourself for the crowds. The greatest treasures—the Velázquez, Murillo, Zurbarán, El Greco, and Goya galleries—are all on the upstairs floor. Two of the best works are Velázquez's *Surrender of Breda* and his most famous work, *Las Meninas*, which occupies a privileged position in a room of its own. The Goya galleries contain the artist's none-too-flattering royal portraits—Goya believed in painting the truth—his exquisitely beautiful *Marquesa de Santa Cruz*, and his famous *Naked Maja* and *Clothed Maja*, for which the 13th duchess of Alba was said to have posed. Goya's most moving works, the *2nd of May* and the *Fusillade of Moncloa* or *3rd of May*, vividly depict the sufferings of Madrid patriots at the hands of Napoleon's invading troops in 1808. Before you leave, feast your eyes on the fantastic flights of fancy of Hieronymus Bosch's *Garden of Earthly Delights* and his triptych *The Hay Wagon*, both downstairs on the ground floor. *Admission: 400 ptas., no charge Wed. Open Tues.–Sat. 9–7, Sun. 9–2.*

Across the street is the **Ritz**, the grand old lady of Madrid's hotels, built in 1910 by Alfonso XIII when he realized that his cap-

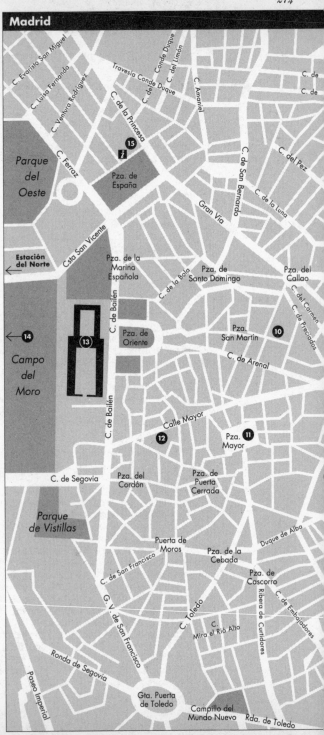

Major Attractions

Other Attractions

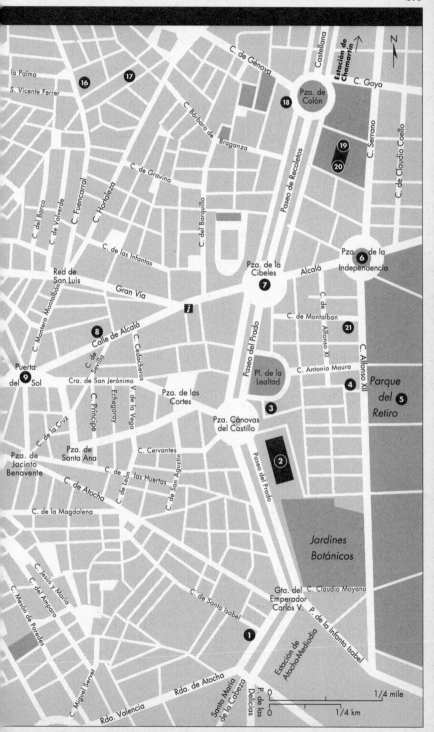

ital had no hotels elegant enough to accommodate the guests at his wedding in 1906. The Ritz garden is a delightfully aristocratic place to lunch in summer—men always need ties.

4 In the **Casón del Buen Retiro,** entrance on Calle Alfonso XII, Picasso's *Guernica* hangs behind bulletproof glass, a haunting expression of the artist's anguish and outrage at the German bombing of this small Basque town in April 1937. *Open same hours as Prado and visited on same ticket.*

5 The **Retiro,** once a royal retreat, is today Madrid's prettiest park. Visit the beautiful rose garden, **La Rosaleda,** and enjoy the many statues and fountains. You can hire a carriage, row a boat on **El Estanque,** gaze up at the monumental **statue to Alfonso XII,** one of Spain's least notable kings though you wouldn't think so to judge by its size, or wonder at the **Monument to the Fallen Angel**—Madrid claims the dubious privilege of being the only capital to have a statue dedicated to the Devil. The **Palacio de Velázquez** and the beautiful steel and glass **Palacio de Cristal,** built as a tropical plant house in the 19th century, now host art exhibits.

6 Leaving the Retiro via its northwest corner, you come to the Plaza de la Independencia, dominated by the **Puerta de Alcalá,** a grandiose gateway built in 1779 for Charles III. A customs post once stood beside the gate, as did the old bullring until it was moved to its present site at Ventas in the 1920s. At the turn of the century, the Puerta de Alcalá more or less marked the eastern limits of Madrid.

Time Out The **Café León** (Alcalá 57), with its marble-topped tables and charming Old World air, is an ideal place for some light refreshment.

Continue to the **Plaza de la Cibeles,** one of the great landmarks of the city, at the intersection of its two main arteries, the Castellana and Calle de Alcalá. If you can see it through the roar and fumes of the thundering traffic, the square's center is the **7** **Cibeles Fountain,** the unofficial emblem of Madrid. Cybele, the Greek goddess of fertility, languidly rides her lion-drawn chariot, overlooked by the mighty **Palacio de Comunicaciones,** a splendidly pompous cathedral-like building often jokingly dubbed Our Lady of Communications. In fact, it's the main post office, erected in 1918. The famous goddess looks her best at night when she's illuminated by floodlights.

Now head down the long and busy Calle de Alcalá toward the Puerta del Sol, resisting the temptation to turn right up the Gran Vía, which beckons temptingly with its mile of stores and cafés. Before you reach the Puerta del Sol, art lovers may want **8** to step inside the **Real Academia de Bellas Artes** at Alcalá 13. This recently refurbished fine arts gallery boasts an art collection second only to the Prado's and features all the great Spanish masters: Velázquez, El Greco, Murillo, Zurbarán, Ribera, and Goya. *Open Tues.–Sat. 9–7, Sun. and Mon. 9–2.*

Time Out A small detour down Sevilla, then right down San Jerónimo, brings you to two atmospheric places for a drink or light lunch. **Lhardy** (San Jerónimo 8, tel. 91/522–2207) is a veritable old Madrid institution that opened as a pastry shop in 1839. Today it combines the roles of expensive restaurant and delicatessen. *Closed Sun. evening and in Aug.*

Next door, at No. 6, on the corner of Espoz y Mina, is the more moderately priced **Museo de Jamón,** a relative newcomer on the Madrid scene, with hundreds of hams hanging from its ceilings. It's ideal for a beer or glass of wine and a generous plate of cheese or ham.

9 The **Puerta del Sol** is at the very heart of Madrid. Its name means Gate of the Sun, though the old gate disappeared long ago. It's easy to feel you're at the heart of things here—indeed, of all of Spain—for the kilometer distances for the whole nation are measured from the zero marker in front of the Police Head-quarters. The square was expertly revamped in 1986 and now accommodates both a copy of **La Mariblanca** (a statue that 250 years ago adorned a fountain here) and, at the bottom of Calle Carmen, the much loved statue of the **bear and *madroño*** (straw-berry tree). The Puerta del Sol is inextricably linked with the history of Madrid and of the nation. Here, half a century ago, a generation of literati gathered in the long-gone cafés to thrash out the burning issues of the day; and if you can cast your thoughts back almost 200 years, you can conjure up the heroic deeds of the patriots' uprising immortalized by Goya in the *Second of May*.

This is a good place to break the tour if you've had enough sight-seeing for one day. Head north up Preciados or Montera for some of the busiest and best shopping streets in the city or southeast toward Plaza Santa Ana for tavern-hopping in Old Madrid.

Time Out If it's teatime (6–7 PM), don't miss **La Mallorquina** (Calle Mayor 2, tel. 91/521–1201), an old pastry shop between Calle Mayor and Arenal. Delicious pastries are sold at the downstairs count-er; the old-fashioned upstairs tea salon offers an age-old tea rit-ual and unbeatable views over the Puerta del Sol.

10 Art lovers will want to make a detour to the **Convento de las Descalzas Reales** on Plaza Descalzas Reales just above Arenal. It was founded by Juana de Austria, daughter of Charles V, and is still inhabited by nuns. Over the centuries the nuns, daughters of the royal and noble, endowed the convent with an enormous wealth of jewels, religious ornaments, superb Flem-ish tapestries, and the works of such great masters as Titian and Rubens. A bit off the main tourist track, it's one of Madrid's better kept secrets. Your ticket includes admission to the nearby, but less interesting, **Convento de la Encarnación.** *Admission: 300 ptas., no charge Wed. Guided tours only. Open Tues.–Thurs., Sat. 10:30–12:30 and 4–5:15; Fri. 10:30–12:30; Sun. 11–1:15.*

Walk up **Calle Mayor,** the Main Street of Old Madrid, past the shops full of religious statues and satins for bishops' robes, to **11** the **Plaza Mayor,** the capital's greatest architectural show-piece. It was built in 1617–19 for Philip III—that's Philip on the horse in the middle. The plaza has witnessed the canoniza-tion of saints, burning of heretics, fireworks and bullfights, and is still one of the great gathering places of Madrid.

Time Out In summer you can relax over a drink in any of the delightful sidewalk cafés that adorn the square; in winter, head for the **Mesón del Corregidor** (tel. 91/266–5066) at No. 8, near the

Cuchilleros arch. This colorful tavern restaurant has typical dishes and tapas.

If you're here in the morning, take a look inside the 19th-century steel-and-glass San Miguel market, a colorful provisions
12 market, before continuing down Calle Mayor to the **Plaza de la Villa.** The square's notable cluster of buildings includes some of the oldest houses in Madrid. The **Casa de la Villa,** the Madrid city hall, was built in 1644 and has also served as the city prison and the mayor's home. Its sumptuous salons are now open to the public on Mondays at 5 PM. The free guided visits are usually in Spanish, but English tours can be arranged with advance notice. An archway joins the Casa de la Villa to the **Casa Cisneros,** a palace built in 1537 for the nephew of Cardinal Cisneros, primate of Spain and infamous inquisitor general. Across the square, the **Torre de Lujanes** is one of the oldest buildings in Madrid. It once imprisoned Francis I of France, archenemy of the Emperor Charles V.

Time Out If it's lunchtime, close by is a moderately priced restaurant that is a long-standing Madrid tradition: **Casa Ciriaco** on Calle Mayor 84 (tel. 91/248–0620).

The last stop on the tour, but Madrid's second most important
13 sight, is the **Royal Palace.** This magnificent granite and limestone residence was begun by Philip V, the first Bourbon king of Spain, who was always homesick for his beloved Versailles, the opulence and splendor of which he did his best to emulate. His efforts were successful, to judge by the 2,800 rooms with their lavish Rococo decorations, precious carpets, porcelain, time pieces, mirrors, and chandeliers. From 1764, when Charles III first moved in, till the coming of the Second Republic and the abdication of Alfonso XIII in 1931, the Royal Palace proved a very stylish abode for Spanish monarchs. Today King Juan Carlos, who lives in the far less ostentatious Zarzuela Palace outside Madrid, uses it only for official state functions. The Palace can be visited only on guided tours, available in English. Allow 1½–2 hours for a visit. A *visita completa* (full visit), including the Royal Carriage Museum (below), costs 500 ptas.; most visitors opt for the *Salones Oficiales* (State Rooms) ticket at 300 ptas. The museum is free on Wednesdays. *Open Mon.– Sat. 9:30–12:45 and 4–6 (3:30–5:15 in winter), Sun. 9:30–1. Closed during official functions.*

14 The **Royal Carriage Museum,** which belongs to the palace but has a separate entrance on Paseo Vírgen del Puerto, can be visited on an all-inclusive or separate ticket. One of its highlights is the wedding carriage of Alfonso XIII and his English bride, Victoria Eugenia, granddaughter of Queen Victoria, which was damaged by a bomb thrown at it in the Calle Mayor during their wedding procession in 1906; another is the chair that carried the gout-stricken old Emperor Charles V to his retirement at the remote monastery of Yuste. *Admission: 150 ptas., or 500 ptas. joint ticket to Royal Palace. Open Mon.–Sat. 9:30–12:45 and 4–6 (3:30–5:15 in winter), Sun. 9:30–1 only. Closed during official functions.*

Shopping

Gift Ideas There are no special regional crafts associated with Madrid itself, but traditional Spanish goods are on sale in many stores. The **Corte Inglés** and **Galerías Preciados** department stores both stock good displays of Lladró porcelain, as do several specialist shops on the Gran Vía and behind the Plaza hotel on Plaza de España. Department stores stock good displays of fans, but for really superb examples, try the long-established **Casa Diego** in Puerta del Sol. Two stores opposite the Prado on Plaza Cánovas del Castillo, **Artesanía Toledana** and **El Escudo de Toledo,** have a wide selection of souvenirs, especially Toledo swords, inlaid marquetry ware, and pottery.

Antiques The main areas to see are the Plaza de las Cortes, the Carrera San Jerónimo, and the Rastro flea market, along the Ribera de Curtidores and the courtyards just off it.

Boutiques Calle Serrano has the largest collection of smart boutiques and designer fashions. Another up-and-coming area is around Calle Argensola, just south of Calle Génova. **Loewe,** Spain's most prestigious leather store, has boutiques on Serrano 26 and Gran Vía 8. **Adolfo Domínguez**, one of Spain's top designers, has several boutiques in Salamanca, and another on Calle Orense in the north of town.

Shopping Districts The main shopping area in the heart of Madrid is around the pedestrian streets of **Preciados** and **Montera,** between Puerta del Sol and Plaza Callao on Gran Vía. The smartest and most expensive district is the **Barrio de Salamanca** northeast of Cibeles, centered around Serrano, Velázquez, and Goya. **Calle Mayor** and the streets to the east of **Plaza Mayor** are lined with fascinating old-fashioned stores straight out of the 19th century.

Department Stores **El Corte Inglés** is the biggest, brightest, and most successful Spanish chain store. Its main branch is on Preciados, just off the Puerta del Sol. **Galerías Preciados** is its main rival, with branches on Plaza Callao right off Gran Vía, Calle Arapiles, Goya corner of Conde de Peñalver, Serrano and Ortega y Gasset, and its newest branch at La Vaguada. Both stores are open Monday–Saturday 10–8, and neither closes for the siesta.

Food and Flea Markets **The Rastro,** Madrid's most famous flea market, operates on Sundays from 9 to 2 around the Plaza del Cascorro and the Ribera de Curtidores. A **stamp and coin** market is held on Sunday mornings in the Plaza Mayor, and there's a **secondhand book** market most days on the Cuesta Claudio Moyano near Atocha Station.

Bullfighting

The Madrid bullfighting season runs from March to October. Fights are held on Sunday, and sometimes also on Thursday; starting times vary between 4:30 and 7 PM. The pinnacle of the spectacle may be seen during the three weeks of daily bullfights held during the San Isidro festivals in May. The bullring is at Ventas, Alcalá 237 (metro Ventas). You can buy your ticket there shortly before the fight, or, with a 20% surcharge, at the agencies that line Calle Victoria, just off Carrera San Jeronimo and Puerta del Sol.

Dining

Visitors have a choice of restaurants, tapas bars, and cafés. Restaurants are strictly for lunch and dinner; they do not serve breakfast. Tapas bars are ideal for a glass of wine or beer accompanied by an array of savory tidbits *(tapas)*. Cafés, called *cafeterías*, are basically coffeehouses serving snacks, light meals, tapas, pastries, and coffee, tea, and alcoholic drinks. They also serve breakfast and are perfect for afternoon tea.

Mealtimes Mealtimes in Spain are much later than in any other European country. Lunch begins between 1 and 3:30, with 2 being the usual time, and 3 more normal on Sunday. Dinner is usually available from 8:30 onward, but 10 PM is the usual time in the larger cities and resorts. An important point to remember is that lunch is the main meal, not dinner. Tapas bars are busiest between noon and 2 and from 8 PM on. Cafés are usually open from around 8 AM to midnight.

Precautions Tap water is said to be safe to drink. However, most Spaniards drink bottled mineral water; ask for either *agua sin gas* (without bubbles) or *agua con gas* (with). A good paella should be served only at lunchtime and should be prepared to order (usually 30 minutes); beware the all-too-cheap version.

Typical Dishes Paella—a mixture of saffron-flavored rice with seafood, chicken, and vegetables—is Spain's national dish. Gazpacho, a cold soup made of crushed garlic, tomatoes, and olive oil and garnished with diced vegetables, is a traditional Andalusian dish and is served mainly in summer. The Basque Country and Galicia are the gourmet regions of Spain, and both serve outstanding fish and seafood. Asturias is famous for its *fabadas* (bean stews), cider, and dairy products; Extremadura for its hams and sausages; and Castile for its roasts, especially *cochinillo* (suckling pig), *cordero asado* (roast lamb), and *perdiz* (partridge). The best wines are those from the Rioja and Penedés regions. Valdepeñas is a pleasant table wine, and most places serve a perfectly acceptable house wine called *vino de la casa*. Sherries from Jerez de la Frontera make fine aperitifs; ask for a *fino* or a *manzanilla;* both are dry. In summer you can try *horchata*, a sweet white drink made from ground nuts, or *granizados de limón* or *de café*, lemon juice or coffee served over crushed ice. *Un café solo* is a small, black, strong coffee, and *café con leche* is coffee with cream, cappuccino-style; weak black American-style coffee is hard to come by.

Dress In Very Expensive and Expensive restaurants, jacket and tie are the norm. Elsewhere, casual dress is appropriate.

Ratings Spanish restaurants are officially classified from five forks down to one fork, with most places falling into the two- or three-fork category. In our rating system, prices are per person and include a first course, main course, and dessert, but not wine or tip. Sales tax (IVA) is often included in the menu price; check the menu for *IVA incluído* or *IVA no incluído*. When it's not included, an additional 6% (12% in the fancier restaurants) will be added to your bill. Most restaurants offer a fixed-price menu called a *menú del día*. This is usually the cheapest way of eating; *à la carte* dining is more expensive. Service charges are never added to your bill; leave around 10%, less in inexpensive restaurants and bars. Major centers such as Madrid tend to be a bit more expensive. Best bets are indicated by a ★.

Category	Cost
Very Expensive	over 6,500 ptas.
Expensive	4,300 ptas.–6,500 ptas.
Moderate	2,100 ptas.–4,300 ptas.
Inexpensive	850 ptas.–2,100 ptas.

Very Expensive **Irízar Jatetxea.** Owned by the famous Basque restaurateur
★ Luis Irízar, this is one of Madrid's most luxurious and renowned restaurants. It's opposite the Teatro Zarzuela (next to
Armstrong's) and the cuisine is Basque, but much influenced
by nouvelle cuisine from France and Navarre. Definitely a
place for a treat. *Jovellanos 3, tel. 91/531–4569. Reservations
essential. AE, DC, V. Closed Sat. lunch, Sun.*

Zalacaín. The ambience in this modern building attempts to du-
plicate that of a private villa, with plush decor and alcove-sepa-
rated rooms. Located just off the Castellana and María de
Molina, it is one of only two Spanish restaurants to be awarded
three Michelin stars. *Alvarez de Baena 4, tel. 91/261–4840.
Reservations required. AE, DC. Closed Sat. lunch, Sun., Holy
Week, Aug.*

Expensive **El Cenador del Prado.** This elegant and stylish restaurant just
★ off Plaza Santa Ana offers beautiful decor and an imaginative
menu with more than a hint of nouvelle cuisine. The chef
learned his trade in New York, and specialties include *caracoles
con setas en hojaldre* (snails and mushrooms en croute) and
salmón marinado a la pimienta verde (salmon marinated in
green peppers). *Calle del Prado 4, tel. 91/429–1561. Reservations advised. AE, DC, MC, V. Closed Sat. lunch, Sun., 2
weeks in Aug.*

La Dorada. One of Madrid's most outstanding fish restaurants,
the seafood here is flown in daily in the owner's private plane
from the Costa del Sol. Its sister restaurants in Barcelona and
Seville are equally esteemed. It's located in the modern north
of town, near the Azca Center and Holiday Inn. *Orense 64, tel.
91/270–2004. Reservations required. AE, DC, V. Closed Sun.,
Aug.*

New Yorker. This fashionable restaurant, popular with businesspeople, opened in 1985. The ambience is elegant, and contemporary Spanish paintings adorn the walls. The menu offers
international specialties and service that's highly professional.
*Amador de los Ríos 1, to the west of the Castellana just above
the Plaza Colón, tel. 91/410–1522. Reservations required. AE,
V. Closed Sat. lunch, Sun.*

Solchaga. Here you can choose between several dining rooms,
each with its own distinctive character. Pot-bellied stoves and
ornate gilt mirrors help convey the atmosphere of an old-fashioned private house rather than a restaurant; a charming find.
*Plaza de Alonso Martínez 2, tel. 91/447–1496. Reservations
advised. AE, DC, MC, V. Closed Sat. lunch, Sun.*

Moderate **Armstrong's.** This charming English-owned restaurant opposite the Teatro Zarzuela is bright and modern with refreshing
pink decor and is quite a change from the usual Madrid scene.
Its imaginative menu mixes French and Spanish nouvelle cuisine with English and American favorites, and there's a good
choice of salads, brunch on weekends, and a special teatime
menu. It stays open unusually late—until 1AM! *Jovellanos 5,*

tel. 91/522–4230. Reservations advised. AE, DC, MC, V. Closed Sun. evening and Mon.

La Barraca. A Valencian restaurant with cheerful blue-and-white decor, colorful windowboxes, and ceramic tiles, this is the place to go for a wonderful choice of paellas. Located just off Gran Vía (Alcalá end), behind Loewe, it's popular with businesspeople and foreign visitors. Try the *paella reina* or the *paella de mariscos. Reina 29, tel. 91/532–7154. Reservations advised. AE, DC, MC, V.*

Botín. Madrid's oldest and most famous restaurant, just off the Plaza Mayor, has been catering to diners since 1725. Its decor and food are traditionally Castilian. *Cochinillo* (suckling pig) and *cordero asado* (roast lamb) are its specialties. It was a favorite with Hemingway; today it's very touristy and a bit overrated, but fun. Insist on the *cueva* or upstairs dining room. *Cuchilleros 17, tel. 91/266–4217. Reservations advised, especially at night. AE, DC, MC. V.*

Carmencita. Dating to 1850, this charming restaurant is small and intimate, with ceramic wall tiles, brass hat racks, and photos of bullfighters. The menu recounts the famous who have dined here and their life stories. The cuisine is part traditional, part nouvelle with an emphasis on *pasteles* (a kind of mousse) both savory and sweet. *Libertad 16, on the corner of San Marcos in the Chueca area above Gran Vía; tel. 91/531–6612. Reservations advised. V. Closed Sun.*

Casa Ciriaco. In this atmospheric old standby only a few paces from the Plaza Mayor and city hall, the Madrid of 50 years ago lives on. You won't find many foreigners here—just businesspeople and locals enjoying traditional Spanish cooking and delicious *fresones* (strawberries) for dessert. *Mayor 84, tel. 91/248–0620. Reservations accepted. No credit cards. Closed Wed., and Aug.*

★ **Fuente Real.** Dining here is like eating in a turn-of-the-century home. Tucked away between Mayor and Arenal, it's brimming with personal mementoes such as antique dolls, Indian figures, and Mexican Christmas decorations. The cuisine is French and Spanish with an emphasis on high-quality meats and crêpes. Try the *pastel de espinacas* (spinach mousse) or *crêpes de puerros* (leeks). *Fuentes 1, tel. 91/248–6613. Reservations not necessary. AE, MC, V. Closed Sun. PM and Mon.*

Inexpensive **El Cuchi.** "Hemingway *never* ate here" is the sign that will lure
★ you inside this colorful tavern at the bottom of the Cuchilleros steps off the Plaza Mayor. A fun-packed experience awaits. The ceilings are plastered with photos of Mexican revolutionaries, huge blackboards announce the menu and list the calories in the irresistible desserts, and home-baked rolls are lowered in baskets from the ceiling to your table. Salads are on the house. This is a place you shouldn't miss. *Cuchilleros 3, tel. 91/266–4424. Reservations advised. AE, DC, MC, V.*

El Luarqués. One of many budget restaurants on this street, El Luarqués is decorated with photos of the port of Luarca on Spain's north coast, and it's always packed with Madrileños who recognize its good value. *Fabada asturiana* (bean and meat stew) and *arroz con leche* (rice pudding) are two of its Asturian specialties. *Ventura de la Vega 16, tel. 91/429–6174. No reservations. No credit cards. Closed Sun. evening, Mon., and Aug.*

Lodging

Hotels around the center in the midst of all the sights and shops are mostly located in old 19th-century houses; many of these are currently undergoing restoration to bring them up to standard. Most of the newer hotels that conform to American standards of comfort are located in the northern part of town on either side of the Castellana and are a short metro or bus ride from the center. There are hotel reservation desks in the national and international terminals of the airport, and at Chamartín station. Or you can contact **La Brújula** (tel. 91/248–9705) on the sixth floor of the Torre de Madrid in Plaza de España, which is open 9–9. It has English-speaking staff and can book hotels all over Spain.

All hotels and hostels are listed with their rates in the annual *Guía de Hoteles* available from bookstores and kiosks for around 500 ptas., or you can see a copy in local tourist offices. Rates are always quoted per room, and not per person. Single occupancy of a double room costs 80% of the normal price. Breakfast is rarely included in the quoted room rate; always check. The quality of rooms, particularly in older properties, can be uneven; always ask to see your room *before* you sign the acceptance slip. If you want a private bathroom in a less expensive hotel, state your preference for shower or bathtub; the latter usually costs more though many hotels have both. Local tourist offices will provide you with a list of accommodations in their region, but they are not allowed to make reservations for you. In Madrid hotel booking agencies are found at the airports and railroad stations.

Hotels and Hostels Hotels are officially classified from five stars (the highest) to one star, hostels from three stars to one star. Hostels are usually a family home converted to provide accommodations that often occupy only part of a building. If an R appears on the blue hotel or hostel plaque, the hotel is classified as a *Residencia*, and full dining services are not provided, though breakfast and cafeteria facilities may be available. A three-star hostel usually equates with a two-star hotel; two- and one-star hostels offer simple, basic accommodations. The main hotel chains are Husa, Iberotel Melia, Sol, and Tryp, and the state-run *paradores* (tourist hotels). Holiday Inn, InterContinental, and Trusthouse Forte also own some of the best hotels in Madrid, Barcelona, and Seville; only these and the paradores have any special character. The others mostly provide clean, comfortable accommodation in the two- to four-star range.

In many hotels rates vary according to the time of year. The hotel year is divided into *estación alta, media,* and *baja* (high, mid, and low season); high season covers the summer and usually Easter and Christmas periods, plus the major fiestas. IVA is rarely included in the quoted room rates, so be prepared for an additional 6%, or, in the case of luxury four- and five-star hotels, 12%, to be added to your bill. Service charges are never included.

Paradors There are about 80 state-owned-and-run paradors, many of which are located in magnificent medieval castles or convents or in places of great natural beauty. Most of these fall into the four-star category and are priced accordingly. All have restaurants that specialized in local regional cuisine and serve a full breakfast. The most popular paradors (Granada's San Francisco parador, for example) are booked far in advance, and many close for a month or two in winter (January or February) for renovations.

Ratings Prices are for two people in a double room and do not include breakfast. Best bets are indicated by a star ★.

Category	Cost
Very Expensive	over 19,000 ptas.
Expensive	12,000–19,000 ptas.
Moderate	7,000–12,000 ptas.
Inexpensive	4,200–7,000 ptas.

Very Expensive **Fénix.** Located just off the Castellana near the Plaza Colón and convenient for the Salamanca shopping district, this is fast becoming Madrid's leading four-star hotel. It's a favorite with influential businesspeople and conveys a feeling of style and luxury. Its bar and cafeteria are popular meeting places. *Hermosilla 2, tel. 91/431–6700. 216 rooms. AE, DC, MC, V.*

Palace. This dignified turn-of-the-century hotel opposite parliament and the Prado is a slightly less dazzling step-sister of the nearby Ritz but is full of charm and style. Long a favorite of politicians and journalists, its Belle Epoque decor—especially the glass dome over the lounge—is superb. *Plaza de las Cortes 7, tel. 91/429–7551. 500 rooms, 20 suites. AE, DC, MC, V.*

★ **Ritz.** Spain's most exclusive hotel is elegant and aristocratic with beautiful rooms, spacious suites, and sumptuous public salons furnished with antiques and handwoven carpets. Its palatial restaurant is justly famous, and its garden terrace is the perfect setting for summer dining. Features are brunches with harp music on weekends and tea or supper chamber concerts from February through May. Close to the Retiro Park and overlooking the famous Prado Museum, it offers pure unadulterated luxury. It is substantially more expensive than most other hotels in this category. *Plaza Lealtad 5, tel. 91/521–2857. 156 rooms. AE, DC, MC, V.*

Villamagna. Second in luxury only to the Ritz, the Villamagna's modern facade belies a palatial interior exquisitely furnished with 18th-century antiques. Set in a delightful garden, it offers all the facilities one would expect in a hotel of international repute. It is substantially more expensive than most other hotels in this category. *Paseo de la Castellana 22, tel. 91/261–4900. 182 rooms. AE, DC.*

Expensive **Alcalá.** Close to the Retiro Park and Goya shopping area, this
★ comfortable hotel has long been recognized for high standards. Bedrooms are well furnished, each with TV and minibar, and the cafeteria serves a good lunch menu for around 900 ptas. The hotel restaurant, Le Basque (closed Sun. and Mon. lunch), is owned by Luis Irízar of the famous Irízar Jatetxea restaurant, and its Basque culinary delights are well known to Madrileños. *Alcalá 66, tel. 91/435–1060. 153 rooms. AE, DC, MC, V.*

Emperador. This older hotel on the corner of San Bernardo has been renovated throughout, and storm windows now help to shut out the roar of Gran Vía traffic. All the rooms have TV and VCR, and a special feature is the rooftop pool and terrace with superb views. *Gran Vía 53, tel. 91/247–2800. 231 rooms. AE, DC, MC, V.*

Plaza. This elegant hotel at the bottom of Gran Vía has long been a favorite with American visitors. New storm windows cut down the traffic noise, security safes have been installed in each room, and the mattresses have all been replaced with firmer ones more suited to American tastes. The view from its legendary rooftop pool is a favorite with Spanish and foreign photographers. *Plaza de España, tel. 91/247–1200. 306 rooms. AE, DC, MC, V.*

Sanvy. Backing onto the Fénix, the Sanvy, located just off the Plaza Colón on the edge of the Salamanca district, is a comfortable, well-renovated hotel with a swimming pool on the top floor. Its Belagua Restaurant is gaining prestige. *Goya 3, tel. 91/276–0800. 141 rooms. AE, DC, MC, V.*

Moderate **Capitol.** If you like being right in the center of things, then this hotel on the Plaza Callao is for you. It's an older hotel, but four floors have been renovated; the rooms on these floors are more comfortable indeed, but also 30% more expensive. There's a well-decorated reception area and a pleasant cafeteria for breakfast. *Gran Vía 41, tel. 91/521–8391. 145 rooms. AE, DC, V.*

Mayorazgo. This is an older hotel that has yet to be renovated, but it's comfortable as long as you're not seeking all the conveniences of home. Advantages include its friendly, old-fashioned service and its prime location right in the heart of town, tucked away in a quiet back street off Gran Vía that leads down to Plaza de España. *Flor Baja 3, tel. 91/247–2600. AE, DC, MC, V.*

Rex. This is a sister hotel to the Capitol next door, and both belong to the Tryp chain. It's located on the corner of Silva just down from Callao, and the lobby, bar, restaurant, and two floors have so far been completely refurbished. The unrenovated rooms are considerably cheaper, but you'll be much more comfortable in one of the newer ones. *Gran Vía 43, tel. 91/247–4800. 147 rooms. AE, DC, V.*

Inexpensive **Cliper.** This simple hotel offers good value for the cost-conscious traveler. It's tucked away in a side street off the central part of Gran Vía between Callao and Red San Luis. *Chinchilla 6, tel. 91/531–1700. 52 rooms. AE, MC, V.*

★ **Inglés.** The exterior may seem shabby but don't be deterred. The Inglés is a long-standing budget favorite. Its rooms are comfortable, with good facilities, and the location is a real bonus: You're a short walk from the Puerta del Sol one way, and from the Prado the other; inexpensive restaurants and atmospheric bars are right at hand. *Echegaray 10, tel. 91/429–6551. 58 rooms. AE, DC, MC, V.*

Paris. Overlooking the Puerta del Sol, the Paris is a stylish hotel full of old-fashioned appeal. It has an impressive turn-of-the-century lobby and a restaurant where you can dine for around 1,500 ptas. Recently refurbished, the hotel has managed to retain its character while adding modern amenities. *Alcalá 2, tel. 91/521–6496. 123 rooms. MC, V.*

Bars and Cafés

Bars **The Mesones.** The most traditional and colorful taverns are on Cuchilleros and Cava San Miguel just west of Plaza Mayor, where you'll find a whole array of mesones with names like **Tortilla, Champiñón,** and **Huevo.**

Old Madrid. Wander the narrow streets between Puerta del Sol and Plaza Santa Ana, which are packed with traditional tapas bars. Favorites here are the **Cervecería Alemana,** Plaza Santa Ana 6, a beer hall founded more than 100 years ago by Germans and patronized, inevitably, by Hemingway; **Los Gabrieles,** Echegaray 17, with magnificent ceramic decor; **La Trucha,** Manuel Fernández y González 3, with loads of atmosphere; and **Viva Madrid,** Fernández y González 7, a lovely old bar.

Calle Huertas. Fashionable wine bars with turn-of-the-century decor and chamber or guitar music, often live, line this street. **La Fídula** at No. 57 and **El Hecho** at No. 56 are two of the best.

Plaza Santa Barbara. This area just off Alonso Martínez is packed with fashionable bars and beer halls. Stroll along Santa Teresa, Orellana, Campoamor, or Fernando VI and take your pick. The **Cervecería Santa Barbara** in the plaza itself is one of the most colorful, a popular beer hall with a good range of tapas.

Cafés If you like cafés with an old-fashioned atmosphere, dark wooden counters, brass pumps, and marble-topped tables, try any of the following: **Café Comercial,** Glorieta de Bilbao 7; **Café Gijón,** Paseo de Recoletos 21, a former literary hangout and the most famous of the cafés of old, now one of the many café-terraces that line the Castellana; **Café León,** Alcalá 57, just up from Cibeles; **Café Roma** on Serrano; and **El Espejo,** Paseo de Recoletos 31, with art-nouveau decor and an outdoor terrace in summer. And don't forget **La Mallorquina** tearooms on Puerta del Sol (*see* Exploring, above).

The Arts

Details of all cultural events are listed in the daily newspaper *El País* or in the weekly *Guía del Ocio.*

Concerts and Opera The main concert hall is the new **Auditorio Nacional de Madrid** (tel. 91/248–1405), Príncipe de Vergara 136 (metro, Cruz del Royo), which opened at the end of 1988. The old **Teatro Real** (tel. 91/248–1405) on the Plaza de Oriente opposite the Royal Palace is being converted into Madrid's long-needed opera house.

Zarzuela and Dance Zarzuela, a combination of light opera and dance ideal for non-Spanish speakers, is held at the **Teatro Nacional Lírico de la Zarzuela,** Jovellanos 4, tel. 91/429–8225. The season runs from October to July.

Theater If language is no problem, check out the fringe theaters in Lavapiés and the **Centro Cultural de la Villa** (tel. 91/575–6080) beneath the Plaza Colón, and the open-air events in the Retiro Park. Other leading theaters—you'll also need reasonable Spanish—include the **Círculo de Bellas Artes,** Marqués de Casa Riera 2, just off Alcalá 42 (tel. 91/531–7700); the **Teatro Español,** Príncipe 25 on Plaza Sta. Ana (tel. 91/429–9193) for Spanish classics; and the **Teatro María Guerrero,** Tamayo y Baus 4 (tel. 91/319–4769), home of the Centro Dramático Nacional, for plays by García Lorca. Most theaters have two curtains, at 7 and 10:30 PM, and close on Mondays. Tickets are inexpensive and often easy to come by on the night of performance.

Films Foreign films are mostly dubbed into Spanish, but movies in English are listed in *El País* or *Guía del Ocio* under "V.O.," meaning *versión original*. A dozen or so theaters now show films in English; some of the best bets are **Alphaville** and **Cines Renoir,** both in Martín de los Heros, just off Plaza España, and the **Filmoteca Español** (Santa Isabel 3), a city-run institution where first-rate V.O. films change daily.

Nightlife

Cabaret **Florida Park** (tel. 91/573-7805), in the Retiro Park, offers dinner and a show that often features ballet, Spanish dance, or flamenco and is open Monday to Saturday from 9:30 PM with shows at 11 PM. **Berlin** (Costanilla de San Pedro 11, tel. 91/266-2034) opens at 9:30 PM for a dinner that is good by most cabaret standards, followed by a show and dancing until 4 AM. **La Scala** (Rosario Pino 7, tel. 91/571-4411), in the Meliá Castilla hotel, is Madrid's top nightclub, with dinner, dancing, cabaret at 8:30, and a second, less expensive show around midnight. This is the one visited by most night tours.

Flamenco Madrid offers the widest choice of flamenco shows in Spain; some are good, but many are aimed at the tourist trade. Dinner tends to be mediocre and overpriced, but it ensures the best seats; otherwise, opt for the show and a drink *(consumición)* only, usually starting around 11 PM and costing around 2,500 ptas. **Arco de Cuchilleros** (Cuchilleros 7, tel. 91/266-5867), behind the Plaza Mayor, is one of the better, cheaper ones. **Café de Chinitas** (Torija 7, tel. 91/248-5169) and **Corral de la Morería** (Morería 17, tel. 91/265-8446) are two of the more authentic places where well-known troupes perform. **Venta del Gato** (Avda de Burgos 214, tel. 91/202-3427) is authentic, too, but it's to the north. **Zambra** (Velázquez 8, tel. 91/435-5164), in the Hotel Wellington, is one of the smartest (jacket and tie essential), with a good show and dinner served into the small hours.

Jazz The leading club of the moment is **Café Central** (Plaza de Angel 10), follc.ed by **Clamores** (Albuquerque 14). Others include **Café Jazz Populart** (Huertas 22) and **El Despertar** (Torrecilla del Leal 18). Excellent jazz frequently comes to Madrid as part of city-hosted seasonal festivals; check the local press for listings and venues.

Casino **Madrid's Casino** (tel. 91/856-1100) is 28 kilometers (17 miles) out at Torrelodones on the N-VI road to La Coruña. *Open 5 PM-4 AM. Free transportation service from Plaza de España 6.*

15 Milan

Arriving and Departing

As Lombardy's capital and the most important financial and commercial center in northern Italy, Milan is well connected with Rome and Florence by fast and frequent rail and air service, though the latter is often delayed in winter by heavy fog.

By Plane   Linate Airport, 11 kilometers (7 miles) outside Milan, handles mainly domestic and European flights (tel. 02/7485–2200). Malpensa, 50 kilometers (30 miles) from the city, handles intercontinental flights (tel. 02/7485–2200).

Between the Airport and Downtown   Buses connect both airports with Milan, stopping at the central station and at the Porta Garibaldi station. Fare from Linate is 2,200 lire on the special airport bus or 800 lire on municipal bus no. 73 (to Piazza San Babila); from Malpensa 7,000 lire. A taxi from Linate to the center of Milan costs about 35,000 lire, from Malpensa about 100,000 lire.

By Train   The main train terminal is the central station in Piazzale Duca d'Aosta (tel. 02/67500). Several smaller stations handle commuter trains. There are several fast Intercity trains between Rome and Milan, stopping in Florence. A nonstop Intercity leaves from Rome or Milan morning and evening, taking about four hours to go between the two cities.

By Car   From Rome and Fmorence, take the A1 Autostrada. From Venice, take the A4. With bans on parking throughout the center of Milan, it's easier to park on the outskirts and use public transportation.

Getting Around

By Subway   Milan's subway network, the Metropolitana, is modern, fast, and easy to use. "MM" signs mark Metropolitana stations. There are at present two lines, with another scheduled to open soon. The ATM (city transport authority) has an information office on the mezzanine of the Duomo Metro station (tel. 02/875494). Tickets are sold at newsstands at every stop, and in ticket machines *for exact change only*. The fare is 800 lire, and the subway runs from 6:20 AM to midnight.

By Bus and Streetcar   Buy tickets at newsstands, tobacco shops, and bars. Fare is 800 lire. One ticket is valid for 75 minutes on all surface lines, and one subway trip. Daily tickets valid for 24 hours on all public transportation lines are on sale at the Duomo Metro station ATM Information Office, and at Stazione Centrale Metro station.

By Taxi   Use yellow cabs only. They wait at stands or can be telephoned in advance (tel. 6767, 8585, or 8388).

Guided Tours

City Tours   Three-hour morning or afternoon sightseeing tours depart from Piazzetta Reale, next to the Duomo; the cost is about 40,000 lire and can be purchased at some travel agencies or aboard the bus.

Excursions   CIT (Galleria Vittorio Emanuele, tel. 02/866661, or central station, tel. 02/220224) offers an all-day tour of Lake Maggiore, including a boat trip to the Borromean Islands and lunch. There is a brief stop at Lake Como. The cost is about 95,000 lire.

Personalized Tours Arrange for guide service and interpreters through the **Centro Guide Turistiche** (Via Marconi 1, tel. 02/863210).

Tourist Information

APT information offices (Via Marconi 1, tel. 02/870016; Central Station, tel. 02/669–0432). **Municipal Information Office** (Galleria Vittorio Emanuele at the corner of Piazza della Scala, tel. 02/870545).

Exploring Milan

Numbers in the margin correspond to points of interest on the Milan map.

The center of Milan is the Piazza del Duomo. The massive ❶ **Duomo** (cathedral) is one of the largest churches in the world, a mountain of marble fretted with statues, spires, and flying buttresses. The interior is a more solemn Italian Gothic. Take the elevator or walk up 158 steps to the roof, from which—if it's a clear day—you can see over the city to the Lombard plain and the Alps beyond, all through an amazing array of spires and statues. The **Madonnina,** a gleaming gilt statue on the highest spire, is a Milan landmark. *Entrance to elevator and stairway outside the cathedral, to the right. Admission: 3,500 lire. Open Mar.–Oct., daily 9–5:45; Nov.–Feb. 9–4:15.*

Outside the cathedral to the right is the elegant, glass-roofed ❷ **Galleria,** where the Milanesi and visitors stroll, window-shop, and sip pricey cappuccinos at trendy cafés. At the other end of ❸ the Galleria is **Piazza della Scala,** with Milan's city hall on one ❹ side and **Teatro alla Scala,** the world-famous opera house, opposite.

Via Verdi, flanking the opera house, leads to Via Brera, where ❺ the **Pinacoteca di Brera** houses one of Italy's great collections of paintings. Most are of a religious nature, confiscated in the 19th century when many religious orders were suppressed and their churches closed. *Via Brera 28, tel. 02/808387. Admission: 8,000 lire. Open Tues., Wed., Thurs. 9–5:30, Fri.–Sat. 9–1:20, Sun. 9–12:30.*

Time Out A pleasant café with tables outdoors in fair weather is open to Brera visitors, just inside the entrance to the gallery.

After an eyeful of artworks by Mantegna, Raphael, and many other Italian masters, explore the Brera neighborhood, dotted with art galleries, chic little restaurants, and such offbeat cafés ❻ as the **Jamaica** (Via Brera 26), once a bohemian hangout. Take Via dei Fiori Chiari in front of the Brera and keep going in the ❼ same direction to the moated **Castello Sforzesco,** a somewhat sinister 19th-century reconstruction of the imposing 15th-century fortress built by the Sforzas, who succeeded the Viscontis as lords of Milan in the 15th century. It now houses wide-ranging collections of sculptures, antiques, and ceramics, including Michelangelo's *Rondanini Pietà,* his last work, left unfinished at his death. *Piazza Castello, tel. 02/6236 ext. 3947. Admission free. Open Tues.–Sun. 9:30–12:15 and 2:30–5:15.*

From the vast residence of the Sforzas it's not far to the church ❽ of **Santa Maria delle Grazie.** Although portions of the church were designed by Bramante, it plays second fiddle to the **Refec-**

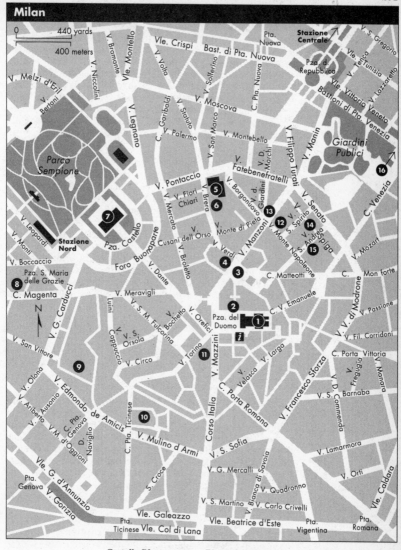

Milan

Castello Sforzesco, **7**
Corso Buenos
Aires, **16**
Duomo, **1**
Galleria, **2**
Jamaica, **6**

Piazza della Scala, **3**
Pinacoteca di Brera, **5**
San Lorenzo
Maggiore, **10**
San Satiro, **11**
Santa Maria delle
Grazie, **8**
Sant'Ambrogio, **9**

Teatro alla Scala, **4**
Via Manzoni, **13**
Via Monte
Napoleone, **12**
Via Sant'Andrea, **15**
Via Spiga, **14**

tory next door, where, over a three-year period, Leonardo da Vinci painted his megafamous fresco, *The Last Supper*. The fresco has suffered more than its share of disaster, beginning with the experiments of the artist, who used untested pigments that soon began to deteriorate. *The Last Supper* is now a mere shadow of its former self, despite meticulous restoration that proceeds at a snail's pace. To save what is left, visitors are limited in time and number, and you may have to wait in line to get a glimpse of this world-famous work. *Piazza Santa Maria delle Grazie 2, tel. 02/498–7588. Admission: 8,000 lire. Open Tues.–Sat. 9–1:15 and 2–6:15, Sun.–Mon. 9–1:15.*

If you are interested in medieval architecture, go to see the medieval church of **Sant'Ambrogio** (Piazza Sant'Ambrogio). Consecrated by St. Ambrose in AD 387, it's the model for all Lombard Romanesque churches, and contains some ancient works of art, including a remarkable 9th-century altar in precious metals and enamels, and some 5th-century mosaics. On December 7, the feast day of St. Ambrose, the streets around the church are the scene of a lively flea market. Another noteworthy church is **San Lorenzo Maggiore** (Corso di Porta Ticinese), with 16 ancient Roman columns in front and some 4th-century mosaics in the Chapel of St. Aquilinus. Closer to Piazza del Duomo on Via Torino, the church of **San Satiro** is another architectural gem in which Bramante's perfect command of proportion and perspective, a characteristic of the Renaissance, made a small interior seem extraordinarily spacious and airy.

Time Out Stop in at the **Peck** shops a few steps from San Satiro. One is a gourmet delicatessen; the other has a tempting array of snacks to eat on the premises. *Via Spadari 9; Via Cantù 3.*

Now head for Milan's most elegant shopping streets: **Via Monte Napoleone, Via Manzoni, Via Spiga,** and **Via Sant'Andrea.** The **Café Cova** (Monte Napoleone 8) is famous for its pastries; Hemingway loved them. And the **Sant'Ambroeus,** not far away, is the epitome of a genteel tearoom (Corso Matteotti 7). If the chic goods of this area are a shock to your purse, make your way to **Corso Buenos Aires,** near the central station, which has hundreds more shops and accessible prices, too.

Dining

Generally speaking, a *ristorante* pays more attention to decor, service, and menu than does a *trattoria*, which is simpler and often family-run. An *osteria* used to be a lowly tavern, though now the term may be used to designate a chic and expensive eatery. A *tavola calda* offers hot dishes and snacks, with seating. A *rosticceria* has the same, to take out.

The menu is always posted in the window or just inside the door of an eating establishment. Check to see what is offered, and note the charges for *coperto* (cover) and *servizio* (service), which will increase your check. A *menu turistico* includes taxes and service, but beverages are extra.

Mealtimes Lunch hour lasts from 1 to 3, dinner from 8 to 10. Practically all restaurants close one day a week; some close for winter or summer vacation.

Precautions Tap water is safe unless noted *Non Potabile*. Bottled mineral water is available everywhere, *gassata* (with bubbles) or *non gassata* (without). If you prefer tap water, ask for *acqua semplice*.

Dress Except for restaurants in the Very Expensive and occasionally in the Expensive categories, where jacket and tie are advisable, casual attire is acceptable.

Ratings Prices are per person and include first course, main course, dessert or fruit, and house wine, where available. Best bets are indicated by a star ★.

Category	Cost
Very Expensive	over 100,000 lire
Expensive	60,000–100,000 lire
Moderate	40,000–60,000 lire
Inexpensive	under 40,000 lire

Expensive **Biffi Scala.** The elegant Biffi Scala caters mainly to the after-opera crowd that pours in around midnight. Built in 1861, it features a high ceiling and polished wood walls. Specialties include *crespelle alle erbette* (pancakes stuffed with wild mushrooms and other vegetables) and *carpaccio alla biffi scala* (thin slices of cured raw beef with a tangy sauce). *Piazza della Scala, tel. 02/866651. Dinner reservations required, especially after the opera. AE, DC, MC, V. Closed Sun., Aug. 10–20, and Dec. 24–Jan. 6.*

★ **Boeucc.** Milan's oldest restaurant is situated not far from La Scala and is subtly lighted, with fluted columns, chandeliers, thick carpet, and a garden for warm-weather dining. In addition to the typical Milanese foods, it also serves such exotica as *penne al branzino e zucchine* (pasta with sea bass and zucchini sauce) and *gelato di castagne con zabaglione caldo* (chestnut ice cream with hot zabaglione). *Piazza Belgioioso 2, tel. 02/790224. Reservations required. Closed Sat., Sun. lunch, and Aug. AE.*

Don Lisander. This 17th-century chapel has been drastically redecorated, and now features designer lighting, abstract prints, and a modern terra-cotta tile floor, creating an uncompromisingly contemporary effect. Try the *terrina di brasato alle verdure* (terrine of braised beef with vegetables), or else go for the *branzino al timo* (sea bass with thyme). *Via Manzoni 12A, tel. 02/790130. Reservations required. AE, DC, MC, V. Closed Sat. dinner, Sun., 2 weeks in mid-Aug., and 2 weeks at Christmas.*

Giannino. You'll find great character and style at this roomy, old-fashioned restaurant, with oak beams, stained-glass windows, and a huge lobster aquarium. If it's on the menu, be daring and try the *dadolata di capriolo* (venison in cream sauce) or *quaglie con risotto* (quails with rice). *Via A. Sciesa 8, tel. 02/545–2948. Dinner reservations required. AE, DC, MC, V. Closed Sun., Aug.*

Gualtiero Marchesi. Owner Gualtiero Marchesi has written several books on *nuova cucina* (nouvelle cuisine). Your eye, as well as your taste buds, should relish his spaghetti salad with caviar and chives or the *costata di manzo bollita alle piccole verdure* (thinly sliced boiled pork with steamed vegetables). Portions are minuscule. *Via Bonvesin de la Riva 9, tel. 02/*

741246. Reservations advised. AE, DC, MC, V. Closed Sun., Mon. lunch, Aug., and holidays.

★ **Savini.** Red carpets and cut-glass chandeliers characterize the classy Savini, a typical, Old World Milanese restaurant whose dining rooms spread over three floors. There's also a "winter garden" from which patrons can people-watch shoppers in the Galleria. The *risotto al salto* (rice cooked as a pancake, tossed in the pan, a Milanese specialty) is excellent here, as is the *costoletta di vitello* (fried veal cutlets). *Galleria Vittorio Emanuele, tel. 02/805–8343. Dinner reservations advised. AE, DC, MC, V. Closed Sun., 3 weeks in Aug., and 2 weeks at Christmas.*

Moderate **Antica Brasera Meneghina.** A huge fireplace, ornate mirrors,
★ black-and-white tiled floor, and bentwood chairs lend this restaurant a 17th-century air, while the long garden, shaded by a 450-year-old wisteria and containing fig trees, fountains, and frescoes, make it absolutely delightful in the summer. The menu features typical Milanese dishes such as *rustin negàa* (veal cooked in white wine with ham, bacon, sage, and rosemary) and *cassoeula* (casserole of pork, sausage, and cabbage). *Via Circo 10, tel. 02/808108. Winter reservations advised. AE, DC, MC, V. Closed Mon., Aug.*

Al Buon Convento. The granite columns and oak beams here date back to the 15th century, when a bevy of nuns occupied the premises. Expect genuine, home-style cooking served up in an intimate, candlelighted ambience. Don't miss the *spaghetti alla lucana* (spaghetti with a tomato and chili sauce). *Corso Italia 26, tel. 02/805–0623. Reservations advised. V. Closed Sun., Aug.*

Opera Prima. If you've always imagined yourself dining by candlelight, from silver plates, and with strains of classical music lilting in the background—well, then, Opera Prima is the place you've been searching for. The *crespelle alla vaniglia e al cioccolato* (vanilla and chocolate pancakes) are sinfully good, and the *tagliolini opera prima* (pasta with chicken, vegetables, and a cream and chili sauce) is a good way to start off your meal. *Via Rovello 3, tel. 02/865235. Reservations advised. AE, DC, MC, V. Closed Sun. and Aug.*

★ **Tencitt.** This chic ultra-1980s restaurant is decorated in stark black and white, with suffused wall lighting and a striped tent effect on the ceiling. Dishes that sit well with the professional/academic clientele (it's near the university) are the *risotto con zucche e scampi* (rice with squash and scampi) and the *storione all'erba e cipolline* (sturgeon with herbs and spring onions). *Via Laghetto 2, tel. 02/795560. Reservations required. AE, DC, MC, V. Closed Sat. lunch, Sun., Aug.*

Inexpensive **La Bruschetta.** A winning partnership of Tuscans and Neapolitans run this tiny, busy, and first-class pizzeria near the Duomo. It features the obligatory wood-burning stove, so you can watch your pizza being cooked, though there are plenty of other dishes to choose from as well—try the *spaghetti alle cozze e vongole* (spaghetti with clams and mussels). *Piazza Beccaria 12, tel. 02/802494. Reservations advised, but service is so fast you don't have to wait long. No credit cards. Closed Mon., 3 weeks in Aug.*

Al Cantinone. Operagoers still come to the Cantinone bar for a drink after the final curtain, just as they did a century ago. The decor is basic, the atmosphere lively, the service fast, and the food reliable. The proprietor stocks 240 different wines. Try the *costolette al Cantinone* (veal cutlets with mushrooms, olives, and a cream and tomato sauce). *Via Agnello 19, tel. 02/807666. Reservations advised. AE, MC, V. Closed Sat. lunch, Sun., Aug., Christmas, and Easter.*

La Piazzetta. A popular lunch spot in the Brera quarter, it's usually crowded with journalists, actors, and politicians. There's a salad bar, but you'll find hot dishes, too, such as the typically Milanese *ossobuco con risotto* (braised veal shanks with white wine and tomato. *Via Solferino 25, tel. 02/659–1076. No reservations. No credit cards. Closed Sun., Easter, and Aug.*

Lodging

Make reservations well in advance, particularly when trade fairs are on, which can be most of the year except for August (when many hotels close) and mid-December to mid-January. March and October are months with the highest concentration of fairs, and it's virtually impossible to find a room at this time. Should you arrive without reservations, there's a booking service at Via Palestro 24 (tel. 02/782072).

Italy offers a good choice of accommodations. Room rates are on a par with other European capitals, and porters, room service, and in-house cleaning and laundering are disappearing in Moderate and Inexpensive hotels. Taxes and service are included in the room rate. Breakfast is an extra charge, and you can decline to take breakfast in the hotel, though the desk may not be happy about it; make this clear when booking or checking in. Air-conditioning also may be an extra charge. In older hotels, room quality may be uneven; if you don't like the room you're given, ask for another. This applies to noise, too; some front rooms are bigger and have views but get street noise. Specify if you care about having either a bath or shower, as not all rooms have both. In Moderate and Inexpensive places, showers may be the drain-in-the-floor type guaranteed to flood the bathroom. Major cities have hotel reservation service booths in the rail stations.

Hotels   Italian hotels are officially classified from five-star (deluxe) to one-star (guest houses and small inns). Prices are established officially and a rate card on the back of the door of your room or inside the closet door tells you exactly what you will pay for that particular room. Any variations should be cause for complaint and should be reported to the local tourist office. CIGA, Jolly, Space, Atahotels, and Italhotels are among the reliable chains or groups operating in Italy, with CIGA among the most luxurious. Sheraton hotels are making an impact in Italy in a big way, though most, located in Rome, Florence, Bari, Padua, and Catania, tend to be geared toward convention and business travel. There are a few Relais et Châteaux member hotels that are noted for individual atmosphere, personal service, and luxury; they are also expensive. The AGIP chain is found mostly on main highways.

Good-value accommodations can be found at one-star hotels and *locande* (inns). Rooms are usually spotlessly clean but basic, with shower and toilets down the hall.

Rentals   More and more people are discovering the attractions of renting a house, cottage, or apartment in the Italian countryside. These are ideal for families or for groups of up to eight people looking for a bargain—or just independence. Availability is subject to change, so it is best to ask your travel agent or the nearest branch of ENIT, the Italian tourist board, about rentals.

Ratings   The following price categories are determined by the cost of two people in a double room. Best bets are indicated by a ★.

Category	Cost
Very Expensive	over 400,000 lire
Expensive	200,000–400,000 lire
Moderate	130,000–180,000 lire
Inexpensive	under 110,000 lire

Very Expensive
★

Duomo. Just 20 yards from the cathedral, this hotel's first-, second- and third-floor rooms all look out onto the church's Gothic gargoyles and pinnacles. The rooms are spacious and snappily furnished in contemporary style. *Via San Raffaele 1, tel. 02/8833, fax 02/877552. 160 rooms with bath. Facilities: restaurant, bar. MC, V. Closed Aug.*

Excelsior Gallia. This vast circa-1930 mock-Victorian hotel is located near the central station. It should be emerging from a major renovation, due to be completed by 1992, featuring all-new decor and up-to-the-minute comforts. *Piazza Duca d'Aosta 9, tel. 02/6785, fax 02/656306. 252 rooms with bath. Facilities: sauna, Turkish bath, health club, restaurant. AE, DC, MC, V.*

Galileo. In spite of its location on busy Corso Europa, this hotel is surprisingly quiet. The rooms have chic designer lighting, tartan carpets, and original modern prints on the walls. The bathrooms are particularly grand, with two basins each. *Corso Europa 9, tel. 02/7743. 76 rooms with bath. Facilities: grill room. AE, DC, MC, V.*

Pierre. No expense was spared to furnish each room of Milan's newest luxury hotel in a different style, using the most elegant fabrics and an assortment of modern and antique furniture. Electronic gadgetry is rife: You can open the curtains, turn off the lights, and who knows what else, merely by pressing buttons on a remote-control dial. The Pierre is located near the medieval church of Sant'Ambrogio. *Via De Amicis 32, tel. 02/805–6220, fax 02/805–2157. 47 rooms with bath. Facilities: restaurant, bar. AE, DC, MC, V.*

Principe di Savoia. The most fashionable and glitzy hotel in Milan is the Principe di Savoia. This is where fashion buyers and expense-account businesspeople stay. Dark wood paneling and period furniture, brass lamps, and a stucco lobby are all reminiscent of early 1900s Europe. *Piazza della Repubblica 17, tel. 02/6230, fax 02/545–6043. 245 rooms with bath. Facilities: restaurant, bar. AE, DC, MC, V.*

Expensive   **Carlton-Senato.** Visitors who intend to spend lots of time shopping in nearby high-fashion streets (Via della Spiga, Via Sant'Andrea, and Via Monte Napoleone) will find this place ideally located. The atmosphere is very light and airy, and there are lots of little touches (such as complimentary chocolates and liqueurs in the rooms) to make up for the rather functional room furnishings. *Via Senato 5, tel. 02/798583. Fax 02/864–60861. 79 rooms with bath. Facilities: restaurant, bar, garage. AE, MC, V. Closed Aug.*

Moderate **Canada.** This friendly, small hotel is close to Piazza del Duomo on the edge of a district full of shops and restaurants. Recently renovated, it offers good value; all rooms have TV, air-conditioning, and fridge-bar. *Via Santa Sofia 16, tel. 02/583–04844, fax 02/583–00282. 35 rooms with bath. AE, DC, MC, V.*

Centro. The fragments of a Roman column and bust in the entrance lead you to expect something more old-fashioned and classier than is the case: The rooms are decorated in 1960s modern, with floral wallpaper and bare wood floors. Avoid rooms on the Via Broletto side—cars rumbling over cobblestones sound like thunder. *Via Broletto 46, tel. 02/875232, fax 02/875578. Facilities: bar, coffee shop. AE, DC, MC, V.*

Gritti. This bright, clean hotel has a cheerful atmosphere. Rooms are adequate, with picturesque views from the upper floors over the tiled roofs to the gilt Madonnina on top of the Duomo, only a few hundred yards away. *Piazza Santa Maria Beltrade (north end of Via Torino), tel. 02/801056, fax 02/890–10999. 48 rooms with bath. AE, DC, MC, V.*

King. Within easy walking distance of Leonardo's *Last Supper* at Santa Maria delle Grazie, the King has high ceilings and an imposing mock–Louis XV lobby. Built in 1966, it was restored in 1986 in pseudo-antique style, with aptly regal red rugs, armchairs, and bedsteads. *Corso Magenta 19, tel. 02/874432. 48 rooms, 44 with bath. AE, MC, V.*

Inexpensive **Antica Locanda Solferino.** Make reservations well in advance for this one: The rooms are few, and provide excellent value. The building is 19th century, but the rooms were all recently redecorated with delightful peasant-print bedspreads, low bedside tables draped with lace-edge cloths, attractive dried-flower arrangements on the tables, and 19th-century prints on the walls. *Via Castelfidardo 2, tel. 02/657–0129, fax 02/656460. 11 rooms with bath. V. Closed 10 days mid-Aug. and another 10 days at Christmas.*

Pensione Rovello. Accommodations here are simple and spanking clean, with warm terra-cotta tile floors and plain white walls. It's a favorite with younger travelers and American fashion models. Expect to pay in advance. *Via Rovello 18A, tel. 02/873956. 12 rooms, 10 with bath. No credit cards.*

The Arts

The most famous spectacle in Milan is **La Scala Opera,** which presents some of the world's most impressive operatic productions. The house is invariably sold out in advance; ask at your hotel whether tickets can be found for you. You can also book tickets at CIT travel agencies elsewhere in Italy and in foreign countries, but no more than 10 days before the performance. The opera season begins early in December and ends in May. The concert season runs from May to the end of June and from September through November. There is a brief ballet season in September. Programs are available at principal travel agencies and tourist information offices in Italy and abroad. *Box Office, Teatro alla Scala, Piazza della Scala, tel. 02/809126. Open Tues.–Sun. 10–1 and 3:30–5:30. Tickets for same evening's performance on sale from 5:30.*

16 Munich

Arriving and Departing

By Plane A new, bigger airport for Munich is scheduled to open in spring 1992 to replace the smaller, overcrowded Riem airport, but at press time an opening date had not been announced and full service details were not available. Riem airport is about 6 miles from the city center. The new airport is farther, 18 miles northeast near Erding, or about 35 minutes by train.

Between the Airport and Downtown An extension of the S3 suburban train line will link the new airport directly with Munich's main train station (Hauptbahnhof). A fast motorway will also link the airport with Munich. A city-to-airport bus service will also operate from the train station, but at the time of writing its frequency and price had not been determined. If Riem airport is still operating when you visit, buses run approximately every 20 minutes each way linking the train station (Arnulfstr.) and two airport terminals; service runs between 5 AM and 9 PM, then afterward to meet arriving and departing flights until the 11 PM shutdown. A one-way journey takes about 25 minutes and costs DM 5.50. A taxi will cost about DM 25.

By Train All long-distance services arrive at and depart from the main train station, the Hauptbahnhof. Trains to and from destinations in the Bavarian Alps use the adjoining Starnbergerbahnhof. For information on train times, tel. 089/592991; English is spoken by most information office staff. For tickets and information, go to the station or to the ABR travel agency right by the station on Bahnhofplatz.

By Bus Munich has no central bus station. Long-distance buses arrive at and depart from the north side of the train station. A taxi stand is 20 yards away.

By Car From the north (Nuremberg, Frankfurt), leave the autobahn at the Schwabing exit and follow the "Stadtmitte" signs. The autobahn from Stuttgart and the west ends at Obermenzing; again, follow the "Stadtmitte' signs. The autobahns from Salzburg and the east, from Garmisch and the south, and from Lindau and the southwest all join up with the city beltway, the Mittlere Ring. The city center is well posted.

Getting Around

Downtown Munich is only about one mile square, so it can easily be explored on foot. Other areas—Schwabing, Nymphenburg, the Olympic Park—are best reached on the efficient and comprehensive public transportation network. Munich's public transportation system is, in fact, a model of its kind: clean, fast, and ultra-reliable. It incorporates buses, streetcars, subways (U-Bahn), and suburban trains (S-Bahn). Tickets are good for the entire network, and you can break your trip as many times as you like using just one ticket, provided you travel in one direction only and within a given time limit. If you plan to make only a few trips, buy strip tickets (Streifenkarten). The blue strip is for adults and allows up to five journeys for DM 9.50. The red strip is for children and costs DM 4.50. All tickets must be validated by time-punching them in the automatic machines at station entrances and on all buses and streetcars. Otherwise, buy the Tageskarte, which costs DM 7.50 for the inner-city area and DM 12.50 for the entire system. Up to two adults and three children can use this excellent-value

ticket for unlimited journeys between 9 AM and the end of the
day's service (about 2 AM). Holders of a Eurail Pass, a Youth
Pass, an Inter-Rail Card, or a DB Tourist Card travel free on all
S-Bahn trains.

By Taxi Munich's cream-colored taxis are numerous. Hail them in the
street or call 089/21611 (there's an extra charge for the drive to
the pickup point). Rates start at DM 2.90 and rise by DM 1.70
per kilometer (about DM 2.75 per mile). There are additional
charges of 50 pf for each piece of luggage. Figure on paying DM
7 to DM 10 for a short trip within the city.

Important Addresses and Numbers

Tourist The address to write to for information in advance of your visit
Information is Fremdenverkehrsamt München, Postfach, 8000 München 1.
This address also deals with lodging questions and bookings.
Two other offices provide on-the-spot advice: at the Hauptbahnhof (tel. 089/239–1256), daily between 8 AM and 10 PM, and
at the Rathaus on Marienplatz (no phone calls), open weekdays
9 AM–5 PM.

Consulates **U.S. Consulate General** (Königstrasse 5, tel. 089/23011). **British
Consulate General** (Amalienstrasse 62, tel. 089/394–015). **Canadian Consulate** (Tal 29, tel. 089/222–661).

Emergencies **Police** (tel. 089/110). **Ambulance** and **emergency medical attention** (tel. 089/558661). **Dentist** (tel. 089/723–3093). **Pharmacies:**
The **Internationale Inter-Apotheke,** corner of Luisenstrasse
and Elisenstrasse, stocks American and British products; tel.
089/595444. Open weekdays 8–5:30, Saturday 8–1. Outside
these hours, call 089/594475.

English Bookstores The **Anglia English Bookshop** (Schellingstrasse 3, tel. 089/
283642) has the largest selection of English-language books in
Munich. A library of English-language books is kept in
Amerika Haus (Karolinenplatz 3, tel. 089/595369). American
and British newspapers can be bought at the **International
Presse** shop at the Hauptbahnhof.

Travel Agencies **American Express** (Promenadenplatz 6, tel. 089/21990). **ABR,**
the official Bavarian travel agency, has outlets all over Munich;
tel. 089/12040 for information.

Guided Tours

Orientation Tours City bus tours are operated by **Münchner Fremden-Rundfahrten** (Arnulfstr. 8, tel. 089/591–504). Tours run daily and
take in the city center, the Olympic Park, and Nymphenburg.
Departures are at 10 AM and 2:30 PM from outside the Hertie
department store across from the train station, and the cost is
between DM 13 and DM 23 per person, depending on the duration of the tour.

Walking Tours The Munich tourist office (*see* Important Addresses and Numbers, above) organizes guided walking tours for groups or individuals on demand, but no regular walking tours are offered.
Tours can be tailored to suit individual requirements; costs
vary accordingly. Bike tours of the city, including bike rentals,
are offered through **City Hopper Touren** (tel. 089/272–1131).
They run Tuesday–Sunday from 10 AM to 6 PM. Organized
walking and cycling tours of the old city take place daily from
the Hauptbahnhof. The assembly point is "Radius Touristik am

Münchner Hauptbahnhof" beside train track No. 35. Tel. 089/596113.

Excursions **Münchner Fremden-Rundfahrten** (*see* above) organizes bus trips to most leading tourist attractions outside the city. A tour of the royal palaces of Ludwig II, for example, costs DM 62 per person. All tours leave from outside the Hertie department store. Other tours are offered by **Reisebüro Autobus Oberbayern** (Lenbachplatz 1, tel. 089/558061). Among the offerings is a "Late Riser's Excursion," which departs at 10 AM. All tours leave from Elisenstrasse, in front of the Old Botanical Garden.

Exploring Munich

Even in Bonn—the official capital of Germany—they grudgingly call Munich the nation's "secret capital." This sly compliment may reflect the importance of Munich—it's the number-one tourist destination in Germany, as well as the most attractive major German city—but there's nothing "secret" about the way Münchners make this brave claim. Indeed, the noise with which the people of Munich trumpet the attractions of their city could be dismissed as so much Bavarian bombast were it not for the fact that it is so enthusiastically endorsed by others. Flamboyant, easygoing Munich, city of beer and Baroque, is light-years away from the dour Prussian glumness of Berlin, the gritty industrial drive of Hamburg, or the hard-headed commercial instincts of high-rise Frankfurt. This is a city to visit for its good-natured and relaxed charm—*Gemütlichkeit* they call it here—and for its beer halls, its museums, its malls, its parks, and its palaces.

Munich is a crazy mix of high culture (witness its world-class opera house and art galleries) and wild abandon (witness the vulgar frivolity of the Oktoberfest). Its citizenry seems determined to perpetuate the lifestyle of 19th-century king Ludwig I, the Bavarian ruler who brought so much international prestige to his home city after declaring: "I want to make out of Munich a town which does such credit to Germany that nobody knows Germany unless he has seen Munich." He kept his promise with an architectural and artistic renaissance—before abdicating because of a wild romance with a Spanish dancing girl, Lola Montez.

The Historic Heart *Numbers in the margin correspond to points of interest on the Munich map.*

❶ Begin your tour of Munich at the **Hauptbahnhof,** the main train station and an important orientation point. The city tourist office is here, too, ready with information and maps. Cross the street and you're at the start of a kilometer (1½ miles) of pedestrian shopping malls. Facing you are **Hertie,** Munich's leading **❷** department store, and **Karlsplatz** square, known locally as *Stachus,* and one of Europe's busiest traffic intersections. The huge, domed building on your left is the late-19th-century **Justizpalast** (Palace of Justice), now fresh from a seven-year clean-up. It's one of Germany's finest examples of *Gründerzeit,* the display of 19th-century reproductions of Medieval and Renaissance architectural styles.

Head down into the pedestrian underpass—it's another extensive shopping area—to reach the other side and one of the origi-

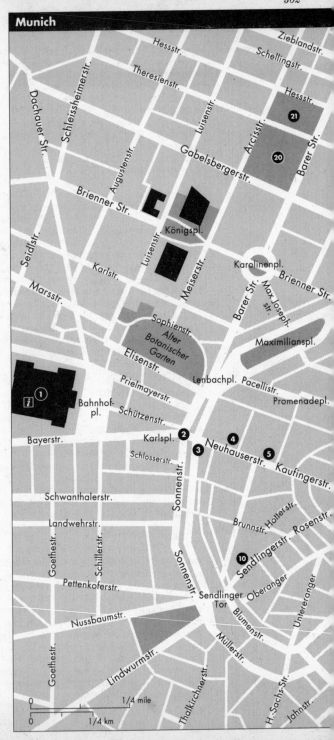

Munich

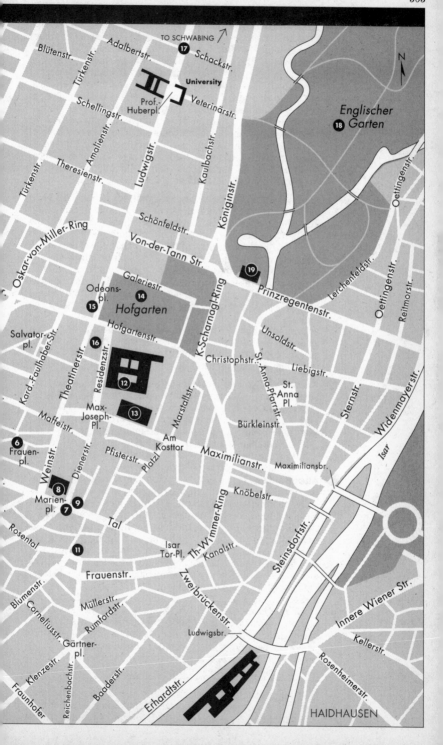

TO SCHWABING

17 Schackstr.

Adalbertstr.

Blütenstr.

Türkenstr.

Schellingstr.

University

Prof.-
Huberpl.

Veterinärstr.

Amalienstr.

Theresienstr.

Türkenstr.

Ludwigstr.

Kaulbachstr.

Königinstr.

**Englischer
Garten**

18

Oettingenstr.

Schönfeldstr.

Oskar-von-Miller-Ring

Von-der-Tann Str.

K.-Scharnagl-Ring

Prinzregentenstr.

19

Lerchenfeldstr.

Oettingenstr.

Reitmorstr.

Galeriestr.

Odeons-
pl.

15

14

Hofgarten

Hofgartenstr.

Unsoldstr.

Liebigstr.

Salvator-
pl.

Kard.-Faulhaber-Str.

Theatinerstr.

Residenzstr.

16

Residenzstr.

12

Christophstr.

St.-Anna-Pfarrstr.

St.
Anna
Pl.

Sternstr.

Maffeistr.

Max-
Joseph-
Pl.

13

Marstallstr.

Bürkleinstr.

6

Frauen-
pl.

Weinstr.

Dienerstr.

Pfisterstr.

Am
Kosttor

Platzl

Maximilianstr.

Maximiliansbr.

Widenmayerstr.

Isar

8

Marien-
pl. **7** **9**

Tal

Knöbelstr.

Th.-Wimmer-Ring

Rosental

11

Isar
Tor-Pl.

Kanalstr.

Steinsdorfstr.

Frauenstr.

Müllerstr.

Rumfordstr.

Zweibrückenstr.

Ludwigsbr.

Innere Wiener Str.

Blumenstr.

Corneliusstr.

Gärtner-
pl.

Klenzestr.

Reichenbachstr.

Baaderstr.

Erhardtstr.

Kellerstr.

Rosenheimerstr.

Fraunhofer

HAIDHAUSEN

N

③ nal city gates, **Karlstor.** The city's two principal shopping streets—**Neuhauserstrasse** and **Kaufingerstrasse**—stretch away from it on the other side. Two of the city's major churches **④ ⑤** are here, too: the **Bürgersaal** and the **Michaelskirche.** The latter is one of the most magnificent Renaissance churches in Germany, a spacious and handsome structure decorated throughout in plain white stucco. It was built for the Jesuits in the late 16th century and is closely modeled on their church of the Gesù in Rome. The intention was to provide a large preaching space, hence the somewhat barnlike atmosphere. Ludwig II is buried here; his tomb is in the crypt. The large neoclassical tomb in the north transept is the resting place of Eugène de Beauharnais, Napoleon's stepson. The highly decorated Rococo interior of the Bürgersaal makes a startling contrast with the simplicity of the Michaelskirche.

A block past the Michaelskirche to your left is Munich's 14th-**⑥** century cathedral, the **Frauenkirche,** or Church of Our Lady. Towering above it are two onion-shaped domes, symbols of the city (perhaps because they resemble brimming beer mugs, cynics claim). They were added in 1525 after the body of the church had been completed. Step inside and you'll be amazed at the stark simplicity of the church; it's very different from the darkly mysterious interiors of other Gothic cathedrals. In part, this is the result of the terrible damage the church suffered in the war: A series of photographs at the main entrance show the building as it was just after the war, a gaunt skeleton filled with rubble. Look for the Baroque tomb of Ludwig the Bavarian by the west door, put up in 1662. In the crypt, you'll find an assortment of other Wittelsbach tombs (the Wittelsbachs were the ruling dynasty for seven centuries).

⑦ From the Frauenkirche, walk to the **Marienplatz** square, the heart of the city, surrounded by shops, restaurants, and cafés. It takes its name from the 300-year-old gilded statue of the Virgin in the center. When it was taken down to be cleaned in 1960, workmen found a small casket containing a splinter of wood said to have come from the cross of Christ. The square is domi-**⑧** nated by the 19th-century **Neues Rathaus,** the new town hall, built in the fussy, turreted style so loved by Ludwig II. The **⑨** **Altes Rathaus,** or old town hall, a medieval building of great charm, sits, as if forgotten, in a corner of the square. At 11 daily (plus May–Oct., 5 PM and 9 PM), the **Glockenspiel,** or chiming clock, in the central tower of the town hall, swings into action. Two tiers of dancing and jousting figures perform their ritual display. It can be worthwhile scheduling your day to catch the clock. Immediately after the war, an American soldier donated some paint to help restore the battered figures and was rewarded with a ride on one of the knight's horses, high above the cheering crowds.

Time Out Duck into the arcades at **Donisl** (Weinstr. 1), on your left as you face the town hall, for the first beer of your Munich visit. This is one of the most authentically Bavarian of the city's beer halls, where the beer flows freely all day—and all night long during the city's *Fasching* (carnival) celebration before Ash Wednesday. You can grab a bite to eat, too.

Heading south down Rosenstrasse to Sendlingerstrasse, you **⑩** come to the **Asamkirche** on your right. Some consider the Asamkirche a preposterously overdecorated jewel box; others consider it one of Europe's finest late-Baroque churches. One thing is certain: If you have any interest in church architecture, this is a place you shouldn't miss. It was built around 1730 by the Asam brothers—Cosmas Damian and Egid Quirin—next door to their home, the Asamhaus. They dedicated it to St. John Nepomuk, a 14th-century Bohemian monk who was drowned in the Danube. Pause before you go in to see the charming statue of angels carrying him to heaven from the rocky riverbank. Inside, there is a riot of decoration: frescoes, statuary, rich rosy marbles, billowing clouds of stucco, and gilding everywhere. The decorative elements and the architecture merge to create a sense of seamless movement and color.

⑪ Go back to Marienplatz and turn right for the **Viktualienmarkt,** the food market. Open-air stalls sell cheese, wine, sausages, fruit, and flowers. Fortified with Bavarian sausage and sauer-
⑫ kraut, plunge into local history with a visit to the **Residenz,** home of the Wittelsbachs from the 16th century to their enforced abdication at the end of World War I. From Max-Joseph-Platz you'll enter the great palace, with its glittering Schatzkammer, or treasury, and glorious rococo theater, designed by court architect François Cuvilliès. Also facing the
⑬ square is the stern neoclassical portico of the **Nationaltheater,** built at the beginning of the 19th century and twice destroyed. *Residenz and Residenz Museum, Max-Joseph-Platz 3. Admission: DM 3.50, children free. Open daily 10–4:30.*

⑭ To the north of the Residenz is the **Hofgarten,** the palace gardens. Two sides of the gardens are bordered by sturdy arcades designed by Leo von Klenze, whose work for the Wittelsbachs in the 19th century helped transform the face of the city. Dominating the east side of the Hofgarten are the bombed-out ruins of what was once the War Museum. Next to its gaunt silhouette, work is proceeding apace on one of the most controversial building projects Munich has seen for many years, the new State Chancellery.

Time Out Munich's oldest café, the **Annast,** is located on Odeonsplatz, right by the west entrance to the Hofgarten. Sit at one of the tables under the Hofgarten trees at the back of the café and the downtown bustle can seem far away.

Odeonsplatz itself is dominated by two striking buildings. One
⑮ is the **Theatinerkirche,** built for the Theatine monks in the mid-17th century, though its handsome facade, with twin eye-catching domes, was added only in the following century. Despite its Italian influences, the interior, like that of the Michaelskirche, is austerely white. The other notable building here is
⑯ the **Feldherrnhalle,** an open loggia built by Ludwig I and modeled on the Loggia dei Lanzi in Florence. Next to it is the site of Hitler's unsuccessful *putsch* of 1923, later a key Nazi shrine.

The Feldherrnhalle looks north along one of the most imposing boulevards in Europe, the **Ludwigstrasse,** which in turn becomes the **Leopoldstrasse.** Von Klenze was responsible for much of it, replacing the jumble of old buildings that originally stood here with the clean, high-windowed lines of his restrained Italianate buildings. The state library and the university are lo-
⑰ cated along it, while, halfway up it, is the **Siegestor,** or Arch of Victory, modeled on the Arch of Constantine in Rome. Beyond it is **Schwabing,** once a sort of combination Latin Quarter and

Greenwich Village. It's much glossier these days but still has an unmistakable vigor and spontaneity. Explore the streets around Wedekindplatz to get the feel of the place.

Back on Leopoldstrasse, wander down to the university, turn on to Professor-Huber-Platz (he was a Munich academic executed by the Nazis for his support for an anti-Hitler movement), and take Veterinärstrasse. It leads you to Munich's **⑱** largest park, the magnificent **Englischer Garten.** You can rent a bike from Dr. Buss's stand at the entrance to the park on summer weekends. The cost is DM 3 per hour and DM 15 for the day.

The Englischer Garten, 4½ kilometers (3 miles) long and over a ½ kilometer (1 mile) wide, was laid out by Count Rumford, a refugee from the American War of Independence. He was born in England, but it wasn't his English ancestry that determined the park's name as much as its open, informal nature, a style favored by 18th-century English aristocrats. You can rent boats, visit beer gardens—the most famous is at the foot of a Chinese Pagoda—ride your bike (or ski in winter), or simply stroll around. Ludwig II used to love to wander incognito along the serpentine paths. What would he say today, now that so much of the park has been taken over by Munich's nudists? This is no misprint. Late-20th-century Germans have embraced nature worship with almost pagan fervor, and large sections of the park have been designated nudist areas. The biggest is be- **⑲** hind the **Haus der Kunst,** Munich's art gallery and one of the few Hitler-era buildings left in the city. If you prefer the idealized version of the human body to the real thing, head inside. Unusually, the museum also houses one of the city's most exclusive discos, the PI. *Haus der Kunst, Prinzregentenstr. 1. Admission: DM 3.50 adults, 50 pf children; Sun. and holidays free. Open Tues.–Sun. 9–4:30, Thurs. 7–9.*

You'll find more culture in Munich's two leading picture galleries, the Alte (meaning "old") and the Neue (meaning "new") Pinakothek. They are located on Barerstrasse, just to the west **⑳** of the university. The **Alte Pinakothek** is not only the repository of some of the world's most celebrated old masters but an architectural treasure in its own right, though much scarred from wartime bomb damage. It was built by von Klenze at the beginning of the 19th century to house Ludwig I's collections. Early Renaissance works, especially by German painters, are the museum's strongest point, but there are some magnificently heroic works by Rubens, too, among much else of outstanding quality. *Barerstr. 27. Admission: DM 4, adults, 50 pf children; free Sun. and holidays. Open Tues.–Sun. 9–4:30; Tues. and Thurs. 7 PM–9 PM.*

㉑ The **Neue Pinakothek** was another of Ludwig I's projects, built to house his "modern" collections, meaning, of course, 19th-century works. The building was destroyed during World War II, and today's museum opened in 1981. Whatever you think of the low, brick structure—some have compared it with a Florentine palazzo—it is an unparalleled environment in which to see one of the finest collections of 19th-century paintings in the world. *Barerstr. 29. Admission: DM 4 adults, 50 pf children; free Sun. and holidays. Open Tues.–Sun. 9–4:30, and Tues. and Thurs. 7–9 PM. Take the No. 18 streetcar from Karlsplatz for both the Alte and Neue Pinakothek.*

There are two trips you can take to attractions just out of the city center. One is to the **Olympic Park,** a 10-minute U-Bahn ride north; the other is to Nymphenburg, 6 kilometers (4 miles) northwest and reached by the No. 12 streetcar or No. 41 bus.

Suburban Attractions **Schloss Nymphenburg** was the summer palace of the Wittelsbachs. The oldest parts date from 1664, but construction continued for more than 100 years, the bulk of the work being undertaken in the reign of Max Emmanuel between 1680 and 1730. The gardens, a mixture of formal French *parterres* (trim, ankle-high hedges and gravel walks) and English parkland, were landscaped over the same period. The interiors are exceptional, especially the Banqueting Hall, a rococo masterpiece in green and gold. Make a point of seeing the Schönheits Galerie, the **Gallery of Beauties.** It contains more than 100 portraits of women who had caught the eye of Ludwig I; duchesses rub shoulders with butchers' daughters. Among them is Lola Montez. Seek out the **Amalienburg,** or Hunting Lodge, on the grounds. It was built by Cuvilliés, architect of the Residenz Theater in Munich. That the lodge was designed for hunting of the indoor variety can easily be guessed by the sumptuous silver and blue stucco and the atmosphere of courtly high life. The palace also contains the **Marstallmuseum** (the Museum of Royal Carriages), containing a sleigh that belonged to Ludwig II, among the opulently decorated vehicles, and, on the floor above, the **Nymphenburger Porzellan,** with examples of the porcelain produced here between 1747 and the 1920s. *Schloss Nymphenburg. Admission: Combined ticket to Schloss, Amalienburg, and Marstallmuseum is DM 4; separate tickets, DM 2 each. Accompanied children free. Porzellan factory nearby (see Shopping, below). Open Apr.–Sept., Tues.–Sun. 9–12:30 and 1:30–5; Oct.–Mar., 10–12:30 and 1:30–4.*

Of all the controversial buildings that mark Munich's skyline, none outdoes the circus tent-shaped roofs of the **Olympic Park.** Built for the 1972 Olympics, the park, with its undulating, transparent tile roofs and modern housing blocks, represented a revolutionary marriage of technology and visual daring when first unveiled. Sports fans might like to join the crowds in the Olympic stadium when the local soccer team, Bayern Munich, has a home game. Call 089/3061–3577 for information and tickets. There's an amazing view of the stadium, the Olympic Park, and the city from the Olympic tower. An elevator speeds you to the top in seconds. *Admission: DM 5 adults; DM 2.50 children; combined tower and park tour (until 5 PM) DM 7 adults, DM 4 children. Open mid-Apr.–mid-Oct., daily 8 AM–midnight; mid-Oct.–mid-Apr., daily 9–midnight.*

Shopping

Gift Ideas Munich is a city of beer, and beer mugs and coasters make an obvious gift to take home. There are many specialist shops in downtown Munich, but **Ludwig Mory,** located in the town hall on Marienplatz, is about the best. Munich is also the home of the famous Nymphenburg porcelain factory; its major outlet is on Odeonsplatz. You can also buy direct from the factory located on the half-moon–shaped road—Schlossrondell—in front of Nymphenburg Palace. *Tel. 089/172439. Salesroom open weekdays 8 AM–noon and 12:30 PM–5 PM.*

Shopping Districts From Odeonsplatz you are poised to plunge into the heart of the huge pedestrian mall that runs through the center of town. The first street you come to, **Theatinerstrasse**, is also one of the most expensive. In fact, it has only one serious rival in the money-no-object stakes: **Maximilianstrasse,** the first street to your left as you head down Theatinerstrasse. Both are lined with elegant shops selling desirable German fashions and other high-priced goods from around the world. Leading off to the right of Theatinerstrasse is **Maffeistrasse,** where **Loden-Frey** has Bavaria's most complete collection of traditional wear, from green "loden" coats to Lederhosen. Maffeistrasse runs parallel to Munich's principal shopping streets: **Kaufingerstrasse** and **Neuhauserstrasse,** the one an extension of the other.

Department Stores All the city's major department stores—other than **Hertie** (*see* Exploring, above)—are along Maffeistrasse, Kaufingerstrasse, and Neuhauserstrasse. **Kaufhof** and **Oberpollinger** are probably the best. Both have large departments stocking Bavarian arts and crafts, as well as clothing, household goods, jewelry, and other accessories.

Antiques Antique hunters should make for **Karlstrasse, Ottostrasse, Türkenstrasse,** and **Westenriederstrasse.** Also try the open-air Auer Dult fairs held on Mariahilplatz at the end of April, July, and October (streetcar No. 25).

Dining

It's hard to generalize about German food beyond saying that standards are high and portions are large. In fact, the range of dining experiences is vast: everything from highly priced nouvelle cuisine to hamburgers. As a visitor, you should search out local restaurants if atmosphere and regional specialties are your priority. Throughout the country you'll find *Gaststätten* and/or *Gasthöfe*—local inns—where atmosphere and regional specialties are always available. Likewise, just about every town will have a *Ratskeller,* a cellar restaurant in the town hall, where exposed beams, huge fireplaces, sturdy tables, and immense portions are the rule.

Germans like to nibble at roadside or market snack stalls, called *Imbisse.* Hot sausages, spicy meatballs *(Fleischpflanzerl),* Leberkas (in the south), and sauerkraut are the traditional favorites. But foods eaten on the hoof are creeping in, too: french fries, pizzas, gyros, and hamburgers. In eastern Germany, the old state-run self-service worker cafeterias may still be operating in some towns, but these are rapidly being replaced by commercial enterprises. For late breakfasts or good-value lunches, try the restaurants of the main department stores across the country: Hertie, Karstadt, Kaufhof.

The most famous German specialty is sausage. Everyone has heard of frankfurters, but if you're in Munich, try *Weisswurst,* a delicate white sausage traditionally eaten only between midnight and noon. Nuremberg's sausage favorite is the *Nürnberger Bratwurst;* its fame is such that you'll find restaurants all over Germany serving it. Look for the "Bratwurststube" sign. Dumplings*(Knödel)* can also be found throughout the country, though their natural home is probably Bavaria; farther north, potatoes often take their place.

The natural accompaniment to German food is either beer or wine. Munich is the beer capital of Germany, though there's no part of the country where you won't find the amber nectar. Say "Helles" or Export if you want light beer; "Dunkles" if you want dark beer. Germany is a major wine-producing country, also, and much of it is of superlative quality. You will probably be happy with the house wine in most restaurants or with one of those earthenware pitchers of cold Moselle wine. If you want something more expensive, remember that all wines are graded in one of three basic categories: *Tafelwein* (table wine); *Qualitätswein* (fine wines); and *Qualitätswein mit Prädikat* (top-quality wines).

Münchners love to eat just as much as they love their beer, and the range of food is as varied and rich as the local breweries' output. Some of Europe's best chefs are to be found here, purveyors of French nouvelle cuisine in some of the most noted—and pricey—restaurants in Germany. But these restaurants are mainly for the gourmet. For those in search of the local cuisine, the path leads to Munich's tried-and-true wood-paneled, flagstone beer restaurants and halls where the food is as sturdy as the large measure of beer that comes to your table almost automatically. Provided your pockets are deep enough, the choice is limitless—from a mountainous roast pork knuckle with dumplings to delicate slivers of salmon and truffle salad. The high-brow restaurants offer a low-key, library-quiet atmosphere; while many of the lower-brow establishments provide ear-splitting conviviality. Try the *Weisswurst* (white veal sausages with herbs), brought to your table in a tureen of boiling water to keep them fresh and hot. They are served with a sweet mustard and pretzels and are a breakfast or midmorning favorite. Equally good is *Leberkäs*, wedges of piping-hot meat loaf with a fried egg on top and pan-fried potatoes.

Mealtimes Lunch is served from around 11:30 (especially in rural areas) to around 2; dinner is generally from 6 until 9:30 PM, or earlier in some quiet country areas. Big city hotels and popular restaurants serve later. Lunch tends to be the main meal, a fact reflected in the almost universal appearance of a lunchtime *Tageskarte*, or suggested menu; try it if you want maximum nourishment for minimum outlay. This doesn't mean that dinner is a rushed or skimpy affair, however; the Germans have too high a regard for food for any meal to be underrated. Breakfast, served anytime from 6:30 to 10, is often a substantial meal, with cold meats, cheeses, rolls, and fruit. Many city hotels offer Sunday "brunch," and the custom is rapidly catching on.

Dress Jacket and tie are recommended for restaurants in the Very Expensive and Expensive categories. Casual dress is appropriate elsewhere.

Ratings Prices are per person and include a first course, main course, dessert, and tip and tax. Best bets are indicated by a star ★.

Category	Cost
Very Expensive	over DM 100
Expensive	DM 75–DM 100

Moderate	DM 50–DM 75
Inexpensive	DM 25–DM 50

Very Expensive **Aubergine.** German gourmets swear by the upscale nouvelle cuisine of Eckart Witzigmann, chef and owner of this sophisticated restaurant. The decor is streamlined modern—white and glittery. The service is appropriately polished. If you want a gastronomic experience on the grand scale, try the turbot in champagne or the breast of pigeon with artichoke and truffle salad. *Maximilianplatz 5, tel. 089/598171. Reservations required. MC. Closed Sun., Mon., Christmas and New Year's Day, and first 3 weeks of Aug.*

Boettner's. This is the oldest of Munich's classy restaurants, in business since 1905. There's a time-honored and quiet quality to its gracious bar and dark, wood-paneled dining room. Seafood dominates the menu; try the lobster and sole served on a bed of tomato-flavored pasta. *Theatinerstr. 2, tel. 089/221210. Reservations required. AE, DC, MC, V. Closed Sat. for dinner, Sun., and holidays.*

Sabitzer's. Further evidence of upscale Munich's love affair with nouvelle cuisine, though with Bavarian influences, is provided by the classy offerings at Sabitzer's. Within its elegant gold-and-white 19th-century interior, you'll dine on such specialties as wild salmon with stuffed goose livers and lamb with venison. *Reitmorstr. 21, tel. 089/298584. Reservations required. AE, DC, MC. Closed weekends, July and Aug.*

Tantris. Chef Heinz Winkler presides almost regally over what some consider Munich's top restaurant. Here, too, nouvelle cuisine, served with great panache, reigns supreme. Try the pigeon breast for a remarkable gastronomic experience. The downside is the setting, which bears an uncanny resemblance to an airport departure lounge, albeit one for VIPs. *Johann-Fichter-Str. 7, tel. 089/362061. Reservations required. AE, DC, MC. Closed Sat. lunch, Sun., Mon., first week in Jan., and 3 weeks in Aug.*

Expensive **Austernkeller.** The nautical decor of this centrally located,
★ vaulted cellar-restaurant provides an appropriate setting for the classy seafood specialties of the Austernkeller. Oysters—*Austern* in German—dominate the menu, but there's a wide range of other shellfish featured, too. *Stollbergstr. 11, tel. 089/298787. Reservations advised. AE, DC, MC, V. Closed Mon. and Christmas.*

Bouillabaisse. There's little point eating here if your tastes run to German specialties. Pungent and rich *bouillabaisse*, the garlicky fish stew from Provence in the south of France, is the star attraction here. The decor is striking, with imposing chandeliers to lighten up the otherwise somber and heavy-beamed dining room. *Falkenturmstr. 10, tel. 089/297909. Reservations advised. AE, DC, MC, V. Closed Sun., Mon. lunch, and Aug.*

Le Gourmet. Imaginative combinations of French and Bavarian specialties have won the little Gourmet substantial praise from local critics. Try chef Otto Koch's oxtail in champagne sauce or his zucchini and truffle salad. *Ligsalzstr. 46, tel. 089/503597. Reservations advised. AE, DC, MC. Closed Sun. and first week in Jan.*

Käferschanke. Fresh fish, imported daily from the south of France, is the attraction here. Try the grilled prawns in a sweet-sour sauce. The rustic decor, complemented by some fine antique pieces, is a delight. The restaurant is located in the classy Bogenhausen suburb, a 10-minute taxi ride from downtown. *Schumannstr. 1, tel. 089/41681. Reservations advised. AE, DC, MC. Closed Sat. and holidays.*

★ **Preysing Keller.** Devotees of all that's best in modern German food—food that's light and sophisticated but with recognizably Teutonic touches—will love the Preysing Keller, a hotel/restaurant. It's in a 16th-century cellar, though this has been so overrestored that there's practically no sense of its age or original character. Never mind; it's the food, the extensive wine list, and the perfect service that make this place special. Try the fixed-price seven-course menu—at DM 100 per person—for best value and an all-around taste of one of the best dining venues in Munich. *Innere-Wiener-Str. 6, tel. 089/481015. Reservations required. No credit cards. Closed Sun., Christmas, and New Year's Day.*

Moderate **Bistro Terrine.** The name may make you think that this is no more than a humble, neighborhood French-style restaurant. In fact, excellent classic French dishes are served within its appealing Art Nouveau interior. Order the fixed-price menu to keep the check low; à la carte dishes are appreciably more expensive. *Amalienstr. 40, tel. 089/281780. Reservations advised. AE, MC. Closed Sun.*

★ **Nürnberger Bratwurst Glöckl.** This is about the most authentic old-time Bavarian sausage restaurant in Munich, and it's always crowded. Wobbly chairs, pitch-black wooden paneling, tin plates, monosyllabic waitresses, and, downstairs, some seriously Teutonic-looking characters establish an unbeatable mood. If you want undiluted atmosphere, try for a table downstairs; if you want to hear yourself speak, go for one upstairs. The menu is limited, with *Nürnberger Wurst*—finger-size Nürnberg sausages—taking pride of place. The beer, never in short supply, is served straight from wooden barrels. The restaurant is right by the Frauenkirche—the entrance is set back from the street and can be hard to spot—and makes an ideal lunchtime layover. *Frauenplatz 9, tel. 089/220385. Reservations advised. No credit cards.*

Welser Küche. Here you'll eat in medieval style, in a redbrick vaulted banqueting hall and with only a dagger to tackle the roast meat. It sounds like tourist-trail fare, but in fact it's fun and the food's good. *Residenzstr. 27, tel. 089/296565. Reservations advised. AE, DC, MC, V.*

Inexpensive **Donisl.** Ranking high among the beer restaurants of Munich, Donisl is located just off Marienplatz, and in summer, its tables spill out onto the sidewalk. But the real action is inside. The large central hall, with garlands of dried flowers and painted and carved booths lining the walls, is animated night and day. The atmosphere can be boisterous. Traditional music from 5 PM. *Weinstr. 1, tel. 089/220184. No reservations. AE, DC, MC, V.*

Dürnbräu. A fountain plays outside this picturesque old Bavarian inn. Inside, the mood is crowded and noisy. Expect to share a table; your fellow diners will range from millionaires to students. The food is resolutely traditional. Try the cream of spinach soup and the boiled beef. *Dürnbräugasse 2, tel. 089/222195. Reservations advised. AE, DC, MC, V.*

Franziskaner. Vaulted archways, cavernous rooms interspersed with intimate dining areas, bold blue frescoes on the walls, and long wooden tables create a spick-and-span medieval atmosphere—the look without the dirt. This is the place for an early morning Weisswurst and a beer; the Bavarians swear it will banish all trace of that morning-after feeling. *Perusastr. 5, tel. 089/645548. No reservations. No credit cards.*

★ **Haxnbauer.** This is about the most sophisticated of the beer restaurants. There's the usual series of interlinking rooms—some large, some small—and the usual sturdy/pretty Bavarian decoration. But there is much greater emphasis on the food than in other similar places. Try Leberkäs or *Schweinshaxe*, pork shank. *Münzstr. 2, tel. 089/221922. Reservations advised. MC, V.*

Hofbräuhaus. The heavy stone vaults of the Hofbräuhaus contain the most famous of the city's beer restaurants. Crowds of singing, shouting, swaying beer drinkers fill the atmospheric and smoky rooms. Picking their way past the tables are hefty waitresses in traditional garb bearing frothing steins. Make no mistake—this is a place where beer takes precedence over food. Go upstairs, where there's greater emphasis on eating, for a less raucous time. It's located between Marienplatz and Maximilianstrasse. *Platzl 9, tel. 089/221676. No reservations. No credit cards.*

Hundskugel. This is Munich's oldest tavern, dating to 1640; history positively drips from its crooked walls. The food is surprisingly good. If *Spanferkel*—roast suckling pig—is on the menu, make a point of ordering it. This is simple Bavarian fare at its best. *Hotterstr. 18, tel. 089/264272. Reservations advised. No credit cards.*

★ **Pfälzer Weinprobierstube.** A warren of stone-vaulted rooms of various sizes, wooden tables, glittering candles, dirndl-clad waitresses, and a vast range of wines add up to an experience as close to your picture of timeless Germany as you're likely to get. The food is reliable rather than spectacular. Local specialties predominate. *Residenzstr. 1, tel. 089/225628. No reservations. No credit cards.*

Zum Brez'n. A hostelry bedecked in the blue-and-white checked colors of the Bavarian flag. The eating and drinking are spread over three floors and cater to a broad clientele—from local business lunchers to hungry night owls emerging from Schwabing's bars and discos looking for a bite at 2 AM. Brez'n offers a big all-day menu of traditional roasts, to be washed down with a choice of three draft beers. *Leopoldstrasse 72, tel. 089/390092. Reservations not necessary. No credit cards.*

Lodging

Make reservations well in advance and be prepared for higher-than-average rates. Though Munich has a vast number of hotels in all price ranges, most are full year-round; this is a major trade and convention city, as well as a prime tourist destination. If you plan to visit during the "fashion weeks" (Mode Wochen) in March and September or during the Oktoberfest at the end of September, make reservations at least several months in advance. Munich's tourist offices will handle only written or personal requests for reservations assistance. Write to: Fremdenverkehrsamt, Postfach, 8000 Munich 1, fax 089/2391313. Your best bet for finding a room if you haven't reserved is the tourist office at the Hauptbahnhof, by the Bayerstasse entrance. The staff will charge a small fee, but they are supremely well organized.

The closer to the city center you stay, the higher the price. Consider staying in a suburban hotel and taking the U-Bahn or S-Bahn into town. Rates are much more reasonable, and a 15-minute train ride is no obstacle to serious sightseeing. Check out the city tourist office "Key to Munich" packages. These include reduced-rate hotel reservations, sightseeing tours, theater visits, and low-cost travel on the U- and S-Bahn. Write to the tourist office (see above).

The standard of German hotels is generally excellent. Prices can be high, but not disproportionately so in comparison to other northern European countries. You can expect courteous service; clean and comfortable rooms; and, in rural areas especially, considerable old-German atmosphere.

In addition to hotels proper, the country also has numerous *Gasthöfe* or *Gasthäuser* (country inns); pensions or *Fremdenheime* (guest houses); and, at the lowest end of the scale, *Zimmer*, meaning, quite simply, rooms, normally in private houses. Look for the sign "Zimmer frei" or "zu vermieten," meaning "for rent." A red sign reading "Besetzt" means there are no vacancies.

Lists of hotels are available from the German National Tourist Office and from all regional and local tourist offices. Tourist offices will also make reservations for you—they charge a nominal fee—but may have difficulty doing so after 4 PM in peak season and on weekends. A reservations service is also operated by the Deutsche Zentrale für Tourismus (DTZ) (Beethovenstr. 69, Frankfurt/Main, tel. 069/75720). The reservation fee is DM 3 per person.

Most hotels have restaurants, but those describing themselves as *Garni* will provide breakfast only.

Romantik Hotels Among the most delightful places to stay and eat in Germany are the aptly named Romantik Hotels and Restaurants. All are in historic buildings—this is a precondition of membership—and are personally run by the owners. The emphasis generally is on solid comfort, good food, and style. A detailed listing of all Romantik Hotels is available from **Romantik Hotel Reservations,** Box 1278, Woodinville, WA 98072, tel. 800/826-0015.

Youth Hostels Germany's youth hostels—*Jugendherberge*—are probably the most efficient, up-to-date, and proportionately most numerous of those in any country in Europe. There are more than 500 in all, many located in castles, adding a touch of romance to otherwise utilitarian accommodations. There are no restrictions, though those under 20 take preference if space is limited. You'll need an International Youth Hostel card to stay in a German youth hostel; write **American Youth Hostels Association** (Box 37613, Washington, DC 20013) or **Canadian Hostelling Association** (333 River Rd., Ottawa, Ontario K1L 8H9). For full listings, write **Deutsches Jugendherbergswerk Hauptverband** (Bismarckstr. 8, D-4930 Detmold, tel. 05231/74010) or contact the German National Tourist Office.

Rentals Apartments and hotel homes, most accommodating from two to eight guests, can be rented throughout Germany. Rates are low, with reductions for longer stays. Charges for gas and electricity, and sometimes water, are usually added to the bill. There is normally an extra charge for linen, but not if you bring your own. Local and regional tourist offices have lists of apartments in their areas; otherwise write the **German Automobile Association** (ADAC), Am Westpark 8, 8000 Munich 70, tel. 089/76760.

Ratings Service charges and taxes are included in all quoted room rates. Similarly, breakfast is usually, but not always, included—large breakfasts are always extra—so check before you book in. Rates are often surprisingly flexible in German hotels, varying considerably according to demand. Major hotels in cities often have lower rates on weekends or other periods when business is quiet. If you're lucky, you can find reductions of up to 60%. Likewise, rooms reserved after 10 PM will often carry a discount, on the basis that an occupied room at a reduced rate is better than an empty one. Although it's worthwhile to ask if your hotel will give you a reduction, don't count on finding rooms at lower rates late at night, especially in the summer. Prices are for two people in a double room. Best bets are indicated by a star ★.

Category	Cost
Very Expensive	over DM 250
Expensive	DM 180–DM 250
Moderate	DM 120–DM 180
Inexpensive	under DM 120

Very Expensive **Bayerischer Hof.** This is one of Munich's most traditional luxury hotels. Public rooms are decorated with antiques, fine paintings, marble, and painted wood. Old-fashioned comfort and class abound in the older rooms; some of the newer rooms are rather functional. *Promenadeplatz 2–6, tel. 089/2120900. 440 rooms with bath. Facilities: 3 restaurants, nightclub, rooftop pool, garage, sauna, masseur, hairdresser. AE, DC, MC, V.*

City Hilton. Munich's second Hilton is right next door to the Gasteig cultural center. Ticket bookings are no problem. The hotel has all the expected Hilton comforts and services—it even has a selection of track suits and shoes for joggers. *Rosenheimerstr. 15, tel. 089/48040. 680 rooms and suites with bath. Facilities: restaurant, piano bar, access to body-building center and public pool. AE, DC, MC, V.*

★ **Vier Jahreszeiten.** The Vier Jahreszeiten—it means the Four Seasons—has been playing host to the world's wealthy and titled for more than a century. It has an unbeatable location on Munich's premier shopping street and is only a few minutes' walk from the heart of the city. Elegance and luxury set the tone throughout; many rooms have handsome antique pieces. Dine in one of Munich's finest restaurants, the Walterspiel. *Maximilianstr. 17, tel. 089/230390. (Reservations in the U.S. from Kempinski International, tel. 800/426–3135). 341 rooms with bath, 25 apartments, presidential suite. Facilities: restaurant, nightclub, rooftop pool, sauna, garage, car rental, Lufthansa check-in desk. AE, DC, MC, V.*

Expensive **Eden Hotel Wolff.** Chandeliers and dark wood paneling in the public rooms underline the old-fashioned elegance of this downtown favorite. It's directly across the street from the train station and the airport bus terminal. The rooms are comfortable, and most are spacious. Dine on excellent Bavarian specialties in the intimate Zirbelstube restaurant. *Arnulfstr. 4, tel. 089/*

551150. 210 rooms with bath. Facilities: restaurant. AE, DC, MC, V.

Excelsior. The Excelsior is very much a businessperson's hotel, with a sense of functional comfort and a pedestrian mall location, close by the train station, that makes it ultraconvenient for downtown. Renovations in 1986 have helped maintain its reputation for efficiency and good service. *Schützenstr. 11, tel. 089/551370. 116 rooms with bath or shower. Facilities: restaurant, bar. AE, DC, MC, V.*

Palace. This hotel opened in 1986, but the decor and mood lean toward old-fashioned elegance, with the accent firmly on Louis XVI styles and plush luxury. Most rooms overlook the little courtyard. The hotel is located in Alt-Bogenhausen, 6½ kilometers (4 miles) from the airport. Downtown Munich is a 10-minute tram ride away. *Trögerstr. 21, tel. 089/4705091. 73 rooms and suites with bath. Facilities: bar, roof garden, Jacuzzi, sauna, gym. AE, DC, MC, V.*

Prinzregent. An air of Bavarian rusticity pervades this small, new hotel. Carved wood, gilt angels, rococo-style sconces and mirrors, and rough white plaster walls predominate. There's no restaurant, but the breakfast room is decked out with woods taken from an old farmhouse. The hotel is just a 10-minute ride from downtown. *Ismaningerstr. 42–44, tel. 089/4702081. 70 rooms with shower. Facilities: sauna, pool, bar. AE, DC, MC, V.*

★ **Splendid.** Chandelier-hung public rooms, complete with antiques and Oriental rugs, give the small Splendid something of the atmosphere of a spaciously grand 19th-century hotel. The service is attentive and polished. Have breakfast in the small courtyard in summer. There's no restaurant, but the bar serves snacks as well as drinks. It's close to classy shops and the Isar River. *Maximilianstr. 54, tel. 089/296606. 37 rooms with bath and 1 suite. Facilities: bar. AE, MC, V.*

Platzl. This is a Bavarian-rustic–style but modern hotel in a building dating to 1573 and located in the heart of Munich's historic quarter—opposite the famous Hofbräuhaus beer hall. In fact, the Platzl is owned by an out-of-town brewery, Ayingerbräu. The rooms are smallish but comfortable. *Sparkassenstr. 10, tel. 089/237030 (toll-free booking in the U.S., tel. 800/448–8355). 170 rooms with bath. Facilities: equipped for physically disabled guests, sauna, solarium, fitness rooms, rooftop terrace, restaurant, bar, underground garage. AE, MC, V.*

Moderate **Adria.** A modern and comfortable hotel, the Adria is located on the edge of Munich's museum quarter, in the attractive Lehel district, a short walk from the Isar River and the Englischer Garten. There's no restaurant, but there's a large and bright breakfast room. *Liebigstr. 8, tel. 089/293081. 51 rooms with bath. AE, DC, MC, V. Closed Dec. 24–Jan. 6.*

Domus. Head here for home comforts and friendly, personal service. All the rooms have balconies. There's no restaurant, but drinks and snacks are available in the Tyrolean Room bar, decked out in rough-hewn and snug Alpine style. The hotel is close to many museums and the Englischer Garten. *St. Anna-Str. 31, tel. 089/221704. 45 rooms with bath. Facilities: bar, garage. AE, DC, MC, V. Closed Christmas.*

★ **Gästehaus am Englischer Garten.** Despite the slightly basic rooms, you need to reserve well in advance to be sure of getting one in this converted, 200-year-old watermill. The hotel, complete with ivy-clad walls and shutter-framed windows, stands right on the edge of the Englischer Garten, no more than a five-minute walk from the bars and shops of Schwabing. Be sure to ask for a room in the main building; the modern annex down the road is cheaper but charmless. There's no restaurant, but in summer, breakfast is served on the terrace. *Liebergesellstr. 8, tel. 089/392034. 34 rooms, some with bath. No credit cards.*

Intercity. Despite its proximity to the train station, double-glazing of all the windows ensures peace in this longtime downtown favorite. Try for one of the Bavarian-style rooms; others are basic and little more than adequate. There's an excellent restaurant offering good-value Bavarian specialties. *Bahnhofplatz 2, tel. 089/558571. 208 rooms and 4 apartments with bath. Facilities: restaurant, bar, skittle alley. DC, MC, V.*

Königen Elizabeth. Housed in a 19th-century neoclassical building, which was completely restored and opened for the first time as a hotel in 1989, the Elizabeth is modern and bright, with an emphasis on pink decor. The restaurant offers Hungarian specialties. The Elizabeth is a 10-minute streetcar ride northwest of the city center en route to Nymphenburg. *Leonrodstr. 79, tel. 089/12686. 80 rooms with bath. Facilities: bar, beer garden, sauna, solarium, and keep-fit equipment. AE, DC, MC, V.*

Inexpensive
★ **Monopteros.** There are few better deals in Munich than this little hotel. It's located just south of the Englischer Garten, with a tram stop for the 10-minute ride to downtown right by the door. The rooms may be basic, but the excellent service, warm welcome, and great location more than compensate. There's no restaurant. *Oettingenstr. 35, tel. 089/292348. 11 rooms, 3 with shower. No credit cards.*

Pension Beck. One of the best-located, budget-priced hostelries in Munich, the Beck is located between the Haus der Kunst art gallery and Deutsches Museum. Streetcar No. 18 stops outside. Mrs. Beck runs this rambling family pension with a matronly touch, and her sometimes abrasive exterior belies a heart of gold. *Thierschstr. 36, tel. 089/225–768. 50 rooms, most with bath. No credit cards.*

Uhland. This is a cozy, family-run hotel full of Old-World charm, in a mid-19th-century building to match. It's very close to the site of the Oktoberfest, so if you're planning a visit about that time, book well in advance. No restaurant, but breakfasts are noteworthy. *Uhlandstr. 1, tel. 089/539277. AE, DC, MC, V.*

The Arts

Details of concerts and theater performances are available from the *Vorschau* or *Monatsprogramm* booklets obtainable at most hotel reception desks. Some hotels will make ticket reservations; otherwise use one of the ticket agencies in the city center: **Hieber Max,** Liebfrauenstr. 1 (tel. 089/226571) or the **Residenz Bücherstube** (concert tickets only, tel. 089/220868), both on Theatinerstrasse. You can also book tickets at the kiosk on the concourse below Marienplatz.

Concerts Munich's Philharmonic Orchestra entertains in Germany's biggest concert hall, the recently built **Gasteig Cultural Center.** Tickets can be bought directly at the box office (the Gasteig center is on Rosenheimerstrasse, on a hill above the Ludwigsbrücke Bridge). The Bavarian Radio Orchestra performs Sunday concerts here. In summer, concerts are held at two Munich palaces, **Nymphenburg** and **Schleissheim,** and in the open-air interior courtyard of the **Residenz.**

Opera Munich's **Bavarian State Opera** company is world-famous, and tickets for major productions in its permanent home, the State Opera House, are difficult to obtain. Book far in advance for the annual opera festival held in July and August. The box office, (Maximilianstr. 11, tel. 089/221316) takes reservations one week in advance. It's open weekdays 10:30–1 and 3:30–5:30, Saturday 10–12:30.

Dance The ballet company of the Bavarian State Opera performs at the **State Opera House.** Ballet productions are also staged at the attractive late-19th-century **Gärtnerplatz Theater** (tel. 089/2016767).

Film Munich has an annual film festival, usually held in June. English-language films are shown regularly at the Europa film theater in the **Atlantik Palast** (Schwantalerstr. 2–6), **Cinema** (Nymphenburgerstr. 31), the **Film Museum** (St. Jakobs Platz), and the **Museum Lichtspiele** (Ludwigsbrücke).

Theater There are two state theater companies, one of which concentrates on the classics. More than 20 other theater companies (some of them performing in basements) are to be found throughout the city. An English-speaking company called the **Company** (tel. 089/343827) presents about four productions a year.

Nightlife

Bars, Cabaret, Nightclubs Although it lacks the racy reputation of Hamburg, Munich has something for just about all tastes. For spicy striptease, explore the regions south of the train station (Schillerstrasse, for example) or in the neighborhood of the famous Hofbräuhaus (Am Platzl).

Jazz The best jazz can be heard at the **Allotria** (Türkenstr. 33), the **Unterfahrt** (Kirchenstr. 96), and the **Podium** (Wagnerstr. 1). Or try **Jenny's Place in the Blue Note** (Moosacherstr. 24, tel. 351–0520), named for an English singer who settled in Munich.

Discos Schwabing is disco-land. Try the **Circo Valentino** on Occamstrasse (a fun street at all times of day).

For singles Every Munich bar is singles territory. Three you might like to try are **Schumann's** (Maximilianstr. 36) anytime after the curtain comes down at the nearby opera house; **Alter Simpl** (Türkenstr. 57) but not before midnight; and **Harry's New York Bar** (Falkenturmstr. 9), which offers an escape from the German bar scene *and* serves genuine Irish Guinness. For the student, beards, and pipe scene, try **Bunte Vogel** in Schwabing (Herzogstr. 44), which also features an unusual collection of table lamps.

17 Paris

Arriving and Departing

By Plane International flights arrive at either Charles de Gaulle Airport (Roissy), 24 kilometers (15 miles) northeast of Paris, or at Orly Airport, 16 kilometers (10 miles) south of the city. For information on arrival and departure times, call individual airlines.

Between the Airport and Downtown **From Charles de Gaulle:** Buses leave every 12 minutes from 5:45 AM to 11 PM. The fare is 30 frs and the trip takes 40 minutes (up to 1½ hours during rush hour). You arrive at Porte Maillot, on the Right Bank by the Hotel Concorde-Lafayette, a half-mile west of the Champs-Elysées (two stops by métro).

From Orly: Buses leave every 12 minutes from 6 AM to 11 PM and arrive at the Air France terminal near Les Invalides on the Left Bank. The fare is 30 frs, and the trip takes between 30 and 60 minutes, depending on traffic.

Both airports provide free bus shuttles to the nearest train stations, where you can take the RER service to Paris. The advantages of this are speed, price (28 frs to Paris from Charles de Gaulle in Roissy, 22 frs from Orly), and the fact that the RER trains link up directly with the métro system. The disadvantage is having to lug your bags around. Taxi fares from airports to Paris range from 150 to 200 frs.

By Train Paris has five international stations: Gare du Nord (for northern France, northern Europe, and England via Calais or Boulogne); Gare de l'Est (for Strasbourg, Luxembourg, Basle, and central Europe); Gare de Lyon (for Lyon, Marseille, the Riviera, Geneva, Italy); Gare d'Austerlitz (for the Loire Valley, southwest France, Spain); Gare St-Lazare (for Normandy, England via Dieppe). The Gare Montparnasse serves western France (mainly Nantes and Brittany) and is the terminus for the new TGV Atlantic service from Paris to Bordeaux. For train information, tel. 45–82–50–50. You can reserve tickets at any Paris station regardless of the destination. Go to the Grandes Lignes counter for travel within France or to the Billets Internationaux (international tickets) desk if you're heading out of France.

By Bus Long-distance bus journeys within France are uncommon, which may be why Paris has no central bus depot. The two leading Paris-based bus companies are **Eurolines Nord** (3 av. de la Porte de la Villette, 19e, tel. 40–38–93–93) and **L'Autobus** (2 rue Tiquetonne, 2e, tel. 42–33–86–72).

By Car It is no surprise in a country as highly centralized as France that the highway system fans out from Paris. You arrive from the north (England/Belgium) via A1; from Normandy via A13; from the east via A4; from Spain and the southwest via A10; from the Alps, the Riviera, and Italy via A7. Each of these expressways connects with the *Périphérique* (beltway) that encircles Paris. Note that exits here are named by "Porte" and are not numbered. The "Périphe" can be extremely fast—but it gets very busy and is best avoided between 8 and 10 AM and between 5 and 7:30 PM.

Getting Around

Paris is relatively small as capital cities go, and most of its prize monuments and museums are within walking distance of one another. A river cruise is a pleasant way to get an introductory overview. The most convenient form of public transportation is the métro, with stops every few hundred yards; buses are a slower alternative, though they do allow you to see more of the city. Taxis are not expensive but not always easy to hail, either. Car travel within Paris is best avoided because parking is chronically difficult.

By Métro There are 13 métro lines crisscrossing Paris and the nearby suburbs, and you are seldom more than a five-minute walk from the nearest station. It is essential to know the name of the last station on the line you take, since this name appears on all signs within the system. A connection (you can make as many as you please on one ticket) is called a *correspondance*. At junction stations, illuminated orange signs, bearing the names of each line terminus, appear over the corridors leading to the various correspondances. Illuminated blue signs, marked *sortie*, indicate the station exit.

The métro service starts out from each terminus at 5:30 AM and continues until 1:15 AM—when the last métro on each line reaches its terminus. Some lines and stations in the seedier parts of Paris are a bit risky at night—in particular Line 2 (Porte-Dauphine–Nation) and the northern section of Line 13 from St-Lazare to St-Denis/Asnières. The long, bleak corridors at Jaurès and Stalingrad are a haven for pickpockets and purse snatchers. But the Paris métro is a relatively safe place, as long as you don't walk around with your wallet hanging out of your back pocket or travel alone (especially women) late at night.

The métro network connects at several points in Paris with RER trains that race across Paris from suburb to suburb: RER trains are a sort of supersonic métro and can be a great time-saver. All métro tickets and passes are valid for RER and bus travel within Paris. Second-class métro tickets cost 5.20 frs each, though a *carnet* (10 tickets for 32.80 frs) is a far better value. Alternatively, you can buy a *coupon jaune* (weekly) or *carte orange* (monthly) ticket, sold according to zone. Zones 1 and 2 cover the entire métro network (cost: 51 frs per week or 180 frs per month). If you plan to take a suburban train to visit monuments in the Ile de France, you should consider a four-zone ticket (Versailles, St-Germain-en-Laye; 92 frs per week) or a five-zone ticket (Rambouillet, Fontainebleau; 112 frs per week). For these weekly or monthly tickets, you need to obtain a pass (available from train and major métro stations) and provide two passport-size photographs.

The *Formule 1* ticket is valid for one day's second-class travel (22–66 frs, depending on the number of zones), while the *Paris–Visite* card is valid for first-class travel over 3 days (75 frs Paris only, 145 frs with suburbs) or 5 days (120/180 frs).

Access to métro and RER platforms is through an automatic ticket barrier. Slide your ticket in flat and pick it up as it pops up farther along. Keep your ticket; you'll need it again to leave the RER system.

By Bus Most buses run from around 6 AM to 8:30 PM; some continue until midnight. Night buses operate from 1 AM to 6 AM between Châtelet and nearby suburbs. They can be stopped by hailing them at any point on their route. The buses and the métro use the same tickets, but they must be bought either from métro stations or tobacco shops. You need to show weekly/monthly/

special tickets to the driver as you get on; if you have individual yellow tickets, you should state your destination and be prepared to punch one or more tickets in the red and gray machines on board the bus.

By Taxi There is no standard vehicle or color for Paris taxis, but all offer good value. Daytime rates (7 AM to 7:30 PM) within Paris are about 2.70 frs per kilometer, and nighttime rates are around 4.10 frs, plus a basic charge of 10 frs. Rates outside the city limits are about 40% higher. It is best to ask your hotel or restaurant to call for a taxi, since cruising cabs can be hard to find. There are numerous taxi stands, but you have to know where to look. Note that taxis seldom take more than three people at a time.

Important Addresses and Numbers

Tourist Information Paris Tourist Office (127 av. des Champs-Elysées, tel. 47–23–61–72). Open daily 9 AM–8 PM. (Closed Dec. 25, Jan 1.) Offices in major train stations are open daily 8–8.

Embassies U.S. (2 av. Gabriel, 75008 Paris, tel. 42–96–12–02). Canada (35 av. Montaigne, 75008 Paris, tel. 42–25–99–55). U.K. (35 rue du Faubourg St-Honoré, 75008 Paris, tel. 42–66–91–42).

Emergencies Police: dial 17 for emergencies. Automatic phone booths can be found at various main crossroads for use in police emergencies *(Police-Secours)* or medical help *(Services Medicaux);* Ambulance (tel. 18 or 43–78–26–26); Doctor (tel. 47–07–77–77); Hospitals: American Hospital (63 blvd. Victor-Hugo, Neuilly, tel. 47–47–53–00); British Hospital (48 rue de Villiers, Levallois-Perret, tel. 47–58–13–12); Dentist (tel. 43–37–51–00; open 24 hours). Pharmacies: Dhéry (Galerie des Champs, 84 av. des Champs-Elysées, tel. 45–62–02–41; open 24 hours); Drugstore (corner of blvd. St-Germain and rue de Rennes, 6e; open until 2 AM); Pharmacie des Arts (106 blvd. Montparnasse 6e; open until midnight).

English Bookstores W. H. Smith (248 rue de Rivoli); Galignani (224 rue de Rivoli); Brentano's (37 av. de l'Opéra); Shakespeare & Co. (rue de la Bûcherie).

Most newsstands in central Paris sell *Time, Newsweek,* and the *International Herald Tribune,* as well as the English dailies.

Travel Agencies American Express (11 rue Scribe 75009 Paris, tel. 42–66–09–99). Wagons-Lits (106 rue Danton, 92300 Levallois-Perret, tel. 42–68–24–00).

Guided Tours

Orientation Tours Bus tours of Paris offer a good introduction to the city. The two largest operators are Cityrama (tel. 42–60–30–14) and Paris Vision (tel. 42–60–30–01). Tours start from their respective offices, 4 pl. des Pyramides and 214 rue de Rivoli. Both addresses are in the first *arrondissement* (ward), opposite the Tuileries Gardens (toward the Louvre end). Tours are generally given in double-decker buses with either a live guide or a tape-recorded commentary (English, of course, is available). They last three hours and cost about 150 frs. The same operators also offer a variety of other tours with a theme (Historic Paris, Modern Paris, Paris by Night, etc.) lasting from 2½ hours to all day and costing between 120 and 300 frs.

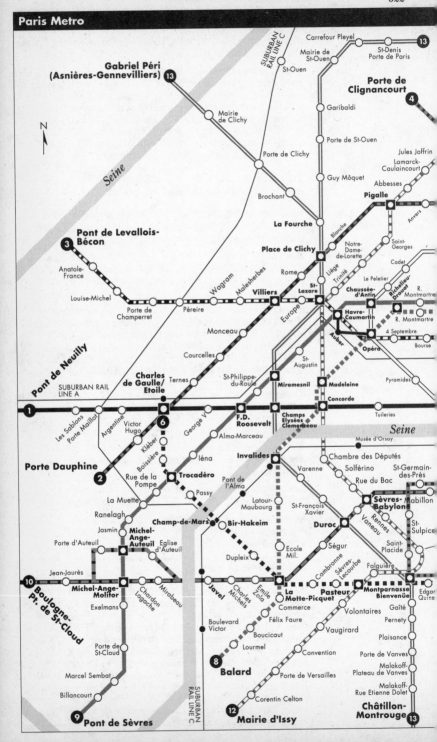

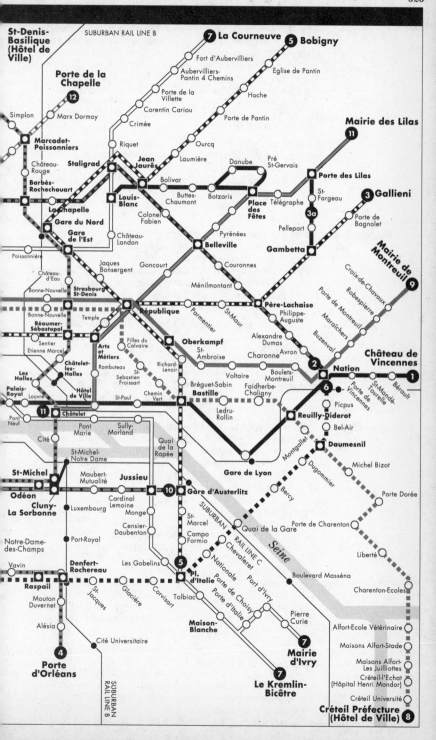

Boat Trips Boat trips along the Seine are a must for first-time Paris visitors. The two most famous services are the **Bâteaux Mouches,** which leaves from the Pont de l'Alma, at the end of the avenue George V, and the **Vedettes du Pont-Neuf,** which sets off from the square du Vert Galant, on the western edge of the Ile de la Cité. Price per trip is around 30 frs. Boats depart in season every half-hour from 10:30 AM to 5 PM (slightly less frequently in winter). Evening cruises are available most of the year and, thanks to the boats' powerful floodlights, offer unexpected views of Paris's riverbanks.

Canauxrama (tel. 46–07–13–13) organizes canal tours in flat-bottom barges along the picturesque but relatively unknown St-Martin and Ourcq Canals in East Paris. Departures from 5 bis quai de la Loire, 19e (métro Jaurès), or the Bassin de l'Arsenal, opposite 50 blvd. de la Bastille, 12e (métro Bastille). Times vary, so phone to check hours. Tours cost from 70 frs, depending on the time of day and length of trip.

Walking Tours There are numerous special-interest tours concentrating on historical or architectural topics. Most are in French, however. Charges vary between 30 and 50 frs, depending on fees that may be needed to visit certain buildings. Tours last about two hours and are generally held in the afternoon. Details are published in the weekly magazines *Pariscope* and *L'Officiel des Spectacles* under the heading "Conférences."

Excursions The **RATP** (Paris Transport Authority) organizes many guided excursions in and around Paris. Ask at its tourist service on the place de la Madeleine (north of place de la Concorde), or at the RATP office at St-Michel (53 quai des Grands-Augustins). **Cityrama** and **Paris Vision** *(see* Orientation Tours, above) organize half- or full-day trips to Chartres, Versailles, Fontainebleau, the Loire Valley, and Mont St-Michel at a cost of between 150 and 750 frs.

Personal Guides **Espaces Limousines** (48 rue Sarrette, 14e, tel. 45–45–53–30) and **Executive Car** (29 rue d'Astorg, 8e, tel. 42–65–54–20) have limousines and minibuses that take up to seven passengers around Paris or to surrounding areas for a minimum of three hours. The cost is about 200 frs per hour. Phone for details and reservations.

Exploring Paris

Paris is a compact city. With the possible exception of the Bois de Boulogne and Montmartre, you can easily walk from one sight to the next. Paris is divided in two by the River Seine, with two islands (Ile de la Cité and Ile St-Louis) in the middle. The south—or Left—Bank has a more intimate, bohemian flavor than the haughtier Right Bank. The east–west axis from Châtelet to the Arc de Triomphe, via the rue de Rivoli and the Champs-Elysées, is the principal thoroughfare for sightseeing and shopping on the Right Bank.

Monuments and museums are sometimes closed at lunchtime (usually noon–2) and one day a week (Monday or Tuesday): Check before you make the trip. A special **Carte Musées** pass, covering access to Paris museums and monuments, can be obtained from museums or métro stations (price: one-day pass, 50 frs; three days, 100 frs; five days, 150 frs). And remember that cafés stay open all day, making them the goal of foot-weary tourists in need of coffee, a beer, or a sandwich. Bakeries are another reliable source of sustenance.

Though attractions are grouped into four logical touring areas, there are several "musts" that most first-time visitors will not want to miss: the Eiffel Tower, the Champs-Elysées, the Louvre, and Notre-Dame. If time is a problem, you can explore Notre-Dame and the Latin Quarter; head to place de la Concorde and enjoy the vista from the Champs-Elysées to the Louvre; then take a boat trip along the Seine for a waterside rendezvous with the Eiffel Tower and a host of other monuments. You could finish off with dinner in Montmartre and consider it a day well spent.

Numbers in the margin correspond to points of interest on the Paris map.

Notre-Dame and the Left Bank
❶

The most enduring symbol of Paris, and its historical and geographical heart, is **Notre-Dame Cathedral,** around the corner from Cité métro station. This is the logical place from which to start any tour of the city—especially as the tour starts on the Ile de la Cité, one of the two islands in the middle of the Seine, where Paris's first inhabitants settled around 250 BC. Notre-Dame has been a place of worship for more than 2,000 years; the present building is the fourth on this site. It was begun in 1163, making it one of the earliest Gothic cathedrals, although it was not finished until 1345. The facade seems perfectly proportioned until you notice that the north (left) tower is wider than the south. The interior is at its lightest and least cluttered in the early morning. Bay-by-bay cleaning is gradually revealing the original honey color of the stone. Window space is limited and filled with shimmering stained glass; the circular rose windows in the transept are particularly delicate. The 387-step climb up the towers is worth the effort for a perfect view of the famous gargoyles and the heart of Paris. *Admission: 27 frs adults, 12 frs children. Towers open daily 10–5. Treasury (religious and vestmental relics) open 10–6, Sun. 2–6. Admission: 15 frs adults, 10 frs students, 3 frs children.*

The pretty garden to the right of the cathedral leads to a bridge that crosses to the city's second and smaller island, the **Ile St-Louis,** barely 550 meters (600 yards) long and an oasis of inner-city repose.

❷ The rue des Deux Ponts bisects the island. Head left over the Pont de la Tournelle. To your left is the **Tour d'Argent,** one of the city's most famous restaurants (*see* Dining, below).

❸ Continue along quai de la Tournelle past Notre-Dame, then turn left at rue St-Jacques. A hundred yards ahead, on the right, is the back end of the **Eglise St-Séverin,** an elegant and unusually wide 16th-century church. Note the spiraling column among the forest of pillars behind the altar.

❹ Turn left out of the church, cross the bustling boulevard St-Germain, and take rue de Cluny to the left. This leads to the **Hôtel de Cluny.** Don't be misled by the name. This is a museum devoted to the late Middle Ages and Renaissance. Look for the *Lady with the Unicorn* tapestries and the beautifully displayed medieval statues. *6 pl. Paul-Painlevé. Admission: 15 frs. Open Wed.–Mon. 9:45–12:30 and 2– 5:15.*

❺ Head up rue de la Sorbonne to the **Sorbonne,** Paris's ancient university. Students here used to listen to lectures in Latin,

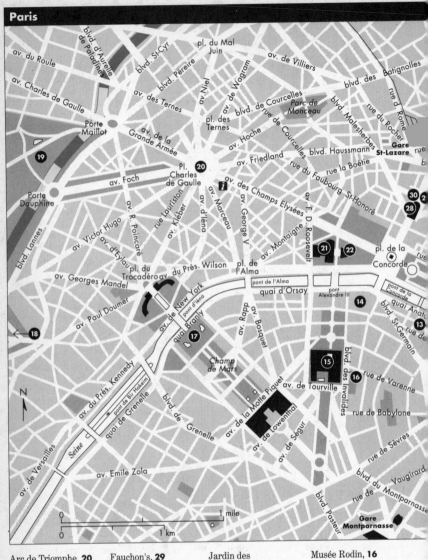

which explains why the surrounding area is known as the *Quartier Latin* (Latin Quarter). The Sorbonne is the oldest university in Paris—indeed, one of the oldest in Europe—and has for centuries been one of France's principal institutions of higher learning.

❻ Walking up rue Victor-Cousin and turning left into rue Cujas, you come to the **Panthéon.** Its huge dome and elegant colonnade are reminiscent of St. Paul's in London but date from a century later (1758–89). The Panthéon was intended to be a church, but during the Revolution it was swiftly earmarked as a secular hall of fame. Its crypt contains the remains of such national heroes as Voltaire, Rousseau, and Zola. The interior is empty and austere, with principal interest centering on Puvis de Chavanne's late 19th-century frescoes, relating the life of Geneviève, patron saint of Paris. *Admission: 23 frs adults, 12 frs senior citizens, 5 frs children. Open daily 10–noon and 2–5.*

Behind the Panthéon is **St-Etienne du Mont,** a church with two claims to fame: its ornate facade and its curly Renaissance rood-screen (1521–35) separating nave and chancel—the only one of its kind in Paris. Don't forget to check out the fine 17th-century glass in the cloister at the back of the church.

❼ Take the adjoining rue Clovis, turn right into rue Descartes, then left at the lively place de la Contrescarpe down rue Rollin. Cross rue Monge to rue de Navarre. On the left is the **Arènes de Lutèce** (always open during daylight hours, admission free), a Gallo-Roman arena rediscovered only in 1869; it has since been landscaped and excavated to reveal parts of the original amphitheater, and counts as one of the least-known points of interest in Paris.

❽ Rue de Navarre and rue Lacépède lead to the **Jardin des Plantes** (Botanical Gardens), which have been on this site since the 17th century. The gardens have what is reputedly the oldest tree in Paris, a robinia planted in 1636 (allée Becquerel), plus a zoo, alpine garden, hothouses, aquarium, and maze. Natural science enthusiasts will be in their element at the various museums, devoted to insects (Musée Entomologique), fossils and prehistoric animals (Musée Paléontologique), and minerals (Musée Minéralogique). *Admission: 12–18 frs. Museums open Wed.–Mon. 2–5.*

Head back up Rue Lacépède from the Jardin des Plantes. Turn left into rue Gracieuse, then right into rue Ortolan, which soon crosses the rue Mouffetard—site of a colorful market and many restaurants. Continue along rue du Pot-de-Fer and rue Rataud. At rue Claude-Bernard, turn right; then make your first left up rue St-Jacques.

❾ Set slightly back from the street is the **Val de Grâce,** a domed church designed by the great architect Jules Hardouin-Mansart and erected in 1645–67 (after the Sorbonne church but before the Invalides). Its two-tiered facade, with capitals and triangular pedestals, is directly inspired by the Counter-Reformation Jesuit architectural style found more often in Rome than in Paris. The Baroque style of the interior is epitomized by the huge twisted columns of the baldachin (ornamental canopy) over the altar.

Time Out If you're feeling thirsty (and rich), continue to the **Closerie des Lilas** along nearby boulevard de Port-Royal. This celebrated brasserie retains more style than some of its cousins farther down the once bohemian, now unexciting, boulevard du Montparnasse, whose modern landmark, the 203-meter (656-foot) Tour Montparnasse, is visible in the distance. *171 blvd. du Montparnasse, tel. 43–26–70–50. Reservations advised for meals. AE, DC, V.*

From the crossroads by the Closerie des Lilas, there is an enticing view down the tree-lined avenue de l'Observatoire toward the **Palais du Luxembourg.** The palace was built by Queen Maria de' Medici at the beginning of the 17th century in answer to Florence's Pitti Palace. It now houses the French Senate and is not open to the public. In the surrounding gardens, mothers push their baby carriages along tree-lined paths among the majestic fountains and statues.

Head through the gardens to the left of the palace into rue de Vaugirard. Turn left, then right into rue Madame, which leads down to the enormous 17th-century church of **St-Sulpice.** Stand back and admire the impressive, though unfinished, 18th-century facade, with its unequal towers. The interior is overwhelmingly impersonal, but the wall paintings by Delacroix, in the first chapel on the right, are worth a visit.

Rue Bonaparte descends to boulevard St-Germain. You can hardly miss the sturdy pointed tower of **St-Germain-des-Prés,** the oldest church in Paris (begun around 1160, though the towers date to the 11th century). Note the colorful nave frescoes by the 19th-century artist Hippolyte Flandrin, a pupil of Ingres.

Time Out The spirit of writers Jean-Paul Sartre and Simone de Beauvoir still haunts the **Café de Flore** opposite the church, though this, and the neighboring **Aux Deux Magots,** have more tourists than literary luminaries these days. Still, you can linger over a drink while watching what seems to be all of Paris walking by. *Blvd. St-Germain. No credit cards.*

Rue de l'Abbaye runs along behind St-Germain-des-Prés to place Fürstemberg, a charming little square where fiery Romantic artist Eugène Delacroix (1798–1863) had his studio. If you go there on a summer evening, you'll sometimes find young Frenchmen singing love songs to guitar accompaniment. Turn left into rue Jacob and continue along rue de l'Université. You are now in the heart of the Carré Rive Gauche, the Left Bank's district of art dealers and galleries.

About a quarter of a mile along rue de l'Université, turn down rue de Poitiers. Ahead is the sandstone bulk of the **Musée d'Orsay.** Follow it around to the left to reach the main entrance. The new Musée d'Orsay—opened in late 1986—is already one of Paris's star tourist attractions, thanks to its imaginatively housed collections of the arts (mainly French) spanning the period 1848–1914. Exhibits take up three floors, but the visitor's immediate impression is one of a single, vast hall. This is not surprising: The museum was originally built in 1900 as a train station. The combination of hall and glass roof with narrow, clanky passages and intimate lighting lends Orsay a human, pleasantly chaotic feel. You may get lost inside, but you won't mind too much.

The chief artistic attraction, of course, is the Impressionist collection, transferred from the inadequate Jeu de Paume museum across the river. Other highlights include Art Nouveau furniture, a faithfully restored Belle Epoque restaurant (formerly part of the station hotel), and a model of the Opéra quarter beneath a glass floor. *62 rue de Lille, tel. 40–49–48–14. Admission: 23 frs, 12 frs Sun. Open Tues., Wed., Fri., Sat. 10–5:30; Thurs. 10–9:15; Sun. 9–5:30.*

If the lines outside the Musée d'Orsay prove daunting, take a peek into the **Légion d'Honneur** museum across the way, a stylish mansion with a collection of French and foreign medals and decorations. *Admission: 10 frs. Open Tues.–Sun. 2–5.*

⑭ Farther along on rue de l'Université is the 18th-century **Palais Bourbon,** home of the French National Legislature (Assemblée Nationale). The colonnaded facade commissioned by Napoleon is a sparkling sight after a recent cleaning program (jeopardized at one stage by political squabbles as to whether cleaning should begin from the left or the right). There is a fine view from the steps across to place de la Concorde and the Madeleine.

Follow the Seine down to the exuberant **Pont Alexandre III.** The Grand and Petit Palais are to your right, across the river. To the **⑮** left, the silhouette of **L'Hôtel des Invalides** soars above expansive if hardly manicured lawns. The Invalides was founded by Louis XIV in 1674 to house wounded (or "invalid") war veterans. Although only a few old soldiers live here today, the military link remains in the form of the **Musée de l'Armée**—a vast collection of arms, armor, uniforms, banners, and pictures. The **Musée des Plans-Reliefs** contains a fascinating collection of scale models of French towns made by the military architect Vauban in the 17th century.

The museums are far from being the only reason for visiting the Invalides. It is an outstanding Baroque ensemble, designed by Bruand and Mansart, and its church possesses the city's most elegant dome as well as the tomb of Napoleon, whose remains are housed in a series of no less than six coffins within a tomb of red porphyry. A *son-et-lumière* (sound and light) performance in English is held in the main courtyard on evenings throughout the summer (Admission: 30 frs). *Admission to museums and church: 25 frs adults, 13 frs children. Open daily 10–6 (10–5 in winter).*

⑯ Alongside is the **Musée Rodin.** Together with the Picasso Museum in the Marais, this is the most charming of Paris's individual museums, consisting of an old house (built 1728) with a pretty garden, both filled with the vigorous sculptures of Auguste Rodin (1840–1917). The garden also has hundreds of rosebushes, with dozens of different varieties. *77 rue de Varenne. Admission: 20 frs, 10 frs Sun. Open Tues.–Sun. 10–5.*

Take avenue de Tourville to avenue de La Motte-Picquet. Turn left, and in a few minutes you will come face-to-face with the **⑰** **Eiffel Tower.** It was built by Gustave Eiffel for the World Exhibition of 1889. Recent restorations haven't made the elevators any faster—long lines are inevitable—but decent shops and two good restaurants have been added. Consider coming in the evening, when every girder is lit in glorious detail. Such was Eiffel's engineering precision that even in the fiercest winds the tower never sways more than 11½ centimeters (4½ inches). Today, of course, it is the best-known Parisian landmark. Standing beneath it, you may have trouble believing that it nearly became 7,000 tons of scrap-iron when its concession expired in 1909. Only its potential use as a radio antenna saved the day; it now bristles with a forest of radio and television transmitters. If you're full of energy, you can stride up the stairs as far as the tower's third floor, but only the elevator will take you right to the top. The view from 1,000 feet up will enable you to appreciate the city's layout and proportions. *Admission: on foot, 8 frs; elevator, 16–47 frs, depending on the level. Open July–Aug., daily 10 AM–midnight; Sept.–June, Sun.–Thurs. 10 AM–11 PM, Fri., Sat. 10 AM–midnight.*

West Paris and the Louvre
18 Our second itinerary starts at the **Musée Marmottan.** To get there, take the métro to La Muette, then head down chaussée de la Muette, through the small Ranelagh park to the corner of rue Boilly and avenue Raphaël. The museum is a sumptuous early 19th-century mansion, replete with many period furnishings, and probably is the most underestimated museum in Paris. It houses a magnificent collection of paintings by Claude Monet—including some of his huge, curving *Waterlily* canvasses—along with other Impressionist works and some delicately illustrated medieval manuscripts. *2 rue Louis-Boilly. Admission: 25 frs adults, 10 frs children and senior citizens. Open Tues.–Sun. 10–5:30.*

19 Continue along rue Boilly and turn left on boulevard Suchet. The next right takes you into the **Bois de Boulogne.** Class and style have been associated with "Le Bois" (The Woods) ever since it was landscaped into an upper-class playground by Haussmann in the 1850s. The attractions of this sprawling 891-hectare (2,200-acre) wood include cafés, restaurants, gardens, waterfalls, and lakes. You could happily spend a day or two exploring, but for the moment we suggest that you pass Auteuil racetrack on the left and then walk to the right of the two lakes. An inexpensive ferry crosses frequently to an idyllic island. Rowboats can be rented at the far end of the lake. Just past the boathouse, turn right on the route de Suresnes and follow it to Porte Dauphine, a large traffic circle.

20 Cross over to avenue Foch, with the unmistakable silhouette of the Arc de Triomphe in the distance. Keep an eye out for the original Art Nouveau iron-and-glass entrance to Porte Dauphine métro station, on the left. Then continue along avenue Foch, the widest and grandest boulevard in Paris, to the **Arc de Triomphe.** This 51-meter (164-foot) arch was planned by Napoleon to celebrate his military successes. Yet when Empress Marie-Louise entered Paris in 1810, it was barely off the ground and an arch of painted canvas had to be strung up to save appearances. Napoleon had been dead for more than 20 years when the Arc de Triomphe was finally finished in 1836. In 1988–89 it underwent a thorough face-lift to ward off signs of decay.

Place Charles de Gaulle, referred to by Parisians as **L'Etoile** (The Star), is one of Europe's most chaotic traffic circles. Short of a death-defying dash, your only way to get over to the Arc de Triomphe is to take the pedestrian underpass from either the Champs-Elysées (to your right as you arrive from avenue Foch) or avenue de la Grande Armée (to the left). France's Unknown Soldier is buried beneath the archway; the flame is rekindled every evening at 6:30.

From the top of the Arc you can see the "star" effect of Etoile's 12 radiating avenues and admire two special vistas: one, down

the Champs-Elysées toward place de la Concorde and the Louvre, and the other, down avenue de la Grande-Armée toward
La Tête Défense, a severe modern arch surrounded by imposing glass and concrete towers. Halfway up the Arc there is a
small museum devoted to its history. *Museum and platform.*
Admission: 27 frs adults, 15 frs senior citizens, 5 frs children.
Open daily 10–5 (4:30 in winter).

The Champs-Elysées is the site of colorful national ceremonies
on July 14 and November 11; its trees are often decked out with
French tricolors and foreign flags to mark visits from heads of
state. It is also where the cosmopolitan pulse of Paris beats
strongest. The gracefully sloping 2-kilometer (1¼-mile) boulevard was originally laid out in the 1660s by André Le Nôtre as a
garden sweeping away from the Tuileries. There is not much
sign of that as you stroll past the cafés, restaurants, airline offices, car showrooms, movie theaters, and chic arcades that oc-
㉑ cupy its upper half. Farther down, on the right, is the **Grand
Palais,** which plays host to Paris's major art exhibitions. Its
glass roof makes its interior remarkably bright. *Admission
varies. Usually open 10:30–6:30.*

The Grand Palais also houses the **Palais de la Découverte,** with
scientific and mechanical exhibits and a planetarium. Entrance
is in the avenue Franklin-Roosevelt. *Admission: 20 frs adults,
10 frs students; additional 13 frs (9 frs students) for planetarium. Open Tues.–Sun. 10–6.*

Directly opposite the main entrance to the Grand Palais is the
㉒ **Petit Palais,** built at the same time (1900) and now home to an
attractively presented collection of French paintings and furniture from the 18th and 19th centuries. *Admission: 12 frs
adults, 6 frs students. Open Tues.–Sun. 10–5:40.*

The flowerbeds, chestnut trees, and sandy sidewalks of the
lower section of the Champs-Elysées are reminders of its original leafy elegance. Continue down to place de la Concorde, built
around 1775 and scene of more than a thousand deaths at the
guillotine, including those of Louis XVI and Marie-Antoinette.
The obelisk, a gift from the viceroy of Egypt, was erected in
1833.

㉓ To the east of the place de la Concorde is the **Jardin des Tuileries:** formal gardens with trees, ponds, and statues. Standing
guard on either side are the **Jeu de Paume**—former home of an
Impressionist collection and now planned to house temporary
exhibitions—and the **Orangerie,** recently restored to contain
some early 20th-century French works by Monet, Renoir, Marie Laurencin, and others. *Admission: 23 frs, 12 frs Sun. Open
Wed.–Mon. 9:45–5.*

Pass through the Tuileries to the Arc du Carrousel, a rather
small triumphal arch erected more quickly (1806–08) than its
big brother at the far end of the Champs-Elysées. Towering be-
㉔ fore you is the **Louvre,** with its glass pyramids. The Louvre,
originally a royal palace, is today the world's largest and most
famous museum. I. M. Pei's pyramids are the highlight of a major modernization program; in the course of their construction
the medieval foundations of the palace were unearthed and are
maintained and displayed as an integral part of the museum's
collection. The pyramids stand as the easternmost landmark of
a majestic vista stretching through the Arc du Carrousel, Tuileries, place de la Concorde, the Champs-Elysées, and the Arc

de Triomphe all the way to the giant arch of La Défense, 4 kilometers (2½ miles) west of the capital.

The Louvre was begun as a fortress in 1200 (the earliest parts still standing date from the 1540s) and completed under Napoleon III in the 1860s. The Louvre used to be even larger; a wing facing the Tuileries Gardens was razed by rampaging revolutionaries during the bloody Paris Commune of 1871.

Whatever the aesthetic merits of Pei's new-look Louvre, the museum has emerged less cramped and more rationally organized. Yet its sheer variety can seem intimidating. The main tourist attraction is Leonardo da Vinci's *Mona Lisa* (known in French as *La Joconde*), painted in 1503. The latest research, based on Leonardo's supposed homosexuality, would have us believe that the subject was actually a man! The *Mona Lisa* may disappoint you; it's smaller than most imagine, it's kept behind glass, and it's invariably encircled by a mob of tourists.

Turn your attention instead to some of the less-crowded rooms and galleries nearby, where Leonardo's fellow Italians are strongly represented: Fra Angelico, Giotto, Mantegna, Raphael, Titian, and Veronese. El Greco, Murillo, and Velázquez lead the Spanish; Van Eyck, Rembrandt, Frans Hals, Brueghel, Holbein, and Rubens underline the achievements of northern European art. English paintings are highlighted by works of Lawrence, Reynolds, Gainsborough, and Turner. Highlights of French painting include works by Poussin, Fragonard, Chardin, Boucher, and Watteau—together with David's *Coronation of Napoleon*, Géricault's *Raft of the Medusa*, and Delacroix's *Liberty Guiding the People*.

Famous statues include the soaring *Victory of Samothrace* (3rd century BC), the celebrated *Venus de Milo* (end of 2nd century BC), and the realistic Egyptian *Seated Scribe* (C. 2000 BC). Be sure to inspect the Gobelins tapestries, the Crown Jewels (including the 186-carat Regent diamond), and the 9th-century bronze statuette of Emperor Charlemagne. *Admission 27 frs adults, 14 frs students and Sun., under 18 free. Open Wed.–Mon. 9–6 (9–9:45 PM Mon. and Wed.).*

Montmartre If you start at the Anvers métro station and head up rue de Steinkerque, with its budget clothing shops, you will be greeted by the most familiar and spectacular view of the Sacré Coeur basilica atop the Butte Montmartre. The **Sacré-Coeur** was built in a bizarre, mock-Byzantine style between 1876 and 1910. It is no favorite with aesthetes, yet it has become a major Paris landmark. It was built as an act of national penitence after the disastrous Franco-Prussian War of 1870—a Catholic show of strength at a time when conflict between Church and State was at its most bitter.

The large, rather gloomy interior is short on stained glass but long on golden mosaics; *Christ in Glory*, above the altar, is the most impressive. The basilica's many cupolas are dominated by a dome and an 80-meter (260-foot) bell tower that contains the Savoyarde, one of the world's largest bells, cast in Annecy, Savoy, in 1895. The view from the dome is best on a clear day, when all the sights of Paris are spread out before you.

26 Around the corner is the **place du Tertre,** full of would-be painters and trendy, overpriced restaurants. The painters have been setting up their easels on the square for years; don't be talked into having your portrait done unless you really want to—in which case, check the price first.

Despite its eternal tourist appeal and ever-growing commercialization, Montmartre has not lost all its traditional bohemian color. Walk down rue Norvins and descend the bustling rue Lepic to place Blanche and one of the favorite haunts of Toulouse-Lautrec and other luminaries of the Belle Epoque—the **(27)** legendary **Moulin Rouge** cabaret.

Montmartre is some distance from the rest of the city's major attractions, so go left up boulevard de Clichy as far as **place Pigalle,** then take the métro to Madeleine.

Central Paris The **Eglise de la Madeleine,** with its array of uncompromising **(28)** columns, looks like a Greek temple. The only natural light inside comes from three shallow domes; the walls are richly but harmoniously decorated, with plenty of gold glinting through the dim interior. The church was designed in 1814 but not consecrated until 1842, after efforts to turn the site into a train station were defeated. The portico's majestic Corinthian colonnade supports a huge pediment with a sculptured frieze of the *Last Judgment.* From the top of the steps you can admire the vista down rue Royale across the Seine. Another vista leads up boulevard Malesherbes to the dome of **St-Augustin,** a mid-19th-century church notable for its innovative use of iron girders as structural support.

Place de la Madeleine is in the heart of Paris's prime shopping **(29) (30)** district: Jewelers line rue Royale; **Fauchon's** and **Hédiard's,** behind the Madeleine, are high-class delicatessens.

Continue down boulevard de la Madeleine and turn right into rue des Capucines. This nondescript street leads to rue de la **(31)** Paix. Immediately to the right is **place Vendôme.** This is one of the world's most opulent squares, a rhythmically proportioned example of 17th-century urban architecture that shines in all its golden-stoned splendor since being sandblasted several years ago. Other things shine here, too, in the windows of jewelry shops that are even more upscale (and discreet) than those **(32)** in rue Royale—fitting neighbors for the top-ranking **Ritz** hotel. The square's central column, topped by a statue of Napoleon, is made from the melted bronze of 1,200 cannons captured at the Battle of Austerlitz in 1805.

Time Out Rue de la Paix leads, logically enough, to the **Café de la Paix** on the corner of the place de l'Opéra. There are few grander cafés in Paris, and fewer places where you can perch with as good a tableau before you.

Dominating the northern side of the square is the imposing **(33)** **Opéra,** the first great work of the architect Charles Garnier, who in 1860 won the contract to build the opera house. He used elements of neoclassical architecture—bas reliefs on facades and columns—in an exaggerated combination that borders on parody. The lavishly upholstered auditorium, with its delightful ceiling painted by Marc Chagall in 1964, seems small—but this is because the stage is the largest in the world, accommodating up to 450 players. *Admission: 17 frs. Open daily 11–4:30.*

(34) Behind the Opéra are **les grands magasins,** Paris's most venerable department stores. The nearer of the two, the **Galeries Lafayette,** is the more outstanding because of its elegant turn-of-the-century glass dome. But **Printemps,** farther along boulevard Haussmann to the left, is better organized and has an excellent view from its rooftop cafeteria.

Take the métro at Chaussée d'Antin, near the Galeries Lafayette, and travel three stops (direction Villejuif) as far as
35 **Palais-Royal.** This former royal palace, built in the 1630s, has a charming garden, bordered by arcades and boutiques, that many visitors overlook.

36 On the square in front of the Palais-Royal is the **Louvre des Antiquaires,** a chic shopping mall full of antiques dealers. It deserves a browse whether you intend to buy or not. Afterward, head east along rue St-Honoré and left into rue du Louvre. Skirt the circular **Bourse du Commerce** (Commercial Ex-
37 change) and head toward the imposing church of **St-Eustache,** (1532–1637), an invaluable testimony to the stylistic transition between Gothic and Classical architecture. It is also the "cathe-
38 dral" of **Les Halles**—the site of the central market of Paris until the much-loved glass-and-iron sheds were torn down in the late '60s. The area has since been transformed into a trendy—and already slightly seedy—shopping complex, Le Forum.

Head across the topiary garden and left down rue Berger. Pass the square des Innocents, with its Renaissance fountain, to boulevard de Sébastopol. Straight ahead lies the futuristic,
39 funnel-topped **Centre Pompidou** (Pompidou Center)—a must for lovers of modern art. The Pompidou Centre, also known as the Beaubourg, was built in the mid-1970s and named in honor of former French president Georges Pompidou (1911–74). This "cultural Disneyland" is always crowded, housing a **Museum of Modern Art,** a huge library, experimental music and industrial design sections, a children's museum, and a variety of activities and exhibitions. Musicians, magicians, fire-eaters, and other street performers fill the large forecourt near the entrance. *Admission: Museum of Modern Art, 23 frs, free Sun.; 50 frs for daily pass covering all sectors of the center. Open Mon., Wed.–Fri. noon–10; weekends 10–10.*

Continue east to the **Marais,** one of the most historic quarters of Paris. The spacious affluence of its 17th-century mansions, many restored to former glory, contrasts with narrow winding streets full of shops and restaurants. Rue de Rambuteau leads from the Centre Pompidou into rue des Francs-Bourgeois. Turn left on rue Elzivir to rue Thorigny, where you will find
40 the Hôtel Salé and its **Musée Picasso.** This is a convincing experiment in modern museum layout, whether you like Picasso or not. Few of his major works are here, but many fine, little-known paintings, drawings, and engravings are on display. *5 rue Thorigny. Admission: 21 frs. Open Thurs–Mon. 9:15–5:15; Wed. 9:15 AM–10 PM.*

Double back down rue Elzivir and turn left along rue des
41 Francs-Bourgeois until you reach the **place des Vosges.** Built in 1605, this is the oldest square in Paris. The square's harmonious proportions, soft pink brick, and cloisterlike arcades give it an aura of calm. In the far corner is the **Maison de Victor Hugo,** containing souvenirs of the great poet's life and many of his surprisingly able paintings and ink drawings. *6 pl. des Vosges. Admission: 12 frs. Open Tues.–Sun. 10–5:40.*

Time Out The shops on nearby rue St-Antoine (*see* below) have all the makings for a first-class picnic, which you can have in the shade of the square inside place des Vosges.

Rue Birague leads from the middle of the place des Vosges down to rue St-Antoine. About 250 yards along to the left is the **place de la Bastille.** Unfortunately, there are no historic vestiges here; not even the soaring column, topped by the figure of Liberty, commemorates the famous storming of the Bastille in 1789 (the column stands in memory of Parisians killed in the uprisings of 1830 and 1848). Only the new **Opéra de la Bastille,** which opened in 1989, can be said to mark the bicentennial.

Retrace your steps down rue St-Antoine as far as the large Baroque church of **Saint-Paul-Saint-Louis** (1627–41). Then continue down the rue de Rivoli to the **Hôtel de Ville.** This magnificent city hall was rebuilt in its original Renaissance style after being burned down in 1871, during the violent days of the Paris Commune. The vast square in front of its many-statued facade is laid out with fountains and bronze lamps.

Avenue de Victoria leads to place du Châtelet. On the right is the **Tour St-Jacques.** This richly worked 52-meter (170-foot) stump is all that remains of a 16th-century church destroyed in 1802.

From Châtelet take the pont-au-Change over the Seine to the Ile de la Cité and the **Palais de Justice** (law courts). Visit the turreted **Conciergerie,** a former prison with a superb vaulted 14th-century hall (Salles des Gens d'Armes) that often hosts temporary exhibitions. The **Tour de l'Horloge** (clock tower) near the entrance on the quai de l'Horloge has a clock that has been ticking off time since 1370. Around the corner in the boulevard du Palais, through the imposing law court gates, is the **Sainte-Chapelle,** built by St-Louis (Louis IX) in the 1240s to house the Crown of Thorns he had just bought from Emperor Baldwin of Constantinople. The building's lead-covered wood spire, rebuilt in 1854, rises 77½ meters (250 feet). The somewhat garish lower chapel is less impressive than the upper one, whose walls consist of little else but dazzling 13th-century stained glass. *Conciergerie and Sainte-Chapelle. Admission: joint ticket 36 frs; single ticket 23 frs. Open daily 10–6; winter 10–5.*

From boulevard du Palais turn right on quai des Orfèvres. This will take you past the quaint place Dauphine to the **square du Vert Galant** at the westernmost tip of the Ile de la Cité. Here, above a peaceful garden, you will find a statue of the Vert Galant: gallant adventurer Henry IV, king from 1589 to 1610.

Shopping

Gift Ideas Paris is the home of fashion and perfume. Old prints are sold in *bouquinistes* (stalls) along the Left Bank of the Seine. For state-of-the-art home decorations, the shop in the **Musée des Arts Décoratifs** in the Louvre (107 rue de Rivoli) is well worth visiting.

Antiques Antiques dealers proliferate in the **Carré Rive Gauche** between St-Germain-des-Prés and the Musée d'Orsay. There are also several dealers around the Drouot auction house near Opéra (corner of rue Rossini and rue Drouot; métro: Richelieu-

Drouot). The **Louvre des Antiquaires,** near the Palais-Royal *(see* Exploring, above), and the **Village Suisse,** near the Champ de Mars (78 av. de Suffren), are stylish shopping malls dominated by antiques.

Boutiques Only Milan can compete with Paris for the title of Capital of European Chic. The top shops are along both sides of the Champs-Elysées and along the avenue Montaigne and the rue du Faubourg St-Honoré. If you're on a tight budget, search for bargains along the shoddy streets around the foot of Montmartre *(see* Exploring, above), or near **Barbès-Rochechouart** métro station. The streets to the north of the Marais, close to **Arts-et-Métiers** métro, are historically linked to the cloth trade, and many shops offer garments at wholesale prices.

Department Stores The most famous department stores in Paris are **Galeries Lafayette** and **Printemps,** on boulevard Haussmann. Others include **Au Bon Marché** near Sèvres-Babylone (métro on the Left Bank) and the **Samaritaine,** overlooking the Seine east of the Louvre (métro Pont-Neuf).

Food and Flea Markets The sprawling **Marché aux Puces de St-Ouen,** just north of Paris, is one of Europe's largest flea markets. Best bargains are to be had early in the morning (open Sat.–Mon.; métro Porte de Clignancourt). There are smaller flea markets at the Porte de Vanves and Porte de Montreuil (weekends only).

Dining

Eating out in Paris should be a pleasure, and there is no reason why choosing a less expensive restaurant should spoil the fun. After all, Parisians themselves eat out frequently and cannot afford five-star dining every night, either.

Mealtimes Dinner is the main meal and usually begins at 8. Lunch begins at 12:30 or 1.

Dress Jacket and tie are recommended for Very Expensive and Expensive restaurants, and at some of the more stylish Moderate restaurants as well. When in doubt, it's best to dress up. Otherwise casual dress is appropriate.

Precautions Tap water is perfectly safe, though not always very appetizing (least of all in Paris). Mineral water is a palatable alternative; there is a vast choice of *eau plate* (plain) as well as *eau gazeuse* (fizzy).

Ratings Prices are per person and include a first course, main course, and dessert plus taxes and service (which are always included in displayed prices), but not wine. Best bets are indicated by a star ★.

Category	Cost
Very Expensive	over 400 frs
Expensive	250–400 frs
Moderate	150–250 frs
Inexpensive	under 150 frs

Left Bank **Jules Verne.** The sensational view from this restaurant on the
Very Expensive third floor of the Eiffel Tower is a fitting accompaniment to the

subtle flavors of Alain Bariteau's cuisine. The elegant gray-and-black decor is at its best at night, but prices are most accessible on a weekday at lunch, when there is a good fixed-price menu. *Eiffel Tower, 7e, tel. 45–55–61–44. Reservations required. AE, DC, MC, V.*

★ **Tour d'Argent.** Discretion is the key at this temple of French gastronomy, on the Left Bank opposite the Ile St-Louis. The restaurant's exterior is plain; inside, however, a plush elevator whisks you to the top and to a memorable view of Notre-Dame and the Ile de la Cité. Waiters materialize in anticipation of your slightest wish. Parisians are relieved that the food has maintained its high standards under new chef Manuel Martinez. There is a fixed-price lunch menu (365 frs) every day except Saturday and Sunday. *15 quai de la Tournelle, 5e, tel. 43–54–23–31. Reservations required. AE, DC, MC, V. Closed Mon.*

Expensive **Le Coupe-Chou.** Uneven floors, bare stone walls, and candlelit alcoves make this many-roomed restaurant, in a rickety old town house near the Panthéon, popular for its atmosphere. The service can seem desultory, but the competent cuisine and magical setting compensate. Coffee amid the cushions and flickering shadows of the after-dinner lounge makes a romantic end to the evening. *11 rue de Lanneau, 5e, tel. 43–54–36–54. Reservations advised. V. Closed Sun. lunch.*

Moderate **Petit Zinc.** This is a long-established haunt on the lively rue de Buci. Its imperturbable white-aproned waiters and unpretentious Belle Époque decor lend it an authentically Parisian atmosphere, especially on the bustling, green-walled first floor; the room upstairs is larger but more discreetly lit. The seafood is good here; *pintade* (guinea fowl) is recommended, and game and poultry are served in robust sauces. It is open until 3 AM. *25 rue de Buci, 6e, tel. 46–33–51–66. Reservations advised. AE, DC, MC, V.*

Suffren. Next to the Ecole Militaire at the far end of the Champ de Mars, is this archetypal brasserie: lively, good value, with oysters, fish, and other seafood in abundance. Foreigners are treated with a welcome lack of condescension. *84 av. de Suffren, 15e, tel. 45–66–97–86. Reservations accepted. V. Closed Mon.*

Vagenende. Dark wood, gleaming mirrors, and obsequious waiters take the Vagenende dangerously close to turn-of-the-century pastiche. It claims to be a bustling brasserie, but don't believe it: Service is far too unhurried and the dining room far too cozy. You can be sure of having a copious and enjoyable meal (foie gras, oysters, and chocolate-based desserts are outstanding), with a stroll outside along the cheerful boulevard St-Germain to walk it off. *142 blvd. St-Germain, 6e, tel. 43–26–68–18. Reservations advised. AE, DC, MC, V. Closed Feb. 1–8.*

West Paris **Maxim's.** Eating here is a once-in-a-lifetime experience for two
Very Expensive reasons: first, the plush velvet interior, with its curly riot of Art Nouveau furnishings; second, Maxim's international reputation for luxurious abandon. Unfortunately, the check—and not the cuisine—is the most lasting reminder of a dinner here, but that doesn't seem to bother most customers. *3 rue Royale, 8e, tel. 42–65–27–94. Reservations required. AE, DC, MC, V. Closed Sun. in July, Aug.*

★ **Robuchon.** Virtuoso chef Joël Robuchon is a cult figure in epicurean circles and a worthy successor to the great Jamin, previous owner of this elegant restaurant near the Trocadero. To get a table here—there are only 45 seats—you need to make a reservation well in advance, but it is worth it: The menu changes constantly as Robuchon concocts new works of edible art. *32 rue de Longchamp, 16e, tel. 47–27–12–27. Reservations required. MC, V. Closed Sat., Sun., July.*

Expensive **Chez Edgard.** Some come here for the reliable French cuisine, accompanied by a fine wine list. But most are eavesdroppers, picking up the crumbs from the whispered conversations of senior politicians and journalists amid the discreet warmth of the restaurant's deep red decor. It is a place to watch Paris power brokers in action—with a handy address close to the Champs-Elysées. *4 rue Marbeuf, 8e, tel. 47–20–51–15. Reservations advised. AE, DC, MC, V. Closed Sun.*

Inexpensive **Relais de la Sabretèche.** It's worth traveling deep into the residential 16th arrondissement, near the Porte de St-Cloud, for a restaurant that offers both unbeatable value and appealing, country-house decor. Consider the four-course set menu (served lunchtime and at dinner until 9 PM) for about 100 frs. For a similar sum, you can wash the meal down with a St-Estèphe or Châteauneuf-du-Pape (ask for a bottle from the cellar or it will be too warm). The service is discreet to the point of forgetfulness. *183 blvd. Murat, 16e, tel. 46–47–91–39. Reservations advised. V. Closed Sun. dinner, Mon.*

Montmartre and Central Paris *Expensive* **Coconnas.** The irresistible combination of summer dining beneath the 16th-century arcades of the place des Vosges and traditional, high-quality food based on duck, steak, and chicken have rapidly made the Coconnas a hit with tourists and Parisians alike. The inside dining room is tastefully decked out with old prints and sturdy wooden furniture. *2 bis pl. des Vosges, 4e, tel. 42–78–58–16. Reservations advised. MC, V. Closed Mon., Tues., mid-Dec.–mid-Jan. Moderate.*

Escargot Montorgueil. Traditional French favorites—such as snails, of course—help the Escargot Montorgueil maintain its reputation as one of the most reliable restaurants in Les Halles. The extravagant turn-of-the-century decor, with mirrors and traditional wall sofas, recalls the time before this area underwent its dramatic face-lift. *38 rue Montorgueil, 1er, tel. 42–36–83–51. Reservations advised. AE, DC, MC, V. Closed Mon. and most of Aug.*

Moderate ★ **Brasserie Flo.** Flo is an authentic, bustling brasserie that effortlessly recaptures the spirit of 1900. Sausages and sauerkraut are served with large glasses of Alsatian beer. The atmosphere gets livelier (some would say noisier) throughout the evening. Closing time is 1:30 AM. *7 cour des Petites-Ecuries, 10e, tel. 47–70–13–59. Reservations advised. AE, DC, V.*

Clodenis. A small, elegant restaurant down the slope from the Sacré Coeur, Clodenis serves excellent fish dishes and has some fixed-price menus for less than 200 frs. The decor—soft lighting, small tables, and beige wallpaper—is easy on the eye. *57 rue Caulaincourt, 18e, tel. 46–06–20–26. Reservations advised. AE, DC, MC, V. Closed Sun., Mon.*

Inexpensive **Chartier.** This is the down-to-earth Belle Epoque cousin of the Vagenende (*see* Left Bank). Again, there are mirrors and fancy lamps, but here you'll be rushed and crowded; the waiter's white apron will be stained; and your check will be written on the tablecloth. This is the gastronomic equivalent of roughing it, but as this is Paris, you can have steak, fries, and a glass of wine for almost the same price as the burger meal at the fast-food places nearby. The good food belies the price. *7 rue du Faubourg-Montmartre, 9e, tel. 47–70–86–29. No reservations. No credit cards. Closes 9:30 PM.*

Jo Goldenberg. The doyen of Jewish eating places in Paris, Jo Goldenberg is in the heart of that most Jewish district, the Marais. Its two-level restaurant, with modern paintings, is always good-natured and crowded. The food is solid and cheap and heavily influenced by Central Europe (ground beef and salami). This makes it a great place to dine on a winter evening, but a bit heavy going in summer. The Israeli and Eastern European wines are rarely available elsewhere in France. *7 rue Rosiers, 4e, tel. 48–87–20–16. Reservations advised. AE, DC, V.*

Lodging

Paris is popular throughout the year, so make reservations early. The cost of renovating many hotels for the 1989 bicentennial celebrations has been passed on to the consumer, so be prepared for higher prices.

Prices must, by law, be posted at the hotel entrance and should include taxes and service. Prices are always by room, not per person. Ask for a *grand lit* if you want a double bed. Breakfast is not always included in this price, but you are usually expected to have it and often are charged for it whether you have it or not. In smaller rural hotels, you may be expected to have your evening meal at the hotel, too.

The quality of rooms, particularly in older properties, can be uneven; if you don't like the room you're given, ask to see another. If you want a private bathroom, state your preference for *douche* (shower) or *baignoire (bath)*—the latter always costing more. Tourist offices in major train stations can reserve hotels for you, and so can tourist offices in most towns.

Hotels   Hotels are officially classified from one-star to four-star-deluxe. France has—but is not dominated by—big hotel chains: Examples in the upper price bracket include Frantel, Holiday Inn, Novotel, and Sofitel. The Ibis and Climat de France chains are more moderately priced. Chain hotels, as a rule, lack atmosphere, with the following exceptions:

Logis de France. This is a group of small, inexpensive hotels that can be relied on for comfort, character, and regional cuisine. Look for its distinctive yellow and green sign. The Logis de France paperback guide is widely available in bookshops (cost: around 50 frs) or from Logis de France (83 av. d'Italie, 75013 Paris).

France-Accueil is another chain of friendly low-cost hotels. You can get a free booklet from France-Accueil (85 rue Dessous-des-Berges, 75013 Paris).

Relais et Châteaux. You can stay in style at any of the 150 members of this prestigious chain of converted châteaux and manor houses. Each hotel is distinctively furnished, provides top cuisine, and often stands in spacious grounds. A booklet listing members is available in bookshops or from Relais et Châteaux (9 av. Marceau, 75016 Paris).

Rentals *Gîtes Ruraux* offers families or small groups the opportunity for an economical stay in furnished cottage, chalet, or apartment. These can be rented by the week or month. Contact either the **Fédération Nationale des Gîtes de France**, 35 rue Godot de Mauroy, 75009 Paris (indicate the region that interests you), or the French Government Tourist Office in New York or London (*see* Before You Go in Chapter 1, Essential Information).

Bed-and-Breakfasts These are known in France as *chambers d'hôte* and are increasingly popular in rural areas. Check local tourist offices for details.

Youth Hostels With inexpensive hotel accommodations in France so easy to find, you may want to think twice before staying in a youth hostel—especially as standards of French hostels don't quite approximate those in neighboring countries. Contact **Fédération Unie des Auberges de Jeunesse** (10 rue Notre-Dame de Lorette, 75009 Paris).

Rating Prices are for double rooms and include all taxes. Best bets are indicated by a star ★.

Category	Cost
Very Expensive	over 850 frs
Expensive	450–850 frs
Moderate	250–450 frs
Inexpensive	under 250 frs

Left Bank and Ile St-Louis
Very Expensive

Lutétia. Situated across the square from the Bon Marché department store, the Lutétia maintains its excellent reputation for old-fashioned service. The building was renovated from top to bottom only a few years ago, under the eagle eye of top fashion designer Sonia Rykiel. The facade shines again, and the elegant interiors are full of Art Deco touches. *45 blvd. Raspail, 6e, tel. 45–44–38–10. 300 rooms with bath. AE, DC, MC, V.*

Expensive
★

Hôtel d'Angleterre. Some claim the Hôtel d'Angleterre is the ultimate Left Bank hotel: a little shabby, but elegant, small, and perfectly managed. The 18th-century building was originally the British ambassador's residence; later, Ernest Hemingway made it his Paris home. Room sizes and rates vary greatly, and all rooms are individually decorated. Some are imposingly formal, others are homey and plain. Ask for one overlooking the courtyard. There's no restaurant, but a small bar has been installed. *44 rue Jacob, 6e, tel. 42–60–34–72. 30 rooms with bath. Facilities: bar. AE, DC, MC, V.*

Marronniers. There are few better places in Paris for great value and great atmosphere. Located on appealing rue Jacob, the hotel is reached through a small courtyard. All the rooms are light and full of character. Those on the top floor have sloping ceilings, uneven floors, and terrific views over the church of St-Germain-des-Prés. The vaulted cellars have been converted into two atmospheric lounges. *21 rue Jacob, 6e, tel. 43–25–30–60. 37 rooms with bath or shower. Facilities: bar. No credit cards.*

St-Louis. This is another of the Ile-St-Louis's elegantly converted 17th-century town houses, and antique furniture and oil paintings decorate the public areas. The bedrooms are elegantly simple, with exposed beams and stone walls. Blue-gray or light brown tiles add a classy accent to the bathrooms. Breakfast is served in the ancient cellar, but there's no restaurant or bar. *75 rue St-Louis-en-l'Isle, 4e, tel. 46–34–04–80. 21 rooms with bath. No credit cards.*

Moderate **Esméralda.** You'll find this delightful 17th-century inn just across the river Seine from Notre-Dame. The rooms are small but full of character: Don't be afraid to ask for one with a view of the cathedral. There are also three inexpensive singles in the eaves. *4 rue St-Julien-le-Pauvre, 5e, tel. 43–54–19–20. 19 rooms, with bath or shower. Facilities: sauna. No credit cards.*

Inexpensive **Vieux Paris.** Low rates and a handy location on a side street leading to the Seine make the Vieux Paris a winner. The hotel is tiny and is set in a late 15th-century building. You won't find great comfort in the rooms—some of them are *very* small—but the combination of age and slightly musty French charm is hard to resist. *9 rue Gît-le-Coeur, 6e, tel. 43–54–41–66. 21 rooms, 11 with bath. MC, V.*

West Paris **Le Bristol.** Luxury and discretion are the Bristol's trump
Very Expensive cards. The understated facade on rue du Faubourg St-Honoré
★ might mislead the uninformed, but the Bristol ranks among Paris's top four hotels. The spaciously elegant and air-conditioned rooms all have authentic (or good imitation) Louis XV and Louis XVI furniture. Moreover, the management has filled the public room with paintings, sculptures, sumptuous carpets, and tapestries. The marble bathrooms are magnificent. Nonguests can have tea in the vast garden or dine in the summer restaurant; the piano bar is open till 1 AM. For hotel guests, there's a pool on the roof, complete with solarium and sauna. Service throughout is impeccable. *112 rue du Faubourg St-Honoré, 8e, tel. 42–66–91–45. 155 rooms and 45 suites with bath. Facilities: 2 restaurants, bar, pool, sauna, solarium, parking, conference facilities for 400. AE, DC, MC, V.*

Crillon. There can surely be no more sumptuous hotel than this regal mansion overlooking place de la Concorde. The Crillon was founded in 1909 by the Champagne family Taittinger, with the express intention of creating the best hotel in the city. They chose as their setting two adjoining town houses built by order of Louis XV. Renovations in the '80s have seen great additional comforts—all rooms are air-conditioned—though not at the expense of the original imposing interior. Mirrors, marble, tapestries, sculptures, great sprays of flowers, and glistening floors are found in all the public rooms. The expansive bedrooms have a judicious mixture of original and reproduction antiques and are hung with beige velvet. The bathrooms, of course, are marble. Of the three restaurants, the best is Les Ambassadeurs, offering some of the best hotel food in the city. *10 place de la Concorde, 8e, tel. 42–65–24–24. 189 rooms and suites with bath. Facilities: 3 restaurants, bars, private reception rooms. AE, DC, MC, V.*

George V. Some say that the George V lacks the style of its super deluxe Parisian counterparts. Others value its unashamedly international atmosphere. There's no lack of authentic period furniture or of highly trained staff. All the rooms are imposing, though the penthouse suites are the only ones to enjoy a commanding view over the city. There are a number of restaurants, the best of which is Les Princes; in summer, you can eat on the leafy patio. *31 av. George V, 8e, tel. 47–23–54–00. 292 rooms and 42 suites with bath. Facilities: 3 restaurants, bars,* shopping mall, hairdresser, conference facilities. AE, DC, MC, V.

Expensive   **Bradford.** The Bradford prides itself on providing slightly old-fashioned, well-polished service in a homey atmosphere, the kind that has guests coming back year after year. An old wooden elevator takes you from the flower-filled lobby up to the rooms. Some are vast, with brass beds and imposing fireplaces. None have TV; that's not the Bradford style. Drinks are served in the soothing Louis XVI-style lounge on the first floor; there's no restaurant. *10 rue St-Philippe-du-Roule, 8e, tel. 43-59-24-20. 46 rooms with bath or shower. MC, V.*

Moderate   **Queen's Hotel.** Queen's is one of only a handful of hotels located in the desirable residential district around rue la Fontaine, within walking distance of the Seine and the Bois de Boulogne. The hotel is small and functional, but standards of comfort and service are high. Flowers on the facade add an appealing note. *4 rue Bastien-Lepage, 16e, tel. 42-88-89-85. 22 rooms with bath or shower. AE, MC, V.*

Montmartre and Central
Very Expensive

Grand. After the cleaning of the majestic, honey-colored facade, renovation at the Grand goes on—with the reception area and Second Empire dining room set to gleam afresh by 1992. All rooms at this 19th-century palace backing onto place de l'Opéra have been lavishly redecorated in Art Nouveau style and are air-conditioned. Of its three restaurants, the Opéra is the most formal and imposing, while the Relais Capucines offers less intimidatingly grand meals. Le Patio serves buffet lunches and breakfast. *2 rue Scribe, 9e, tel. 42-68-12-13. 515 rooms and suites with bath. Facilities: 3 restaurants, 2 bars, 13 conference rooms, secretarial services, travel agency, shops, parking. AE, DC, MC, V.*

Régina. The historic place des Pyramides is the location of this late 19th-century hotel. The building is somewhat old-fashioned and formal, but the rooms are spacious and the service is excellent—friendly but efficient. Ask for a room overlooking the Louvre and the Tuileries Gardens. *2 pl. des Pyramides, 1er, tel. 42-60-31-10. 130 rooms and 15 suites with bath. Facilities: restaurant, bar. AE, DC, MC, V. Restaurant usually closed in Aug.*

Ritz. The Paris Ritz is one of the world's most famous hotels, located on the most famous and elegant square in the city, place Vendôme. Millions of dollars have been lavished on the hotel by Egyptian-born owner Mohammed al-Fayed (the owner of Harrods in London). The building is a sumptuous 18th-century town house, a delightful combination of elegance and comfort. The luxurious suites are named after just some of the guests who have stayed here—Coco Chanel, Marcel Proust, and Edward VII among them. The restaurant L'Espadon maintains the luxurious note. *15 pl. Vendôme, 1er, tel. 42-60-38-30. 143 fully equipped rooms and 46 suites. Facilities: 2 restaurants, health and sports complex. AE, DC, MC, V.*

Expensive   **Bretonnerie.** You'll find this small, three-star hotel on a tiny street in the Marais, a couple of minutes' walk from the Beaubourg. The rooms are decorated in elegant Louis XIII-style but vary considerably in size. The largest is room No. 1, a duplex; others are definitely cramped. The bar and breakfast rooms in the vaulted cellar have been completely renovated, but there is no restaurant. *22 rue Ste-Croix-de-la-Bretonnerie,*

4e, tel. 48–87–77–63. 27 rooms with bath or shower. Facilities: bar. MC, V.

Moderate **Family.** A few minutes' walk from the Tuileries Gardens will get you to this small two-star hotel near the Madeleine. It was entirely renovated in 1988, but the rooms have kept their stylish '30s look. There's no restaurant, but breakfast and snacks can be served in your room. Service is exceptionally friendly. *35 rue Cambon, 1er, tel. 42–61–54–84. 24 rooms and 1 suite with bath. AE, MC, V.*

Place des Vosges. A loyal American clientele swears by this historic little hotel, located on a charming street just off the exquisite square of the same name. The grand entrance hall is decorated in Louis XIII style; some of the rooms, however, are little more than functional, and a number of the smaller ones fall into the inexpensive category. There's no restaurant, but there's a welcoming little breakfast room. *12 rue de Birague, 4e, tel. 42–72–60–46. 11 rooms with bath or shower. AE, DC, MC, V.*

Regyn's Montmartre. Despite small rooms (all recently renovated), this small, owner-run hotel in Montmartre's place des Abbesses is rapidly gaining an enviable reputation for simple but stylish accommodation. A predominantly young clientele and a correspondingly relaxed atmosphere have made the hotel very popular. Try for one of the rooms on the upper floors for great views over the city. *18 pl. des Abbesses, 18e, tel. 42–54–45–21. 22 rooms with bath or shower. DC, MC, V.*

The Arts

The monthly magazine *Passion* (in English) and the weekly magazines *Pariscope, L'Officiel des Spectacles,* and *7 à Paris* give detailed entertainment listings. The best place to buy tickets is at the place of performance. Otherwise, try hotels, travel agencies (try **Paris-Vision** at 214 rue de Rivoli), and special ticket counters (in the **FNAC** stores at 26 av. de Wagram, near the Arc de Triomphe and the Forum des Halles). Half-price tickets for same-day theater performances are available at the ticket stand at the west side of the Madeleine church.

Theater There is no Parisian equivalent to Broadway or the West End, although a number of theaters line the grand boulevards between Opéra and République. Shows are mostly in French; classical drama is at the distinguished **Comédie Française** (by Palais-Royal). A completely different charm is to be found in the tiny **Théâtre de la Huchette,** near St-Michel, where Ionesco's short modern plays make a deliberately ridiculous mess of the French language.

Concerts The principal venues for classical music are the **Salle Pleyel** (252 rue du Faubourg St-Honoré), near the Arc de Triomphe, and the new **Opéra de la Bastille**. You can also attend one of the many inexpensive organ or chamber music concerts in churches throughout the city.

Opera The **Opéra** itself is a splendid building, and, with Rudolf Nureyev as artistic director, its dance program has reached new heights. Getting a ticket for an opera or ballet performance is not easy, though, and requires either luck, much preplanning, or a well-connected hotel receptionist. The **Opéra Comique** (the French term for opera with spoken dialogue), close by in the rue Favart, is more accessible. The new **Opéra de la Bastille**

opened in 1989 and stages both traditional opera and symphony concerts.

Film There are hundreds of movie theaters in Paris and some of them, especially in principal tourist areas such as the Champs-Elysées and the boulevard des Italiens near Opéra, run English films marked "V.O." *(version originale*—i.e., not dubbed). Admission is around 35–40 frs, with reduced rates on Monday. Movie fanatics should check out the **Centre Pompidou** and **Musée de Cinéma** at Trocadéro, where old and rare films are often screened.

Nightlife

Cabaret This is what Paris is supposed to be all about. Its nightclubs are household names—more so abroad than in France, it would seem, judging by the hefty percentage of foreigners present at most shows. Prices range from 200 frs (basic admission plus one drink) up to 600 frs (dinner included). For 300–400 frs, you can get a good seat plus half a bottle of Champagne.

The **Crazy Horse** (12 av. George V, tel. 47–23–32–32) is one of the field leaders in pretty women and dance routines: It features lots of humor and a lot less clothes. The **Moulin Rouge** (place Blanche, tel. 46–06–00–19) is an old favorite at the foot of Montmartre. Nearby is the **Folies-Bergère,** (32 rue Richer, tel. 42–46–77–11), not as it once was but still renowned for its glitter and vocal numbers. The **Lido** (116 bis av. des Champs-Élysées, tel. 45–63–11–61) is all razzle-dazzle.

Bars and Nightclubs Upscale nightclubs are usually private, so unless you have a friend who is a member, forget it. A good bet, though, for drinking and dancing the night away, is the **Club 79** (79 av. des Champs-Elysées). For a more leisurely evening in an atmosphere that is part bar and part gentlemen's club, try an old haunt of Hemingway, Fitzgerald, and Gertrude Stein: **Harry's Bar** (5 rue Danou), a cozy wood-paneled spot for Americans, journalists, and sportsmen.

Jazz Clubs The Latin Quarter is a good place to track down Paris jazz, and the doyen of clubs is the **Caveau de la Huchette** (5 rue de la Huchette), where you can hear Dixieland in a hectic, smoke-filled atmosphere. **Le Slow Club** (130 rue de Rivoli), another favorite, tries to resurrect the style of early Bourbon street, and nearly succeeds.

Rock Clubs **Le Sunset** (60 rue des Lombards) is a small, whitewashed cellar with first-rate live music and a clientele that's there to listen. **New Morning** (7 rue des Petites Ecuries) is a top spot for visiting American musicians and good French bands.

Discos **Club Zed** (2 rue des Anglais off bd. St. Germain), is the best place for lively dancing. **Memphis** (3 impasse Bonne-Nouvelle) boasts some impressive lighting and video gadgetry.

18 Prague

Arriving and Departing

By Plane All international flights arrive at Prague's Ruzyně Airport, about 20 kilometers (12 miles) from downtown. For arrival and departure times, tel. 02/367814 or 02/367760.

Between the Airport and Downtown Czechoslovak Air Lines (ČSA) provides bus services linking the airport with Town Terminal Vltava (Revoluční 25). Buses depart every 20 minutes during the day, every half hour evenings and on weekends. The trip costs 6 Kčs. and takes about 30 minutes. A special shuttle service serves main hotels and costs 50 Kčs.; buy the ticket before boarding. The cheapest way to get into Prague is by regular bus No. 119; the cost is 2 Kčs., but you'll need to change to the subway at the Dejvícká station for the last leg of the trip. By taxi, expect to pay 200–250 Kčs.

By Train The main station for international and domestic routes is Hlavni nádraží (tel. 02/229252), ul. Vítězného unora, not far from Wenceslas Square.

By Bus The main bus station is Florenc (at Na Florenci, tel. 02/221445), not far from the train station.

Getting Around

Public transportation is a bargain. From special "blue ticket" machines you can buy a one-day ticket for 8 Kčs. and have unlimited use of all public transportation. Otherwise, tickets cost 1 Kčs. and should be obtained before boarding at newsstands, tobacco shops, various stores and hotels, or subway stations. Punch your ticket in the machine as you board.

By Subway Prague's three modern subway lines are easy to use and spotlessly clean. They provide the simplest and fastest means of transportation, and most new maps of Prague mark the routes.

By Tram/Bus You need to buy a new ticket every time you change vehicles. Express buses (marked with green badges) serve the suburbs and cost 4 Kčs.

By Taxi Taxis (tel. 02/202951 or 02/203941) are inexpensive but can be difficult to find other than in the center of town. The basic charge of 25 Kčs. is increased by 5 Kčs. per kilometer (surcharge at night). Rates are a little higher from the airport and some Interhotels.

Important Addresses and Numbers

Tourist Information Čedok (Na příkopě 18, tel. 02/212711) is very near Wenceslas Square. For its **Department of Accommodation Services,** go to Panská 5 (tel. 02/227004) just around the corner. Almost next door to Čedok is the **Prague Information Service** (Na příkopě 20, tel. 02/544444). Across the road, **Pragotur** (U Obecního domu 2, tel. 02/2317281), near the Powder Tower, provides a variety of services, including reservations in non-Čedok hotels and private accommodations.

Embassies U.S. (Tržiště 15, Malá Strana, tel. 02/536641). **Canadian** (Mickiewiczova 6, Hradčany, tel. 02/326941). **U.K.** (Thunovská 14, Malá Strana, tel. 02/533347).

Emergencies Police (tel. 158), **Ambulance** (tel. 155), **Doctor: Fakultní poliklinika** (Karlovo náměstí 32, tel. 02/299381). **24-Hour Pharmacy** (Na příkopě 7, near Wenceslas Sq., tel. 02/220081).

English Bookstores Many bookstores now carry English books. Try Vodičkova ulice 41 for a good selection. English-language newspapers are available in most hotels and on street stands in the city center.

Guided Tours

Čedok arranges a variety of tours in and around Prague; they can either be arranged before you leave or booked in Prague. Call 02/2318255 or 02/2316619 for any of the following:

Orientation Tours The "Historical Prague" tour, departing at 10 AM from Čedok (Bílkova 6) opposite the Hotel Inter-Continental, covers all the major sites, including Prague Castle, in three hours. During the summer there is also a nighttime tour that includes dinner and a visit to a wine tavern.

Special-Interest Tours The "U Fleku" brewery and beer-tasting tour departs on Friday mornings from Wenceslas Square 24 and lasts 1½ hours. For cultural tours, call Čedok (*see* above). These include performances of folklore, Laterna Magika (*see* The Arts, below), opera, and concerts. You can save money by buying tickets—if any are available—at box offices, but this will take time.

Excursions Čedok's one-day tours out of Prague cover principal historic and scenic sights and include lunch. The "Bohemian Paradise and Garnet Jewelry" tour should yield attractive buys as well as good scenery. The "Beauty Spots of South Bohemia" tour focuses on history and medieval architecture among woods and lakes. Other tours include visits to famous spa towns and castles.

Personal Guides Contact **Čedok** (Na příkopě 18, tel. 02/2127640) or the **Prague Information Service** (Na příkopě 20, tel. 02/544444).

Exploring Prague

Prague is one of the most enchanting cities in Europe. Like Rome, far to the southwest, Prague is built on seven hills, sprawling within the confines of a broad loop of the Vltava River. The riverside location, enhanced by a series of graceful bridges, makes a great setting for two of the city's most notable features: its extravagant, fairy-tale architecture and its memorable music. Mozart claimed that no one understood him better than the citizens of Prague, and he was only one of several great masters who lived or lingered here.

It was under Charles IV (Karel IV) during the 14th century that Prague briefly became the seat of the Holy Roman Empire—virtually the capital of Western Europe—and acquired its distinctive Gothic imprint. At times you'll need to look quite hard for this medieval inheritance; it's still here, though, under the overlays of graceful Renaissance and exuberant Baroque.

Prague escaped serious wartime damage, but it didn't escape neglect. Because of the long-term restoration program now under way, some part of the city is always under scaffolding. But what's completed—which is nearly all that's described in the following itineraries—is hard to find fault with as an example of sensitive and painstaking restoration.

Numbers in the margin correspond to points of interest on the Prague map.

The Nové Město and Staré Město

① ② ③

Václavské náměstí (Wenceslas Square) is the Times Square of Prague. Confusingly, it's not actually a square at all but a broad boulevard sloping down from the **Národní muzeum** (National Museum) and the equestrian **statue of Wenceslas.** The lower end is where all the action is. Na příkopě, once part of the moat surrounding the Old Town, is now an elegant pedestrian mall. Čedok's main office and Prague Information Service **④** are along here, on your way to the **Prašná brána** (Powder Tower), a 19th-century neo-Gothic replacement of the medieval original.

⑤

Turn into Celetná and you're on the old **Royal Route,** once followed by coronation processions past the foreboding Gothic **⑥** spires of the Týn Church through **Staroměstské náměstí** (Old **⑦** Town Square), down **Karlova,** across **Karlův most** (Charles Bridge), and up to the castle. Along this route, you can study every variety or combination of Romanesque, Gothic, Renaissance, and Baroque architecture. Two good examples are the town buildings at 12 Celetná and 8 Karlova. On Staroměstske náměstí, the crowds regularly gather below the famous **Clock Tower,** where, on the hour, the complex 16th-century mechanism activates a procession that includes the Twelve Apostles. Note the skeleton figure of Death that tolls the bell.

⑧

In the **Old Jewish Cemetery** in **Josefov** (Joseph's Town, the old Jewish quarter), ancient tombstones lean and jostle each other; below them, in a dozen layers, are 12,000 graves. As you stand by the tomb of the scholar Rabbi Low, who died in 1609, you may see, stuffed into the cracks, scraps of paper bearing prayers and requests. It's said that many Jews hid their valuables here before being transported to the concentration camps. Be sure to visit the tiny Gothic **Staronová synagóga** (Old-New Synagogue), which, along with the cemetery, forms part of the **⑨** **State Jewish Museum** (Státní Židovské muzeum). *Červená 101. Admission: 10 Kčs. Open Sun.–Fri. 9–4:30 (9–5 in summer); closed Sat. and religious holidays.*

When you stand on Charles Bridge, you'll see views of Prague that would still be familiar to the 14th-century architect Peter Parler and to the sculptors who added the 30 Baroque statues in the early 18th century (a few have been replaced). They're worth a closer look, especially the 12th on the left (St. Luitgarde, by Matthias Braun, circa 1710), and the 14th on the left (in which a Turk guards suffering saints, by F. M. Brokoff, circa 1714).

⑩

The **museum** devoted to Prague composer **Bedřich Smetana,** located nearby at Novotného lávka, is small, and its exhibits mainly documentary. But it's a lovely quiet oasis in which to listen to tapes of Smetana's music—and admire the views across the Vltava and up to the castle. *Novotného lávka. Admission: 7 Kčs. Open Wed.–Mon. 10–5.*

⑪

The **Betlémska kaple** (Bethlehem Chapel) has been completely reconstructed since Jan Hus thundered his humanitarian teachings from its pulpit in the early 15th century to congregations that could number 3,000. But the little door through which he came to the pulpit is original, as are some of the inscriptions on the wall. *Betlémské náměstí. Open daily 9–6.*

Prague

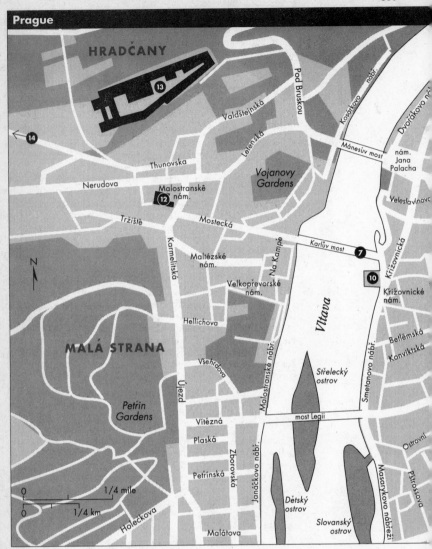

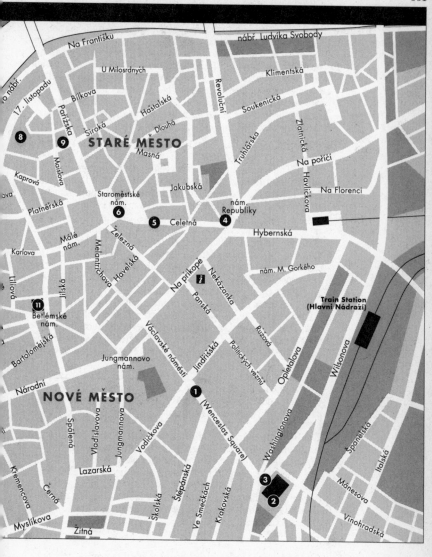

Malá Strana and Hradčany (Lesser Quarter and Castle)
⑫ Cross Charles Bridge and follow Mostecká up to Malostranské náměstí. After the turbulence of the Counter-Reformation at the end of the 16th century, Prague witnessed a great flowering of what became known as Bohemian Baroque. The architects (Dientzenhofer, father and son) of the **Chram svatého Mikuláše** (Church of St. Nicholas) were among its most skilled exponents. If you're in Prague when a concert is being given in this church, fight for a ticket. The lavish sculptures and frescoes of the interior make for a memorable setting. *Malostranské náměstí. Open daily 10–4 (9–6 in summer).*

⑬ The monumental complex of **Hradčany** (Prague Castle) has witnessed the changing fortunes of the city for more than 1,000 years. The scaffolding has only recently been removed from the latest restoration of the castle's **Cathedral of St. Vitus.** It took from 1344 to 1929 to build, so you can trace the whole gamut of styles from Romanesque to Art Nouveau. This is the final resting place for numerous Bohemian kings. Charles IV lies in the crypt. Good King Wenceslas has his own chapel in the south transept, studded with semiprecious stones. Knightly tournaments often accompanied coronation ceremonies in the castle, hence the broad **Riders' Staircase** leading up to the grandiose Vladislav Hall of the Third Courtyard. Oldest of all the buildings, though much restored, is the Romanesque complex of **St. George's Church and Monastery.** Behind a Baroque facade, it houses a superb collection of Bohemian art from medieval religious sculptures to decadent Baroque paintings. *Hradčanské náměstí. All museum buildings in the castle are open Tues.–Sun. 10–5. Admission to each: 10 Kčs.*

Time Out At the small, pleasant snack bar of U Ševce Matouše (At the Cobblers) on Loretánské náměstí, you can get your shoes repaired while you have refreshments.

⑭ The Baroque church and shrine of **Loreto** is named for the Italian town to which the Virgin Mary's House in Nazareth was supposedly transported by angels to save it from the infidel. The crowning glory of its fabulous treasury is the glittering monstrance of the *Sun of Prague*, set with 6,222 diamonds. Arrive on the hour to hear the 27-bell carillon. *Loreta 12. Admission: 10 Kčs. Open Tues.–Sun. 9–noon and 1–4:30.*

Shopping

Tuzex Stores Ask Čedok for the latest list of these hard-currency-only outlets and their specialties. One of the main ones, at Železná 18, sells imported goods, glass, and porcelain. The branch at Štěpánská 23 specializes in fashion and leather goods.

Specialty Shops Look for the name **Dilo** for objets d'art and prints; **ULUV** or **UVA** for folk art. At Na příkopě 12 you'll find excellent costume jewelry. **Moser** (Na příkopě 12) is the most famous for glass and porcelain.

Shopping Districts Many of the main shops are in and around Wenceslas Square (Václavské náměstí) and Na příkopě, as well as along Celetná and Pařížská.

Department Stores Three central stores are **Bilá Labut** (Na poříčí 23), **Družba** (Václavské nám. 21), and **Kotva** (nám. Republiky 8).

Dining

Independent travelers with prepaid meal vouchers (nonrefundable) are now able to use them at any Čedok hotel or restaurant in the city or region where they are staying. For meals not limited by vouchers, you can choose among restaurants, wine cellars *(vinárna)*, the more down-to-earth beer taverns *(pivnice)*, cafeterias, and a growing number of coffee shops and snack bars. Eating out is popular, and it's wise to make reservations whenever possible.

Prague ham makes a favorite first course, as does soup, which is less expensive. The most typical main dish is roast pork (or duck or goose) with sauerkraut and dumplings. Dumplings in various forms, generally with a rich gravy, accompany many dishes. Fresh green vegetables are rare, but there are plenty of the pickled variety.

Mealtimes Lunch is usually from 11:30 to 2 or 3; dinner from 6 to 9:30 or 10.

Dress In Prague, a jacket and tie are recommended for Very Expensive and Expensive restaurants, as well as for some of the stylish establishments in the Moderate category. Informal dress is appropriate elsewhere.

Ratings Prices are reasonable by American standards, even in the more expensive restaurants. Czechs dont's normally go in for three-course meals, and the following prices apply only if you're having a first course, main course, and dessert (excluding wine and tip). Best bets are indicated by a star ★.

Category	Cost
Very Expensive	over 150 Kčs.
Expensive	100–150 Kčs.
Moderate	50–100 Kčs.
Inexpensive	under 50 Kčs.

Very Expensive **U Malířů.** This is one of Prague's most picturesque wine taverns. Since being taken over by the French, "At the Painters" now offers an unusual mixture of Czech and French food at Western prices. *Maltézské náměstí 11, Malá Strana, tel. 02/531883. Reservations required. No credit cards. Closed Sun.*

★ **U Zlaté Hrušky.** Careful restoration has returned this restaurant to its original 18th-century style. It specializes in Moravian wines, which go down well with fillet steaks and goose liver. Some dishes are Moderate. *Nový Svět 3, Castle area, tel. 02/531133. Reservations required. No credit cards. Dinner only.*

Expensive **Klášterní Vinárna.** You'll find this wine restaurant in a former Ursuline convent in the city center. The emphasis is on Czech home cooking—try the house goulash. The menu includes some Moderate dishes. *Národní 8, tel. 02/290596. Reservations required. No credit cards. Closed Sun.*

★ **Opera Grill.** Though called a grill, this is one of the most stylish small restaurants in town, complete with antique Meissen candelabra and Czech specialties. *K. Světlé 35, Staré Město, tel. 02/*

265508. Reservations required. AE, DC, MC, V. Closed week-ends. Dinner only.

U Labutí. Located in tastefully remodeled stables in the castle area, "At the Swans" has a stylish—if slightly rich and heavy—menu (haunch of venison, goose liver with ham and almonds), which includes some Expensive dishes. The place is rich in atmosphere, too. *Hradčanské náměstí 11, tel. 02/536962. Reservations required. AE, DC, MC, V. Dinner only.*

★ **U Mecenáše.** This wine restaurant manages to be both medieval and elegant despite the presence of an ancient gallows! Try to get a table in the back room. Moussaka is one of the specialties from an international menu. *Malostranské náměstí 10, Malá Strana, tel. 02/533881. Reservations required. AE, DC, MC, V. Closed Sat. Dinner only.*

Moderate **U Lorety.** Sightseers will find this an agreeable spot—peaceful except for the welcoming carillon from neighboring Loreto Church. The service here is discreet but attentive, the tables are private, and the food is consistently excellent. Venison and steak are specialties. *Loretánské náměstí 8, near the Castle, tel. 02/536025. Reservations advised. AE, DC, MC, V. Closed Mon. (and Tues. in winter).*

U Pastýřky-Koliba. It's worth the trek from the center to enjoy the folk-style decor and specialty dishes of Slovakia here, complete with open fire for spit roasts. *Bělehradská 15, Prague 4, tel. 02/434093. Reservations required. No credit cards. Closed Sun. Dinner only.*

Vikárka. This was an eating house beside St. Vitus Cathedral as far back as the 16th century. It offers good-value local cooking in a historic setting. *Vikářská 6, in the Castle, tel. 02/535158. Reservations accepted. AE, DC, MC, V. Open only until 7:30. Closed Mon. in winter.*

Inexpensive **U Medvídků.** Enjoy South Bohemian and old Czech specialties here in a noisy but jolly atmosphere. Try the goulash with sliced bread dumplings. *Na Perštýně 7, Staré Město, tel. 02/2358904. Reservations not necessary. No credit cards. Closed Sun.*

U Pinkasů. The two great attractions here are the draught beer and the goulash—you can also add your signature to the wall with the countless others before you. *Jungmannovo náměstí 15 Staré Město, tel. 02/265770. Reservations not necessary. No credit cards.*

★ **U Sv. Tomáše.** Although it's touristy, this restored ancient tavern overflows with atmosphere. Try the famous dark ale and such good, down-to-earth fare as roast pork with cabbage and dumplings. *Letenská 12, Malá Strana, tel. 02/530064. Reservations advised. No credit cards. Closed Sun.*

U Zlatého Tygra. This is a favorite with not-so-young beer connoisseurs—a typical no-frills Prague pub. The pork fillet in potato pancake with sauerkraut salad makes a good foundation for the beer. *Husova 17, Staré Město, tel. 02/265219. Reservations not necessary. No credit cards. Closed Sun.*

Lodging

There's a choice of hotels, motels, limited private accommodations, and campsites. Many older properties are gradually being renovated, and the best have great character and style. There is still an acute shortage of rooms during the peak season, so make reservations well in advance. The standards of facilities and services hardly match those in the West, so don't be surprised by faulty plumbing or indifferent reception clerks. The prices at least compare favorably.

Hotels These are officially graded with from one to five stars. Prices include obligatory half-board, except for five-star hotels, where only breakfast is included. Most hotels used by foreign visitors—Interhotels—belong to Čedok and are mainly in the three- to five-star categories. These will have all or some rooms with bath or shower. Čedok can also handle reservations for some non-Čedok hotels, such as those run by Balnea (the spa treatment organization); CKM (the Youth Travel Bureau); and municipal organizations, some of which are excellent.

Hotel bills can be paid in crowns, though some hotels still try to insist on hard currency.

Private Accommodations The best private accommodation service is AVE in the main train station. They keep a list of over 2,000 rooms; the average cost is $25–$40 for a double. The office is open daily from 6 AM to 10:30 PM. Pragotur and Čedok also offer private room services.

Ratings Prices are for double rooms, generally not including breakfast. Prices at the lower end of the scale apply to low season. At certain periods, such as Easter or during festivals, there may be an increase of 15%–25%. Best bets are indicated by a star ★.

Category	Cost
Very Expensive	over $200
Expensive	$100–$200
Moderate	$50–$100
Inexpensive	under $50

Very Expensive
★ **Diplomat.** Completed in 1990 as part of a joint venture with an Austrian company, the Diplomat succeeds in fusing elegance with "Western" efficiency. The effect is marred only by an unfortunate location, outside of the center on the road to the airport. *Edvarda Beneše 15, tel. 02/3314111. 387 rooms with bath. Facilities: sauna, nightclub. AE, DC, MC, V.*

Esplanade (Interhotel). Facing a park near the National Museum, this is another favorite with Americans seeking a traditional atmosphere. An old town house, it was last renovated in 1980. The nightclub, Est Bar, has a good local reputation. *Washingtonova 19, tel. 02/226056. 65 rooms with bath. AE, DC, MC, V.*

★ **Palace Praha** (Interhotel). Beautifully renovated in art nouveau style, the newly reopened Palace is Prague's most elegant and luxurious hotel. Its central location just off Wenceslas Square makes this an excellent choice. *Panská 12, tel. 02/2359394. 125 rooms with bath. Facilities: saunas, health club, nightclub. AE, DC, MC, V.*

Expensive
Forum (Interhotel). Prague's latest high rise is near ancient Vyšehrad Castle, away from the city center. Prices include half-board. *Kongresová ul., tel. 02/410111. 531 rooms with bath. Facilities: saunas, pool, bowling alleys, miniature golf, gym, nightclub, roulette. AE, DC, MC, V.*

Jalta (Interhotel). The Jalta has a plum location on Wenceslas

Square. Despite its five-star status, it's on the shabby side but is comfortable nevertheless. *Václavské náměstí 45, tel. 02/ 265541. 90 rooms with bath. Facilities: 2 nightclubs. AE, DC, MC, V.*

★ **Paříž** (Interhotel). Although some of the rooms are small, this is a delightful hotel. Its turn-of-the-century Art Nouveau style was tastefully restored in 1985, while the hotel's Old Town location is ideal. The Paříž was reputedly a great favorite of Alexander Dubček. Rooms without bath are Moderate. *U Obecního domů 1, tel. 02/2322051. 86 rooms, 75 with bath. AE, DC, MC, V.*

Moderate **Ambassador** (Interhotel). This is another oldie from the turn of the century, renovated in 1983. It's right on Wenceslas Square. *Václavské náměstí 5, tel. 02/2143111. 170 rooms with bath. Facilities: disco. AE, DC, MC, V.*

International (Interhotel). Situated about 4.8 kilometers (3 miles) from the center, the International is known as the Russian Ritz for its 30-year-old architectural pretensions! High-season prices can edge this one up into the Expensive category. *Náměstí Družby 1, tel. 02/321051. 327 rooms with bath. Facilities: garden, miniature golf, nightclub. AE, DC, MC, V.*

Panorama (Interhotel). Out in the sticks in an ugly building, the Panorama has two saving graces: it is on a subway line and it has a top-floor swimming pool with a great view. *Milevská 7, tel. 02/416111. 432 rooms with bath. Facilities: saunas, pool, solarium, nightclub. AE, DC, MC, V.*

The Arts

Prague's cultural life is one of its top attractions and its citizens like to dress up for it, but performances are usually booked far ahead. You can get a monthly program of events from the Prague Information Service, Čedok, or many hotels. **Čedok** (Bílkova, tel. 02/2318255) is the main ticket agency for foreigners, but there's a wider choice through **Sluna** (Pasáž Černa Růže, off Na příkopě, tel. 02/265124).

Concerts Performances are held in the **National Gallery** in Prague Castle; the **National Museum;** the **Gardens** below the castle (where music comes with a view); the **Church of St. Nicholas** in Malá Strana; and **St. James's Church** on Malá Stupartská (Staré Město), where the organ plays amid a flourish of Baroque statuary.

Year-round concert halls include **Dvořák Hall** (the House of Artists, náměstí Jana Palacha), **Smetana Hall** (Obecní dum, Náměstí Republiky 5), and **Palác Kultury** (Kvetna 65).

Opera and Ballet Opera is of an especially high standard in Czechoslovakia. The main venues in the grand style of the 19th century are the beautifully restored **National Theater** (Národní třida 2, tel. 02/ 205364) and **Smetana Theater** (Vitezného února 8, tel. 02/ 269746). The even older **Týl Theater** is under restoration until 1993.

Theater You won't need to know the language at **Divadlo na Zábradlí** (Theater on the Balustrade, Anenské náměstí 5, tel. 02/ 2360449), home of the famous Black Theater mime group when it is (rather rarely) in Prague. **Laterna Magika** (Magic Lantern, Národní třída 40, tel. 02/260033) is a popular extravaganza combining live actors, mime, and sophisticated film techniques.

Puppet Shows These are brought to a high art form at the **Špejbl and Hurvínek Theater** (Římská 45).

Nightlife

Cabaret **The Alhambra** (Václavské náměstí 5, tel. 02/220467) has a three-part floor show. More moderately priced is **Variété Praha** (Vodičkova 30, tel. 02/24018). You'll find plenty of fellow foreigners at both.

Discos The best-known and most crowded is at the **Ambassador** hotel (*see* Lodging, above). There's one at each of the three hotels on the Vltava River: **Admirál** (Hořejši nábřeží), **Albatros** (nábřeží L. Svobody), and **Racek** (Dvorecká louka).

19 Rome

Arriving and Departing

By Plane Rome's principal airport is at Fiumicino, 29 kilometers (18 miles) from the city. Though its official name is Leonardo da Vinci Airport, everybody calls it Fiumicino. For flight information, tel. 06/6012–3640. The smaller military airport of Ciampino is on the edge of Rome and is used as an alternative by international and domestic lines, especially for charter flights.

Between the Airport and Downtown The new express-train link between Leonardo da Vinci Airport and the Ostiense railway station in downtown Rome offers frequent departures from both ends. The ride takes about 30 minutes. The fare is 5,000 lire. At the Ostiense station you can get a bus or taxi or take the *metro* (subway). Centrally located hotels are a fairly short taxi ride from the Ostiense station. If you need to get to Termini station or thereabouts, the fastest way is to take Metro Line B; follow the signs at the Ostiense station to the Piramide station of the metro.

A taxi to or from the airport at Fiumicino costs about 60,000 lire, including supplements. At a booth inside the terminal you can hire a car with driver for a little more. If you decide to take a taxi, use only yellow cabs, which must wait outside the terminal; make sure the meter is running. Gypsy drivers solicit your trade as you come out of customs; they're not reliable, and their rates may be rip-offs.

Ciampino is connected with the Subaugusta station of the Metro Line A by bus. A taxi between Ciampino and downtown Rome costs about 35,000 lire.

By Train Termini station is Rome's main train terminal, while Tiburtina and Ostiense stations are used principally by commuters. For train information, try the English-speaking personnel at the Information Office in Termini, or at any travel agency. Tickets and seats can be reserved and purchased at travel agencies bearing the FS (Ferrovia dello Stato) emblem. Short-distance tickets are also sold by tobacconists.

By Bus There is no central bus station in Rome; long-distance and suburban buses terminate either near Termini station or near strategically located metro stops.

By Car The main access routes from the north are the Autostrada del Sole (A1) from Milan and Florence, and the Aurelia highway (SS 1) from Genoa. The principal route to or from points south, such as Naples, is the southern leg of the Autostrada del Sole (A2). All highways connect with the GRA (Grande Raccordo Anulare), a beltway that encircles Rome and funnels traffic into the city. Markings on the GRA are confusing; take time in advance to study which route into the center best suits you.

Getting Around

The best way to see Rome is to choose an area or a sight that you particularly want to see, reach it by bus or Metro (subway), then explore the area on foot, following one of our itineraries or improvising one to suit your mood and interests. Wear comfortable, sturdy shoes, preferably with thick rubber soles to cushion you against the cobblestones. Heed our advice on security, and try to avoid the noise and polluted air of heavily trafficked streets, taking parallel byways wherever possible.

You can buy transportation route maps at newsstands and at ATAC information and ticket booths.

By Metro The subway, or Metro, provides the easiest and fastest way to get around. The Metro opens at 5:30 AM, and the last train leaves each terminal at 11:30 PM. Line A runs from the eastern part of the city to Termini station and past Piazza di Spagna and Piazzale Flaminio to Ottaviano, near St. Peter's and the Vatican Museums. Line B serves Termini, the Colosseum, and the Piramide station (air terminal). The fare is 700 lire. There are change booths and/or ticket machines on station mezzanines; it's best to buy single tickets or books of 5 or 10 (the latter only 6,000 lire) ahead of time at newsstands and tobacco shops. A daily tourist ticket known as a **BIG** is good on buses as well, costs 2,800 lire, and is sold at ATAC ticket booths.

By Bus Orange city buses (and two streetcar lines) run from about 6 AM to midnight, with skeleton *(notturno)* services on main lines throughout the night. The fare is 700 lire; you must buy your ticket before boarding. They are sold singly or in books of five or 10 (latter only 6,000 lire) at tobacco shops and newsstands. A **Biglietto Orario** is good on all ATAC lines for 90 minutes and costs 1,000 lire. Weekly tourist tickets cost 10,000 lire and are sold at ATAC booths. When entering a bus, remember to board at the rear and exit at the middle.

By Taxi Taxis wait at stands and, for a small extra charge, can also be called by telephone. The meter starts at 3,500 lire; there are supplements for service after 10 PM, on Sundays and holidays, and for each piece of baggage. Use yellow cabs (with meters) only, and be very sure to check the meter. To call a cab, tel. 3570, 3875, 4994, or 8433.

By Bicycle Bikes provide a pleasant means of getting around when traffic isn't heavy. There are bike-rental shops at Via del Pellegrino 89, near Campo dei Fiori, and at Piazza Navona 69, next to Bar Navona. Rental concessions are at the Metro stop of Piazza di Spagna, Piazza del Popolo, Largo San Silvestro, and Largo Argentina. There are also two in Villa Borghese, at Viale della Pineta and Viale del Bambino on the Pincio.

By Moped You can rent a moped or scooter and mandatory helmet at **Scoot-a-Long** (Via Cavour 302, tel. 06/678–0206) or **Scooters For Rent** (Via della Purificazione 66, tel. 06/465485).

Important Addresses and Numbers

Tourist Information The main **EPT** (Rome Provincial Tourist) office is at Via Parigi 5 (tel. 06/463748, open Mon.–Sat. 9–1:30 and 2–7). There are also EPT booths at Termini station and Leonardo da Vinci Airport. A booth on the main floor of the **ENIT** (National Tourist Board) building at Via Marghera 2 (tel. 06/4971222, open weekdays 9–1, Wed. also 4–6) can provide information on destinations in Italy outside Rome.

Consulates U.S. (Via Veneto 121, tel. 06/46741). **Canadian** (Via Zara 30, tel. 06/844–1841. **U.K.** (Via Venti Settembre 80a, tel. 06/475–5441).

Emergencies **Police** (tel. 06/4686); **Carabinieri** (tel. 06/112); **Ambulance** (tel. 06/5100 Red Cross). **Doctor:** Call your consulate, the private **Salvator Mundi Hospital** (tel. 06/586041), or the **American Hospital** (tel. 06/25671), which has English-speaking staff members, for a recommendation. **Pharmacies:** You will find

American and British medicines or their equivalents and English-speaking personnel at **Farmacia Internazionale Capranica** (Piazza Capranica 96, tel. 06/679–4680), **Farmacia Internazionale Barberini** (Piazza Barberini 49, tel. 06/462996), and **Farmacia Doricchi** (Via Venti Settembre 47, tel. 06/474–1471), among others. They are open 8:30–1 and 4–8; some stay open all night.

English Bookstores You'll find English-language books and magazines at newsstands in the center of Rome, especially on Via Veneto. Also try the **Economy Book and Video Center** (Via Torino 136, tel. 06/474–6877); the **Anglo-American Bookstore** (Via della Vite 57, tel. 06/679–5222), or the **Lion Bookshop** (Via del Babuino 181, tel. 06/322–5837).

Travel Agencies **American Express** (Piazza di Spagna 35, tel. 06/67641). **CIT** (Piazza Repubblica 64, tel. 06/47941). **Wagons-Lits Travel** (Via Boncompagni 25, tel. 06/481–7545). **Thomas Cook** (6 Via Paolo Mercuri, tel. 06/6868941).

Guided Tours

Orientation Tours **American Express** (tel. 06/67641), **CIT** (tel. 06/479–4372), and **Appian Line** (tel. 06/464151) offer three-hour tours in air-conditioned buses with English-speaking guides, covering Rome with four separate itineraries: "Ancient Rome" (including the Roman Forum and Colosseum), "Classic Rome" (including St. Peter's Basilica, Trevi Fountain, and the Janiculum Hill, with its panorama of the city), "Christian Rome" (some major churches and the Catacombs), and the "Vatican Museums and Sistine Chapel." Most tours cost about 32,000 lire, though the Vatican Museums tour is about 41,000 lire. American Express tours depart from Piazza di Spagna, CIT from Piazza della Repubblica, and Appian Line picks sightseers up at their hotels.

American Express can provide a car for up to three persons, limousine for up to seven, and minibus for up to nine, all with English-speaking driver. Guide service is extra. A minibus costs about 300,000 lire for three hours. Almost all operators offer "Rome by Night" tours, with or without dinner and entertainment. Reservations can be made through travel agents.

Special-Interest Tours You can arrange to attend a public papal audience in the Vatican or at the Pope's summer residence at Castelgandolfo through **CIT** (tel. 06/47941), **Appian Line** (tel. 06/464151), or **Carrani** (tel. 06/460510).

Excursions Most operators offer half-day excursions to Tivoli to see Villa D'Este's fountains and gardens; Appian Line's morning tour to Tivoli also includes Hadrian's Villa and its impressive ancient ruins. Most operators have all-day excursions to Assisi, to Pompeii and/or Capri, and to Florence. CIT also offers excursions to Anzio and Nettuno; its "Etruscan Tour" takes in some fascinating old towns and lovely countryside northwest of Rome.

Personal Guides Visitors can arrange for a personal guide through **American Express** (tel. 06/67641), **CIT,** or the main **EPT** tourist office (tel. 06/463748).

Exploring Rome

Antiquity is taken for granted in Rome, where successive ages have piled the present on top of the past—building, layering, and overlapping their own particular segments of Rome's 2,500 years of history to form a remarkably varied urban complex. Most of the city's major sights are located in a fairly small area known as the *centro*. At its heart lies ancient Rome, where the Forum and Colosseum stand. It was around this core that the other sections of the city grew up through the ages: medieval Rome, which covered the horn of land that pushes the Tiber toward the Vatican and extended across the river into Trastevere; and Renaissance Rome, which was erected upon medieval foundations and extended as far as the Vatican, creating beautiful villas on what was then the outskirts of the city.

The layout of the centro is highly irregular, but several landmarks serve as orientation points to identify the areas that most visitors come to see: the Colosseum, the Pantheon and Piazza Navona, St. Peter's, the Spanish Steps, and Villa Borghese. You'll need a good map to find your way around; newsstands offer a wide choice. Energetic sightseers will walk a lot, a much more pleasant way to see the city now that some traffic has been barred from the centro during the day; others might choose to take taxis, buses, or the Metro. The important thing is to relax and enjoy Rome. Don't try to see everything, but do take time to savor its pleasures. If you are in Rome during a hot spell, do as the Romans do: Start out early in the morning, have a light lunch and a long siesta during the hottest hours, then resume sightseeing in the late afternoon and end your evening with a leisurely meal outdoors, refreshed by cold Frascati wine and the *ponentino*, the cool evening breeze.

Ancient Rome *Numbers in the margin correspond to points of interest on the Rome map.*

❶ Start your first tour at the city's center, in **Piazza Venezia.** Behind the enormous marble monument honoring the first king of
❷ unified Italy, Victor Emmanuel II, stands the **Campidoglio** (Capitol Square) on the Capitoline Hill. The majestic ramp and beautifully proportioned piazza are Michelangelo's handiwork, as are the three palaces. **Palazzo Senatorio** at the center is still the ceremonial seat of Rome's city hall; it was built over the Tabularium, where ancient Rome's state archives were kept.

❸ The palaces flanking Palazzo Senatorio contain the **Capitoline Museums.** On the left, the **Museo Capitolino** holds some fine classical sculptures, including the *Dying Gaul*, the *Capitoline Venus*, and a fascinating series of portrait busts of ancient philosophers and emperors. In the courtyard of the **Palazzo dei**
❹ **Conservatori** on the right of the piazza, you can use the mammoth fragments of a colossal statue of the emperor Constantine as amusing props for snapshots. Inside you will find splendidly frescoed salons, as well as sculptures and paintings. *Piazza del Campidoglio, tel. 06/678–2862. Admission: 5,000 lire (ticket valid for both museums). Open Tues.–Sat. 9–1:30, Tues. and Thurs., also 5–8; Sat. (May–Sept.) also 8 PM–11 PM; Sun. 9–1; closed Mon.*

The Campidoglio is also the site of the very old church of the
❺ **Aracoeli,** which you can reach by way of the stairs on the far side of the Museo Capitolino. Stop in to see the medieval pavement; the Renaissance gilded ceiling that commemorates the victory of Lepanto; some Pinturicchio frescoes; and a much-revered wooden statue of the Holy Child. The Campidoglio gardens offer some good views of the heart of ancient Rome, the

Imperial Fora, built when the original Roman Forum became too small for the city's burgeoning needs.

6 In the valley below the Campidoglio, the **Roman Forum,** once only a marshy hollow, became the political, commercial, and social center of Rome, studded with public meeting halls, shops, and temples. As Rome declined, these monuments lost their importance and eventually were destroyed by fire or the invasions of barbarians. Rubble accumulated, much of it was carted off by medieval home-builders as construction material, and the site reverted to marshy pastureland; sporadic excavations began at the end of the 19th century.

You don't really have to try to make sense of the mass of marble fragments scattered over the area of the Roman Forum. Just consider that 2,000 years ago this was the center of the then-known world. Wander down the Via Sacra and climb the Palatine Hill, where the emperors had their palaces and where 16th-century cardinals strolled in elaborate Italian gardens. From the belvedere you have a good view of the Circus Maximus. *Entrances on Via dei Fori Imperiali, Piazza Santa Maria Nova and Via di San Gregorio, tel. 06/679–0333. Admission: 10,000 lire. Open Apr.–Sept., Mon., Wed.–Sat. 9–6, Tues., Sun. 9–1; Oct.–Mar., Mon., Wed.–Sat. 9–3, Tues., Sun. 9–1.*

7 Leave the Forum from the exit at Piazza Santa Maria Nova, near the Arch of Titus, and head for the **Colosseum,** inaugurated in AD 80 with a program of games and shows that lasted 100 days. On opening day alone 5,000 wild animals perished in the arena. The Colosseum could hold more than 50,000 spectators; it was faced with marble, decorated with stuccoes, and had an ingenious system of awnings to provide shade. Try to see it both in daytime and at night, when yellow floodlights make it a magical sight. The Colosseum, by the way, takes its name from a colossal, 36-meter (115-foot) statue of Nero that stood nearby. You must pay a fee to explore the upper levels, where you can also see a dusty scale model of the arena as it was in its heyday. *Piazza del Colosseo, tel. 06/7004261. Admission: 3,000 lire to upper levels. Open Mon., Tues., and Thurs.–Sat. 9–one hour before sunset; Sun. and Wed. 9–1.*

Time Out Facing the Colosseum is **Il Gladiatore,** a handy place for a good, moderately priced lunch. *Piazza del Colosseo 15. Closed Wed.* For delicious ice cream try **Ristoro della Salute,** one of Rome's best *gelaterie. Piazza del Colosseo 2a.*

8 Stroll past the **Arch of Constantine.** The reliefs depict Constantine's victory over Maxentius at the Milvian Bridge. Just before this battle in AD 312, Constantine had a vision of a cross in the heavens and heard the words, "In this sign thou shalt conquer." The victory led not only to the construction of this majestic marble arch but, more important, was a turning point in the history of Christianity: Soon afterward a grateful Constantine decreed that it was a lawful religion and should be tolerated throughout the empire.

9 A fairly long but pleasant walk takes you to the **Baths of Caracalla,** which numbered among ancient Rome's most beautiful and luxurious, inaugurated by Caracalla in 217 and used until the 6th century. An ancient version of a swanky athletic club, the baths were open to the public; citizens could bathe, socia-

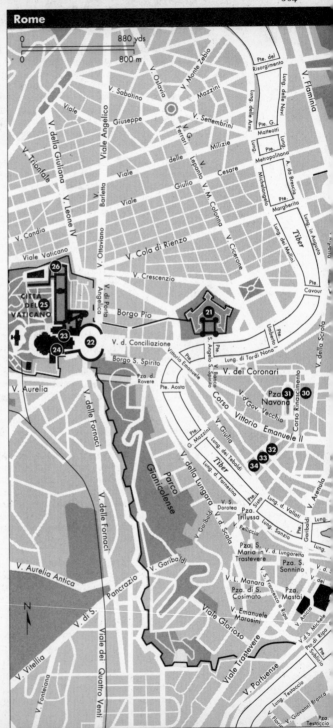

Rome

lize, and exercise in huge pools and richly decorated halls and libraries, now towering ruins. An open-air opera performance here can be an exciting experience, especially if the opera is *Aïda*, but dress warmly because the night air is cool and damp. *Via delle Terme di Caracalla. Admission: 6,000 lire. Open Apr.–Sept., Tues.–Sat. 9–6, Sun. and Mon. 9–1; Oct.–Mar., Tues.–Sat. 9–3, Sun.–Mon. 9–1.*

Piazzas and Fountains
10
11

Piazza del Popolo is one of Rome's most vast and airy squares, but for many years it was just an exceptionally beautiful parking lot with a 3,000-year-old obelisk in the middle. Now most traffic and parking has been barred, and the piazza is open to strollers. The church of **Santa Maria del Popolo** over in the corner of the piazza near the arch stands out more, now that it has been cleaned, and is rich in art, including two stunning Caravaggios in the chapel to the left of the main altar.

Time Out
Rosati is a café that has never gone out of style, forever a rendezvous of literati, artists, and actors. Its sidewalk tables, tearoom, and upstairs dining room can revive you with an espresso, snack, lunch, or dinner—all with a hefty price tag. *Piazza del Popolo 4. Closed Tues.*

12
13

If you're interested in antiques, stroll along **Via del Babuino.** If trendy fashions and accessories suit your fancy, take Via del Corso and turn into **Via Condotti,** Rome's most elegant and expensive shopping street. Here you can ogle fabulous jewelry, designer fashions, and accessories in the windows of Buccellati, Ferragamo, Valentino, Gucci, and Bulgari.

Time Out
The **Antico Caffè Greco** is a 200-year-old institution, haunt of writers, artists, and well-groomed ladies toting Gucci shopping bags. With its small marble-topped tables and velour settees, it's a nostalgic sort of place—Goethe, Byron, and Liszt were regulars here, and even Buffalo Bill stopped in when his road show came to town. Table service is expensive. *Via Condotti 86. Closed Sun.*

14
15

Via Condotti gives you a head-on view of the Spanish Steps in **Piazza di Spagna,** and of the church of **Trinità dei Monti.** In the center of the piazza is Bernini's **Fountain of the Barcaccia** (Old Boat) around which Romans and tourists cool themselves on hot summer nights. The 200-year-old **Spanish Steps,** named for the Spanish Embassy to the Holy See, opposite the American Express office, is a popular rendezvous, especially for the young people who throng this area. On weekend afternoons, Via del Corso is packed with wall-to-wall teenagers, and McDonald's, tucked away in a corner of Piazza di Spagna beyond the American Express office, is a mob scene. In contrast, **Babington's Tea Room,** to the left of the Spanish Steps, is a stylish institution that caters to an upscale clientele.

To the right of the Spanish steps is the **Keats and Shelley Memorial House.** Once the home of these romantic poets, it's now a museum. *Piazza di Spagna 26, tel. 06/678–4235. Admission: 4,500 lire. Open Apr.–Sept., weekdays 9–1 and 3–6; Oct.–Mar., weekdays 9–1 and 2:30–5:30.*

Time Out
In a corner of Piazza Mignanelli behind the American Express office is **La Rampa,** one of the best restaurants in this area. It's

usually crowded, however, and you may have to wait for a table. *Piazza Mignanelli 18. Closed Sun., Mon. lunch.*

Head for Via del Tritone and cross this heavily trafficked shopping street into narrow Via della Stamperia, which leads to the
⑯ Fontana di Trevi, a spectacular fantasy of mythical sea creatures and cascades of splashing water. Legend has it that visitors must toss a coin into the fountain to ensure their return to Rome, but you'll have to force your way past crowds of tourists and aggressive souvenir vendors to do so. The fountain as you see it was completed in the mid-1700s, but there had been a drinking fountain on the site for centuries. Pope Urban VIII almost sparked a revolt when he slapped a tax on wine to cover the expenses of having the fountain repaired.

⑰ At the top of Via del Tritone, **Piazza Barberini** boasts two fountains by Bernini: the jaunty **Triton** in the middle of the square and the **Fountain of the Bees** at the corner of Via Veneto. Decorated with the heraldic Barberini bees, this shell-shaped fountain bears an inscription that was immediately regarded as an unlucky omen by the superstitious Romans, for it erroneously stated that the fountain had been erected in the 22nd year of the reign of Pope Urban VIII, who had commissioned it, while in fact the 21st anniversary of his election was still some weeks away. The wrong numeral was hurriedly erased, but to no avail: Urban died eight days before the beginning of his 22nd year as pontiff.

⑱ A few steps up Via Quattro Fontane is **Palazzo Barberini,** Rome's most splendid 17th-century palace, now surrounded by rather unkempt gardens and occupied in part by the **Galleria Nazionale di Arte Antica.** Visit the latter to see Raphael's *Fornarina,* many other good paintings, some lavishly frescoed ceilings, and a charming suite of rooms decorated in 1782 on the occasion of the marriage of a Barberini heiress. *Via Quattro Fontane 13, tel. 06/481-4591. Admission: 6,000 lire. Open Mon.–Tues. 9–2, Wed.–Sat. 9–7, Sun. 9–1.*

⑲ One of Rome's oddest sights is the **crypt** of the church of **Santa Maria della Concezione** on Via Veneto, just above the Fountain of the Bees. In four chapels under the main church, the skeletons and scattered bones of some 4,000 dead Capuchin monks are arranged in decorative motifs, a macabre practice peculiar to the bizarre Baroque Age. *Via Veneto 27, tel. 06/462850. Admission free, but a donation is encouraged. Open daily 9–noon and 3–6.*

The lower reaches of Via Veneto are quiet and sedate, but at the intersection with Via Bissolati, otherwise known as "Airline Row," the avenue comes to life. The big white palace on the right is the U.S. Embassy, and the even bigger white palace beyond it is the luxurious **Hotel Excelsior.** Together with Doney's next door and the Café de Paris across the street, the Excelsior was a landmark of La Dolce Vita, that effervescent period during the 1950s when movie stars, playboys, and exiled royalty played hide-and-seek with press agents and *paparazzi,* ducking in and out of nightclubs and hotel rooms along the Via Veneto. The atmosphere of Via Veneto is considerably more sober now, and its cafés cater more to tourists and expensive pickups than to barefoot cinema *contesse.*

Via Veneto ends at **Porta Pinciana,** a gate in the 12-mile stretch of defensive walls built by Emperor Aurelian in the 3rd century; 400 years later, when the Goths got too close for comfort, Belisarius reinforced the gate with two massive towers. Beyond is **Villa Borghese,** most famous of Rome's parks, studded with tall pines that are gradually dying off as pollution and age take their toll. Inside the park, strike off to the right toward the **Galleria Borghese,** a pleasure palace created by Cardinal Scipione Borghese in 1613 as a showcase for his fabulous sculpture collection. In the throes of structural repairs for several years, the now-public gallery is, at press time, only partially open to visitors. It's still worth a visit to see the seductive reclining statue of Pauline Borghese by Canova, and some extraordinary works by Bernini, among them the unforgettable *Apollo and Daphne* in which marble is transformed into flesh and foliage. With restorations dragging on, interminably, a few of the best works, including Casavaggio's, have been moved downstairs from the picture gallery, which is now closed. *During reconstruction the entrance is on Via Raimondi, reached from Via Pinciana. Via Pinciana (Piazzale Museo Borghese–Villa Borghese), tel. 06/858577. Admission free for the duration of the renovations. Open Tues.–Sat. 9–1, Sun. 9–1, Mon. 9–2.*

Castel Sant'Angelo– St. Peter's– Vatican Museums **Ponte Sant'Angelo,** the ancient bridge across the Tiber in front of Castel Sant'Angelo, is decorated with lovely Baroque angels designed by Bernini and offers fine views of the castle and of St. Peter's in the distance. **Castel Sant'Angelo,** a formidable fortress, was originally built as the tomb of Emperor Hadrian in the 2nd century AD. It looked much like the **Augusteo,** or Tomb of Augustus, which still stands more or less in its original form across the river. Hadrian's Tomb was incorporated into the town walls and served as a military stronghold during the barbarian invasions. According to legend it got its present name in the 6th century, when Pope Gregory the Great, passing by in a religious procession, saw an angel with a sword appear above the ramparts to signal the end of the plague that was raging. Enlarged and fortified, the castle became a refuge for the popes, who fled to it along the **Passetto,** an arcaded passageway that links it with the Vatican. Inside the castle you see ancient corridors, medieval cells and Renaissance salons, a museum of antique weapons, courtyards piled with stone cannonballs, and terraces with great views of the city. There's a pleasant bar with outdoor tables on one level. The highest terrace of all, under the newly restored bronze statue of the legendary angel, is the one from which Puccini's heroine, Tosca, threw herself. *Lungotevere Castello 50, tel. 06/687–5036. Admission: 8,000 lire. Open Apr.–Sept., Mon. 3–8, Tues., Wed., Fri. 9–2, Thurs., Sat. 9–7, Sun. 9–1; Oct.–Mar., Tues.–Sat. 9–1, Sun. 9–noon, Mon. 2–6:30.*

Via della Conciliazione, the broad avenue leading to St. Peter's Basilica, was created by Mussolini's architects by razing blocks of old houses. This opened up a vista of the basilica, giving the eye time to adjust to its mammoth dimensions, and thereby spoiling the effect Bernini sought when he enclosed his vast square (which is really oval) in the embrace of huge quadruple colonnades. In **Piazza San Pietro** (St. Peter's Square), which has held up to 400,000 at one time, look for the stone disks in the pavement halfway between the fountains and the obelisk.

From this point the colonnades seem to be formed of a single row of columns all the way around.

When you enter Piazza San Pietro (completed in 1667), you are entering Vatican territory. Since the Lateran Treaty of 1929, **Vatican City** has been an independent and sovereign state, which covers about 44 hectares (108 acres) and is surrounded by thick, high walls. Its gates are minded by the Swiss Guards, who still wear the colorful dress uniforms designed by Michelangelo. Sovereign of this little state is John Paul II, 264th Pope of the Roman Catholic Church. At noon on Sunday, the Pope
㉓ appears at his third-floor study window in the **Vatican Palace,** to the right of the basilica, to bless the crowd in the square. (Note: Entry to St. Peter's and the Vatican Museums is barred to those wearing shorts, miniskirts, sleeveless T-shirts, and otherwise revealing clothing. Women should carry scarves to cover bare shoulders and upper arms or wear blouses that come to the elbow. Men should dress modestly, in slacks and shirts.)

㉔ **St. Peter's Basilica** is one of Rome's most impressive sights. It takes a while to absorb the sheer magnificence of it, however, and its rich decoration may not be to everyone's taste. Its size alone is overwhelming, and the basilica is best appreciated when providing the lustrous background for ecclesiastical ceremonies thronged with the faithful. The original basilica was built in the early 4th century AD by the Emperor Constantine, over an earlier shrine that supposedly marked the burial place of St. Peter. After more than a thousand years, the old basilica was so decrepit it had to be torn down. The task of building a new, much larger one took almost 200 years and employed the architectural genius of Alberti, Bramante, Raphael, Peruzzi, Antonio Sangallo the Younger, and Michelangelo, who died before the dome he had planned could be completed. Finally, in 1626, St. Peter's Basilica was finished.

The basilica is full of extraordinary works of art. Among the most famous is Michelangelo's *Pietà* (1498), seen in the first chapel on the right just as you enter from the square. Michelangelo has four *Pietà*s to his credit. The earliest and best known can be seen here. Two others are in Florence, and the fourth, the *Rondanini Pietà*, is in Milan.

At the end of the central aisle is the bronze statue of **St. Peter,** its foot worn by centuries of reverent kisses. The bronze throne above the altar in the apse was created by Bernini to contain a simple wood and ivory chair once believed to have belonged to St. Peter. Bernini's bronze *baldacchino* (canopy) over the papal altar was made with metal stripped from the portico of the Pantheon at the order of Pope Urban VIII, one of the powerful Roman Barberini family. His practice of plundering ancient monuments for material to implement his grandiose schemes inspired the famous quip, *"Quod non fecerunt barbari, fecerunt Barberini"* (What the barbarians didn't do, the Barberini did).

As you stroll up and down the aisles and transepts, observe the fine mosaic copies of famous paintings above the altars, the monumental tombs and statues, and the fine stucco work. Stop at the **Treasury** (Historical Museum), which contains some priceless liturgical objects, and take the elevator up to the roof of the basilica. From here you can climb a short interior staircase to the base of the dome for an overhead view of the interior of the basilica. Only if you are in good shape should you attempt the strenuous climb up the narrow, one-way stairs to the balcony of the lantern atop the dome, where the view embraces the Vatican Gardens as well as all of Rome.

The entrance to the **Crypt of St. Peter's** is in one of the huge piers at the crossing. It's best to leave this visit for last, as the crypt's only exit takes you outside the church. The crypt contains chapels and the tombs of many popes. It occupies the area of the original basilica, over the **grottoes,** where evidence of what may be St. Peter's burial place has been found. You can book special tours of the grottoes. *St. Peter's Basilica, tel. 06/ 698–4466. Open daily 7–7. Treasury (Museo Storico-Artistico): entrance in Sacristy. Admission: 3,000 lire. Open Apr.–Sept., daily 9–6; Oct.–Mar., daily 9–3. Roof and Dome: entrance between Gregorian Chapel and right transept. Admission: 4,000 lire, including use of elevator to roof, 3,000 lire if you climb the spiral ramp on foot. Open Apr.–Aug., daily 8–6; Sept.–Mar., daily 8–5. Crypt (Tombs of the Popes): entrance alternates among the piers at the crossing. Admission: free. Open Apr.–Sept., daily 7–6; Oct.–Mar., daily 7–5. Grottoes: Apply several days in advance to Ufficio Scavi, left beyond the Arco delle Campane entrance to the Vatican, left of the basilica, tel. 06/698–5318. Admission: 5,000 lire for 2-hour guided visit, 3,000 lire with tape cassette. Ufficio Scavi office hours: Mon.–Sat. 9–noon and 2–5; closed Sun. and religious holidays.*

For many visitors, a **papal audience** is the highlight of a trip to Rome. The Pope holds mass audiences on Wednesday morning; during the winter they take place in a modern audience hall (capacity 7,000) off the left-hand colonnade. From March to October they are held in **St. Peter's Square,** and sometimes at the papal residence at **Castel Gandolfo.** *You can pick up free tickets 4–6 at the North American College, Via dell'Umiltà 30 (tel. 06/ 678–9184), or apply to the Papal Prefecture (Prefettura), which you reach through the Bronze Door in the right-hand colonnade, tel. 06/698–4466. Open Tues. 9–1, Wed. 9–shortly before audience commences. Or arrange for tickets through a travel agent: Carrani Tours, Via V.E. Orlando 95, tel. 06/ 460510; Appian Line, Via Barberini 109, tel. 06/464151. Admission: about 30,000 lire (including transportation) if booked through an agent or hotel concierge.*

25 Guided minibus tours through the **Vatican Gardens** show you some attractive landscaping, a few historical monuments, and the Vatican mosaic school, which produced the mosaics decorating St. Peter's. These tours give you a different perspective on the basilica itself. From March through October, you can choose a garden tour that includes the Sistine Chapel, which you would otherwise see as part of a tour of the Vatican Museums. *Vatican Gardens. Tickets at information office, on the left side of St. Peter's Square, tel. 06/698–4466. Open Mon.–Sat. 8:30–6:30. Garden tour cost: 12,000 lire. Available Oct.–Mar., Tues., Fri., and Sat.; Nov.–Feb., Tues., Thurs., and Sat. Garden and Sistine Chapel tour cost: 21,000 lire. Available Oct.– Mar., Mon. and Thurs. All tours begin at 10 AM.*

From St. Peter's Square information office you can take a shuttle bus (cost: 2,000 lire) direct to the Vatican Museums. This operates every morning, except Wednesday and Sunday, and saves you the 15-minute walk that goes left from the square and continues along the Vatican walls.

26. The collections in the **Vatican Museums** cover nearly 8 kilometers (5 miles) of displays. If you have time, allow at least half a day for Castel Sant'Angelo and St. Peter's and another half-day for the museums. Posters at the museum entrance plot out a choice of four color-coded itineraries; the shortest takes about 90 minutes, the longest more than four hours, depending on your rate of progress. All include the **Sistine Chapel.**

In 1508, Pope Julius II commissioned Michelangelo to fresco the more than 930 square meters (10,000 square feet) of the chapel's ceiling. For four years Michelangelo dedicated himself to painting over fresh plaster, and the result was his masterpiece. The cleaning operations, now completed, have revealed its original and surprisingly brilliant colors.

You can try to avoid the tour groups by going early or late, allowing yourself enough time before the closing hour. In peak season, the crowds definitely detract from your appreciation of this outstanding artistic achievement. Buy an illustrated guide or rent a taped commentary in order to make sense of the figures on the ceiling. A pair of binoculars helps.

The Vatican collections are so rich that unless you are an expert in art history, you will probably want only to skim the surface, concentrating on a few pieces that strike your fancy. If you really want to see the museums thoroughly, you will have to come back again and again. Some of the highlights that might be of interest on your first tour include the *Laocoön,* the *Belvedere Torso,* and the *Apollo Belvedere,* which inspired Michelangelo. The Raphael Rooms are decorated with masterful frescoes, and there are more Raphaels in the Picture Gallery *(Pinacoteca).* At the Quattro Cancelli, near the entrance to the Picture Gallery, a rather spartan cafeteria provides basic nonalcoholic refreshments. *Viale Vaticano, tel. 06/698–3333. Admission: 10,000 lire, free on last Sun. of the month. Open Easter period and July–Sept., weekdays 8:45–4, Sat. 8:45–1; Oct.–June, Mon.–Sat. 8:45–1. Ticket office closes 45 minutes before museums close. Closed Sun., except last Sun. of the month, and on religious holidays.*

Old Rome 27. Take Via del Plebiscito from Piazza Venezia to the huge **Church of the Gesù.** This paragon of Baroque style is the tangible symbol of the power of the Jesuits, who were a major force in the Counter-Reformation in Europe. Encrusted with gold and precious marbles, the Gesù has a fantastically painted ceiling that flows down over the pillars, merging with painted stucco figures to complete the three-dimensional illusion.

28. On your way to the Pantheon you will pass **Santa Maria Sopra Minerva,** a Gothic church built over a Roman temple. Inside there are some beautiful frescoes by Filippo Lippi; outside there is a charming elephant by Bernini with an obelisk on its back.

29. Originally built in 27 BC by Augustus's general Agrippa and rebuilt by Hadrian in the 2nd century AD, the **Pantheon** is one of Rome's most perfect, best-preserved, and perhaps least appreciated ancient monuments. Romans and tourists alike pay little attention to it, and on summer evenings it serves mainly as a backdrop for all the action in the square in front. It represents a

fantastic feat of construction, however. The huge columns of
the portico and the original bronze doors form the entrance to a
majestic hall covered by the largest dome of its kind ever built,
wider even than that of St. Peter's. In ancient times the entire
interior was encrusted with rich decorations of gilt bronze and
marble, plundered by later emperors and popes. *Piazza della
Rotonda. Open Oct.–June, Mon.–Sat. 9–5, Sun. 9–1; July–
Sept., daily 9–6.*

Time Out There are several sidewalk cafés on the square in front of the
Pantheon, all of which are good places to nurse a cappuccino
while you observe the scene. On a nearby square is the **Bar
Sant'Eustachio** (Piazza Sant'Eustachio 82), famous for its coffee (which is served with plenty of sugar; if you prefer, tell the
counterman you want it without *(senza)* or with only a little
(poco) sugar *(zucchero)*. Serious coffee drinkers also like **Tazza
d'Oro** (Via degli Orfani 84), just off Piazza della Rotonda. And
for a huge variety of ice cream in natural flavors, **Giolitti** (Via
Uffizi del Vicario 40; closed Mon.) is generally considered by
gelato addicts to be the best in Rome. It also has good snacks
and a quick-lunch counter.

---

30 Stop in at the church of **San Luigi dei Francesi** on Via della
Dogana Vecchia to see the three paintings by Caravaggio in the
last chapel on the left; have a few hundred-lira coins handy for
the light machine. The clergy of San Luigi considered the artist's roistering and unruly lifestyle scandalous enough, but his
realistic treatment of sacred subjects was just too much for
them. They rejected his first version of the altarpiece and
weren't particularly happy with the other two works either.
Thanks to the intercession of Caravaggio's patron, an influential cardinal, they were persuaded to keep them—a lucky
thing, since they are now recognized to be among the artist's
finest paintings. *Open Fri.–Wed. 7:30–12:30 and 3:30–7,
Thurs. 7:30–12:30.*

31 Just beyond San Luigi is **Piazza Navona,** an elongated 17th-cen-
tury piazza that traces the oval form of the underlying Circus of
Diocletian. At the center, Bernini's lively **Fountain of the Four
Rivers** is a showpiece. The four statues represent rivers in the
four corners of the world: the Nile, with its face covered in allu-
sion to its then unknown source; the Ganges; the Danube; and
the River Plate, with its hand raised. And here we have to give
the lie to the legend that this was Bernini's mischievous dig at
Borromini's design of the facade of the church of **Sant'Agnese in
Agone,** from which the statue seems to be shrinking in horror.
The fountain was created in 1651; work on the church's facade
began some time later. The piazza dozes in the morning, when
little groups of pensioners sun themselves on the stone benches
and children pedal tricycles around the big fountain. In the late
afternoon the sidewalk cafés fill up for the aperitif hour, and in
the evening, especially in good weather, the piazza comes to life
with a throng of street artists, vendors, tourists, and Romans
out for their evening *passeggiata* (promenade).

Time Out The sidewalk tables of the **Tre Scalini** café (Piazza Navona 30;
closed Wed.) offer a grandstand view of this gorgeous piazza.
Treat yourself to a *tartufo*, the chocolate ice-cream specialty
that was invented here. The restaurant is a pleasant place for a
moderately priced lunch. For a salad or light lunch, go to **Cul de**

Sac (Piazza Pasquino 73, just off Piazza Navona) or to **Insalata Ricca** (Via del Paradiso, next to the church of Sant'Andrea della Valle). Both are informal and inexpensive.

㉜ Across Corso Vittorio is **Campo dei Fiori** (Field of Flowers), the site of a crowded and colorful daily morning market. The hooded bronze figure brooding over the piazza is philosopher Giordano Bruno, who was burned at the stake here for heresy.

㉝ The adjacent **Piazza Farnese,** with fountains made of Egyptian granite basins from the Baths of Caracalla, is an airy setting for **㉞** **Palazzo Farnese,** now the French Embassy, one of the most beautiful of Rome's many Renaissance palaces. There are several others in the immediate area: **Palazzo Spada,** a Wedgwood kind of palace encrusted with stuccoes and statues; **Palazzo della Cancelleria,** a massive building that is now the Papal Chancellery, one of the many Vatican-owned buildings in Rome that enjoy extraterritorial privileges; and the fine old palaces along Via Giulia.

This is a section to wander through, getting the feel of daily life carried on in a centuries-old setting, and looking into the dozens of antiques shops. Stroll along Via Arenula into a rather gloomy part of Rome bounded by Piazza Campitelli and Lungotevere Cenci, the ancient Jewish ghetto. Among the most interesting sights here are the pretty **Fountain of the Tartarughe** (Turtles) on Piazza Mattei, the **Via Portico d'Ottavia,** with medieval inscriptions and friezes on the old buildings, and the **Teatro di Marcello,** a theater built by Julius Caesar to hold 20,000 spectators.

㉟ A pleasant place to end your walk is on **Tiberina Island.** To get **㊱** there, walk across the ancient **Fabricio Bridge,** built in 62 BC, the oldest bridge in the city.

Shopping

Shopping is part of the fun of being in Rome, no matter what your budget. The best buys are leather goods of all kinds, from gloves to handbags and wallets to jackets; silk goods; and high-quality knitwear. Shops are closed on Sunday and on Monday morning; in July and August, they close on Saturday afternoon as well.

Antiques A well-trained eye will spot some worthy old prints and minor antiques in the city's fascinating little shops. For prints, browse among the stalls at **Piazza Fontanella Borghese;** at **Casali,** Piazza della Rotonda 81a, at the Pantheon; and **Tanca,** Salita de'Crescenzi 10, also near the Pantheon. For minor antiques, **Via dei Coronari** and other streets in the **Piazza Navona** area are good. The most prestigious antiques dealers are situated in **Via del Babuino** and its environs.

Boutiques **Via Condotti,** directly across from the Spanish steps, and the streets running parallel to Via Condotti, as well as its cross streets, form the most elegant and expensive shopping area in Rome. Lower-price fashions may be found on display at shops on **Via Frattina** and **Via del Corso.**

Shopping Districts In addition to those mentioned, Romans themselves do much of their shopping along **Via Cola di Rienzo** and **Via Nazionale.**

Religious Articles These abound in the shops around St. Peter's, on **Via di Porta Angelica** and **Via della Conciliazione,** and in the souvenir shops tucked away on the roof and at the crypt exit in St. Peter's itself.

Department Stores You'll find a fairly broad selection of women's, men's, and children's fashions and accessories at the **Rinascente** stores on Piazza Colonna and at Piazza Fiume and at the **Coin** department store on Piazzale Appio near San Giovanni Laterno. The **UPIM** and **Standa** chains have shops all over the city that offer medium-quality, low-price goods. The **Croff** chain features housewares.

Food and Flea Markets The open-air markets at **Piazza Vittorio** and **Campo dei Fiori** are colorful sights. The flea market held at **Porta Portese** on Sunday morning is stocked mainly with new or second-hand clothing. If you go, beware of pickpockets and purse snatchers.

Dining

There are plenty of fine restaurants in Rome serving various Italian regional cuisines and international specialties with a flourish of linen and silver, as well as a whopping *conto* (check) at the end. If you want family-style cooking and prices, try a *trattoria*, a usually smallish and unassuming, often family-run place. Fast-food places and Chinese restaurants are proliferating in Rome; very few can be recommended. Fixed-price tourist menus can be scanty and unimaginative. The lunch hour in Rome lasts from about 1 to 3 PM, dinner from 8 or 8:30 to about 10:30, though some restaurants stay open much later. During August many restaurants close for vacation.

Generally speaking, a *ristorante* pays more attention to decor, service, and menu than does a *trattoria*, which is simpler and often family-run. An *osteria* used to be a lowly tavern, though now the term may be used to designate a chic and expensive eatery. A *tavola calda* offers hot dishes and snacks, with seating. A *rosticceria* has the same, to take out.

The menu is always posted in the window or just inside the door of an eating establishment. Check to see what is offered, and note the charges for *coperto* (cover) and *servizio* (service), which will increase your check. A *menu turistico* includes taxes and service, but beverages are extra.

Mealtimes Lunch hour in Rome lasts from 1 to 3, dinner from 8 to 10. Practically all restaurants close one day a week; some close for winter or summer vacation.

Precautions Tap water is safe in large cities unless noted *Non Potabile*. Bottled mineral water is available everywhere, *gassata* (with bubbles) or *non gassata* (without). If you prefer tap water, ask for *acqua semiplice*.

Dress Except for restaurants in the Very Expensive and occasionally in the Expensive categories, where jacket and tie are advisable, casual attire is acceptable.

Ratings Prices are per person and include first course, main course, dessert or fruit, and house wine, where available. Best bets are indicated by a star ★.

Category	Cost
Very Expensive	over 100,000 lire
Expensive	60,000–100,000 lire
Moderate	40,000–60,000 lire
Inexpensive	under 40,000 lire

Very Expensive **Le Restaurant.** The resplendent dining room of the Grand ho-
★ tel's restaurant is a model of 19th-century opulence, lavish
with fine damasks and velvets, crystal chandeliers, and oil
paintings. The menu varies with the seasons; there is always a
daily recommended menu. Among the specialties are *carpaccio
tiepido di pescatrice* (brill with thin slices of raw beef) and
medaglioni di vitello al marsala con tartufo (veal medallions
with marsala wine and truffles). The wine list offers some majestic vintages. *Via Vittorio Emanuele Orlando 3, tel. 06/4709.
Reservations advised. AE, DC, MC, V.*

La Terrazza dell'Eden. The Eden Hotel's rooftop restaurant is a
favorite haunt of Italian politicians and other powerbrokers
drawn by the classic regional Italian cooking and breathtaking
views. Entirely redecorated in soft colors and period furnishings, the dining room and adjacent bar have acquired new elegance and style. Terrace space has been doubled for outdoor
dining and for gourmet buffet brunches on balmy weekends.
The menu offers a wide range of fine Italian specialties and
some strictly Roman dishes. The wine list is exceptionally
good. *Eden Hotel, Via Ludovisi 49; tel. 06/474–3551, ext. 437.
Reservations advised. AE, DC, MC, V.*

★ **El Toulà.** On a little byway off Piazza Nicosia in Old Rome, El
Toulà has the warm, welcoming atmosphere of a 19th-century
country house, with white walls, antique furniture in dark
wood, heavy silver serving dishes, and spectacular arrangements of fruits and flowers. There's a cozy little bar off the entrance where you can sip a *prosecco*, the aperitif best suited to
the chef's Venetian specialties, among them the classic *pasta e
fagioli* (bean soup), risotto with radicchio, and *fegato alla
veneziana* (liver with onions). *Via della Lupa 29/b, tel. 06/687–
3750. Reservations required. AE, DC, MC, V. Closed Sat.
lunch, Sun., Aug., and Dec. 24–26.*

Expensive **Alberto Ciarla.** Located on a large square in Trastevere, the
★ scene of a busy morning food market, Alberto Ciarla is one of
Rome's best seafood restaurants. In contrast with its workaday location, the ambience is upscale, with red-and-black
decor. Bubbling aquariums, a sure sign that the food is super-
fresh, are set around the wall. Seafood salads are a specialty.
Meat eaters will find succor in the house pâté and the lamb. *Piazza San Cosimato 40, tel. 06/581–8668. Reservations required. AE, DC, MC, V. Closed lunch, all day Sun., Aug. 5–
25, and Christmas.*

★ **Andrea.** Ernest Hemingway and King Farouk used to eat here;
FIAT motors supremo Gianni Agnelli and other Italian
powerbrokers still do. A half-block off Via Veneto, Andrea offers classic Italian cooking in an intimate, clubby ambience in
which snowy table linens gleam against a discreet background
of dark green paneling. The menu features delicacies such as
homemade *tagliolini* (thin noodles) with shrimp and spinach
sauce, spaghetti with seafood and truffles, and mouth-water-

ing *carciofi all'Andrea* (artichokes simmered in olive oil). *Via Sardegna 26, tel. 06/482–1891. Reservations advised. AE, DC, MC, V. Closed Sun. and Mon. lunch and most of Aug.*

Coriolano. The only tourists who find their way to this classic restaurant near Porta Pia are likely to be gourmets looking for quintessential Italian food—that means light homemade pastas, choice olive oil, and market-fresh ingredients, especially seafood. Although seafood dishes vary, *tagliolini all'aragosta* (thin noodles with lobster sauce) is usually on the menu, as are *porcini* mushrooms (in season) cooked to a secret recipe. The wine list is predominantly Italian but includes some French and California wines. *Via Ancona 14, tel. 06/861122. Reservations advised. AE, DC, MC, V. Closed Sun. and Aug. 1–25.*

Piperno. Located in the old Jewish ghetto next to historic Palazzo Cenci, Piperno has been in business for more than a century. It is *the* place to go for Rome's extraordinary *carciofi alla giudia*, crispy-fried artichokes, Jewish-style. You eat in three small, wood-paneled dining rooms or, in fair weather, at one of a handful of tables outdoors. Try *filetti di baccala* (very salty fried cod), *pasta e ceci* (a thick soup of pasta tubes and chickpeas), and *fiori di zucca* (stuffed zucchini flowers)—but don't miss the *carciofi*. *Monte dei Cenci 9, tel. 06/654–2772. Reservations advised. AE, DC, MC, V. Closed Sun. dinner, Mon., Christmas, Easter, and Aug.*

★ **Ranieri.** On a quiet street off fashionable Via Condotti near the Spanish Steps, this historic restaurant was founded by a former chef of Queen Victoria. It remains a favorite with tourists for its traditional atmosphere and decor, with damask-covered walls, velvet banquettes, crystal chandeliers, and old paintings. Among the many specialties on the vast menu are *gnocchi alla parigina* (souffléed gnocchi with tomato and cheese sauce) and *mignonettes alla Regina Vittoria* (veal with pâté and cream). *Via Mario de' Fiori 26, tel. 06/679–1592. Reservations advised. AE, DC, MC, V. Closed Sun.*

Il Veliero. The attractive sailing ship decor of this top fish restaurant near Piazza Farnese sets the scene for seafood feasts accompanied by fresh-baked bread from a wood-burning oven. There are many types of pasta and risotto, with shellfish or squid to follow the splendid choice of seafood *antipasti*. For your main course, try grilled or baked fish, or succulent Mediterranean crayfish, scampi, or shrimp. Have the bluefish if it's on the menu. *Via Monserrato 32, tel. 06/654–2636. Reservations advised. AE, DC, V. Closed Mon.*

Moderate **Colline Emiliane.** Located near Piazza Barberini, the Colline Emiliane is an unassuming trattoria offering exceptionally good food. Behind an opaque glass facade, there are a couple of plain little dining rooms where you are served light homemade pastas, a very special chicken broth, and meats ranging from pot roast to *giambonetto di vitella* (roast veal) and *cotoletta alla bolognese* (veal cutlet with cheese and tomato sauce). *Via degli Avignonesi 22, tel. 06/481–7538. Reservations advised. No credit cards. Closed Fri.*

Mario. This Tuscan trattoria in the center of Rome's shopping district has been run by Mario for 30 years. Usually crowded, it has a friendly, relaxed atmosphere and a faithful clientele, including many journalists from the Foreign Press headquarters nearby. Hearty Tuscan specialties, such as *pappardelle alla lepre* (noodles with hare sauce) and *coniglio* (rabbit), are featured on the menu. Try *panzanella* (Tuscan bread salad with tomatoes) and the house Chianti. *Via della Vite 55, tel. 06/678-3818. Dinner reservations advised. AE, DC, MC, V. Closed Sun. and Aug.*

Pierluigi. Pierluigi, in the heart of Old Rome, is a longtime favorite. On busy evenings it's almost impossible to find a table, so make sure you reserve well in advance. Seafood predominates—if you fancy a splurge, try the lobster—but traditional Roman dishes are offered, too, such as *orecchiette con broccoli* (disk-shaped pasta with greens) or just simple spaghetti. In warm weather ask for a table in the piazza. *Piazza dei Ricci 144, tel. 06/686-1302. Reservations advised. AE. Closed Mon. and 2 weeks in Aug.*

★ **Romolo.** Generations of Romans have enjoyed the romantic garden courtyard and historic dining room of this charming Trastevere haunt, reputedly once home of Raphael's ladylove, *La Fornarina*. In the evening, a guitarist serenades diners. The cuisine is appropriately Roman; specialties include *mozzarella alla fornarina* (deep-fried mozzarella with ham and anchovies) and *braciolette d'abbachio scottadito* (grilled baby lamb chops). Alternatively, try one of the new vegetarian pastas featuring *carciofi* (artichokes) or radicchio. *Via di Porta Settimiana 8, tel. 06/581-8284. Reservations advised. AE, DC, V. Closed Mon. and Aug. 2-23.*

★ **Vecchia Roma.** The frescoed walls of this historic restaurant located in a onetime palace in Old Rome, and the specialties—among them *fettucine verdi* (spinach-flavored pasta with cream sauce) and *petti pollo con gamberi di fiume* (chicken breasts with freshwater shrimp)—have long made this a classic choice of resident foreigners and sophisticated travelers. In summer you dine under white umbrellas. *Piazza Campitelli 18, tel. 06/656-4604. Reservations advised. No credit cards. Closed Wed. and Aug.*

Inexpensive **Abruzzi.** This simple trattoria off Piazza Santi Apostoli near Piazza Venezia specializes in regional cooking of the Abruzzi, a
★ mountainous region southeast of Rome. The straightforward menu and reasonable prices make it a lunchtime favorite for politicians, priests, and both students and professors from the nearby Gregorian papal university. Specialties include *tonnarelli Abruzzi* (square-cut pasta with mushrooms, peas, and ham) and *abbacchio* (roast lamb). *Via del Vaccaro 1, tel. 06/679-3897. Lunch reservations advised. V. Closed Sat and Aug.*

Baffetto. Rome's best-known inexpensive pizza restaurant is plainly decorated and *very* popular; you'll probably have to wait in line outside on the *sampietrini*—the cobblestones. The interior is mostly given over to the ovens, the tiny cash desk, and the simple paper-covered tables. *Bruschetta* (toast) and *crostini* (mozzarella toast) are the only variations on the pizza theme. Expect to share a table. *Via del Governo Vecchio 114, tel. 06/686-1617. No reservations. No credit cards. Closed lunch, Sun., and Aug.*

Hostaria Farnese. This is a tiny trattoria between Campo dei Fiori and Piazza Farnese, in the heart of Old Rome. Papa serves, Mamma cooks, and depending on what they've picked up at the Campo dei Fiori market, you may find *rigatoni* with tuna and basil, spaghetti with vegetable sauce, *spezzatino* (stew), and other homey specialties. *Via dei Baullari 109, tel. 06/654-1595. Reservations advised. AE, V. Closed Thurs.*

Pollarola. Located near Piazza Navona and Campo dei Fiori, this typical Roman trattoria has flowers (artificial) on the tables and an antique Roman column embedded in the rear wall, evidence of its historic site. You can eat outdoors in fair weather. Try a pasta specialty such as *fettucine alla gorgonzola* (noodles with creamy gorgonzola sauce) and a mixed plate from the temptingly fresh array of antipastos. The house wine, white or red, is good. *Piazza della Pollarola 24 (Campo dei Fiori), tel. 06/654-1654. Reservations advised for groups. AE, V. Closed Sun.*

Lodging

The list below covers mostly those hotels that are within walking distance of at least some sights and that are handy to public transportation. Those in the Moderate and Inexpensive categories do not have restaurants but serve Continental breakfast. Rooms facing the street get traffic noise throughout the night, and few hotels in the lower categories have double glazing. Ask for a quiet room, or bring earplugs.

We strongly recommend that you always make reservations in advance. Should you find yourself in the city without reservations, however, contact one of the following EPT offices: at Fiumicino Airport (tel. 06/601–1255); Termini train station (tel. 06/487–1270); on the A1 autostrada at the Feronia service area (tel. 0765/255465); and on the A2 autostrada at the Roma-Sud Frascati service area (tel. 06/946–4341; summer only).

Rome offers a good choice of accommodations. Room rates are on a par with other European capitals, and porters, room service, and in-house cleaning and laundering are disappearing in Moderate and Inexpensive hotels. Taxes and service are included in the room rate. Breakfast is an extra charge, and you can decline to take breakfast in the hotel, though the desk may not be happy about it; make this clear when booking or checking in. Air-conditioning also may be an extra charge. In older hotels, room quality may be uneven; if you don't like the room you're given, ask for another. This applies to noise, too; some front rooms are bigger and have views but get street noise. Specify if you care about having either a bath or shower, as not all rooms have both. In Moderate and Inexpensive places, showers may be the drain-in-the-floor type guaranteed to flood the bathroom. Major cities have hotel reservation service booths in the rail stations.

Hotels Italian hotels are officially classified from five-star (deluxe) to one-star (guest houses and small inns). Prices are established officially and a rate card on the back of the door of your room or inside the closet door tells you exactly what you will pay for that particular room. Any variations should be cause for complaint and should be reported to the local tourist office. CIGA, Jolly, Space, Atahotels, and Italhotels are among the reliable chains or groups operating in Italy, with CIGA among the most luxurious. Sheraton hotels are making an impact in Italy in a big way, though most, located in Rome, Florence, Bari, Padua, and Catania, tend to be geared toward convention and business travel. There are a few Relais et Châteaux member hotels that are noted for individual atmosphere, personal service, and luxury; they are also expensive. The AGIP chain is found mostly on main highways.

Good-value accommodations can be found at one-star hotels and *locande* (inns). Rooms are usually spotlessly clean but basic, with shower and toilets down the hall.

Rentals More and more people are discovering the attractions of renting a house, cottage, or apartment in the Italian countryside. These are ideal for families or for groups of up to eight people looking for a bargain—or just independence. Availability is subject to change, so it is best to ask your travel agent or the nearest branch of ENIT, the Italian tourist board, about rentals.

Ratings The following price categories are determined by the cost of two people in a double room. Best bets are indicated by a ★.

Category	Cost
Very Expensive	over 400,000 lire
Expensive	200,000–400,000 lire
Moderate	130,000–180,000 lire
Inexpensive	under 110,000 lire

Very Expensive **Cavalieri Hilton.** Though it is outside the main part of Rome and a taxi ride to wherever you are going, this is a large, elegant hotel set in its own park with two excellent restaurants. *Via Cadlolo 101, tel. 06/31511, fax, 06/315–12241. 387 rooms with bath. Facilities: 2 restaurants, pool, terrace. AE, DC, V.*

Le Grand. This 100-year-old establishment, located within walking distance of Via Veneto, caters to an elite international clientele. The spacious guest rooms are decorated in Empire style, with smooth fabrics and thick carpets in blue and pale gold tones. Crystal chandeliers and marble baths add luxurious notes. Afternoon tea is served daily in the split-level main lounge. One of Italy's most beautiful dining rooms, Le Restaurant, is here as well (*see* Dining, above). *Via Vittorio Emanuele Orlando 3, tel. 06/4709, fax 06/474–7307. 170 rooms with bath. Facilities: bar, 2 restaurants. AE, DC, MC, V.*

★ **Hassler-Villa Medici.** Guests can expect a cordial atmosphere and magnificent service at this hotel, just at the top of the Spanish Steps. The public rooms are memorable, especially the first-floor bar (a chic city rendezvous), and the glass-roof lounge, with gold marble walls and hand-painted tile floor. The elegant bedrooms are decorated in a variety of classic styles; some feature frescoed walls. *Piazza Trinità dei Monti 6, tel. 06/ 679–2651, fax 06/678–9991. 101 rooms with bath. Facilities: bar, restaurant. AE, V, MC.*

Lord Byron. The most elegant hotel in Rome is the Lord Byron. Located in the diplomatic residential section of Rome away from its bustling center, the small villa has neat, fresh, and cheerful bedrooms that do, however, tend to be small. The staff offers the best service of any Rome hotel, and its dining room has extremely creative Italian cooking that has earned it two Michelin stars. *Via de Notaris 5, tel. 06/360–9541, fax 06/360– 9541. 55 rooms with bath. Facilities: bar, restaurant, garden. AE, DC, V.*

Expensive **Eden.** Just off Via Veneto, the Eden celebrated its centenary in 1989, having renovated three of its four floors. Further renovations are under way to make this hotel, now a Trusthouse Forte property, one of Rome's most luxurious. Rooms on the upper floors have terrific views (the best is from the penthouse bar and restaurant). *Via Ludovisi 49, tel. 06/474-3551, fax 06/482-1584. 93 rooms with bath. Facilities: bar, restaurant. AE.*

Forum. A centuries-old palace converted into a fine hotel, the Forum is on a quiet street within hailing distance of the Roman Forum and Piazza Venezia. The wood-paneled lobby and street-level bar are warm and welcoming, as are the smallish, pink-and-beige bedrooms. The view of the Colosseum from the roof-top restaurant is superb: Breakfast here—or a nightcap at the roof bar—can be memorable. *Via Tor dei Conti 25, tel. 06/679-2446, fax 06/678-6479. 80 rooms with bath. Facilities: bar, restaurant. AE, DC, MC, V.*

★ **Victoria.** Oriental rugs, oil paintings, welcoming armchairs, and fresh flowers add charm to the public rooms of this hotel, a favorite of American businesspeople who prize the personalized service and restful atmosphere. Some upper rooms and the roof terrace overlook the Villa Borghese. *Via Campania 41, tel. 06/473931, fax 06/679-9319. 150 rooms with bath. Facilities: bar, restaurant. AE, DC, MC, V.*

Moderate **Carriage.** Few hotels in Rome have this combination of excellent location (near the Spanish Steps), Old World elegance, and reasonable rates. The decor is in soft blue and gold, with subdued Baroque accents added for a touch of luxury. The rooms have antique-reproduction closets and porcelain phones. *Via della Carrozze 36, tel. 06/679-4106, fax 06/679-4106. 27 rooms with bath. Facilities: bar. AE, DC, MC, V.*

Gregoriana. Bedroom decor at this former convent near the Spanish Steps is low-key enough, but the owners have gone wild in the public rooms: Two floors have leopard-skin wallpaper; the third has a splashy floral print; and the lobby is decked out in rattan. Reserve well in advance: The Gregoriana is popular with the high-fashion crowd. *Via Gregoriana 18, tel. 06/679-4269, fax 06/678-4258. 19 rooms with bath. No credit cards.*

★ **Internazionale.** Within easy walking distance of many downtown sights, this has long been one of Rome's best midsize hotels. Decor throughout is in soothing pastel tones, with some antique pieces, mirrors, and chandeliers heightening the English country-house look. Guests relax in small, homey lounges downstairs and begin the day in the pretty breakfast room. *Via Sistina 79, tel. 06/679-3047, fax 06/678-4764. 40 rooms with bath. AE, DC, MC, V.*

Inexpensive **Margutta.** Centrally located near the Spanish Steps and Piazza
★ del Popolo, this small hotel has an unassuming lobby but bright, attractive bedrooms and modern baths. Three rooms on the top floor are in demand for their views of Rome's rooftops and domes. *Via Laurina 34, tel. 06/322-3674. 27 rooms with bath. AE, DC, MC, V.*

Suisse. The mood in the Suisse's public rooms may be old-fashioned—the check-in desk is distinctly drab—but the bedrooms, while small, are cheerful enough, with bright bedspreads, framed prints, and some charming old furniture. Some rooms face the (fairly) quiet courtyard. There's an upstairs breakfast room, but no restaurant. *Via Gregoriana 56, tel. 06/678-3649. 28 rooms, half with bath. No credit cards.*

The Arts

Pick up a copy of the *Carnet di Roma* at EPT tourist offices; issued monthly, it's free and has an exhaustive listing of scheduled events and shows. The bi-weekly booklet *Un Ospite a Roma;* free from your hotel concierge, is another source of information. If you want to go to the opera, ballet, or to a concert, it's best to ask your concierge to get tickets for you. They are on sale at box offices only, just a few days before performances.

Opera   The **Teatro dell'Opera** is on Via del Viminale (tel. 06/6759–5725 for information in English; tel. 06/6759–5721 to book tickets in English); its summer season at the **Baths of Caracalla** in July and August is famous for spectacular performances amid the Roman ruins. Tickets are on sale at the opera box office or at the box office at Caracalla (*see* Exploring, above).

Concerts   The main concert hall is the **Accademia di Santa Cecilia** (Via della Conciliazione 4, tel. 06/654–1044). The Santa Cecilia Symphony Orchestra has a summer season of concerts.

Film   The only English-language movie theater in Rome is the **Pasquino** (Vicolo del Piede, just off Piazza Santa Maria in Trastevere, tel. 06/580–3622). The program is listed in Rome daily newspapers.

Nightlife

Rome's "in" nightspots change like the flavor of the month, and many fade into oblivion after a brief moment of glory. The best source for an up-to-date list is the weekly entertainment guide, "Trovaroma," published each Thursday in the Italian daily *La Repubblica.*

Bars   Jacket and tie are in order in the elegant **Blue Bar** of the Hostaria dell'Orso (Via dei Soldati 25, tel. 06/686–4221), and in **Le Bar** of Le Grand hotel (Via Vittorio Emanuele Orlando 3, tel. 06/4709). **Harry's Bar** (Via Veneto 150, tel. 06/474–5832) is popular with American businesspeople and journalists residing in Rome.

Young Romans favor **Calisé** (Piazza Mastai 7, tel. 06/580–9404) in Trastevere, where sandwiches and salads, as well as drinks, are available until 3 AM. Current favorites around the Pantheon, a hub of after-dark activity, include **La Palma** (Via della Maddalena 23, tel. 06/654–0752), where the under-25 crowd hangs out, and **Hemingway** (Piazza delle Coppelle 10, tel. 06/654–4135), which attracts a crowd from the movie, TV, and fashion world. Both are open evenings only, but until very late.

Discos and Nightclubs   There's deafening disco music for an under-30s crowd at the **Kripton** (entrance at Via Luciani 52, tel. 06/870504). Special events such as beauty pageants and theme parties are a feature, and there's a restaurant on the premises. **Casanova** (Piazza Rondanini 36, tel. 06/654–7314), in the Pantheon area, where much of the late-night crowd hangs out, offers disco music and often has theme nights and sometimes cabaret. Sports personalities and other celebrities are attracted to **Veleno** (Via Sardegna 27, tel. 06/493583), one of the few places in Rome to offer black dance music, including disco, rap, funk, and soul.

Singles Scene   Locals and foreigners of all nations and ages gather at Rome's cafés in **Piazza della Rotonda** in front of the Pantheon, at **Piazza**

Navona; and **Piazza Santa Maria** in Trastevere. The cafés on **Via Veneto** and the bars of the big hotels draw tourists mainly and are good places to meet other travelers in the over-30 age group. In fair weather, under-30s will find crowds of contemporaries on the **Spanish Steps,** where it's easy to strike up a conversation.

20 Stockholm

Arriving and Departing

By Plane All international flights arrive at Arlanda Airport, 40 kilometers (25 miles) north of the city. The airport is linked to Stockholm by a fast freeway. For information on arrival and departure times, call the individual airlines.

Between the Airport and Downtown Buses leave both the international and domestic terminals every 10–15 minutes, from 7:10 AM to 10:30 PM, and run to the city terminal at Klarabergsviadukten next to the central train station. A taxi from the airport will cost at least SEK 350, but a useful and flexible alternative is the SAS (Scandinavian Airlines) limousine service to any point in Greater Stockholm. It operates as a shared taxi at between SEK 185 and SEK 280, depending on the distance. If two or three people travel together in a limousine to the same address, only one pays the full rate; all others pay half price.

By Train All major domestic and international services arrive at Stockholm Central Station on Vasagatan, in the heart of the city. This is also the terminus for local commuter services. For 24-hour train information, tel. 08/225060. At the station there is a ticket and information office, where you can make seat or sleeping-car reservations. An automatic ticket-issuing machine is also available. Seat reservation cost SEK 20, couchettes SEK 80, and beds SEK 160.

By Bus Long-distance buses, from such places as Härnösand and Sundsvall, arrive at Norra Bantorget, a few blocks north of the central station, and all others at Klarabergsviadukten, just beside it. Bus tickets can also be bought at the railroad reservations office.

By Car There are two main access routes from the west and south: the E3 main highway from Gothenburg and E4 from Malmö, which continues as the main route to Sundsvall, the far north, and Finland. All routes to the city center are well marked.

Getting Around

The most cost-effective way of getting around Stockholm is to use a **Stockholmskortet** (Key to Stockholm) card. Besides giving unlimited transportation on city subway, bus, and rail services, it offers free admission to 50 museums and several sightseeing trips. The card costs SEK 125 for 24 hours, SEK 250 for two days, and SEK 375 for three days. It is available from the tourist center at Sweden House, at Kungsträdgården, and the Hotellcentralen accommodations bureau at the central station.

Maps and timetables for all city transportation networks are available from the SL information desks at Norrmalmstorg or Sergels Torg. You can also obtain information by phone (tel. 08/236000).

By Bus and Subway The Stockholm Transit Authority (SL) operates both the bus and subway systems. Tickets for the two networks are interchangeable.

The subway system, known as T-banan (the *T* stands for tunnel), is the easiest and fastest way of getting around the city. Some of the stations offer permanent art exhibitions. Station entrances are marked with a blue T on a white background.

The T-banan has about 100 stations and covers more than 60 route-miles. Trains run frequently between 5 AM and 2 AM.

Individual tickets are available at ticket counters, but it is cheaper to buy a special discount coupon that gives a significant saving compared with buying separate tickets each time you travel. The coupons are available at Pressbyrån newsstands. A one-day ticket for the city center alone, valid on both bus and subway, costs SEK 28. A ticket covering the entire Greater Stockholm area costs SEK 50 for 24 hours or SEK 95 for 72 hours. People under 18 or over 65 pay half price. At press time, these prices were scheduled to go up.

The Stockholm bus network is one of the world's largest. Services run not only within the central area but also to out-of-town points of interest, such as Waxholm, with its historic fortress, and Gustavsberg, with its well-known porcelain factory. Within Greater Stockholm, buses run throughout the night.

By Train SL operates conventional train services from Stockholm Central Station to a number of nearby points, including Nynäshamn, a departure point for ferries to the island of Gotland. Trains also run from the Slussen station to the fashionable seaside resort of Saltsjöbaden.

By Taxi Taxis are difficult to come by on the street (although you may find one at an official taxi stand), so they usually have to be ordered. Telephone 08/150000 or 08/150400 if you need to reserve one well in advance. There is an immediate charge of SEK 19 if you hail a taxi in the street, SEK 40 if you order one by phone. A trip of 10 kilometers (6 miles) costs SEK 58.8; between 6 and 7 kilometers, SEK 67 at night and SEK 77 on weekends; there is an additional charge if you book the taxi in advance.

Important Addresses and Numbers

Tourist Information The main tourist center is at **Sweden House** (Kungsträdgården, tel. 08/789–2000 or 789–2490). During the peak tourist season (mid-June to mid-August), it is open weekdays 8:30–6; weekends 8–5. Off-season the hours are 9–5 and 9–2, respectively. Besides providing information, it is the main ticket center for sightseeing excursions. There are also information centers at the central station, in the City Hall (summer only), and in the Kaknäs TV tower.

Embassies U.S. (Strandvägen 101, tel. 08/783–5300). **Canadian** (Tegelbacken 4, tel. 08/237920). **U.K.** (Skarpögatan 6–8, tel. 08/667–0140).

Emergencies **Police** (tel. 08/769–3000; emergencies only: 90000); **Ambulance** (tel. 90000); **Doctor** (Medical Care Information, tel. 08/6449200)—tourists can get hospital attention in the district where they are staying or can contact the private clinic, **City Akuten** (tel. 08/1171776); **Dentist** (tel. 08/6541117); **Pharmacy: C. W. Scheele** (tel. 08/248280) (all are indicated by the sign Apotek).

English Bookstores Most bookstores have a good selection of English books. **Hedengrens Bokhandel** (Sturegallerian, tel. 08/611–5132) offers dictionaries and maps in all languages.

Travel Agencies **American Express** (Birger Jarlsgatan 1, tel. 08/235330). **Thomas Cook** (Vasagatan 22, tel. 08/204990).

Guided Tours

Orientation Tours   A guided sightseeing tour lasting 1½ hours departs from Sweden House in Hamngatan at 11 AM every morning. It covers the
central area and also includes a visit to the Kaknäs TV Tower.
Tickets can be purchased from the Excursion Shop at Sweden
House. A convenient budget-price tour by boat and/or bus is
SL's "Tourist Route" (Turistlinjen). The tour departs every 15
minutes during peak vacation periods and every half hour at
other times; you can get on and off at any one of the 14 stops.
This tour is free for holders of the Key to Stockholm card but is
conducted in Swedish only.

Boat Tours   You'll find a bewildering variety of tours available at Stockholm's quaysides. The **Waxholm Steamship Company** (tel. 08/
140830) operates scheduled services to many of the islands in
the archipelago on its famous white steamers. Trips range from
one to three hours each way. Popular one-day excursions include Waxholm, Utö, Sandhamn, and Möja. Conventional
sightseeing tours include a one-hour circular city tour operated
by the **Strömma Canal Company** (tel. 08/233375). It leaves from
the Nybroplan quay every hour between 10 and 5 during the
summer.

Special-Interest   A Stimulating Stockholm program offers a range of unusual ex-
Tours   cursions. These include tours for those interested in the fur
business or in glass manufacturing. Information on the full
range of excursions is available at the "Stimulating Stockholm"
desk at the tourist center.

Excursions   Not to be missed is the boat trip to the Palace of Drottningholm, the 17th-century private residence of the Royal Family
and a smaller version of Versailles. The boat departs from the
City Hall Bridge (Stadshusbron) every half hour between 10
and 4:30 during the summer. Another popular trip goes from
Stadshusbron to the ancient towns of Sigtuna and Skokloster.
By changing boats you can continue to Uppsala, where you can
catch a train back to Stockholm. Information is available from
the **Strömma Canal Company** (tel. 08/233375) or the tourist
center at Sweden House.

Personal Guides   Contact the **Guide Center** at **Stockholm Information Service**
(tel. 08/240885 or 789–2431).

Exploring Stockholm

*Numbers in the margin correspond to points of interest on the
Stockholm map.*

Because Stockholm's main attractions are concentrated in a
relatively small area, the city itself can be explored in several
days. But if you want to take advantage of some of the full-day
excursions offered, it is worthwhile to devote a full week to
your visit.

The city of Stockholm, built on 14 small islands among open
bays and narrow channels, has been dubbed the "Venice of the
North" by advertising copywriters. It is a handsome, civilized
city, full of parks, squares, and airy boulevards, yet it is also a
bustling, modern metropolis. Glass-and-steel skyscrapers
abound, but in the center you are never more than five minutes'
walk from twisting, medieval streets and waterside walks.

The first written mention of Stockholm dates from 1252, when a powerful regent named Birger Jarl is said to have built a fortified castle here. And it must have been this strategic position, where the calm, fresh waters of Lake Mälaren meet the salty Baltic Sea, that prompted King Gustav Vasa to take over the city in 1523, and King Gustavus Adolphus to make it the heart of an empire a century later.

During the Thirty Years' War (1618–48), Sweden gained importance as a Baltic trading state, and Stockholm grew commensurately. But by the beginning of the 18th century, Swedish influence had begun to wane, and Stockholm's development had slowed. It did not revive until the Industrial Revolution, when the hub of the city moved north from the Old Town area.

City Hall and Old Town Anyone in Stockholm with limited time should give priority to a tour of **Gamla Stan** (The Old Town), a labyrinth of narrow, medieval streets, alleys, and quiet squares just south of the city center. Ideally, you should devote an entire day to this section. But before crossing the bridge, pay a visit to the modern-day ❶ **City Hall,** constructed in 1923 and now one of the symbols of Stockholm. You'll need an early start, since there is only one guided tour per day, at 10 AM (also at noon on Saturday and Sunday). Lavish mosaics grace the walls of the **Golden Hall,** and the **Prince's Gallery** features a collection of large murals by Prince Eugene, brother of King Gustav V. Take the elevator to the top of the 348-foot tower for a magnificent view of the city. *Admission: SEK 20. Tower open May–Sept., daily 11–3.*

❷ Crossing into the Old Town, the first thing you'll see is the magnificent **Riddarholm Church,** where a host of Swedish kings are buried. *Admission: SEK 10. Open Mon.–Sat. 10–3, Sun. 1–3.*

❸ From there proceed to the **Royal Palace,** preferably by noon, when you can see the colorful changing-of-the-guard ceremony. The smartly dressed guards seem superfluous, since tourists wander at will into the castle courtyard and around the grounds. Several separate attractions are open to the public. Be sure to visit the **Royal Armory,** with its outstanding collection of weaponry and royal regalia. The **Treasury** houses the Swedish crown jewels, including the regalia used for the coronation of King Erik XIV in 1561. You can also visit the **State Apartments,** where the king swears in each successive government. *Admission: SEK 25 for Treasury and Armory; SEK 25 for State Apartments. Treasury and Armory open Mon.–Sat. 11–3, Sun. noon–4. State Apartments open Tues.–Sun. noon–3.*

From the palace, stroll down **Västerlånggatan,** one of two main shopping streets in the Old Town. This is a popular shopping area, brimming with boutiques and antiques shops. Walk down to the Skeppsbron waterfront, then head back toward the center over the Ström bridge, where anglers cast for salmon. If ❹ you feel like a rest, stop off at **Kungsträdgården** and watch the world go by. Originally built as a royal kitchen garden, the property was turned into a public park in 1562. During the summer, entertainment and activities abound, and you can catch a glimpse of local people playing open-air chess with giant chessmen.

Djurgården Be sure to spend at least a day visiting the many attractions on the large island of **Djurgården.** Although it's only a short walk from the city center, the most pleasant way to approach it is by

Stockholm

Major Attractions
City Hall, **1**
Gröna Lund Tivoli, **6**
Kungsträdgården, **4**
Museum of National
Antiquities, **9**
Nordic Museum, **8**
Riddarholm Church, **2**
Royal Palace, **3**
Skansen, **7**
Vasamuseet, **5**

Other Attractions
Cathedral, **22**
Concert Hall, **12**
House of Nobles, **20**
Kaknäs Tower, **15**
Museum of Far
Eastern Antiquities, **18**
Museum of Modern
Art, **14**
National Museum, **16**
Parliament, **21**

Royal Dramatic
Theater, **11**
Royal Library, **13**
Royal Opera House, **17**
Supreme Court, **19**
Stock Exchange, **10**

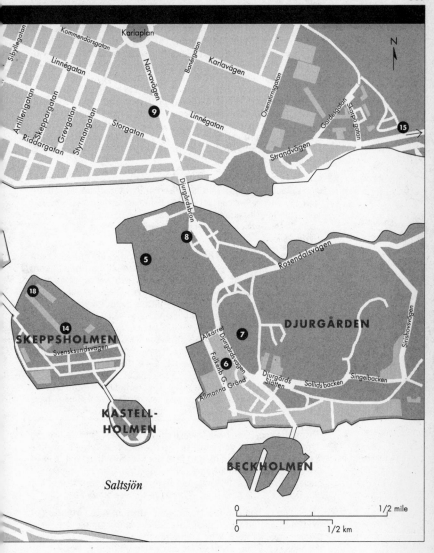

ferry from Skeppsbron, in the Old Town. The ferries drop you off near two of Stockholm's best-known attractions, the Vasa Museum and Gröna Lund Tivoli. The *Vasa*, a restored 17th-century warship, is one of the oldest preserved war vessels in the world and has become Sweden's most popular tourist sight. She sank ignominiously in Stockholm Harbor on her maiden voyage in 1628, reportedly because she was not carrying sufficient ballast. Recovered in 1961, she has been restored to her original appearance and has now been moved into a spectacular new mu-
⑤ seum, the **Vasamuseet,** which opened in 1990. It features guided tours, films, and displays. *Galarvarvet, tel. 08/666-4800. Admission: SEK 25 adults, SEK 10 children. Open daily 10-5.*

⑥ **Gröna Lund Tivoli,** Stockholm's version of the famous Copenhagen amusement park is a favorite family attraction, featuring hair-raising roller coasters as well as tamer delights. *Tel. 08/665-7000. Admission: SEK 25 adults, SEK 15 children. Open Apr. 20 through end of Aug. (opening hours vary widely; check in daily newspapers).*

⑦ Just across the road is **Skansen,** a large, open-air folk museum consisting of 150 reconstructed traditional buildings from Sweden's different regions. Here you can see a variety of handcraft displays and demonstrations. There is also an attractive open-air zoo—with many native Scandinavian species, such as lynxes, wolves, and brown bears—as well as an excellent aquarium. *Tel. 08/663-0500. Admission: May-Aug., SEK 25 adults, group SEK 20; Sept.-Apr., SEK 18 adults, group SEK 13. Children free in 1991. Open Jan.-Apr. and Sept.-Dec., daily 9-5; May-Aug., daily 9 AM-10 PM.*

Time Out   For a snack with a view, try the **Solliden Restaurant** at Skansen. Skansen also offers a selection of open-air snack bars and cafés; Gröna Lund has four different restaurants.

From the zoo, head back toward the city center. Just before the
⑧ Djurgård bridge, you come to the **Nordic Museum,** which, like Skansen, provides an insight into the way Swedish people have lived over the past 500 years. The collection includes displays of peasant costumes, folk art, and Lapp culture. *Admission: SEK 20. Open Tues.-Fri. 10-4, Thurs. 10-8, weekends 11-4.*

⑨ Once you're back on the "mainland," drop into the **Museum of National Antiquities.** Though its name is uninspiring, it houses some remarkable Viking gold and silver treasures. **The Royal Cabinet of Coin,** located in the same building, boasts the world's largest coin. *Narvavägen 13-17. Admission: SEK 20. Open Tues.-Sun. noon-5. (Thurs. open noon-7).*

Off the Beaten Track

Just over 155 meters (500 feet) tall, the **Kaknäs TV Tower** at Djurgården is the highest structure in Scandinavia. From the top you can catch a magnificent view of the city and surrounding archipelago. Facilities include a cafeteria, restaurant, and souvenir shop. *Djurgården, tel. 08/789-2435.*

You can see the world's largest variety of water lily at the **Bergianska Botanical Garden,** just north of the city center. The lily's leaves are more than 2.17 meters (7 feet) in diameter. *Frescati, tel. 08/153912.*

Fjäderholmarna (the Feather Islets), the collective name for a group of four secluded islands in the Stockholm archipelago, have been open to the public only since the early '80s after 50 years as a military zone. There is a museum depicting life in the archipelago, as well as the largest aquarium in Scandinavia, housing many species of Baltic marine life. Boats leave from Slussen, Strömkajen, and Nybroplan in downtown Stockholm. *Fjäderholmarna, tel. 08/718–0100.*

Shopping

Gift Ideas Stockholm is an ideal place to find items that reflect the best in Swedish design and elegance, particularly glass, porcelain, furs, handcrafts, home furnishings, and leather goods. The quality is uniformly high, and you can take advantage of the tax-free shopping service in most stores.

Department Stores The largest is **NK,** on Hamngatan, where you can find just about anything. Other major stores are **PUB,** on Hötorget, and **Ahléns City,** on Klarabergsgatan. All three are open on Sunday. A brand-new shopping complex is **Sturegallerian,** a covered gallery built on the site of the former public baths at Stureplan. There are about 50 shops, plus a number of restaurants and cafés.

Shopping Districts The center of Stockholm's shopping activity has shifted from Kungsgatan to Hamngatan, a wide boulevard along which a huge, covered shopping complex called **Gallerian** has been built. The **Old Town** area is best for handcrafts, antiquarian bookshops, and art shops.

Food and Flea Markets The biggest flea market in northern Europe is located in **Skärholmen** shopping center, a 20-minute subway ride from the downtown area. Market hours are weekdays 11–6, Sat. 9–3, Sun. 10–3. Superior food markets selling such Swedish specialties as marinated salmon and reindeer can be found on **Ostermalmstorg** and **Hötorget.**

Glassware For the best buys, try **Nordiska Kristall,** on Kungsgatan, or **Rosenthal Studio-Haus,** on Birger Jarlsgatan. The latter operates its own shipping service. **Arioso,** on Västerlånggatan in the Old Town, is good for modern crystal and ceramics, and **Önskebutiken,** on the corner of Kungsgatan and Sveavägen, specializes in crystal as well as porcelain.

Handicrafts A good center for all kinds of Swedish handicrafts in wood and metal is **Svensk Hemslöjd,** on Sveavägen. It also sells embroidery kits and many types of weaving and knitting yarn. **Stockholms Läns Hemslöjdsförening,** on Drottninggatan, has a wide selection of Swedish folk costumes and handicraft souvenirs from different parts of Sweden.

Dining

Swedish cuisine used to be considered somewhat uninteresting, but lately it has become much more cosmopolitan. The inevitable fast-food outlets, such as McDonald's and Wimpy, have come on the scene, as well as Clock, the homegrown version. But there is also a good range of more conventional restaurants, ranging from the usual top-class establishments to less expensive places where you can pick up a somewhat cheaper lunch or snack.

Many restaurants all over the country specialize in *Husmanskost*—literally "home cooking"—which is based on traditional Swedish recipes.

Sweden is best known for its *smörgåsbord*, a word whose correct pronunciation defeats non-Swedes. It consists of a tempting buffet of hot and cold dishes, usually with a strong emphasis on seafood, notably herring, prepared in a wide variety of ways. Authentic smörgåsbord can be enjoyed all over the country, but the best is found in the many inns in Skåne, where you can eat as much as you want for about SEK 190. Virtually all Swedish hotels now serve a lavish smörgåsbord-style breakfast, often included in the room price. Do justice to your breakfast and you'll probably want to skip lunch!

Mealtimes The Swedes tend to eat early. Restaurants start serving lunch at about 11 AM, and outside the main cities you may find that they close quite early in the evening (often by 9) or may not even open at all for dinner. Don't wait too long to look for someplace to have a meal.

Dress Except for the most formal restaurants, where a jacket and tie are advisable, casual—or casual chic—attire is perfectly acceptable for restaurants in all price categories.

Ratings Prices are per person and include a first course, main course (Swedes tend to skip desserts), and service charge, but no drinks. A service charge of 13%–15% is added to meal prices, so there is no need to tip. If you want to leave something extra, round the total to the nearest SEK 5 or so. Best bets are indicated by a star ★.

Category	Cost
Very Expensive	over SEK 400
Expensive	SEK 230–SEK 400
Moderate	SEK 120–SEK 230
Inexpensive	under SEK 120

Very Expensive **Erik's.** The authentic marine atmosphere owes much to its location: a restored barge moored in Stockholm Harbor. The emphasis is on Swedish fish and shellfish with a French accent. During the summer, guests enjoy deck-side dining and a pleasant harbor view. *Strandvägskajen 17, tel. 08/660–6060. Reservations advised. AE, DC, MC, V. Closed Sun., Christmas, New Year's Day, and Midsummer Night (June 22).*

★ **Operakällaren.** Located in part of the elegant Opera House building, this is one of Stockholm's best-known traditional restaurants, featuring both Scandinavian and Continental cuisine. It is famed for its smörgåsbord, particularly during the pre-Christmas period. The restaurant faces Kungsträdgården, the waterfront, and the Royal Palace. *Operahuset, tel. 08/ 111125. Reservations advised. AE, DC, MC, V.*

Ulriksdals Värdshus. This is a beautifully located country inn built in 1868 and set in a castle park on the outskirts of town. It offers both Swedish and international cuisines, but is particularly noted for its lunchtime smörgåsbord. *Ulriksdals Slottspark, tel. 08/850815. Reservations advised. AE, DC, MC, V. Closed Sun. dinner and Christmas.*

Expensive **Aurora.** Located in a 300-year-old building complete with authentic cellar vaults, Aurora is one of the best-known restaurants in the Old Town. The cuisine is both Swedish and international. The adjacent Old City Club, under the same management, is open for moderate-price lunch Monday through Friday. *Munkbron 11, tel. 08/219359. Reservations advised. AE, DC, MC, V. Dinner only. Closed Sun.*

★ **Clas på Hörnet.** Located just outside the city center, Clas på Hörnet is a small, intimate establishment occupying the ground floor of a restored 200-year-old town house, now a hotel (*see* Lodging, below). It offers a choice of international or Swedish cuisine. *Surbrunnsgatan 20, tel. 08/165136. Reservations advised. AE, DC, MC, V. Closed Christmas.*

Gourmet. The accent is on French cuisine, but Swiss and Swedish specialties are also available. Seafood figures prominently. Try the house specialty, Sea Crayfish in Love. *Tegnérgatan 10, tel. 08/314398. Reservations advised. AE, DC, MC, V. Closed Sun., July.*

Quarter Deck. Located on the Old Town waterfront near the Royal Palace, the Quarter Deck, part of the Hotel Reisen, offers a superb harbor view. The cuisine is both Swedish and French, with the accent on seafood. *Skeppsbron 12–14, tel. 08/223260. Reservations advised. AE, DC, MC, V. Closed Christmas, New Year's Day, and July.*

★ **Stallmästaregården.** An historic old inn with an attractive courtyard and garden, Stallmästaregården is located in the Haga Park, some distance from the city center. But the fine French and Swedish cuisine is well worth the journey. In the summer meals are served in the courtyard overlooking Brunnsviken Lake. A lower, fixed-price menu is available. *Norrtull, near Haga, tel. 08/243910. Reservations advised. AE, DC, MC, V.*

Moderate **Bakfickan.** The name means "hip pocket" and is appropriate ★ because this restaurant is tucked round the back of the Opera House complex. It's a budget-price alternative to the nearby Operakällaren and is particularly popular at lunchtime, offering Swedish home cooking and a range of daily dishes. Counter and table service are available. *Operahuset, tel. 08/242700. No reservations. AE, DC, MC, V. Closed Sun.*

Glada Laxen. Since the name means "Happy Salmon," it is not surprising that salmon in various guises, from smoked to mousse, is the star attraction here. Centrally located in the Gallerian shopping center near the Sweden House Tourist Center, this is a popular spot. *Regeringsgatan 23, tel. 08/211290. Reservations advised, especially for lunch. AE, DC, MC, V. Closed Sun. during summer. Dinner until 7:30 PM*

Gondolen. Suspended under the gangway of the *Katarina* elevator at Slussen, Gondolen offers a magnificent view over the harbor, Lake Mälaren, and the Baltic Sea. The cuisine is international, and a range of fixed-price menus is available. *Slussen, tel. 08/402021. Reservations advised. AE, DC, MC, V. Closed Christmas and New Year's Day.*

Markurell's. The two separate restaurants, the Wärdshuset and the Bistro, are conveniently located opposite the central station. It's a busy establishment serving international cuisine. *Mäster Samuelsgatan 73, tel. 08/211012. Reservations advised. AE, DC, MC, V.*

Sturehof. Centrally located, with an unpretentious, nautical ambience, Sturehof's specialty is its seafood. It also boasts an

English-style pub. *Stureplan 2, tel. 08/142750. Reservations advised. AE, DC, MC, V. Closed Sat. lunch, Sun., Christmas, New Year's Day, and June 22.*

Inexpensive **Cassi.** This centrally located restaurant specializes in French cuisine at reasonable prices. *Narvavägen 30, tel. 08/661–7461. Reservations advised. MC. Closed Sat.*

★ **Open Gate.** Located near the Slussen locks, on the south side of Stockholm Harbor, this is a popular, trendy Art Deco Italian-style trattoria. Pasta dishes are the house specialty. *Högbergsgatan 40, tel. 08/439776. No reservations. AE, DC, MC, V.*

Örtagården. This all-vegetarian, no-smoking restaurant is located one floor up from the Östermalmshallen market hall. It offers an attractive buffet, with soups, salads, and hot dishes, served in a turn-of-the-century atmosphere. *Nybrogatan 31, tel. 08/662–1728. MC, V. Closed Christmas and New Year's Day.*

Lodging

You can get a good idea of the facilities and prices at a particular hotel by consulting the official annual guide, *Hotels in Sweden*, obtainable free of charge from the Swedish National Tourist Office. There is a good selection of hotels in all price categories in every town and city, though major international chains such as Sheraton have made only small inroads in Sweden thus far. The main homegrown chains are SARA, Scandic, and RESO. The Sweden Hotels group has about 100 independently owned hotels and offers a central reservation office. The group also has its own classification scheme—A, B, or C—based on the facilities available at each establishment. CountrySide Sweden is a group of 35 handpicked resort hotels, some of them restored historic manor houses or centuries-old inns. Most have been family-run for generations. Apart from the more modest inns and the cheapest budget establishments, private baths and showers are now standard features, although it is just as well to double-check when making your reservation. Whatever their size, virtually all Swedish hotels provide scrupulously clean accommodations and courteous service.

Stockholm has plenty of hotels in most price brackets, although relatively few in the Inexpensive category. Many hotels cut their rates in high season, however, when business travelers are on vacation, so that during the summer even a hotel classified as Very Expensive can become affordable. The major hotel chains also have a number of bargain schemes available on weekends throughout the year and daily during the summer.

Almost 50 hotels offer the "Stockholm Package," providing accommodations for one night, costing between SEK 380 and SEK 610 per person, including breakfast and a Stockholmskortet (Key to Stockholm) card (*see* Getting Around, above). Details of the Stockholm Package can be obtained from the **Stockholm Information Service** (Excursion Shop, Box 7542, S-103 93 Stockholm). Also, you can call **The Hotel Center** (tel. 08/240880) or reserve the package through travel agents.

If you arrive in Stockholm without a hotel reservation, the **Hotellcentralen** in the central station will arrange accommodations for you. The office is open daily 8 AM–9 PM, June–September; weekdays 8:30–5 the rest of the year. There's a small fee for each reservation. Or phone one of the central reservations offices run by the major hotel groups: RESO (tel. 08/235700), SARA (tel. 08/753–7350), Scandic (tel. 08/345550), Sweden Hotels (tel. 08/204311), or Best Western (tel. 08/300420).

Ratings   Prices are for two people in a double room, based on high-season rates. Best bets are indicated by a star ★.

Category	Cost
Very Expensive	over SEK 1,200
Expensive	SEK 970–SEK 1,200
Moderate	SEK 725–SEK 970
Inexpensive	under SEK 725

Very Expensive   **Amaranten.** Only five minutes' walk from the central station, Amaranten is a large, modern hotel, built in 1969 and refurbished in 1988. The "executive tower" offers a roof garden and 52 rooms. Guests enjoy a gourmet restaurant and brasserie, and piano bar. *Kungsholmsgatan 31, tel. 08/541060. 410 rooms with bath. Facilities: sauna, pool, restaurants, piano bar, and solarium. AE, DC, MC, V.*

★   **Continental.** Located in the city center across from the central station, the Continental is popular with American guests. It was first opened about 25 years ago and is now undergoing renovation that's scheduled for completion in 1992. It offers three restaurants in different price brackets, all of which have recently been renovated. *Klara Vattugränd 4, tel. 08/244020. 250 rooms, with bath. Facilities: 4 restaurants. AE, DC, MC, V.*

★   **Diplomat.** This is an elegant hotel located within easy walking distance of Djurgården Park and Skansen and offering magnificent views over Stockholm Harbor. The building itself is a turn-of-the-century town house that was converted into a hotel in 1966. The teahouse is a popular spot for light meals. *Strandvägen 7C, tel. 08/663–5800. 130 rooms with bath. AE, DC, MC, V. Closed Christmas and New Year's Day.*

Grand. Located on the waterfront in the center of town, the Grand is a large, gracious, Old World-style hotel dating back to 1874. It faces the Royal Palace. The two restaurants—French and Swedish—offer harbor views. The bar serves light snacks. *S. Blasieholmshamnen 8, tel. 08/221020. 319 rooms with bath, most with waterfront views. Facilities: sauna, restaurant, beauty salon. AE, DC, MC, V.*

★   **Lady Hamilton.** Considered one of Stockholm's most desirable hotels, the Lady Hamilton, in the Old Town, was built as a private home in 1470 and has been a hotel only since 1980. It houses an extensive collection of antiques, including one of George Romney's portraits of Lady Hamilton. *Storkyrkobrinken 5, tel. 08/234680. 34 rooms with bath. Facilities: sauna, pool, cafeteria. AE, DC, MC, V. Closed Christmas.*

Reisen. The building dates from 1819, although it was refurbished several years ago. It's situated in a waterfront sector of the Old Town and offers a fine restaurant, a grill, and what is reputed to be the best piano bar in town. The swimming pool is built under medieval arches. *Skeppsbron 12–14, tel. 08/223260. 113 rooms with bath. Facilities: sauna, pool, library. AE, DC, MC, V. Closed Christmas and New Year's Day.*

SAS Royal Viking. This is a large modern hotel adjoining the central train station and the airport bus terminal. Some rooms are on the small side. The restaurant was modernized in 1990, and another new amenity is the SkyJazz bar on the top floor. There is an SAS check-in counter in the lobby. *Vasagatan 1, tel. 08/141000. 340 rooms with bath. Facilities: sauna, pool, rooms for disabled guests. AE, DC, MC, V. Closed Christmas.*

SAS Strand. Acquired in 1986 by the SAS group, this is a gracious, Old World hotel. It was built in 1912 but was recently modernized. No two rooms are the same; many are furnished with antiques. An SAS check-in counter adjoins the main reception area. The Piazza is an indoor restaurant with an outdoor feel to it. Its specialty is Italian cuisine, and there is a superb wine list. *Nybrokajen 9, tel. 08/222900. 138 rooms with bath. Facilities: sauna, function rooms. AE, DC, MC, V.*

Sergel Plaza. Opened in 1984, the modern Sergel Plaza incorporates part of an older building located in the city center and is entirely decorated in the style of the 1700s. Its distinctive feature is its glass-roof lobby, which houses a piano bar. *Brunkebergstorg 9, tel. 08/226600. 406 rooms with bath. Facilities: restaurant, sauna, health club. AE, DC, MC, V.*

Expensive **Birger Jarl.** A short subway ride from the city center, Birger Jarl is a modern, characteristically Scandinavian hotel that opened in 1974. There is no full-service restaurant. *Tulegatan 8, tel. 08/151020. 252 rooms with bath. Facilities: sauna, pool, coffee shop. AE, DC, MC, V. Closed Christmas and New Year's Day.*

★ **Clas på Hörnet.** An 18th-century inn converted into a small hotel in 1982, Clas på Hörnet is just outside the city center. Its rooms, furnished with antiques of the period, go quickly. If you can't manage to reserve one, at least have a meal in the gourmet restaurant (*see* Dining, above). *Surbrunnsgatan 20, tel. 08/165130. 10 rooms with bath. AE, DC, MC, V.*

Karelia. A turn-of-the-century building on one of the main shopping streets, Karelia has a Finnish atmosphere. There is a Finnish restaurant for dining and dancing plus a separate restaurant specializing in Russian cuisine. *Birger Jarlsgatan 35, tel. 08/247660. 103 rooms with bath. AE, DC, MC, V. Closed Christmas.*

Lord Nelson. This companion hotel to the Lady Hamilton was built in much the same style. Its location on a busy pedestrian street in the Old Town makes it rather noisy at night. The atmosphere throughout is distinctly nautical—even down to the cabin-size rooms. The café is open until 8 PM daily. *Västerlånggatan 22, tel. 08/232390. 31 rooms with bath. AE, DC, MC, V. Closed Christmas and New Year's Day.*

Mornington. Although it is not particularly imposing from the outside, Mornington is a comfortable, quiet hotel, situated near the indoor market at Östermalmstorg and within walking distance of the city center. The dining bar offers a small but varied menu. *Nybrogatan 53, tel. 08/663–1240. 140 rooms with bath. AE, DC, MC, V. Closed Christmas and New Year's Day.*

Moderate **Alfa.** About 20 minutes from the city center, Alfa is a medium-size, medium-class hotel. Opened in 1972, it has recently been refurbished. *Marknadsvägen 6, tel. 08/810600. 104 rooms with bath. Facilities: restaurant. AE, DC, MC, V.*

City. A large, modern-style hotel built in the 1940s but modernized in 1982–83, City is located near the city center and the Hötorget market. It is owned by the Salvation Army, so alcohol is not served. Breakfast is served in the atrium Winter Garden. *Slöjdgatan 7, tel. 08/222240. 300 rooms with bath. Facilities:*

restaurant, café, sauna, rooms for disabled guests. AE, DC, MC, V.

Stockholm. This hotel has an unusual location—the upper floors of a downtown office building. The mainly modern decor is offset by traditional Swedish furnishings that help create its family atmosphere. Breakfast is the only meal served. *Norrmalmstorg 1, tel. 08/221320. 92 rooms with bath. AE, DC, MC, V. Closed Christmas and New Year's Day.*

Inexpensive   **Alexandra.** Although it is in the Södermalm area, to the south of the Old Town, the Alexandra is only five minutes by subway from the city center. It is a small, modern hotel, opened 20 years ago and renovated in 1988. Only breakfast is served. *Magnus Ladulåsgatan 42, tel. 08/840320. 79 rooms with bath. Facilities: sauna, solarium. AE, DC, MC, V. Closed Christmas and New Year's Day.*

Gustav af Klint. A "hotel ship" moored at Stadsgården quay, near Slussen subway station, the Gustav af Klint is divided into two sections—a hotel and a hostel. It was refurbished in 1989. There is a cafeteria and restaurant, and you can dine on deck in summer. *Stadsgårdskajen 153, tel. 08/404077. 28 cabins, none with bath. AE, MC, V. Closed Christmas and New Year's Day.*

Långholmen. This former prison, built in 1724, was converted into a combined hotel and hostel in 1989. It is located on the island of Långholmen, which has popular bathing beaches. The Inn, next door, serves Swedish home cooking, and the wine cellar offers light snacks. *Långholmen, tel. 08/668–0500. 101 rooms. AE, DC, MC, V.*

The Arts

Stockholm's main theater and concert season runs from September through May or June, so there are not many major performances during the height of the tourist season. But for a list of events, pick up the free booklet *Stockholm This Week*, available from hotels and tourist information offices. You can get last-minute tickets to theaters and shows at the cut-price ticket booth on Norrmalmstorg Square. Tickets sold here are priced 25% below box office rates. The booth is open Monday noon–5 and Tuesday–Saturday noon–7. There is also a **central reservation office** for regular-price tickets (tel. 08/108800).

Concerts   The city's main concert hall is the **Concert House** (Konserthuset) at Hötorget 8, home of the Stockholm Philharmonic Orchestra. The main season runs from mid-September to mid-May. In addition to full-scale evening concerts, there are "coffee break" or lunchtime concerts some days. During the summer, free concerts are given in many city parks. For information, phone 08/102110.

Opera   The season at the **Royal Opera House,** just across the bridge from the Royal Palace, runs from mid-August to early June and offers performances at top-class international standards (tel. 08/248240). And from early June to early September, there are performances of opera, ballet, and orchestral music at the exquisite **Drottningholm Court Theater,** which was the setting for Ingmar Bergman's film *The Magic Flute.* The original 18th-century stage machinery is still used in these productions. You can get to Drottningholm by subway and bus or by special theater-bus (leaving from the Grand Hotel or Vasagatan, opposite the central station). For tickets, call 08/660–8225.

Theater Stockholm has about 20 top-rank theaters, but dramatic productions are unlikely to interest those who don't understand Swedish. A better option is to go to a musical; several city theaters hold regular performances. Plays in English are featured at the **Regina Theater** (Drottninggatan 71A, tel. 08/207000).

Film English and American films predominate, and they are screened with the original soundtrack and Swedish subtitles. Programs are listed in the local evening newspapers, though titles are usually in Swedish. Movie buffs should visit **Filmstaden** (Film City), Mäster Samuelsgatan 25 (tel. 08/225420), where 11 cinemas under one roof show a variety of films from noon until midnight.

Nightlife

Cabaret Stockholm's biggest nightclub, **Börsen** (Jakobsgatan 6, tel. 08/ 249210), offers high-quality international cabaret shows. Another popular spot is the **Cabaret Club,** Barnhusgatan 12 (tel. 08/110608). Although it can accommodate 450 guests, reservations are advised.

Bars and **Café Opera** (tel. 08/110026) is a popular meeting place for young
Nightclubs and old alike. It has the longest bar in town, plus dining and roulette, and dancing after midnight. Piano bars are also an important part of the Stockholm scene. **Riche** is another popular watering hole in the city center. Try the **Anglais Bar** at the Hotel Anglais (tel. 08/249900) or the **Clipper Club** at the Hotel Reisen, Skeppsbron (tel. 08/223260).

Jazz Clubs **Fasching** (Kungsgatan 63, tel. 08/216267) is Stockholm's largest, but another popular spot is **Stampen** (Grämunkegränd 7, tel. 08/205793). Get here in good time if you want a seat, and phone first to be sure the establishment hasn't been reserved for a private party.

Discos **Galaxy** (Strömsborg, tel. 08/215400) is one of the most popular night spots, catering to a variety of musical tastes. There is an outdoor bar and dining area in summer. Others are **Downtown** (Norrlandsgatan 5A, tel. 08/119488) and **Karlsson** (Kungsgatan 65, tel. 08/119298).

21 Venice

Arriving and Departing

By Plane Marco Polo International Airport is situated about 10 kilometers (6 miles) northeast of the city on the mainland. For flight information, tel. 041/661111.

Between the Airport and Downtown ATVO and ACTV (Venice City Transit) buses make the 25-minute trip in to Piazzale Roma, going through the city's unappealing outlying regions; the cost is around 4,000 lire. From Piazzale Roma visitors will most likely have to take a *vaporetto* (water bus) to their hotel (*see* Getting Around, below). The Co-operative San Marco motor launch is only slightly more costly (13,000 lire) and presents a far more attractive introduction to the city; it runs direct from the airport, dropping passengers across the lagoon at Piazza San Marco. (It works on a limited schedule in winter.) Land taxis are available, running the same route as do the buses; the cost is about 40,000 lire. Water taxis (slick high-power motorboats) are a real rip-off: Negotiate the fare in advance, usually upward of 100,000 lire.

By Train Make sure your train goes all the way to Santa Lucia train station in Venice's northeast corner; some trains leave passengers at the Mestre station on the mainland, from which you must connect with a local to Santa Lucia. The EPT-AAST information booth (open daily 8–8) and the baggage depot in the station are usually festooned with long lines of tourists. If you need a hotel room, go to the AVA hotel association desk (open daily 9–9); there are others at the airport and at the city garage at Piazzale Roma. The deposit (10–30,000 lire, depending on the hotel category) is discounted on your hotel bill. Vaporetto landing stages are directly outside the station. *Make sure you know how to get to your hotel before you arrive.* Don't take water taxis, since they are expensive and probably can't take you right to the door of your hotel. By water taxi or vaporetto you'll have to walk some distance anyway. For this reason, try to obtain a map of Venice before you arrive—and take a luggage cart; porters are hard to find.

By Car You will have to leave your car in the Piazzale Roma garage, on the Tronchetto parking island, or even on the mainland. Some visitors park in Padua or Mestre and then take the train into Venice. From Tronchetto take ACTV bus No. 17 to Piazzale Roma, where you can get a vaporetto, or take the Line 34 water bus direct to St. Mark's.

Getting Around

First-time visitors find that getting around Venice presents some unusual problems: the complexity of its layout (the city is made up of more than 100 islands, aml linked by bridges); the bewildering unfamiliarity of waterborne transportation; the illogical house numbering system and duplication of street names in its six districts; and the necessity of walking whether you enjoy it or not. It's essential you have a good map showing all street names and water bus routes; buy one at any newsstand.

By Vaporetto ACTV water buses run the length of the Grand Canal and circle the city. There are several lines, some of which connect Venice with the major and minor islands in the lagoon; Line 1 is the Grand Canal local. Timetables are posted on all landing stages, where ticket booths are located (open early morning–9 PM).

081- 9685018

Buy single tickets or books of 10 and count your change carefully; shortchanging is a nasty habit in these parts. The fare is 1,800 lire on most lines, 2,500 lire for the Line 2 express between the train station, Rialto, San Marco, and the Lido. Stamp your ticket in the machine on the landing stage. A daily tourist ticket costs 10,000 lire. Vaporetti run every 10 minutes or so during the day; Lines 1, 2, and 5 run every hour between midnight and dawn. Landing stages are clearly marked with name and line number and serve boats going in both directions.

By Water Taxi Known as *motoscafi*, or *taxi*, these are excessively expensive, and the fare system is as complex as Venice's layout. A minimum fare of about 35,000 lire gets you nowhere, and you'll pay three times as much to get from one end of the Grand Canal to the other. *Always agree on the fare before starting out.* To avoid arguments, overcharging, and rip-offs, avoid motoscafi altogether.

By Traghetto Few tourists know about the two-man gondolas that ferry people across the Grand Canal at various fixed points. It's the cheapest and shortest gondola ride in Venice, and it can save a lot of walking. The fare is 400 lire, which you hand to one of the gondoliers when you get on. Look for "Traghetto" signs.

By Gondola Don't leave Venice without treating yourself to a gondola ride, preferably in the quiet of the evening when the churning traffic on the canals has died down, the palace windows are illuminated, and the only sounds are the muted splashes of the gondolier's oar. Make sure he understands that you want to see the *rii*, or smaller canals, as well as the Grand Canal. They're supposed to charge a fixed minimum rate of about 50,000 lire for 50 minutes, but in practice they ask for 80,000–100,000 lire for a 30- to 40-minute ride. Come to terms with your gondolier *before* stepping into his boat.

On Foot This is the only way to reach many parts of Venice, so wear comfortable shoes. Invest in a good map that names all the streets, and count on getting lost more than once.

Important Addresses and Numbers

Tourist Information The main Venice **AAST Tourist Office** (tel. 041/522–6356) is at Calle Ascensione 71C, just off Piazza San Marco, under the arcade in the far left corner opposite the basilica. Open Mon.–Sat., Nov.–Mar., 8:30–1:30; Apr.–Oct., 8:30–7:30. There are EPT-AAST information booths at the Santa Lucia station (tel. 041/715016); in the bus terminal at Piazzale Roma (tel. 041/522–7402), open summer only; at Marco Polo airport; and at Tronchetto parking lot.

Consulates U.K. (Campo Santa Maria della Carità 1051, Dorsoduro, tel. 041/522–7207). U.S. (The nearest U.S. Consulate is in Milan, at Largo Donegani 1, tel. 02/652841).

Emergencies Police (tel. 113). **Ambulance** (tel. 041/523–0000). **Doctor:** Try the emergency room at Venice's hospital (tel. 041/523–0000), or call the British Consulate (*see* above) and ask for recommendations. **Pharmacies: Farmacia Italo-Inglese** (Calle della Mandola, tel. 041/522–4837). **International Pharmacy** (Calle Lunga San Marco, tel. 041/522–2311). Pharmacies are open weekdays 9–12:30 and 4–7:45; Saturday 9–12:45; Sunday and night service by turns.

Travel Agencies **American Express** (San Moise 1471, tel. 041/520–0844). **CIT** (Piazza San Marco 4850, tel. 041/528–5480). **Wagons-Lits Travel** (Piazzetta dei Leoncini 289, tel. 041/522–3405). **Thomas Cook** (Rialto 5126, tel. 041/528–7358).

Guided Tours

Orientation Tours **American Express** (tel. 041/520–0844) and **CIT** (tel. 041/528–5480) offer two-hour walking tours of the San Marco area, taking in the basilica and the Doge's Palace. The cost is about 35,000 lire. American Express also has an afternoon walking tour from April to October that ends with a gondola ride and glass-blowing demonstration. The cost is about 40,000 lire.

Special-Interest Tours **American Express, CIT,** and other operators offer group gondola rides with serenade. The cost is about 40,000 lire. During July and August free guided tours of the Basilica di San Marco are offered by the Patriarchate of Venice; information is available at a desk in the atrium of the church (tel. 041/520–0333). Some tours are in English, and there are several daily, except Sunday.

Excursions Don't take organized tours to the islands of Murano, Burano, and/or Torcello. These tours are annoyingly commercial and emphasize glass factory showrooms, pressuring you to buy. You can easily do these islands on your own. **American Express** offers a bus trip to the Venetian Villas and Padua. The cost is about 60,000 lire, and they run from April to October on Tuesday, Thursday, and weekends. **CIT** runs an excursion on the Burchiello motor launch along the Brenta Canal, with return by bus.

Personal Guides **American Express** and **CIT** can provide guides for walking or gondola tours of Venice, or cars with driver and guide for excursions on the mainland. Pick up a list of licensed guides and their rates from the **AAST** Information Office in Piazza San Marco (tel. 041/522–6356).

Exploring Venice

Venice—La Serenissima, the Most Serene—is disorienting in its complexity, an extraordinary labyrinth of narrow streets and waterways, opening now and again onto some airy square or broad canal. The majority of its magnificent palazzi are slowly crumbling; though this sounds like a recipe for a down-at-the-heels slum, somehow in Venice the shabby, derelict effect is magically transformed into one of supreme beauty and charm, rather than horrible urban decay. The place reeks with atmosphere, especially at night when the lights from the vaporetti and the stars overhead pick out the gargoyles and arches of the centuries-old facades. For hundreds of years Venice was the unrivaled mistress of trade between Europe and the Orient, and the staunch bulwark of Christendom against the tide of Turkish expansion. Though the power and glory of its days as a wealthy city-republic are gone, the art and exotic aura remain.

To enjoy the city, you will have to come to terms with the crowds, which take over from May through September. Hot and sultry in the summer, Venice is much more welcoming in early spring and late fall. Romantics like it in the winter when prices are much lower, the streets are deserted (well, nearly), and the sea mists impart a haunting melancholy to the *campi* (squares) and canals. Piazza San Marco (St. Mark's Square) is the pulse of Venice, crowded with people and pigeons no matter what time of year. But after joining with the crowds to visit the Basilica di San Marco and the Doge's Palace, strike out on your own and just follow where your feet take you—you won't be disappointed.

Numbers in the margin correspond to points of interest on the Venice map.

Piazza San Marco and the Accademia

❶ Even the pigeons have to fight for space on **Piazza San Marco,** and pedestrian traffic jams clog the surrounding byways. Despite the crowds and because it is the most famous piazza in Venice, San Marco is the logical starting place of each of our various itineraries. Pick up pamphlets and a copy of *A Guest in Venice,* a free information booklet, at the **AAST Information Office** in the far left corner of Piazza San Marco, opposite the basilica. The information office is in the wing built by order of Napoleon to complete the much earlier palaces on either side of the square, enclosing it to form what he called "the most beautiful drawing room in all of Europe." Upstairs is the **Museo Correr,** with eclectic collections of historical objects and a picture gallery of fine 15th-century paintings. *Piazza San Marco, Ala Napoleonica, tel. 041/522–5625. Admission: 5,000 lire. Open Mon., Wed.–Sat. 10–4, Sun. 9–12:30.*

❸ The **Basilica di San Marco** (St. Mark's Cathedral) was begun in the 11th century to hold the relics of St. Mark the Evangelist, the city's patron saint, and its richly decorated facade is surmounted by copies of the four famous gilded bronze horses (the originals are in the basilica's upstairs museum). Inside, golden mosaics sheathe walls and domes, lending an extraordinarily exotic aura, half Christian church, half Middle Eastern mosque. Be sure to see the **Pala d'Oro,** an eye-filling 10th-century altarpiece in gold and silver, studded with precious gems and enamels. From the atrium, climb the steep stairway to the museum: The bronze horses alone are worth the effort. *The Basilica is open from early morning, but tourist visits are allowed Mon.–Sat. 9:30–5:30, Sun. 2:30–5:30. No admission to those wearing shorts or other revealing clothing. Pala d'Oro and Treasury. Admission: 2,000 lire. Open Apr.–Sept., Mon.–Sat. 9:30–5:30, Sun. 2–5:30. Oct.–Mar., Mon.–Sat. 10–5, Sun. 2–5. Gallery and Museum. Admission: 2,000 lire. Open Apr.–Sept., daily 9:30–5:30; Oct.–Mar., daily 10–5.*

❹ Next to St. Mark's is the **Palazzo Ducale** (Doge's Palace), which, during Venice's prime, was the epicenter of the Serene Republic's great empire. More than just a palace, it was a combination White House, Senate, Supreme Court, torture chamber, and prison. The building's exterior is striking; the lower stories consist of two rows of fragile-seeming arches, while above rests a massive pink-and-white marble wall whose solidity is barely interrupted by its six great Gothic windows. The interior is a maze of vast halls, monumental staircases, secret corridors, state apartments, and the sinister prison cells and torture chamber. The palace is filled with frescoes, paintings, carvings, and a few examples of statuary by some of the Renaissance's greatest artists. Don't miss the famous view from the balcony, overlooking the piazza and St. Mark's Basin and the church of San Giorgio Maggiore across the lagoon. *Piazzetta San Marco, tel. 041/522–4951. Admission: 10,000 lire. Open daily 8:30–7.*

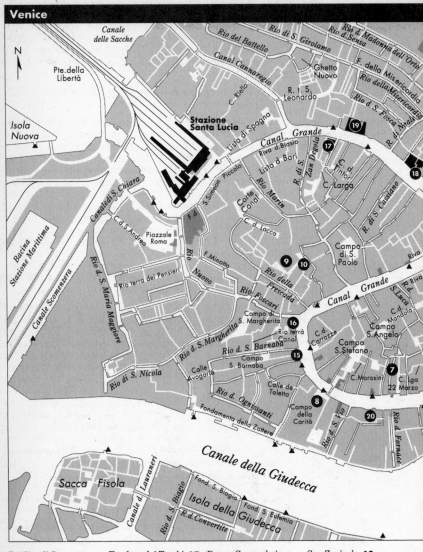

Venice

Sacca
della
Misericordia

Canale delle Navi

San
Michele

0 ——————— 440 yards
0 ——————— 400 meters

Ci. Racchetta
Fondamente
Rio S. Caterina
R. d.
Gesuiti Nuove

Strada
Nuova

Rio d. Santi Apostoli

Rio della Panada
C.d. Squero

Campo d.
Pescheria

Erberia

del Vin

C.d.Testa

R. dei Mendicanti

Campo Santi
Giovanni e Paolo

12

13

R. Barbaria delle Tole

R. d. S. Cristina

Rio d. S. Marina

14

R. d. Fava

Sal. d. S. Lio

Rugo

C.d. Bande

11

R. S. Severo

R. d. S. Lorenzo

Ruga
Giuffa

C. Lion

C. d.
Furlani

R. d. S.
Francesco

Canale d. Galeazze

Darsena
Grande

Rio d. Vergini

del Carbon

Campo
Manin

Fabbri

Frezzaria

2   **1**

5   **3**
       4

R. d. Palazzo

Molo

Riva degli

Fond.
Osmarin

R. d. Greci

R. d. Pietà

Schiavoni

R. d. Scudi

R. d. Corna

R. d. Arsenale

Rio della Tana

V. Garibaldi

Rio d. S. Daniele

Rio d. S. Anna

di S. Pietro

i

6

R. d.

S. Moisè

**Piazza
San Marco**

Riva dei Sette Martiri

Rio d. S. Giuseppe

R. d. S. Giuseppe

Canale di S. Marco

Isola di
S. Giorgio
Maggiore

Fond.
delle Zitelle

Calle
Michelangelo

ci

Viale Trieste

Rio dei Giardini

▲ Boat stop

⑤ For a pigeon's-eye view of Venice take the elevator up to the top of the **Campanile di San Marco** (St. Mark's bell tower) in Piazza San Marco, a reconstruction of the 1,000-year-old tower that collapsed one morning in 1912, practically without warning. Fifteenth-century clerics found guilty of immoral acts were suspended in wooden cages from the tower, sometimes to live on bread and water for as long as a year, sometimes to die of starvation and exposure. (Look for them in Carpaccio's paintings of the square that hang in the Accademia.) *Piazza San Marco, tel. 041/522–4064. Admission: 3,000 lire. Open Apr.–Oct., daily 9:30–7:30; Nov.–Mar. 10–4.*

Time Out **Caffè Florian** is a Venetian landmark located on the square. It's a great place to nurse a Campari or a cappuccino. The pleasure of relaxing amid so much history does not come cheap. A pot of hot chocolate indoors runs about $10, and outside on the piazza, which is really where you want to sit, prices are even higher—and there's an extra charge if you're served when the orchestra is playing.

⑥ Armed with a street map, head west out of San Marco (in the opposite direction of the basilica), making your way past **San Moisè**'s elaborate Baroque facade and by the American Express office, on to Calle Lunga 22 Marzo, where the inconspicuous **La Caravella** restaurant of the hotel Saturnia Internazionale (*see* both Dining and Lodging, below) is one of the **⑦** city's best. Continue on to the church of **Santa Maria del Giglio**, behind the **Gritti Palace hotel** (also considered tops). Across the bridge behind the church, **Piazzesi** on Campiello Feltrina is famous for its handprinted paper and desk accessories. In the next little square, **Norelene** (Campo San Maurizio 2606) has stunning handprinted fabrics in opulent Fortuny designs.

Time Out You must cross yet another bridge to get to Campo Santa Stefano, also known as Campo Morosini, where you can indulge yourself with some of the best ice cream you've ever eaten, at **Paolin,** a tiny bar whose outdoor tables occupy a good chunk of the vast campo.

⑧ Join the stream of pedestrians crossing the Grand Canal on the wooden **Accademia Bridge,** and head straight on for the **Galleria dell'Accademia** (Academy of Fine Arts), Venice's most important picture gallery and a must for art lovers. Try to spend at least an hour viewing this remarkable collection of Venetian art, which is attractively displayed and well lighted. Works range from 14th-century Gothic and Bellini's 15th-century oils to the Golden Age of the 16th century, represented by Titian, including his last work, the *Pietà;* Tintoretto, including his *Virgin of the Treasures* and *Miracles of St. Mark;* and Veronese. *Campo della Carità, tel. 041/522–2247. Admission: 8,000 lire. Open Mon.–Sat. 9–2, Sun. 9–1.*

Once again consulting your map, make your way through Calle Contarini, Calle Toeletta, and Campo San Barnaba to Rio Terra Canal, where **Mondonovo** ranks as one of the city's most interesting mask shops (Venetians love masks of all kinds, from gilded lions to painted sun faces and sinister death's heads). Just around the corner is Campo Santa Margherita, which has a homey feel.

Time Out **Antico Capon** is a good, simple trattoria whose tables spill out onto the square in fair weather. Stop in for a pizza, or just relax with a beer at the nearby sidewalk café. *Campo Santa Margherita.*

Continue past Campo San Pantalon to Campo San Rocco, just **9** beside the immense church of the Frari. The **Scuola di San Rocco** was embellished with more than 50 canvases by Tintoretto in the 1500s; they are an impressive sight, dark paintings aglow with figures hurtling dramatically through space amid flashes of light and color. *The Crucifixion* in the Albergo (the room just off the great hall) is held to be his masterpiece. *Campo di San Rocco. Admission: 5,000 lire. Open daily 10–1 and 3:30–6:30.*

The church of Santa Maria Gloriosa dei Frari (known simply as **10** the **Frari**) is one of Venice's most important churches, a vast soaring Gothic building of brick. Since it is the principal church of the Franciscans, its design is suitably austere to reflect that order's vows of poverty, though paradoxically it contains a number of the most sumptuous pictures in any Venetian church. Chief among them are the magnificent Titian altarpieces, notably the immense *Assumption of the Virgin* over the main altar. Titian was buried here at the ripe old age of 88, the only one of 70,000 plague victims to be given a personal church burial. *Campo dei Frari. Admission: 500-lire donation "for lighting expenses."*

San Zanipolo and Backtracking once again to the Piazza San Marco, go to the **the Rialto** arch under the Torre dell'Orologio (Clock Tower) and head northeast into the **Merceria,** one of Venice's busiest streets and, with the **Frezzeria** and **Calle Fabbri,** part of the shopping area that extends across the Grand Canal into the **Rialto district.** At Campo San Zulian, turn right into Calle Guerra and Calle delle **11** Bande to the graceful white marble church of **Santa Maria Formosa;** it's situated right on a lively square (of the same name) with a few sidewalk cafés and a small vegetable market on weekday mornings.

Use your map to follow Calle Borgoloco into Campo San Marina, where you turn right, cross the little canal, and take Calle **12** Castelli to **Santa Maria dei Miracoli** (Calle Castelli). Perfectly proportioned and sheathed in marble, this late-15th-century building embodies all the classical serenity of the early Renaissance. The interior is decorated with marble reliefs by the church's architect, Pietro Lombardo, and his son Tullio.

Retrace your steps along Calle Castelli and cross the bridge into Calle delle Erbe, following signs for "SS. Giovanni e Paolo." The massive Dominican church of Santi Giovanni e **13** Paolo—**San Zanipolo,** as it's known in the slurred Venetian dialect—is the twin (and rival) of the Franciscan Frari. The church is a kind of pantheon of the doges (25 are buried here), and contains a wealth of artworks. Outside in the campo stands Verrocchio's equestrian statue of Colleoni, who fought for the Venetian cause in the mid-1400s.

Cross the canal in front of the church (keeping an eye out to the left for the pop-eyed, tongue-lolling gargoyle at head height), and continue along Calle Larga, crossing a pair of bridges to Campiello Santa Maria Nova. Take Salita San Canciano to Salita San Giovanni Crisostomo to find yourself once again in

⓮ the mainstream of pedestrians winding their way to the **Rialto Bridge.** Street stalls hung with scarves and gondolier's hats signal that you are entering the heart of Venice's shopping district. Cross over the bridge, and you'll find yourself in the market district. Try to visit the Rialto market when it's in full swing, with fruit and vegetable vendors hawking their wares in a colorful and noisy jumble of sights and sounds. Not far beyond is the fish market, where you'll probably find sea creatures you've never seen before (and possibly won't want to see again). A left turn into Ruga San Giovanni and Ruga del Ravano will bring you face to face with scores of shops: At **La Scialuppa** (Calle Saoneri 2695) you'll find hand-carved wooden models of gondolas and their graceful oar locks known as *forcole.*

The Grand Canal Just off the Piazzetta di San Marco (the square in front of the Doge's Palace) you can catch Vaporetto Line 1 at either the San Marco or San Zaccaria landing stages (on Riva degli Schiavoni), to set off on a boat tour along the **Grand Canal.** Serving as Venice's main thoroughfare, the canal winds in the shape of an "S" for more than 3½ kilometers (2 miles) through the heart of the city, past some 200 Gothic-Renaissance palaces. This is the route taken by vaporetti, gondolas, water taxis, mail boats, police boats, fire boats, ambulance boats, barges carrying provisions and building materials, bridal boats, and funeral boats. See it both when traffic is at a peak (preferably from a vantage point such as the Rialto Bridge), and again when it's calm and quiet. Your vaporetto tour will give you an idea of the opulent beauty of its palaces and a peek into the side streets and tiny canals where the Venetians go about their daily business. *Vaporetto Line 1. Cost: 1,800 lire.*

Here are some of the key buildings that this tour passes. The **Galleria dell'Accademia,** with its fine collection of 14th- to 18th-century Venetian paintings, that were visited earlier. The **⓯** **Ca'Rezzonico** was built in 1680 and is now a museum with Vene- **⓰** tian paintings and furniture. **Ca'Foscari** is a 15th-century Gothic building that was once the home of Doge Foscari, who was unwillingly deposed and died the following day! Today it's part **⓱** of Venice's university. The **Fondaco dei Turchi** was an original Byzantium "house-warehouse" of a rich Venetian merchant, but the building has suffered some remodeling during the past **⓲** 100 years. **Ca'd'Oro** is the most flowery palace on the canal; it **⓳** now houses the Galleria Franchetti. The **Palazzo Vendramin Calergi** is a Renaissance building where Wagner died in 1883. It's also the winter home of the municipal casino. Last but not **⓴** least, there is the **Peggy Guggenheim Museum,** which usually has excellent exhibitions.

Shopping

Glass Venetian glass is as famous as the city's gondolas, and almost every shop window displays it. There's a lot of cheap glass for sale; if you want something better, among the top showrooms are **Venini** (Piazzetta dei Leoncini 314), **Pauly** (Calle dell' Ascensione 72, opposite the AAST information office), **Salviati** (Piazza San Marco 78 and 110), **Cenedese** (Piazza San Marco 139), and **Isola** (Campo San Moisè and Mercerie 723). On the island of Murano, where prices are generally no lower than in Venice, **Domus** (Fondamenta dei Vetrai) has a good selection.

Shopping District The main shopping area extends from the Piazza San Marco through the Mercerie and Calle Fabbri toward the Rialto.

Department Stores The **Coin** store (Campo San Bartolomeo) specializes in fashion and accessories. **Standa** has stores on Campo San Luca and Strada Nuova, where you can pick up medium-price goods of all kinds.

Dining

Venetian restaurants are expensive. Beware of the tourist traps around the Piazza San Marco: prices here are higher than most, and the food isn't up to par. City specialties include *pasta e fagioli*, a thick bean soup; risotto and all kinds of seafood; and the delicious *fegato alla veneziana*, thin strips of liver cooked with onions, served with grilled *polenta*, cornmeal cakes.

Generally speaking, *a ristorante* pays more attention to decor, service, and menu than does a *trattoria*, which is simpler and often family-run. An *osteria* used to be a lowly tavern, though now the term may be used to designate a chic and expensive eatery. A *tavola calda* offers hot dishes and snacks, with seating. A *rosticceria* has the same, to take out.

The menu is always posted in the window or just inside the door of an eating establishment. Check to see what is offered, and note the charges for *coperto* (cover) and *servizio* (service), which will increase your check. Q *menu turistico* includes taxes and service, but beferages are extra.

Mealtimes Lunch hour in Venice last from 12:30 to 2:30, dinner from 7:30 to 9:30. Practically all restaurants close one day a week; some close for winter or summer vacation.

Precautions Tap water is safe unless noted *Non Potabile*. Bottle mineral water is available everywhere, *gassata* (with bubbles) or *non gassata* (without). If you prefer tap water, ask for *acqua semplice*.

Dress Except for restaurants in the Very Expensive and occasionally in the Expensive categories, where jacket and tie are advisable, casual attire is acceptable.

Ratings Prices are per person and include first course, main course, dessert or fruit, and house wine, where available. Best bets are indicated by a star ★.

Category	Cost
Very Expensive	over 120,000 lire
Expensive	80,000–120,000 lire
Moderate	40,000–80,000 lire
Inexpensive	under 40,000 lire

Very Expensive ★ **Danieli Terrace.** Seafood is the star here: Try the *branzino al forno* (baked sea bass) if it's on the menu; otherwise the scampi is almost as good as that at the Gritti. Such desserts as *zabaglione* (a fluffy confection combining egg yolk, sugar, and dry marsala) are fabulous—it's worth bearing this in mind as you order the main course. Fair weather sees patrons dining on the candlelighted terrace; otherwise you'll be seated in the opulent pastel-toned dining room—either way you'll be treated to a view of San Giorgio and the lagoon. *Hotel Danieli, Riva degli Schiavoni 4196, tel. 041/522–6480. Reservations advised. AE, DC, MC, V.*

Gritti. The dining room of the Gritti Palace hotel is one of Venice's most elegant eating spots. Its flower-trimmed terrace overlooking the Grand Canal is magical in the evening when the traffic dies down and the white dome of Santa Maria della Salute gleams across the way. The *risotto con scampi* is delicious as prepared by the Gritti's talented chef, and the sole is well worth trying, too. *Hotel Gritti, Campo Santa Maria del Giglio 2467, tel. 041/522–6044. Reservations advised. AE, DC, MC, V.*

Expensive **Antico Martini.** This Venetian institution is both chic and discreet, and its menu is made up mostly of Venetian specialties, with a few concessions to international palates. The *San Pietro* (fish) with shellfish sauce is first-class, the creamy *tiramisù* (a coffee-flavored sponge cake with soured cream cheese) is an admirable end to any meal. There are outdoor tables in the summer, and a softly lighted wood-paneled winter dining room. *Campo San Fantin 1983, tel. 041/522–4121. Reservations advised. AE, DC, MC, V. Closed Tues., Wed. lunch, mid-Nov. to mid–Mar. but open for Christmas and Carnival.*

★ **La Caravella.** Tiny and intimate, La Caravella is decorated like the dining saloon of an old Venetian sailing ship, with lots of authentic touches. The menu is huge and slightly intimidating, though the highly competent mâitre d' will advise you well. The *granseola* (crab) is marvelous in any of several versions. *Calle Larga XXII Marzo 2397, tel. 041/520–8901. Reservations required. AE, DC, MC, V. Closed Wed. from Nov.–Apr.*

Moderate **Da Arturo.** The tiny Da Arturo is a refreshing change from the numerous seafood restaurants of which Venetians are so fond. The cordial proprietor prefers, instead, to offer antipasti with seasonal vegetables and such meat dishes as the excellent *braciolona di maiale* (pork chop in vinegar). *Calle degli Assassini 3656, tel. 041/528–6974. Reservations required. No credit cards. Closed Sun., Aug., and Dec. 20–31.*

★ **Fiaschetteria Toscana.** This is one of the city's best Moderate restaurants, which is why you'll see so many Venetians in the pleasant upstairs dining room or under the arbor in the square out front. Courteous, cheerful waiters serve such specialties as *rombo* (turbot) with capers and an exceptionally good *pasta alla buranella* (pasta with shrimp, au gratin). Some seafood dishes can be expensive. *Campo San Giovanni Crisostomo, tel. 041/528–5281. Reservations advised. AE, MC, V. Closed Tues. and first 2 weeks in July.*

Locanda Montin. Though unlikely to win any gastronomic awards, Montin is friendly and fun and enjoys a considerable reputation. You'll find all sorts of patrons sharing white linen-clothed tables, from the neighborhood locals to Viscount Linley, nephew of England's Queen Elizabeth. The garden out back is used as a flower-filled extension during summer months. At any time of year, try the *fegato alla veneziana* (liver and onions) or the delicious veal escalope. *Fondamenta Eremite 1147, tel. 041/522–7151. Reservations advised. AE, DC, MC, V, Closed Tues. eve. and Wed.*

Inexpensive **Da Ignazio.** A smiling waiter will welcome you to this attractive little trattoria in the Rialto district, where you'll find a tempting display of fruits and vegetables fresh from the nearby market. Specialties include *pasta e fagioli* (bean soup) and *seppie* (squid) Venetian-style. *Calle dei Saoneri, near San Polo, tel. 041/523–4852. Dinner reservations advised. No credit cards. Closed Sat.*

Al Milion. You'll mix with Venetians at this popular bistro-type place behind San Giovanni Crisostomo. Be prepared to choose quickly from the handwritten menu; lingering is not encouraged. You'll enjoy such hearty local fare as *pasta e fagioli* (thick bean soup). *Campo San Giovanni Crisostomo, tel. 041/522–9302. No reservations. No credit cards. Closed Wed.*

★ **Vino al Vino.** This is an informal annex of the upscale Antico Martini around the corner, and it's one of the few places where you can eat lightly and well at almost any time of the day (it's open 10 AM–1 AM). The place has a 1920s look: cream-colored walls covered with small prints and ceramic plates, marble tables, and café chairs. Venetians stop in for snacks and a glass of wine from an impressive assortment. *Calle del Cafetier 2007/a (San Fantin), tel. 041/523–7027. No reservations. AE, DC, MC, V. Closed Tues.*

Lodging

Venice is made up almost entirely of time-worn buildings, so it stands to reason that the majority of hotels are in renovated palaces. Top hotels may still contain palatial trappings, though some Cinderella-type rooms may be small and dowdy. Rooms in Moderate and Inexpensive hotels are often cramped and spartanly decorated, with thin walls and little or no lounging space. Air-conditioning is essential for survival in summer heat, and many hotels charge a hefty supplement for it. The main tourist season runs from mid-March through October, December 20 to New Year's Day, and the two-week Carnival period in mid-February. Make reservations well in advance at all times, but especially so for these periods.

Venice offers a good choice of accommodations. Room rates are on a par with other European capitals, but porters, room service, and in-house cleaning and laundering are disappearing in Moderate and Inexpensive hotels. Taxes and services are included in the room rate. Breakfast is an extra charge, and you can decline to take breakfast in the hotel, though the desk may not be happy about it; make this clear when booking or checking in. Air-conditioning also may be an extra charge. In older hotels, room quality may be uneven; if you don't like the room you're given, ask for another. This applies to noise, too; some front rooms are bigger and have views but get street noise. Specify if you care about having either a bath or shower, as not all rooms have both. In Moderate and Inexpensive places, showers may be the drain-in-the-floor type guaranteed to flood the bathroom. Major cities have hotel reservation service booths in the rail stations.

Hotels Italian hotels are officially classified from five-star (deluxe) to one-star (guest houses and small inns). Prices are established officially and a rate card on the back of the door of your room or inside the closet door tells you exactly what you will pay for that particular room. Any variations should be cause for complaint and should be reported to the local tourist office. CIGA, Jolly, Space, Atahotels, and Italhotels are among the reliable chains or groups operating in Italy, with CIGA among the most luxurious. Sheraton hotels are making an impact in Italy in a big way, though most, located in Rome, Florence, Bari, Padua, and Catania, tend to be geared toward convention and business travel. There are a few Relais et Châteaux member hotels that are noted for individual atmosphere, personal service, and luxury; they are also expensive. The AGIP chain is found mostly on main highways.

Good-value accommodations can be found at one-star hotels and *locande* (inns). Rooms are usually spotlessly clean but basic, with shower and toilets down the hall.

Rentals More and more people are discovering the attractions of renting a house, cottage, or apartment in the Italian countryside. These are ideal for families or for groups of up to eight people looking for a bargain—or just independence. Availability is subject to change, so it is best to ask you travel agent or the nearest branch of ENIT, the Italian tourist board, about rentals.

Camping Italy has a wide selection of campgrounds, and the Italians themselves are taking to camping by the thousands, which means that beach or mountain sites will be crammed in July and August. It's best to avoid these peak months and to send for the (necesssary) camping license for **Federazione Italiana del Campeggio,** Casella Postale 649, 50100 Firenze.

Ratings The following price categories are determined by the cost of two people in a double room. Best bets are indicated by a star ★.

Category	Cost
Very Expensive	over 400,000 lire
Expensive	220,000–400,000 lire
Moderate	100,000–220,000 lire
Inexpensive	under 100,000 lire

Very Expensive **Cipriani.** A sybaritic oasis of stunningly decorated rooms and suites with marble baths and Jacuzzis, the Cipriani is located across St. Mark's Basin on the island of Giudecca (pronounced JOO-dek-ka), offering a panorama of romantic views of the entire lagoon. The hotel launch whisks guests back and forth to the Piazza San Marco at any hour of the day or night. Cooking courses and fitness programs are offered as special programs to occupy the guests. Then, for sheer dining pleasure, there is the excellent Cipriani restaurant. Some rooms have pretty garden patios. *Guidecca 10, tel. 041/520–7744, fax 041/520–3930. 98 rooms with bath. Facilities: pool, gardens, tennis, health club. AE, DC, MC, V. Closed Nov. 1–Feb. 28.*
Danieli. A 15th-century palazzo is the hub of this exceptionally gracious and opulent hotel, surrounded by a cluster of modern, balconied wings. Sumptuous Venetian decor and atmosphere predominates, though some lower-price rooms can be drab. Celebrities love the Danieli, and it's a special favorite of English-speaking visitors. The restaurant (*see* Dining, above) and bar are unashamedly swanky; and the terrace has a fantastic view of St. Mark's Basin. *Riva degli Schiavoni 4196, tel. 041/522–6480, fax 041/520–0208. 230 rooms with bath. AE, DC, MC, V.*

★ **Gritti Palace.** The atmosphere of an aristocratic private home is what the management is after here, and they succeed beautifully. Fresh-cut flowers, fine antiques, sumptuous appointments, and Old World service make this a terrific choice for anyone who wants to be totally pampered. The dining terrace (*see* Dining, above) overlooking the Grand Canal is best in the evening when boat traffic dies down. *Campo Santa Maria del Giglio 2467, tel. 041/794611, fax 041/520–0942. 98 rooms with bath. AE, DC, MC, V.*

Expensive **Londra Palace.** You get the obligatory view of San Giorgio and St. Mark's Basin at this distinguished hotel whose rooms are decorated in dark paisley prints, with such sumptuous touches as canopied beds. French chefs preside over Les Deux Lions restaurant, now a haven of *cuisine française*, and the piano bar is open late. The hotel offers a complimentary Mercedes for one-day excursions and free entrance to the casino. *Riva degli Schiavoni 4171, tel. 041/520–0533, fax 041/520–0533. 69 rooms with bath. Facilities: terrace solarium. AE, DC, MC, V.*

★ **Metropole.** Guests can step from their water taxi or gondola into the lobby of this small hotel just five minutes from the Piazza San Marco. Many rooms have a view of the lagoon and all rooms are furnished with style. Ask for one of the quiet spacious rooms on the garden (room 141 is the nicest). *Riva degli Schiavoni 4149, tel. 041/520–5044, fax 041/522–3679. 65 rooms with bath. Facilities: restaurant, bar and grill room. AE, DC, MC, V.*

Saturnia Internazionale. Beamed ceilings, damask-hung walls, and authentic Venetian decor impart real character and charm to the solid comfort of the Saturnia's rooms and salons. Many rooms, among them nos. 80, 82, and 84, have been redecorated in chic style and endowed with glamorous bathrooms. The historic palace-hotel is centrally located near Piazza San Marco. *Calle Larga XXII Marzo 2398, tel. 041/520–8377, fax 041/520–7131. 95 rooms with bath. Facilities: 2 restaurants, bar. AE, DC, MC, V.*

Moderate **Accademia.** There's plenty of atmosphere and a touch of the romantic in this delightful hotel in a 17th-century villa. Rooms
★ are comfortable and brightly furnished, as are the sitting rooms on the ground floor. Many rooms overlook the gardens, where you can sit in warm weather. *Fondamenta Bollani 1058, Dorsoduro, tel. 041/523–7846. 27 rooms, most with bath. Facilities: gardens, bar. AE, DC, MC, V.*

La Residenza. A Gothic palace makes a delightful setting for this charming hotel, conveniently close to both San Marco and the San Zaccaria landing stage. Breakfast is served in a real antique-furnished Venetian salon, and rooms on the lower floor are especially good. Make reservations well in advance. *Campo Bandiera e Moro 3608, tel. 041/528–5315. 19 rooms, some with bath. AE, DC, MC, V. Closed 2nd week Jan.–mid-Feb., mid-Nov.–2nd week Dec.*

Scandinavia. Despite its curiously un-Italian name, this hotel indulges heavily in traditional—and somewhat overpowering—Venetian decor, with cut-glass chandeliers and dizzying combinations of damask patterns. The entrance is just off the lively Campo Santa Maria Formosa (near the San Zaccaria landing stage). A steep staircase leads to the rooms upstairs. *Campo Santa Maria Formosa 5240, tel. 041/522–3507. 29 rooms, 27 with bath. Facilities: restaurant. AE, DC, MC, V.*

Inexpensive
★ **Alboretti.** Redecorated in 1988, this small hotel is simply but attractively furnished. Despite its size and central location, the Alboretti has a little garden courtyard off the breakfast room and a lounge upstairs from the tiny lobby and bar area. There is no elevator. Together with its moderately priced restaurant, the Alboretti is a good value. *Rio Terra Sant'Agnese 882, tel. 041/523–0058. 19 rooms with bath. Facilities: restaurant. AE, MC, V.*

Galleria. Guests won't find much in the way of luxury here, but low prices, friendly staff (definitely no English spoken, but lots of smiles and nods), and a fine location hard by the Accademia Bridge make this a strong favorite. Ask for a room overlooking the Grand Canal—the view is one of the best in Venice. *Accademia 878–A, Dorsoduro, tel. 041/520–4172. 10 rooms, most with bath. No credit cards.*

★ **San Stefano.** This is a hotel in miniature, from the tiny reception area to the minuscule courtyard and breakfast room; even the elevator is skinny. The rooms are well furnished in Venetian style, with optional air-conditioning and TV. All in all, it's an excellent value, and centrally located, too. *Campo San Stefano 2957, tel. 041/520–0166, fax 041/522–4460. 11 rooms, all with bath. MC, V.*

The Arts

For a program of events, pick up the free *Guest in Venice* booklet at the AAST tourist office in Piazza San Marco, or at most hotel desks. Your hotel may also be able to get you tickets for some events.

Concerts A **Vivaldi Festival** is held in September, and concerts are held year-round in the city's churches; contact the **Kele e Teo Agency** (Piazza San Marco 4930, tel. 041/520–8722), which supplies tickets for many of the city's musical events.

Opera The opera season at **Teatro La Fenice** (Campo San Fantin, tel. 041/521–0161) runs from December to May. The box office is open September to July, Mon.–Saturday 9:30–12:30 and 4–6.

Nightlife

You won't find much in the way of organized nightlife in this city. The **Martini Scala Club** (Calle delle Veste, near Teatro La Fenice, tel. 041/522–4121) is an elegant piano bar with late-night restaurant. The bars of the top hotels stay open as long as their customers keep on drinking. **El Souk** disco (Calle Contrarini 1056, near the Accademia, tel. 041/520–0371) draws a fairly sophisticated young crowd. **Ai Speci** (Calle Specchieri 648, tel. 041/520–9088) is an intimate American-style bar.

22 Vienna

Arriving and Departing

By Plane All flights use Schwechat Airport, about 16 kilometers (10 miles) southwest of Vienna (tel. 0222/71110–2231).

Between the Airport and Downtown Buses leave from the airport for the city air terminal by the Hilton on Wien Mitte-Landstrasse Hauptstrasse every half hour from 6 to 8:30 AM and every 20 minutes from 8:50 AM to 10:10 AM. Thereafter, buses run according to aircraft arrivals. Buses also run every hour from the airport to the Westbahnhof (west train station) and the Südbahnhof (south train station). Be sure you get on the right bus! The one-way fare for all buses is AS50. A taxi from the airport to downtown Vienna costs about AS330; agree on the price in advance. Cabs (legally) do not meter the drive, as fares are more or less fixed (legally again) at about double the meter fare. A seat in a limousine costs less; book at the airport. **Mazur** (tel. 0222/604–9191 or 604–2530) offers cheaper pickup and delivery service by arrangement. If you are driving from the airport, follow signs to "Zentrum."

By Train Vienna has four train stations. The principal station, Westbahnhof, is for trains to and from Linz, Salzburg, and Innsbruck. Trains from Germany and France arrive here, too. The Südbahnhof is for trains to and from Graz, Klagenfurt, Villach, and Italy. Franz-Josefs-Bahnhof is for trains to and from Prague, Berlin, and Warsaw. Go to Wien Mitte (Landstrasse) for local trains to and from the north of the city. Budapest trains use the Westbahnhof and Südbahnhof, so check.

By Bus If you arrive by bus, it will probably be at the central bus terminal, Wien Mitte, opposite the city air terminal (and the Hilton).

By Boat All Danube riverboats dock at the DDSG terminal on Mexikoplatz. There's an awkward connection with the U-1 subway from here. Some boats also make a stop slightly upstream at Heiligenstadt, Nussdorf, from which there is an easier connection to the U-4 subway line.

By Car Main access routes are the expressways to the west and south (Westautobahn, Südautobahn). Routes to the downtown area are marked "Zentrum."

Getting Around

Vienna is fairly easy to explore on foot; as a matter of fact, much of the heart of the city—the area within the Ring—is largely a pedestrian zone. The Ring itself was once the city ramparts, torn down just over a century ago to create today's broad, tree-lined boulevard. Public transportation is comfortable, convenient, and frequent, though not cheap.

Tickets for bus, subway, and streetcar are available in most stations. Tickets in multiples of five are sold at cigarette shops, known as Tabak-Trafik, or at the window marked "Vorverkauf" at central stations such as Karlsplatz or Stephansplatz. A block of five tickets costs AS75, a single ticket AS20. If you plan to use public transportation frequently, get a **24-hour ticket** (AS45), a **three-day tourist ticket** (AS115), or an **eight-day ticket** (AS235). Maps and information are available at Stephansplatz, Karlsplatz, and Praterstern U-Bahn stations.

By Bus or Streetcar Inner-city buses are numbered 1A through 3A and operate weekdays to 7:40 AM, Saturday until 2 PM. Reduced fares (buy a

Kurzstreckenkarte; it gives four trips for AS30) are available for these routes as well as designated shorter stretches (roughly two to four stops) on all other bus or streetcar lines. Streetcars and buses are numbered according to route, and they run until about midnight. Night buses marked N follow special routes every hour; the fare is AS25. The central terminal point is Schwedenplatz. The Nos. 1 and 2 streetcar lines run the circular route around the Ring, clockwise and counterclockwise, respectively.

By Subway Subway lines (U-Bahn; stations are marked with a huge blue "U") are designated U-1, U-2, U-3, U-4, and U-6 and are clearly marked and color-coded. Additional services are provided by a fast suburban train, the S-Bahn, indicated by a stylized blue "S" symbol. Both are tied into the general city fare system.

By Taxi Cabs can be flagged on the street if the "Frei" (free) sign is illuminated. Alternatively, dial 60160, 91011, or 40100 to call for one. All rides are metered. The basic fare is AS22, but expect to pay AS60 for an average city ride. There are additional charges for luggage and a night surcharge of AS10.

Important Addresses and Numbers

Tourist Information City Tourist Office (Kärntnerstr. 38, behind the opera, tel. 0222/513–8892). Open daily 9–7.

Embassies U.S. (Gartenbaupromenade [Marriott Bldg.], tel. 0222/51451). **Canadian** (Dr. Karl Lueger-Ring, tel. 0222/533–3691). **U.K.** (Jauresg. 12, tel. 0222/713–1575).

Emergencies Police (tel. 133); Ambulance (tel. 144); Doctor (American Medical Society of Vienna (Lazaretteg. 13, tel. 0222/424568); **Pharmacies:** open weekdays 8–6, Sat. 8–noon.

English Bookstores Big Ben Bookshop (Porzellang. 24, tel. 0222/316412), **British Bookshop** (Weihburgg. 8, tel. 0222/512–1945), **English Book Shop** (Plankeng. 7, tel. 0222/512–2993), **Shakespeare & Co.** (Sterng. 2, tel. 0222/535–4376).

Travel Agencies American Express (Kärntnerstr. 21–23, tel. 0222/51540; Parkring 10, tel. 0222/515–1180), **Austrian Travel Agency** (Kärntner R 3–5, tel. 0222/588000), **Wagons-Lits** (Kärntner Ring 2, tel. 0222/50160).

Guided Tours

Orientation Tours Vienna Sightseeing Tours (tel. 0222/712–4683) offers a short highlights tour or a lengthier one to the Vienna Woods, Mayerling, and other areas surrounding Vienna. Tours start in front of or beside the opera house. **Cityrama** (tel. 0222/534130) provides city tours with hotel pickup; tours assemble opposite the InterContinental Hotel. All hotels and travel agencies have details.

Special-Interest Tours Tours are available to the Spanish Riding School, the Vienna Boys Choir, operettas and concerts, the wine suburb of Grinzing, nightclubs, and Vienna by night. Check with the city tourist office or your hotel for details.

Walking Tours *Vienna from A to Z* (in English) is available at most bookstores; it explains the numbered plaques attached to all major buildings in Vienna. *Vienna: Downtown Walking Tours* by Henriette Mandl outlines suggested routes and provides information on sights. For organized walking tours with English-speaking guides, check with the tourist office or your hotel.

Excursions Day bus trips are organized to the Danube Valley, the Hungarian border, the Alps south of Vienna, Salzburg, and Budapest; get information from the city tourist office.

Exploring Vienna

Vienna has been described as an "old dowager of a town," not a bad description for this onetime center of empire. It's not just the aristocratic and courtly atmosphere, with monumental doorways and stately facades of former palaces at every turn. Nor is it just that Vienna has a higher proportion of middle-aged and older citizens than any other city in Europe, with a concomitant sense of stability, quiet, and respectability. Rather, it's these factors, combined with a love of music; a discreet weakness for rich food (especially cakes); an adherence to old-fashioned and formal forms of address; a high, if unadventurous, regard for the arts; and a gentle mourning for lost glories, that to produce a stiff but elegant, slightly other-worldly, sense of dignity.

The Heart Most main sights are in the inner zone, the oldest part of the
of Vienna city, encircled by the **Ring**, once the city walls and today a broad boulevard. Before setting out, be sure to check opening times of museums carefully; they can change unpredictably. If you will be visiting a number of museums, you can save money by purchasing an AS150 Museum Pass, which will give you entries worth AS210 (get it at the first museum you visit). Carry a ready supply of AS10 coins, too; many places of interest have coin-operated tape machines that provide English commentaries. As you wander around, train yourself to look upward; some of the most memorable architectural treasures are on upper stories and roof lines.

Numbers in the margin correspond to points of interest on the Vienna map.

Vienna's role as imperial city is preserved in the complex of buildings that make up the former royal palace. Start your tour at Albertinaplatz, behind the opera house. Head down Augustinerstrasse. To the right is the "Memorial to Victims of Fascism," disputed in part because the sculptor was once an admitted Communist. On your left is the **Albertina**, home to the world's largest collection of drawings, sketches, engravings, and etchings. There are works here by Dürer—these are perhaps the highlight of the collection—Rembrandt, Michelangelo, Correggio, and many others. The holdings are so vast that only a limited number can be shown at one time. Some original works are so delicate that they can be shown only in facsimile. *Augustinerstr. 1, tel. 0222/534830. Admission: AS30. Open Mon., Tues., Thurs. 10–4; Wed. 10–6; Fri. 10–2; weekends 10–1; closed Sun. in July and Aug.*

Beethoven was a regular visitor at the Palais Lobkowitz across the street on Lobkowitz Platz. The renovated palace now houses the **Theater Museum**. Exhibits cover the history of theater in Vienna and the rest of Austria. A children's museum in the basement is reached by a slide! *Lobkowitzpl., tel. 0222/512–2427. Admission: AS30. Open Wed.–Mon. 9–6.*

❸ Go back to Augustinerstrasse to the 14th-century **Augustinerkirche,** a favorite on Sundays, when the 11 AM mass is sung
❹ in Latin. Nearby is the **Nationalbibliothek** (the National Library), with its stunning Baroque great hall. *Josefsplatz 1, tel.
0222/534100. Admission: AS15. Open May–Oct., Mon.–Sat.
10–4; Nov.–Apr., Mon.–Sat. 11–noon.*

Josefsplatz is where much of *The Third Man* was filmed, specifically in and around the Palais Pallavicini across the street. The
❺ entrance to the **Spanische Reitschule,** the Spanish Riding
School, is here, too, though the famed white horses are actually
stabled on the other side of the square. For tickets, write the
Austrian Tourist Office (Friedrichstr. 7, A-1010 Vienna) *at
least* three months in advance. There are performances on Sunday at 10:45 AM and Wednesday at 7 PM year-round. Mid-April
through October, there are additional performances on Saturday at 9 AM.

From here you're only a few steps from Michaelerplatz, the cir-
❻ cular square that marks the entrance to the **Hofburg,** the royal
palace. On one side of the square, opposite the entrance, on the
corner of Herrengasse and Kohlmarkt, is the **Loos building**
(1911), designed by Adolf Loos. Step inside to see the remarkable restoration of the foyer. Outside, it's no more than a simple
brick-and-glass structure, but architectural historians point to
it as one of the earliest "modern" buildings in Europe—a building where function determines style. In striking contrast is the
Baroque **Michaelertor,** opposite, the principal entrance to the
Hofburg.

Time Out Some insist that no visit to Vienna is complete without a visit to
Demel, on the left just down the Kohlmarkt. Others find the
café-pastry shop overpriced—it is expensive even by Vienna
standards—and complain of the service. The choice is yours.

Head under the domed entrance of the Michaelertor to visit the
❼ **imperial apartments** of Emperor Franz Josef and Empress
Elisabeth. Among the exhibits is the exercise equipment used
by the beautiful empress. Here, too, is the dress she was wearing when she was stabbed to death by a demented Italian anar-
chist on the shores of Lake Geneva in 1898; the dagger marks
are visible. *Michaelerplatz 1, tel. 0222/587–5540. Admission:
AS25. Open Mon.–Sat. 8:30–noon, 12:30–4; Sun. 8:30–12:30.*

❽ Be sure to see the **Schatzkammer,** the imperial treasury, home
of the magnificent crown jewels. *Hofburg, Schweizerhof, tel.
0222/934–5410. Admission: AS45. Open Nov.–Mar., Mon. and
Wed.–Fri. 10–4, weekends 9–4 (Apr.–Oct. until 6).*

❾ The **Hofburgkapelle,** the court chapel, is where the Vienna
Boys Choir sings mass at 11 AM on Sunday. You'll need tickets
to attend; they are available at the chapel from 5 PM Friday (expect long lines) or by writing to Burgkapelle, Hofburg,
Schweizerhof, A-1010 Vienna. The city tourist office can sometimes help with ticket applications.

Head south to Heldenplatz, the open square in front of the
Neue Hofburg Museums, a ponderously ornate 19th-century
⑩ edifice housing a series of museums. Highlights are the Waffen-
sammlung (the weapons collection), the collections of musical
instruments, the ethnographic museum, and the exciting
Ephesus museum, with finds from the excavations at that an-

Albertina, **1**
Augustinerkirche, **3**
Donner Brunnen, **18**
Hofburg, **6**
Hofburgkapelle, **9**
Hoher Markt, **27**
Imperial Apartments, **7**
Kapuzinerkirche, **17**
Karlskirche, **14**
Kirche am Hof, **24**
Kunsthistorisches Museum, **12**
Maria am Gestade, **26**
Mozart Erinnerungsräume, **22**
Nationalbibliothek, **4**
Naturhistorisches Museum, **11**
Neue Hofburg Museums, **10**
Pestsäule, **19**
Peterskirche, **20**
Ruprechtskirche, **28**
Sacher Hotel, **16**
Schatzkammer, **8**
Schloss Belvedere, **30**
Schönbrunn Palace, **29**
Schottenkirche, **23**
Spanische Reitschule, **5**
Staatsoper, **15**
Stephansdom, **21**
Tabak Museum, **13**
Theater Museum, **2**
20th Century Museum, **31**
Uhrenmuseum, **25**

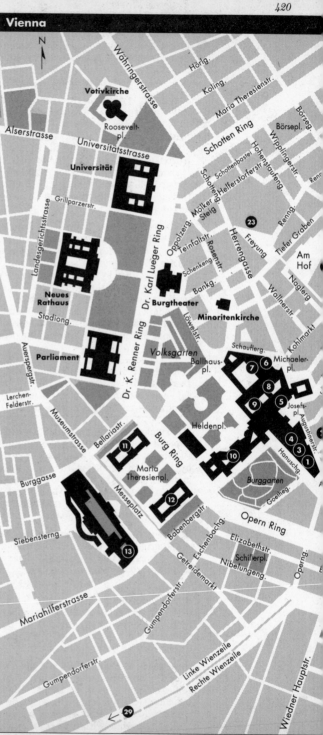

Vienna

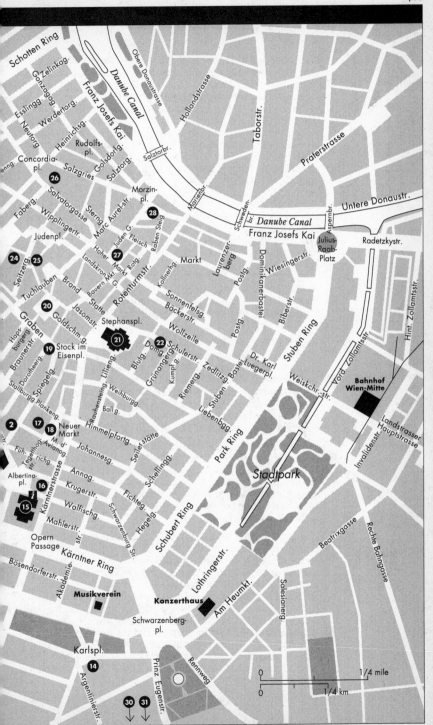

cient site. *Neue Hofburg, Heldenplatz 1, tel. 0222/934–5410. Admission: AS30; free first Sun. of each month. Open Wed.– Mon. 9–4.*

Walk west again across the Ring, the broad boulevard encircling the inner city, to the imperial museum complex. The **Naturhistorisches Museum** (Natural History Museum) is on your right, the **Kunsthistorisches Museum** (Art History Museum) is on your left. The latter is one of the great art museums of the world; this is not a place to miss. The collections focus on old-master painting, notably Brueghel, Cranach, Titian, Canaletto, Rubens, and Velazquez. But there are important Egyptian, Greek, Etruscan, and Roman exhibits, too. *Burgring 5, tel. 0222/934–5410. Admission: AS45; free first Sun. of each month. Open Wed.–Mon. 9–6.*

Time Out Across the Messeplatz stretches Messepalast, the building that now serves as a fair and exhibit space. Inside is one of Vienna's better-kept secrets, the **Glacis-Beisl** restaurant. The garden under the vine-clad arbors has to be experienced. *Tel. 0222/ 930–7374. Reservations advised. No credit cards. Closed Jan.– Feb.*

At the Mariahilferstrasse end of the Messepalast complex is the small and fascinating **Tabak Museum,** the Tobacco Museum. *Mariahilfstr., tel. 0222/961716. Open Wed.–Fri. 10–3, Tues. 10–7, weekends 9–1.*

Head east down the Ring, with the Kunsthistorisches Museum on your right. Looming up to the right, over Karlsplatz, is the heroic facade and dome, flanked by vast twin columns, of the **Karlskirche.** It was built around 1715 by Fischer von Erlach. The oval interior is surprisingly small, given the monumental facade: One expects something more on the scale of St. Peter's in Rome. The ceiling has airy frescoes, and stiff shafts of gilt radiate like sunbeams from the altar.

Take the pedestrian underpass back under the Ring to Opernplatz. This is the site of the **Staatsoper,** one of the best opera houses in the world and a focus of Viennese social life. Tickets are expensive and rare, so you may have to settle for a backstage tour. The tour schedule for the day is usually posted outside the doors on the Operngasse side and will depend on the activities going on inside.

Head up Kärntnerstrasse, Vienna's main thoroughfare, now an elegant and busy pedestrian mall. On your left is the creamy facade of the **Sacher Hotel.** Take a look inside at the plush red-and-gilt decor, a *fin de siècle* masterpiece. The hotel is also the home of the original Sachertorte—the ultimate chocolate cake. Back on Kärntnerstrasse, around the corner from the Sacher, is the city tourist office. Leading off Kärntnerstrasse, to the left, is the little street of Marco d'Aviano-Gasse. Follow it to **Kapuzinerkirche,** in whose crypt, called the **Kaisergruft** or the imperial vault, the serried ranks of long-dead Hapsburgs lie. The oldest tomb is that of Ferdinand II; it dates from 1633. The most recent tomb is that of Empress Zita, widow of Austria's last kaiser, dating from 1989.

In the center of the square is the ornate 18th-century **Donner Brunnen,** the Providence Fountain. The figures represent main rivers that flow into the Danube; Empress Maria Teresa thought the figures were obscene and wanted them removed or properly clothed.

Time Out Coffee or tea and what are said, even by the French and Belgians, to be the best pastries in the world are available in staggering quantity at the **Konditorei Oberlaa.** *Neuer Markt 16. Open weekdays 9–7, Sat. 9–2.*

19 Continue north through Seilergasse to reach pedestrians-only Graben. The **Pestsäule,** or Plague Column, shoots up from the middle of the street, looking like a geyser of whipped cream touched with gold. It commemorates the Black Death of 1697; look at the graphic depictions of those who fell victim to the ravages of the terrible disease. A small turning to the right, **20** just past the column, leads to the Baroque **Peterskirche.** The little church, the work of Johann Lukas von Hildebrandt, finished in about 1730, has what is probably the most theatrical interior in the city. The pulpit is especially fine, with a highly ornate canopy, but florid and swirling decoration is everywhere. Many of the decorative elements are based on a tent form, a motif suggested by the Turkish forces that camped outside the city walls during the great siege of Vienna at the end of the 17th century.

21 Walk down Goldschmiedgasse to Stephansplatz, site of the **Stephansdom** (St. Stephen's Cathedral). Its towering Gothic spires and gaudy 19th-century tiled roof are still the dominant feature of the Vienna skyline. The oldest part of the building is the 13th-century entrance, the soaring **Riesentor,** or Giant Doorway. Inside, the church is mysteriously dark, filled with an array of monuments, tombs, sculptures, paintings, and pulpits. Despite extensive wartime damage—and numerous Baroque additions—the building radiates an authentically medieval atmosphere. Climb up the 345 steps of **Alte Steffl,** Old Steven, the south tower, for a stupendous view over the city. An elevator goes up the north tower to **Die Pummerin,** the Boomer, a 22-ton bell first cast in 1711 from cannons captured from the Turks. Take a 30-minute tour of the crypt to see the entrails of the Hapsburgs, carefully preserved in copper jars.

22 On a narrow street east of the cathedral is the house where Mozart lived from 1784 to 1787. Today it's the **Mozart Erinnerungsräume,** the Mozart Museum. It was here that the composer wrote *The Marriage of Figaro,* and here, some say, that he spent the happiest years of his life. *Domgasse 5, tel. 0222/513–6294. Admission: AS15. Open Tues.–Sun. 10–12:15 and 1–4:30.*

Other Corners of Vienna Walk back down the Graben and the narrow Naglergasse and turn left into the Freyung. On your left is the **Palais Ferstl,** now a stylish shopping arcade. At the back is the skillfully restored **Café Central,** once headquarters for Vienna's leading literary **23** figures. Cross the Freyung to the dominant **Schottenkirche.** The monks who were brought to found it were actually Irish, not Scottish. They started a school as well, which shares the courtyard to the left with a pleasant garden restaurant in summer. Turn back through the Freyung to **Am Hof,** a remarkable square with the city's Baroque central fire station, possibly the **24** world's most ornate. Cross the square to the **Kirche am Hof.** The interior is curiously reminiscent of many Dutch churches.

Time Out For a typical meal or just a beer or coffee, stop at **Gustlbauer.** The restaurant is a regular stop for the Fiaker coachmen, who leave their livery and passengers briefly for a quick Schnapps. The waiter will help you decipher the handwritten menu. Vienna's mayor, who lives nearby, often appears. *Am Hof, Drahtgasse 2, tel. 0222/533–5889. Open weekdays 10–midnight, Sat. 10–3.*

Continue to Judenplatz and turn right into Parisergasse to the ㉕ **Uhrenmuseum** (Clock Museum), located in a lovely Renaissance house. *Schulhof 2, tel. 0222/533–2265. Admission: AS15; free Fri. morning. Open Tues.–Sun. 9–12:15 and 1–4:30.*

Turn down the Kurrentgasse and, via Fütterergasse, cross the Wipplingerstrasse into Stoss im Himmel (literally, a "thrust to ㉖ heaven"). To your left down Salvatorgasse is **Maria am Gestade,** originally a church for fishermen on the nearby canal. Note the ornate "folded hands" spire. Return along Wip- ㉗ plingerstrasse, across Marc Aurel-Strasse, to **Hoher Markt,** with a central monument celebrating the betrothal of Mary and Joseph. Roman ruins are displayed in the museum on the south side of the square. *Hoher Markt 3, tel. 0222/535–5606. Admission: AS15; free on Fri. morning. Open Tues.–Sun. 10–12:15 and 1–4:30.*

On the north side of Hoher Markt is the amusing **Anker-Uhr,** a clock that tells time by figures moving across a scale. The figures are identified on a plaque at the lower left of the clock; it's well worth passing by at noon to catch the show. Go through ㉘ Judengasse to the **Ruprechtskirche** (St. Rupert's). The oldest church in Vienna is small; damp; dark; and, unfortunately, usually closed, though you can peek through a window.

Vienna Environs It's a 15-minute ride from center city on subway line U-4 (stop ㉙ either at Schönbrunn or Hietzing) to **Schönbrunn Palace,** the magnificent Baroque residence built between 1696 and 1713 for the Hapsburgs. Here Kaiser Franz Josef I was born and died. His "office" (kept as he left it in 1916) is a touching reminder of his spartan life; other rooms, however, reflect the elegance of the monarchy. The ornate public rooms are still used for state receptions. A guided tour covers 45 of the palace's 1,441 rooms; among the curiosities are the Chinese room and the gym fitted out for Empress Elisabeth, where she exercised daily to keep her figure. *Schönbrunner Schlosstr., tel. 0222/81113–238. Admission: AS50. Open Oct.–Apr., daily 9–noon and 1–4; May–Sept., daily 9–noon and 1–5.*

Once on the grounds, don't overlook the **Tiergarten** (Zoo). It's Europe's oldest menagerie and, when established in 1752, was intended to amuse and educate the court. It contains an extensive assortment of animals, some of them in their original Baroque enclosures. *Tel. 0222/821236. Admission: AS30. Open daily 9–dusk, 6 PM latest.*

Follow the pathways up to the **Gloriette,** that Baroque ornament on the rise behind Schönbrunn, and enjoy superb views of the city. Originally this was to have been the site of the palace, but projected construction costs were considered too high. *Admission: AS10. Open May–Oct., daily 8–6.*

The **Wagenburg** (Carriage Museum), near the entrance to the palace grounds, holds some splendid examples of early transportation, from children's sleighs to funeral carriages of the emperors. *Tel. 0222/823244. Admission: AS30. Open Oct.–Apr., Tues.–Sun. 10–4; May–Sept., Tues.–Sun. 10–5.*

㉚ Take the D streetcar toward the Südbahnhof to reach **Schloss Belvedere** (Belvedere Palace), a Baroque complex often compared to Versailles. It was commissioned by Prince Eugene of Savoy and built by Johann Lukas von Hildebrandt in 1721–22. The palace is made up of two separate buildings, one at the foot and the other at the top of a hill. The lower tract was first built as residential quarters; the upper buildings were reserved for entertaining. The gardens in between are among the best examples of natural Baroque ornamentation found anywhere. The buildings have contemporary significance: The State Treaty that gave Austria its independence in 1955 was signed in the great upper hall. The composer Anton Bruckner lived in an apartment to the north of the upper building until his death in 1896. Both sections now house outstanding art museums: the gallery of 19th- and 20th-century art in the Upper Belvedere (Klimt, Kokoschka, Schiele, Waldmüller, Markart) and the Baroque museum (including medieval Austrian art) in the Lower Belvedere. *Prinz-Eugen-Str. 27, tel. 0222/784158. Admission: AS30. Open Tues.–Sun. 10–4.*

Continue across the Gürtel from the Upper Belvedere south-
㉛ ward to the **20th Century Museum,** containing a small but extremely tasteful modern art collection. *Schweizer Garten, tel. 0222/782550. Admission: AS30. Open Thurs.–Tues. 10–4.*

You can reach a small corner of the **Vienna Woods** by streetcar and bus: Take a streetcar or the subway U-2 to Schottentor/University and, from there, the No. 38 streetcar (Grinzing) to the end of the line. Grinzing itself is out of a picture book; alas, much of the wine offered in the taverns is less enchanting. (For better wine and ambience, try the village of Nussdorf, reached by streetcar D.) To get into the woods, change in Grinzing to the No. 38A bus. This will take you to Kahlenberg, which provides a superb view over the Danube and the city. You can take the bus or hike to Leopoldsberg, the promontory over the Danube from which Turkish invading forces were repulsed during the 16th and 17th centuries.

Shopping

Antiques The best (and most expensive) shops are in the inner city, but there are good finds in some of the outer districts, particularly among the back streets in the **Josefstadt** (eighth) district.

Boutiques Name brands are found along the **Kohlmarkt** and the side streets off the Kärntnerstrasse.

Folk Costumes A good selection at reasonable prices is offered by the **NÖ Heimatwerk** (Herrengasse 6); also try **Trachten Tostmann** (Schottengasse 3a) or **Loden-Plankl** (Michaelerplatz 6).

Shopping Districts Tourists gravitate to the **Kärntnerstrasse,** but the Viennese do most of their shopping on the **Mariahilferstrasse.**

Department Stores **Gerngross, Herzmansky,** and **Stafa** (all on Mariahilferstr.) are the major outlets.

Food and The **Naschmarkt** (between Rechte and Linke Wienzeile; week-
Flea Markets days 6 AM–mid-afternoon, Sat. 6–1) is a sensational open-food market, offering specialties from around the world. The **Floh-markt** (flea market) operates year-round beyond the Nasch-

markt (subway U-4 to Kettenbrückengasse) and is equally fascinating (Sat. 8–4). Bargaining here goes on in any number of languages. An **Arts & Crafts Flea Market** with better offerings operates on Saturday and Sunday afternoons from about 2 to 7 alongside the Danube Canal near the Salztorbrücke. One of the best seasonal local markets for handicrafts is on **Spittelberggasse,** particularly just before Christmas.

Dining

In contrast to many cities, the leading Viennese hotels are in competition for the country's best cooks and therefore offer some of the city's best dining. Even the chain hotels have joined in the effort to see which can win over the leading chefs. The results are rewarding; you may not even have to leave your hotel to enjoy outstanding food and service.

Take your choice of sidewalk *Wurstl* (frankfurter) stands, quick-lunch stops *(Imbissstube)*, cafés, Heuriger wine restaurants, self-service restaurants, modest *Gasthäuser* neighborhood establishments with local specialties, and full-fledged restaurants in every price category. Most establishments post their menus outside. Shops that sell coffee beans (such as Eduscho) also offer coffee by the cup at prices that are considerably lower than those in a café.

Mealtimes Austrians often eat up to five meals a day: a very early Continental breakfast of rolls and coffee; a slightly more substantial breakfast *(Gabelfrühstück)* with eggs or cold meat, possibly even a small goulash, at mid-morning (understood to be 9, sharp); a main meal at noon; afternoon coffee *(Jause)* with cake at teatime; and, unless dining out, a light supper to end the day. Cafés offer breakfast; most restaurants open somewhat later. Lunches usually cost more in cafés than in restaurants.

Dress A jacket and tie are generally advised for restaurants in the top price categories. Otherwise casual dress is acceptable, although formal dress is preferred in some moderate restaurants at dinner. When in doubt, it's best to dress up.

Ratings Prices are per preson and include soup and a main course, usually with salad, and a small beer or glass of wine. Meals in the top-priced categories will include a dessert or cheese and coffee. Prices include taxes and service (you may wish to leave small change, in addition). Best bets are indicated by a star ★.

Category	Cost
Very Expensive	over AS800
Expensive	AS500–AS800
Moderate	AS200–AS500
Inexpensive	under AS200

Very Expensive **Rotisserie Prinz Eugen.** "New Vienna Cuisine"—the Austrian
★ version of nouvelle cuisine—is combined successfully with more usual dishes at the Hilton's Rotisserie Prinz Eugen, which has managed to sustain its initial reputation for outstanding decor, service, and food. There is piano accompaniment in the evening. *Hilton Hotel, Am Stadtpark, tel. 0222/*

71700–305. Reservations advised. AE, DC, MC, V. Closed Sat. lunch.

Steirer Eck. One food editor tapped the Steirer Eck in 1991 as Vienna's best restaurant, but the judgment is not unanimous. Some of the standard dishes are more successful than the forays into the "New Vienna Cuisine." No one denies the elegance of the ambience, however. *Rasumofskygasse 2, tel. 0222/713–3168. Reservations advised. AE. Closed weekends and holidays.*

Zu den Drei Husaren. This is one of Vienna's enduring monuments to tradition, complete with candlelight and live piano music (except on Sundays). Casual visitors (as opposed to the "regulars") may have to settle for more atmosphere than service, however. The hors d'oeuvre trolleys are intentionally enticing and can easily double the lunch or dinner bill. *Weihburggasse 4, tel. 0222/512–1092. Reservations required. AE, DC, MC, V.*

Expensive **da Conte.** The newest Italian restaurant on the scene is also the best, set in a series of charming, arched-ceiling rooms. The same management is responsible for the cheaper, smaller restaurant next door, as well as the Italian gourmet deli on the corner. *Kurrentgasse 12, tel. 0222/533–6464. Reservations advised. AE, DC, MC, V. Closed Sun.*

Demel. One of Vienna's most famous pastry shops offers magnificent snacks of delicate meats, fish, and vegetables, as well as the expected cakes and other goodies. The stuffed mushrooms and vegetable-cheese combinations are especially tempting—as is the hot chocolate. *Kohlmarkt 14, tel. 0222/533–5516. No reservations. AE, DC, MC, V. Closed after 6 PM.*

★ **Korso.** You'll find outstanding food and atmosphere at this gourmet temple of "New Vienna Cuisine." Not everyone agrees with the kitchen's approach to experiments—some say the restaurant really was created for the cook—but few are disappointed. *Mahlerstr. 2, tel. 0222/5151–6546. Reservations advised. AE, DC, MC, V. Closed Sat. lunch and Sun.*

Le Salut. This intimate restaurant offers the best French cuisine in town, with a price tag to match. In summer, the tables outside add to the pleasure. *Wildpretmarkt 3, tel. 0222/533–1322. Reservations advised. AE, DC, MC, V. Closed Sun., also Sat. in July and Aug.*

★ **Vier Jahreszeiten.** This restaurant effortlessly manages to achieve that delicate balance between food and atmosphere. The service is attentive without being overbearing. The lunch buffet offers both excellent food and value. Evening dining includes grill specialties and live piano music (except on Sunday). *Hotel Intercontinental, Johannesgasse 28, tel. 0222/711–22143. Reservations advised. AE, DC, MC, V.*

Moderate **Bastei-Beisl.** A comfortable, wood-paneled restaurant offering good traditional Viennese fare. Outdoor tables are particularly pleasant on summer evenings. *Stubenbastei 10, tel. 0222/512–4319. Reservations usually not necessary. AE, DC, MC, V. Closed Sun.*

★ **Gigerl.** It's hard to believe you're right in the middle of the city at this imaginative and charming wine restaurant that serves hot and cold buffets. The rooms are small and cozy but may get smoky and noisy when the place is full—which it usually is. The food is typical of wine gardens on the fringes of the city: roast meats, casserole dishes, cold cuts, salads. The wines are excellent. The surrounding narrow alleys and ancient buildings add to the charm of the outdoor tables in summer. *Rauhen-steingasse 3, tel. 0222/513–4431. Reservations advised. AE, DC, MC, V.*

Melker Stiftskeller. This is one of the city's half-dozen genuine wine taverns, or kellers; the food selection is limited but good, featuring pig's knuckle. House wines from the Wachau are excellent. *Schottengasse 3, tel. 0222/533–5530. Reservations usually not necessary. MC. Evenings only; closed Sun.*

★ **Ofenloch.** This place is always packed, which speaks well not only of the excellent specialties from some Viennese grandmother's cookbook but also of the atmosphere. Waitresses are dressed in appropriate period costumes, and the furnishings add to the color. At times the rooms may be too smoky and noisy for some tastes. If you like garlic, try *Vanillerostbraten,* a rump steak with as much garlic as you request. *Kurrentgasse 8, tel. 0222/533–8844. Reservations required. AE, MC, V. Closed Sun.*

Stadtbeisl. Good standard Austrian fare is served at this popular eatery, which is comfortable without being pretentious. The service gets uneven as the place fills up, but if you are seated outside in summer, you probably won't mind. *Naglergasse 21, tel. 0222/533–3323. Reservations advised. V.*

Zu den drei Hacken. This is one of the few genuine Viennese *Gasthäuser* in the city center; like the place itself, the fare is solid if not elegant. Legend has it that Schubert dined here; the ambience probably hasn't changed much since then. There are tables outside in summer, although the extra seating capacity strains both the kitchen and the service. *Singerstr. 8, tel. 0222/5125895. No reservations. No credit cards. Closed Sat. dinner and Sun.*

Zu ebener Erde und erster Stock. Ask for a table upstairs in this exquisite, tiny, utterly original Biedermeier house, which serves good, standard Austrian fare; the downstairs space is really more for snacks. *Burggasse 13, tel. 0222/936254. Reservations advised. AE, DC, MC, V. Closed Sun.*

Zur Himmelpforte. This high-quality restaurant has a deserved reputation for reasonably priced gourmet meals. Its standards may not reach the heights of some other Viennese establishments, but then neither do the prices! The house offers the *real* Budweiser beer as well. *Himmelpfortgasse 24, tel. 0222/513–1967. Reservations usually not necessary. AE, DC, MC, V. Closed Sun.*

Inexpensive

★ **Figlmüller.** Known for its Schnitzel, Figlmüller is always packed. Guests share the benches, the long tables, and the experience. Food choices are limited, but nobody seems to mind. Only wine is offered to drink, but it is good. The small "garden" is now enclosed and is just as popular as the tables inside. *Wollzeile 5 (passageway), tel. 0222/512–6177. No reservations. No credit cards. Closed Sat. dinner and Sun.*

Ilona-Stüberl. Head to Ilona-Stüberl for a cozy Hungarian atmosphere—without the gypsy music. Be prepared to douse the fire if you ask for a dish with hot peppers! The tables outside in summer are pleasant but somewhat public. *Bräunerstr. 2, tel. 0222/533–9029. Reservations advised. AE, DC, MC, V. Closed Sun.*

Lodging

Vienna's inner city is the best base for visitors because it's so close to most of the major sights, restaurants, and shops. This accessibility translates, of course, into higher prices.

Austrian hotels and pensions are officially classified using from one to five stars. These grades broadly coincide with our own four-way rating system. No matter what the category, standards for service and cleanliness are high. All hotels in the upper three categories have either a bath or shower in the room; even the most inexpensive accommodations provide hot and cold water.

Ratings All prices quoted here are for two people in a double room. Though exact figures vary, a single room generally costs more than 50% of the price of a comparable double room. Breakfast—which can be anything from a simple roll and coffee to a full and sumptuous buffet—is usually included in the room rate. In the top five-star hotels, however, it is extra (and expensive). Best bets are indicated by a star ★.

Category	Cost
Very Expensive	over AS2,300
Expensive	AS1,250–AS2,300
Moderate	AS850–AS1,250
Inexpensive	under AS850

Very Expensive **Bristol.** Opposite the opera house, the Bristol is classic Viennese, preferred by many for the service as well as the location.
★ The bar is comfortable, though not overly private; the restaurants associated with the hotel are outstanding, especially Korso. Back and upper guest rooms are quieter. *Kärntner Ring 1, tel. 0222/515160. 152 rooms with bath. Facilities: restaurants, bar. AE, DC, MC, V.*

★ **Imperial.** This former palace represents elegant old Vienna at its best, with such features as heated towel racks in some rooms. The location could hardly be better, although being on the Ring sometimes makes the front and lower rooms a bit noisy. The bar is intimate and pleasant. Lunch in the café is both reasonable and good; the hotel restaurant is excellent. *Kärntner Ring 16, tel. 0222/501100. 151 rooms with bath or shower. Facilities: beauty parlor, conference rooms. AE, DC, MC, V.*

★ **InterContinental.** Vienna's modern InterContinental has the reputation of being one of the chain's very best. The rooms are spacious; the main restaurant, exceptional. But whereas the hotel succeeds in acquiring some Viennese charm, the bar fails hopelessly, as does the Brasserie. Rooms in front overlooking the park are quieter, particularly in winter when the ice-skating rink at the back is in operation. *Johannesgasse 28, tel. 0222/ 711–220. 500 rooms with bath. Facilities: sauna, health club, laundry, dry cleaning service, barber, hair stylist, complimentary limo, parking. AE, DC, MC, V.*

Marriott. The only Viennese aspect here is the service; all else is global modern. The atrium lobby, while pleasant, is anything but intimate. The restaurants are good, and Sunday brunch at the Marriott has become immensely popular (book at least a week in advance). *Parkring 12A, tel. 0222/515180. 304 rooms with bath. Facilities: sauna, health club, pool, shops, garage. AE, DC, MC, V.*

Palais Schwarzenberg. The rooms are incorporated into a quiet wing of a Baroque palace, a 10-minute walk from the opera. The restaurant enjoys an excellent reputation; the view out over the formal gardens is glorious. *Schwarzenbergplatz 9, tel. 0222/784515. 38 rooms with bath. Facilities: bar. AE, DC, MC, V.*

Sacher. The hotel's reputation has varied considerably during recent years, but it remains one of the legendary addresses in Europe, with its opulent decor highlighted by original oil paintings, sculptures, and objets d'art. The Blue and Red bars are intimate and favored by nonguests as well, as is the café, particularly in summer when tables are set up outside. Guest rooms are spacious and elegantly appointed. *Philharmonikerstr. 4, tel. 0222/514560. 117 rooms with bath or shower. Facilities: coffee shop, bar. AE, DC, MC, V.*

Expensive ★

Astoria. Though the Astoria is one of Vienna's traditional old hotels, the rooms have been modernized considerably. The paneled lobby, however, has been preserved and retains an unmistakable Old World patina. The location is central, but because of the street musicians and the late-night crowds in the pedestrian zone, rooms overlooking the Kärntnerstrasse tend to be noisy in summer. *Kärntnerstr. 32–34, tel. 0222/515770. 108 rooms with bath or shower. Facilities: restaurant. AE, DC, MC, V.*

Capricorno. This establishment overlooks the Danube Canal in a fairly central location. Although its facade is modern and somewhat short on charm, the hotel nonetheless represents good value. *Schwedenplatz 3–4, tel. 0222/533–3104. 46 rooms with bath or shower. AE, DC, MC, V.*

Central. This older hotel doesn't have quite the downtown location its name suggests, but it is reasonably central, although across the canal. *Taborstr. 8a, tel. 0222/21105. 60 rooms, 41 with bath or shower. AE, DC, MC, V.*

Europa. The location—midway between the opera house and the cathedral—is ideal, but the rooms on the Kärntnerstrasse side are noisy in summer; ask for a room overlooking Neuer Markt. The building is postwar modern and lacks the charm of older hotels, but the staff is friendly and helpful. The café is popular, particularly in summer when tables are put outdoors. *Neuer Markt 3, tel. 0222/515940. 102 rooms with bath. Facilities: restaurant, coffee shop, bar. AE, DC, MC, V.*

★ **König von Ungarn.** This utterly charming, centrally located hotel is tucked away in the shadow of the cathedral. The historic facade belies the modern efficiency of the interior, from the atrium lobby to the guest rooms themselves. The restaurant (just next door in a house that Mozart once lived in) is excellent, though not inexpensive, and is always packed at noon. *Schulerstr. 10, tel. 0222/515840. 32 rooms with bath or shower. AE, DC, MC, V.*

Mailberger Hof. This is a favorite of opera stars, conductors, and those who want a central but quiet location. Some rooms have limited kitchenette facilities. The arcaded courtyard is very pretty. *Annagasse 7, tel. 0222/512–0641. 80 rooms with bath or shower. AE, DC, MC, V.*

Moderate ★

Austria. This older hotel is on a quiet side street in a historic area. It is popular with tourists. *Wolfengasse 3/Fleischmarkt,* *tel. 0222/51523. 51 rooms, 40 with bath or shower. Facilities: bar. DC, MC.*

★ **Kärntnerhof.** Though tucked away in a tiny, quiet side street, Kärntnerhof is nevertheless centrally located. It's known for its particularly friendly staff. The rooms are functionally decorated but clean and serviceable. *Grashofgasse 4, tel. 0222/512–1923. 45 rooms, 34 with bath or shower. AE, DC, MC, V.*

Pension Christine. This quiet pension, just steps from Schwedenplatz and the Danube Canal, offers mainly smallish modern rooms, warmly decorated with attractive dark-wood furniture set off against beige walls. Room 524 is particularly spacious and inviting. *Hafnersteig 7, tel. 0222/533–2961. 32 rooms with bath or shower. MC.*

★ **Pension Zipser.** This 1904 house, with an ornate facade and gilt-trimmed coat of arms, has become a favorite with regular visitors to Vienna. It is slightly less central than some others on our list, but very comfortable. *Lange Gasse 49, tel. 0222/420828. 46 rooms with bath or shower. Facilities: bar. AE, DC, MC, V.*

★ **Post.** Taking its name from the city's main post office, opposite, this is an older but updated hotel that offers a fine location, a friendly staff, and a good café. *Fleischmarkt 24, tel. 0222/515830. 107 rooms, 77 with bath or shower. AE, DC, MC, V.*

Schweizerhof. This is more of a pension than a hotel, but the location is excellent and the smallish rooms are certainly adequate. *Bauernmarkt 22, tel. 0222/533–1931. 55 rooms with bath or shower. AE, DC, MC, V.*

Wandl. The house is old and some of the rooms are small, but the Wandl's location and reasonable prices compensate for most of its deficiencies. *Petersplatz 9, tel. 0222/534550. 134 rooms with bath or shower. No credit cards.*

The Arts

Theater and Opera Check the monthly program published by the city; posters also show opera and theater schedules. Tickets for the Opera, Volksoper, and the Burg and Akademie theaters are available at the central ticket office to the left rear of the Opera (**Bundestheaterkassen,** Hanuschgasse 3, tel. 0222/514440; open weekdays 9–5, weekends 9–1). Tickets go on advance sale a week before performances. Unsold tickets can be obtained at the evening box office. Plan to be there at least one hour before the performance; students can buy remaining tickets at lower prices, so they are usually out in force. Tickets can be ordered six days in advance from anywhere in the world by phone (tel. 0222/513–1513; AE, DC, MC, V). Theater is offered in English at **Vienna English Theater** (Josefsgasse 12, tel. 0222/402–1260) and **International Theater** (Porzellangasse 8, tel. 0222/316272).

Music Most classical concerts are in either the **Konzerthaus** (Lothringerstr. 20, tel. 0222/712–1211) or **Musikverein** (Dumbastrasse 3, tel. 0222/505–8190). Tickets can be bought at the box offices (AE, DC, MC, V). Pop concerts are scheduled from time to time at the **Austria Center** (Am Hubertusdamm 6, tel. 0222/236–9150; U-4 subway to VIC stop).

Film Films are shown in English at **Burg Kino** (Opernring 19, tel. 0222/587–8406), **de France** (Schottenring 5, tel. 0222/345236), and **Film Museum** (Augustinerstr. 1, tel. 0222/533–7054). To find English-language movies, look for "OF" (Originalfassung) or "OmU" (original with subtitles) in the newspaper listings.

Nightlife

Cabarets Most cabarets are expensive and unmemorable. Two of the best are **Casanova** (Dorotheergasse 6, tel. 0222/512–9845), which emphasizes striptease, and **Moulin Rouge** (Walfischgasse 11, tel. 0222/512–2130).

Discos The **Splendid** (Jasomirgottstr. 3, tel. 0222/533–1515) is the city's oldest dance-bar, open daily to 4 AM. **Queen Anne** (Johannesgasse 12, tel. 0222/512–0203) is central, popular, and always packed. The **P1** disco (Rotgasse 3, tel. 0222/535–9995) vies with the **U-4** (Schönbrunnerstr. 222, tel. 0222/858307) for top ranking among the young set. Live bands, dancing, and snacks are offered at **Chattanooga** (Graben 29, tel. 0222/533–5000).

Nightclubs A casual '50s atmosphere pervades the popular **Café Volksgarten** (Burgring 1, tel. 0222/630518), situated in the city park of the same name; tables are set outdoors in summer. The more formal **Eden Bar** (Liliengasse 2, tel. 0222/512–7450) is considered one of Vienna's classiest night spots; don't expect to be let in unless you're dressed to kill.

Wine Taverns For a traditional Viennese night out, head to one of the city's atmospheric wine taverns, which sometimes date as far back as the 12th century. You can often have full meals at these taverns, but the emphasis is mainly on drinking. **Melker Stiftskeller** (*see* Dining, above) is one of the friendliest and most typical of Vienna's wine taverns. Other well-known ones: **Antiquitäten-Keller** (Magdalenenstr. 32, tel. 0222/566–9533; closed Aug.), which has a backdrop of classical music; **Augustinerkeller** (Augustinerstr. 1, tel. 0222/533–1026), open at lunchtime as well as during the evenings, in the same building as the Albertina collection; **Esterhazykeller** (Haarhof 1, tel. 0222/533–3482), a particularly mazelike network of rooms; **Piaristenkeller** (Piaristengasse 45, tel. 0222/429152), with zither music; and **Zwölf-Apostelkeller** (Sonnenfelsgasse 3, tel. 0222/512–6777), near St. Stephen's Cathedral.

23 Zürich

Arriving and Departing

By Plane Kloten (tel. 01/8121212) is Switzerland's most important airport and is among the most sophisticated in the world. Several airlines fly directly to Zürich from major cities in the United States, Canada, and the United Kingdom.

Between the Airport and Downtown Beneath the air terminals, there's a train station with an efficient, direct service into the Hauptbahnhof (main station) in the center of Zürich. Fast trains run every 20 minutes, and the trip takes about 10 minutes. The fare is 4.60 Fr. and the ticket office is in the airport. There are express trains to most Swiss cities at least every hour. Trains run from 6 AM to midnight.

Taxis are very expensive: about 40 Fr. into town. Some hotels provide their own bus service. Cars can be rented at the airport.

By Bus All bus services to Zürich will drop you at the Hauptbahnhof.

By Car There are direct highways from the border crossings with France, Germany, and Italy. The German frontier is the nearest.

Getting Around

Although Zürich is Switzerland's largest city, it has a population of only 362,000 and is not large by European standards. That's one of its nicest features: You can explore it comfortably on foot.

By Bus and Streetcar The city's transportation network is excellent. **VBZ Züri-Line** (Zürich Public Transport) buses run from 5:30 AM to midnight, every six minutes on all routes at peak hours, and about every 12 minutes at other times. Before you board the bus, you must buy your ticket from the automatic vending machines (instructions appear in English) found at every stop. A money-saving ticket for all travel for 24 hours is a good buy at 5 Fr. Free route plans are available from VBZ offices.

By Taxi Taxis are very expensive, with a 6 Fr. minimum, and should be avoided unless you have no other means of getting around.

Important Addresses and Numbers

Tourist Information The tourist office is located at Bahnhofplatz 15 (Main Station), tel. 01/2114000. Open Mar.–Oct., weekdays 8 AM–10 PM, weekends 8 AM–8:30 PM; Nov.–Feb., Mon.–Thurs. 8–8, Fri. 8 AM–10 PM, weekends 9–6.

Consulates U.S. (Zollikerstr. 141, tel. 01/552566). U.K. (Dufourstr. 56, tel. 01/471520).

Emergencies Police (tel. 117). **Ambulance** (tel. 144). **Doctor** (tel. 01/2616100); poisoning cases, 01/2515151. **Dentist** (tel. 01/2616100). **Pharmacy: Bellevue** (Theaterstr. 14, tel. 01/2524411) offers an all-night service.

English Bookstores Payot (Bahnhofstr. 9). **Travel Book Shop** (Rindermarkt 20).

Travel Agencies American Express (Bahnhofstr. 20, tel. 01/2118370). **Kuoni** (Bahnhofplatz 7, tel. 01/2213411).

Guided Tours

Orientation Tours There are three bus tours available. The daily "Sights of Zürich" tour (22 Fr. adults, 11 Fr. children) gives a good general idea of the city in two hours. "In and Around Zürich" goes farther and includes an aerial cableway trip to Felsenegg. This is also a daily tour that takes 2½ hours; it costs 30 Fr. adults, 15 Fr. children. There is a May-to-October tour, "Zürich by Night," that takes in everything from folklore to striptease in 3½ hours (65 Fr.). All tours start from the main station. Contact the tourist office for reservations.

Walking Tours From June to October, conducted walking tours (12 Fr.) start from the tourist office and take roughly two hours.

Excursions There are many bus excursions to other areas, such as the Bernese Oberland, St. Gotthard, the Ticino, Lucerne, and Geneva. Since these depend on the season and weather, it's best to book them after you arrive and can check with the tourist office.

Exploring Zürich

Zürich is not at all what you'd expect. Stroll around on a fine spring day and you'll ask yourself if this can really be one of the great business centers of the world: The lake glistening and blue in the sun, the sidewalk cafés, swans gliding in to land on the river, the hushed and haunted old squares of medieval guildhouses, and elegant shops. There's not a gnome (a mocking nickname for a Swiss banker) in sight, not a worried business frown to be seen. The point is that for all its economic importance, Zürich is a place where people enjoy life. Hardworking, inventive, serious when need be, the Swiss love the good things in life, and they have the money to enjoy them.

Zürich started in 15 BC as a Roman customs post on the Lindenhof overlooking the river Limmat, but its growth really began around the 10th century AD. It became a free imperial city in 1336, a center of the Reformation in 1519, and then gradually assumed commercial importance during the 19th century. Today there is peace as well as prosperity here, and since Zürich is so compact, you can take in its variety in a morning's stroll.

Numbers in the margin correspond to points of interest on the Zürich map.

❶ Collect your map (it's essential) from the tourist office (Bahnhofplatz 15), then start your walk from the nearby **Bahnhofstrasse,** famous for its shops and cafés and as the center of the banking network, though you'd be unlikely to guess it. Take Rennweg on your left, and then turn left again into the For-
❷ tunagasse, a quaint medieval street leading to the **Lindenhof,** a square where there are remains of Zürich's Roman origins. The fountain commemorates the ingenuity of the Zürich women who, when the city was besieged by the Habsburgs in 1292, donned armor and marched around the walls. The invaders thought they were reinforcements and beat a hasty retreat.

❸ An alley on the right leads to a picturesque square dating from the Middle Ages, with the **Peterskirche,** Zürich's oldest parish church (13th century), which also happens to have the largest clockface in Europe. Walk down to the river and follow it to the
❹ 13th century **Fraumünster** (church), which has modern stained-glass windows by Chagall. There are two handsome guildhalls

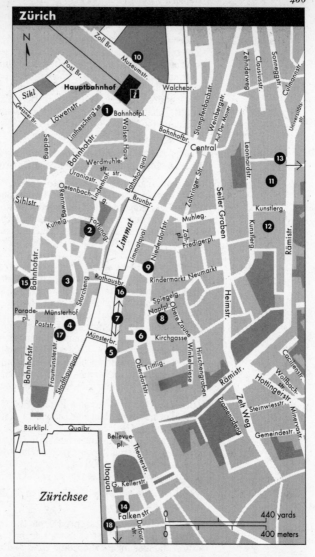

nearby: the **Zunfthaus zur Waag** hall of the linen weavers (Münsterhof 8), built in 1637, and the **Zunfthaus zur Meise** (Münsterhof 20), built during the 18th century for the wine merchants.

Time Out Head away from the river to the Bahnhofstrasse, then to Paradeplatz to visit **Sprüngli**, the famous café/sweets shop where glossy Zürichers gather to see and be seen. The chocolate truffles are sinfully rich.

Continue along Bahnhofstrasse to Bürkliplatz and cross the **Quai Bridge** to take in the impressive views of the lake and town. Now head left to the **Wasserkirche** (Water Church), dating from the 15th century and a lovely example of late-Gothic architecture. It is attached to the **Helmhaus,** originally an 18th-century cloth market.

6 Now turn right toward the **Grossmünster** church, which dates from the 11th century. During the 3rd century AD, St. Felix and his sister Regula were martyred by the Romans. Legend maintains that having been beheaded, they then walked up the hill carrying their heads and collapsed on the spot where the Grossmünster now stands. On the south tower you can see a statue of Charlemagne (768–814), emperor of the West. During the 16th century, the Zürich reformer Huldrych Zwingli preached sermons here that were so threatening in their promise of fire and brimstone that Martin Luther himself was scared.

7 Back at the river on the **Limmatquai** are some of Zürich's most enchanting old buildings. Today most of them are restaurants. In the **Haus zum Ruden,** a 13th-century noblemen's hall, you will eat under a 300-year-old wooden ceiling. Other notable buildings here are the **Zunfthaus zur Saffran** (built in 1723 for haberdashers) and the **Zunfthaus zur Zimmerleuten** (built in 1708 for carpenters). The 17th-century Baroque **Rathaus** (Town Hall) is nearby.

8 Turn right into the **Old Town,** and you will enter a maze of fascinating medieval streets where time seems to have stood still. The Rindermarkt, Napfplatz, and Kirchgasse all have their charming old houses.

9 Head back to the river through **Niederdorf** (Zürich's nightlife district) and cross the bridge to the Hauptbahnhof. On the **10** northern edge of the Hauptbahnhof, go to the **Schweizerisches Landesmuseum,** housed in a curious 19th-century building, for a look at Swiss history. There are fascinating pre-Romanesque and Romanesque church art, glass paintings from the 15th to the 17th century, splendid ceramic stoves, gold and silver from Celtic times, and weapons from many ages. *Museumstr. 2, tel. 01/2211010. Admission free. Open Tues.–Fri. and Sun. 10–noon, 2–5; Sat. 10–noon and 2–4.*

Shopping

Gift Ideas Typical Swiss products, all of the highest quality, include watches in all price categories, clocks, jewelry, music boxes, embroidered goods, wood carvings, and the famous multiblade Swiss army pocket knife.

Shopping Districts The **Bahnhofstrasse** is as fine a shopping street as you'd come upon in Paris. Here you'll find **Jelmoli** (Seidengasse 1), Switzerland's largest department store, carrying a wide range of tasteful Swiss goods. **Heimatwerk** (Bahnhofstr. 2) specializes in handmade Swiss crafts, all of excellent quality. For high fashion, go to **Trois Pommes** (Storchengasse 6/7) and **Grieder** (Bahnhofstrasse 30), and for the finest porcelain, glass, and silverware, visit **Sequin-Dormann** (Bahnhofstr. 69a). If you have a sweet tooth, stock up on truffles at **Sprüngli** (Paradeplatz).

In the **Old Town** and off the **Limmatquai,** you'll find boutiques, antiques shops, bookstores, and galleries in picturesque byways. The **Löwenstrasse** has such a diversity of shops that it has been nicknamed "Shopville." The **Langstrasse** is another good shopping area and often has slightly lower prices.

Food and Flea Markets

In many parts of town, there are lively markets where fruit, vegetables, and flowers are competitively priced. The best are at **Bürkliplatz, Helvetiaplatz,** and **Milkbuckstrasse** (open Tues. and Fri. 6 AM–11 AM) and at **Marktplatz,** on the way to the airport (open Wed. and Sat. 6 AM–11 AM).

At Bürkliplatz, at the lake end of the Bahnhofstrasse, there's a flea market that's open May through October, and a curio market is held at **Rosenhof** every Thursday between April and Christmas.

Dining

Options range from luxury establishments to modest cafés, *stübli* (cozy little pubs), and restaurants specializing in local cuisine.

Because the Swiss are so good at preparing everyone else's cuisine, it is sometimes said that they have none of their own, but there definitely is a distinct and characteristic Swiss cuisine. Switzerland is the home of great cheeses—Gruyère, Emmentaler, Appenzeller, and Vacherin—which form the basis of many dishes. *Raclette* is cheese melted over a fire and served with potatoes and pickles, *Rösti* are hash brown potatoes, and *fondue* is a bubbling pot of melted cheeses flavored with garlic and kirsch, into which you dip chunks of bread. Other Swiss specialties to look for are *geschnetzeltes Kalbfleisch* (veal bits in cream sauce), *polenta* (cornmeal mush) in the Italian region, and fine game in autumn. A wide variety of Swiss sausages make both filling and inexpensive meals, and in every region the breads are varied and superb.

You're likely to be served seconds in Zürich's generous restaurants, where the rest of your *Rösti* and *Geschnetzeltes Kalbfleisch nach Zürcher Art* (veal pieces in mushroom-cream sauce) simmer in copper pans by your table while you relish the hefty first portion. This is a Germanic city, after all, though its status as a minor world capital means that most international cuisines are represented as well. But brace yourself: The cash register rings portentiously when the waiter places your order. Watch for posted *tagesteller* specials, a good source of savings.

Mealtimes

At home, the main Swiss meal of the day is lunch, with a snack in the evening. Restaurants, however, are open at midday and during the evening; often limited menus are offered all day.

Watch for *Tagesteller* (fixed-price lunch menus), which enable you to experience the best restaurants without paying high à la carte rates.

Dress

Jacket and tie are suggested for restaurants in the Very Expensive and Expensive categories; casual dress is acceptable elsewhere.

Ratings

Prices are per person, without wine or coffee, but including tip and taxes. Best bets are indicated by a star ★.

Category	Cost
Very Expensive	over 80 Fr.
Expensive	50 Fr.–80 Fr.

Moderate	30 Fr.–50 Fr.
Inexpensive	under 30 Fr.

Very Expensive **Agnes Amberg.** Every meal is a dégustation, a parade of exquisitely presented nouvelle delights, including sautéed foie gras in cabbage leaves with rock salt and Szechuan pepper and guinea fowl on leek fondue with honey-vinegar sauce. Though the decor may seem excessive, the service is unpretentious and usually impeccable. *Hottingerstr. 5, tel. 01/2512626. Reservations required. Jacket and tie advised. AE, DC, MC, V. Closed Mon. and Sat. noon and Sun.*

★ **Chez Max.** Owner Max Kehl deserves his reputation as one of the leading chefs of Switzerland, combining French and Japanese techniques to create unique, imaginative nouvelle dishes. Just over three kilometers (two miles) out of the city on the road to Rapperswil, it's worth the trip. *Seestr. 53, Zollikon, tel. 01/3918877. Reservations required. Jacket and tie advised. AE, DC, MC, V. Open evenings only. Closed Sun., Mon, and 3 weeks in July–Aug.*

★ **Petermann's Kunststuben.** This is one of Switzerland's gastronomic meccas, and while it's south of the city's center, in Küssnacht on the lake's eastern shore, it's well worth the trip. Chef Horst Petermann presides over an evolving menu that may include tempura of lobster tail in vanilla butter, turbot roasted in veal juice with confit of shallots, or sweetbreads with caper sabayon. *Seestrasse 160, Küsnacht, tel. 01/9100715. Reservations required. Jacket and tie advised. AE, DC, MC, V. Closed Sun. and Mon.*

Piccola Accademia. This extraordinary restaurant serves world-class Italian cuisine to a loyal clientele of theater and arts personalities, whose photos and grateful testimonies line the walls. *Rotwandstr. 48, tel. 01/2416243. Reservations required. Jacket advised. AE, DC, MC, V.*

Expensive **Haus zum Ruden.** In addition to serving the most ambitious cuisine of Zürich's many guildhouse restaurants, this fine restaurant—dating in part from 1295—is also the most architecturally spectacular, combining river views with a barrel-vaulted ceiling and 30-foot beams. Kitchen specialties include tartare of smoked salmon and prunes, *paupiettes* (stuffed slices) of sole and salmon with saffron, and veal with foie-gras cream. *Limmatquai 42, tel. 01/2619566. Reservations advised; required at night. Jacket advised. AE, DC, MC, V.*

Hummer und Austernbar. In a fin de siècle setting of polished wood, candles, and soft pastels, you can have your fill of impeccably fresh lobsters and oysters (*hummer* means "lobster," *austern*, "oysters"), or sample Brittany lobsters poached in Champagne sauce and St. Pierre flambéed with fennel. There's a long wine list, but Champagne seems to be the drink of choice with Zürichers, who come here in hordes. *Hotel St. Gotthard, Bahnhofstrasse 87, tel. 01/2115500. Reservations advised. Jacket and tie advised. AE, DC, MC, V.*

★ **Kronenhalle.** Owned by the Zumsteg family (silk barons and patrons of the arts) for most of this century, this lively, genial old dining hall doubles as a gallery, its wainscoted walls crowded with personalized works by Picasso, Matisse, Bonnard, and Chagall. The hefty French cuisine with a local accent includes duck, trout, and lamb specialties. *Le tout* Zürich eats here and drinks prize-winning cocktails hip to hip in the bar.

Rämistr. 4, tel. 01/2510256. Reservations advised. Jacket and tie advised. AE, DC, MC, V.

★ **Veltliner Keller.** Though its rich, carved-wood decor borrows from Alpine culture, this ancient and atmospheric dining spot is no tourist-trap transplant: The house, built in 1325 and functioning as a restaurant since 1551, has always stored Italian-Swiss Valtellina wines, which were carried over the Alps and imported to Zürich. There is a traditional emphasis on heavy meat standards, but the kitchen is flexible and reasonably deft with seafood as well. Specialties include grilled salmon, veal steak with Gorgonzola, and delicious dessert mousses. Try the house version of *schoppa da giuotta*, or barley soup, a traditional Alpine dish. *Schlüsselgasse 8, tel. 01/2213228. Reservations advised. Jacket and tie advised. AE, DC, MC, V.*

Moderate **Zunfthaus zur Schmiden.** Of Zürich's several grand old guildhouses that have been converted to restaurants, this 570-year-old blacksmith's hall is the loveliest, all burnished wood and leaded glass. Its typical menu of veal dishes and Rösti is also the least expensive. *Marktgasse 20, tel. 01/2515287. Reservations advised. Dress: neat but casual. AE, DC, MC, V.*

Zunfthaus zur Waag. Another, airier guildhall, its woodwork whitewashed, its windows looking out to the Fraumünster, this one offers generous portions of fine Swiss specialties, though rather formally served. *Münsterhof 8, tel. 01/2110730. Reservations advised. Jacket advised. AE, DC, MC, V.*

Inexpensive **Bierhalle Kropf.** Under the giant boar's head, businessmen, ★ workers, and shoppers crowd shared tables to feast on generous hot dishes and a great selection of sausages. The *Leberknödli* (liver dumplings) are terrific. The florid murals and woodwork of this establishment (more than 100 years old) have been recently restored. *Gassen 16, tel. 01/2211805. Reservations advised. Dress: casual. AE, DC, MC, V.*

Hiltl Vegi. As the German eating world takes its cholesterol count, more and more vegetarian restaurants are catching on, including this popular old landmark, founded during the late 19th century. The ambience these days is all-contemporary, with color photos posted of daily specials, which include soups, curries, and variations on ratatouille. *Sihlstrasse 28, tel. 01/2213870. Reservations not necessary. Dress: casual. No credit cards.*

Mère Catherine. This is a popular French-style bistro, with a dark and unselfconscious old-style decor and specials listed on the blackboard. You can have onion soup, duck-liver terrine, seafood, and a few meat dishes—even *steak de cheval* (horse steak). The clientele is young and sociable. *Nägelihof 3, tel. 01/2622250. Reservations not necessary. Dress: casual. No credit cards.*

★ **Odeon.** In an atmosphere that's as Parisian as this Prussian town can get, this historic café/restaurant once sheltered a pre-revolutionary Lenin, who nursed a coffee and read the house's daily papers. Now the crowd is just as intense, with a tonic air of counterculture chic mixed with the no-filter cigarette smoke. You can nurse a coffee, too, or have a plate of pasta, a sandwich, or dessert from the limited menu. It's open daily until 2 AM, weekends until 4 AM. *Am Bellevue, tel. 01/2511650. Reservations not necessary. Dress: casual. AE, DC, MC, V.*

★ **Zeughauskeller.** Built as an arsenal in 1487, this enormous stone-and-beam hall offers hearty meat platters and a variety of beers and wines in comfortable and friendly chaos. It's great

for families. *Bahnhofstr. 28a, off Paradeplatz, tel. 01/2112690.*
Reservations advised at lunch. Dress: casual. No credit cards.

Lodging

Switzerland's accommodatons cover a broad range, from the
most luxurious hotels to the more economical rooms in private
homes. Pick up the *Schwiezer Hotelführer (Swiss Hotel Guide)*
from the SNTO before you leave home. The guide is free and
lists all the members of the Swiss Hotel Association (comprising nearly 90% of the nations's accommodations); it tells you
everything you'll want to know.

Most hotel rooms today have private bath and shower; those
that don't are usually considerably cheaper. Single rooms are
generally about two-thirds the price of doubles, but this can
vary considerably. Remember that the no-nonsense Swiss
sleep in separate beds or, at best, a double with separate bedding. If you prefer more sociable arrangements, ask for the
rare "matrimonial" or "French" bed. Service charges and taxes
are included in the price quoted and the bill you pay. Breakfast
is included unless there is a clear notice to the contrary. In resorts especially, half pension (choice of a noon or evening meal)
may be included in the room price. If you choose to eat à la carte
or elsewhere, the management will generally reduce your
price. Give them plenty of notice, however.

All major towns and train stations have hotel-finding services,
which sometimes charge a small fee. Local tourist offices will
also help.

Hotels
Zürich has an enormous range of hotels, from some of the most
chic and prestigious in the country to modest guest houses.
Prices tend to be higher than they are anywhere else in Eu-
rope, but you can be sure that you will get what you pay for:
Quality and good service are guaranteed.

Hotels are graded from one star (the lowest) to five stars. Always confirm what you are paying before you register, and
check the posted price when you get to your room. Major credit
cards are generally accepted, but, again, make sure beforehand.

Two important hotel chains are the Romantik Hotels and Restaurants and Relais & Châteaux, with premises that are generally either in historic houses or houese that have some special
character. Another chain that has a good reputation is Best
Western, affiliated with the familiar American chain. The
Check-In E and G Hotels is a voluntary group of small hotels,
boardinghouse, and mountain lodges that offer accommodations at reasonable prices. Details are available from the
SNTO, which also offers pamphlets recommending family hotels and a list of hotels and restaurants that cater specifically to
Jewish travelers.

Rentals
Rentals are available from the **Swiss Touring Club** (rue Pierre
Fatio 9, CH-1211 Geneva 3) or from **Uto-Ring AG** (Beeth-
ovenstr. 24, 8002 Zürich). In the United States, write to
Interhome (36 Carlos Dr., Fairfield, NJ 07006). In Britain, con-
tact **Interhome** (383 Richmond Rd., Twickenham, Middlesex
TW1 2EF).

Ratings · Prices are for two people in a double room with bath or shower, including taxes, service charges, and breakfast. Best bets are indicated by a star ★.

Category	Cost
Very Expensive	over 400 Fr.
Expensive	250 Fr.–400 Fr.
Moderate	120 Fr.–250 Fr.
Inexpensive	under 120 Fr.

Very Expensive ★ **Baur Au Lac.** Have a pedicure and borrow the Rolls at this most magnificent of European luxury hotels, owned by the same family since 1844. The rooms are posh but discreet; the sumptuous lounges and restaurants teem with the rich and famous. The staff of 300 is courteous but rarely stuffy. It's steps from the Bahnhofstrasse and lake, with a private park and Alpine views. *Talstr. 1, CH-8022, tel. 01/2211650. 156 rooms with bath. Facilities: restaurants, grillroom, American bar, disco, summer restaurant and terrace bar, beauty shop, Rolls-Royce limo service, parking. AE, DC, MC, V.*

★ **Dolder Grand.** High on the wooded hill over Zürich, this sprawling Victorian fantasy-palace provides quarters for bodyguards, nannies, and harems. The public areas are splendid; the recently decorated rooms spacious; and the views magnificent, whether from the original structure or the sleek new wing. *Kurhausstr. 65, CH-8032, tel. 01/2516231. 207 rooms with bath. Facilities: French restaurant, swimming pool with wave machine, 9-hole golf course, tennis courts, ice-skating rink, terrace, café, bar, garage. AE, DC, MC, V.*

★ **Savoy Baur en Ville.** The oldest hotel in Zürich, built in 1838, this luxurious downtown landmark was gutted in 1975 and reconstructed as an airtight urban gem. It's directly on the Paradeplatz and at the hub of the banking, shopping, and sightseeing districts. The rooms have a warm, postmodern decor, with pearwood cabinetry, brass, and chintz, and there are two fine restaurants—one French, the other Italian—as well as a city-slick café. *Am Paradeplatz, CH-8022, tel. 01/211536. 112 rooms with bath. Facilities: 2 restaurants, café. AE, DC, MC, V.*

Expensive ★ **Neues Schloss.** Step off the busy street and past the cold, modern exterior and you'll find a warm welcome. This fine establishment is run by a member of the venerable Seiler family, experienced Swiss hoteliers who specialize in comfort, discretion, and personal service. It's close to the main shopping district. *Stockerstr. 17, CH-8022, tel. 01/2016550. 59 rooms with bath. Facilities: restaurant. AE, DC, MC, V.*

Splügenschloss. Constructed at the turn of the century as luxury apartments, this Relais & Châteaux property maintains an ornate and historic decor, with antiques in rooms as well as throughout public spaces. Some rooms have been paneled completely in Alpine-style pine, others in fussy florals. Its location southeast of the Neues Schloss may be a little out of the way for tourists, but atmosphere buffs will find it worth the effort. *Splügenstrasse 2, CH-8002, tel. 01/2010800. 55 rooms. Facilities: restaurant, bar. AE, DC, MC, V.*

★ **Zum Storchen.** In a stunning central location, tucked between

Fraumünster and St. Peter on the gull-studded banks of the Limmat, this airy 600-year-old structure houses an impeccable modern hotel. It has warmly appointed rooms, some with French windows that open over the water. *Weinplatz 2, CH-8001, tel. 01/2115510. 77 rooms with bath. Facilities: restaurant, terrace café, snack bar, bar. AE, DC, MC, V.*

Moderate   **City.** Close to the Bahnhofstrasse, train station, and Löwen-strasse shopping district, this is a hotel in miniature, with small furnishings and baths and a high proportion of single rooms. It's recently been renewed to a chic pastel polish, and some rooms fall in the Expensive category. *Löwenstrasse 34, CH-8021, tel. 01/2112055. 83 rooms. AE, DC, MC, V.*

Rothus. It's a trade-off: You get a private shower at bargain rates, but there's a strip joint on the ground floor. (Avoid it by using the side entrance.) It's functional and tidy, with modern baths, and has a great Niederdorf location. Breakfast is extra. *Marktgasse 14, CH-8001, tel. 01/2521530. 50 rooms, some with bath/shower. Facilities: restaurant. AE, DC, MC, V.*

★ **Sonnenberg.** If you're traveling by car and want to avoid the urban rush, escape to this hillside refuge east of town. There are breathtaking views of the city, lake, and mountains, and the wood, stone, and beam decor encourages the resort atmosphere. Train travelers take tram No. 3 or No. 8 to Klusplatz, then walk 10 minutes uphill—or catch a cab. *Aurorastr. 98, CH-8030, tel. 01/2620062. 35 rooms with bath. Facilities: restaurant, summer dining pavilion. AE, DC, MC, V.*

Inexpensive   **Limmathof.** Austere and dormlike but ideally placed, it's minutes from the bahnhof on the edge of the Niederdorf nightlife district. Despite the no-frills decor, all rooms have tile baths. It's excellent value. *Limmatquai 142, CH-8023, tel. 01/474220. 65 rooms with bath. Facilities: restaurant. No credit cards.*

Linde Oberstrasse. Near the university, in a sterile residential area, this small hotel, built as a guildhouse in 1628, offers a handful of modest but agreeable rooms. The baths are down the hall, but you get a sink, TV, and minibar to compensate. There's a tram to the city center that stops out front. *Universitätstr. 91, CH-8033, tel. 01/3622109. 10 rooms, none with bath. Facilities: restaurant. AE, DC, MC, V.*

★ **Vorderer Sternen.** On the edge of the old town and near the lake, this plain but adequate establishment takes in the bustle (and noise) of the city. It's steps from the opera house, theaters, art galleries, cinemas, and a shopping area; it's also close to a tram junction. It serves breakfast, and there's a restaurant downstairs—but treat yourself at the nearby Kronenhalle. *Theaterstr. 22, tel. 01/2514949. 15 rooms, none with bath. AE, DC, MC, V.*

The Arts

Pick up *Zürich News*, published each week by the tourist office, to check what's on. Ticket reservations can be made through the **Billetzentrale.** *Werdmühleplatz, tel. 01/2212283. Open weekdays 10–6:30, Sat. 10–2.* **Musik Hug** (Limmatquai 26, tel. 01/471600) and **Jecklin** (Rämistrasse 30, tel. 01/2515900) are good ticket sources as well.

The **Zürich Tonhalle Orchestra** (Claridenstr. 7, tel. 01/2011580) ranks among Europe's best. The **Opernhaus** (Falkenstr., tel. 01/2516922) is renowned for its adventurous opera, operetta, and ballet productions. The **Schauspielhaus** (Rämistr. 34, tel. 01/2511111) is one of the finest German-speaking theaters in the world. Zürich has 40 movie theaters, with English-language films appearing regularly. The city boasts many art galleries of interest. Among them is **Sammlung E. G. Bührle** (Zollikerstr. 172, tel. 01/550086), which specializes in 19th-century French masters. Take streetcar No. 2 or No. 4 to Wildbachstrasse. *Admission: 6.60 Fr. Open Tues. and Fri. 2–5 and the first Fri. of each month, 2–8.*

Nightlife

Zürich has a lively nightlife scene, largely centered in the Niederdorf, parallel to the Limmat, across from the Hauptbahnhof. Many spots are short-lived, so check in advance. Informal dress is acceptable in most places, but again, check to make sure. The hotel porter is a good source of information.

Bars and Lounges The narrow bar at the **Kronenhalle** (Rämistrasse 4, tel. 01/2516669) draws mobs of well-heeled locals and internationals for its prize-winning cocktails. **Champagnertreff** in the Hotel Central (Central 1, tel. 01/2515555) is a popular Deco-look piano bar with several champagnes available by the glass. **Odeon** (Am Bellevue, tel. 01/2511650) serves a young, arty set until 4 AM. Some beer halls, including **Bierhalle Kropf** (In Gassen 16, tel. 01/2211805) and **Zeughauskeller** (Bahnhofstrasse 28, tel. 01/2112690), serve a variety of draft beers in an old-Zürich atmosphere.

Cabaret/Nightclubs There are strip shows all over town, as well as the traditional nightclub atmosphere at **Le Privé** (Stauffacherstrasse 106, tel. 01/2416487), **Moulin Rouge** (Mühlegasse 14, tel. 01/690730), and **Terrace** (Limmatquai 3, tel. 01/2511074). There's a variety show (no strip) at **Polygon** (Marktgasse 17, tel. 01/2521110).

Discos **Mascotte** (Theaterstrasse 10, tel. 01/2524481) is, at the moment, popular with all ages on weeknights, but caters to young crowds on weekends. **Nautic Club** (Wythenquai 61, tel. 01/2026676) opens onto the lakefront on summer nights. **Le Petit Prince** (Bleicherweg 21, tel. 01/2021739) attracts an upscale crowd. **Birdwatcher's Club** (Schützengasse 16, tel. 01/2115058) requires jackets and a membership card. Even more exclusive is **Diagonal**, at the Hotel Baur au Lac (Talstrasse 1, tel. 01/2211650), where you must be a hotel guest—or the guest of one.

Jazz **Casa Bar** (Münstergasse 30, tel. 01/472002) is the exclusive domain of jazz, with music until 2 AM.

Folklore If you're passing through Switzerland quickly and want the regional experience in a nutshell—even if it's inappropriate to this cosmopolitan and distinctly non-Alpine city—head for the **Kindli Swiss Chalet** (Oberer Rennweg, tel. 01/2114182), which offers evenings of yodeling, horn playing, dancing, and fondue.

Index

Personal Itinerary

Departure   *Date*

             Time

Transportation

Arrival   *Date*   *Time*

Departure   *Date*   *Time*

Transportation

Accommodations

Arrival   *Date*   *Time*

Departure   *Date*   *Time*

Transportation

Accommodations

Arrival   *Date*   *Time*

Departure   *Date*   *Time*

Transportation

Accommodations

Personal Itinerary

Arrival *Date*   *Time*

Departure *Date*   *Time*

Transportation

Accommodations

Arrival *Date*   *Time*

Departure *Date*   *Time*

Transportation

Accommodations

Arrival *Date*   *Time*

Departure *Date*   *Time*

Transportation

Accommodations

Arrival *Date*   *Time*

Departure *Date*   *Time*

Transportation

Accommodations

Personal Itinerary

Arrival	*Date*	*Time*
Departure	*Date*	*Time*
Transportation		
Accommodations		

Arrival	*Date*	*Time*
Departure	*Date*	*Time*
Transportation		
Accommodations		

Arrival	*Date*	*Time*
Departure	*Date*	*Time*
Transportation		
Accommodations		

Arrival	*Date*	*Time*
Departure	*Date*	*Time*
Transportation		
Accommodations		

Addresses

Name	*Name*
Address	*Address*
Telephone	*Telephone*
Name	*Name*
Address	*Address*
Telephone	*Telephone*
Name	*Name*
Address	*Address*
Telephone	*Telephone*
Name	*Name*
Address	*Address*
Telephone	*Telephone*
Name	*Name*
Address	*Address*
Telephone	*Telephone*
Name	*Name*
Address	*Address*
Telephone	*Telephone*
Name	*Name*
Address	*Address*
Telephone	*Telephone*
Name	*Name*
Address	*Address*
Telephone	*Telephone*

Fodor's Travel Guides

U.S. Guides

Alaska
Arizona
Boston
California
Cape Cod, Martha's
  Vineyard, Nantucket
The Carolinas & the
  Georgia Coast
The Chesapeake
  Region
Chicago
Colorado
Disney World & the
  Orlando Area
Florida
Hawaii

Las Vegas, Reno,
  Tahoe
Los Angeles
Maine, Vermont,
  New Hampshire
Maui
Miami & the
  Keys
National Parks
  of the West
New England
New Mexico
New Orleans
New York City
New York City
  (Pocket Guide)

Pacific North Coast
Philadelphia & the
  Pennsylvania
  Dutch Country
Puerto Rico
  (Pocket Guide)
The Rockies
San Diego
San Francisco
San Francisco
  (Pocket Guide)
The South
Santa Fe, Taos,
  Albuquerque
Seattle &
  Vancouver

Texas
USA
The U. S. & British
  Virgin Islands
The Upper Great
  Lakes Region
Vacations in
  New York State
Vacations on the
  Jersey Shore
Virginia & Maryland
Waikiki
Washington, D.C.
Washington, D.C.
  (Pocket Guide)

Foreign Guides

Acapulco
Amsterdam
Australia
Austria
The Bahamas
The Bahamas
  (Pocket Guide)
Baja & Mexico's Pacific
  Coast Resorts
Barbados
Barcelona, Madrid,
  Seville
Belgium &
  Luxembourg
Berlin
Bermuda
Brazil
Budapest
Budget Europe
Canada
Canada's Atlantic
  Provinces

Cancun, Cozumel,
  Yucatan Peninsula
Caribbean
Central America
China
Czechoslovakia
Eastern Europe
Egypt
Europe
Europe's Great Cities
France
Germany
Great Britain
Greece
The Himalayan
  Countries
Holland
Hong Kong
India
Ireland
Israel
Italy

Italy 's Great Cities
Jamaica
Japan
Kenya, Tanzania,
  Seychelles
Korea
London
London
  (Pocket Guide)
London Companion
Mexico
Mexico City
Montreal &
  Quebec City
Morocco
New Zealand
Norway
Nova Scotia,
  New Brunswick,
  Prince Edward
  Island
Paris

Paris (Pocket Guide)
Portugal
Rome
Scandinavia
Scandinavian Cities
Scotland
Singapore
South America
South Pacific
Southeast Asia
Soviet Union
Spain
Sweden
Switzerland
Sydney
Thailand
Tokyo
Toronto
Turkey
Vienna & the Danube
  Valley
Yugoslavia

Wall Street Journal Guides to Business Travel

Europe   International Cities   Pacific Rim   USA & Canada

Special-Interest Guides

Bed & Breakfast and
  Country Inn Guides:
  Mid-Atlantic Region
  New England
  The South
  The West

Cruises and Ports
  of Call
Healthy Escapes
Fodor's Flashmaps
  New York

Fodor's Flashmaps
  Washington, D.C.
Shopping in Europe
Skiing in the USA &
  Canada

Smart Shopper's
  Guide to London
Sunday in New York
Touring Europe
Touring USA